INTERNATIONAL
ASSOCIATION
OF ADMINISTRATIVE
PROFESSIONALS®

COMPLETE

OFFICE

HANDBOOK

Third Edition

The Definitive Reference for Today's Electronic Office

Susan Jaderstrom, Leonard Kruk, and Joanne Miller

GENERAL EDITOR: *Susan W. Fenner*

RANDOM HOUSE REFERENCE   NEW YORK

Complete Office Handbook, Third Edition

This book is available for special purchases in bulk by organizations and institutions, not for re-sale, at special discounts. Please direct your sales inquiries to Random House Premium Sales, toll-free 800-800-3264 or fax 212-572-4961.

Please address inquiries about electronic licensing of reference products, for use on a network or in software or on CD-ROM, to the Subsidiary Rights Department, Random House Reference, fax 212-940-7352.

For all other inquiries, please visit the Random House Reference Web site: www.randomwords.com

This is a revised and completely retypeset edition of the *Professional Secretaries International®
Complete Office Handbook,* originally published in 1992 by Random House, Inc. The second edition of this book was published in 1997 by Random House, Inc.

Excerpt from *The Columbia Guide to Online Style* on p. 562 is ©1998 Janice R. Walker and Todd Taylor. Reprinted with permission from Columbia University Press.

Typeset and printed in the United States of America.
Cover design by Heidi North
Interior book design by Nancy Etheredge, REM Studio
Page Composition by Allentown Digital Services, an R. R. Donnelly & Sons company.

Library of Congress Cataloging-in-Publication Data is available.

Third Edition
0 9 8 7 6 5 4 3 2 1
August 2002

ISBN **0-375-70929-0**

New York Toronto London Sydney Auckland

CONTENTS

LIST OF ILLUSTRATIONS

PART I

PROFESSIONAL

DEVELOPMENT

AND

HUMAN

RELATIONS

Career options for office professionals at all levels are rapidly expanding as more technology is introduced into office tasks. The Information Age has changed the way offices operate and the way information is handled, affording new opportunities for professional growth.

Computer and telecommunication technologies will continue as engines of change, constantly redefining the role of the office professional. As requirements become increasingly complex, office professionals will need to have strong technical and interpersonal skills and function as integral parts of the management team. In addition, office-support positions will require lifelong education and training to keep pace with changing office technology and to be responsive to global marketplace demands.

CHAPTER 1

GROWING

PROFESSIONALLY

CHANGING ROLES: FROM
SECRETARY TO EXECUTIVE ASSISTANT

The earliest recorded mention of a secretary dates from the sixteenth century. At that time, a secretary was usually a man with the ability to read, write, and calculate; he wrote all manuscripts, letters, and records by hand.

Not until the late nineteenth and early twentieth centuries did the mechanized office come into being. The invention of the typewriter, telephone, duplicating equipment, and calculating machine helped to speed up information processing within business. As a result, the male secretary's support role evolved into management as he became an understudy for the executive and the executive's successor in managing the business. With that change, more and more women were hired and trained to perform clerical support tasks for this male-dominated management.

The twenty-first-century office, however, is very different from the one that existed in the twentieth century. Several important factors have contributed to this change.

One factor is technology. The computer has replaced the typewriter. The ease of having facts and figures accessible and able to be manipulated by electronic tools means that more workers in the office have a link to vital information and makes computer literacy essential for everyone in business today.

Business is also increasing in size and complexity. The economic need to reduce office costs through greater individual productivity and restructuring to eliminate or combine positions has made the secretarial role emerge as a major responsible position within the office.

No longer is the secretary necessarily a woman, nor is the secretary viewed as a lowly clerk. Both men and women are opting for administrative support careers. These office positions are recognized as significant contributions to the efficient operation of an organization, especially given the emphasis on projects and work teams. The position of office professional has thus become a viable career with nearly unlimited opportunities.

The recent evolution of the secretary to administrative or executive assistant to project manager is significant. Although expert keyboarding and language skills are still critical, the role is evolving to one of a professional who supports management and work teams in the processing, organizing, and interrelating of business information.

The International Association of Administrative Professionals® (IAAP®) defines today's office professional as "an executive assistant who possesses a mastery of office skills, demonstrates the ability to assume responsibility without direct supervision, exercises initiative and judgment, and makes decisions within the scope of assigned authority."

Job titles and responsibilities vary dramatically from organization to organization. The title *secretary* is rapidly being replaced by other terms, such as *administrative professional, desktop publishing specialist, project coordinator,* and *office manager,* to reflect the changing office environment and responsibilities of today's office support staff.

The greatest challenge in today's workplace will be to accept change, adapt, learn new computer skills, and share this information with others. A "change enabler" is one who facilitates the acceptance, implementation, and evolution of change. Become a change enabler by following these steps:

1. Determine the types of changes that are having the greatest impact on your organization. Embrace these changes, update your skills, and help others who may be having difficulties.

2. Create a short- and long-term plan for yourself. This may include enrolling in seminars or computer courses, or obtaining a postsecondary degree. It is also a good idea to keep current by reading appropriate trade magazines and journals. Photocopy relevant articles and distribute them to your work group.

3. Recommend the formation of a change-enablers team. Ask if you can be the team leader. This interdisciplinary group should meet at least quarterly, preferably monthly, to discuss your company's organizational focus and work processes. Each team member should become an avid reader in at least one area, for example, technology, distance collaboration, project management, e-commerce, and work teams. Communicate the discussion and recommendations of the team meetings to all employees via the company newsletter or e-mail.

4. Become an active member of your local IAAP® chapter. This association will help you to identify future trends, provide you a network of colleagues, and help you become more professional. (See page TK for information on contacting IAAP®.)

ENTRY-LEVEL OPPORTUNITIES

As more positions are evolving, the term *secretary* is now increasingly applied to entry-level or clerical positions. There is no standardization within this field, nor is there a single, clear definition for specific job titles. However, a number of entry-level opportunities exist for office professionals to begin their careers in the office-support field.

It is relatively easy to enter this profession. At least a high school education with an emphasis on computer skills, effective written and oral communication, and information management is necessary. Knowledge of office procedures and familiarity with office technology software are needed.

IAAP® conducted an entry-level competency study and found that beginning office workers should know how to manage records; schedule appointments and maintain calendars; keyboard; write and format correspondence; and effectively use language skills. In addition, the ability to use word processing, spreadsheet, database, presentation, and e-mail software packages is important; so too, is projecting a professional image and self-direction in learning.

Persons in entry-level positions must be prepared to perform a variety of office functions, with broad emphasis on professional attitudes, behaviors, and skills rather than on particular job titles or stereotyped roles. Since each organization is different, job titles may vary and may include:

Administrative support (AS): This generally includes most of the nonclerical functions previously performed by the traditional secretary. Skills and characteristics needed within the area of administrative support include ability to work as part of a team, good communication and organization skills, initiative, and computer skills.

Beginning positions include the following:

Switchboard operator: Handles incoming calls and processes outgoing calls, has a good telephone personality, takes messages, answers inquiries, and may perform other clerical functions.

Receptionist: Welcomes, orients, and directs visitors, handles phone system or switchboard, may do some filing and correspondence, may control petty cash, distributes mail, and controls courier and messenger dispatch.

Secretary: Performs a variety of office tasks such as handling mail and composing correspondence, organization, maintaining files, and supporting multiple team members.

Customer service representative: Interfaces with customers by phone, e-mail, help lines and/or in person regarding the company's product(s) and customers' accounts.

Telemarketing representative: Calls prospective customers to determine their interest in purchasing a company's product(s).

With new technology being used in business almost as quickly as it is introduced, nearly all medium- to large-sized businesses use integrated office systems, that is, office equipment, including computers, connected via a communications network. These systems require specially-trained personnel with traditional basic skills as well as new skills to manage office work.

Skills and characteristics needed for those interested in a secretarial career include the ability to work independently, a technical orientation, a knowledge of computer hardware and software, a team spirit, accuracy, language arts and grammatical skills, and the ability to proofread, edit, and prioritize tasks.

Records management has become a specialized field, but it offers numerous entry-level opportunities.

Entry-level job opportunities include:

Records clerk/trainee: Performs simple sorting and retrieving of information.

Junior file clerk: Processes material already classified by a senior clerk.

Archival technician: Prepares information for storage and archives.

Skills and characteristics needed for this field include having a team orientation and being detail-minded, logical, systematic, and security conscious.

Several other entry-level opportunities exist in office services. Among them is:

Data entry: Inputs information from a variety of sources into a computer database. May take, enter, and track orders.

Mail Assistant: Sorts and distributes incoming and outgoing mail. Operates manual and electronic equipment.

ADVANCED-LEVEL OPPORTUNITIES

Advancement from an entry-level position within an organization largely depends on the perseverance and hard work of the entry-level professional. Each organization varies in how far it will advance its office-support personnel. Titles such as *administrative assistant, executive assistant,* and *executive secretary* are often used interchangeably to describe office professionals performing higher-level office tasks or working for higher-level executives. Other titles may be *marketing assistant, office manager, technology specialist,* and *project coordinator.*

Entry-level professionals often advance into administrative support, which generally involves the following:

- Providing support services to upper-level executives or teams
- Performing office duties in addition to purchasing and interacting with vendors
- Conducting research on the Internet
- Managing projects

Other important skills and abilities for office administrators to have include:

- Interpersonal skills
- Problem-solving abilities
- Analytical and decision-making abilities

- Computer literacy
- Supervisory and managerial techniques
- Communication skills, including speaking, listening, and writing
- Research skills
- Meeting planning

These skills may also qualify office professionals for other positions.

Administrative support supervisor: Interviews, hires, evaluates, and trains new personnel; creates job descriptions; delegates and assigns work; coordinates work schedules; keeps attendance and payroll records; evaluates new office technology; develops, writes, and implements office procedures; establishes and maintains work production standards; supervises and motivates personnel.

Information manager: Manages records, paper and electronic files, and databases; organizes and retrieves information, troubleshoots hardware/software problems; does computer training; develops e-policy.

HINT: *According to Nancy Flynn, executive director of The ePolicy Institute (www.epolicyinstitute.com) and author of* The ePolicy Handbook, Writing Effective E-Mail *and other e-related books, "Whether you employ one part-time worker or 10,000 full-time professionals, any time you allow employees access to your organization's e-mail and Internet system, you put your assets, reputation, and future at risk. Regardless of industry or size, every employer who wants to reduce the risk of workplace lawsuits and other e-related liabilities should implement a comprehensive e-policy program. A written e-policy clearly spells out what employees may and may not say and do via the organization's e-mail, Internet, and intranet systems, and is one of the most effective ways to keep on-line employees in line."*

Communications manager: Manages communications technologies, such as servers, multifunction image processors, and local area networks (LANs); works with Web site development and updating.

Records manager: Manages information and personnel documents; assumes responsibility for records protection and security; coordinates work flow; determines priorities; manages the budget; converts paper to electronic documents.

Meetings or travel manager: Coordinates meetings; plans agendas; secures speakers; negotiates hotel contracts; makes business travel arrangements; familiar with on-line research/booking.

Employee relations manager: Works in a human resources department, interviews and makes recommendations on hiring new employees; assists with employee benefits, work schedules, and personal concerns of employees.

Other advanced-level duties that you may be asked to perform include:

- Managing data and follow-up reports in a computerized accounting system
- Monitoring reports generated by electronic data interchange
- Disseminating press releases and other types of internal and external communications
- Assisting in research and gathering information for special projects
- Training personnel and others on computer hardware and software, as well as office procedures
- Facilitating e-meetings using technologies

SPECIALIZED OFFICE CAREER OPPORTUNITIES

Just as in any career, office professionals have an opportunity to specialize in many fields. In the fields of law, medicine, education, government, and technology, numerous career opportunities exist for the office professional.

Although the basic duties within each specialized field may be similar and the use of office technology the same, terminology, applications, and procedures vary greatly from area to area. A quick look at each field will help to clarify some of the differences.

The Legal Office Professional

Accuracy and speed are important requirements for a career in the legal field. Whether in a one-lawyer office or a large firm, the work of a law office is detailed and exacting. Terminology is precise; timing, organization, and confidentiality are essential.

Duties include keying and transcription. A knowledge of legal documents and legal terminology as well as good oral and written skills are important. The work is highly varied, ranging from managing the office to preparing legal documents and court papers; it also includes extensive contact with clients.

Many kinds of positions are available within the legal profession. They include opportunities in single-attorney offices; in partnerships; in large law firms; in the legal departments of major corporations; and in the local, state, and federal court systems. Legal practices vary from general law to specialization in such areas as real estate, corporate law, tax law, criminal law, estate planning, marital law, or labor law.

The Medical Office Professional

The medical office professional's special duties include managing the office, scheduling patients, quoting and collecting fees, preparing and processing insurance claim forms, ordering and maintaining supplies and equipment, transcribing dictation, maintaining patients' records, assisting and supporting patients, and performing clinical duties. Confidentiality of patient records must always be maintained.

Opportunities within the medical profession exist in physicians' offices, medical clinics, public health facilities, hospitals, health maintenance organizations, nursing homes, research centers, medical centers, foundations, laboratories, insurance agencies, private agencies, medical departments of large companies, educational institutions, companies that manufacture medical supplies and equipment, and medical transcription service companies.

The Educational Office Professional

A career in the educational field can be multifaceted regardless of the educational level. This office professional must have excellent communication skills and the ability to work under established policies and practices as well as to plan and organize work schedules. Computer skills are important, as is familiarity with other office equipment. The educational office professional must serve as liaison between students, teachers, administrators, coworkers, parents, and the local community, so good interpersonal skills are essential.

The duties of educational office professionals vary from institution to institution. Opportunities for such personnel exist from the preschool to the graduate level and can be in public, private, or church-affiliated schools, large or small. Specialized schools for special need students, vocational schools, and correctional schools also need office professionals. Many not-for-profit organizations, such as the National Education Association and the American Association of School Administrators, offer job opportunities.

The Government Office Professional

The largest employer in the United States is the federal government, which offers numerous opportunities for office professionals both here and abroad. To become eligible for most government positions, you must take a written civil service examination. Promotions are usually made from within based on the availability, demonstrated skills, and seniority of those applying.

Other positions are available in state, county, and municipal governments as well as in quasi-governmental agencies. Contact the Office of Personnel Management in the region in which you desire employment; it is the best source for checking available jobs in the public sector.

The Technical Office Professional

Aerospace, pharmaceuticals, engineering, environmental protection, life sciences, mathematics, and the physical sciences are just some of the career fields available to the technical office professional.

Knowledge of electronic office equipment is essential in these fields. Technical documents such as scientific reports and abstracts require proper formatting. Office professionals must have the ability to key technical data accurately and to proofread text that includes mathematical equations, symbols, and related data. A strong background in mathematics or science and a knowledge of technical terminology are definite assets. Confidentiality is also a critical element for this field.

The growth of research and technology, within both government and private companies, has created many opportunities for office professionals who have the ability to deal with technical terms and symbols.

PART-TIME, TEMPORARY, AND HOME OFFICE CAREERS

Changes in the demographics of the workforce, labor shortages, and the advancement of technology have made the options for office professionals more flexible. While most are employed on a full-time basis in a particular workplace, today's office professional also works part-time, as a temporary, or even from home.

Some businesses prefer hiring on a part-time rather than a full-time basis. An individual or firm may require only a few hours of work each day or a few days of work per week in order to fulfill necessary requirements. For some companies, dividing a full-time job between two part-time employees (job sharing) is a plus and has added flexibility. Part-time work enables individuals to maintain important career connections while allowing them to pursue other responsibilities and interests.

Temporary Career Options

Millions of temporary workers (temps) are used by businesses every day. Businesses outsource for a variety of reasons: to handle seasonal peak workloads better; to avoid problems recruiting and training permanent workers; or as a way to maintain lean permanent staffs. For various reasons, the temp career may be a viable option for today's office professional.

Two economic trends are also contributing to the use of temps. The first is a shortage of qualified workers. According to *The Occupational Outlook Handbook*, an annual publication from the U.S. Department of Labor, the demand for skilled clerical and technical help is forecasted to grow significantly faster than the demand for the workforce as a whole. For details, see www.bls.gov and look for career outlook.

The second trend is the changing lifestyles of the workforce itself. Factors such as downsizing, the aging of the workforce, fewer potential workers, and increased mobility have created a labor shortage.

As a result of these trends, a temporary office career fits with many career goals. Temps come in all ages and both genders and are highly trained. To keep pace with the growing demand for computer-literate workers, outsourcing services provide training to sharpen computer skills and to provide knowledge of current hardware and software. This not only helps the employer, but can also provide temps with skills that might otherwise never be learned or upgraded.

The Home Office Career and Telecommuting

For many millions of Americans, technology has allowed work to shift from offices to homes or off-site locations, part time or full time. The trend toward working at home is driven by the personal computer, which can be connected to the main work area so a worker can "telecommute." Increasingly, clerical workers use this option to do tasks formerly performed in offices, as do home-based entrepreneurs who provide services to numerous organizations. A home office career allows professionals to maintain skills and pursue a career. They can contribute to the organization while following other interests or while managing the household, all without having to leave home.

Here are some guidelines to follow when working at home:

- Establish a work schedule, specific hours when you plan to do your tasks, with "to do" and "follow-up" lists as if you were in the office. Good home office workers or telecommuters are people who are able to manage their own time and workload well, solve many of their own problems, and find satisfaction in completing tasks with minimal supervision.

- Establish with your manager(s) the hours when you will be available by phone or e-mail or call in at specified times.

- Organize your work schedule so most of the individual work is reserved for telecommuting days and collaborative work for times when everyone is in the office. But even when you are working at home, telecommunication tools—such as phones, e-mail, conference calls, and faxes—can be used to connect to your work team.

- Determine with your manager issues of security and which files you may take home. Be sure to log all files that you take out of the office. Electronic records-management systems that can be accessed from remote locations with proper security codes are the best solution for home office workers who need access to information.

- Be sure you have appropriate technology and home office furniture. For example, a mobile telecommuter who will be working in many locations should have a laptop or PDA (personal digital assistant). A person who spends a lot of time in a home office inputting data into a computer should have a PC, an ergonomic chair, and keyboard support to minimize potential injuries. (See Chapter 10—the same guidelines given there apply to setting up a home office workstation.) High speed transmission is essential if you will be spending considerable time on the Internet up- or downloading files. Also, fax capability is essential for many telecommuting employees. Many employers will provide the technology for the employee, and some will help defray the cost of the home office furniture.

- Consult your organization's policies regarding an employee's personal use of company-owned computer and equipment, as well as maintaining the integrity of information (i.e., formatted, filed, categorized) stored on paper and in electronic form.

• Sign an agreement that summarizes your organization's expectations. This agreement should include the days and hours you will be working at home, work assignments, reimbursement policy for phone calls and supplies, management contact expectations, company equipment and furniture to be provided, telecommunications hookup, equipment maintenance, and any additional conditions you feel are pertinent.

• Know that there is no "right" number of days for telecommuting. On the average, one to three days a week seems to be the practice. More time away can give you the feeling of being "out of the loop" and create morale problems, as well as make it hard for teams to schedule meetings.

• Remember that telecommuting is not a perk, an entitlement, or a benefit. It is an alternative way to work that is not for everyone. Not all jobs or personalities are suited for this type of work.

• Keep in mind that working at a distance is, in some respects, similar to working in the office. Good employees set expectations, give feedback to their team, and do all the other required tasks no matter where they work.

• You can contact the International Telework Association & Council (ITAC) (204 E Street NE, Washington, DC 20002, 202–547–6157 voice, 202–547–6348 fax, www.telecommute.org) for more information about telecommuting programs. TAC comprises individuals, corporations, educators, consultants, and vendors involved in telecommuting in both the private and public sectors.

PREPARATION FOR OTHER CAREERS

Unlike many other professions, the office profession offers many career options. Neither extensive preparation nor a degree in business administration or a technical or scientific field is necessary, but such degrees may be useful.

For example, an office professional who is interested in a career in the communications industry might take a position at a television station or public relations firm to gain firsthand experience. With that background, an office worker could advance to an account executive or a sales position. An office professional interested in law might train as a legal secretary, obtain a position in a law firm, and then advance to a paralegal position.

With the increased knowledge needed to use office technology, office professionals have found positions as equipment salespersons and as marketing support representatives. They have also become customer service representatives.

Traditional furniture vendors are expanding and diversifying their marketing horizons to include office furniture that is especially designed to meet the needs of the electronic office. Managers of such vendors often seek marketing representatives who are knowledgeable about the furniture required by the integrated office, its effects on personnel, and the expectations of users.

Other advanced office career options in the computer field include training directors, who train personnel in various software applications such as word processing, spreadsheet, or desktop publishing; programmers, who write the software that tells computers what operations to perform; systems analysts, who develop appropriate programs, systems, and applications for users; and equipment technicians, who repair and service computer hardware and accessories. Another option is to become an independent contractor, who works at home for firms that have no computer equipment or that need additional support during peak periods.

The likelihood that today's office professional will advance to an operational or managerial job is great, thanks to technology. Technology has freed the office professional to make more decisions and receive more recognition. Within this profession, you can guide your career in a direction that will be in harmony with your own talents. Growing numbers of office professionals find their careers following a path into technology, finance, desktop publishing, administration, personnel, and management.

No matter what field you decide to pursue, certifying your computer skills can be a plus. For more information on the various Microsoft Office User Specialist (MOUS) certifications available, go to www.mous.net or call 800–933–4493.

PROFESSIONAL DEVELOPMENT AND GROWTH

To advance in your career, it is important to continue education in your field. Reading is the best and easiest way to grow professionally. Current news magazines, business-oriented publications, and trade publications such as IAAP®'s *OfficePRO* magazine can keep you informed about events, trends, policies, and procedures.

If possible, enroll in continuing education courses. Colleges offer evening, weekend, and on-line courses; many give credit for life experiences. Take advantage of company-sponsored workshops and seminars. In addition, many professional organizations offer seminars to help office professionals understand and perform better.

Another good step is to join professional organizations, such as the International Association of Administrative Professionals® (IAAP®); the National Association of Legal Secretaries (NALS); the American Association for Medical Assistants (AAMA); the American Association for Medical Transcription (AAMT); and many others. These groups provide a wealth of information on information processing and evolving technologies. Most offer newsletters, magazines, seminars, workshops, and equipment exhibits.

Other groups, such as consultants, retailers, and manufacturers, offer seminars and information on such topics as how to integrate software and how to increase office productivity, as well as training in time management, office organization, and on-line services.

See About IAAP® on page 596.

PROFESSIONAL DEVELOPMENT THROUGH CERTIFICATION

IAAP® administers two business-oriented certification programs in the office professional field. Receiving these certifications is indicative of meeting the highest professional standards. The registered service marks for the ratings that measure administrative proficiency are the Certified Professional Secretary® (CPS®) and Certified Administrative Professional^{cm} (CAP^{cm}) rating. These ratings are obtained by (1) completing and verifying educational and employment experience requirements and (2) passing examinations administered each May and November by the Institute for Certification (IC), a department of IAAP®.

Working secretaries, students, and business educators are eligible to take the CPS® examination. Many colleges and universities grant academic credit hours to those with the CPS® rating who are enrolled in a degree program.

The CPS® examination is divided into three parts:

1. *Finance and Business Law:* 30% economics, 35% accounting, 35% business law (135 questions; 2 hours and 30 minutes).
2. *Office Systems and Administration:* 50% office technology, 25% office administration, 25% business communications (165 questions; 2 hours).
3. *Management:* 36% behavioral science in business, 19% human resources management, 45% organizations and management (165 questions; 2 hours).

The four-part CAP^{cm} exam is available to administrative professionals who have completed all experience and education requirements. The CAP^{cm} exam parts are:

1. *Finance and Business Law:* 30% economics, 35% accounting, 35% business law (135 questions; 2 hours and 30 minutes).
2. *Office Systems and Administration:* 50% office technology, 25% office administration, 25% business communications (165 questions; 2 hours).
3. *Management:* 36% behavioral science in business, 19% human resources management, 45% organizations and management (165 questions; 2 hours).
4. *Organizational Planning:* team skills, planning, and advanced administration. Scenario-based questions cover all areas (100–150 items; 3 hours and 30 minutes).

Certification is also possible in certain specialized fields. A legal secretary may become a Professional Legal Secretary (PLS). This is the only certification program for legal secretaries; it provides a standard measurement of legal secretarial knowledge and skills. Additional information can be obtained by contacting the National Association of Legal Secretaries.

Medical assistants are eligible to join the American Association of Medical Assistants (AAMA). The AAMA offers a certifying examination that upon successful passing leads to certification as a Certified Medical Assistant (CMA). This can be achieved through continuing education or through reexamination. For more information, contact the American Association of Medical Assistants.

Certification as a medical transcriptionist can be obtained through the American Association for Medical Transcription (AAMT). Their examination leads to certification as a Certified Medical Transcriptionist (CMT). Additional information can be obtained by contacting the American Association for Medical Transcription.

Office personnel in the educational field can obtain certification through the National Association of Educational Office Personnel (NAEOP). Their Professional Standards Program leads to the distinction of a Certified Educational Office Employee. This is awarded to those who meet established criteria.

Organizations for office professionals include:

General
International Association of Administrative Professionals®
10502 NW Ambassador Drive
Box 20404
Kansas City, MO 64195-0404
816–891–6600
Fax number: 816–891–9118
E-mail: service iaap-hq.org
Homepage: www.iaap-hq.org
Certifications: Certified Professional Secretary (CPS); Certified Administrative Professional (CAP).

Legal
NALS℠ Inc.
314 East Third Street, Suite 210
Tulsa, OK 74120
918–582–5188
Homepage: www.nals.org
Certifications: ALS basic certification; PLS advanced certification.

Educational
National Association of Educational Office Personnel
Box 12619
Wichita, KS 67277-2619
316–942–4822
Fax number: 316–342–7100
Homepage: www.naeop.org
Certifications: Numerous—check the Web site under the Professional Standards section.

Medical
American Association of Medical Assistants
20 North Wacker, Suite 1575
Chicago, IL 60606
312–899–1500
800–228–2262
Homepage: www.aama-ntl.org
Certifications: Certified Medical Assistant.
American Association for Medical Transcription
100 Sycamore Avenue
Modesto, CA 95354
800–578–9823
Homepage: www.aamt.org
Certifications: Certified Medical Transcriptionist (CMT).

SEMINARS, WORKSHOPS, AND TRAINING

In addition to certification, office professionals today must rely on seminars, workshops, and other training programs to achieve ongoing career development and to keep up with changing technology in the digital office.

Many companies provide in-house training programs to their employees as a means of keeping their workforce's skills at optimum levels. Some programs are taught by instructors from within the organization, such as administrative professionals. Others are hired from outside the company for their expertise in particular topics.

Other training programs are independent study. They may use manuals; an on-line program; tutorials; audiotapes; videotapes; or interactive video instruction. Interactive video instruction allows the trainee to become actively involved with the computer screen and keyboard. The trainee in effect directs the lesson by "dialoguing" with the computer.

SETTING PERSONAL GOALS

The growth in jobs for office professionals represents a major percentage of the total growth in jobs for white-collar workers. The office and all its related support areas offer great growth potential. As an office professional you have a better chance to achieve your personal goals if you know your own goals as well as the goals of your organization.

In order to set personal goals, know what you want out of life and how hard you are willing to work for it. Identify where you want to go and how to get there. Goals are benchmarks by which you can measure your progress. By setting goals, high achievers are able to seize opportunities to make goals realities.

Every job you hold is a critical step in the development of your career. A career requires long-term planning and commitment to reach your professional potential. A master career plan should consist of long-range goals and short-range, more immediate objectives. An inventory of the skills you have—the things you do well and enjoy—is the core of a plan for your career.

To build a successful career, you also must know the basic skills and components of your career. For example, if your goal is to become a technology trainer, you must know hardware and software, and the procedures involved to be an effective teacher. Such knowledge is usually gained through work experience and continuing education. The development of job and career objectives is an ongoing process.

When planning goals for your career, decide what role you want to pursue in the offices of both today and tomorrow. Be open-minded to maintain the flexibility needed for this ever-changing environment.

CAREER PATHS AND CAREER LADDERS

The average American today will work for 10 different employers, keep each job only 3.6 years, and change entire careers at least three times before retirement. Many will adopt new careers after retirement. These statistics may sound somewhat astonishing, but they show that career paths and career ladders are important elements in this process.

A career path addresses goals that have been established. Through a succession of positions, a person gains skills to achieve a career goal. Movement may be vertical or lateral, but continues in a particular direction.

Climbing the career ladder, on the other hand, begins when one has determined a career path and is advancing up the "rungs" through promotion. In any career, several career ladders exist. Within an office, a career ladder for word processing may exist as well as one for administrative services. Only you can determine which ladder you want to climb and create opportunities to climb the ladder.

FUTUREVISIONEERING™ YOUR CAREER

Technology has forever changed the way offices operate and the way information is handled. You can begin FutureVisioneering™ your career path by identifying emerging computer and communications technologies that can significantly impact how you work and can lead to expanded job opportunities.

Emerging information technology will produce revolutionary changes in all organizations. Workers will become even more dependent on desktop videoconferencing, artificial intelligence (AI), and voice recognition. Networking technology, both local area networks (LANs) and wide area networks (WANs), has made transmission of voice, data, and images faster, less expensive, and more widespread. Interactive three-dimensional video, very-high-bandwidth communication channels, virtual reality as a communications medium, and shape-recognition cameras may be part of an office assistant's future.

New technologies will also revolutionize how workers share information. More workers will individually manage information, making group knowledge increasingly important, through sharing face-to-face or by electronic means. Portable laptop computers, video/audio teleconferencing equipment, visualizers, optical scanners, smart electronic information display boards that connect to computers, and input tablets that process handwriting are examples of standard equipment for the modern business meeting. In addition, new electronic communication feedback systems and video WEBbing technology will be integrated into some of the more sophisticated meeting and training rooms.

One thing is certain—machines are not replacing the office professional in the office. If anything, they are enhancing and expanding the position to one of greater importance than ever. The future will be dominated by a new discipline, termed "knowledge management." As the office environment becomes electronic, the key to the office professional's career success lies in his or her ability to connect—people, information, and data—and to put them together for a particular use. Administrative support personnel are the gatekeepers of electronic channels. As these channels become more prevalent and better developed, the role of controlling and making sense of all this e-traffic will become even more important.

Staying up to date with the latest technologies and incorporating them into your work routine is necessary for both job security and job enhancement. Executive-search firms are reporting an increased demand for people with strong technology and telecommunications skills. They also report that because of technology, new supervisory jobs, such as videoconferencing specialists, desktop publishing specialists and coordinators, and Web site coordinators are arising in most organizations, especially growing companies. Continue to keep current by attending seminars, reading technology and communications magazines, and learning the latest versions of software applications. Become the office expert on software and in finding valuable business-related information on the Internet. Keeping everyone in your department up to date and serving as an end-user technology resource person ensures that you will be of great value to your organization.

Actively reengineering your job description must be an ongoing activity. Professionals can no longer continue to accept the status quo but must create future career opportunities. Perhaps it is time to become a FutureVisioneer™ by looking ahead, seeing the future, and creating the pathway to it.

Career advancement can be a job promotion or new job within your present company or a new position with another firm. To prepare for career opportunities, you must be able to:

- Prepare a resume
- Write a cover letter
- Fill out an employment application
- Interview successfully
- Follow up on the interview
- Complete employment tests
- Determine when to use employment agencies or other support networks

CHAPTER 2

CAREER

ADVANCEMENT

THE RESUME

A resume is a written summary of abilities, accomplishments, and work history. The purpose of the resume is to get an interview, not a job. Employers do not hire on the basis of a resume alone, but the resume should motivate an employer to meet you. Successful job seekers should prepare at least two versions of their resume. One version is read by people in 6 to 8 seconds. The other version is designed to be electronically examined and analyzed by a computer. Both resumes should have the following qualities:

- Resumes should be well organized. The preferred length is one or two pages of 8½-by-11-inch paper, no matter how many previous jobs or how much experience and education a candidate has.
- Resumes should emphasize strengths and accomplishments and show that the candidate is qualified for the available job. It should demonstrate excellent writing skills, with perfect grammar, spelling, and punctuation. A well-written resume is tailored to the available job, showing a knowledge of the necessary skills, talents, and background. A resume is not a life history, lengthy job description, or detailed listing of irrelevant earlier jobs.

All resumes should also have the following components:

- Heading
- Job objective
- Highlights of qualifications
- Work experience
- Education

Hard Copy and Electronic Resumes

Many companies use electronic methods to collect, screen, and file resumes. These electronic methods include scanning of resumes, accepting e-mail resumes, accessing Internet home page resumes, or having applicants complete on-line resume forms. If you have a choice, avoid having your resume scanned because of the errors that scanning software may introduce.

If you send your resume electronically, you may wish to add, "A formatted hard copy of this resume is available upon request," or follow up by postal mail with an attractively formatted resume.

Heading

The heading includes your name, address (including ZIP code), home, cell, and/or work telephone numbers (including area codes), and a professional sounding e-mail address. Do not include a personal Web page address unless the Web page supplements your resume. If a home telephone answering machine is used, the recording should be professional and to the point. If your present employer is aware of your job search, then include your work number. If it is impossible to talk with a prospective employer at a work phone, then omit it.

HINT: *Don't include pager numbers; employers dislike pagers and often won't call pager numbers.*

Some suggested styles for resume headings are shown in the sample resumes. (See Figures 2-1, 2-2, and 2-3 for examples.) See Figure 2-4 for an example of an optically scannable resume.

Job Objective

Start with a clear job objective that can be stated in five or six words. The job objective lets the employer know that you have gone through a thorough self-analysis and know what you want in your career. Tailor the objective to each employer being targeted and to each job being sought. If possible, the objective should match the wording of the advertisement.

The job objective immediately follows the heading and states a job title or specific occupational field.

Here are some possible job objectives:

- Administrative assistant to the director of sales
- Legal secretary for a law firm specializing in litigation
- Office support in the insurance industry
- Medical transcriptionist in a metropolitan hospital
- Records management specialist for a manufacturing firm

Highlights of Qualifications

Immediately after the objective comes a "profile" that states, in five or six lines, why you are the ideal person for this particular position. This section can also be called "Summary of Skills" or "Qualifications and Skills."

This section can include skills, years of experience, character traits, schools attended, fluency in languages, hardware and software you are proficient in, or anything else the employer might find important. Below is a list of suggestions for qualifications, which will work well in either a traditional or scanned resume.

- Ability to work well under pressure
- Ability to work well with all levels of management and personnel
- Able to learn new tasks quickly
- Bilingual; fluent in English and Spanish
- Innovative in developing workflow systems
- Proficient in use of Microsoft Office™ software

Professional Highlights

This is the core of the resume. Experience is listed in reverse chronological order or according to job functions. Reverse chronological order is preferable if you are staying in the same field, especially if your job history shows growth and development and no gaps in work history. Reverse chronological resumes list the most recent job first. (See Figures 2-1 and 2-3.) If there are many jobs to list, select the last four or five.

Listing experience by job functions is useful if you are changing careers, entering the job market for the first time, reentering the job market after an absence, have an irregular work history, or need to highlight volunteer experience. This type of resume describes your responsibilities over the years, starting with the most important work-related tasks. Your employers are listed separately.

Marcia Hernandez_____

38 South Hawthorne Way • Washington, DC 20009
202–555–7236 mhernandez@sonic.net

Job Objective   Administrative assistant with sales firm

QUALIFICATIONS AND SKILLS

- Sixteen years of office support experience, including customer relations
- Excellent time-management and organizational skills
- Self-motivated, dependable, and goal-oriented employee
- Skilled in written and verbal communications
- Professional appearance and high professional standards

PROFESSIONAL EXPERIENCE

2000–present   SENIOR SALES ASSISTANT
Bigelow Publishing Co., Washington, D.C.

Primary focus of this position is marketing and technical support for six sales representatives in Florida, West Virginia, Virginia, North Carolina, South Carolina, and Pennsylvania.
- Develop specialized education materials.
- Coordinate regional sales exhibits and conferences.
- Serve as liaison among central office, editorial staff, customers, and sales representatives.
- Research and compose correspondence for representatives.
- Coordinate city and county textbook adoptions, and develop and maintain production information.
- Access and update computerized inventory and customer database.

1995–2000   DISPATCHER
3M Business Products Sales, Inc., Reston, Virginia

Routed and dispatched 20 service representatives for copy machines in the greater Washington, D.C., area.

1990–1995   ORDER CLERK
3M Business Products Sales, Inc., Reston, Virginia

Received orders for 300 businesses over the telephone for office and school supplies in the greater Washington, D.C., area.

Figure 2-1 A reverse chronological resume for a person who is looking for work in the same field and who has no education beyond a high school diploma.

Joanne Jacobson CPS/CAP
3948 Grove Street • Kansas City, MO 64112
816–555–4930
jjacobson@aol.com

Objective: Position as an administrative assistant involving information services with a high degree of public contact.

HIGHLIGHTS OF QUALIFICATIONS

- Ten years of experience as an administrative assistant.
- Familiar with the PC and Macintosh plus a variety of word processing, database, and spreadsheet software.
- Learn new computer systems quickly.
- Consistently earned outstanding performance evaluations.
- Achieved the Certified Professional Secretary (CPS) rating, 1999.
- Earned Certified Administrative Professional (CAP) designation in 2001.

PROFESSIONAL EXPERIENCE

Organizational and Planning Skills
- Conducted in-house systems training on the computer network for 200 employees.
- Developed office procedures, including office manuals.
- Planned and supervised yearly national sales meetings for 200 employees, including choosing the meeting site, confirming speakers, and arranging for support services.
- Prepared all reports for the Board of Directors' monthly meetings.

Interpersonal/Communication Skills
- Served as a liaison with computer systems manager and outside consulting firm to coordinate the network.
- Coordinated payroll preparation with outside processing firm.
- Developed press releases.
- Prepared correspondence.

Computer Skills
- Researched, proposed, and supervised the installation of a $150,000 purchase of telecommunications and computer equipment.
- Prepared income and expense spreadsheets using Excel on the PC.
- Designed company newsletter on the Macintosh using Word and Photoshop software.

—Continued—

Figure 2-2 A resume highlighting job duties for a person with similar work experience in a variety of firms.

JOANNE JACOBSON CPS/CAP

Page 2 of 2

EMPLOYMENT HISTORY

1994–present	Administrative Assistant	First Interstate Bank Kansas City, Missouri
1991–1994	Administrative Assistant	Valley Bank Overland Park, Kansas
1988–1991	Office Support	Kellogg and Sons Blue Springs, Kansas
1986–1988	Office Support	Borden Foods Company East Point, Georgia

EDUCATION AND PROFESSIONAL AFFILIATIONS

Enrolled in Administrative Management program at Mission College, Kansas City, Missouri.

Member of International Association of Office Professionals

Figure 2-2 (continued).

KATHLEEN GLENN
102 Rancho Coati Drive
White Plains, NY 10604
914–555–9999
kglenn@aol.com

Objective   Office Assistant

QUALIFICATIONS

- Five years' experience in office environment; familiar with office procedures.
- Two years experience on the PC using word processing, spreadsheet, and desktop publishing software.
- Developed and implemented alphabetic and numeric filing systems.
- Excellent telephone communication skills; patient, personable, and loyal.
- Demonstrated ability to work independently and as a cooperative team member.

EXPERIENCE

1998–present   GABLER SALES COMPANY, White Plains, New York

Administrative Assistant: Duties include communicating with customers by telephone and scheduling appointments, creating and maintaining a database of customers, organizing an accurate alphabetic filing system, keyboarding correspondence and generating price lists and brochures, processing mail and shipping, preparing bank deposits, and maintaining records for taxes.

VOLUNTEER EXPERIENCE

1995–1998   THE PRACTICAL PRESS, White Plains, New York

Office assistant: Duties included answering marketing questions for telephone customers. Handled mail order of books, processed invoices, implemented bookkeeping procedures.

EDUCATION

Currently attending White Plains Community College, White Plains, New York

Working toward Administrative Assistant Certificate. To be completed May 20__.

Figure 2-3 A resume highlighting qualifications and accomplishments for a person with recent work experience.

Stella Anderson
1280 Ward Road
Penngrove, CA 94951
707–792–9026
sander@wco.com

Keyword Summary
PC, Word, Excel, PowerPoint, Access, Photoshop, QuickBooks, Outlook, Windows, Keyboard 50 wpm, 10 Key 10,000 kph, Telephone Skills, Spanish Fluency, Alphanumeric Filing, Dean's List, Team Player, Competitive, Communication Skills, Customer Oriented, Flexible, Industrious, Organizational Skills

Objective
Seeking an administrative assistant position that will utilize my computer and communications skills

Education
Santa Rosa Junior College, Petaluma, California
Administrative Assistant Certificate, 2001
3.25/4.0 GPA

Computer Experience and Training: Hardware: PC; Software: MS Word, Excel, Access, PowerPoint, Photoshop, QuickBooks, e-mail, Outlook

Relevant Coursework: Communication Skills, Business English, Business Math, Computerized Bookkeeping, Filing and Records Management

Experience
Interim Services, Santa Rosa, CA
Office Support and Receptionist
Answered up to a 4-line telephone system, organized appointment calendars, created and updated files, filed documents, prepared special mailings, distributed mail, handled customer inquiries, gave instructions in Spanish.

DeMartini Steak House, San Francisco, CA
Server
Nightly sales of $1,000–$2,000. Consistently won sales contests. Demonstrated excellent customer service skills.

Figure 2-4 An optically scannable resume.

Any major accomplishment can be included under the job function without stating the name of the employer. (See Figure 2-2.) Separating the job functions from employer names is particularly useful when changing from one type of business to another (for example, applying for a job in a nonprofit association after working for a manufacturer).

Whether the resume lists jobs reverse chronologically or by job functions, all descriptions should be clear. Phrases such as "worked as acting administrative assistant" or "worked as accountant" are too vague and will not give employers an idea of the work performed. Even the phrase "responsible for" does not give a good idea of job duties.

Employers want to know what you accomplished on the job, not just what your job description was. If you are writing a resume to be read by a person, you should use action verbs, which are verbs that help create a well-defined image of contributions and accomplishments. Listed below are some action verbs you could use to describe your accomplishments:

Analyze	Evaluate	Present
Assist	Examine	Process
Calculate	Generate	Produce
Collect	Implement	Purchase
Compose	Instruct	Recommend
Conduct	Interpret	Represent
Consult	Maintain	Research
Coordinate	Manage	Review
Create	Order	Save
Design	Organize	Schedule
Develop	Perform	Supervise
Diagnose	Plan	Train
Direct	Prepare	Write

If you are writing a scannable resume, keywords are important. Keywords are more of the noun or noun-phrase type, such as total quality management, customer support, cash-flow management, payroll, computerized systems, or documentation of patient charts. A keyword can also be the words listed in advertisements or job descriptions for the type of job that you want.

Numbers and figures should be included whenever possible. Money-saving techniques should be stated. "Managed yearly operating budget of $170,000" is more impressive than "managed budget." Supervisory experience should be emphasized, stating how many people were hired, trained, and supervised. If all work experience is with one employer, list each position separately to show job progression.

The following are additional suggestions for writing about your experience:

- Avoid long sentences. A description of a job or job duty should be ten lines long or less and list the accomplishments most relevant to the position you would like to fill. Omit accomplishments that have nothing to do with the target job.

- Prioritize descriptions by importance, impressiveness, and relevance to the job being sought.
- Avoid using "I," for example, "I was responsible for supervising five employees. In this position I did . . . " Instead, use action verbs without a pronoun: "Managed and maintained local area network of 15 office computers. Recommended selection and purchase of new database software."
- Use years instead of months and days: 2000–present or 2001–2003.
- Write "continued" on the bottom of the first page of a two-page resume and your full name and "page two" on the second page. (See Figure 2-2.)
- Omit jobs that go back 10 or 15 years. It is not necessary to list every position ever held. Jobs can be summarized with a statement such as "Prior Relevant Experience" without mentioning dates.
- Describe duties in detail only once if several jobs involved similar responsibilities. Avoid giving several examples of work performed when one is adequate.
- Omit company addresses; the name and location of the company are adequate.
- Include home-based and volunteer work if job experience is limited. (See Figure 2-3 for an example of how to include volunteer work on a resume.) Volunteer work and part-time jobs should not be included if work experience is extensive.

Education

If your education occurred within the last five years and is related to the job, it can be emphasized by placing the information about it (including the years) immediately after the job objective. If you have been out of school for some time or your education is not related to the job, you may decide to deemphasize it by placing this information at the bottom of the resume and omitting the years. However, most scanning software programs are not programmed to read education if the dates are omitted.

Providing graduation years will give an employer an idea of your age, which could be used to eliminate qualified candidates. Omit reference to high school if you attended college or hold post-high school degrees. List each associate, bachelor's, or master's degree separately unless they were earned from the same institution. The date should be included if a degree was earned recently.

If an associate, bachelor's, or master's degree has been earned, list the degrees as follows:

▲ Santa Rosa Junior College, Santa Rosa, CA
  Associate Degree in Business Office Technology
▲ Dana College, Blair, NE
  Bachelor's Degree in Business Administration
▲ University of Wyoming, Laramie, WY
  Master of Business Administration

If you want or need a job for which you might appear overqualified, list only the level of education expected for the position.

If you have taken classes beyond high school but have not earned a degree, list the institution and courses relevant to the prospective job. Include seminars or other job training. It is also appropriate to list professional certifications such as the Certified Professional Secretary® (CPS®) rating. The following are examples:

▲ College of Marin, Kentfield, CA
   Completed courses include: Computerized Accounting, Word, and Excel.
▲ Findlay University, Findlay, OH
   Will receive a Bachelor of Science degree in Accounting, August 20__ .
   Achieved a 3.8 grade point average (out of a possible 4.0).
▲ San Francisco State University, San Francisco, CA
   Completed 10 hours graduate work in Business Administration.
▲ Achieved the Certified Professional Secretary® (CPS®) rating, 20__ .
▲ Attended Certified Professional Secretary® (CPS®) Seminar, June 20__ , Savannah, GA
   Received 2.1 CEU for the Local Area Network courses.

If you have completed no education beyond high school, high school can be either included or omitted. The year of graduation is not necessary unless it was recent. The following is an example:

▲ Graduated from Petaluma High School, Petaluma, CA

Here are some other resume preparation techniques:

- Include academic awards and grade point average if they are impressive.
- Include major awards if they are relevant to your profession. For example, "Won a national award for designing a computerized loan amortization program."
- Include leadership roles, such as holding an office in a professional association or an important club. This information is stated under a "Professional Associations" heading. For example, "President of the Dallas chapter, International Association of Administrative Professionals™, 2000–2001."
- Omit hobbies unless they are relevant to the job.
- Do not include references. They can be given when the employer is serious about a candidate. It is not necessary to say "References provided upon request."
- Avoid buzzwords and abbreviations unless they are related to the industry to which you are applying. If the employer uses jargon and detailed technical terms to describe required qualifications, it is acceptable to use such words.
- Omit salary requirements; they will be discussed during the interview.

- Do not give reasons for leaving previous jobs. This information will come up either on the employment application or during the interview.
- Never include personal information such as height, age, weight, sex, health, and status. It is illegal for a job interviewer to ask you about such matters.

THE COVER LETTER

A cover letter is sent to a prospective employer with the resume. A personalized cover letter gives applicants an additional opportunity to sell themselves. It usually describes how the qualifications and skills listed on the resume correspond with those required for the job. A three-paragraph letter will be sufficient in most cases. Your cover letter should cover the following points:

- It should be readable, to the point, and refer to the specific job. Some job openings attract hundreds of responses, so the cover letter should be so well-written as to place it in the category of applicants the firm "definitely will interview."
- It should be keyed, no longer than one page ($8\frac{1}{2}$ by 11 inches), and printed on paper that matches the paper used for the resume. Perfect spelling, grammar, and punctuation are necessary, because they show the care you put into your work. Format the letter using short paragraphs, bullets, and white space to make the letter easy to read.
- It should be addressed to a specific individual. If an individual's name is not listed in an advertisement or job announcement, phone the company to find out the name of the person making the hiring decision, the correct spelling of the name, and the person's title. If there is no company name or phone number listed in an advertisement, address your letter "Dear Manager" or "Dear Selection Committee."
- Do not use an envelope from your current company to mail your letter. Always affix the correct postage.

First Paragraph

The first paragraph is the introduction and answers the following questions:

- Why are you writing?
- Where or how did you learn about the job?
- What is your most important qualification for the job?

Avoid starting out in an unconventional or annoying way. A direct statement is more positive and professional than a question, such as "Are you looking for a dynamic and talented administrative assistant?" The following is an example of an opening for a job advertised in a newspaper. It is not necessary to repeat the exact words of an advertisement.

Maralee Shadle
394 East Forest Avenue
Sonoma, CA 95476
707–555–4883
mshadle@aol.com
May 8, 20–

Mr. Richard Herndon, Director
Valley of the Moon Hospital
384 Oak Leaf Lane
Sonoma, CA 95476

Dear Mr. Herndon:

I am applying for the administrative assistant's position advertised on May 7 in
The Press Democrat. I am skilled on the PC, detail oriented, and able to work
well under pressure.

With five years of experience as an administrative assistant in the advertising
department of a Fortune 500 firm, I know the importance of meeting
deadlines and following through on details. I am exceptionally well organized
and have a wide range of experience, including supervising and training a staff
of 20. My computer skills include expertise in Excel, Word, PowerPoint, Access,
and Photoshop.

Valley of the Moon is well known in Sonoma County for its contributions to
the community. I feel that I have much to offer the hospital and would enjoy
discussing my qualifications and your needs in person. Please contact me at
707–555–4883 to schedule an appointment.

Sincerely,

Maralee Shadle

Figure 2-5 Cover letter showing work experience correlating closely with the job opening.

Peggy Girardi
4390 Olive Street
Pasadena, CA 91104
818–555–9938
pgirardi@earthlink.net
June 23, 20–

Ms. Christie Rummler
Personnel Manager
Lifetime, Inc.
Department 2093, Box 24
Pasadena, CA 91109-7237

Dear Ms. Rummler:

I am applying for the administrative position advertised on June 22 in the *Los Angeles Times*. I have extensive experience in office procedures and support functions and have several years of management responsibilities.

My last five years have been spent as an administrative assistant to an executive vice president. Some of my accomplishments include complete organization and management of procedures for our division of 50 support staff. I have designed Web sites, brochures, and flyers using a wide variety of software. Although the enclosed resume states some of my skills, it does not take into consideration my willingness to take on new tasks, ability to learn quickly, and desire to succeed.

I welcome the opportunity to talk with you about the position and my interest in working for Lifetime, which provides outstanding health care products. I can be reached at 818–555–9938.

Sincerely,

Peggy Girardi

Figure 2-6 Cover letter showing a willingness to take on new responsibilities.

▲ I am applying for the bookkeeping position advertised in the May 10 edition of the *San Francisco Chronicle.*

If an instructor, friend, or employee of the firm told you of a job opening, state that fact also.

▲ Carol Starnes, instructor at Glendale College, suggested I contact you about the office support position available at XYZ Company.

▲ Richard Kerry of Interstate Bank told me a new branch bank was opening in Fremont.

The second part of the first paragraph indicates your main qualifications for the job and should be dynamic. Select one fact that justifies suitability for the job.

▲ I have ten years' experience as an office manager for the national headquarters of an insurance agency.

▲ I have been an administrative assistant to the president for the past five years.

▲ I am a recent graduate of San Jose State University, with a degree in accounting.

Second Paragraph

The second paragraph emphasizes education and work background and creates interest in you as an applicant. It may be six or seven sentences long and it must relate your education and experience directly to the available job. It should describe exactly how schoolwork and job experience qualify you to function in the job advertised. Your goal is to create interest in you as an applicant. State your knowledge about the company in the opening sentence to show your interest in a job with that firm. Use terms and phrases that are meaningful to the employer. The following is an example of an opening statement about the company:

▲ Because Company X is well known for its technical expertise, you are looking for employees who are experienced in handling technical information.

The work experience description indicates how your experience will be valuable to an employer and does not describe your desire for a job. (See Figures 2-5 and 2-6.) For example, avoid this kind of sentence when replying to an advertisement for a position requiring word processing skills: "I have worked with Word software before, and this experience will give me the edge in operating it. I can adjust quickly to any working environment." The following sentence is more meaningful to an employer, because it describes what you can do for him or her:

▲ I am a highly motivated self-starter with three years' experience using Microsoft Office software on a PC. My work experience includes writing and editing customer reply letters, keying and formatting the company newsletter, developing promotional brochures and flyers, and producing the company's annual report.

Third Paragraph

The third paragraph asks for an interview and indicates your availability for one. This paragraph is usually only two or three sentences long. The following is an example:

▲ I would like to schedule an interview to further discuss the possibilities of our working together. I can be reached at 415–555–3994 after 4 P.M. during the week.

Some people recommend stating that you will call in a week to ten days to set up a meeting. This tactic may or may not work. Depending on the size of the company and the number of applications received, employers might not accept calls from a prospective employee. Employers who travel may not be available at the time the call is made.

TRANSMITTING A RESUME AND COVER LETTER

Resumes Screened by an Individual

Resumes screened by an individual (as opposed to being scanned by a computer) should be attractive to the eye. Word-processed resumes may be easily and quickly customized, changed, or corrected. The following are suggestions for this style of resume:

- Use no more than two or three different typefaces and type sizes.
- Do not overuse type styles such as bold, italic, and uppercase.
- Use wide margins, proportional spacing, and indentions.
- Select off-white or white 16- to 20-pound bond paper.
- Use a printer that provides a high resolution.

Faxing

If an employer has asked for a faxed resume, include a cover sheet indicating the name of the person requesting the resume and a brief message stating why the resume is being faxed. If you have the address, mail the original resume immediately with a cover letter explaining that the resume has been faxed. If you are called for an interview, take a copy of your resume with you to the appointment.

HINT: *Before you send your resume electronically to any company or service, be sure that the organization is credible. There have been incidents in which individuals have stolen other people's identities by using resumes obtained fraudulently through electronic sources.*

E-Mailing

If the resume is sent by e-mail, include the cover letter as part of the e-mail message and limit the content to three short paragraphs so it runs no longer than about one screen. Use plain text and make certain the lines are no more than 60 characters in length. Include a salutation ("Dear Ms. Rummler") and a standard closing (such as "Sincerely"). Leave blank lines between paragraphs. Test the message by sending it to a friend or to your own e-mail account.

Optically-Scannable Resumes

Many companies scan resumes so their computers can search using keywords. Keywords are words or phrases that define the requisites of a job. Because computer-read resumes are designed to be scanned and not read by an individual, use the following guidelines:

- Align the entire document along the left margin, with 1½-inch left and right margins.
- Place name, address, phone number, fax number, and e-mail address on separate lines.
- Use plain, standard sans serif fonts such as Arial or Helvetica or serif fonts such as Times Roman or Courier in a 12- to 14-point size.
- Avoid tabs, which can cause an error for the optical scanning equipment.
- Avoid italic text, script, underlining, columns, graphics or pictures, shadowing, and shading. Bold can be scanned but it too tends to cause errors.
- Avoid horizontal and vertical lines as well as parentheses and brackets.
- Use a paper clip, not a staple, to hold more than one page together. Be sure to include name, telephone number, and date at the top of each page. Also, label pages out of total number of pages sent (e.g., page 1 of 2, page 2 of 2, etc.).
- Use 20-pound white paper with black ink printed on a laser or ink-jet printer. A photocopy or fax may not scan.
- Send the resume unfolded and flat in a large envelope.

Converting a Resume into an Electronic Format

Instead of rekeying your existing resume, you may convert your resume into ASCII, or plain text format with line breaks, by using your word processing program's Save As option. Converting your file will remove formatting commands such as boldfacing, centering, bullets, and graphic lines. After saving the resume, carefully check and correct all errors and compare the new resume to the guidelines listed above.

E-mailing a Resume

Do not send a resume as an attachment without knowing the employer's required format. Carefully follow the employer's instructions. A recipient may be reluctant to open attachments for fear of viruses. If your resume is in an HTML format, look at it with several different browsers. Always send a test copy of your e-mail resume to yourself or someone else to check the formatting.

Resumes for On-line Employers and Internet Resume Banks

Many Internet resume banks and some employers offer on-line inputting of resumes into databases. Before completing the on-line forms, print the forms to study them. Assume that all on-line resume banks will scan and sort the resumes by keywords.

Web Page

Developing a Web page is a way to demonstrate the ability to use audio, video, and interactive features. Several free Web page builders are available on the Internet that allow experimentation. A Web page is a supplement, not a replacement, for the more traditional resume.

Many employers accept electronic or e-mail resumes, make available on-line resume forms, and receive resumes directly or through or a resume bank service.

Keyword resumes should include nouns and verbs that reflect skills and experiences. Examples of keywords include:

- Skills: Programming Experiences, Systems Analysis, Establishing an Electronic Records System, Computer Applications
- Job titles: Administrative Manager, Administrative Assistant, Executive Assistant, Research Coordinator, Human Resource Specialist, Executive Secretary to the President
- Unique experiences: Team Facilitator for New Product Launch, Meeting Coordinator for Video Conferences, Project Manager for National Sales Meeting
- Industry terminology: Windows XP®, Desktop Publishing, Computer Aided Design (CAD), Computer-Based Training (CBT), International Association of Administrative Professionals™ (IAAP™)
- Education: BS in Business Administration, MBA, AS in Administrative Studies
- Certifications: CPS® (Certified Professional Secretary®), CAP (Certified Administrative Professional), Microsoft Office User Specialist® (MOUS)

A keyword summary at the beginning of a resume increases the number of hits a resume generates. Keywords should also be included in the cover letter.

Some job applicants use Web-based resumes, which often reside on a personal home page. Web-based resumes can range from quite ordinary to very elaborate. Web resumes are often longer than one or two pages. Links to portfolio items of interest to employers are usually included. Prospective employers have the advantage of choosing to concentrate on those topics of information that interests them.

Some of the more popular sites that post jobs on the Web include:

America's Job Bank (www.ajb.dni.us). This computerized network links state employment service offices to provide job seekers with the country's largest pool of active job opportunities and nationwide exposure for their resumes. For employers, it provides rapid, national exposure for job openings and an easily accessible pool of candidates.

America's Talent Bank (www.ajb.dni.us/html/atb__home.html). Supported by the Department of Labor, America's Talent Bank (ATB) is a product of state employment service agencies and is provided as an additional service to the public. It also provides a nationwide electronic resume system.

Job Source Network (www.jobsourcenetwork.com). Thousands of U.S. and international job sites are linked on this site, which also publishes career resource publications.

Additionally, on-line job postings, a resume databank, and other employment-related information are available on **Headhunter** (www.headhunter.net) and **Monster Board** (www.monster.com).

THE EMPLOYMENT APPLICATION

Many employers ask a prospective employee to complete an employment application. Applications are hard copies obtained either from the employer or downloaded from an employer's Web page or an on-line application filled out on the computer.

Hard Copy Employment Application: It is important that the employment application be filled out neatly and accurately. If the application can be completed at home, where there are fewer distractions, there will be less possibility of error. Make a copy of the application and fill it out as practice before completing the actual application. Answer all questions truthfully and as accurately as possible.

Read the directions carefully. If it says to print or type all responses, a keyboarded copy will make the most favorable impression, assuming corrections can easily be made. If a typewriter is not available, use a pen with dark ink that will not smear. Do not use a pencil.

Fill in all blanks. If an item does not apply, write "N/A," which means "not applicable," or use a dash (—). Usually an application requires more information than is on a resume. There may be questions about salary, your reason for leaving your last job, and references.

On-line Application: If possible, print out the on-line application before actually completing it on-line. Once an on-line application is started, it may take up to 30 or more minutes to complete. To save keying time and to ensure accuracy, also have an electronic version of the resume open and use the copy (ctrl + c) and paste (ctrl + v) functions to transfer information from the resume into the on-line application. Before submitting the application, double-check the application for accuracy.

Personal Information

Your name, address (including ZIP code), and home phone number will always be requested. Other items may include work telephone number and e-mail address.

Unless height and weight directly relate to a job requirement (police officer, for example), these questions are illegal. Nor should an employer ask about marital status, number and ages of children, or date of birth. Asking for proof of age after hiring is acceptable. (For other illegal questions that should not be asked on an application form, see the section Illegal Questions later in this chapter.)

Candidates for civic appointments or government positions may be asked to waive the privilege of confidentiality of information on file at federal, state, or city agencies. To know ahead of time what is in those records, contact the Federal Information Center in the nearest city.

Education

Most applications have a section for education. Unless the application states otherwise, list the most recent education first and work backwards. Information requested often includes the name of the educational institution, dates attended, grade point average, credits completed, and the full address.

Job Experience

This section will ask for the names and addresses (including ZIP codes) of current and previous employers and dates employed. Usually the current job is listed first. The application may ask the name of your supervisor, his or her phone number, and job title.

If a job description is asked for, use action verbs. There will probably only be room for a few words, so use the ones most relevant to the job. If you prefer that the interviewer not contact your present employer without your permission, a note to that effect can be placed in the margin of the hard copy application.

You may be asked your reason for leaving past jobs. If the reason is that you received a promotion, make certain the next job listed actually is a promotion. Try to avoid using the term "fired"; reword to "looking for a more responsible position" or "prefer to discuss in interview." "To raise a family" and "to return to school" are also possible responses.

If the application has a blank for "salary requested," you can either list a salary range or write "negotiable" or "open." It is also appropriate to leave this item blank if you wish. If you fill in an amount, however, be sure it is accurate.

References

The best references are former employers or teachers who can relate positive information about you. Friends and relatives are not appropriate although coworkers are acceptable. All references should be contacted ahead of time so they are not surprised by phone calls. Their names, addresses, phone numbers, and occupations will probably be requested.

Researching the Company

If you learn as much as possible about the company, its products, and the interviewer prior to the interview, you will show the interviewer how interested you are in the job. The reference librarian at a public library is a good source of information. Information about many companies is available on-line. Go to the company's Web page, enter the company's name into a search engine, and search local and on-line newspapers for information about the company and its industry.

Before going to the job interview, you should:

- Secure a copy of the company's annual report, if possible, through the company, the public library, or the Chamber of Commerce. Try to determine the goals of the company from your research.
- Know the company's major products and services.
- Be aware of the company's competition.
- Find out about the company's reputation.
- Ask others about the organization and the interviewer. Try to find someone who works for the company and talk with them to determine the company's culture. Try to find someone who has been interviewed by the person who will be interviewing you.
- Know the supervisory role of the person doing the interviewing.

THE JOB INTERVIEW

Preparing for the Interview

A job interview is an opportunity for you to learn more about a company and a job and for the employer to see if you match the needs of the company. Some positions may require two or three interviews. The higher the job level and the more bureaucratic the organization, the more interviews there will be.

A successful job interview calls for a candidate to do the following:

- Dress conservatively and appropriately.
- Arrive on time.
- Maintain eye contact.
- Greet interviewer with a firm handshake.
- Demonstrate enthusiasm and initiative.
- Use good speech and grammar and the same kind of action verbs used in the resume.
- Indicate specific job goals.
- Bring extra resumes, samples of work, educational transcripts, or performance reviews.
- Listen carefully to questions.
- Think before you answer.
- Act naturally.
- Be informed about the company.
- Have questions to ask about the position.
- Be realistic about salary.

Appearance and Behavior

Research shows that most interviewers decide whether to hire someone in the first 10 to 30 seconds of the interview. The goal of a prospective employee is to make that first impression positive.

One of the ways to make a good first impression is to be well-groomed and appropriately dressed. Your clothes must be clean, pressed, in good condition and comfortable. When interviewing, you should wear the kinds of clothes that would be worn in the office. When in doubt, ask the recruiter or hiring manager before the interview.

Good manners require eye contact and a firm handshake. Eye contact is absolutely essential, and a lack of it may cost you the job. A firm handshake is also important. If you get nervous, hold a cotton handkerchief in your hands to absorb any moisture before shaking hands.

It is best to act self-confident, rather than shy. Most employers are looking for someone who is assertive, self-assured, and competent. Even if you desperately need or want the job, you should not convey this during the interview.

Interview Questions

An effective interviewer evaluates skills, abilities, and experience. At the same time, the interviewer makes judgments about a candidate's motivation, enthusiasm, and ability

to fit into the organization. Keep your answers on a professional, not a personal, level. Some possible interview questions may include:

Q: Tell me something about yourself.

HINT: *Outline several strong work-related points and accomplishments; make a summary statement and then stop talking.*

Q: Tell me about your professional experience. What are your most important achievements?

HINT: *Mention the most impressive achievement first; prepare success stories ahead of time.*

Q: What are your goals?

HINT: *Be general and mention that you see yourself gaining increased responsibility, if the firm has opportunities for advancement.*

Q: What are your major strengths?

HINT: *Highlight qualities that will help you succeed in the job available (for example, you work hard, learn quickly, and are conscientious).*

Q: What are your major weaknesses? What areas do you need to improve?

HINT: *Disguise weaknesses as strengths (for example, "I like to stick with a problem until I solve it"; "Sometimes I have ignored my family to finish a project"); select a minor weakness that you discovered early in your career and describe how you overcame it.*

Q: Why are you looking for a new position? Why did you leave Company X?

HINT: *Indicate a desire for greater responsibility and challenge or an opportunity to use talents not used in the present position; avoid mentioning money, personality conflicts, or anything that is not a major component of the job. Never deride a former employer.*

Q: Why do you want to work for this company?

HINT: *Show familiarity with the company; draw on the research you did. By asking open-ended questions such as these, the employer can learn about a prospective employee's communication skills and thought processes.*

The following are some suggestions for answering open-ended questions:

- Listen to the question and answer all parts of it.
- Show that the question has been anticipated by answering questions directly.
- Describe education and work experience in a clear, concise way.
- Describe the most important results and accomplishments of your career or experiences.
- Ask the interviewer to clarify the question if you are in doubt about its meaning.
- Let the interviewer set the pace of the discussion. An interviewer should be in control.
- Avoid giving either lengthy answers or simple "yes" or "no" answers. Keep your answers to the point.
- Discuss problem areas briefly and honestly.
- Do not criticize former employers. Avoid displaying bitterness and a negative attitude.

Illegal Questions

When applying for a job, a person cannot be discriminated against because of race, color, national origin, religion, sex, age, or, in many cases, physical or mental handicaps. The following questions are illegal:

- Are you married (single, divorced)?
- Do you have children? How old are they? What are your child care arrangements?
- Are you planning a family?
- How old are you?
- Do you have any handicaps?
- Have you ever received psychiatric or psychological treatment?
- What race are you?
- Where were you born? Where were your parents (spouse) born?
- Of what country are you a citizen?
- Have you ever been arrested?
- What is your credit rating?
- What is your religion?
- You went to St. Michael's College. Is that a religiously affiliated school?
- Do you belong to any unions?

If an illegal question is asked, there are several options available:

- If the job is interesting and the answer will help rather than hurt your chances, answer the question. After you are hired, bring the illegal question to the attention of the interviewer.
- Do not answer immediately. After a long pause, quietly ask, "Why did you ask that question?"
- Ask politely what the question has to do with job performance. Explain that the question does not pertain to your ability to do the job.
- State that you would like to discuss the job to see whether you are interested and that after that discussion, you would be willing to talk about other things.

Advice and assistance on job discrimination issues are available from state labor and rights agencies or from an office of the Equal Employment Opportunity Commission.

Panel Interviews

This type of interview is becoming common and is used frequently by government employers, schools, banks, and consulting firms. Usually each interviewer will have a specialty or concern that he or she feels is important and will ask more technical questions. Because several people are involved, you may feel more pressure.

The following are techniques for dealing with a panel interview:

- Rephrase the question to give yourself more time to think of an answer.
- If you do not know the answer to a question, say so.
- Write down the first name of each interviewer and arrange the names according to where each person is sitting. Use the list to address the panel members individually.
- Make eye contact with all members of the panel, not just the one who has asked you the question. Do not ignore anyone in the group. Start and finish each answer with the person who asked the question.
- Include the information you want the group to know. Do not merely respond; treat the group interview as if it were a regular interview.
- Avoid the tendency to feel overconfident if you know one or two members of the panel. Approach each question as if the members of the panel know nothing about your work experience and background.
- Use the name of each interviewer at the end of the interview, shake hands, smile, make eye contact, and say words such as, "Thank you for your time," or "I enjoyed meeting with you" to each interviewer.

Computer Interview

Some companies conduct screening interviews by computer. Applicants answer carefully selected questions on the computer. The human interviewer reviews the report generated by the computer, which includes contradictory responses and highlights any potential problem areas. The report also generates a list of structured interview questions to ask, should the applicant be invited back for a face-to-face interview.

Research has shown that applicants respond more honestly to computer-generated questions and are less likely to provide socially acceptable responses. Be careful to be consistent and not to divulge too much information during a computer interview but be honest and do not write or select answers that you think the company wants to hear.

Video Interview

Some companies are recognizing the cost benefits of screening or interviewing an out-of-state candidate using video technology. The candidate visits a branch office or public video-conference facility. The technology allows for two-way viewing and listening. One or more corporate interviewers participates. Except for the fact that the candidate is not physically in the same room as the interviewer, the process is about the same as a face-to-face interview. Another video interview technique is to have the candidate answer a series of questions and submit the video. Some job candidates incorporate video presentations into employment materials.

Voice Mail Interview

Some employers use voice mail systems to screen applicants. Typically an applicant is asked a series of questions, such as "What can you tell us about yourself?" or "Identify four characteristics that others use in describing you."

The best way to handle a voice mail interview is to hang up after you hear the questions, think about what you want to say, and call back. Have your resume, cover letter, and an outline of answers to the questions in front of you as you complete the voice mail interview.

Telephone Interview

To increase effectiveness in a telephone interview, prepare an agenda in advance. Plan to have a comfortable area to take the calls and take notes while you talk. Keep paper, pens, and the agenda by the telephone. If your telephone skills are not as strong as you wish, ask a friend to call you and ask you typical interview questions. Plan a strong closing, ask what the next step will be, and ask whether you can meet with the interviewer in person.

Problem Areas

Several problem areas may come up in the interview. However, they can be neutralized with the right strategy. Major problem areas are discussed below.

Being fired, although problematic, is not the worst thing that can happen. The reason for being fired is important. If you were fired because you were unqualified for a job, you have a serious problem to overcome. A response might be: "I realized after I took the job it was wrong for me. I tried to stay with it, but they asked me to leave. Now I have a better idea of the kind of job that would be best for me."

If the firing resulted from a personality conflict, indicate that to the interviewer. Give the employer names of people who can describe the work you did and the circumstances of the dismissal. Do not go into lengthy details but do offer an honest perspective.

If you were dismissed as part of a major change in the company, explain that. Mergers and acquisitions have made layoffs common.

Emotional problems can be another area of concern. Use your own judgment before discussing emotional, alcohol, or drug problems. Some companies may understand, but others may hold these problems against job candidates. Unless such a problem became an issue in a previous job, it may be better to refrain from discussing it.

Health problems can also raise questions. An employer may ask whether applicants have any health problems or handicaps that may affect work performance. If you do have physical limitations (such as the inability to lift more than 20 pounds) that will affect your ability to do the job, mention this during the interview. If your limitation does not affect your work performance, do not discuss it during the interview.

Past criminal activity can present difficulties. Some employers will ask whether you have been convicted of a crime other than a minor traffic violation. The key word is "conviction." If you were arrested but not convicted, then the arrest requires no further discussion.

It is illegal for an employer to check a person's arrest, court, or conviction record if it does not substantially relate to the responsibilities of the prospective job. Any lawful questions about past encounters with the law should be answered truthfully. If a record has been sealed, a conviction has been reversed, or you have been pardoned, it is legal to answer any questions about the conviction in the negative.

Gaps in work history may raise a few eyebrows. Do not be defensive. Explain that the job market was tight or that you took time off to go back to school, travel, take care of your children, or define career objectives.

Job hopping, too, can be an issue. Explain that it was necessary to change jobs frequently because of factors beyond your control, such as company layoffs or company moves. Mention your eagerness to make a long-term commitment to the next employer.

Questions to Ask the Interviewer

An important goal of the job interview is to discover whether you are interested in the job. Here are some questions to ask the prospective employer:

- Why is this job open?
- Would you describe a typical day?
- Why did the person who previously held this job leave?
- What are your expectations for this job?
- To whom would I be reporting?
- What are the promotional and career opportunities in the organization?
- With what kind of team will I work?
- Does the company promote or sponsor advanced education for its employees?
- Are my background and experience a good match for this job?
- When do you expect to make a decision on this position?
- When can I expect to hear from you?

Salary Negotiation

You should know the salary range for the open position or for similar jobs before going to the interview. Researching the company and the job often reveals this type of information. If your research shows that the salary is significantly below what you are willing to accept, it is best to decline the interview.

Here are some ways to negotiate salary:

- Let the interviewer introduce the subject of money.
- Avoid disclosing your present salary until it looks like the company is serious about hiring you.
- Turn a direct question to you about salary into a question to the interviewer, such as, "What is your standard salary range for this position?"
- Be prepared to answer any questions about salary. Be honest about previous salaries.
- Start negotiating as high in the range as possible, preferably toward the top of the range.
- Never react with anger or surprise. Pause to think.
- Take 24 hours to think about every job offer.
- If the salary is lower than you are willing to accept, look for other areas for negotiation, such as vacation time, shorter working hours, tuition for additional school or training, bonuses, stock options, matching retirement funds, and other perks. It may also be possible to negotiate a performance review and salary increase in three months.

THE FOLLOW-UP LETTER

Follow up on every job interview to each person who interviewed you. A follow-up letter is usually more effective than a telephone call because the employer can review the letter during the decision-making process. The letter can also bring up any additional information you may have omitted during the interview, although there is no need to restate information already on the resume or in the cover letter. In the follow-up letter, you can express interest in the job or indicate otherwise. (See Figure 2-7.)

Here are some tips for the follow-up letter:

- Handwrite or keyboard. Use professional stationery.
- Send it within 24 hours of the interview.
- Keep it short and to the point.
- Proofread it carefully so there are no errors in grammar, spelling, or punctuation. Spell the interviewer's name and company name correctly and use the exact title of the interviewer. Call the company to get this information if necessary.
- Thank the interviewer for taking the time to interview you and to explain the job.
- Express interest in the position (or explain why you are no longer interested).
- Reemphasize why your skills match the job.
- Give a phone number where you can be reached.

EMPLOYMENT TESTING

Some companies use employment tests to screen applicants further. If the applicant wants a job, taking the tests is necessary. When the interview is arranged, ask whether any tests will be given. Tests may analyze personality, determine skill level, assess knowledge about a subject, or test for illegal drug use or health conditions; some companies may also perform credit checks, honesty testing, and handwriting analyses.

Personality Tests

Some employers test personality in order to determine whether the applicant's personal and behavioral preferences match the job. Some companies use standardized tests such as the Minnesota Multiphasic Personality Inventory (MMPI) and others use tests they have developed themselves. Sometimes companies administer personality tests to current employees as one factor in making promotion decisions.

There is no way to prepare for this kind of test. When taking a personality test, it is best to be honest and mark the first reaction to the question. A possible question on a personality test might be, "What would you prefer? (a) stay home and read a book; (b) go to a party; (c) don't know."

Marilyn Meyer
638 Sixth Street Petaluma, CA 94952
meyer@msn.com
June 1, 20–

Ms. Mona Chan
Personnel Director
Transamerica Insurance
384 Sutter Street
San Francisco, CA 94132

Dear Ms. Chan:

Thank you for the opportunity to discuss the administrative assistant position
with Transamerica. The position seems to be very challenging, requiring
flexibility, initiative, and imagination. I am very interested in the position and
would welcome the opportunity to discuss my qualifications further with you.

After talking with you, I feel that my skills and abilities would help you meet the
goals that you are trying to accomplish in your department. When you
mentioned the purchase of a new network system, I started thinking about all
of the preparations that could be done ahead of time to make the transition
smooth. My previous experience developing manuals and procedures would be
very helpful.

Again, thank you for your time. I look forward to hearing from you soon.

Sincerely,

Marilyn Meyer

Figure 2-7 A follow-up letter should be sent after every interview.

Skill Tests

The purpose of skill testing is to determine whether the applicant has the skill level needed to perform the job. Skill tests may include the following:

- Knowledge of computer software, including word processing, spreadsheet, and desktop publishing applications.
- Proofreading.
- Spelling, grammar, and punctuation.
- Using the 10-key machine or calculator.
- Keyboarding speed and accuracy.
- Record keeping and filing.
- Transcription of dictated material.
- Composition and transcription of correspondence.
- General math, including fractions, percentages, and decimals.

If the skill being tested is something used every day on your present job, little review is necessary. If, however, you feel insecure about any skill area, it is best to postpone the test for a few days and spend time preparing for it.

To review, go to an on-line testing site, a bookstore or an on-line bookstore, a library, or a temporary agency. Review skills using books or software. Use assessment software to analyze and test keyboarding and software skills.

To feel confident about taking a skill test, you need to know details of the testing procedure. Some questions to ask before the interview are:

- What kind of test is it—multiple choice? true/false? problem-solving? fill in the blank?
- How much time does each test take?
- Will there be an opportunity to repeat any test?
- For computers and software: Is the computer a Mac or PC? Is it a hard disk or floppy disk system? What is the operating system? What is the software? What version is the software? Is spell-checker software allowed? Can the software reference manual be used during the testing?
- Are dictionaries or reference manuals allowed?

Subject-Matter Tests

Some professional positions require either oral or written tests or a combination of both. The purpose of the tests is to find out how much you know about a subject or how well you can analyze and solve hypothetical cases in a subject area, such as management, sales, personnel, or training.

Try to get as many details as possible about the test from the interviewer or others who have taken the test. Often it is difficult to review or prepare ahead of time, but it builds confidence to know what to anticipate. If the questions are written ones about a specific subject, practice writing out answers. Review important aspects of the particular field. Find out how long the test takes to complete.

Drug Tests

Some employers test prospective employees for the use of illegal drugs. Some people have expressed concern about drug testing because, among other issues, the tests may not be accurate. Unless you are willing to go to court, you will probably have to submit to drug testing to get a job at a company that has a policy of testing new employees. Also, be aware that some prescriptions and over-the-counter medications may cause a false positive test result.

LOCATING JOB OPPORTUNITIES THROUGH EMPLOYMENT AGENCIES AND OTHER MEANS

Employment agencies, or placement firms, as they are also called, work as intermediaries between employers and prospective employees. Their job is to match the talents and interests of the prospective employee with the company and the job. Most placement firms prefer to work with candidates who have solid job experience or training.

Agencies may deal with permanent or temporary positions, or both, and usually specialize in specific fields, such as accounting, marketing, office support, engineering, chemical, heavy industry, or technology. If an agency does not specialize in one particular field, it may employ counselors who do.

Placement Firms

A placement firm is useful when you have a good idea of the career area you are interested in, although some agencies provide career information and counseling. As a part of their service, agencies usually provide help with interviewing techniques, resumes, and salary negotiations. They also conduct appropriate skill testing.

Placement firms depend on the premise that they can get you a better job than you can get on your own. Often the jobs are listed only with the firm. A fee is charged for this service. In most cases, the company doing the hiring pays the fee. In some cases, however, the new employee and the company split the fee or the employee pays the entire fee. The fee varies and may be a percentage of salary. Sometimes the employee may pay the fee on an installment basis.

The placement firm arranges all interviews. A prospective employee may interview at several companies before accepting a job. To increase job opportunities, some people use more than one placement firm. Even if you use a placement firm, you should still watch the want ads and network with your coworkers and friends.

The following questions may assist you in deciding whether to use placement firms:

- In what areas does the firm specialize?
- Is the office well organized?
- Is the placement firm well known? Does it have a good reputation? Do you know of anyone who has used its service?

HINT: *Phone the personnel departments of major employers and ask with which agencies they work and which ones have a good reputation. Check with the Better Business Bureau to see whether there have been any complaints against them.*

- How many people work for the firm? How long have they worked there?

HINT: *If a counselor has no business cards, assume he or she is new. Ask the agency manager to switch you to another counselor.*

- Does the counselor seem really interested in your background and career goals? Is the counselor familiar with the job market?
- Does the firm do career counseling and testing? Does it help with resumes? Does it help with interviewing skills?
- Is there a fee involved? If so, who pays? If you pay, could you get the job on your own? If you quit the job after a short period, will any part of the fee be refunded?

HINT: *Never pay a fee unless an employer has offered you a job and you have accepted. Get all promises in writing.*

Other types of firms also provide services to job hunters. Headhunters, executive search firms, and consultants are paid to find people to fill positions that may or may not be open. They usually deal with high-level administrative assistants and executives. Headhunters typically contact job candidates themselves, although people looking for jobs also contact headhunters.

Resume services help write and print resumes. For an additional fee, they will send out resumes to a list of companies they have compiled.

Career counselors charge a fee to provide testing and career counseling. They also give advice on a job search. They do not make job placements, and they charge a fee whether a job is secured or not. Career counselors can be located in the Yellow Pages under "Career and Vocational Counseling." Free career counseling may be offered through college and business schools to students and graduates. Some schools have a lifetime commitment to counsel and/or place graduates.

Temporary Employment Agencies

Temporary employment agencies quickly find jobs for people on a temporary basis. These jobs may range in length from one day to several months or even years. The temporary agency serves as your employer. It interviews and evaluates the skills and preferences of temporary employees, tests employees' skills, trains employees on software packages, and finds prospective employers. A company uses temporary employees for peak work periods, temporary replacements, one-time projects, specialized work, or vacation replacements.

The skills, capabilities, and requirements requested by the company determine the level of pay. Temporary employees submit time cards each week and receive paychecks from the temporary agency. The agency bills the company for salary and fees. There are no fees or deductions from wages other than legally required payroll taxes that all employees must pay. After a period of time, paid vacation or sick leave may become available. Many temporary agencies make health benefits and 401(k) plans available to their workers.

Temping is recommended for the following situations:

- You have little or no experience in your targeted position.
- The company you want to work for is not hiring at the present time.
- You are changing careers or reentering the labor market, or you are a student or a recent graduate.

Temping lets you get inside a company so you can sell yourself in person rather than on paper. Numerous networking opportunities are available through temping, especially if you make people aware of your qualifications and ambitions.

A growing number of office professionals are choosing temporary work as a career. Advantages include pay increases without extensive performance reviews, vacations when desired, and opportunities to experience a wide variety of people and companies. Career temps typically avoid assignments of indefinite length so they do not feel the same obligation as a permanent employee. Pay raises, negotiated through the agency by the temp, can occur after a temp has been requested back by customers on a few assignments. The highest rates are paid for the most current skills.

Many temps register with a number of agencies, try them out, then narrow them down to their favorite two or three. This method is ethical and expected by most temp agencies.

Ask the following questions when deciding whether to choose temporary work:

- In what areas does the temporary agency specialize?
- Is it well known? Does it have a good reputation? Do you know of anyone who has been a temporary worker for this firm?
- How often will you be called for work?
- Do you have enough financial security to go without work if you are not called?

- Are there enough jobs available so you can work as much as you want?
- How often can you turn down jobs if they do not interest you?
- What is the pay period? Can the check be mailed? How promptly will you receive it? Can your salary be directly deposited into your bank account?
- Are insurance benefits available? If not, where can you get insurance and what will it cost?
- Can you accept a full-time position if one is offered?
- Is workers' compensation available if you are injured on the job?
- Are there any bonus incentives, such as holiday pay, for working for a temporary agency for a long period of time?

Networking

Networking is a way to use friends and colleagues in the job search. It is estimated that up to 90 percent of jobs are filled by word of mouth. The aim of networking is to expand your list of contacts until you reach the ones who are hiring.

Start by talking with friends and close business associates; then contact people you have met at associations and professional organizations, people in different departments at your present company, and people in other companies or organizations. The goal is to get names of other people you can contact. It is important to remember that you are asking for information, not a job.

Evening classes at local colleges can connect you with other employees. Often the instructor works professionally in the field in which he or she teaches and can direct you to people and companies. Another technique is to find out where employees of a company you are interested in go for lunch and after work. Often a relaxed atmosphere is a good context in which to meet people from a company and get a feeling about a company or industry. If you are unemployed, working as a temporary is a quick way to acquire contacts in and knowledge of a company before interviews or applications take place; in addition, many openings are posted on internal bulletin boards or e-mail systems before they are publicly advertised.

On-line Resumes and Positions

The Internet and commercial on-line services are the fastest-growing employment marketplace in the world. Thousands of employment recruiters and companies recruit on-line exclusively because it is faster, less expensive, and global. The cost of going on-line varies widely, as do fees for specific databases or areas.

Computerized job databases let a job seeker access up-to-date information on employment opportunities throughout the world. These computerized job openings are like electronic classified ads.

Software programs are available to help develop a resume for use in keyword searches. Multimedia resumes can be developed with sound, video, text, and graphics. Resumes may either be scanned to databases by a service company or uploaded through a modem.

On-line resumes can be searched by anyone who has access to the database. Resume databases have been developed by associations, groups, and companies. Often the resumes are searched by another computer, which is looking for particular keywords. The computer finds a "hit" when resumes match the keyword criteria.

Preparing for Advancement

Developing a personal portfolio is an excellent tool for preparing for advancement or a career change. A portfolio is organized according to what you consider important for advancing your career. The following are suggestions for inclusion in the portfolio:

- Forms or templates you designed
- Printouts of software macros you created
- Style sheets and memo or letter formats you use
- Time- and money-saving ideas the company adopted; include appreciation letters and awards, which prove that others value your work
- Copies of certificates, academic degrees; a list of courses and seminars attended
- Documentation of self-directed computer training
- Management tasks and responsibilities you handle on a regular basis
- Documentation on helping others with specialized computer features and software and hardware troubleshooting
- Examples of situations that demonstrate you are a team player

Organize the portfolio with dividers so your accomplishments are easy to review. If you are preparing the portfolio for an in-house evaluation, organize the dividers according to the categories that are used in your performance evaluation.

CAREER ADVICE AFTER A LAYOFF

Layoffs are a frequent reason to look for a new position. The following are steps to take immediately after finding out about a layoff:

- Apply for unemployment compensation. It typically takes between three and five weeks to get the first unemployment check, which will amount to only a fraction of your normal salary.
- Consider health insurance options. The COBRA law requires that companies allow former employees to stay on their health plan for up to 18 months, provided the worker pays the insurance premiums.

- Examine retirement account savings. See if you can borrow from your 401(k) or pension. These loans are not considered distributions, so they usually do not incur a tax liability on the amount borrowed.

- Suggest "consulting" for your former employer. Your work still may need to be done, and you are the most qualified person to do it. Your former employer may have more flexibility in hiring consultants, and consultants cost the company less money than a full-time employee.

- Consider doing temporary work, part-time work, or contract work—the biggest growth industry for the recently unemployed. The benefits of temporary or contract work include autonomy, flexibility, and variety. Such work also brings in money, builds self-esteem, and develops contacts. The major disadvantage is the uncertain cash flow.

- If your former employer has not offered the services of an outplacement firm, request it or seek out nonprofit organizations that offer career counseling, interviewing, resume-writing, and networking workshops for a nominal fee. Community colleges also offer career testing, placement services, and computer classes at reasonable fees.

- Some employers are willing to provide office space during the transition period when terminated employees are seeking another job. Individuals may have access to computers, telephones, and sometimes even support staff to assist them in the job search.

CHAPTER 3

TIME

MANAGEMENT

AND

PROBLEM

SOLVING

Businesses view time as an extremely valuable resource. Applying effective time management principles to office tasks is crucial for office professionals because many businesses are downsizing their operations and implementing new technologies to remain competitive.

Effective time management requires that important tasks and projects be identified and completed in the time available and that they be done well. Ineffective use of time results in unnecessary confusion and last-minute upheavals, personnel misunderstandings, disgruntled customers, and stress. To avoid these pitfalls, office professionals must *analyze, plan, schedule,* and *control* the use of their time.

ANALYZING CURRENT USE OF WORK TIME

Analyzing your current use of work time allows you to adopt more realistic approaches to planning time use and to find alternative ways to do certain tasks.

Daily Time Log

To begin, prepare a chart that lists the typical tasks you do each day. Divide the day into 15-minute blocks and record the amount of time you spend on each task. You may wish to indicate the priority status (Rush [R], Same Day [SD], Next Day [ND], Later [L]) of these tasks. You will also find it helpful to record the interruptions (I) that occur. It is important to keep a log for each day. (A sample log appears in Figure 3-1.)

Maintain this log for one week and repeat the process quarterly. Review the answers to the following questions. Your responses may provide you with valuable insights about the current use of your time.

- What time period or time periods during the day were the most productive? the least productive? Why?
- During what hours of the day did the most interruptions occur? Who caused the interruptions? Supervisors, coworkers, outside visitors, or callers?
- How much time was spent on crises that materialized during the day?

TIME	Entering Information on Computer	Proofreading/Editing Copy	Copying/Faxing/Broadcasting Documents	Tracking Budgets/Recording Financial Data	Filing Records (paper & electronic)	Greeting Clients/Managing Calendars	Handling Incoming/Outgoing Mail (including e-mail)	Attending Meetings	Composing/Designing Communications	Answering the Phone/Troubleshooting	Coordinating Conference Calls, Video/Computer Meeting	Conferring with Supervisor	Organizing/Scheduling Projects	Arranging Meetings/Travel	Interviewing/Hiring/Supervising/Training Staff	Researching Information, Including Internet Searches	Coordinating/Managing Projects	Other
A.M. 7:45–8:00																		
8:00–8:15																		
8:15–8:30																		
8:30–8:45																		
8:45–9:00																		
9:00–9:15																		
9:15–9:30																		
9:30–9:45																		
9:45–10:00																		
10:00–10:15																		
10:15–10:30																		
10:30–10:45																		
10:45–11:00																		
11:00–11:15																		
11:15–11:30																		
11:30–11:45																		
11:45–12:00																		
P.M. 12:00–12:15																		
12:15–12:30																		
12:30–12:45																		
12:45–1:00																		
1:00–1:15																		
1:15–1:30																		
1:30–1:45																		
1:45–2:00																		
2:00–2:15																		
2:15–2:30																		
2:30–2:45																		
2:45–3:00																		
3:00–3:15																		
3:15–3:30																		
3:30–3:45																		
3:45–4:00																		
4:00–4:15																		
4:15–4:30																		
4:30–4:45																		
4:45–5:00																		
5:00–5:15																		
5:15–5:30																		
5:30–5:45																		
5:45–6:00																		

EVALUATION

Tasks to simplify _____

Tasks to modify _____

Tasks to group _____

Interruptions/with whom _____

Tasks to delegate _____

Figure 3-1. Sample daily log.

- How much of the day was spent handling your personal concerns? your supervisor's?
- Were there any daily routines or tasks that could have been streamlined, combined with other tasks, or delegated?
- Were the tasks requiring 15 minutes (or less) "Rush" tasks or were these tasks to fill time? Could large tasks have been broken down into smaller daily segments?
- Could the "Rush" tasks have been started sooner?
- Were there times in the day when the pace was slow? Were there specific times when the stress level was particularly high? Were there specific times when you needed extra assistance? When are you most productive?

Special Considerations for Analyzing Time

It is important to analyze, evaluate, and make comments about your use of time on *each* day's log. Record tasks on your time log as you work on them; do not wait until the end of the day to reconstruct your time. Analyze your time log to identify the bottlenecks and potential problems. Attempt to solve only one problem at a time, but set a realistic deadline for solving it.

Your supervisors may be able to recommend suggestions for more effective use of your time. Share the time log you have completed with them. In addition to asking for their input, present a tentative list of suggestions for improvement.

The time logs may indicate that there are slow- and fast-paced time periods. Determine if these periods are predictable. Use the analyses to determine when you will need extra assistance, overtime, or outsourcing services during peak periods. Include these needs as part of the normal budgetary process so you are not caught unprepared during a peak period.

TAKING TIME TO PLAN

A written plan can assist you in directing your efforts to reach predetermined goals. Completing random tasks without a plan can be expensive and inefficient. On the other hand, adhering to a plan so rigidly that it does not allow for interruptions or special requests can be self-defeating.

A simple planning technique that most time management experts recommend involves a master list and a "to do" list. Tasks that need to be accomplished that week and tasks that should be done daily are listed on these forms.

Master Lists

A weekly master list allows you to record projects or tasks as you think of them or as your supervisor requests them. Do not set priorities for these activities; just record them as you become aware of them. Estimate the amount of time that you will require to complete each activity and indicate the due date. Use project management software to assist you in meeting target dates for each subactivity. See the section in this chapter on Project Management Software.

If a task is large, break it down into smaller segments. Before leaving work each day, select several of the tasks or subtasks and place them on the next day's "to do" list. Use the following headings on your master list:

- Week of ____
- Activity description
- Starting date
- Due date
- Estimated time to complete

"To Do" Lists

From the master list, calendar, and the tasks that come up during the day, prepare the daily "to do" list by using task manager software or by writing the tasks in a special notebook. Although there is no one right way to prepare "to do" lists, several suggestions include:

- Organize the next day's "to do" list at the end of each day if possible; if not, do the day's list first thing each morning. Preparing the list before you leave for the day shows what you accomplished, and the next day's priorities may be clearer.
- Prioritize each task; label each task A (must do), B (should do), or C (nice to do). Category A tasks are important and must be done without delay; category B tasks should be completed as soon as possible, preferably the same day; and category C tasks may be completed the same day, if there is time, or later. All items listed on a "to do" list are not of equal value; therefore, treat each task individually.
- Highlight the three most important A items on the "to do" list to signify that these tasks should take precedence over the other A tasks. This is especially useful when there are numerous A tasks on the "to do" list. Using a combination letter and number system is another method that identifies precedence (A-1, A-2).
- Keep the list visible. If you tape it to a reading stand or place it in a desktop planner holder, it will not get lost on your desk. Cross out tasks that are completed; add tasks to the list when necessary. Indicate those tasks that you delegate or that are in progress.
- Redo the list at the end of the day, and carry forward those tasks that were not completed to the next day's "to do" list. Reorder the priorities of the tasks. Limit the number of daily tasks to 10 or 12 depending on their complexity.

HINT: *Do not place too many tasks in Category A; overscheduling the A tasks can cause stress and fatigue.*

- Include names of people to contact and their telephone numbers. Use a "to do" list format that allows a place to record telephone calls you must make. If you highlight the names of the people who cannot be reached, you will be reminded to try them again at a later time. Indicate "VM" if you left a voice mail message or "EM" if you sent an e-mail.

HINT: *Leave a voice mail message that is current and that refers a caller to someone else if you are away from the office.*

- Use a calendar to record monthly and yearly events; e.g., dates for payroll reports, staff meetings, sales conferences, and budget deadlines. These reminders can then be worked into the planning of the master lists and "to do" lists.
- Divide a major project, such as planning a conference, into many subparts. Prioritize these subparts; keep a project notebook with a page for each subpart; list all contacts, phone numbers, and sources of information associated with that subpart; establish feasible deadlines for each subpart; check the notebook regularly and include the appropriate subtasks on the daily "to do" list.

Special Considerations for Planning Time

Interruptions happen; be flexible when listing tasks and their priorities on your "to do" list. You can achieve this flexibility by adding 10 to 20 percent to your estimated time. Adopt a realistic attitude toward planning. Do not list *all* the long-range projects in need of completion. The result will be too overwhelming, and you will only become frustrated. Listing the subtasks involved with a long-range project will help you *get started* on complicated or lengthy tasks.

When you do not complete all the tasks on the list, there is no need for you to criticize yourself. If the tasks are identified realistically, the process will work. However, if a task appears on a "to do" list three or four times, try to determine why. If you are avoiding the task because it is too difficult or uninteresting, handle it immediately or at least begin it rather than take the time to keep transferring it to the next day's list. Sometimes it is better to just do the task and eliminate writing it on a list. If too much time is spent in listing minor items, the tasks may never get done.

Planning *how* to do a project requires time. When reviewing your master list, identify alternative methods for completing tasks in case the original plan goes awry. Be sure to include sufficient time for organizing the materials and collecting the resources you will need. Allow at least half an hour of planning time for new projects. Consult with the people involved to see what they need and when you can expect information from them. If you don't receive the information on time, begin the project anyway. Do a draft and fill in the blank information when it arrives.

MAKING A REALISTIC SCHEDULE

A plan requires action in order for it to be useful. If you schedule tasks realistically, you can expect to accomplish the *important* things within the time available. Before determining your schedule, you need to consider several questions:

- Who is requesting the work? Usually, the more important or senior the person, the higher the priority of the task.
- When must each task be completed?
- What types of materials must be available before starting each task? Do you need someone's approval?
- Where does the work go after it is completed? If it goes to another department, how much time must be allowed for completion there?
- What tasks require service outside the company; e.g., printing?
- What tasks can best be accomplished by others?
- Which of the tasks will take the longest to complete? Are there subtasks that can be identified and started immediately?
- Are there similar activities in any of the tasks that may be subgrouped and done at the same time?

Scheduling Time to Spend on Each Task

Here are some ways to schedule the time you need to spend on each task:

- Estimate the time it takes to complete a task; then compare the estimated time to the actual time. Review your estimate in the future to better reflect the actual time.

HINT: *If you are a perfectionist, ask yourself whether the job has to be done perfectly or whether something less than perfect will be acceptable to finish the task on schedule. Perfectionists need to watch their priorities and make adjustments.*

- Set more specific, self-imposed deadlines. Instead of deciding to finish a task today, set a deadline of late morning or early afternoon.
- Determine the best time of your day to do creative work or work that requires concentration. Use "your best" time for thinking and planning or for tackling your most difficult task.

HINT: *Try to begin your work as soon as you arrive; work for 30–45 minutes before you get coffee, make telephone calls, or check e-mails.*

- Complete routine tasks such as handling mail at the same time each day. Schedule blocks of time for completing similar tasks.

HINT: *Try to return and place calls during a single block of time rather than to make them periodically throughout the day.*

HINT: *Schedule time to check e-mail messages rather than interrupt your work for each message. Delete junk mail immediately.*

- Refine your Internet search techniques by reviewing the advanced search suggestions of your particular search engine. Be specific in choosing search keywords. Efficient searching saves time because you will not be easily sidetracked to irrelevant Web sites.
- Play games with unpleasant or routine tasks. For example, set aside 15 minutes before a break or before lunch to file, so you will get a "reward" at the end. Try to complete routine tasks five minutes before the self-imposed deadline.
- Place work with the highest priority in a brightly colored folder in the center of your desk before you leave the office.
- Collect ideas of things to do to keep busy during slow days or hours. Examples of such tasks include purging files from the hard disk, ordering supplies, or reviewing infrequently used computer procedures.
- Schedule time for self-improvement. Review your career goals to determine if you are making progress in reaching these goals. Inquire about company-paid tuition plans, or check the possibility of getting time off from work to take additional coursework.

Special Considerations for Scheduling Time

Don't put off long, complex projects. Concentrating on tasks that are simple and quick to complete may bring a quick sense of accomplishment, but little tasks should not replace long-term projects. Also, it is important to perform high-priority tasks—those in category A on your "to do" list—first.

Without a schedule, you will easily become sidetracked. Concentrate on one task at a time. Finish a task rather than place it aside, thinking it will just take 15 minutes to finish and, therefore, can be done later. Unfinished tasks can create chaos on days that suddenly become filled with crises. If you prefer having several projects underway at one time, be sure you schedule your time so you meet each project's deadline. Completing a subtask early in the day often gives you the psychological motivation you need.

There is no one right way to get started. Some people begin a project by doing the most difficult parts first. Others begin with the easiest parts and work into the project. Waiting for "free time" to do a lengthy project is not wise.

CONTROLLING WORK TIME

There are two important steps to take to make your work time efficient and productive: organize your work and minimize interruptions.

Procedures for Organizing Work

The following suggestions are a few ways to organize work to make the best use of your time. Additional suggestions may be found in each of the chapters covering specific topics.

- Clear the working area of distractions and clutter. Arrange equipment, such as the computer and printer, so each piece can be comfortably reached. Keep frequently used supplies within close reach.
- Handle each piece of paper as few times as possible. When handling a piece of paper, try to take at least one step in moving it to its appropriate destination. Sort materials into action folders such as "Urgent," "To Read," "To Sign," and "To Check Later." Identify the file name in the upper right-hand corner of the document. Designate with an asterisk or colored pencil whether the item must be retained for tax or legal purposes.
- Prepare form letters, form paragraphs, frequently used phrases, and formats for computer storage. Create macros to minimize keystrokes. Note the date each form letter was used and the person to whom the letter was sent so the same items are not used in the next mailing. Prepare checklists that outline the steps required for procedures you do frequently; e.g., travel details or conference planning.
- Keep samples of previously completed forms as references. Attach a description of how the data were obtained, what sources were used, and who should receive copies.

HINT: *In case of your absence, a temporary worker will find these samples as well as information about the location of the necessary data helpful.*

- Prepare a list of facts for future reference. Some of this information, however, should not be readily available to everyone.
    - ▲ Temporary agencies—contact persons; fee schedules; and, if applicable, the names of individuals who have done excellent work on previous assignments.
    - ▲ Bank names—account numbers, hours, and names of people to contact.
    - ▲ Organizations—dues, current contact person, and meeting dates, times, and locations.
    - ▲ Supervisor's credit card names and numbers, expiration dates, and telephone numbers to call in case the cards are lost or stolen.

▲ Supervisor's preferences for rental cars, hotels, restaurants, airline carriers, airline seating, and flight times. Include telephone numbers and addresses where appropriate.

▲ Conference or meeting room availability, contact person, and room capacity.

▲ Computer network hotline sources—numbers to call and hours of operation.

▲ Equipment repair contacts—numbers to call, hours, warranties, notes on repairs already made, and signatures required to authorize repairs.

• Know your organization. Identify sources of assistance; express your appreciation to those who have helped you. Most people will willingly assist you in a crisis, especially if you have taken the time to recognize their previous efforts.

• Organize a tickler file to avoid missing deadlines. Label 12 folders with the months of the year, 31 folders for the days of the month, and one folder for the next year. Decide on what day a document should be handled and place the item in that day's tickler folder. If a document needs to be handled in a future month, place it in that month's folder; then at the end of the current month, remove the items and place them in the appropriate daily tickler folders. Check the files daily and place tasks that need to be completed on your "to do" list. It is helpful to place some tasks in a tickler file labeled a day or two before the deadline to be sure they are handled on time.

HINT: *To avoid placing material in tickler files with weekend or holiday dates, use colored adhesive circles to identify those dates.*

• Plan outgoing calls carefully. Have the information needed for each call and a checklist of questions available. For the people you call frequently, make a list of the things you want to ask or tell them. When the list is a few items long, make the call. If you do not reach a person, leave a detailed message so a return call is not needed. If you do need to talk to the person, indicate a precise time frame (e.g., 1:30 to 2:30 P.M.) that you will be available for the call. Note this time so you are indeed present for the return call.

• Prepare a list of frequently used e-mail addresses and indicate their corporate relationships.

Minimizing Interruptions

An analysis of your time log (see section on analyzing time in this chapter) can be helpful in determining whether interruptions are interfering with your getting the necessary work completed. You also should understand why people are interrupting you and come up with a solution to keep this from happening so frequently. Interruptions are a part of a normal day; however, the effects of interruptions may be minimized by taking some of the following steps:

- Block a period of "quiet time" when you ask a coworker to cover your telephone and greet clients. Reciprocate by doing the same for your coworker. Schedule activities that require concentration for this uninterrupted time.
- Listen attentively to telephone calls and take complete notes so additional time will not be wasted making another call.
- Keep a telephone message pad, pencil, and notebook within reach at all times for telephone messages, directions, or notes. If your supervisor is not available to speak with a caller, ask the caller the best time for your supervisor to return the call.

HINT: *Maintain a record of the time of day when you can most easily reach those people with whom you have frequent contact.*

- Discourage lengthy telephone conversations and excessive socializing with coworkers, personal friends, and clients. Suggest that the discussions be continued during break or lunch periods, or indicate that it is necessary to complete your present task within the hour to meet a deadline.
- Use your own discretion in handling interruptions. Is it something that requires immediate attention or is it a matter you or your supervisor can handle later?
- Demonstrate the way to complete a task or use the technology to managers or coworkers so you are not always interrupted to show them the operations.

Special Considerations for Controlling Time

It is more impressive to do a task right the first time than to use additional time, including overtime, to redo it. Listen attentively to instructions and think through the strategies for completing tasks. Ask questions when instructions are not clear or discrepancies exist in the materials. Take enough time to understand the assignment. Being too hasty in getting started often results in more serious problems later.

Refrain from interrupting others. Do not just "drop in" for a chat with your colleagues.

If you cannot complete work by the time requested, communicate this to the person making the request. It is more prudent to say "no" and suggest an alternative solution than to accept an impossible deadline.

Decide when a job has been sufficiently completed. High standards are necessary, but constant striving for perfection can lead to workaholism.

SCHEDULING A SUPERVISOR'S TIME

Office professionals not only have their own time to manage, they often must schedule the time of their supervisors. Here are some ways to schedule the time of your supervisor.

Suggestions for Scheduling a Supervisor's Time

- Understand thoroughly the goals of your organization and your supervisor. Determine how you and the personnel you supervise can assist in meeting those goals.
- Determine how your supervisor prefers you to schedule appointments, handle interruptions, and take messages. Ask about these matters the first week you are in a new position.
- Schedule a time to discuss goals, priorities, and changes with your supervisor for 5 to 10 minutes each day. This time is useful for clarifying instructions so you will not have to interrupt your supervisor repeatedly. Throughout each day write your questions, ideas, and suggestions in a notebook so you can refer to them the next time you meet.

HINT: *When a problem arises, evaluate the situation carefully before you discuss it with your supervisor. Try to have a concrete suggestion for solving the problem in mind.*

- Use an electronic organizer or personal information manager (PIM) software to remind your supervisor of things to do, meetings, and appointments. If software is not available or appropriate, prepare an appointment reminder form that highlights important events scheduled for the next day and give it to your supervisor before you leave the office. Schedule time daily to compare calendars.
- If you and your supervisor agree to do so, underline, circle, highlight, or summarize information in documents that may be of interest to your supervisor. If the material is to be read at a later time, identify it by topic and prepare a file for each.
- Keep track of where your supervisor is throughout the day in case you need to contact him or her on an urgent matter. Be persistent in reminding your supervisor of meetings or deadlines.

HINT: *Inform your supervisor when you leave your desk area. Forward your telephone calls to an appropriate location if you will be away from your desk for 15 minutes or longer.*

- Maintain a list of your supervisor's projects. Keep track of where the materials are kept and the progress of the projects daily.

Special Concerns About Scheduling a Supervisor's Time

Your assumptions about what items have high priority may be incorrect; therefore, check with your supervisor to determine the relative importance of projects.

Several warning signs may indicate impending time crises—a supervisor's procrastination, equipment malfunctions, or missed intermediate deadlines by people to whom work has been delegated. When you notice such warning signs, stay ahead of your own schedule so these last-minute crises can be handled with a minimum of frustration.

Request assistance before a rush period occurs. Monitor work schedules and check for assignments to other departments so you can estimate more accurately the amount of assistance and the amount of time you will need.

Keep abreast of sources of help or costs of outsourcing. If you need assistance for rush jobs, you will have the information available and save your own and your supervisor's time.

Keep your supervisor apprised of your workload. If you see overscheduling about to occur, request a review of priorities. One approach is to say "I'm willing to try to finish it by the deadline, but I have several other projects that also require immediate attention. What would you suggest I do first?"

WORKING FOR MORE THAN ONE MANAGER

Reengineering and downsizing will continue to create changes for office professionals. You may find you are now handling work for more than one manager or for an entire department or work group. A work group may not be permanent since it may change with the project.

Suggestions for Handling Work Flow

To avoid chaos and conflicts, here are some suggestions for working for more than one manager.

- Use different-colored folders containing completed work or messages for each supervisor. Place these folders in a stand on the corner of your desk so managers can take them without interrupting your work on other tasks. Stacked individual outboxes may also work, but they become unwieldy if you have five or more people in your work group.

HINT: *Use preprinted page flags that extend off a page to alert managers about what needs to be done. Such flags as "Sign Here," "Approval Needed," "Copy," and "Rush" are especially helpful when interruptions are not appropriate and communication must be timely.*

- Maintain a checkout board so you know if people are in or out of the area. Keep reminding people to use the board. If necessary, explain how this helps you respond to customer/client needs and, in turn, improves the image of the firm.

- Prepare a master calendar showing everyone's days away from the office, such as those involving vacations, travel, conference attendance, and work-at-home time. With appropriate software, you can get a daily update on when people in your work group will be away from the office. This information is vital for planning your work schedule and deadlines.

- Create a work priority form for each manager to use when requesting work. Information to include on the form consists of current date, project deadline date and time, notes from the originator, and the account or accounts to charge. These completed forms are helpful in preparing your master lists and "to do" lists.

HINT: *Schedule at least five minutes each day with individual managers or leaders of work groups to go over the day's priorities or to discuss an impending crisis or deadline. Demonstrate a cooperative and confident attitude that you can handle the tasks. However, if the timeline is not feasible, indicate this at the beginning of a project.*

- Become familiar with the working habits of individual managers. By recognizing the perfectionist, procrastinating, detail-oriented, organized/disorganized type of worker, you will be in a position to accommodate your own work schedule more effectively. Above all, avoid playing favorites.

HINT: *Maintain a list of other office professionals from whom you will be able to obtain various types of information when you need it.*

Special Concerns When Working for More Than One Manager

Working for more than one manager requires multiple skills. If you do not understand a set of instructions, ask for help. Do not say, "I do not understand this." Instead say, "I know what to do with the first section, but I am not clear about the section on recording your expenses. This is what I understood you to say, but I want to be sure I have all the details."

Meeting a deadline may not always be feasible. When you discover that you cannot complete a task by the due date, inform the manager soon enough so other arrangements can be made. Try to suggest an alternative plan. For example, "I have these tasks [indicate your master list] to complete by this Friday, but I'll be able to complete this project by next Wednesday." Do not wait until the last minute and then give an excuse or produce incomplete or poor work.

Working for more than one manager also may cause problems with prioritizing your work. In general, do work from the manager with the most seniority or authority first. In many work groups, managers are on an equal basis. If this is the case, use the first-in, first-out method. If two managers have equal authority and have a rush job at the same time, ask the managers involved to make the decision. Refrain from mediating such disputes.

SCHEDULING TIME OF SUPERVISEES

Office professionals often find they must schedule and supervise the work of others, such as other office professionals, temporary workers, independent contractors, interns, or work-study students. In addition, office professionals may schedule training or actually do the training as well as schedule and monitor work that is outsourced. The following suggestions may help you in scheduling the time and work of your supervisees:

- Review your strengths and weaknesses. Are there tasks others can do or become trained to do? A review of your daily "to do" list can help you answer that question. Obtain your supervisor's approval before you delegate the work to another office professional or to an outside firm.
- Select carefully the people to whom you delegate tasks. Do not always delegate the work you do not like to do or delegate to the same person each time. Those you supervise must also have the opportunity to progress professionally. Let them know they are capable.
- Provide sufficient information about doing the job and be very specific about what you need and when you need it. Do not assume everyone knows what is expected.
- Introduce new skills slowly. Break a complicated task into subtasks. You will save time if the trainee practices the skill soon after you give instructions. Be there when the trainee does the task the first time.
- Follow up on the progress of the delegated tasks periodically.
- Create a form to keep track of work that you delegate. Include space for such items as name of the worker, date delegated, description of work delegated, date due, follow-up, problem areas, and strengths. Keep notes on the tasks so you can refer to them the next time a similar situation arises.

HINT: *Be very specific about timelines for completing the tasks.*

- Use the above information to provide feedback to the worker or source of service. Always give the worker some concrete suggestions for ways to improve.

HINT: *Be specific about why you are satisfied or dissatisfied with the results. Concentrate on the behavior, not on personality or character.*

- Follow precisely the IRS guidelines for hiring independent contractors.
- Keep notes on the work completed by temporary workers. Ask temporary agencies how they test, screen, and guarantee satisfaction. Request a temp who has done satisfactory work for you previously. If you are not satisfied with a temporary worker, intern, or student worker, inform the recruiter or appropriate placement coordinator.

HINT: *Maintain professional working relationships with representatives from temporary agencies, colleges, and schools.*

Special Considerations for Scheduling the Time of Others

You may think that no one does the task as well as you do. However, your supervisees may become defensive and eventually fail to cooperate if you cannot curb your need for perfection. However, under no circumstances should you allow slovenly work. You are still accountable for the final results.

Interns and work-study students require additional training time and a specific space where they can work. Weigh the pros and cons of their presence carefully. Are you able to schedule the time needed to adequately supervise them? Is there enough room for them to have sufficient space to work?

Some of the work that you believed to be "yours" to do may be outsourced to an outside business service. You may be the liaison between your office and this service. Maintain a schedule of work that leaves the office. Work out completion schedules with the service center that allow for breakdowns or other unforeseen incidents.

The Human Resources Department in your company may offer training sessions for office professionals to become trainers. Take advantage of these opportunities. The sessions will not only help you schedule improved training sessions for your supervisees but may also provide an opportunity for you to train others in the firm.

BALANCING WORK AND LIFE AT HOME

Many office professionals work long hours to meet their company's demands. Their work involves meeting others' expectations, which is often stressful. These extended hours, along with high stress levels, often contribute to employee burnout. To avoid this type of emotional and physical exhaustion, try to correct it by following some of these suggestions. These suggestions do not require a great deal of time and can be fit into a typical workday.

- Review your priorities. Perhaps you have too many tasks identified as A's on your "to do" list.
- Spend some time alone to regain your perspective. Take a walk during your break. Move away from your desk, if only for a few minutes.

- Try meditation or yoga. Take an exercise class during the lunch hour. Enroll in a stress management workshop.
- Each day plan something you will enjoy; for example, read a chapter in a favorite book, lunch with a friend, or watch a family member's sporting event. Anticipate an upcoming event that you will enjoy; for example, a minivacation or a night at the theater.
- Say "no" to outside demands on your time. You cannot help everyone.
- Concentrate on the positive aspects of your life. Keep a list of these close by, and when you feel a "burnout moment" coming, review your list. Purchase an inspirational quotations book and read a quote or two throughout the day. Select several quotes to post in an easily viewed site.
- Maintain a sense of humor. Browse in your local bookstore or library for a book with humorous one-liners.
- Eat a light lunch. Obtain sufficient sleep. Find a quiet place and take a 20-minute nap.
- Avoid negative groups and company-related gossip during breaks and lunchtimes. Talk about your concerns with a trusted friend. Do not consistently suppress your emotions.
- Realize that you cannot "do it all." Accept your limitations and do not criticize yourself.
- Some employers recognize that stressed employees are not productive and that these employees will continue their search for other jobs that meet their needs. Personnel turnover and morale problems are costly; therefore, companies will have to assist in creating a realistic balance between their employees' lives and work. With this assistance, employees may stay on the job longer and burnout may not be so great a problem. These employee "perks" or benefits, however, will have to consist of more than bonuses or pension gifts.
- As office professionals, you may be asked to research ways that other companies attract and retain employees, or recommend ways that your company can improve in this area.
- In planning for benefits, consideration must be given to all employees.

HINT: *The "cafeteria" plan (a benefits menu in which employees choose their own benefits within designated monetary amounts set by their company) is one that often seems the fairest and most beneficial to companies and employees.*

Here are some suggestions:

Child-care facilities on-site
Personal leaves/extended leaves of absence
Maternity and paternity benefits

Flextime opportunities
Health screening
Financial consulting services
Gyms or fitness programs on-site
Flexible vacation times
Telecommuting opportunities
Computer and Internet access for employees
Company cars
Company discount shopping Web site
Insurance services on-site
Discounted travel services
Elder-care leave
Game rooms
Bookmobiles on site
Paid sabbaticals
Medical and dental care on-site
Education assistance
Unlimited sick leave
Legal services
Smoking cessation programs
Club memberships
Dry cleaning services
Company-purchased tickets for sporting or cultural events

MANAGING TIME IN A HOME OFFICE

Telecommuting—working for a company away from the office in a mobile office, home office, or outlying work area—has increased in popularity. The right technology combined with the right people working away from the office can result in increased productivity. Workers save time because they are not commuting, and they don't have to deal with interruptions or office politics.

Becoming the sole proprietor of a home-based business is a goal for many office professionals. For some, a home-based business is a second-income generator or the result of company downsizing; for others, it is a chance to test their expertise and gain financial security. Although home-based businesses are not new, they have become more popular because of technology and the expertise office professionals have in using this technology. For additional information on home-based businesses, refer to Chapter 13.

Telecommuters and home-based business owners require time management skills. Here are some suggestions:

• Plan how to set up your home office in advance. Once you begin working with clients, your focus will be on providing service. Read the trade journals. Check the "home office" information sections on the Internet. Talk with others who have set up businesses to find out about their successes and failures. Seek assistance from the Small Business Administration (SBA) in your area.

HINT: *To contact the Small Business Administration, check the local telephone book, contact the public library, or check with the Chamber of Commerce.*

- Analyze your strengths and weaknesses. Invest the time to brush up on skills that need improvement; for example, small business bookkeeping practices. Good legal and accounting advice may be helpful, but you need to understand every part of your company's business. Invest the time before you begin your business.
- Prepare a detailed list of equipment specifications so the equipment you buy fits in your home office space and is compatible with your company's equipment or your clients' needs. If you are telecommuting, be sure your home office is adequately insured and that it meets your company's safety requirements.

HINT: *Be sure that your home office is well-lighted. Buy a sturdy desk and a chair that is well-built and comfortable for you. A good office chair is the most important piece of furniture in a home office.*

HINT: *To avoid clutter and excess cords, investigate multifunction products—those that combine a fax, printer, scanner, and copier.*

- Keep sufficient supplies on hand. Running out of toner cartridge at 10 P.M. with a project due at 9 A.M. the next day is stressful and wastes time.
- Install a separate telephone line (aside from your personal line) for your office telephone (with voice mail or an answering machine), your fax, and your computer.

HINT: *If you do not have a separate line, use call screen or distinctive ring features for your business calls. Then have non-work-related calls go to voice mail.*

- Develop self-discipline by keeping regular work hours in your office at home. Keep family interruptions to a minimum. Having a separate area (preferably a room that is separated by walls from the other areas of the house) is more conducive to making efficient use of your time.

HINT: *Hang a "Do Not Disturb" sign on the door or let members of the family know that a closed door means no interruptions unless there is an emergency.*

- If you are telecommuting, let your supervisor know that you will be available during certain hours. It is easy to become so involved with a project that you forget to take scheduled breaks. Move about the room or do stretching exercises every hour if you work at the computer for long time periods.

- Use e-mail, since you can read it or send it at any time. If you are a telecommuter and already have an e-mail address at your company, maintain that address. Home-based businesses can obtain access to e-mail through local Internet access providers. Inexpensive or free e-mail software is also available.
- Remain in touch with the people in your office. The lack of social contact is a major disadvantage of a home office. If you are a member of a team, set your goals for the week and communicate these to the other team members. Take time to report on each day's progress. Schedule a regular weekly meeting at the office. By maintaining communication with your supervisor, you are less likely to feel that those who are physically present in the office are more likely to be promoted or given more interesting tasks. Continue your networking efforts if you are a home-based-business owner.

HINT: *Keep in touch with your friends and have lunch with business associates. Join a service organization or offer to do a program for a school or community group.*

- Evaluate your goals and services every six months. If your business is not generating a profit after two years, it is time to review your procedures. You may be spending too much time on tasks that generate limited revenue or you may need to find another niche for service. Set aside sufficient funds to see you through the difficult times.

USING TECHNOLOGY TO MANAGE TIME

Software and other tools are helpful in such areas as scheduling, making appointments, prioritizing tasks, and managing projects. The software varies in capabilities, complexity, and power.

Personal Information Managers (PIMS)

Personal information manager (PIM) software is multifunctional. It manages business-related details such as calendars, addresses, "to do" lists, appointment books, file drawers, fax machines, telephone calls, and notepads.

The three basic modules found in PIM software are contact management, scheduling, and task management. **Contact management software** allows you to list names and multiple addresses and telephone numbers. It can remind you to call and give you information on why you are calling; e.g., follow-up referrals. You can search the directory in several ways; e.g., by company, city, or product. Notes can be added to any contact. **Scheduling software** allows you to record meeting times and the people with whom you are meeting. The program automatically checks for conflicts, records regularly scheduled meetings, includes reminders of meeting times, and prints your schedule in a daily, weekly, or monthly format. **Task management software** allows you to list tasks, make notes, prioritize the tasks, and sort by due date, priority, or person to whom assigned. It may also identify any task that is off schedule.

SELECTING PIM SOFTWARE

Large companies have an information systems department that selects software. You learn the program and use it. In smaller companies, you often have input in the selection process. Answers to the following questions will assist your selection analysis:

- Which tasks need the most help in your office? Is your biggest bottleneck managing your supervisor's calendars and your own, keeping an up-to-date client address list, or completing tasks on time? Do you need a stand-alone program for the bottleneck, or do you want to integrate the functions?
- Where does your information come from now? How do you access it? What type of fingertip information do you need to access daily? How do you link your data?
- Do you keep detailed notes on your clients or contacts? How large a field do you need for a notepad?
- In what format do you want your information? For example, do you want a weekly calendar only, or do you want a weekly, monthly, and yearly format? Do you prefer a program format that looks like your "to do" list, or do you prefer an outline, free-form format? Do you have the graphics capability to produce calendars?
- Can the software print labels and Rolodex® cards? Is there sufficient space for multiple addresses and telephone numbers, such as home, work, e-mail, and fax?
- Is the software capable of rescheduling a task if the task does not get done that day? Is there a scheduling option to handle rooms and equipment?
- What reports do you need to prepare from the data collected?
- Do you need a program with network capabilities? Do you want access to external word processors or printers? Will the software be used for work-group functions?
- Are you away from your computer a great amount of time during working hours? Do you need software for a laptop computer?

SPECIAL CONSIDERATIONS FOR USING PIM SOFTWARE

Personal information managers are not magic. You must be self-motivated to enter the data and maintain the information regularly. Software packages vary in features and price. Some allow more freedom to customize fields and on-screen views than others. For example, if you do not want 15-minute intervals for calendaring, you will want the flexibility to customize your own program.

Individual personalities and working styles should determine the software you and your supervisor eventually use. If you use a program that does not "work" like you prefer working, you will be frustrated. Before selecting PIM software, ask for a demonstration of each function and see how the modules work together. Request a demonstration disk or check with other office professionals to see what works best for them. Check product reviews in current trade magazines. Be aware that the complexity of PIM software also determines the learning time.

Access to your PIM software is not always going to be convenient. You may be at your desk most of the day; your supervisor may not. It is important to set aside time to coordinate schedules and tasks.

Personal Digital Assistants (PDAs)

Personal digital assistants (PDAs), also referred to as palmtops or hand-helds, are small computers that can be held in the palm of your hand. Palmtops are especially useful to someone who is away from the office for long periods. Most PDAs do the same things as full-sized PCs: they can track appointments and project due dates; store telephone numbers, addresses, and messages; create multiple lists; and record notes. They can word-process, browse Web sites, and handle e-mail and voice mail. Some PDAs have color screens, which are useful for accessing graphics or highlighting information. Most electronic organizers can be linked to microcomputers, allowing notes and calculations to be easily transferred, updated, and printed.

Information is entered into a PDA using a keyboard, handwriting, or the voice. The keyboard is very small. Voice-recognition software allows you to format, print, or e-mail voice directions. You will have to spend time programming the software to recognize your voice.

Integrated Software

Office professionals no longer have to learn individual software programs, such as word processing, spreadsheet, database, and graphics. An integrated software program combines several of these applications, along with e-mail and Internet functions. When office professionals use integrated software, they save learning time because the commands for the various applications are the same. They can also easily move data from one application to another without rekeying or reorganizing the material.

PROJECT MANAGEMENT

Project management requires organization and time management skills. Individuals who work on lengthy projects require information about the completion time for a project and the chances that it will be finished in that time. They must break down the project and identify specific tasks, estimate starting and ending times for each task, request the people and materials needed, and operate within a budget. If delays occur, they need to know what effects these delays can cause for a company. Gantt charts, PERT (Program Evaluation and Review Technique) programs, and project management software provide assistance with these tasks.

Gantt Chart: A Gantt chart is a scheduling tool that project managers use to monitor small projects. The bar chart shows scheduled and actual progress for each task; managers can use this information to see if scheduled tasks are on schedule or if problems need to be solved. The project manager needs a breakdown of the work and starting and ending times for each step. To obtain realistic subtask deadlines, begin with the due date and work backwards.

HINT: *Monitor the progress of the project regularly. Never assume that each subtask is being completed according to schedule.*

You can also use a simple paper form to keep track of your projects. Keep information on each project in a separate folder or separated in a single notebook. Some items you will need to record are: name of project, start date, due date, project description, subtasks, individuals responsible for each subtask, action to be taken on each subtask, date due for each subtask, and date completed for each subtask. Build some flexibility into your deadlines by estimating maximum and minimum times that each subtask may take.

PERT: The PERT chart helps project managers find the best way to complete a project. It requires managers from all departments involved with the project to plan together. Managers use the technique not only to determine how long it will take to complete a project but also to indicate problem tasks that may affect the date of completion. PERT allows plans to be updated as the project moves along. The chart includes (1) project activities or tasks (represented by arrows) and (2) events or completions of activities (represented by circles). The path is a line that connects the activities; the longest path is the critical path. If an activity on the critical path falls behind schedule, it causes a delay in the project.

Project Management Software

Project management software also creates a graphic timeline for a project and can display information for keeping track of deadlines in Gantt chart formats. Your first step is to arrange your tasks and subtasks in order of importance. The software allows you to change personal deadline dates or budget items easily. You can review selected portions of a schedule, such as time period or one person's schedule. Doing project management electronically enables you to keep everyone informed and on schedule and assists you in identifying problem areas before they are out of control.

HINT: *Identify everyone involved in each subtask. List all the supplies needed to complete the project and order them in advance.*

A PROCESS FOR SOLVING PROBLEMS

Problems can result from uncertainty, disagreement, and unanswered questions. Ignoring problems or solving problems only when they become emergencies usually creates chaos. Problems require solutions that will bring about change. Bringing about change requires special skills, and office professionals with effective problem-solving skills are valuable employees.

Whether office professionals are working alone or in a work group, one systematic process for solving problems involves the following steps:

1. Define and analyze the problem.
2. Consider possible solutions.
3. Select the best solution and defend it.
4. Evaluate the results.

Define and Analyze the Problem

To define and analyze a problem may be the most difficult step in solving it. The symptoms of a problem are often more evident than its causes. Everyone may have a different perception of the problem. To define the underlying problem accurately, answers to several questions may be helpful.

- From your perspective, is there really a problem?
- Has this problem occurred before? If so, were the conditions similar? Is the conflict about values, methods of work, or personality styles? How was the problem solved before? Did that solution work or is a new approach needed?
- How can you learn more about the problem?
- With whom can the problem be discussed? Are there other viewpoints?
- What are the specific circumstances surrounding this problem?
- What company policies and procedures are involved? What are the legal implications? Are there budget limitations?
- What is the desired outcome?

Consider Possible Solutions

The second step is to explore numerous possible approaches to solving the problem. Brainstorming is one effective technique for seeking creative solutions to problems. It is a technique that does not restrict or judge any suggestions so as many ideas as possible are generated. Mind mapping is another problem-solving technique that is easily completed on your own or in a group. You begin by writing a word or drawing a picture of the problem on a large piece of paper. Draw a circle around the problem. Then as you begin to think of ideas to solve the problem, you draw lines from the circle and write a word or phrase on the line. You may even have branches from these lines. You may use colored markers. The purpose of mind mapping is to keep the ideas flowing so you have a basis for solving the problem.

Include the people who are involved in the solution-generating process. If only one other person is involved, meet and express your concerns sincerely and nonjudgmentally. Listen to the other person's viewpoint. Try to find areas of agreement and arrive at a mutually satisfying solution.

Several questions that will assist you in generating alternative solutions include:

- What is the first solution that you considered?
- What would be the easiest solution? What would you *like* to occur?
- What are the conventional approaches to solving the problem?
- What other ideas (workable or not) can be used as alternative solutions?

HINT: *Use suggestions that others have used to solve similar problems or modify these suggestions to work for you.*

- How did another supervisor solve the problem?

Select the Best Solution and Defend It

After identifying all the possible solutions, the next step is to list the likely consequences of each solution, select the best solution, and prepare to defend it. In most situations, some factors will have an impact on those decisions, such as time, money, convenience, and impact on personnel. Although each solution will have strengths and weaknesses, the best solution should be selected on the basis of all the factors that you have identified and ranked. Here are some questions to help select the best solution:

- What individual department or company limitations must be considered? What solutions are eliminated because of these restraints?
- What are the weaknesses and strengths of each solution?
- What factors are used to judge all solutions? Rank the factors by importance.
- What justification can be made for a decision? How will it solve the problem? What will be the outcome if applied?

Evaluate the Results

After you have identified the best solution, try out the solution and evaluate the results. Establish some timelines and follow up on the outcome. If successful, the solution will be helpful in solving similar problems and eliminating a recurrence of the same problem. The answers to the following questions may be helpful in evaluating the problem-solving process:

- What step-by-step tasks were involved in trying out the solution? Were all the subtasks identified and approved?

- Was the solution successful? Was it necessary to put a second solution into effect? What were the positive and negative consequences? What improvements were needed?

- What experiences with this process could be applied to other problems? What changes would be recommended if these solution procedures were used again?

Special Concerns About Problem Solving

Frustration with a problem may cause it to be blown out of proportion. After you go through the steps in solving a problem, focus your attention on the solution selected; do not waste time imagining every horrible consequence that may result.

Personnel need frequent updates. Do not forget to keep those employees with vested interests informed of your decisions.

It often helps to write a sentence or two describing the desired goal. The focus of your problem definition should not be on who or what gets the blame. How you present the problem will remain in people's memories for a long time. Always communicate with respect for others in the group.

When the problem involves a group, you need each member to at least accept the solution and the process. This can be a lengthy, tedious task; therefore, do not give up and handle it yourself.

If a solution doesn't work, review the mistakes. Obtain more feedback or use another approach.

Some problems are difficult to solve and may need input from your supervisor. Ask for assistance if the authority to solve a problem rests with another department or a colleague. Do whatever is necessary to handle a problem, but if it becomes too complex, consult with your supervisor before the situation becomes unmanageable.

USING TECHNOLOGY TO SOLVE PROBLEMS

There is a wide range of software to aid management in solving problems. The array of products increases as companies reorganize and struggle to maintain their competitive edge. Office professionals will find it helpful to understand some of the technology.

Decision-Making Software (Groupware)

Groupware is software that requires a multiuser environment. In that type of environment, the software allows work groups to manage and share information, solve problems, and develop collaborative applications with a minimum of paperwork exchange. In addition to e-mail and other messaging services, groupware can support such functions as bulletin boards, group calendaring and scheduling, task management, project management, workflow routing, electronic document exchange and tracking, forms routing, desktop videoconferencing, and access to a database. Groupware can also support remote users. Desktop videoconferencing adds another dimension to groupware. This growth technology has implications for work groups who need face-to-face feedback.

Desktop Asset Management

Managing the various hardware and software assets in a firm of any real size creates problems because in large companies there are so many pieces of equipment and software packages in use. The location of the equipment changes because of its mobility. Remote offices and home offices cause additional concerns. Companies are not only concerned about the type and location of equipment and software; they also want to know these details: internal configurations, purchase and warranty agreements, depreciation, cost basis, maintenance, software licensing agreements, and replacement schedules. Managing this type of inventory is costly in both time and money. Desktop asset management software concentrates on personal computers and other easily transportable items such as audiovisual aids. Software features vary in power and sophistication. Companies often decide to use an outsource firm to handle the growing volume of desktop assets that require management.

Artificial Intelligence (AI)

Artificial intelligence (AI) is a broad scientific field that involves making machines more like human intelligence and therefore more useful. In making machines smarter, AI researchers also try to study and understand the human intellect.

An intelligent computer is more than a storage area for facts or programmed instructions. AI researchers want to find more effective ways that allow the computer to reason, link facts, and solve problems. As computer power increases, perhaps additional applications for computers that think like humans will emerge.

Expert Systems

Developing expert systems is a branch of artificial intelligence. Expert system software is based on the knowledge of experts and is used in supporting decisions and in problem solving rather than in developing applications.

Expert-system engineers ask experts what they know and how they use that expertise to solve problems relevant to a specific task. The amount of knowledge gained from these experts must be large, and the questioning technique requires skill and quick comprehension of the experts' reasoning processes. After the questioning period, the developers of the expert system include the acquired knowledge in a computer program. Businesses can use that software to assist them in their problem solving.

Alien Intelligence

Alien intelligence is a new form of computer intelligence that is very different from human intelligence. Alien intelligence is so complex that humans cannot understand its logic in that its capabilities are millions of times more powerful than human capabilities. Alien intelligence techniques involve the analyzing of undefinable quantities of data and taking action based on the knowledge obtained through the process. Often the data available is insurmountable, and humans cannot identify the patterns that exist.

Data mining software is able to search for patterns that help decision makers; for example, data mining software identifies customers who have certain traits, who live in certain areas of the country, who are in specific economic ranges, or who may be planning to change to a competitor. With this massive amount of data, data mining software can then find patterns that are helpful to marketers in narrowing their marketing strategies.

The possibilities for using these advanced problem-solving/decision-making tools in businesses are endless.

Organizational structures vary widely from company to company, even in the same industry. Within any given company, especially a large one, the relationships between functions and subfunctions undergo continual change, reflecting external changes in market demands, corporate objectives, and employee needs. Organizations usually develop a chart indicating what positions exist and how these positions are related to each other. The authority and responsibilities of personnel are also shown. Understanding the office professional's place, authority, and responsibilities in an organization can contribute to your overall effectiveness in the company.

ORGANIZATIONAL PRINCIPLES

All organizations are built on a number of principles. Among them are:

1. *Lines of authority:* An organization plan makes one person responsible for each worker and/or group of workers in an organization.
2. *Responsibility and authority:* Each position must be clearly defined through job descriptions.
3. *Equating responsibility and authority:* Responsibility is coupled with corresponding authority.
4. *Delegation:* Authority needs to be delegated as far down as possible. However, the delegator remains fully responsible and accountable for what has been delegated.
5. *Simple structure:* An organizational structure should be kept as simple as possible, with minimal levels of authority.

ORGANIZATIONAL STRUCTURES

Based on these principles, businesses develop an organizational structure and an organization chart to depict the organization graphically. In an organization with a **line structure,** management has direct authority over, and is responsible for, the performance of all workers reporting to them. This is the most common structure. A line organization chart usually takes the form of a pyramid, with the president or CEO at the apex. (See Figure 4-1.)

CHAPTER 4

ORGANIZATIONAL STRUCTURES AND OFFICE RELATIONSHIPS

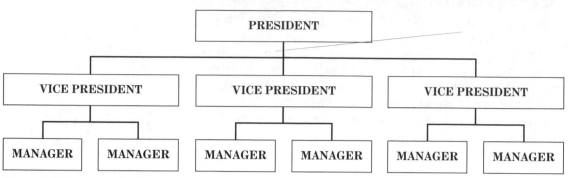

Figure 4-1 Line organization.

In a **line and staff** organization, assistants are assigned to executives. These assistants handle specific advisory responsibilities, such as research, planning, accounting, distribution, public relations, and industrial relations. Staff personnel have advisory or support positions with no direct authority over workers down the line. Staff positions are usually designated by a dotted line on the organization chart. (See Figure 4-2.)

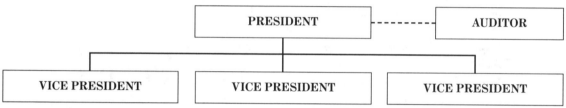

Figure 4-2 Line and staff organization.

Charting Activities Within an Organization

Office professionals are occasionally called upon to chart an organization's structure. There are four general ways to chart the activities of an organization:

1. ***By function, activity, or process:*** An organization chart arranged by function breaks the enterprise into groups involved in a single class of activity, such as finance or sales. (See Figure 4-3.) Such a chart can use either broad categories, such as sales, or a specific activity, such as sales promotion.

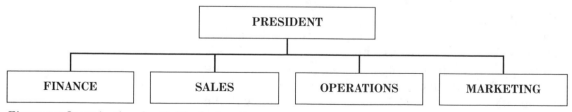

Figure 4-3 Organizational activities by function.

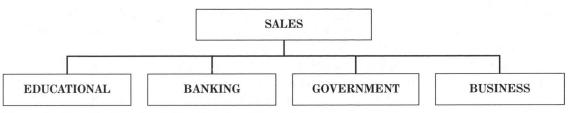

Figure 4-4 Organizational activities structured by customer.

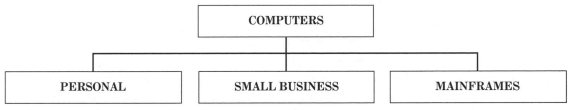

Figure 4-5 Organizational activities structured by product.

Figure 4-6 Organizational activities structured by geography.

2. *By customer or type of customer:* In this kind of chart, workers can be listed alphabetically by customer name or by the customer's type of business, e.g., insurance, banking, transportation, or government. (See Figure 4-4.) Such an organization fits products more closely with customer needs.

3. *By product:* A chart in which activities are grouped by product is useful for an organization that focuses on a specialized product and has experts about that product. (See Figure 4-5.)

4. *By geography:* A chart structured by geographical location permits special attention to local conditions and requirements. It is particularly important in sales and marketing, where local traditions and habits have great influence on success. However, such an organization may duplicate common activities, such as accounting and marketing. (See Figure 4-6.)

The Matrix Structure

An alternative to these four structures is the matrix structure. In a matrix structure, each person reports to two executives: the person in charge of the particular project or product on which the employee is working, and the person in charge of the particular area in which the employee works. For example, in a high-tech company, a software design specialist may report to both the manager of the product on which the specialist is working and the manager of software for the organization. (See Figure 4-7.)

This structure is complex. It often works best when employees and management are well educated and professionally oriented, and the company is small and entrepreneurial. Many companies use a matrix structure as a transition between being functionally organized and being organized by product or market.

THE MODERN OFFICE STRUCTURE

Because each organization is different, there is no ideal way to place administrative support personnel in the organizational structure. In fact, many businesses are restructuring to better suit their needs and to maximize productivity. Business costs have increased, partly because white-collar workers now comprise more than 60 percent of the total workforce. As a result, the office is now viewed as a professional environment where skilled people perform functions vital to the smooth operation of an organization. Businesses are placing more emphasis on the management of office support, and in the process they are creating new career opportunities.

Traditional Office Support

Traditionally, offices have been organized so upper-level managers have private or personal secretaries or executive assistants. Moving down in the organization, middle- and lower-level managers often shared secretaries. Within the traditional structure, executives have immediate access to secretarial support. There is more flexibility in sched-

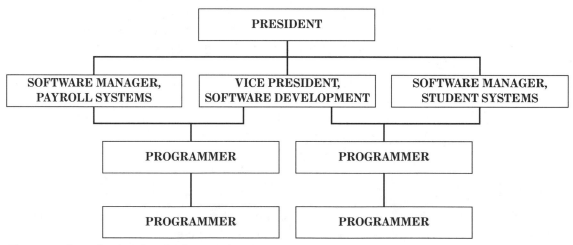

Figure 4-7 Organizational activities as a matrix structure.

uling and prioritizing managerial work. The executive assistant works with his or her boss on a one-to-one basis and does a variety of tasks.

The disadvantage of a traditional secretarial/administrative support structure is that there is often an uneven workload, with some periods when the work is overwhelming and others when there may be little or nothing to do. Interruptions may cause priorities to change, which could result in poor-quality work and lowered productivity. (See Figure 4-8.)

Centralized Administrative Support

A **centralized administrative support center** can be an effective use of technology and people. All document preparation—memos, reports, proposals, and letters—is completed by word processing specialists on text-editing equipment in one central location. (See Figure 4-9.) This type of structure consolidates all word processing equipment and personnel into one central location. A centralized word processing center provides sophisticated equipment for complex documents. The disadvantage is that there may be delays in producing documents if many departments all demand that work be done at the same time.

In some organizations, administrative support specialists are also located in a centralized location. These specialists perform all tasks other than producing documents,

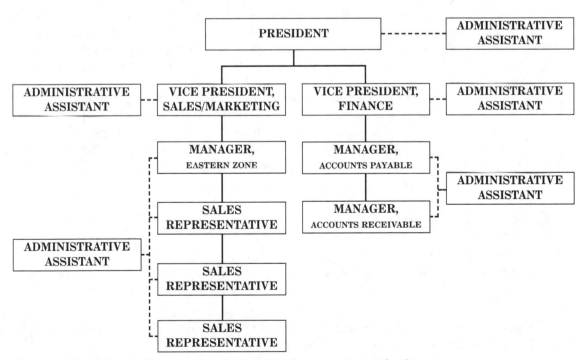

Figure 4-8 Traditional office secretarial/administrative support organization structure.

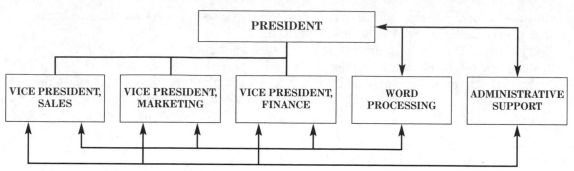

Figure 4-9 Centralized administrative support organization.

such as scheduling meetings, customer relations, making travel arrangements, and research. Work in an organization with this structure comes to the administrative group from each department as well as from the word processing center.

Decentralized Administrative Support

In other organizations, the word processing center may be centralized, but the administrative support staff is **decentralized.** Staff may be located in several locations near users. For example, departments such as sales, marketing, or personnel may each have an administrative secretary. The word processing center, however, remains centralized for all departments to use for document-producing tasks. The advantage of this structure is that there is a cost-effective word processing center, but managers have easier access to administrative support personnel. The disadvantage is that the work flow may be inconsistent. (See Figure 4-10.)

Finally, both document support and administrative support may be **decentralized,** in which case document and administrative support staff are assigned to each department. However, most organizations use a combination of centralized and decentralized structures. In that case, a main word processing center can store data for the departmental word processing centers, which are known as **satellite centers.**

ORGANIZATIONAL CHARTS

An organizational chart is a schematic representation of an organizational structure, showing lines of authority and the relationships among employees. A properly constructed chart:

- Provides a view of the general structure of the company's work by showing relationships and areas of responsibilities.
- Serves as a historical record of organizational changes.

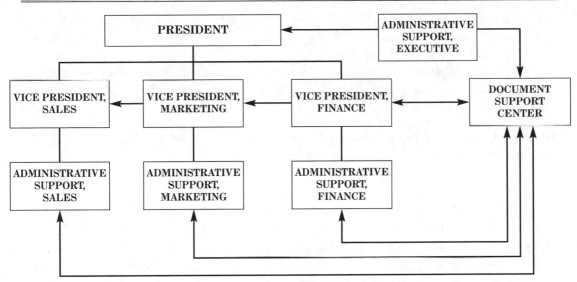

Figure 4-10 Centralized document support with decentralized administrative support organization.

- Serves as information for orienting new employees.
- Can be a work plan for expanding a business and an information source for the general public or special groups.

The design of an organization chart can range from a simple line chart of job titles to a more detailed chart that includes titles, job responsibilities, and photos of the top company executives.

Computer programs are available for use in creating organization charts. Lines can be automatically drawn with the use of the cursor or mouse, and boxes can be formatted with the use of a menu. Charts can be created with an unlimited number of levels. In most cases, changes can be made easily by modifying the chart onscreen before printing. When selecting a software charting program, look for the following features:

- Creates charts in any size, shape, style, or color.
- Generates wall maps and charts with indexes.
- Accommodates a large database of people or positions that can be displayed in a single chart.
- Has the capability to include any database field in the chart, e.g., performance rating, salary grade, and so on.
- Provides for automatic updating of charts to reflect current information in the company database.
- Can build "what-if" scenarios or hypothetical charts of possible organizational changes.

- Has a batch printing feature allowing integration of any number of charts into one master chart with a consolidated index; any number of people or positions can be included.
- Has relationship paths that allow for cross-referencing information about candidates, supervisors, next planned positions, etc., with incumbent data in the same box.

After creating an organization chart, whether it is done via a software program or manually, the following questions should be answered:

- Are titles correct and up to date?
- Are names spelled correctly?
- Is the reporting structure correct?
- Is the organization chart dated to show latest revision?
- Has management reviewed the chart and approved its distribution?
- Has the organization chart been revised according to an established schedule, e.g., semiannually or annually?

OFFICE RELATIONSHIPS AND TEAMS

As today's companies merge, downsize, and invest in technology to meet the changing demands of business, team management is emphasized more than ever before. The team approach allows management to share responsibility for implementation of corporate goals. The team approach also helps office professionals to build a framework for professional and greater efficiency.

Teams of people may work together in common facilities or may be physically separated from one another. For example, key team members may be located in different offices in different parts of the country or world and be connected by means of a telecommunications network. A team may be composed of members from the same department or may be interdisciplinary, with members from various departments. Teams are generally assigned to work on a specific goal or project. The team's assignment may run for as little as one month or as much as a year and a half. A project room is often made available to facilitate the work. The most common type of team is a **linear team,** which is generally organized by function and is process-oriented. An example is a health and safety team organized to review office workstation ergonomics. Team members have fixed roles, such as chairperson, secretary, and so forth. A team focusing on solving a problem, such as developing a new customer service software program in the next year, is referred to as a **parallel team.** This type of team will have members with specialized skills that contribute toward a directed goal. Another type of team is called a **circular team.** Such a team usually consists of highly creative individuals who function democratically and even set their own goals. A new product development team is an example.

A team has the following characteristics:

Results: A team's purpose is to accomplish something.

Goals: A team must have a common purpose that is understood and pursued by the whole group.

Energy: An extra dimension of energy is created as a team works together to achieve an end result.

Structure: An organization should be orderly and members should respond to workflow in a uniform way. However, the structure should be flexible as the team tries to accomplish its goals.

Spirit: Team spirit reflects the quality of the team's work.

Identity: Having a sense of belonging is important.

Collective learning: Because teams learn together as they answer difficult questions and solve hard problems, their collective knowledge will become part of the team as well as part of each individual member.

The relationship between manager and office professional is the most common team within the office. This unit is motivated by the goal of making the workplace more efficient. Managers and office professional must address face-to-face such issues as trust, joint problem solving, giving and receiving feedback, time management, and behavioral styles. Team building commands the presence of all the players.

Everyone in an office works together in a team effort, whether formally or informally, at some level. Acting as a team member:

- Maximizes work distribution for the organization.
- Allows an interchange of office professionals when one person is out ill or on vacation.
- Provides a career path and opportunities for career development for the office professional.
- Maximizes productivity through fall utilization of human resources and technology.

To be an effective team member, you must:

- Understand the group's objective. What is the group expected to achieve? Is the purpose of a particular meeting to exchange information or to solve a conflict? Ask questions to help clarify the purpose, but do so in a nonthreatening way. For example, you might ask, "Am I correct in my understanding of our goal? As I see it we are . . ." "As I see it" is a useful phrase because it implies you are receptive to other viewpoints.
- Focus on the objective. Keep to the subject and try not to deviate.
- Be economical with words. Do not ramble. Try to use strong nouns and active verbs.

- Listen carefully. Concentrate on ideas, not just facts. Watch for nonverbal cues from the speaker. Reserve judgment until the speaker has finished. Be open-minded.
- Interact informally. Important information exchanges are often made in informal settings. Informal interactions offer opportunities to express opinions, influence others, compare information, and learn about decisions not yet been made.

To work effectively in a team-managed organization and enhance your opportunities for career advancement, you should:

1. Assess the needs of each member of the team for computer skills, education, experience, and certification. Such an assessment will pinpoint the technical, administrative, and interpersonal skills needed by members of the team.
2. Focus on developing and improving communication skills such as writing, speaking, and listening.
3. Understand and keep informed about the organization's goals, products, and competition. Be aware of changes within the company and industry.
4. Develop initiative.
5. Learn to delegate.
6. Be organized and manage your time well, not only for yourself but for others in the team.

COMMUNICATION IN THE OFFICE

Effective communication helps create a desirable work climate in which individuals can cooperate to accomplish personal, group, and organizational goals. In organizations, communication occurs between overlapping and interdependent groups as well as individuals. Organizations rely on communication to work effectively. For that reason, they develop communication networks to facilitate the flow of messages. An office professional is often the controller of the communication network and therefore must have good communication skills.

Finally, keep in mind that office professionals also communicate and interact with clients, customers, stockholders, financial institutions, and civic and community groups. How an office professional responds to people outside the organization reflects on the organization's image.

PERSONAL NETWORKING

Developing personal contacts in a company can be very helpful in getting information for your managers as well as for your personal advancement. Since it isn't possible to network with everyone, apply your efforts to the people who can help you the most, that is, those who have information you or your manager may need in the decision process. Remember that it takes time to build relationships with people whom you can count on and trust to provide you with reliable information. Ask yourself these questions:

- Which people in the organization have information my executive or I may need from time to time?
- How can I help others in the organization by providing useful information to them?
- What is the best method of contacting others: telephone, e-mail, or personal visit?
- Can I build relationships with people outside the organization via the Internet? (Although this can be an excellent way to network, be careful you do not become involved in a conflict-of-interest situation whereby you provide confidential and critical information to someone unauthorized to receive it.)

EMERGING CHARACTERISTICS OF MODERN ORGANIZATIONS

New forms of organization are geared to make organizations more receptive and adaptive. The following characteristics are typical of changing organizational structures:

1. *Strong employee involvement:* Input to the system starts from those closest to the accomplishment of assigned objectives. In other words, those most in the know about whether the organization is achieving its preferred outcomes with its stakeholders or not have a say in how the system works. This way, the organization stays attuned and adaptive to the needs of those with a vested interest or stakeholders.
2. *Organic nature:* Fewer rules and regulations, often with no clear boundaries and constantly changing forms, make the company more flexible.
3. *Alliances:* Through collaboration, networks, and strategic alliances, authority with commensurate responsibility is earned and sometimes shared by two or more people.
4. *Linear decentralized organization:* Middle management is more involved in the decision process, resulting in top management exchanging more feedback with those providing products and services.
5. *Teams:* Two or more people may work together on special projects or assignments. In doing so, all team members accept the responsibility for accomplishing the team's assigned objectives.
6. *Learning organizations:* Managers facilitate the workers' applying new information and learning from their experiences. They also work on generating consensus on direction. Time is provided to exchange feedback, to inquire, and to reflect about the feedback.

7. ***Virtual organizations:*** These organizations may consist of a federation of specialists who work together on common projects, but do not work in the same physical location.

An example of a virtual group is a national sales team distributed throughout the United States. Another example could be a small software development group of people telecommuting to their office.

   Both hardware and software is required to support a virtual team. The Internet often electronically connects the members of the virtual organization via teleconferencing and e-mail. General hardware requirements include telephones, PCs, modems or equivalent, and communication links such as the public switch network (telephone system) and local area networks. Software requirements include groupware products such as electronic mail, meeting facilitation software, and group time management systems.

8. ***Self-managed teams (SMT):*** Work groups that operate with varying degrees of autonomy and without an appointed director/manager are referred to as self-managed teams. These teams learn and share job responsibilities usually performed by a manager. In a fully functioning SMT, control comes from within the group, rather than from outside it. Rather than directing and giving orders the team leader becomes a facilitator to assist the team, mediate and resolve conflicts among team members, and interact with other teams and managers in other parts of the organization.

As a supervisor, overseeing, assisting, and monitoring the work of those reporting to you is only one aspect of your job. Other responsibilities include interviewing and hiring, training new and temporary employees, conducting performance appraisals, and administering discipline.

THE HIRING PROCESS

Hiring good people can be a long and difficult process or a short and simple one. There are many steps involved, from writing the job description to interviewing potential candidates to checking references. As today's office professionals advance to supervisory positions, they are increasingly involved in hiring others to work for them.

Writing a Job Description

Organizations require division of responsibilities. As more and more people are added to the organization, this division becomes greater. Job descriptions have several important advantages. They help the manager analyze and improve organization structure and determine whether all company responsibilities are fully covered. They can also help in the reallocation of responsibilities to achieve a better balance, if necessary. An effective job description does more than simply list specific duties and responsibilities. It also indicates the relative importance of each duty and responsibility.

(See Chapter 11, Office Manuals and Publications.)

Writing a Job Advertisement

Once the decision has been made to create a new job, a job advertisement may have to be written for the newspaper or for posting within the company. The human resources department (if one exists in the organization) is the best source of assistance in writing the ad. (See Figure 5-1.) However, if it is left to you or your supervisor, the following considerations should be noted:

- An advertisement should explain as succinctly as possible what the job is.

CHAPTER 5

SUPERVISION

AND

TRAINING

Blind ad (no listing of company's name, only post office box number):

Educational organization needs organized, outgoing person with strong word processing and interpersonal skills to coordinate production and planning of public presentations and management seminars. Desktop publishing and graphic arts a plus. Send resume to this newspaper, P.O. Box 1011.

Open company ad:

Detail-oriented individual needed with minimum 2 yrs. exp. to handle work analysis. Write job descriptions, conduct surveys, and assist in personnel screening. Send resume to the XYZ Corp., 91 Victor St., Scotch Plains, NJ 07091.

Figure 5-1 Sample job advertisements.

- Job requirements or prerequisites should be stated to screen out unsuitable applicants.
- The advertisement should reflect the legal issues in hiring, such as stating that your organization is an equal employment opportunity employer.
- Being creative in the advertisement can help attract a higher quality of applicant.
- The advertisement should not misrepresent the job but rather explain it, indicating the most important points of the job. Beware of the ad that promises too much.
- Use a post office box if the company wants to protect its identity, or to avoid a possible flood of applicants.
- The ad can be placed in trade magazines and newsletters as well as in the classified section of local newspapers (usually placed on Sunday and running for three to five days), business newspapers, and professional association publications.

Interviewing

Conducting a successful interview involves a number of steps. First, screen the written applications. The basic screening device is the application form or resume. Once you have done this, talking to candidates by phone is also a good way to narrow the field further. Try to turn such conversations into mini-interviews.

Before each interview, familiarize yourself with the candidate's application form or resume. Jot down some questions that you want to ask to make sure you control the conversation. The eight most common questions asked during an interview are:

1. What are your major strengths?
2. What are your major weaknesses?
3. How is your previous experience applicable to the work we do here?
4. Why are you changing jobs?
5. Is there someone we can contact who is familiar with your work activities?
6. Where do you see yourself in this company five, ten years from now?
7. What kind of work are you looking for?
8. What kind of compensation do you expect?

During the initial interview, which should last about 30 minutes, you should acquaint the applicant with the company and position(s) available and try to learn as much as possible about his or her background. A good rule of thumb is for the interviewer to talk about 20 percent of the time and the applicant 80 percent.

Write down your impressions during and after the interview. This can help you begin further to narrow down the list of applicants. An initial interview helps in gathering factual information about the applicant's background, attitudes, reasoning process, motives, and personal goals.

Certain questions that are illegal to ask during the interview are shown in Table 5-1. Here are some additional interviewing techniques:

- Create a proper interview environment by holding the interview in a place free from interruptions.
- Put the candidate at ease. This helps to generate a useful flow of information; it also indicates to the candidate this could be a good place to work.
- Perfect your questioning techniques. Vary your use of questions from those that require a simple "yes" or "no" and to those that require more explanation so that the end result is a conversation, not a grilling session.
- Give the applicants feedback to their responses; this encourages more in-depth answers.
- Keep your reactions to yourself; stay in control and maintain a professional rapport.
- Be honest. Conclude the interview by letting the candidates know whether they are being considered for the position and will be called for additional interviews.

If you know after the interview that this is not the candidate for the job, write to the applicant indicating your decision to hire someone else and thank him or her for applying. If the applicant calls, this information should be conveyed orally.

Finally, when choosing one candidate over another ask yourself the following questions:

Table 5-1
UNACCEPTABLE AND ACCEPTABLE QUESTIONS TO ASK IN AN INTERVIEW

CATEGORY	UNACCEPTABLE	ACCEPTABLE
Name	The fact of a change of name or the original name of an applicant whose name has been legally changed Whether the applicant has ever worked for the employer under a different name	Maiden name of a married woman
Birthplace	Birthplace of applicant Birthplace of applicant's parents Requirement that applicant submit birth certificate or naturalization and/or baptismal record	Applicant's place of residence Length of applicant's residence there
Religion	Applicant's religious affiliation Church, parish, or religious holidays observed	
Race/color	Applicant's race Color of applicant's skin, eyes, hair, and so on	
Age	Date of birth, except when information is needed for: 1. Apprenticeship requirements based on a reasonable minimum age 2. Satisfying the provisions of either state or federal minimum age statutes 3. Verifying that applicant is above the minimum legal age 4. Avoiding interference with the operation of the terms and conditions and administration of any bona fide retirement, pension, or employee benefit program	
Citizenship	Any inquiries concerning citizenship	Can applicant produce documentation of eligibility to work in this country
National origin/ancestry	Applicant's lineage, ancestry, and so on Nationality of applicant's parents or spouse	
Language	Applicant's primary language Language used at home How the ability to read, write, or speak a foreign language was acquired	Language(s) the applicant speaks fluently

(continued)

Table 5-1 *(cont.)*

CATEGORY	UNACCEPTABLE	ACCEPTABLE
Relatives	Name and address of any relative	Names of relatives employed by company Person to be notified in case of emergency
Military experience	Applicant's military experience, other than 1. U.S. National Guard or Reserve 2. Draft classification 3. Dates and conditions of discharge	Military experience in United States Whether applicant has received any notice to report for duty
Organizations	Membership in any club, social fraternity, society, or lodge	Membership in any union or professional, trade, or service organization
References	Name of pastor or religious leader	Names of persons willing to provide professional and/or character references
Sex and marital status	Sex of applicant Marital status Dependents	Maiden name
Arrest	Number and kinds of arrests	
Height	Only if it is a bona fide occupational requirement	

1. Does this candidate fit in with the people already here? Does this person have compatible perspectives, integrity, and a desire to work as part of the team?
2. Does this candidate show enthusiasm for this particular job?
3. Does this candidate project a good image?
4. Would this candidate go the extra distance to get the work done?
5. Does this candidate have a genuine enthusiasm for this organization and its goals?

Following the initial screening and interview process, the top candidates can be invited back for further interviews with other members of the staff. If the position requires certain skills, such as keyboarding or dictation proficiency, tests may be given.

Hiring Temporary Help

Temporary help is used to fill in for unplanned absences (such as illness), planned leaves, vacations, and seasonal or short-term workloads. Before you can effectively use temporaries, however, you must:

- Identify what positions can be filled by temporaries and specific duties the temporaries will be performing.
- Summarize skills needed for each position, being as specific as possible.
- Compile a short outline of company-specific procedures, based on job descriptions. Give copies to the agency for its reference and be sure they are available to temporaries when they arrive for work.

In selecting a temporary agency, make appointments for interviews with several firms. Evaluate according to:

Prompt and accurate response: The agency should confirm requests quickly and provide the names of other qualified agencies should it not be able to accommodate your request.

Feedback and quality control: The agency should monitor the temporary the first day to ensure that the temporary has the proper skills and should be ready to respond if problems occur.

Adequate insurance coverage: The agency should provide insurance in several areas to protect both the employee and your employer. Bonded personnel should be available if required.

Solid references: An agency should provide references from other clients and employees.

The key to working with temporary agencies is to develop a long-term relationship.

Checking the Resume and References

In the process of selecting a candidate, you should thoroughly review the resume and check the candidate's references. According to national personnel surveys, 33 percent of the resumes submitted contain false information. Employment dates, salary levels, job responsibilities and titles, and reasons for termination are the most frequent areas where the truth gets stretched.

A starting point for detecting dishonest resumes is to question such things as omissions, abbreviations, peculiar wording, and ambiguous information. Copies of transcripts, W-2 forms, and letters of reference in conjunction with thorough interviews are also common means to counter resume fraud. However, heavy workloads compounded by understaffing may not give you enough time to check resumes.

In an effort to save valuable time and money, many employers are using searchable computer databases to screen and refer suitable candidates. This process, known as electronic applicant tracking, uses special software to scan resumes into a computer system as images. The computer reads each resume and creates a database or **resume bank** of the applicant's relevant skills, educational qualifications, and achievements in the form of keywords. Employers access a candidate's resume by searching for keywords that are relevant to the position being filled. A candidate will be chosen for an interview if he or she matches the requirements submitted by the employer. Employers may also use a resume matching service that searches their own resume banks and refers candidates based on the employer's requirements. (See Chapter 2 for more information on resumes.)

Giving References

As a supervisor or as a colleague, you may be called on to give potential employers references on people you have worked with or trained. In today's litigious society, this is not always as easy as it seems.

Because of the threat of lawsuits, many companies refuse to give references unless they are positive ones. Often employers will have employees sign a waiver granting the company permission to give references. Despite these seemingly careful measures, companies that refuse to give references or give them with employees' permission may still end up being sued.

The best way to approach references is to assume your information will be heard in court and be prepared to defend what you say as fact. Consult your company's legal representative to determine the best policy in providing references.

Some guidelines to follow in giving references:

Check your company policy to find out what information you may provide. This policy should be stated in writing as part of any waiver that employees sign granting the company permission to give information to potential new employers.

If you give a telephone reference, maintain a written record of who called you, when they called, and what you said. If you provide a letter of reference, keep a copy for your files.

Provide only information regarding verified and documented job performance. References are not the place to advertise a personal grudge against a past employee.

If you do make a personal statement, it should begin with the phrase "in my opinion" or "I believe" to make it clear it is your personal opinion and not a fact. Trying to prove objectively that a person lacks motivation or has a difficult personality is extremely hard.

Provide only the information asked of you. If you give information beyond that requested by the caller, make it clear that this information should be treated as confidential. One way to convey that the information you are providing is not intended to damage an employee's reputation is to qualify it. Use phrases such as, "This information is for professional use only."

SEXUAL HARASSMENT

Sexual harassment in the workplace is difficult to define and it is not confined to males harassing females. The Equal Employment Opportunity Commission (EEOC) provides the following guideline:

Unwelcome sexual advances, requests for sexual favors, and other verbal or physical conduct of a sexual nature constitutes sexual harassment when 1. Submission to such conduct is made either explicitly or implicitly a term or condition of an individual's employment; 2. Submission to or rejection of such conduct by an individual is used as the basis for employment decisions affecting such individual; or 3. Such conduct has the purpose or effect of substantially interfering with an individual's work performance or creating an intimidating, hostile, or offensive working environment (Federal Register, 1980:25025).

A study by the International Association of Administrative Professionals™ (IAAP™) and Nan DeMars' CPS reported that office workers considered behaviors related to sex in the workplace—including certain physical contact, verbal discussion of sex, and the display of pornographic material—to be a basis for a formal complaint or a lawsuit. Based on this study and good management sense, follow these guidelines:

- Document all complaints and give each of the parties involved an opportunity to clearly state the case.
- Stop inappropriate behaviors before they become pervasive. Doing so can help improve an employee's performance as well as minimize the threat of lawsuits.
- Become familiar with your company's sexual harassment policy.

EMPLOYMENT DISCRIMINATION BASED ON RELIGION, ETHNICITY, OR COUNTRY OF ORIGIN

Title VII of the Civil Rights Act of 1964 prohibits workplace discrimination based on religion, national origin, race, color, or sex.

The law's prohibitions include harassment or any other employment action based on any of the following:

- *Affiliation:* Harassing or otherwise discriminating because an individual is affiliated with a particular religious or ethnic group. For example, harassing an individual because she is Arab or practices Islam, or paying an employee less because he or she is black.
- *Physical or cultural traits and clothing:* Harassing or otherwise discriminating because of physical, cultural, or linguistic characteristics, such as accent or dress associated with a particular religion, ethnicity, or country of origin. For example, harassing a woman wearing a *hijab* (a body covering and/or head scarf worn by some Muslims), or not hiring a man who is of American Indian descent.
- *Perception:* Harassing or otherwise discriminating because of the perception or belief that a person is a member of a particular racial, national origin, or religious

group whether or not that perception is correct. For example, failing to hire a Hispanic person because the hiring official believed that he was from Pakistan, or harassing a Sikh man wearing a turban because it was thought he was Muslim.

- *Association:* Harassing or otherwise discriminating because of an individual's association with a person or organization of a particular religion or ethnicity. For example, harassing an employee whose husband is from Afghanistan, or refusing to promote an employee because he attends a mosque.

- *Religious Accommodation:* Title VII requires an employer to reasonably accommodate the religious practices of an employee or prospective employee, unless doing so would create an undue hardship for the employer. Some reasonable religious accommodations that employers may be required to provide workers include leave for religious observances, time and/or place to pray, and ability to wear religious garb.

Other Federal Laws Prohibiting Job Discrimination

- *Equal Pay Act of 1963 (EPA):* Protects men and women who perform substantially equal work in the same establishment from sex-based wage discrimination.

- *Age Discrimination in Employment Act of 1967 (ADEA):* Protects individuals who are 40 years of age or older.

- *Title I and Title V of the Americans with Disabilities Act of 1990 (ADA):* Prohibit employment discrimination against qualified individuals with disabilities in the private sector and in state and local governments.

- *Sections 501 and 505 of the Rehabilitation Act of 1973:* Prohibit discrimination against qualified individuals with disabilities who work in the federal government.

- *Civil Rights Act of 1991:* Among other things, the act provides monetary damages in cases of intentional employment discrimination.

Discriminatory Practices Prohibited by These Laws

Under Title VII, the ADA, and the ADEA, it is illegal to discriminate in any aspect of employment, including:

- hiring and firing
- compensation, assignment, or classification of employees
- transfer, promotion, layoff, or recall
- job advertisements
- recruitment
- testing
- use of company facilities

- training and apprenticeship programs
- fringe benefits
- pay, retirement plans, and disability leave or other terms and conditions of employment
- employment decisions based on stereotypes or assumptions about the abilities, traits, or performance of individuals of a certain sex, race, age, religion, or ethnic group, or individuals with disabilities
- denying employment opportunities to a person because of marriage to, or association with, an individual of a particular race, religion, national origin, or an individual with a disability. Title VII also prohibits discrimination because of participation in schools or places of worship associated with a particular racial, ethnic, or religious group.

Employers are required to post notices to all employees advising them of their rights under the laws EEOC enforces and their right to be free from retaliation. Such notices must be accessible, as needed, to persons with visual or other disabilities that affect reading.

Filing a Charge

Anyone who believes that he or she has been subjected to discrimination may file a charge with the nearest field office of the Equal Employment Opportunity Commission. Persons who file a charge, oppose unlawful employment discrimination, participate in employment discrimination proceedings, or otherwise assert their rights under the laws enforced by the commission are protected against retaliation. An EEOC charge must be filed within 180 days (or 300 days if the state has a fair employment practices agency) of the date of the disputed conduct. Field offices are located throughout the United States. To be connected to the appropriate office, call 800–669–4000. EEOC's TTY number is 800–669–6820.

Publications available at no cost include posters advising employees of their EEO rights, as well as pamphlets, manuals, fact sheets, and enforcement guidance on laws enforced by the commission. For a list of EEOC publications, or to order publications, write, call, or fax The U.S. Equal Employment Opportunity Commission, Publications Distribution Center, Box 12549, Cincinnati, OH 45212-0549, 800–669–3362 (voice), 800–800–3302 (TTY), 513–489–8692 (fax). Information about EEOC and the laws it enforces also can be found at the agency's Web site: www.eeoc.gov.

WORKPLACE VIOLENCE

Violence does occur in the workplace, and companies must have firm policies against it. The U.S. Department of Justice reports that assaults and violent acts in the workplace result in fatalities, injuries, grief-stricken family and friends, and absenteeism because of the emotional impact.

Steps that prevent violent incidents and help employees cope if violence does take place include the following:

1. Establish, print, and distribute a clear policy on workplace violence prevention and security. The policy should be discussed with all employees.
2. Managers must improve hiring practices, implement screening techniques, utilize background checks, encourage employees to report threats or violent behavior, establish termination policies, and provide post-termination counseling.
3. All employees should be trained to recognize the warning signs of aggressive or violent behavior.
4. Managers and supervisory personnel must be trained in threat assessment and de-escalation techniques.
5. Organizations should foster harmonious, supportive work environments in which employees are empowered, as well as encourage empathetic management skills.

TRAINING EMPLOYEES

Because today's office professional is the main interface between management and computer-based office systems, a sound knowledge of office automation is imperative. The office professional is expected to be able to access a database, manipulate financial models, output to graphic displays, and integrate the applications into a comprehensive word processing document. A professional is also expected to apply conceptual and human relations skills within this fast-paced environment. Effective training fills gaps in an individual's skills and knowledge.

Training can be handled through several methods:

- Classroom training
- Self-study manuals, audiotapes, and videotapes
- Seminars, workshops, or structured on-the-job training
- Videodisk training packages
- Computer-based Training (CBT)

Training can be done by the organization's in-house personnel or conducted by outside vendors either on-site or off-site.

Classroom Training

Despite a focus on self-paced training, instructor-led training is still the most popular form. Instructor-led training has the following advantages:

- Trainees receive immediate feedback from an acknowledged leader.
- It is scheduled training with a specific time set aside.
- It is less expensive than one-on-one tutoring.

On-site training is more convergent and eliminates the cost of travel. Off-site training is more concentrated and eliminates office interruptions and having equipment tied up for training purposes. Electronic materials are also available to supplement classroom instruction.

Audiotapes and Videotapes

Through the use of a cassette, a voice prompts the learner through a series of programmed segments. An accompanying diskette controlled from the computer keyboard works along with the tape, displaying additional course materials on the screen and illustrating particular points.

Trainees can also watch a training videotape on a TV screen and may also perform exercises on a personal computer.

Computer-Based Training

Computer-based training (CBT) uses a program encoded onto a diskette along with courseware that introduces features of the program frame by frame. The learner turns on the computer, inserts the disk, and hits the proper start-up keys; the system then takes over, showing and telling the student what to do next. Web-based training is another form of computer-based training.

Distance learning, a form of (CBT), is especially popular with companies that need to regularly retrain their employees because it is less expensive than bringing all the students together in a traditional classroom setting. Students may elect to work at home or at the office and communicate with faculty and other students via e-mail, electronic forums and videoconferencing, and other forms of computer-based communication. The Internet serves as the platform for many distance learning systems.

Training Temporary Help

If a position needs to be filled by temporary help, you must effectively organize the temp's time. Here are some pointers for using temporary help:

- Arrange the work to be done in sequence. Prioritize.
- Set aside a specific place for the temp to work.
- Provide all equipment and supplies needed.
- Prepare instructions and write them out.
- Furnish samples of company brochures, letters, forms, and so forth.

- Assign a full-time employee to assist the temp. Let that person monitor the temp's performance.
- Keep your expectations reasonable.
- Introduce the temp to other office personnel. Make the temp welcome as a team member.
- Keep a list of temps who work out well, and ask the agency to send one of these temps the next time you need one.

Skill Certifications

An excellent method for evaluating or upgrading an employee's skills is through skill certification programs. For example, the Microsoft™ Office User Specialist (MOUS) exams evaluate a person's overall comprehension of Microsoft Office or Microsoft Project programs. The International Association of Administrative Professionals (IAAP)™ administers two certification programs: the Certified Professional Secretary (CPS) rating, and the Certified Administrative Professional (CAP) rating. The CPS and CAP designation programs go beyond a simple evaluation of levels of knowledge and competency to provide a body of knowledge for future use, encourage professional development, and provide a means to keep abreast of change.

SUPERVISING EMPLOYEES

How effectively work is accomplished depends a great deal on the supervision people receive. Good supervision encompasses motivation, performance review, the ability to make decisions and communicate expectations and disappointments, and ordinary common sense.

Managing for Change

A manager's greatest challenge will be motivating a high level of employee morale while maintaining a high level of productivity.

Downsizing, erosion of loyalty, virtual officing, and obsolescence, as well as the need to upgrade hardware/software skills, are among the many factors contributing to increased worker stress. Change often creates uncertainty and fear of the unknown, especially in the initial stages of reorganization or introduction of something new. Some workers may challenge a software upgrade as unnecessary because the old version worked just fine. Managers will have to guard against employees believing they are overworked, unimportant, and unappreciated.

Educating and informing are two of the most effective tools in dispelling misunderstanding and overcoming resistance. Once people are properly informed and are shown how a new system works, resistance will generally decrease, especially as they begin to experience benefits from the change.

A needs assessment is the first step in educating your staff. This will help you to pinpoint the technical, administrative, and interpersonal skills in need of improvement. Assessments may reveal needs in such areas as software applications, self-esteem, career development, stress and time management, and dealing with change. Next, implement an improvement program by providing classroom training, self-study manuals or audio/video tapes, seminars, or structured on-the-job training. Use your own personnel to provide the training or hire a specialist from the outside.

A failure to communicate is often the real problem behind a refusal to accept change. Employees are expected to accept or at least try the proposed change. Simply telling people is only part of an effective communications program. Feedback is critical, and supervisors need to analyze the situation and consider the following:

- What is the level of the employees' technical knowledge and expertise?
- What are the individuals' specific needs and aspirations?
- What is the overall business and social climate?
- What are the ages and other demographics of the group?
- What other changes have occurred recently?
- Will the change cause anyone to lose their job or be demoted?
- How supportive is management of the change?

When a change is proposed, people will react to the message according to their experiences and understanding. If they are uninformed and inexperienced, they will not receive the message the way that you intended.

The Internet can provide a volume of information on the latest thinking pertaining to effective management and supervision practices. Here are some Web sites that may be helpful:

- Wharton School's Center for Leadership and Change Management (http://leadership.wharton.upenn.edu)
- Harvard Business School Publishing (www.hbsp.harvard.edu)
- Booz Allen Hamilton's "Strategy + Business" (www.strategy-business.com)
- Management-First.com (www.managementfirst.com)
- About Management (http://management.about.com)
- Bpubs.com (www.bpubs.com) (a search engine)

Motivating Employees

Motivation is the internal process that moves or energizes you to fulfill various goals. The word *motivation* comes from the Latin word meaning "to move." Motivation techniques are important to your job of supervising others. Such techniques include the following:

Set objectives: Help employees establish challenging, measurable objectives that will motivate them. Supervisors with little experience frequently fail to motivate workers because they are afraid to demand too much. Once you have set the objectives, you must follow through to see that the objectives are achieved.

Give recognition: Recognition should be given through verbal praise, a thank-you letter, the company newsletter, and so forth. Incentives can also include bonuses and stock options.

Enrich the job: Give employees a greater variety of duties to perform, especially if the employee wants them and has the time to do them. By making the job more challenging, you prepare the employee for advancement. Job enrichment can also be achieved through additional education. Seminars, workshops, or classes can provide a greater understanding of the jobs and duties of office professionals. Additional responsibility has been shown to increase the employee's sense of satisfaction. It also contributes to promotional possibilities, since new skills will be acquired by performing additional duties.

Develop a team: Productivity can increase when each person in the group contributes to the effectiveness of the team. Motivation starts when you give your undivided attention to the people you supervise.

Compensate the job appropriately: Yearly or semiannual performance reviews that reward good work can help motivate individuals. A pay increase should be the result of a good review. It not only motivates; it helps to develop loyalty and dedication to the organization.

Delegate: Delegation is the process of entrusting the performance of a specific job to another person. Delegation is one of the keys to effective supervision, but it is also one of the hardest things for most supervisors to do. Some supervisors may not understand their role and therefore cannot delegate what they do not understand. Some believe that the work will not be done properly unless they do it themselves. Some fear competition or loss of credit and recognition. Delegation is important, however, to distribute work fairly and to motivate employees and give them an opportunity to grow.

Conducting a Needs Assessment

Having up-to-date computer hardware and software and providing related training are not all that is required to improve an office worker's productivity. Nor is sufficient motivation. Productivity can often suffer because of procedural and reporting issues. An effective tool for analyzing "productivity bottlenecks" is to conduct a needs assessment. This tool can also be helpful when assessing computer hardware and software requirements for users, since the data gathered can help answer many questions and provide necessary information on which to base decisions. The following points will guide you:

- A positive commitment by management is vital to a successful study. Get the support of both the senior and middle managers in the department to be studied. So-

1. **Communicate clearly; describe what is expected and when the job is to be completed.**

2. **Do not limit the delegation to the jobs you do not want to do.**

3. **Explain the importance of assignments.**

4. **Share power with other office professionals.**

5. **Know your fellow office professionals, their aptitudes, and their interests.**

6. **Delegate work evenly among all office professionals.**

7. **Schedule program checks of delegated tasks.**

8. **Define responsibilities for each office professional and make this information known to others.**

9. **Establish reasonable deadlines.**

10. **Reinforce good performance; offer suggestions to improve unsatisfactory performance.**

Figure 5-2 Ten rules for effective delegation.

licit specific issues they want to have included or outcomes they would like to see result from the study.

- Define the exact scope of the study. For example, "to determine the cost/benefits of an alternative administrative support structure" is a clearly defined, measurable objective. All departments and personnel to be included should be listed, along with the project leaders (if any) for each department.

- Communicate the scope and objectives of the study effectively to the administrative support staff. Gain their support by explaining fully and patiently the reasons for the study and its possible benefits for them and the departmental managers. Let each person know at the outset that the results of the study will not necessarily be used to eliminate jobs; rather, the results will be used to improve the current administrative support system. A good technique is to conduct orientation sessions in which you discuss the purpose of the study, timetables, who will be included in the study, and what is to be expected from each participant.

- Establish a needs assessment team of at least three people to help you design the study instruments, conduct the study, and analyze the findings. Since data may comprise many items, it must be reduced to a meaningful, manageable form. Several approaches to gathering the data may be taken. These include interviews, questionnaires, work measurement, and identification of all tasks. A combination of an interview and a questionnaire is usually successful.

- For managers, use open-ended questions that get at the issues that could increase or decrease administrative support productivity. For example, ask the managers questions about what they like best and least about the current system and the reporting relationships; have them identify tasks they currently delegate and other tasks they might want to delegate; ask how they would reorganize the administrative support to be more effective. Most importantly, help them feel that they are participating in the solution. Be sure to keep the manager's interview to a maximum of 30 minutes.

- Use both open- and closed-ended questions for the administrative support group. The open-ended questions could be similar to those used for the managers. The closed-ended questions should be task-related and elicit the information about telephone activity, time spent at the photocopy and fax machines, messenger/errand services, maintenance of manuals and data libraries, research activities (online and in the corporate library), audiovisual services, mail procedures, filing (both paper and electronic), time spent in meetings with managers or others in the organization, nature of computer activities, time spent performing various software applications, and any other activities pertinent to administrative support in the organization. Time survey sheets and work samplings are also effective approaches to augment and validate the information gathered through interviews and closed-ended questionnaires. And, just as with the managers, help the staff to feel as if they also are participating in coming up with appropriate solutions.

- Activities to perform during an interview include introducing yourself and the other team members, reiterating the objective of the study, reviewing the topics you will discuss, and taking notes. But also listen (ask if it is all right to use a tape recorder), assure them that their input will be kept confidential within the survey team, keep the interview focused, summarize at the end, and thank the interviewees for their time.

- Immediately after the interview, organize your notes with a team member and summarize the findings. Identify points that are still unclear and may require you to ask for a second interview. Evaluate your own performance!

- The analysis of the study should be presented in a final report to the department's senior manager, although others may also be involved when the report is presented. Keep the statistics to a minimum, using them only as needed, such as to clarify the findings in a graph format. Just as in any other type of report, one picture or graph is worth a thousand words. If needed, statistical analysis software with graphic output for inclusion in reports exists. Support each of your recommendations with data from the study. Should your recommendations have an impact on "nuts and bolts" issues, such as adding administrative personnel, reorganizing the office layout, or purchasing more equipment, provide the required budget.

- Urge management to announce the results of the administrative study. Having open lines of communication among departmental members is a basic requisite for productivity improvement.

Conducting Job Evaluations

A job evaluation or performance **review** is a private meeting between an employee and an immediate supervisor to discuss the employee's past, present, and future performance. Through a systematic rating procedure, management should maintain a record of the performance of its personnel and make decisions regarding employment, placement, transfers, promotions, dismissals, and individual salary rewards.

Evaluations answer the basic question, "How am I doing?" A formal evaluation is scheduled at least once a year. Informal evaluations occur on a continuous basis.

Here are a number of suggestions for conducting formal and informal evaluations:

1. Prepare the employee: Do not evaluate without letting the employee know why the appraisal is required.
2. Evaluate on the basis of current behavior and performance.
3. Assess all the facts objectively. Be fair.
4. Be consistent. Do not say one thing in the evaluation and write something else on the evaluation form.
5. Appraisal information should be given only to those who need it. Such information should be kept confidential.
6. Be clear, concise, and accurate in writing the evaluation report.
7. Allow adequate time for the evaluation.
8. Listen to what the employee says in the meeting.
9. Establish attainable objectives. Set down in writing a plan of action for improvement, with dates for achieving each objective.
10. Support these objectives by providing opportunities for professional development such as internal training programs, outside seminars, or classes to build skills and promote career advancement.

The evaluation should be constructive. The main objective of such a process is to improve performance. Keep in mind that you should evaluate an employee as if you were the person being evaluated.

A performance appraisal should include the following elements:

- Quality of work.
- Quantity of work, or productivity under normal daily requirements.
- Performance under stress.
- Knowledge of work, e.g., utilization of training and experience and understanding of the job in the organization.
- Initiative.
- Adaptability and flexibility.
- Judgment.
- Resourcefulness.
- Cooperation or teamwork.
- Job presence, e.g., lateness, absenteeism.
- Administrative ability.
- Professional appearance and behavior.

For those personnel involved in word processing, the performance appraisal would also encompass such skills as typing, dictation, and telephone manners.

Giving and Receiving Criticism

Learning to give and take criticism is an important skill for supervisors. Since no one is perfect, criticism should be expected. The way in which you deliver criticism, however, determines whether its effect will be productive or disastrous. Whether you are receiving or giving criticism, some important points should be remembered and practiced.

If you must criticize, keep the following points in mind:

- Stay calm. Anger creates a physical reaction that can make you tense and unreasonable. Walk away. Sit at your desk or some quiet place and relax. Uncross your legs and arms and close your eyes and think of a peaceful scene. Holding your body in this fashion helps to relieve the anger.
- The best times to criticize someone are early in the morning and at midday. This gives you a chance to speak to your coworker again during the day in a casual manner, reassuring the person that you have found fault with the behavior, not the person.
- Listen to what the other person has to say. Create an open environment for discussion. Use body language and a tone of voice to let the person being criticized know that you are on his or her side. Criticize the person's actions or behavior only.
- Criticize in private but compliment in public. Criticizing in public alienates the person you are criticizing and may lower the opinion of you held by people overhearing your remarks.

- Be specific. Say exactly what the person is doing wrong, such as, "This is what I don't like and here's why."
- Be supportive. Give the sense that the criticism is meant to help the person do better.
- Help solve the problem. Suggest a solution or offer to help find a way to improve things.
- Be timely. Give the message soon after the problem occurs.

These destructive ways to give criticism should be avoided:

- Being vague by offering no specifics, merely making a blanket statement, such as "That was a lousy job."
- Blaming the person by attributing the problem to personality or some other unchangeable trait.
- Being threatening, and making the person feel attacked, by saying things such as, "Next time, you're fired."
- Being pessimistic by offering no hope for change or suggestions for doing better.

If you are being criticized:

- Listen without becoming defensive.
- Remain calm. Remind yourself that you can learn from criticism.
- Take notes and repeat the main points to make sure you understand correctly. Doing so allows you time to calm down and shows the other person that you are considering his or her statements.
- Thank the other person if it is a justified and helpful criticism. But if you feel it is unjustified, present your side.
- Tell the person you would like to consider the criticism and discuss it later.
- Outline your responses to the criticism. Explain why you think the criticism is unjustified (if that is the case) and try to end the discussion on a firm and friendly note.

Not all criticism is negative, however. Criticism can also suggest a better method of doing an assignment or a different approach to handling a situation. Such criticism should be viewed as a growth and learning experience.

Supervising Home-Based Office Employees

Telecommuting, or allowing some employees to work part- or full-time at a site other than their primary location, is increasing in many business organizations. This trend is significantly impacting the day-to-day supervisory role of the manager.

Neither all employees nor all jobs are suitable for telecommuting. Good telecommuters are generally people with a demonstrated ability to manage their own time and workload well, solve many of their own problems, and find satisfaction in completing tasks with minimal supervision. Jobs most appropriate for telecommuting are those that are information-based and require a minimum amount of face-to-face contact. Also suitable are jobs that are mobile or can be performed largely via a phone line and computer, such as sales, auditing, consulting, and customer service.

Here are some guidelines to help you effectively supervise your telecommuters:

- Provide training regarding telecommuting for both supervisors and telecommuters.
- Set the hours that telecommuters are to be available by phone or require them to call in at specified times. Rely on phones and personal pagers for crises.
- Organize the team's work so most of the individual work is reserved for telecommuting days and collaborative work for a time when everyone is in the office.
- Handle issues such as security and access to files by using logs and electronic records management systems that can be accessed from remote locations with proper security codes.
- Provide telecommuters with appropriate technology and home office furniture. For example, a mobile telecommuter who will be working in many locations should have a laptop computer with a docking station in the office rather than a desktop computer. A person who spends a lot of time in a home office inputting data into a computer should have correct ergonomic furniture to minimize workers' compensation liabilities. ISDN phone lines, cable modem, or, at a minimum, a 56 baud computer modem is essential for employees who will spend considerable time on the Internet or up- or downloading files. Also, fax equipment is essential for most telecommuting employees. It is important to establish a policy regarding the employee's personal use of the company-owned computer and fax equipment, as well as to maintain the integrity of information stored on both paper and other media.
- Realize that there is no "right" number of days for telecommuting. On the average, one to three days a week seems to be the practice. More time away can give employees the feeling of being "out of the loop" and create morale problems, as well as make it hard for supervisors to schedule group meetings.
- Experiment with telecommuting and have a few volunteers or selected personnel try working at home for one month. This gives you the option of expanding or contracting the program. When doing so, make it clear that telecommuting is not a perk, an entitlement, or a benefit but an alternative way to work and that it will not be suitable for everyone.
- Have each telecommuting employee sign an agreement that summarizes your organization's expectations. This agreement should address such topics as days and hours, work assignments, reimbursement policy for phone calls and supplies, man-

agement contact expectations, company equipment and furniture, telecommunications hookup, and any additional conditions you feel pertinent.

- You can contact the International Telework Association and Council (ITAC) (204 E Street NE, Washington, DC 20002, 202–547–6157 voice, 202–547–6843 fax, www.telecommute.org) for more information about telecommuting programs.

EMPLOYEE DISCIPLINE

Experts indicate that over the course of a management or supervisory career, there is a 90 percent chance of being confronted with a problem employee. Problem employees can be, among other things, chronic complainers, constant talkers, rumormongers, incompetents, habitual latecomers, persistent arguers, or practical jokers.

Dealing with such employees requires a systematic, legal-awareness approach, particularly with today's lawsuits for discrimination and unfair treatment.

Several elements are involved in determining how to discipline an employee:

Facts: The supervisor must seek to discover the facts—the who, what, when, where, why, and how of the incident.

Reason: The supervisor must act as a counselor and listen directly to the employee's account of the incident. This may mean allowing the employee to give the reasons for his or her absence, explain poor performance, or deny an accusation of theft. If an employer fails to give an opportunity for the employee to give his or her side of the story, an arbitrator can reverse the disciplinary action.

Audit: A review of the employee's personnel file must be made as a means of gathering data. The audit should review past performance evaluations and any disciplinary actions that may have been taken. Not all infractions are documented, however, which can make it difficult to support an allegation. By documenting the infraction, support for the disciplinary action can be upheld later in court, if necessary.

Consequences: The supervisor must analyze the impact of the infraction. An employee's behavior can result, for example, in loss of productivity or delay in getting work done.

Type of infraction: The supervisor must define which policy or procedure has been violated. Some offenses are more serious, resulting in more severe discipline or termination.

Improving the Problem Employee's Performance

The first thing to do when you are having problems with an employee is to find out the cause of the problem. Personal problems as well as work-related ones often result in poor performance. Personal problems that affect work performance range from car trouble to divorce, mortgage problems, or the death of a close friend or family member. Work-related problems range from poor lighting to insufficient training, from smoke in the office to a poor relationship with the manager.

Personal problems often manifest themselves at work through mood swings or attendance problems. A supervisor's involvement in personal problems should be kept to a minimum. It is not your role to act as a therapist; rather, you should counsel the employee on job performance and help resolve the problem, using your authority and leverage to encourage and persuade people to do things they might not be interested in doing on their own.

In dealing with work-related problems, several steps need to be taken:

1. Analyze the employee's performance, taking positive and negative behaviors into account.
2. Develop specific goals for improvement.
3. Meet with the employee for a performance improvement interview. Find out from the employee how things are going on the job, if there are any problems, and what you can do to help.
4. Ask the employee to do a self-analysis in order to identify concrete examples of effective performance and areas needing improvement.
5. Present your own analysis to the employee and negotiate a performance agreement that assigns both of you specific tasks designed to improve the employee's work performance within a three- to six-week period.
6. Follow up with a formal interview within a month to evaluate progress.

Firing is only one of several options at the time of the follow-up. The employee's behavior may have worsened, remained the same, or changed only minimally. Before considering firing, a supervisor should explore the possibility of restructuring the employee's job to take advantage of strengths or transfer the employee to another, more suitable position in the organization. Firing may be the only alternative if these options are not feasible, as well as in cases of dishonesty, excessive absenteeism, substance abuse, insubordination, or general lack of productivity. Thorough documentation of the entire performance improvement process should be made to avoid legal difficulties, and other types of disciplinary action can be taken.

Types of Disciplinary Action

When all else fails with problem employees, disciplinary action generally is taken. Based on the infraction and a review of the steps outlined, the following types of discipline can be administered:

Oral warning: This is used for minor infractions and as a first step in progressive discipline. Documentation of a verbal warning is usually not placed in the employee's personnel file, but the supervisor should keep a record of the discussion.

Written warning: A written warning is given by the employee's supervisor as documentation of an infraction. It clearly states future expectations for the employee and indicates what future action will take place if further infractions occur.

Suspension: Suspension is used when the severity of either the present infraction alone or a combination of the employee's past and present behavior warrants a more severe form of discipline. Loss of pay highlights the seriousness and the fact the employee is in jeopardy of losing his or her job.

Sending an employee home: If an infraction is dangerous to the employee or to others, the best course of action is to have the employee leave work for the day. The employee should be told that he or she is to report to work the next day and that management will then inform him or her of the discipline that will be administered.

Discharge: Discharge, or firing, should happen only when it is no longer possible to correct the employee's behavior. The rationale for discharging is that the employee's actions gave management no other alternative.

The most successful people and companies are those who behave ethically. The leaders of a corporation set the tone for ethical behavior, and this determines how employees, customers, and competitors are treated. Ethical problems in business are not just a matter of knowing right from wrong but involve looking at business questions from a reasonable, responsible, and consistent point of view.

Legality Versus Morality

The legality of an action is determined by law. The morality of an action is determined by ethical rules of right and wrong. Ethical behavior requires following the spirit as well as the letter of the law. An ethical business follows rules and trusts that other businesses and their employees will do the same, despite the fact that some unscrupulous business people take advantage of this trust.

Employees may behave unethically because they do what they are told to do without considering the consequences. They may be afraid of losing their jobs, or they may not understand management expectations. The corporate climate often determines employee behavior. For example, when there are slack internal controls, employees may feel free to use work computers for personal reasons or to make an excessive number of personal telephone calls. Employees may be asked to tell "white lies" to protect their supervisors. On the other hand, when management treats employees as trustworthy adults, employees are more likely to act responsibly.

Corporate Image

The reputation of a company is judged by its image in the public eye. One factor of a corporation's image is the care and upkeep of its building, grounds, and offices. Its logo and letterhead also communicate a message about the company. One of the most important factors in a company's image is the way its employees treat its customers and clients as well as the general public. Finally, the way a company treats its own employees is another important factor in corporate image.

A positive corporate image creates respect and confidence in the company and its product or service. Every

CHAPTER 6

BUSINESS

ETHICS

AND

ETIQUETTE

employee can contribute to a positive image by wearing appropriate business attire, by being courteous in telephone calls and written correspondence, by treating visitors well, and by participating in community activities.

More and more people determine where they want to work and with whom they wish to do business based on corporate ethics. Here are some questions to ask in determining whether or not to work for or do business with a company:

- Does the company make quality products or offer superior service?
- Is the company trusted by customers and employees?
- Is the company comfortable and personal for employees, no matter what the size?
- Does the company sacrifice quality for profit?
- Do employees feel that unethical behavior "goes on all the time"?
- Does the company have a code of ethics?
- Has the company been involved in any sexual harassment or civil rights lawsuits, or in any coverups?
- Does the company contribute to the community through public service, charity, youth activities, or the like?

Handling Ethical Problems

As an employee, you may be faced with a situation that is unethical or illegal or both. You will have to decide how best to handle the problem. Research indicates that most office support workers regularly tell "little white lies" and are often in a position to observe unethical activities done by others. Such situations call for a choice of action. All choices have consequences. When making a choice, you must define the problem and weigh the potential consequences. You need to assess the risks of stepping forward and of keeping silent, and to calculate your chances of being fired, reprimanded, demoted, or of having a promotion withheld. You must also live with the possible stress the situation causes.

To help you best solve such borderline ethical problems, it is helpful to answer the following questions:

- What is the problem?
- Is there a law against it? Is there a company policy against it?

HINT: *If the action is against company policy, repeat the request back: "Do I understand you want me to disclose confidential information?"*

- Who is affected by your decision? How are they affected?
- What are the alternatives? What are the consequences of the alternatives?

HINT: *Try to come up with two or three possible solutions.*

- Who can be consulted for help?
- How will your decision make you feel? How does it relate to your personal values? Does it reflect the kind of person you are or want to be and the kind of company you want to work for?

Loyalty is not to be confused with blind allegiance that compromises integrity. Office professionals are responsible and accountable for their own actions. Most managers encourage office staff to bring ethical issues to their attention. Since the majority of office workers will have to face ethical decisions, prepare yourself ahead of time by analyzing your own principles and ethics. If your personal ethics and those of your manager or company do not match, you will not be comfortable in the position. It may be best to find a new position that matches your personal ethics.

Copying Printed Materials and Software

An important issue of legality in today's office involves copyright law. Copyright law defines the rights of copyright owners to authorize others to use their work. Copyright protection applies to published material, software, musical works, pictures, sound recordings, and motion pictures. Reproducing, displaying, or performing copyrighted work without permission is a copyright infringement.

The courts permit "fair use" in copying protected works. Therefore, copying printed documents for purposes such as criticism, comment, news reporting, teaching, or research usually does not violate copyright laws. For example, an article in a newspaper or magazine can be legally copied and distributed to employees. However, copying an article and using it in a seminar where enrollment fees are charged is illegal.

It is illegal to copy software if it is copyrighted. Although licenses vary, software should be treated as if it were a single item, like a book, and should not be used by more than one individual at a time. Software can be moved from computer to computer, but installing copies of the same program on more than one computer is illegal. The copyright law applies to both copy-protected and non-copy-protected software. (See Chapter 8, Office Computer Software, for a discussion of other sorts of programs, such as shareware.)

In order to help firms with many users, most software producers have reasonable pricing for multiple copies. Software must be installed and distributed within the restrictions defined by licenses or agreements with vendors. Installations must be documented so it is clear what was installed, when it was installed, and who installed it. Backup copies, if permitted, must be made in accordance with licenses or vendor agreements and also documented.

Many Web pages contain photographs and graphics. It is illegal to copy graphics or photographs from Web pages or to scan graphics. For example, most cartoons are copyrighted and should not be scanned without getting prior permission in writing from the publisher or copyright holder. Clip art is the term for graphics that can be purchased and legally scanned. Web sites typically indicate whether graphics and/or pictures are copyrighted material.

Business Versus Personal Business

Each company sets its own policy, either formally in writing or informally by example, regarding conducting personal business at work. Research indicates that many office employees use computers for personal business such as accessing stock quotations or making personal travel arrangements. Because completing personal tasks at work decreases productivity, some employers use software that tracks which sites Web users are accessing. Viewing pornography sites at work or accessing the e-mail accounts of others is unethical.

Charging personal long-distance calls to the company and tying up company phones with personal calls are commonly unacceptable practices. Some companies scrutinize phone bills more closely than others and confront employees about questionable calls.

Employees who take company supplies for their personal use may be accused of stealing. Some businesses have tighter controls than others over the supply area and are able to monitor how many supplies are taken and by whom. If the company uses an honor system for supplies, it is a violation of trust to use supplies for personal use.

To avoid embarrassment or questions about your personal integrity, it is best to ask about company policy when you are hired. Just because "everybody else is doing it" does not make it right. You and your company may be held legally liable for e-mail content such as sexist or ethnic jokes or disparaging remarks made about another company. Even when deleted, they remain recoverable in your hard drive and can be a basis for lawsuits.

Sharing Confidential Information

A key role of office support personnel is safeguarding information, both written and oral. Confidential information involves strategic plans, critical company information, hiring, firing, layoffs, and reorganization plans. The issue of confidentiality is an ethical issue encountered regularly in the workplace.

If you are uncertain whether a topic should be treated confidentially, err on the safe side. If you decide to share confidential information, understand that your actions constitute grounds for dismissal with no recourse if it is discovered.

The following are suggestions for safeguarding confidential information:

- Say, "I can't discuss that since it is confidential."
- Avoid leaving information on the computer screen, on a desk, or in a fax machine. Shred confidential information instead of putting it in a wastepaper basket.
- Use a password (available on software packages) to keep others from accessing computer files. Transfer confidential information to a disk that can be locked in a drawer instead of leaving it on the hard drive or network.
- Create special locked files either in a desk drawer or in a separate file cabinet.

Covering Up a Manager's Absence

Office workers may be asked to lie about their supervisor's absence. Avoid saying the manager is in a meeting or out of the office if this information is not true. Saying "Ms. Manager is unavailable" is the truth.

If a manager specifically asks you to lie about his or her whereabouts, do not go into a lengthy explanation as to why you feel this is unethical. Simply state, "I am sorry. I do not feel comfortable in saying that. If you like, I can say . . . ." Most managers do not expect support staff to carry out unethical requests. Even if a manager disagrees with your assessment of a situation, you probably will not be asked to perform the task again.

Additional Ethical Mistakes to Avoid

In a work setting, it is important to consider the needs of others, not just your own. Listed below are ethical mistakes to avoid:

- Blaming "the company" or manager for your own mistakes or those of other employees.
- Taking credit for another employee's ideas or suggestions.
- Protecting poor performers from corrective discipline or termination.
- Suppressing information about on-the-job accidents or failing to report health and safety hazards.
- Plagiarism of any written material.
- Misstating or exaggerating the truth on a resume.

On-the-Job Harassment

Many companies have a harassment policy, which protects employees from harassment because of race, color, ancestry, national origin, religion, sex, marital status, age, or medical condition or disability. Workplace harassment takes many forms, including the following:

- Verbal conduct such as swearing, derogatory comments, slurs, or inappropriate sexual suggestions.
- Visual conduct such as derogatory posters, cartoons, drawings, or gestures. Visual conduct includes e-mail jokes, electronic pictures, or links and/or references to offensive Web sites. Computer screen savers should be appropriate for a business atmosphere.
- Physical conduct such as assault, blocking normal movement, touching, or unwanted sexual advances.
- Demands to submit to sexual requests in order to keep a job or avoid some other loss as well as offers of job benefits in return for sexual favors.
- Retaliation for having reported harassment.

The victim of harassment has a responsibility to complain. The employer has a responsibility to establish a procedure to handle such complaints.

Corporations are held responsible for sexual harassment by their employees (even if top management was not aware of the problem) and can be forced to pay damages. An employer is legally responsible for preventing sexual harassment and providing a harassment-free environment.

Sexual harassment is not just men harassing females. Men may be harassed by women, and sometimes a person is harassed by someone of the same sex. There are no objective criteria for determining what is or is not sexual harassment. Some situations are more obvious than others (e.g., "If you don't have sex with me, you don't get the promotion or get to keep your job.").

To determine whether you are being harassed, ask the following questions:

- Is the action unwelcome?
- Does the behavior continue on a regular basis?
- Is your job at stake if you speak up about sexual propositions, verbal or emotional harassment, or offensive e-mail or electronic communications?
- Does it affect your ability to function at work?

If you feel that your answers indicate you are being harassed, here is a series of steps to take:

1. Tell the harasser that the behavior is offensive and that you want it to stop. Be specific about the behavior. Say "No" as soon as something happens to make you uncomfortable.
2. Keep a record of the behavior with dates, times, and detailed circumstances, including names of witnesses. Print out any offensive e-mail or electronic communications. Store your journal and printouts in a safe place.
3. Write a letter to the harasser specifying what is objectionable and why. Keep a copy.
4. Keep copies of positive work evaluations and memos or letters of praise. These records can refute allegations by the harasser that your work was poor.
5. Try to get witnesses. Ask them to keep a written record of what is happening to you.
6. Follow the company's complaint procedure, which usually means reporting the problem to your supervisor. If the person is your supervisor, go to the harasser's supervisor.
7. If these steps fail, file a formal complaint with the state's department of labor or human resources, the local human rights commission, or the local EEOC office. It is illegal for the harasser to retaliate by firing or demoting you for these actions.

8. Consider conciliation, such as a transfer to another department. If you have a solid case, you may deserve financial compensation.

9. If conciliation fails, decide whether it is worth suing. The court case may take years to settle, though, so this should be only a final step.

BUSINESS ETIQUETTE

Proper business etiquette is essential for good human relations in the office. Good etiquette sets a high standard for handling daily encounters and situations. Treating others with respect and courtesy increases cooperation and enhances working relationships. Most business etiquette is based on common sense and sensitivity.

Introductions

When introducing yourself, extend your hand and give your name. In social settings, the woman is traditionally introduced first. In business, however, decisions on who is introduced to whom depend on the ranks of the individuals, not their gender. In a formal situation, the higher-ranking person should be named first (e.g., "Ms. Higher Rank, I would like you to meet Ms. Lower Rank").

When making introductions, always use both names in a sentence (e.g., "Ms. Jones, I'd like you to meet Ms. Smith"). It is not necessary to repeat the introduction in reverse (e.g., "Ms. Smith, I'd like you to meet Mr. Jones; Mr. Jones, this is Ms. Smith").

When being introduced, always stand if you are sitting and extend your hand. When someone is introduced to you, stand up, maintain eye contact, and shake hands firmly. The handshake should communicate sincere enthusiasm. When wearing a name tag, pin the name tag on your right shoulder (or lapel) so it will be visible when people reach to shake your hand.

If the other party does not extend a hand, withdraw yours and do not worry about it. Having arthritis or other health problems may make shaking hands uncomfortable. If someone has a disability, take the lead from them on their preferred manner of greeting.

In foreign countries, a handshake is not always the accepted means of greeting. In Japan, the preferred form of greeting is a bow from the waist. Most Japanese businesspeople visiting the United States will bow slightly from the waist, and then shake hands. In India and South Asia, one form of greeting is placing the palms together at chest level or higher and giving a slight bow. Indian customs discourage a man from touching a woman or talking with her alone in public. In Europe, a handshake is used, but it is not as firm as the American handshake. In Northern Africa and Central Europe, greetings may be an embrace and a kiss on one or both checks.

The following are general guidelines for introductions:

- The person making the introduction should give a little information about each person to make small talk easier. This information might include titles and areas of responsibility.

- Whether or not to use first names depends on the location and size of the company. Some cities and companies are more formal than others. Generally a lower-ranking person should not use the first name of a higher-ranking person unless asked or given permission to do so.

- After being introduced, repeat the other person's name and say something like, "I am pleased to meet you, Ms. Senior Executive."

- When introducing a company employee to a client, always name the client first: "Mr. Client, I would like you to meet Bob Green, assistant to the president. Mr. Client is with Jones, Inc."

- Introduce a person individually to each member of a group and leave time to shake hands before going on to the next person in the group. Always name the new person first unless the people in the group outrank the new person: "Jim, I would like to introduce my colleagues—June Cortez, John Baker, and Doris Hing. This is Jim Hernandez, manager of information services."

- When introducing people of equal rank, titles (Mr., Ms., Dr.) are not necessary.

- If you forget a name, introduce the person to those whose names you remember. This should be a cue to the omitted person to give his or her name. If this does not happen, admit lapse of memory and say something like, "I'm sorry I've forgotten your name," or "Your name is—?"

- Present a spouse to someone who outranks you. Always name the higher-ranking person first: "Ms. Senior Executive, I'd like you to meet my husband, Mark."

Responding to Invitations

Any invitation, whether to a party introducing a new product line or from a client celebrating a tenth anniversary, should be responded to promptly, to the person named on the invitation. If an invitation was accepted and at the last minute something prevents attendance, it is important to notify the host immediately. If someone other than the person who received the invitation will attend, the host should be notified of this substitution.

Interrupting a Conference

Occasionally an important client or manager asks to talk with a coworker who is in a meeting or conference. It is the role of the office professional to determine whether or not to interrupt the conference.

If the decision is made to interrupt the meeting, the most unobtrusive method is to wait for a break in the meeting to speak with the manager. If the office professional does not know when the next break will occur, a folded note can be given to the coworker. The office professional waits for a response, typically a nod of the head, before leaving the room.

Business Cards

Every office worker needs a business card that includes his or her name, title, phone (including cell phone if appropriate) and fax numbers, e-mail address, company name, mailing and street address, and company Web site address. The following suggestions apply to business cards:

- Plan ahead so an adequate supply of cards is available.
- Present the card face up so it can easily be read.
- Be selective when distributing cards. It is not appropriate to give out a business card socially.
- Avoid wrinkling and soiling cards.
- Include cards with business correspondence.

When enclosing your business card with a business gift, write a message on the back and sign your first name. When using the business card for forwarding material, clip the card on the upper left side of the material. When exchanging cards, let senior management make the first move.

If business is done internationally, the cards should be in English on one side and in the other country's language on the other.

Never refuse a card that someone gives you. When handed the card, read it, check the pronunciation, and ask for clarification if necessary.

Include professional designations on your business card if appropriate.

When out of the card giver's sight, on the back of the card write the date, where you met, and any personal information that will help you remember the person. The date is helpful when updating contacts.

The Business Lunch

A popular way of entertaining employees or clients is the business lunch, which gives people an opportunity to relax and get to know one another away from the office. When a guest is invited to lunch, careful planning and a caring attitude are important.

Here are some tips on inviting guests to lunch:

- Let guests choose the best time.
- Ask for culinary preferences (Italian, Chinese, vegetarian, and so on).
- Decide on the restaurant. Ask coworkers for suggestions, check on the price range, and make certain the location is convenient for the guest.

- Make a reservation, even though one may not be required. Avoid tables near the kitchen, waiters' station, or door. If the location is unacceptable, request another table before sitting down.
- Check for credit card or cash before leaving for the restaurant. If using a credit card, make certain the restaurant accepts that card.
- Make arrangements with the maitre d' and/or waiter to pay for the guest's parking and coat check if necessary.
- Arrive earlier than the guest (you may be seated or wait just inside the restaurant door).

Here are some suggestions for dining with a business associate:

- Sit opposite each other for best eye contact. Guests should have the best seat.
- Place your briefcase, purse, papers, and so forth, on the floor or under your chair.
- Place the napkin in your lap within the first 10 seconds of sitting down and do not place it back on the table until you are ready to leave. If you need to stand or leave the table during the meal, the napkin should be left on your chair.
- Decide what beverage is appropriate. If the other person has ordered an alcoholic beverage, it is acceptable (but not necessary) also to drink alcohol.
- Avoid eating anything that will distract you from the conversation.
- Wait at least ten minutes before discussing business. Do not expect anyone to do a great deal of reading or note taking during the meal.
- Start with the utensil farthest from the plate and work inward.
- Ask the guest whether there is time for dessert and coffee before ordering them.
- Carefully check the bill. Determine ahead of time whether the tip is included.

Here are some suggestions for handling the check:

- Notify the server during the meal that you are picking up the check. Pick it up quickly and do not make a scene. If the check is presented to your guest, let the guest know the company is paying and ask for the check back.
- Leave a 15 percent tip before tax at a moderate restaurant, 20 percent if the restaurant is expensive. Tip even if the service was not good; bring the problem to the attention of the restaurant's management later.

Smoking and Fragrances

Smokers should always be aware of federal, state, and local laws regarding smoking in public places. Many businesses regulate smoking in the office. If smoking is allowed only in designated areas, it is important to abide by all rules, including not smoking in rest rooms.

When dining with a group and no one is smoking at the table, assume that you may not. When visiting someone's office or conference room where there are no ashtrays, assume smoking is not permitted. Smokers should make certain that their clothes and any paperwork are smoke-free. Many nonsmoking employers, clients, and customers find the smell of smoke distasteful. Fragrances are inappropriate in the workplace because of possible allergic reaction of coworkers to perfume or cologne. In addition, fragrances have a social implication not suitable in a business setting.

The Diverse Workplace

In today's workplace it is important to be able to communicate with an increasingly diverse group of people. A diversity of ethnic groups and cultures exists in nearly every workplace. Diversity includes:

- Gender
- Age
- Ethnicity
- Physical abilities
- Religious affiliation
- Sexual orientation

Conflicts may occur in a work setting because colleagues have different cultural expectations regarding work standards, punctuality, relationships, status, or verbal and nonverbal behaviors. To become an effective communicator, you must be flexible, nonjudgmental, and have respect for others. Complete knowledge about numerous cultures is not possible, but the following strategies will increase your effectiveness in the diverse office environment:

- Learn about values, etiquette, and attitudes of diverse colleagues. Spend time with people of different backgrounds.
- Ask questions of individuals in private to help understand and demonstrate your interest in the other person. Explain why you are asking the questions.
- Read about diversity and attend diversity training workshops. Avoid misinterpreting the information and forming conclusions.
- Do not generalize from one person to the other. See each person as an individual. Identify stereotypes you currently hold and remind yourself that they have little validity as accurate indicators of an individual's character, skills, or personality.
- Use nonprejudicial language and/or humor.
- Find shared interests, goals, and values.
- Avoid using the term *minority* to describe ethnic groups. In many parts of the country, the minority groups and majority groups are changing.

- Work on ways to become more verbal when you are aware of inappropriate behavior by others. Trying to play it safe by remaining silent is often perceived as acceptance.

Bias-Free Language

An office professional cannot afford the risk of communicating an insensitive message that may alienate other employees and customers. Using bias-free language focuses on the message. Below are some suggestions for communicating in a diverse workplace.

- Avoid using the masculine pronouns *he* or *him* when the gender could be either male or female. Use the plural *they* or use *he or she.*
- Do not use male and female pronouns in a way that stereotypes roles and occupations; for example, "The office support person should remember to call security when *she* leaves."
- Substitute gender-free words for gender-biased words.
- Omit unnecessary references to ethnicity. For example, avoid "Our new manager is black and from Detroit." Say instead, "Our new manager is from Detroit."
- Avoid religious references to holidays. For example, say "Our office will be closed on December 25" instead of "Our office will be closed for Christmas."
- Avoid referring to those with disabilities in a negative way. For example, avoid "The ramp is for the handicapped only; normal people should use the steps." Instead say, "The ramp is provided as an alternative to the stairs." The term *disabled* is acceptable, but do not use terms like *victim* or *afflicted.*

The Changing Roles of Men and Women in the Office

Traditional social etiquette suggested that a man should always let women leave elevators first, stand up when a woman enters a room, open doors for women, and walk next to the curb. These rules are considerate, but they no longer apply in today's office.

Office etiquette is now based on rank in the company. Never automatically assume that one person (usually a man) ranks higher than another. The following etiquette is appropriate:

- The person closest to an elevator door should exit first.
- The first person to a door should open it and hold it open until all have passed through. If the door is heavy or if a person is carrying something, it is courteous to help regardless of gender. A visitor to an office should be treated like a guest and be allowed to go through a door first.
- Men and women should help each other with coats.

- A person of either gender can hail a taxi.
- When riding with several people in a car (especially if the car belongs to a person of higher rank), it is best to ask where to sit.
- All staff should rise when a visitor of either sex comes into the office from the outside. Staff should also rise for a higher-ranking executive unless that executive is frequently in the office, in which case the lower-ranking person should stop work and acknowledge the presence of the senior person. It is not necessary to stand when a colleague (man or woman) enters or leaves a room.

Respecting the Privacy of Others

Open-plan offices are popular. Suggestions for respecting others working around you are as follows:

- Set your pager to vibrate and turn off or turn the ringer down on your personal cell phone. Take your cell phone with you or turn it off when you leave your desk. Turn off your cell phone during meetings.
- Talk as quietly as possible. Do not use a speakerphone unless you are in a private room. Request a headset if you need your hands free.
- Do not sit in someone's cubicle while he/she is on the phone. Do not stand outside a cubicle waiting for someone to end a phone call.
- Do not make reference to an overheard conversation unless that person initiates the discussion.
- Wait to be invited into someone's cubicle. Do not walk around the office visiting others instead of working.
- Move away from others if two or more people wish to discuss an issue.
- Turn off your computer speakers and use headphones if you like to listen to the radio while you work.
- Do not eat odorous foods at your desk. Strong food odors are offensive to many people.
- Cover your mouth while sneezing, coughing, or yawning.
- Do not use profanity.
- Avoid annoying personal habits such as humming, pencil tapping, mumbling, and interrupting others before they are finished speaking.
- Keep a neat workstation. Sloppiness is immediately apparent in the office and has a negative impact on visitors.
- Avoid looking at others' computer screens.
- Avoid crying at your desk.
- Do not apply makeup or comb hair at your desk.

- Be considerate of others by making more coffee if you take the last cup, changing the copy machine back to the original setting and filling it with paper, adding paper to the printer or fax machine, cleaning up after using the microwave or sink, and taking only your own food out of the refrigerator.

Office Politics

In any job it is important to know who has the power, who will be inheriting the power, and how to assimilate into the organization. Balance is important in office politics. Being overly political and not concentrating on your work will cause people to notice, and not being politically savvy may mean you get overlooked for promotions. Managers in every organization periodically change; the key to surviving office politics is being respectful to everyone.

Be careful of office gossip. People gossip out of boredom or jealousy. Office gossip can give early warnings about corporate reorganizations, the effect of a competitor's product on corporate sales, or the loss of a major client. However, gossiping about personal or work problems of coworkers is counterproductive and dangerous and should be avoided.

Here are some suggestions for dealing with office politics:

- Avoid sharing confidential information unless you are prepared to have the rest of the office know. Do not use e-mail to share confidential information or to gossip about others.
- Treat all coworkers with respect and interest. Give everyone a chance to express his or her opinion. If you avoid negative remarks, coworkers are more likely to treat you with the same respect.
- Avoid criticizing others. Try to change the tone of the gossip sessions to positive subjects. If this tactic does not work, excuse yourself from the conversation.
- Counteract untruths by mentioning the truth when the subject comes up in a conversation. Avoid arguing or losing your temper.
- Ignore harmless gossip and do not pass it on.
- Challenge gossip about yourself. Confront the person whom you believe is responsible for spreading the gossip. Document the dates, times, and people with whom you have spoken to about the gossip. Discuss the situation with personnel in the human resources department.

It is important to be discreet and not to talk about company business inside or outside the business. An executive must feel secure that all information will be confidential, including any knowledge about financial matters or private life.

Domestic Partners

Domestic partners is a term to describe two adults of the same or opposite gender who live together. Some companies are offering benefits to domestic partners and including them in company activities. The following suggestions avoid discrimination against domestic partners.

- Use *guest* instead of *spouse* when issuing invitations to company activities.
- Avoid asking personal questions about relationships or activities outside the workplace. Do not gossip.
- Treat domestic partners the same way you would treat spouses.

Holiday and Birthday Gifts

Many companies have a standard gift or a set amount of money to give to employees during the holidays, a standard gift for customers or clients, and inexpensive promotional items to give away. Companies vary widely in their holiday gift giving, ranging from none at all to giving a turkey or to having or sponsoring a company party.

Employees are usually not expected to give gifts to their employers during the holidays unless the relationship is longstanding and close. Follow the lead of other employees or rely on tradition. Avoid giving gifts during work hours.

Many businesses send out holiday greeting cards to clients or customers with an imprinted company name. Use a card with "Season's Greetings" to avoid the problem of sending religious cards. Each card should be personalized with a signature and a short message.

Some businesspeople send holiday greetings to employees and their families at their home address. This is a nice gesture but not expected or necessary. Office professionals may wish to remember those who have done them favors throughout the year, such as maintenance or security employees.

Holiday cards should be ordered at least two months in advance, particularly if cards are sent abroad. If company gifts are given to clients and customers, they should also be ordered in advance. In many cultures, gift giving is a sign of trust, and the more elaborate gift, the better. When giving a gift to someone from another country, make certain it cannot be interpreted as a bribe under the definition of the 1977 Foreign Corrupt Practices Act. If you are uncertain about the proper gift to give someone from another country, ask a colleague who is familiar with that country or call that country's embassy. In Argentina, for example, giving a set of knives is interpreted as a desire to cut off the business relationship. In China a clock is a symbol of death. Sometimes the best gift is something inexpensive but hard to find in another country. Know the important gift-giving times of the year.

Ask the recipient of the gift, particularly if the recipient is a government agency, about the policy on receiving gifts. A gift that can be shared by the whole office sometimes is more appropriate. Appropriate gifts include food and gift baskets, gift certificates, books, and office-related products such as calendars or pens.

If you receive a gift that is too personal or expensive, return the gift immediately with a letter explaining that your company has gift guidelines. Keep a copy of the letter.

Many businesses keep a list of employee birthdays and celebrate by bringing in a cake and having employees sign a card. Donations for a gift may be requested from coworkers, but it is perfectly acceptable to politely say "no" when asked to contribute.

Office Parties

An office party is an opportunity for coworkers and managers to enhance relationships and boost morale. The following are tips for office parties:

- Dress appropriately for a business event.
- Be aware of alcohol intake. The company should publish or e-mail in advance the policy on drinking in any work-related situation and office social function to avoid misunderstandings. The company should also anticipate the need for alternative transportation for all partygoers and make special transportation arrangements before the party.
- Avoid talking about work.
- Avoid hugging and kissing. Courts in many states have found that unwanted sexual advances, exhibitionism or other outrageous behavior, improper sexual touching, and sexual innuendo that happen at an office party can constitute sexual harassment for which the employer may be held responsible under Title VII of the Civil Rights Act of 1964.

Procedures for an Employee Illness or Death

If an employee or client has been injured, is seriously ill, or is in the hospital, a card is usually sent. Depending on office policy, flowers may also be sent. Some offices have a special fund for purchasing cards and flowers, or donations may be solicited as needed. Other offices have written procedures describing when cards or flowers are to be sent.

In the case of death, a letter of sympathy should be sent to the family. Flowers may also be sent, if appropriate. Some families prefer that donations be made to charities or other organizations. The family should be consulted to determine their wishes.

PART II

EQUIPMENT

AND

SUPPLIES

In the 1960s, data processing significantly changed the way information was handled in the office; in the 1970s, word processing, or automated text editing, was introduced as a substitute for repetitive typing; in the 1980s, information processing, the integration of data and text, became a reality through the widespread use of the personal computer; and in the 1990s, networks linking computers increased the ability of groups to work together electronically. As a result, the role of the office professional has changed dramatically.

Personal computers (PCs), desktop videoconferencing, voice input, multifunction image processors, multimedia, and other products will continue to impact the processing of information at a faster rate than ever before. The faster computer systems of the future will offer several times the performance of today's PCs, delivering more realistic 3-D graphics, flawless video, and quicker processing of digital images. The PCs will also enable a new wave of software innovation, including richer user interfaces. Universal information appliances, such as a PDAs (personal digital assistants) or a wearable computer, will interact with any application or remotely operate any electronic device. Office workers of the 21st century will be at the center of this information explosion, using technologies that will connect them worldwide. This chapter provides an overview of current and emerging office equipment.

CHAPTER 7

OFFICE

EQUIPMENT

THE COMPUTER

A computer is an electromechanical, programmable machine that accepts, processes, interrelates, and displays data. All digital computers have the following components:

- *A central processing unit (CPU),* the device that contains the central control and arithmetic units used for controlling the system.
- *Memory* for temporary storage of programs and data.
- *Mass storage* for permanent storage of programs and files.
- *A visual display monitor,* usually a cathode-ray tube (CRT), or liquid crystal display (LCD) for viewing text, graphics, and numerical data.

- An *input device* for entering data, e.g. keyboard, microphone, optical scanner, digital camera.
- *Software* to give instructions to the computer. (See Chapter 8, Office Computer Software.)
- An *output device,* usually a printer. (See below under the heading *Printers* for more information.)

Central Processing Unit (CPU)

This is the "brain" of a computer. The CPU accepts data, manipulates it according to programmed instructions, and then can direct storage and output of the data. The CPU consists of a control unit and arithmetic logic unit. The control unit is like a telephone switchboard, controlling and coordinating the parts of the computer system as directed by a set of instructions called a **program.** The arithmetic logic unit does the actual calculating or data processing. The speed of a computer system's CPU clock is rated either in megahertz (MHz) (a measure of frequency in millions of cycles per second), or in gigahertz (GHz) (billions of cycles per second).

Memory

Memory enables a computer to store program instructions, data to be processed, and the intermediate results of the mathematical and logical operations it has performed. The size of a computer's memory is given in bytes. A **byte** is roughly the size of one character (single letter, number, or graphics symbol) and is equal to eight bits. A **bit** is the smallest electrical unit of data and is represented as either 1 or 0 in the electronic circuits making up the computer. Other frequently used terms are **kilobyte (KB),** which is 1,024 bytes of information; **megabyte (MB),** which is 1,084,576 bytes; **gigabyte (GB),** which is 1,000 MB; **terabyte (TB),** which is 1,000,000,000,000 bytes; **petabyte (PB),** which is 1,000,000,000,000,000 bytes; and **exabyte (EB),** which is 1,000,000,000,000,000,000 bytes.

A computer has two types of memory, **read-only memory (ROM)** and **random-access memory (RAM).** Measurements of a computer's memory normally refer to RAM.

READ-ONLY MEMORY (ROM)

ROM is the permanent internal memory of a computer. It contains the computer's instructions for starting up (or "booting") the system and for reading the **operating system** instructions. An operating system controls the input, processing, storage, and output of the computer's operations, by managing the interaction between the computer and its peripheral devices, such as the keyboard, printer, and disk drives. (See the section on Systems Software in Chapter 8.)

ROM instructions are generally nonprogrammable, that is, their contents cannot be altered by the user. The CPU can only access instructions in ROM; it cannot write instructions to ROM.

RANDOM-ACCESS MEMORY (RAM)

RAM is the computer's temporary memory; its contents are erased when the power is turned off. It is used to store programs and information only while the computer is operating. The size of the program and amount of data you are working with are limited by the amount of RAM memory installed in your computer. For example, if your computer has 64 MB of RAM and you want to run multiple software programs, you may need to add more MB of RAM. You can purchase additional RAM memory chips that are installed to expand memory. Some software programs, such as high-end graphics, desktop publishing, and large database programs, may require 128 MB or more of RAM.

Media Storage

A variety of magnetically coated materials are used for data and program storage. The main types include:

Floppy disk (or diskette): This is a magnetically coated disk that comes in 3 ½-inch disks (microfloppies) encased in rigid plastic and commonly store 720K (double-density disks) or 1.44 MB (high-density disks) of information. An extra-high-density 3 ½-inch disk holds 2.88 MB of data. A disk drive with a higher capacity can read from and write to a lower-capacity disk. However, the reverse is not possible. For example, if your system has a 2.88 MB minifloppy drive, you can read and write to a 1.44 MB disk in that drive. You cannot read a 2.88 MB disk in a 1.44 MB drive.

Hard disk: This is a rigid, random-access, high-capacity magnetic storage medium. Disks may be removable, providing off-line archival storage, or nonremovable. The major advantages of a hard disk over a floppy disk are speed, capacity, and permanent storage. Modern hard disks have capacities approaching 100 gigabytes. Also, you do not have to continually insert floppy disks when using a hard drive.

Cartridge: This is a magnetic tape loaded into a cartridge (such as a single reel or reel-to-reel) that holds multiple pages of text and is used to back up data.

Compact disks: Referred to as CD-ROMs (compact disk read-only memory), this medium can store much more information than a floppy disk (700 MB versus 2.88 MB on an extra-high-density floppy disk). The disks can store text, data, images, and sound.

CD drive speed is expressed as a numeral followed by an x, where the x stands for 150k/second. A speed rating listed as 2x/2x/6x means the drive writes and rewrites at a maximum throughput of 300k/sec and reads at a maximum throughput of 900k/second. A 2x drive rating means that you can record 300 kilobytes per second. The higher the speed of your drive, the faster you can "burn" (copy or record) CDs. While a 4x writer/rewriter takes about 20 minutes to create a full CD, an 8x writer takes half as long. CD-ROM media consists of more than one type:

CD-R (compact disk–recorder): This is a write-once, read-many technology (WORM) on which users cannot erase or rewrite once the disk has been used. The advantages of this disk are that you can use it with a standard CD player and CDs are a very stable storage medium. The disadvantage is that you can't reuse a disk. Typical applications include large databases such as encyclopedias, catalogs, or other reference information.

CD-RW (compact disk–rewritable): These disks can be erased and reused just like a floppy disk. However, the CD-RW media doesn't work in all players. CD-Rewritable drives are able to write both CD-R and CD-RW disks. This medium is used typically for backing up data files.

Display Monitors

A monitor is an output device that provides a temporary image of information on a video screen. When combined with a keyboard it is called a **video display terminal (VDT).** A display screen can be like a television or can be a flat panel. Monitors vary in size, type, and quality of resolution.

The television-like display screen is called a **cathode-ray tube (CRT)** and typically comes in sizes ranging from 12 to 30 inches.

The larger CRTs, 19 inches or more, are suitable for such applications as **presentation graphics,** which generate, display, and print line drawings, organization charts, bar graphs, and pie charts; **computer-aided design (CAD),** which generates, displays, and prints standard engineering drawings to assist engineers and designers; and **desktop publishing,** which creates a document of typeset quality using personal computers and appropriate software. Dual-head display adaptors, split-screen monitors, and side-by-side monitors are often used with heavy graphic applications, such as desktop publishing and computer-aided design.

There are two major differences in display technologies: resolution and the number of colors produced at those resolutions. **Resolution** is the number of pixels that are used to draw an image on the screen. For example, if a screen displays 800 pixels horizontally and 600 pixels vertically, the resolution is 800 by 600. Multiply 800 by 600 and you'll get the number of pixels used to draw the image (480,000 pixels, in this example). The monitor must be capable of displaying the resolutions and colors that the video card adapter can produce. On the other hand, if your monitor is capable of displaying a resolution of 1,024 by 768 but your adapter can only produce 640 by 480, then the lower number is the maximum resolution you can get.

The following are among the common display standards:

Monochrome (MDA): These monitors display only one color. The basic text mode is 80 characters horizontally and 25 vertically. Each character is made up of a matrix that is 9 dots wide by 14 dots high, yielding an effective resolution of 720 by 350.

Color Graphics Adapter (CGA): This offers a resolution of 320 by 200 pixels (picture elements) in 4 colors selected from a palette of 16 colors. (A pixel is one or more dots treated as a unit. The pixel can represent as little as one dot for monochrome screens or three dots—red, green, blue—for color screens.)

Enhanced Graphics Adapter (EGA): This offers a resolution of 640 by 360 pixels, with 16 colors that can be selected from a palette of 64 colors.

Video Graphics Array (VGA): This offers greater resolution than EGA—up to 720 by 400 pixels in text mode and, in graphics mode, up to 640 by 480 pixels, in 16 colors that can be selected from a palette of 256.

Super VGA (SVGA): Compatible with the older VGA standard, SVGA offers resolutions from 800 by 600 pixels up to 1,280 by 1,024 pixels with a palette of more than 16 million colors. Acronyms referring to the higher resolutions include *Ultra VGA (UVGA),* with 1,024 by 768 resolution; and *Extended Graphics Array (XGA),* 1,024 by 768 graphics in 256 colors, or 640 by 480 at high color (16 bits per pixel). The smallest PC monitors measure 14 inches, which is an adequate size for viewing applications at 640 by 480 or 800 by 600. For comfortable viewing of 800 by 600 resolution, a 15-inch monitor is better. To see multiple applications on the screen at the same time, or to see the quality in a 1,024 by 768 pixel image, a 17-inch screen will be a better choice. With a 20- or 21-inch monitor, you can comfortably view 1,280 by 1,024 resolution, the maximum supported by the Super VGA standard.

A video card's **refresh** or **vertical scan rate**—that is, the number of complete screens the monitor draws per second—is measured in hertz (Hz). Screen flicker is often caused by a slow vertical refresh rate. A video card should meet the refresh standards of the Video Electronics Standards Association (VESA), which are 72 Hz at 640 by 480 and 800 by 600, and 70 Hz at 1,024 by 768. **Noninterlaced monitors** (which draw all the lines on the screen one by one during each pass versus **interlaced monitors,** which draw every other line, half during one pass and the other half during the next) are available with a refresh rate of 70 Hz to 75 Hz.

The amount of **video memory** required varies with the type of application. Most business users need just 4-bit for 16 or 8-bit for 256 colors. However, if typical applications might include desktop publishing, presentation graphics, or computer-aided design (CAD), then 16-bit for 65,000 colors or 32-bit for 16.7 million colors is recommended. Graphics cards are also available for very high resolutions at 64-bit, 128-bit, and 192-bit. The more expensive and faster boards use video memory (VRAM) or Window RAM (WRAM).

To play digital video clips on screen, your computer must be equipped with hardware or software that allows for the rapid compression and decompression of graphics and sound data. QuickTime® software, developed primarily for the Macintosh®, is one way to generate sound synchronized with moving pictures or animations. Other common standards for audio and moving pictures are provided by **MPEG** (Moving Picture Experts Group). The **MPEG-1** standard, for example, calls for a resolution only slightly less than that provided by a VCR and for a minimum rate of 30 frames per second to produce the effect of full-motion video. Although software decompression is less expensive, hardware **MPEG** provides pictures of a higher quality.

Flat panel displays are classified as follows:

Liquid crystal display (LCD): An LCD forms characters by subjecting a liquid crystal solution to an electrical charge. Unlike traditional CRT monitors, which come in convenient standard sizes like 15, 17, 19, and 21 inches, LCD sizes are more varied. For example, NEC-Mitsubishi offers an 18-inch LCD because its research shows fonts displayed on an 18-inch screen are 13 percent larger than the same font, at the same resolution, on a 17-inch display. Typically, resolution is 1,024 by 768 for 15-inch screens and 1,280 by 1,024 for 17-inch and larger. LCD pixels are either on or off and remain that way with no fading or variation, which reduces eyestrain and means the refresh rate is irrelevant.

Gas plasma display (GASP): A GASP is characterized by an exceptionally clear, flicker-free image. It has a sharper image than the LCD and does not depend on any external light source. GASPs have no image distortion, even at edges and corners, and they display a bright, uniform image in normal room light with an amazing 160-degree viewing area from all sides. Thickness ranges from 3 to 6.5 inches, allowing these screens to hang anywhere without interfering with room traffic. There are primarily two types of plasma displays: **multimedia** displays for high-end image reproduction, such as conference room presentations, boardroom audiovisual systems, broadcast production, video conferencing, training and education, trade shows, and network operating centers. **Public displays** are for large-screen presentation of dynamic messages and content associated with advertising at retail store point-of-purchase and merchandising displays, transportation terminals, stadiums, hotel and bank lobbies, trade shows, and kiosks. Sizes are typically 42 inches and 50 inches. Most, but not all, are compatible with DTV/HDTV and have an XGA resolution of 1,024 by 768 pixels or better.

Head mounted displays (eyeglasses SVGA): These are portable computer monitors that are worn on the eyes like ski goggles. Resolution is 800 by 600 and a 1.44-million-pixel display to create the illusion of a 44-inch screen floating in front of you. Audio may be available as a component of these displays. Most systems accept S-Video, composite video, and VGA input, so you can view images generated by everything from a miniature TV or a VCR, to your laptop or PC.

Input Devices

An input device is a means through which a user can enter data and instructions into the computer. The most common device is a **keyboard.** Computer keyboards are similar to standard typewriter keyboards with the addition of function keys. When a key is pressed down, an electrical pulse is emitted that translates the symbol represented by that key into a digital code that the computer can interpret. The code most often used is **ASCII** (American Standard Code for Information Interchange). This code enables one computer to communicate with other computers.

Most keyboards are arranged in a QWERTY layout, which is the same as for the typewriter and is named after the left portion of the top row of alphabetic keys. An alternative to the QWERTY keyboard is the Dvorak keyboard, named after its designer, August Dvorak. The layout is based on the frequency of use of the letters of the alphabet. Both keyboards are available from many manufacturers.

In addition to alphabetic and numeric characters, keyboards have other special purpose keys:

Function keys are programmable, changeable keys, switches, or buttons that initiate predetermined instructions when depressed, such as storage, insertion, or deletion of characters.

Cursor control keys are used to position the **cursor,** the marker that shows the exact location on the screen where one is working. These keys are usually labeled with arrows, one each pointing up, down, left, and right.

Designated-purpose keys include ctrl, alt, caps-lock, and shift keys and special software program command keys. Some keyboards also have a separate numeric keypad similar to an adding machine.

Other input devices or techniques include:

Touchscreen: A video terminal input device using a clear panel overlaid on the CRT screen. The user simply touches the screen with a finger to select available options.

Mouse: A handheld input device that when rolled across a flat surface moves the cursor to a corresponding location on the display.

Voice input: A means of recognizing spoken words and converting them into digital signals that are then changed into characters. With voice-input or voice-recognition software you can work with your PC entirely by voice or by combining voice with a keyboard and a mouse. You can dictate text or numbers, move around a document, format paragraphs, and even move a mouse with your voice.

Light pen: A pen-shaped light-sensitive device that when touched to the display screen can create or change images on the display.

Digitizer or *scanner:* A device used to transform a graphic image into signals that can be accepted for processing by the computer.

Optical character reader (OCR): A device that can read printed or typed characters and then digitally convert them into text and/or numeric data.

Pen-based computer: Characters are written by hand on an LCD display and converted into text or saved as images.

Digital cameras: There are two kinds of digital cameras: digital still (similar to 35 mm) and digital video camcorders. With traditional cameras, film is used both to record and store images. With digital cameras, separate devices perform these two functions. The image is captured by the image sensor, then stored in the camera on a memory device. Images stored in the camera are transferred (downloaded) to a PC and stored on one of its storage devices—usually a hard drive.

Types of Computers

There are two types of computers: the mainframe and the personal computer (PC) also known as the microcomputer.

Figure 7-1 Personal computer. (Photo reprinted with permission from Micron Electronics, Inc.)

MAINFRAME COMPUTERS

The earliest computers were **mainframes,** developed in the late 1940s. Mainframe computers have CPUs that can process millions of bytes of information at extremely fast speeds. These systems can support hundreds of input terminals tied directly into the computer. Mainframes are used to manipulate large databases and for payroll, inventory, and other large-volume applications in business and science.

PERSONAL COMPUTERS

Personal computers (PCs) are also known as microcomputers. (See Figure 7-1) Developed in the mid-1970s, they are reprogrammable electronic devices that process information. A microcomputer uses a microprocessor, a single chip containing all the elements of a computer's CPU. PCs usually fit on the top of a desk. More and more offices are networking microcomputers together.

Personal computers are available in portable versions. These units use the same basic components as their desktop counterparts and are called **laptops.** They weigh from 2 to 7 pounds and can be powered by electricity or by batteries. Portables provide a wide range of computing power, although they do not always have the memory capacity of a desktop. They may include a flat panel display using LCD. Most can be used with the monitor and printer of a compatible PC.

Personal Digital Assistants (PDAs), or **hand-held computers,** are lightweight and mobile. PDAs use internal RAM storage and removable memory cards for software applications, such as a notepad, "to do" list, datebook, telephone log, personal finance organizer, or spreadsheet. Specialized software applications for such areas as sales, inventory, bar-coding, and medical data collection are available as well. You can also receive wireless messages and alphanumeric pages, as well as send and receive faxes and e-mail or connect with the Internet. Information is entered directly on the screen via a pen or with an onscreen or attachable keyboard. Handwriting recognition software transforms handwriting into typed text. Data can be transferred between a PDA and a desktop computer via a linked cable or infrared technology.

Miniaturization and wireless communications are the basis for **wearable computers,** consisting of a small PC and a battery pack. This type of unit is worn on a belt and includes a head-mounted display consisting of a 0.7-inch diagonal LCD. These systems are used primarily in industrial and field applications for storing documentation, entering inventory data, and similar procedures.

DICTATION EQUIPMENT

Dictating systems integrate dictation, voice processing, and document management and are designed exclusively for the management of information work flow. The systems are built on Microsoft Windows™ NT and SQL Server technologies and allow voice, text, and data to be efficiently created, managed, and moved anywhere on the network (LAN/WAN) or the Internet. Organizations can manage dictated voice input, report transcription and distribution across multiple departments and facilities, while centrally managing system supervisory functions and work flow on an enterprise-wide level. Most systems integrate with the Internet and are built on an open platform, allowing for future upgrading of the technology.

Dictation is stored on computer hard drives. Digital equipment allows for flexibility in retrieving, prioritizing, and managing files. Recordings can be accessed out of order, and portions can be erased without disturbing other parts of the recording. Digital dictation can also be accessed via phone for travelers out of the office. The Digital Speech Standard (DSS), the leading international standard for digital speech recordings, guarantees compatibility of digital audio files. DSS speech files reduce the amount of storage required and transmission (for example, telephone) times by utilizing a high rate of data compression. These systems also provide a LAN-based voice-recognition system, which recognizes dictated speech and sends a transcribed file to the dictator for final editing.

Central Dictation System

A central dictation system provides a telephone-like handset for dictation from each executive's office; it can also be accessed from elsewhere by a touch-tone telephone. A central system permits more than one person to record simultaneously.

Desktop Dictation System

A desktop dictation system is about the size of a desktop telephone and may include a conventional handheld microphone or a telephone-like handset. Desktop systems store and record on tape or disk inside the desktop unit. When the document is ready for transcription, the author must remove the media from the machine and deliver it to the transcriber. The transcriber unit is usually controlled by a foot pedal so the transcriber's hands need not leave the keyboard while typing.

HINT: *A desktop system is useful for offices in which two to four people each dictate for several hours daily.*

Portable Dictation Machines

A portable dictation machine is battery operated and fits in the palm of one's hand. It is about the size of a midsized calculator and has a built-in microphone. The transcriber unit is often controlled by a foot pedal so the transcriber's hands need not leave the keyboard while typing.

REPROGRAPHICS

Reprographics is the reproduction of documents by any process that uses light or photography. A wide variety of reprographics equipment is available. The choice of which process to use depends on the quality and quantity of copies needed, cost, and the time factor involved.

Photocopiers

Photocopiers are the most commonly used office machines for reproducing documents. Two imaging technologies are used: analog and digital. The qualities of copies produced by these technologies are basically the same. The real difference is in the way they copy the original. An analog copier copies the original document each time a copy is made, while a digital copier scans the original once and makes multiple copies of the stored image. Analog copiers are no longer made by some manufacturers and in the future may be replaced entirely by digital copiers.

An analog system reflects light through a series of mirrors and lenses directly to a drum, creating a latent image. The drum is applied to the paper, leaving a pattern created by static electricity. Black powder called *toner* then adheres to the statically charged places, creating a copy.

Digital copier technology, based upon the same binary logic as computers and CDs, allows for higher-quality prints. It also gives the user the ability to manipulate images, making digital copies superior to analog copies.

Most digital copiers can "scan once/print many," limiting wear and tear on both the machine and the originals. Digital copiers can produce two-sided copies, automatically number pages, print watermarks (like "confidential" or "copy") onto copies, and add a date stamp. Most models can be networked to your computer system as a printer and be configured as a fax machine. Digitals usually have a larger zoom range than analogs, some as high as 800 percent and as low as 25 percent. Most digital copiers' print engines also support electronic sorting, so sorter bins are not required to make collated sets of documents. Digital copiers have fewer moving parts, so they are less likely to jam.

Machines that use one or more toner colors are available. They give users a choice of copy color other than the traditional black. More expensive **color copiers** use a photographic process to produce an exact color reproduction of the original. There are also dual-purpose machines that function as either full-color or as black-and-white copiers.

Many copier features are available as options. They are often standard features on high-volume machines. They include:

Automatic document feed (ADF): Multiple originals can be placed in the ADF bin without having to feed one original at a time.

Automatic duplexing: Two-sided copying is done automatically.

Electronic editing: Allows users to manipulate the image of the original document in a cut-and-paste approach to produce modified versions.

Multifunction memory: Preset instructions related to specific types of copying jobs can be set into memory for future recall on frequently run jobs.

Reduction/zoom: Reduces or enlarges a version of the original to fit the image on a standard sheet or concentrate on a blown-up section of the original document.

Multitasking: Capabilities for copying, printing, scanning, and faxing.

Network printing: Compatible with PC- and Mac-based networks and allow users to control operations direct from their desktops.

Sorters: A bin sorter can collate copy sets by feeding the output into individual racks or slots on a peripheral device attached to the main copier.

Stapler: Automatically staples the corner of each sorted set of papers at the end of a run.

Three-hole punch: Punches each copy as it exits the copier.

Multiple paper trays: Trays are available in several sizes so when a different size of paper is needed, one tray can be removed and replaced with the desired size. For example, a three-tray system may use one drawer for holding 8 ½-by-11-inch paper, the second for legal-sized paper, and the third for letterhead, transparencies, or other special stock.

System stand: Offers a total paper capacity of several reams of paper.

Some copiers include built-in electronic information displays to help the user. Some allow for restricted access. Another feature is automatic copy-quality adjustment. Standard serial and parallel interfaces permit the use of copiers with PCs. Other options permit access to local area networks (LANs).

Figure 7-2 A multifunction printer, fax, copier, and scanner. (Left: Courtesy of Hewlett-Packard. Right: Courtesy of Canon Computer Systems, Inc.)

Printers

Printers provide the printed output, or hard copy, from a computer. They vary widely in speed, quality of output, available printing fonts, and cost. When selecting a printer, it is necessary to relate one's office tasks and budget to the available printing hardware. Two categories of printers exist—**impact** and **nonimpact.** Impact printers strike a ribbon, similar to typewriters, whereas nonimpact printers create characters through the use of heat or light or by spraying ink on a page. Laser printers have become the office standard for letters and proposals, but dot matrix printers remain an important part of back-office operations in many firms.

DOT MATRIX PRINTERS

Dot matrix printers strike the ribbon with a series of tiny dots to form a character. They are relatively inexpensive and used when the emphasis is on information and not on the visual quality of the output. A top-line dot matrix printer, often called a near-letter-quality (NLQ) printer, has a larger number of pins in its printhead than the average dot matrix printer, typically 24 rather than 9. Although 24-pin models offer high-quality images, they tend to be slower and more expensive than 9-pin models. In most cases, documents printed on dot matrix printers do not need to offer exceptionally high quality, so 9-pin models do just fine. There is very little quality difference between 9-pin and 24-pin models if the documents are being printed in draft mode.

Dot matrix printers are commonly used for printing invoices, purchase orders, shipping forms, labels, and other multipart forms. Dot matrix printers can print through multipart forms in a single pass, allowing them to produce pages faster than even high-speed laser printers.

NONIMPACT PRINTERS

Nonimpact printers are silent but cannot make carbons. There are three types of nonimpact printers: ink jet printers, laser printers (of which there are several varieties), and plotters.

Ink jet printers: Ink is sprayed onto the paper in the shape of the character intended. Printer speeds range from two to six pages per minute. They can print in both black and multiple colors.

Laser printers: These printers use a laser beam to form images on a light-sensitive drum. These images are then transferred onto the paper a page at a time; thus they are sometimes called page printers. Copies are of the highest quality, approaching typeset quality. Laser printers can use a variety of fonts. They can also produce forms, letterheads, and signatures, and can print in color.

PostScript® printers: These are laser printers that use a page description language, or page-formatting program, called PostScript®, which facilitates the printer's communicating with the computer. High-resolution graphics can be printed on PostScript® printers. They also have a wide range of available typefaces that can be scaled to various sizes.

Desktop publishing laser printers: Essentially business-quality typesetting machines, these printers can handle any amount of graphics and include a range of built-in, high-quality typefaces.

Multifunction printer/copiers: Combining the technology of the microprocessor, laser, and photocopier, multifunction printers have features of both printers and copiers. They print a page at a time at high speeds. A microprocessor allows them to accept text, graphics, and instructions from computers, word processors, or magnetic media. They produce hard copy directly from the digitized information received.

HINT: *Depending on the number and types of fonts available with your laser printer, you may wish to purchase optional font cartridges. These contain the instructions and memory your printer will need to print the fonts. Soft fonts, on the other hand, are fonts that can be loaded from your computer into your printer's memory; they can be used when your printer has adequate internal memory.*

Plotters are used for printing computer graphics and are used in computer-aided design (CAD). High-quality output is created by the movement of ink pens over the paper. A variety of color pens is available.

Offset Printing

Offset printing is of high quality and is used for large-volume production. Usually offset printing is done by a printer or a copy shop, not by someone in the office. Paper, aluminum, or plastic (electrostatic) masters are used for offset printing. Paper masters are good for 25 to 3,000 copies, plastic for up to 5,000 copies, and aluminum for up to 50,000 copies. Before the job can be printed, the document must be converted to film and plates. Film negatives are usually created from digital files. Images from the negatives are transferred to printing plates or masters in much the same way as photographs are developed.

Phototypesetting

Phototypesetting is a photographic printing process that produces high-quality documents. Characters are formed at high speeds on photosensitive paper or film. This film is then developed and proofread. Material can be input directly through the phototypesetting equipment or on a personal computer and sent to the phototypesetter on a disk. Many varieties of type sizes and fonts are available. Brochures, newspapers, promotional materials, and books are generally prepared with this process.

HINT: *One typeset page is often the equivalent of two typed pages.*

Micrographics

The paper bottleneck in many offices can be efficiently handled with micrographic systems. Micrographics is the process of recording and reducing paper documents or computer-generated information onto film for long-term storage and archival. Records are photographed and reduced so many small images in color or black and white will appear on a reel or sheet of film. The micrographic media used to store file information are known as **microforms**. A reader is needed to enlarge the microform image and display it for viewing. Microfilm and microfiche are the best-known types of microform.

Micrographics are usually filed and developed by micrographics service bureaus. These companies can also provide for document pickup, inspection and quality control, duplication of microforms, and the sale or lease of micrographics equipment.

MICROGRAPHICS FORMATS

Roll film: The least expensive form of microfilm, is usually found in 16 mm, 35 mm, or 105 mm sizes. The 16 mm roll is used for storing 8 ½-by-11-inch or 8 ½-by-14-inch records, such as correspondence and legal documents. The 35 mm film is used for large records such as engineering drawings, newspaper pages, and blueprints. Roll film can be stored in cartons or cabinets.

Cartridges: A plastic collar is snapped over the film roll, becoming a magazine that self-threads to film readers. Cartridges are used extensively with automated readers, cameras, and automated retrieval systems.

Aperture cards: Microfilm images are mounted on a small card. Information about the microfilm record or records is printed on or punched into the remainder of the card. Aperture cards are used to store large documents such as maps or engineering drawings.

Film jackets: Clear, plastic carriers with one or more sleeves or channels are designed to hold 16 mm or 35 mm filmstrips, or a combination of the two. Jackets are available in a variety of sizes, the most common being 4 inches by 6 inches. Jackets allow the user to update film files easily and quickly by removing outdated strips and inserting newer material.

Microfiche: Suitable for filming reports, periodicals, catalogs, parts lists, and other collections of pages on a permanent, unitized microform. It contains rows of document on a sheet of film about 4 inches by 6 inches. Full-color or black-and-white images can appear on microfiche. A 4-by-6-inch fiche produced with a 24-times reduction ratio can hold up to 98 document images. One produced with a 48-times reduction ratio can hold up to 270 images.

HINT: *About 200 fiche can be filed per inch of space in a file drawer.*

Ultrafiche: An extension of microfiche, it allows more images per inch than any other type of microform. It is possible to store up to 1,000 pages on a 3-by-5-inch sheet of film.

Film folios: Aperture cards the size of microfiche inserted into jackets.

One roll of 16 mm microfilm (100 ft., 30 meters) (24× reduction) = 2,500 letter size images = 1 box = 125 MB

One roll of 35mm microfilm (100 ft.) (12× reduction, open spacing, normal scan) = 1,000 letter size images (or letter size image equivalents) = 50 MB

One microfiche (105 mm film) (24× reduction) = 100 letter size images; 5MB; 200 microfiche = 20,000 images = 1 GB

METHODS TO PRODUCE MICROFORMS

Three methods exist for producing microforms:

1. Photography by micrographics cameras, either rotary or planetary is one method. Rotary photography produces roll microfilm; planetary photography produces fiche.
2. Computer output microfilm (COM) is a method of microfilming in which computer data are printed on film, processed, and duplicated. The use of computer printouts can be minimized or eliminated with this process.
3. Computer-assisted retrieval (CAR) uses a computer to retrieve documents stored on microfilm. CAR systems can utilize bar coding or optical character recognition for indexing. Records can be accessed in various combinations; for example, accounts with an outstanding balance or clients in a specific geographic location could be accessed.

READERS, READER/PRINTERS, AND RETRIEVAL TERMINALS

Microform readers are categorized as follows:

Handheld or *projection readers:* Simple, inexpensive image magnifiers that are held to the eye for viewing or projecting images onto external screens.

Portable readers: Lightweight, briefcase- or smaller-sized full-screen readers powered by a conventional outlet or rechargeable batteries.

Desk or *console reader/printers:* Stationary readers that are also capable of producing full-sized paper copies of microform originals.

Desk or *console retrieval terminals* and *retrieval terminal/printers:* Stationary reading units with automated image-seeking capabilities. Retrieval terminal/printers produce full-size paper copies of microform originals. On some reader/printers, the printer is an integral part of the reader; in others it is a modular unit that attaches to the reader.

Computer screens or facsimile: Sophisticated microfilm readers can be tied in with computer systems using a device called a "jukebox." The user calls up a file on the PC, then the computer searches for the document and directs the jukebox to select the proper microfilm cassette for loading into the reader. The image is automatically called up, digitized, and output into the user's PC.

Optical Disk Systems

Optical disk storage systems are state-of-the-art devices based on laser beams and precision optics. An optical disk system is made up of a number of components. Scanners are the major input source for optical disk-based systems. Drives record documents in digital form onto WORM (write once, read many times) disks and retrieve documents from all types of disks. Jukeboxes are automated disk libraries. The control computer manages the system by cross-referencing data, keeping audit trails, and providing necessary reports. Software is used for image enhancement, database management, and operating systems. Monitors give high-resolution images, and laser printers give printed output.

The major differences from micrographics systems are the following:

Packing density: Some optical disk systems can hold up to 2 million pages of text on a disk.

Retrieval: Documents can be retrieved in seconds.

Transmission speed: Optical disks store documents in a digital form, which means they can be transmitted on a local area network (LAN) or telephone line in two or three seconds.

Paperwork flow: Optical disk systems manage the paperwork flow and control the pacing and sequencing of paperwork by automatically prompting individuals to the next step.

Integration with other systems: Optical systems can interface with other electronic systems. Different users can simultaneously access data on the same file or document.

An optical disk system performs the following functions:

- It scans images from either paper or microfilm.
- It stores documents containing letters and numbers as well as graphics.
- It displays documents on a CRT terminal.
- It searches and retrieves documents.
- It prints documents on paper and/or microfilm.
- It copies documents to and from computer hard disks and optical disks.

Optical Character Scanning

An **optical character reader (OCR)** is a computer device combined with software that can copy graphics or read text in a variety of typefaces and styles. The copy is stored in the computer and is reproduced immediately on a CRT for correction and revisions. The accuracy rate for text recognition is about 95 percent, and the technology is constantly improving. Photographs, drawings, and charts can be scanned for use in desktop publishing or electronic filing in black and white or color.

TYPES OF SCANNERS

There are two primary types of scanners. A **handheld scanner** may be held in the hand and manually swept across the document or image. These have a scan width 2 to 5 inches.

A **page** or **desktop scanner** can handle a full page at a time. Page scanners are further divided into three categories:

- *Sheet-feed:* These operate by automatically moving the document to be scanned via rollers in much the same manner as a fax machine.
- *Flatbed:* These have a flat top upon which the document to be scanned is placed facedown, in much the same manner as on a photocopier. Typically, they offer the best scan results and are the most expensive.
- *Overhead* or *copyboard:* These look like overhead projectors. They scan documents and objects from above. Documents are placed face-up on the scanner's flat scanning surface.

SCANNER RESOLUTION

A scanner's **resolution** is the number of dots it can sample for each linear inch of the document. Common resolutions are 75, 100, 150, 200, 300, 400, and 600 dots per inch (dpi).

INTELLIGENT DOCUMENTS

DataGlyph® technology enables scanners and papers to carry a library's worth of information on a sheet of paper. The glyphs are small areas on a document marked with tiny dot patterns smaller than a hundredth of an inch wide. Information is compressed in these spaces that would ordinarily cover an entire page and is scanned into a computer to be interpreted.

APPLICATIONS

Scanners have various uses in the office. Among the most important are the following:

- Desktop publishing uses scanners to incorporate images into a computer or onto paper as well as for character recognition of keyed manuscripts.
- Scanners are used with databases to incorporate price lists, tabular data, and other text as well as for image databases such as those used by real estate companies and police departments.
- Scanners are used in information storage to store documents in organizations with intensive paperwork operations, such as banks, hospitals, and government agencies.
- Paper documents can be scanned into a personal computer and transmitted to the Internet or via a facsimile board to a fax machine.

TELECOMMUNICATIONS EQUIPMENT

Telecommunications uses telephone and computer technology to transmit voice, image, data, and textual information from one place to another. The most used telecommunications device today, outside of the telephone, is the facsimile machine, or fax.

Telephones

A variety of telephone equipment is available that can efficiently meet the needs of any organization.

The standard *touch-tone phone* uses a 12-button keypad arrangement. It has ten buttons with the digits 0–9, plus two special buttons, * (star) and # (pound), that activate various automated electronic features. Many touch-tone phones are also equipped with an automated telephone dialer that can store from 15 to 31 numbers. It can dial one of these numbers at the touch of a button.

A *call director* is a desktop switchboard allowing an office professional to pick up calls that come in on 18, 30, or as many as 60 extensions. One receptionist or assistant can be responsible for the phones of a number of people who may not be at their desks.

Call directors usually connect to larger switching system devices in the telephone system.

A *speakerphone set* consists of a microphone and loudspeaker and permits the user to carry on a telephone conversation from anywhere in an office without lifting the receiver from its rest. The microphone picks up the user's voice and the loudspeakers broadcast the voice of the party at the other end of the line. A speakerphone also allows a group of people to talk through one phone.

Cordless *portable telephones* are also available as well as *cellular phones* for use when traveling.

Video phones have been limited to videoconferencing for large corporations and business. However, faster Internet connections, computers, and the use of desktop cameras means the use of these phones will become more widespread.

VOICE MAIL

Voice mail, or *store-and-forward messaging,* combines the technology of a telephone, computer, and recording device. It stores messages for immediate or later delivery. Access to the system is gained by entering a code on a rotary or touch-tone telephone. A recording tells the user to speak the message into the phone and then to dial the voice-mail number of the recipient. The system codes the message into digital data and attempts to deliver it immediately. If the system cannot deliver the message, it is filed in the computer's memory for later delivery. When the recipient dials into the system to get his or her messages, the caller's voice is reconstructed and the message is repeated.

SWITCHING SYSTEMS

Single line telephones are ordinarily used in homes and small offices. They have only a single line available, so it is not possible for two or more people to place calls at the same time.

For larger businesses, however, the routing of calls to and from the public lines of the telephone company to the private lines within an organization is handled through a switching system. These systems include key systems, PBX systems, and Centrex.

Multiline telephones, or *key phones,* allow one person to handle several lines, each with a separate button on the phone. These telephones may be equipped with up to 30 buttons placed above, below, or beside the dial. If a line is in use, a light by the button is lit. To place a call, the caller pushes an unlit line button and dials the number. A flashing light signals an incoming call; to answer it, an individual pushes the flashing line's button and picks up the receiver. If a call comes in on one line while an individual is on another, the second line can be answered after the first caller is put on hold by pressing the hold button. The person on hold cannot hear the other conversation.

PBX systems (private branch exchange) are used by large companies to switch calls between users on local lines. The systems also allow sharing a certain number of external phone lines. Most medium-size and larger companies use a PBX because it is much less expensive than connecting an external telephone line to every telephone in the organization. In addition, it is easier to call someone within a PBX because the number you need to dial is typically just three or four digits. Today's PBX systems use digital technology, converting digital signals to analog for outside calls.

A recent variation of the PBX is called a *Centrex system (central office exchange service).* In this type of PBX, all switching occurs at a local telephone office instead of on the company's premises. Typically, the telephone company owns and manages all the communications equipment necessary to implement the PBX and then sells various services to the company, enabling the customer to rent the latest telecommunications technologies. In many cases, Centrex has now replaced the private branch exchange. A typical Centrex service includes direct inward dialing (DID), which provides a block of telephone numbers for calling into a company's PBX system. Using DID, a company can offer its customers individual phone numbers for each person or workstation within the company without requiring a physical line into the PBX for each possible connection. Other services include sharing of the same system among multiple company locations, self-managed line allocation, and cost-accounting monitoring.

Most systems feature voice mail. Some systems feature voice recognition, which allows a caller to choose among various options within the voice mail by simply saying a number. For example, a user may speak the personal identification number of the mailbox. The system would then transfer the caller to the correct mailbox and offer a list of options, such as to hear, send, or delete messages. The caller says the number of the option and the system responds with the appropriate function.

Fax Machines

A fax machine, also called a facsimile machine, instantaneously transmits a copy (or facsimile) of a document from one location to another. Pages of the document are fed into the transmitting machine, electronically digitized, and sent via phone lines to the designated receiving fax machine. The receiving machine converts the digital transmission back into characters and prints it out on paper.

Several types of fax printing technologies are available:

Most older fax machines employ **thermal printing,** which means that a small heating element within the machine marks specially coated heat-sensitive paper. The downside of thermal printing is the paper, which is stored on rolls that result in curled faxes. The waxy coating on the paper is hard to write on and ink fades with time. If the paper is exposed to too much heat, it will darken. Some thermal machines can print onto plain paper. However, the print quality is mediocre.

Although slow, inkjet fax machines can print using plain paper with relatively sharp print. Another plain-paper fax machine is a laser- or light-emitting diode (LED) printing engine. These are faster than inkjet, function like laser printers, and produce high-quality images.

TYPES OF FAX MACHINES

There are two types of fax technology available: thermal-paper, which uses specially coated paper, and plain paper, which uses regular 8½-by-11-inch copy paper. Thermal paper comes in continuous rolls that are useful for receiving documents of nonstandard lengths.

Faxes can be:

- Stand-alone, desktop units.
- Personal fax units sized to fit into a briefcase and designed for use at home or when traveling.
- Public fax machines, much like a public phone booth, that are available in such places as hotels, shopping malls, airports, and post offices.
- Units that double as desktop copiers, answering machines, and regular telephones.
- Machines that are compatible with cellular phones.
- Color fax units that transmit and receive color photographs, color slides, video images, color images, color documents, and transparencies.
- Voice-to-fax units that allow users to call a fax machine and leave a voice message that will be converted by the machine into a printed document.
- Flatbed scanners, which consist of a flat surface on which a user lays documents to be scanned and subsequently faxed, are particularly effective for bound documents.
- Fax servers are shared fax resources installed on LAN, multiuser, and IP (Internet protocol) computer networks. They typically are installed on a gateway PC or file server and they enable network users to have documents transmitted or received as fax image files—not as computer-editable alphanumerics.

Sending speeds: Transmission standard and compression protocol are the two different ways you can evaluate how fast your fax machine sends a page:

A *transmission standard* called V.17 sends faxes at 14,400 bits per second (bps). The sending time for a single page is 6 to 10 seconds. Faxing at 9,600 bps takes 15 to 60 seconds per page. The majority of fax machines transmit at these speeds.

You can send faxes at 33,600 bps—or about three seconds per page—with the V.34 transmission standard. Receiving fax machines must have similar protocols, i.e., V.17 or V.34, to receive documents at these speeds. A fallback mechanism allows these machines to send and receive at 9,600 bps to ensure compatibility with older machines.

Virtually all fax machines are equipped with a basic *compression protocol* called Modified Huffman (MH). Machines equipped with the more advanced Modified Read (MR) or Modified Modified Read (MMR) protocols can send documents as much as 25 percent faster.

FAX FEATURES AND FUNCTIONS

The following are some of the major features and functions of fax machines:

Autodial: Recalls preset numbers from internal memory and automatically dials the destination number of the receiving facsimile unit.

Automatic reduction: The size of the incoming document can be changed to fit the available paper size. This is important because plain paper fax machines must print on standard 8 ½-by-11-inch paper.

Delayed timer transmission: Documents can be placed into the fax machine, which is then programmed to send the information at a preset time. Newer units have the capability to send to multiple locations at different times.

Fall-back speed: Allows the sending unit automatically to reduce the transmission speed when it senses a problem with the telephone line quality. Note that reducing the speed helps to ensure a better copy quality on the receiving end.

Interfaces: Allows the fax unit to be connected with other equipment to meet special communications needs. Faxes can receive from TWX/Telex, send and receive from personal computers, and send and receive encrypted messages. (Encryption is the conversion of text into code.)

Sender I.D./time date stamp: Prints the telephone number of the sending fax unit on top of each page received. It also prints the time and date.

Transmission log: Records and prints out a list of all transmissions received. It lists the number of pages of each batch of transmitted documents received, date and time, and sending unit telephone number.

PC fax: Faxes can be sent over the Internet to a computer or other fax machine, using one of several Internet fax protocols.

Fax to e-mail address: Pictures and text can be scanned into the fax machine and sent to an e-mail address.

XML and Java® support: Allows organizations to integrate production-level faxing capabilities with these software programming applications and enable queries, notifications, and other actions.

Automated e-document delivery: Enables electronic delivery of critical documents such as purchase orders, invoices, and statements automatically from host or mainframe applications.

Internet fax service: Allows for fax delivery via a secure IP (Internet protocol) connection over the Internet.

Seamless integration with business applications: Integrates with business applications, including e-mail, desktop, document management, and scanning devices, to make delivering documents electronically as simple as printing them out on a network printer.

Broadcasting: Transmits documents for simultaneous delivery to multiple destinations worldwide at peak or off-peak times.

FAX DIRECTORIES

As the use of the fax as a primary form of communication has grown, fax directories have been published, such as the *National Fax Directory* (800–877–4253). They offer a comprehensive listing of companies and private individuals using fax machines to send and receive correspondence. The directories include the company name, fax number, and other pertinent information, such as office hours or street address. Such directories also offer on-line databases with similar listings.

HINT: *An on-line database is useful for PC-fax users, who can use their PCs to review the directory listings.*

PUBLIC FAX SERVICES

Public fax services are available to companies without their own fax machine. Senders must pay a telephone charge, a basic transmittal fee with additional charges for additional pages, and a delivery charge if applicable. The costs and transmission times vary. Recipients may pick up the documents or have them delivered. Delivery in foreign countries is to a business center or designated post office.

Teletypewriters

Another telecommunications device is the teletypewriter; however, it is being replaced by the fax machine. Teletypewriters transmit and receive only alphanumeric information over phone lines; they cannot transmit graphics. Some companies have their own teletypewriter networks. Many companies use one of Western Union's teletypewriter networks, Telex or TWX. "Telex" stands for teleprinter exchange and is generally used for international transmissions. "TWX" stands for teletypewriter exchange. Both systems permit a user to keyboard information and then send it to another Telex or TWX unit over standard telephone lines. The system provides the immediacy of a phone message as well as the documentation of a letter.

Major disadvantages are the following:

- Information must be keyed into the teletypewriter.
- Graphics cannot be sent via Telex.
- The cost is about four times that of a fax.

OTHER ELECTRIC AND ELECTRONIC EQUIPMENT

In addition to the major office equipment outlined in the preceding sections, other equipment includes:

Shredder: Used to shred documents containing sensitive information. Some fit on a desktop while others are large, freestanding units that can handle up to 140,000 sheets of paper an hour.

Electronic copy board: Electronically copies ideas, diagrams, or charts written on the copy board and prints them onto paper for distribution. Used especially for meetings.

Electric copyholder: Allows a line guide to advance down printed copy as a foot pedal or hand switch is operated by a typist. Generally made in four sizes to accommodate letter size, legal size, and two sizes of ledger paper.

Electric collator: Collates pages of material automatically.

Mailing and letter-related equipment: This equipment supports mail-related activities and includes letter opening/folding equipment, postage meters, and postage scales. Postage stamps are also available on-line via the Internet.

SELECTING OFFICE EQUIPMENT

Rapidly evolving technology, the multitude of vendors in the market, technical jargon, announcements of new products nearly every day, and the threat of companies going out of business make selection of office equipment a difficult task. What is brand new today can be obsolete next year.

The following guidelines will help you evaluate prospective equipment for your office:

1. Analyze your office's needs. A thorough needs analysis helps to determine equipment applications, the number of users, frequency of use, and types of documents produced.

2. Identify available products. Match the available products to the information gathered in the needs analysis. Determine the available products by talking to equipment dealers, reviewing sales literature, and reading office-related trade magazines. Ask the following:

   - What are the benefits and negatives that differentiate one brand from another?
   - Will the features meet your departmental needs?
   - Is the equipment easy to use?
   - Is the equipment compatible with other equipment in the office?
   - What software and accessories are available?
   - Is service available after the sale? By whom? Is there a toll-free phone number for troubleshooting problems? What are the terms of the warranty?
   - Are the costs of installing the equipment included in the price?
   - Is training free or is there a charge? What type of training is available?

3. Create a comparative chart of available products. Make a list of the information you have gathered by categories in the first column and put the products you have studied across the other columns. In each column, list the comparative information you have gathered on that product. You may wish to assign both a weight and a score, from a low of 1 to a high of 10, for each item. The weight is an estimate of how important each item is. Multiply the weight by the score for each item and then total the weighted scores. In this way you can quantitatively compare the prospective equipment choices.

HINT: *Consider using a spreadsheet program for this purpose. This will allow you to adjust the size of the rows and columns as needed to accommodate available information. The scores assigned to each item can also be automatically totaled for you.*

4. Ask for a demonstration of the equipment and/or a trial use. A thorough demonstration, or preferably trial use, is important before making a final decision. Some dealers will allow prospective customers to use the equipment for one or two weeks at no cost. Both the demonstration and the trial use will provide valuable insights that are not possible through any other form of evaluation.

5. Make a dealer or vendor comparison. A thorough review of the dealer or vendor is needed to avoid problems after the sale. Ask the following questions:

- How many service technicians are employed?
- What is the average tenure of technicians and number of placements serviced by the firm?
- What is the average response time to a service call?
- Are parts and supplies readily available?
- Is a list of references available that can be randomly called? Ask the references the same questions you are asking the dealer and compare the answers. Ask if the service was as good six or more months after the sale as it was in the beginning. Also ask the reference to identify any major service problems, along with how they were resolved. Are there any patterns to the answers received from the various references you called?

INVENTORY AND MAINTENANCE OF EQUIPMENT

With more electronic equipment entering the office, the responsibility for maintaining it is increasing. Some recommended procedures will help you do this.

1. Make a card record, using appropriate software, for each piece of equipment. The record should contain the name, address, and phone number of the vendor or dealer; date of purchase; model number; serial number; and basic information re-

garding the warranty and/or service contract. These cards should be filed alphabetically and periodically updated as the equipment is serviced. A yearly inventory of each piece of equipment should also be done and noted on the card.

HINT: *A database software program can facilitate this process. You can use one that is part of a spreadsheet program or use a stand-alone program.*

2. Consider purchasing a service or maintenance contract. These are available for an additional monthly or annual fee. A service or maintenance contract extends the warranty on the equipment for a longer period of time. Most contracts include options for either mail-in or carry-in service. Others will offer a pick-up and delivery service or on-site repair. Some will also provide a temporary replacement.

3. Establish a maintenance schedule. Have the equipment serviced on a regular basis. Prevention through proper servicing can help to avoid unnecessary downtime. The maintenance schedule should be maintained by the equipment operator or, in the case of executives, by their administrative assistants. Service contracts are available that include periodic cleaning and/or testing of equipment components.

4. Use cleaning products on a regular basis. These products include cleaning kits for personal computers, glass-cleaning products for copiers and CRT screens, and dusters for electronic typewriters.

HINT: *Weekly cleaning of personal computers is recommended, focusing on the screen, keyboard, disk drive, printer, and housing to remove dust and dirt.*

TROUBLESHOOTING YOUR PC

Personal computing is more than creating document—it is problem solving. Understanding the task at hand, knowing what the task requires, and determining if there really is a problem comprise the one-two-three scenario of problem solving.

Understanding the Task at Hand

Working with computers involves an understanding of:

- The type of processor, that is, Pentium™ or Mac™.
- The amount and type of memory, including RAM and hard disk.
- The number and type of disks, that is, 3 ½-inch floppy disks, CD-ROMs, or read/write optical disks.
- The options and adapters, for example, modems, serial ports, and math coprocessor.

- How to remove and insert the components and operate any switches or change jumpers.

It is critical to both become familiar with your system's documentation and keep the technical support telephone numbers for both your hardware and software easily available. When you call a technical support line for help, be prepared to answer questions about the items listed above and take your time in describing what you perceive to be the problem.

Knowing What the Task Requires

Identify whether it is a hardware or a software problem. If it is hardware-related, first check for loose plugs on the back of the CPU and make sure the power is on for all components. Do not take the CPU apart or remove any of the inner workings. If it is a software problem, don't begin to delete or reinstall the software. You could lose valuable data files. Write down exactly what happened and also any unusual error commands that appeared on the screen. This way you will be better prepared to answer your technical support rep's questions.

Determining If There Really Is a Problem

Shutting down the system and rebooting the computer can often clear up a hardware or a software problem. When it does not, follow these steps:

1. Look for visual clues, such as fan speed, flickering or nonoperational display, broken cables, spilled coffee or other liquids, and so forth. Dirt around the fan inlet or around the fan, a weak power supply to the system, or a short from the spilled liquid are possible culprits.
2. Listen for audible clues, including noises from disk drives, error codes from the speaker, or snapping/popping sounds from inside the power display. Noticeable groaning when the system starts may indicate a weak or insufficient power supply.
3. Wiggle the connectors on the back of the CPU or unplug them and inspect the pins. They may be loose or bent. If this doesn't help, begin disconnecting cables, one at a time, and replacing each with one from another computer.
4. If you can't reboot your computer, the problem may be related to your CONFIG.SYS or SYSTEM.INI files. In this case, use your emergency operating system back-up disks. If you don't have a set, create one as soon as possible. Also, invest in quality utility software—it's good insurance!
5. If your computer is still not working, call your information systems department or the customer support number provided with your equipment.
6. Computer problems can be software problems, particularly if your computer has been infected with a virus. See Chapter 8 for suggestions on protecting your computer from virus attacks.

CHAPTER 8

OFFICE

COMPUTER

SOFTWARE

Computer software consists of programmed instructions that direct and control a computer's operations. Mainframes, minicomputers, and personal computers all use software. Software programs can be purchased from equipment manufacturers, vendors whose specialty is designing software, or retail software stores.

Software falls into two categories: systems software and applications software. Systems software governs the operation of the computer. Applications software includes programs that perform specific applications, such as word processing.

SYSTEMS SOFTWARE

Systems software includes operating systems, programming languages, and utilities. An **operating system** is a group of programs that acts as an interpreter and manager for the computer, display monitor, and any peripherals, such as a printer. The operating system also directs and interprets information moving to and from disk drives. Some operating systems are multitasking systems, that is, they can process more than one task at a time.

Operating systems can be grouped by functionality: operating systems for supercomputing, render farms, mainframes, servers, workstations, desktops, handheld devices, real time systems, and embedded systems:

Supercomputing: Primarily scientific computing, supercomputing usually models real systems in nature. Render farms are collections of computers that work together to render animations and special effects. Work that previously required supercomputers can be done with the equivalent of a render farm.

Mainframes: In the past, mainframes were the primary form of computer. Mainframes are large centralized computers. At one time they provided the bulk of business computing through **time sharing.** Mainframes and **mainframe replacements** (powerful computers or clusters of computers) are still useful for some large-scale tasks, such as centralized billing systems, inventory systems, database operations, and so forth. When mainframes were in widespread use, there was also a class of computers known as **minicomputers,** which were smaller, less expensive versions of mainframes for businesses that couldn't afford true mainframes.

Servers: These are computers or groups of computers used for Internet serving, Intranet serving, print serving, file serving, and/or application serving. Servers are also sometimes used as mainframe replacements.

Desktop operating systems: **Personal computers** use desktop operating systems. **Workstations** are more powerful versions of personal computers. Often only one person uses a particular workstation, which often uses a more powerful version of a desktop operating system. Workstations run on more powerful hardware and often have software associated with larger computer systems.

Handheld: These operating systems are much smaller and less capable than desktop operating systems, so they can fit into the limited memory of handheld devices.

Real time operating systems (RTOS): These systems are specifically designed to respond to events that happen in real time. Examples might include computer systems that run factory floors, computer systems for emergency room or intensive care unit equipment, computer systems for air traffic control, or embedded systems. RTOSs are grouped according to the acceptable response time (seconds, milliseconds, microseconds) and according to whether they involve systems where failure can result in loss of life.

Embedded systems: Combinations of processors and special software inside of another device, such as the electronic ignition system on cars, are called embedded systems.

Operating systems can also be classified according to system types:

GUI: Graphical User Interface operating systems have the capability of using a mouse and are graphical.

Multiuser: Allows multiple users to utilize the computer and run programs at the same time.

Multiprocessing: Operating system that allows multiple processors to be utilized.

Multitasking: Operating systems that allow multiple software processes to be run at the same time.

Multithreading: Operating systems that allow different parts of a software program to run concurrently.

Most operating systems are a combination of the above characteristics.

Microsoft® Corporation sells the dominant desktop operating system for both the office and the home, called Microsoft Windows®. Other popular operating systems include UNIX®, developed by AT&T®; MAC® OS by Apple® Computer; and Linux.

Developed by Linus Torvalds and further elaborated by a number of developers throughout the world, Linux is a freely, available multitasking and multiuser operating system. From the outset, Linux was placed under General Public License (GPL). The system can be distributed, used, and expanded free of charge. In this way, developers have access to all the source codes, thus being able to integrate new functions easily or to find and eliminate programming bugs quickly. As a result, drivers for new adapters (SCSI controller, graphics cards, and so forth) can be integrated very rapidly.

Microsoft®'s current operating system is Microsoft Windows XP®, the successor to Windows 2000. The XP version is available in two formats: Professional Education, for the office and business user, and an abbreviated version for the home user. You can upgrade to Windows XP® if you are using a previous version of Windows that supports upgrading. These include Windows® 98 (including Second Edition); Windows Millennium® (Me); Windows NT® 4.0 (Service Pack 6 or later); Windows 2000 Professional; or Windows XP® Home Edition. (Windows 95 and earlier versions do not support upgrade to Windows XP® Professional.)

Features of XP not available in previous versions include built-in instant messaging, support for recordable optical drives, simpler interface that can be customized for multiple users of the same machine, built-in support for wireless networking, links to Microsoft's Web services and a product activation scheme to eliminate illegal copying. You must contact Microsoft® via either the Internet or telephone to unlock the program. Other significant features include the capability to access your computer remotely, run multiple applications concurrently, and greater security, including the ability to encrypt files and folders.

A complete list of features is posted at www.microsoft.com/windowsxp/pro/evaluation/features.asp.

Although Windows XP® is more stable than previous versions, care must be taken when installing the software. Always run Microsoft's Upgrade Advisor before installation. It is available from the XP CD or from www.microsoft.com/windowsxp. The advisor will create a list of hardware/software blocking issues that may impede a successful installation. Earlier versions of software applications and hardware drivers may not be compatible with XP, and you will have to contact the manufacturers of these products for updated software patches. Go to www.microsoft.com/windowsxp/pro/using/howto/default.asp for detailed information on how to successfully install Windows XP®, including backing up your important files prior to installing.

Other suggestions to help improve the operation of Windows XP® include:

Tune Visual Performance: You can adjust the color depth, desktop animations, and visual effects. Right-click your mouse on any empty portion of your desktop and select *Properties/Settings*. The Color Quality setting should be set to Medium (16 bit) for most normal business applications. Use a higher setting if you wish to do photo/video editing and similar applications. Right-click *Properties/Advanced/Performance Settings* to adjust animation and visual effects. Choose to either *activate/deactivate* individual items or use the *general "best performance/best appearance"* buttons. Experiment until you find the mix of speed and visual effects that works best for your applications.

Improve Folder Views: Open *My Documents* and select the *View Menu/Status Bar, List,* and *Arrange Icons by Name.* Next, right-click on an empty spot in the *My Documents* toolbar and select *Customize.* Choose any of the available toolbar buttons you wish and click *Add.*

Customize the Taskbar: Find the *Task Bar* (located next to the *Start* button) and right-click on an empty spot. Uncheck *Lock the Taskbar.* This will allow you to resize various portions of the taskbar to your individual preferences.

Reset Automatic Updates Tab: This feature allows XP to contact the Microsoft® servers by default to auto-search for patches, downloads, and updates. This can be both an annoyance and, more important, a potential security breach because it provides information on XP's memory contents, snippets of open documents, passwords, and so forth. Right-click on *My Computer,* select *Properties,* and choose the *Automatic Updates Tab.* Select either *Turn Off* or, minimally, *Notify Me.*

Adjust the Recycle Bin and Internet Explorer's Cache: Both of these items are set to consume large amounts of your hard drive space. Right click on the *Recycle Bin,* select *Properties,* and on the *Global Tab,* decide how much space you want the Recycle Bin to consume. Generally, a few hundred megs of space for trash should be sufficient. Next, open Internet Explorer and select *Tools/Internet Options.* Under Temporary Internet Files, click the *Settings* button and select an appropriate size for this cache area. If you have a high-bandwidth, fast connection, 5 to 10 Mb should be sufficient. Allow for approximately 25 Mb with a slower dial-up connection.

Adjust System Restore: This feature also consumes considerable hard drive space. Right-click on *My Computer,* select *Properties,* and *System Restore Tab.* Select your main hard drive, click *Settings,* and move the slider to a more reasonable amount of disk space.

Consider Unlocking the Firewall: A built-in desktop firewall is available with XP. This feature can help to provide desktop security, but it is turned off by default. To turn it on, right-click on *My Network Places, Properties,* right-click on your connection (e.g. Local Area Conection), select *Properties* again, then *Advanced,* and then click the box for *Protect My Computer.*

Keep a telephone help line handy. Don't spend endless hours trying to solve an installation problem. Call Microsoft® for help! In the United States, call 425–635–7222; in Canada, call 905–568–4494. Text telephone services are available for the hearing-impaired using a TT/TDD modem and dialing 425–635–4948 in the United States and 905–568–9641 in Canada.

Programming languages are special languages that allow users to communicate with computers. The most frequently used are C, a general-purpose programming language; FORTRAN, which was developed by IBM for scientific, engineering, and mathematical operations; COBOL, which was developed especially for business applications and in which English-like statements are used; Pascal, a flexible language useful for scientific programming; RPG (Report Program Generator), which is used on many small computers to generate reports; and BASIC, an interactive language that allows communication directly with the computer. Microprocessors as well as many small, business-oriented computers use BASIC.

Utilities are special programs that perform such tasks as copying files or transferring files from one storage medium to another. Examples of typical utilities include:

System protection utilities: These programs operate in the background constantly, monitoring vital system resources and data integrity and automatically taking corrective action when needed. Generally, tools for system protection and data recovery are provided. For example, Norton Utilities by Symantec optimizes and defragments your disks to improve access times and enhance the chance of full recovery in the event of a crash. Automated 32-bit file optimization supports most common compression formats.

Document transfer utilities: Exchanging data files across different operating system platforms—that is, between MS-DOS, Windows®, Macintosh®, and UNIX®—is complex. In the past, documents were saved in an unformatted ASCII text format or translators were used to convert files. Document transfer software provides portability to documents so you can use them across platforms, networks, and operating systems.

Data compression utilities: Electronic file transfer via a modem can benefit from file compression software. Examples of typical compression applications include e-mail file attachments, Internet file uploads and downloads, files containing voice or video clips, and transfer of slide presentations to duplicating services. To compress a file is to reduce the size of that file without losing any of the information inside it. Compression provides the obvious benefit of reducing the amount of time required to transfer files from one computer to another, saving online phone charges. A popular and reliable compression program is PKZIP® from PKWare®, Inc. In addition to compressing files from 50% to 70%, and in some cases over 90%, you can also create, open, and extract from ZIP archived files. Even files that have been stored over multiple disks can be extracted. The capability to store long Windows file names and to protect a ZIP file by encrypting it with a password are other benefits of this software. PKZIP® for Windows® is compatible with ZIP files created on other PKZIP® platforms. You can download a shareware version from PKWare®'s Web site, www.pkware.com.

APPLICATIONS SOFTWARE

Applications software consists of programs that enable the computer to perform specific office applications. Applications include word processing, spreadsheets, graphics, desktop publishing, accounting, database management, personal information management, desktop management, project management, and records management. Other software used in offices includes integrated software, groupware, shareware, communications, local area network (LAN), and linking software.

Word Processing

Word processing is the single most commonly used PC application. A word processing program allows the user to enter, edit, and print text documents, such as letters and reports. The functions available in a word processing program will vary, depending on the brand and cost of the software as well as the size of the machine's memory.

Selection of a word processing software program should be based on the functions needed to create typical office documents. For example, if you are a Microsoft® Office user, you will find better multitasking versions included in the suite consisting of Word, Excel, PowerPoint®, Access (professional), and Outlook (a component to the suite that manages calendars, tasks, and contacts for one or more people in a group).

Basic features of word processing programs include:

- Automatic correction.
- Bookmarks.
- Collaboration functionality.
- Compact install option.
- Cross-platform compatibility.
- Drag-and-drop editing.
- Envelope and label printing (including irregular sizes).
- File conversion and management.
- Format painter.
- Grammar and spell checkers.
- Headers/footers.
- Help (context-sensitive).
- Hyphenation (automatic).
- Index and table of contents generation.
- Integration with spreadsheets, graphics, databases.
- Language translation.
- Macro capabilities.
- Mail merge.
- Modular installation.
- OLE visual editing.
- Outlining.
- Paragraph and character styles.
- Shrink-to-fit previews and printing support.
- Smart Tags.
- Special characters and symbols.
- Style gallery and style sheets.
- Tabbed dialog boxes with preview windows.
- Table of authorities and figures generation.
- Text wrapping (automatic).
- Thesaurus.
- Voice recognition.
- Wizard assistants.

- Word, character, and line count.
- Writing to World Wide Web with an HTML editor.
- Zoomable editing views.

Spreadsheet Software

A spreadsheet program is an electronic replacement for an accountant's columnar ledger, pencil, and calculator. Spreadsheets can be used to calculate budgets, track sales and budgets, prepare financial statements, and analyze financial problems. They may be used as journals or ledgers and to generate data for management information reports.

Spreadsheets permit data to be moved, changed, inserted, deleted, and formatted without rekeying. Spreadsheets automate calculations so the user enters only a set of numbers and appropriate formulas in order to find totals, averages, percentages, or the like.

There are four basic spreadsheet designs: traditional, linked, three-dimensional, and relational.

Traditional: The simplest form of spreadsheet is the traditional spreadsheet. It is a grid of cells identified by a column letter and a row number. Each cell may contain a number, a label, a formula, or a function. A label is a piece of text that usually functions as a title or the heading for a column or row. A formula is an equation used to calculate an answer given the numbers in the spreadsheet. A function is a common computation that can be invoked with a brief command; for example, many spreadsheets have a function to sum the numbers in a column or row and another function to calculate the average of the numbers in a column or row.

Linked: Linked spreadsheet designs use data from separate spreadsheets without having to copy values or build giant models. Linked spreadsheets have the ability to coordinate information in different spreadsheets. Any changes made in one spreadsheet will be automatically changed in the corresponding cells of each of the connected spreadsheets.

Three-dimensional: A three-dimensional (or 3-D) spreadsheet design adds depth by providing a third axis. Each cell has three coordinates that identify it: row, column, and page.

Relational: A relational spreadsheet design separates data files from the spreadsheets themselves. Data identification is by name, supports more than three dimensions, and provides automatic consolidation.

Determining which spreadsheet design is best in a particular office requires taking a look at the nature of the information to be processed. Adaptability, flexibility, and ease of operation are also important factors to consider.

Basic features of any spreadsheet program include the following:

▲ Automatic calculation assistance.

▲ Error-checking smart tags.

▲ Format option: Indicates how the numbers should be printed, including currency, percent, fixed, and scientific notations.

▲ Function argument tool tips.

▲ Variable column widths.

▲ Move or copy cells and ranges.

▲ Insert or delete columns or rows.

▲ Formula evaluator and auditing.

▲ Functions: Shortcut formulas to make calculations, e.g., SUM (@SUM) to add a series of numbers, AVG (@AVG) to find the average of a series, MAX (@MAX) to find the largest number in a series.

▲ Extract and consolidate data.

▲ Edit a cell.

▲ Store, print, and edit.

▲ What-if table creation: Allows the user to evaluate the alternatives in calculations by changing figures.

▲ Solver function: Allows users to choose a desired result and suggests the best way for them to get it.

▲ Templates: Invoices, expense reports and tracking, and more.

▲ Outlining: Allows the user to view only the most important parts of a worksheet.

▲ Supports add-ins: Software programs that work with spreadsheets to increase capabilities such as word processing, desktop publishing, better two- or three-dimensional graphics, or more cells per screen.

▲ Voice recognition.

▲ Windows: Splits the screen into two or more sections horizontally or vertically to enable the user to see two sections of a long or wide spreadsheet on one screen.

▲ Graphics: Modules that turn numeric data into line, bar, or pie charts.

Accounting Software

Accounting software is used to manage financial data. It serves as a vehicle for inputting information about business transactions and organizing that information into meaningful management reports.

Accounting software packages can be broken into modules, or they can be fully integrated to include any or all of the following: accounts payable, accounts receivable, general ledger, order entry, sales analysis, invoicing, inventory control, job costing, purchasing, payroll, fixed assets, and report writing.

Features of accounting software include the following:

▲ Production of reports.
▲ File export: can exchange data with spreadsheets and databases.
▲ Audit trail.
▲ Multiuser operation.
▲ Network support.
▲ Security.
▲ Customization of system for the business.

Graphics Software

Graphics software permits the display of graphs, charts, and other line artwork whether on screen or on paper. It adds visual interest to reports and presentations.

Presentation graphics are images generated by computer that can be printed on overhead transparency film or photographed for 35 mm slides. Graphic images can also be printed on paper, with varying degrees of quality, using computer printers or plotters. Some software packages allow the user to project the images electronically through a liquid crystal display (LCD) panel or show them directly on a PC screen. (Additional information on graphics software can be found in Chapter 19, Office Publishing.)

Common graphics programs include the following:

Graphics interchange format (GIF): A graphics file format that handles 8-bit color (250 colors). GIF files include a color table, which includes the most representative 256 colors used in the image. GIF file sizes are based on the actual number of colors used. Thus images with fewer colors take up less space in the computer.

Joint photographic experts group (JPEG): A standard for compressing images with a high compression capability. JPEG++ is an extension of JPEG that allows picture areas to be selected in different ratios, e.g., the background image could be compressed higher than the foreground.

Musical Instrument Digital Interface (MIDI): A standard protocol for the interchange of musical information among musical instruments, synthesizers, and computers; it is used for storing music on digital media. A MIDI interface on a multimedia computer can record a musical session.

Moving Picture Experts Group (MPEG). A standard for compressing video used in CD-ROMs and video CDs. Some MPEG boards can magnify the image to fill a full screen. MPEG-2 is a full-screen video standard.

Paint programs: A series of dots are "painted" on the screen from a palette of available colors. Paint programs are the easiest graphics programs to use. However, they do not allow the degree of editing that other graphics programs offer.

PICT (Macintosh draw format): Such programs work like CGM programs to generate objects.

Sound files: These come in either WAV or VOC formats: The VOC format is an unofficial standard for DOS programs; it is limited in the duration and range of sounds it can represent. The WAV format is used with Windows; it provides a much wider range of sounds than VOC. Sounds are often used to alert the user that a program is booting or that a nonfunctioning key has been struck.

Spreadsheet graphics files: These are graphics modules within spreadsheet programs that turn numeric data into bar, line, pie, or X-Y charts. There are also a number of separate charting programs that permit charts to be generated from worksheet data.

Tagged image file format (TIFF): Through the process of scanning, photographs, artwork, and letters are captured and saved as a tagged image file that can be manipulated by any program that works with TIFF files.

Before investing in graphics software, the following factors should be taken into consideration:

1. Most graphics software will run better on newer, more advanced computers with faster processors.
2. Most packages are more productive on a hard disk machine.
3. A super video graphics array (SVGA) card is the most helpful in running graphics programs. (See the Display Monitors section of Chapter 7.)
4. Most software programs require a windowing environment, such as that on a Macintosh computer or on a PC using Microsoft Windows.
5. A pointing device such as a mouse or light pen is needed if the software runs under a windowing environment or if the user intends to make illustrations that resemble freehand drawings.
6. Access to an ink jet or color laser printer will increase options in producing color visuals with graphics software.
7. The ability to import or export files from or to other programs is an important feature.

Major features of graphics software include the following:

▲ Animation schemes.
▲ Graph, text chart, and drawing tools.
▲ Ability to crop, rotate, re-size drawings.
▲ Picture compression.
▲ Templates.
▲ Macros.
▲ Ability to import and export various files to and from other programs.
▲ Standard symbols.
▲ Multimedia: text, data, voice, video, graphics.

▲ Drag and drop.

▲ Web integration.

▲ Multiple slide masters.

Desktop Publishing Software

Desktop publishing is defined as the writing, assembling, and designing of publications, such as business reports, newsletters, brochures, and trade journals, with the use of a personal computer. Through the use of desktop publishing software (DTP), pictures or graphics are combined electronically with words on the same page. DTP software includes draw or paint programs, clip-art programs, and page layout programs. (See Chapter 19, Office Publishing, for more details on desktop publishing software.)

Features of desktop publishing software include the following:

▲ Clip art images.

▲ Text creation and editing.

▲ Graphics creation and editing.

▲ Different fonts and character sizes.

▲ Interactive page layout (usually utilizing a mouse) and a graphic display of the page.

▲ Output devices support.

▲ Batch composition: All pages are automatically composed according to preset page and typographic specifications.

▲ Ability to import text and graphics from other programs.

▲ Control over hyphenation, justification, leading (fine spacing), kerning (intercharacter spacing), and so forth.

▲ Tools for document creation and distribution on the Internet, e.g., HyperText Markup Language (HTML), Dynamic HTML (DHTML), and Extensible Markup Language (XML).

▲ Automatic page numbering.

▲ Automatic repagination once a document has been edited.

▲ Wizard assistance guides.

▲ Design templates.

▲ Web integration.

The major information components of a document are text and graphic data. Desktop publishing applications view documents as including any kind of information—the output from a database query, a printed document, an on-line diagnostic manual, an illustrated parts catalog, a collection of video clips, or a home page on the World Wide Web (Internet).

A markup language is a mechanism to identify structures in a document. All desktop publishing programs rely on tagged documents of one kind or another. The most prevalent markup languages include:

Standard Generalized Markup Language (SGML): This markup language organizes and tags the elements of a document. SGML allows you to manage information as data objects instead of as characters on a page. In other words, SGML allows you to set up hierarchical models for each type of document you produce, such as "chapter," "title," and "paragraph," to fit the logical, predictable structure of your document. SGML permits you to use your information for applications beyond traditional publishing, for example Web pages, information databases, e-mail, hypermedia and hypertext documents, and database and CD-ROM publishing.

HTML (Hypertext Markup Language): This is another example of a markup language. It is a non-proprietary format based upon SGML, and can be created and processed by a wide range of tools, from simple text editors (where you type in tags) to sophisticated authoring tools. HTML uses bracketed tags to structure text into headings, paragraphs, lists, hypertext links, and so forth.

Dynamic HTML: This is typically used to describe the combination of HTML, style sheets, and scripts that allows documents to be animated. Dynamic HTML allows a Web page to change after it is loaded into the browser without further communication with the Web server for an update. You can think of it as "animated" HTML. For example, a piece of text can change from one size or color to another, or a graphic can move from one location to another, in response to some kind of user action, such as clicking a button.

XML (Extensible Markup Language): Yet another markup language for documents, this one contains structured information. Structured information contains both content (words, pictures, and so forth) and some indication of what role that content plays (for example, content in a section heading has a different meaning from content in a footnote, which means something different than content in a figure caption or content in a database table). Almost all documents have some structure.

Database Management Software

A database is a collection of information. Database management software is the set of instructions used with a computer to organize, store, and retrieve data.

Data are placed into files relating to a particular subject, such as customer lists, accounts receivable, and inventory or personnel records. Within the files are individual records pertaining to individuals or groups. Information in each record is broken down into different blocks, such as name and address, which are called fields.

Database programs are used by businesses to maintain inventories and process customer orders. Banks use databases to handle checking and savings accounts. The use and purpose of databases is limited only by your imagination.

Database management software can be placed into four categories: flat-file, relational, programmable, and library.

Flat-file databases: These menu-driven programs work with only one data file at a time. They are designed for people who need to organize facts in a very simple manner. These are the easiest databases to use.

Relational databases: Multiple forms and multiple disk files store information in relational databases. Information that appears on different forms is entered only once into the computer.

Programmable databases: These systems are designed for computer programmers who need to construct large and complex systems.

Library databases: Routines allow a user to manipulate data files and maintain records and keys in stored order. These are intended for sophisticated users.

Features of database management software include the following:

- ▲ Input forms and queries.
- ▲ Report generation.
- ▲ Onscreen creation of forms.
- ▲ Rearrangement of files without destroying existing data.
- ▲ Security mechanisms.
- ▲ Math capability.
- ▲ Menu-driven operations.
- ▲ Documentation.
- ▲ Onscreen interactive tutorials.
- ▲ Onscreen help.
- ▲ Networking capability.
- ▲ Record locking: Allows only one user at a time to make changes to a record in a database file.
- ▲ Multiuser capability.
- ▲ Application templates, e.g., contact manager, inventory control, and so forth.
- ▲ Wizard assistance guides.
- ▲ Voice recognition.
- ▲ Web integration.

Personal Information Management and Desktop Management

Personal Information Management (PIM) software and Desktop Management Software programs help organize and manage the details of daily office life. Both categories of software generally provide notepads for composing letters or lists, a text editor, electronic calendars, calculators, alarms, onscreen lists of things to do, and pop-up directories for names, addresses, and telephone numbers. PIM software also aids in decision making by recognizing patterns, pointing out relationships, assigning priorities, and providing for cross-referencing the data between categories. For example, a customer contact can be cross-referenced with a particular salesperson, a territory, or a product category. ACT and Sales Suite are examples of popular PIM software programs.

On the other hand, typical Desktop Management Software programs, such as Lotus Organizer® and Sidekick®, are patterned after paper-based organizers or desktop planners. Capability is generally provided for storing phone numbers and messages, creating multiple lists, keeping track of appointments, and recording notes. When keeping track of each department member's appointments, they can also be useful for scheduling meetings. This category of software is usually less complicated and generally easier to learn than PIM software.

Project Management Software

Projects are not the typical ongoing administrative activities, such as opening the mail, preparing information for the payroll, or processing invoices. A project generally consists of a set of nonroutine tasks performed in a specific sequence leading to a goal. It usually has distinct start and finish dates and a limited set of resources. Planning to move 50 people to a new floor by a specified date or developing a new advertising campaign are examples. Keeping track of the many concurrent activities and preparing periodic status reports can be difficult, time-consuming, and prone to error. Project management software, which can track one or more projects concurrently, is designed to keep track of project schedules and costs. Typical tasks include monitoring needed resources, coordinating and allocating resources, and updating deadlines and budgets. Features of project management software include:

- Capability to share data with other programs and also to incorporate features such as drag-and-drop editing and long file names.
- Unique planning wizards and templates to monitor actions as well as offer suggestions, e.g., a Gantt Chart Wizard for creating a graphic visualization of the key project milestones.
- Planning features to organize the details of a project into a manageable structure and identify the high-risk tasks that could severely impact the project if missed, such as a "baseline chart" for comparing the current schedule with the original plan. A "resource tools" feature keeps management informed of bottlenecks and shortages in advance.
- PERT (Planning Evaluation and Review Technique) chart and resource graph view screens that can be combined to see the information and understand the relationships among tasks. Tracking capability for up to 9,999 tasks per project and 9,999 resources per project.
- Capability to move data easily among spreadsheets, slides, and reports as well as other documents, other programs, and other databases compliant with the Open DataBase Connectivity (ODBC) standard.

- Enhancement of teamwork through capability to route projects to team members via e-mail and to collect task status information via e-mail.
- Preformatted reports showing current activities, costs, assignments, and workloads that are available, or the creation of custom reports.

Records Management Software

Records management involves managing and controlling office information. Typical applications include maintaining a records center, tracking active and inactive records, making note of vital records, creating archives or historical records, and developing a record retention schedule.

No one system is right for all users. Criteria for judging all records management software, however, are: support, vendor stability, quality of documentation, ease of use, error handling ability, and value (how well a package addresses user needs).

Features of records management software include the following:

▲ Keyword search: searches for and selects a word for retrieval.

▲ File management.

▲ Retention maintenance: a system for purging inactive files according to a schedule.

▲ Destruction notification: supplies a form notifying the user of erasure of a document.

▲ Request processing.

▲ Records retrieval and inventory.

▲ File tracking.

▲ Generation of reports.

▲ Space allocation: the assignment of a given number of characters.

▲ Bar coding.

▲ Mixed media: allows more than one type of device for storage of records, e.g., microfilm, microfiche, or floppy disk.

▲ Computer-assisted retrieval (CAR): used with micrographics.

Integrated Software Suites

Integrated software suites are related groups of software programs that can perform more than one function. Functions work together so information can be transferred from one application to another. Integrated software can consist of word processing, database management, spreadsheet, graphics, and desktop management.

Multiuser integrated software operates in a network environment. Such software includes inter-workstation electronic mail, shared file storage, and many business applications.

The following are the two types of integrated software:

All-in-one:* These allow users to move between applications without leaving the program.

Modular:* These provide a "family" or suite of programs produced by the same software house and sharing similar commands. They permit the sharing of information among individual stand-alone programs. When selecting integrated software, it is important to know how the product integrates applications. A file-conversion utility is less desirable than a cut-and-paste approach, because with the former, the application usually must be abandoned when the utility is activated.

Features of integrated software suites include the following:

- Seamless integration with word processing, spreadsheet, graphic presentation, desktop management, and database management programs.
- Online interactive help (wizards, coaches, and so forth) and templates to assist in creating documents, databases, and presentations.
- Capability to share work over a network with team support tools.
- Capability to copy files, worksheets, tables and charts by "dragging and dropping" them into other applications, documents, or e-mail messages.
- Automatic error and spell check correction.

Groupware

Groupware is a term describing software to support people working in groups connected via computer and communications technologies. This software is designed to enable computer users to work together within facilities over local area networks, as well as beyond the walls of a building through telecommunication systems. Typical groupware applications include conferencing, workflow, calendar, e-mail, and distributing data among groups. Another term used to describe this activity is computer-supported cooperative work (CSCW).

Some of the main features of groupware include:

Ready-to-run application templates:* for common groupware applications, such as team issues, customer service, meeting tracking, status reporting, reservation scheduling, and more.

Document database:* Users can access, track, store, and organize any number of objects and data types, including text, numerical data, structured data, images, graphics, and sound and video images.

Electronic messaging:* Users can send and receive e-mail across a variety of mail systems.

Replication technology:* Everyone working on a document is provided with the same up-to-date information. Groupware also performs replication between servers and desktop clients, allowing employees in the field to dial in at regular intervals and have their records updated.

Administrative tools: Network administrators, both local and remote, maintain servers, support users, load software, set up replication schedules, manage disk space, and create new accounts.

Modular construction: Network administrators start with core capabilities and build strategic business process applications for their organizations as needs require.

Shareware

Shareware programs are software programs that can be distributed and copied at little or no cost without violating copyright laws. Shareware is distributed through electronic bulletin boards, on-line information services, user groups, and shareware catalogs from a mail-order company that specializes in shareware programs.

A user who decides to keep a shareware program is expected to register with and pay a fee to the software company that created the program. After registering and paying the fee, the shareware user will receive support and manuals for the shareware.

HINT: *The Public Software Library in Houston maintains one of the largest collections of public domain software and shareware for PC and Macintosh computers. Call 713–610–1432 for details.*

Communications, Network, and Linking Software

Communications, network, and linking software programs enable a computer to transmit and receive information from another computer over telephone lines. They can also link a PC to a mainframe, minicomputer, or other PCs, and transfer files from one application program to another.

To transmit and receive information, a *modem* (Modulator-DeModulator) is needed. A modem is a device that converts digital signals into analog (voice-like) signals for transmission over a telephone line. At the other end of the line, another modem converts the analog signals back into digital form. A modem is also known as a data set.

Local area networks (LANs) distribute information throughout an office via different terminals (called nodes) connected to a central information repository (called a server). The server allows people to share peripherals and data files. The server functions like a traffic cop, managing the flow of information between the computers hooked together on the LAN. Thus, a LAN allows people in a department to share information with each other electronically as well as to share common resources like printers and large hard disks. A LAN electronically ties functions together for better communications among individuals, departments within the office and/or satellite offices or locations, and it reduces equipment costs, since different PC users can share expensive peripherals, such as laser printers.

SELECTING SOFTWARE

The following general guidelines—many of which are also used for selecting hardware—will help you evaluate your prospective software:

1. Perform a needs analysis, either through a survey, questionnaire, or interviews of other users. A thorough needs analysis determines the software applications needed, who the users are, frequency of use, types of documents produced, the operating system currently in use (if applicable), the computer hardware available, and the printer requirements. It can also indicate what your future needs are likely to be.
2. Identify available packages. Determine the available packages by talking to software manufacturers, software dealers, reviewing sales literature, and reading office-related trade magazines. Ask the following questions:
   ▲ What are the benefits that differentiate one brand from another?
   ▲ What tasks need to be done?
   ▲ Will the features meet the needs of the end user?
   ▲ How easy are the package's features to learn in relationship to performing the task?
   ▲ What is the availability and compatibility to other equipment and software already being used? Will the software interface with existing hardware and software?
   ▲ Is support available after the sale? By whom? Is a toll-free phone number available for troubleshooting problems? Is there a user group that you can join? Are there others within the organization who have knowledge of the software to assist when problems occur? What kind of maintenance or upgrading is available for software? Are there add-on packages for the software available?
   ▲ Is training free or is there a charge? What type of training is available?

HINT: *Software decisions drive hardware decisions. Match available packages to the information gathered in the needs analysis.*

3. Establish a comparative grid, or matrix, of available packages. Make a list of the information gathered by categories in the first column and put the packages studied across the tops of the other columns. Fill in the comparative information at the appropriate cell intersections. You may wish to assign both a weight for each category and a score for each package, from a low of 1 to a high of 10. Multiply the weight by the score in each cell and then total the scores in each column. In this way you can quantitatively compare the prospective software package choices.

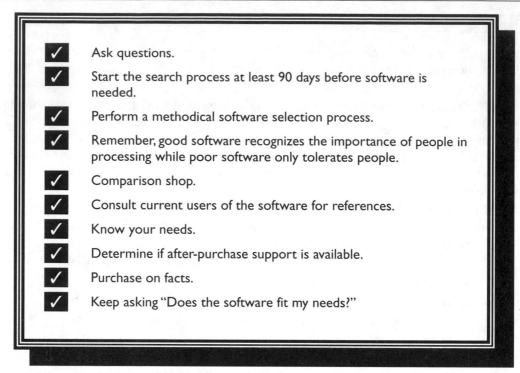

Figure 8-1 Guidelines for buying software.

4. Request a demonstration of the software and/or a trial use. A thorough demonstration, preferably with trial use, is necessary before making a final decision. Both the demonstration and the trial usage will provide valuable insights that are not possible through any other form of evaluation, helping you to determine if the software is easy to use.

HINT: *Small organizations with limited budgets should consider integrated software, which can combine a few categories of tasks. The larger the organization, the more specialized the software usually needs to be.*

ASSORTED SOFTWARE ISSUES

Establishing a Software Inventory

Managing software is an important function of the office professional or network administrator. With the addition of more and more personal computers into the office and home, maintaining an inventory of software has become important. Such an inventory not only shows what software is available but also provides a degree of consistency and standardization in the software used.

A software inventory can be done manually or electronically through a database management system. An inventory sheet (or file, if maintained on the computer) for each software package should be completed. An inventory sheet contains important information concerning the software: name of the software, version number, number of copies, serial numbers, users' names, and vendor information.

By maintaining an inventory sheet, upgrades in the software by the manufacturer can be easily made. Notification of these changes can be quickly incorporated into the appropriate departments. Security and copyright issues can be better managed, protected, and documented.

Backing Up Software

With larger hard drives, the most effective way to back up is to use a tape or CD-ROM backup system. These systems are easy to install and generally include a tape or disk drive, backup software, and one preformatted tape or CD. Files can also be backed up using a ZIP disk, a CD, or a removable hard drive.

Here are some tips on using a tape drive system:

- Tape backup systems are designed to back up data files into the gigabyte range. When purchasing a tape system, you need to relate the capacity of your hard drive to the capacity of the system you are planning to purchase.
- Use the software program's maximum compression command to fit more information on a tape. You can experiment with the compression ratio for optimum results. Text-only files compress better than graphics files or files ending with .EXE.
- Although you can use only one tape, it is recommended that you alternate among three or four tapes. This provides a safety net in case a tape goes bad and also promotes greater tape longevity.
- Create a new tape once a week and store that tape at an off-site facility for additional data protection.
- Keep your tapes stored at room temperature and in a safe place, such as a locked file drawer. Data security is paramount when you have a lot of data stored on something so small that it can fit into a pocket.
- Save hours of time by buying preformatted tapes. The additional cost is minimal.
- Keep your tape heads clean by periodically cleaning them with a cotton swab and rubbing alcohol. Or you can buy a tape backup drive cleaning kit.
- Always match the type of backup tape to your backup drive requirements. Some drives use DC (data cartridge) tapes and others use QIC (quarter-inch cartridge) tapes.

- When your drive fails, assuming the drive is not damaged, you need to restore it initially by using your "emergency" DOS disk. Next, install the tape backup software, replace the backup tape, and select Restore. Be sure to select the option to overwrite all files that were installed with your "emergency" DOS disk.

Computer Viruses

Computer viruses are self-replicating blocks of computer code that enter a computer through a modem or network, or locally through a contaminated diskette. By replicating themselves thousands or millions of times, viruses may tie up the computer's processor and block other functions. Virus "infections" spread just as biological viruses do—by contact. As healthy diskettes and programs come in contact with an infected system, the virus merges into healthy programs or disks, causing an infection. The insertion process takes only a fraction of a second. A virus may destroy data, reformat a disk, wear out its drive, or flash a harmless message on the screen. A virus not only affects PCs, but it can also attack mainframes and minicomputers.

A number of things can indicate that a virus has infected or attempted to infect a system. Unexplained system "crashes," programs that suddenly don't work right, data files or programs that are mysteriously erased, and disks that become unreadable are all possible signs of a virus.

Products are available to help a system recover from a virus attack. There are three categories of antiviral programs:

- Infection prevention products, which stop the virus from repeating and infecting the system.
- Infection detection products, which detect an infection soon after the infection occurs. These products identify the area of the system that has been infected. Such products check the program when it is run for any changes. If a change from the original is detected, the user is notified of the affected area.
- Infection identification products, which identify specific virus strains in systems that are already infected and usually remove the virus and restore the system to its correct state, prior to the infection.

To help prevent the risk of viral contamination, companies should have a data backup procedure scheduled, at least once a week for moderate users and one or more times a day for heavy users. Access to backups should be controlled so their availability and integrity are guaranteed. The backups should be carefully dated and kept for several months, at least. Access to programs and data should be restricted to an "as needed" basis.

Some additional steps you can follow to help keep a good system from becoming infected include the following:

1. Floppy-disk-based systems should be started only with a specific, clearly labeled boot, or startup, diskette. Only one boot diskette should be assigned to each PC. It should be clearly marked as the boot diskette.

2. Never boot a hard disk system from a diskette. If an infected disk is used to boot the system, it can infect the hard disk system.

3. Never put shareware programs into a hard disk's root directory. This protects the root directory, which serves as the base for other subdirectories within the system. Most viruses can affect only the directory from which they are executed. In a LAN, avoid placing shareware in a common file-server directory that makes it accessible to any PC in the network. Viruses can also be downloaded into the system through bulletin boards or via disks from traveling executives who use other computer systems. Disks that have been used elsewhere should be checked prior to use (through the use of an antiviral program).

4. In a shared resource system, where data is transported between PCs or printers, the output data should be put on a floppy disk. No other files including system files should be on the floppy disk.

5. Software should be tested before it is used on the system. Backing up an infected disk will create a second infected disk.

6. There should be strict policies regulating the downloading of software from other systems, since a virus can be transferred from the originating computer.

7. Always treat your e-mail with caution and never open a suspicious attachment or an attachment from a sender you do not know. If uncertain, contact your system administrator for advice. Also, make sure your e-mail system has security protection.

8. Software is available to build a firewall that will help you to keep viruses from penetrating your system. Firewalls create barriers which prevent unauthorized access to a network. Firewalls are the security doors through which some data may pass and some may not.

9. Up-to-date information about new viruses and how to protect against them is available at http://ca.com/virusinfo.

Software Copyright Issues

Copyright infringement is on the rise, primarily because employees do not know the scope of the laws against it. According to the law, an author or creator of a work owns all the rights to any form of it, including the right to copy and distribute it. Title 17 of the U.S. Code states that "it is illegal to make or distribute copies of the copyrighted material without authorization." The only exception is the user's right to make a backup copy for archival purposes.

An employee who makes duplicates of a copyrighted story, book, or report and dis-

1. (Company/Agency) licenses the use of computer software from a variety of outside companies. (Company/Agency) does not own this software or its related documentation, and unless authorized by the software developer, does not have the right to reproduce it.

2. With regard to use on local area networks or on multiple machines, (Company/Agency) employees shall use the software only in accordance with the license agreement.

3. (Company/Agency) employees learning of any misuse of software or related documentation within the company shall notify the department manager or (Company's/Agency's) legal counsel.

4. According to the U.S. Copyright law, persons involved in the illegal reproduction of software can be subject to civil damages of as much as $50,000, and criminal penalties, including fines and imprisonment. (Company/Agency) does not condone the illegal duplication of software. (Company/Agency) employees who make, acquire, or use unauthorized copies of computer software shall be disciplined as appropriate under the circumstances. Such discipline may include termination.

I am fully aware of the software use policies of (Company/Agency) and agree to uphold these policies.

_____

Employee Signature and Date

Figure 8-2 Sample corporate employee agreement: company/agency policy regarding the use of personal computer software.

tributes them to fellow employees is violating the law. Unauthorized duplication of software is a federal crime. Penalties include fines of as much as $100,000 and jail terms of up to five years. In addition, the material in question can be impounded or destroyed.

The Digital Millennium Copyright Act governs both copyright holders and the general public who want access to copyrighted materials on the Internet and Web. The act:

• Mandates protection of digital copyrighted works.

• Prohibits the use of technological devices designed to protect copyrighted works.

- Provides penalties for criminal infringement of digital works on-line.
- Protects service providers from liability in the transmission of copyrighted and/or infringed materials.
- Includes a licensing and royalty scheme for the transmission of copyrighted music over the Internet.

Art forms (graphics, photos, music, and so forth) are protected when copyrighted for use on or off the Internet. The list is extensive, including buttons and graphics, cartoons, illustrations, and original writing found on other people's Web sites.

Management should work with the company's legal department to develop policies related to copyright issues. These policies should be discussed with employees to educate and remind them of the consequences. (See Figure 8-2) The simplest and best policy is to have one authorized copy of a software product for every computer upon which it is run.

Software vendors make application licenses for multiple users available to large organizations. A multiuser license reduces the cost of implementing a particular software program, such as word processing, throughout an organization. Grappling with issues of compliance, new technologies, constantly changing programs, software piracy, employee turnover, and how to reallocate licenses, heterogeneous environments, and management pressures can be a complicated issue and is something best done by someone with expertise in this area.

The Software and Information Industry Association (SIIA) produces a number of publications that describe procedures appropriate for ensuring that a business or organization is "software-legal." The Software and Information Industry Association's address is 1090 Vermont Ave. NW, Sixth Floor, Washington, DC 20005, 202–289–SIIA, fax 202–289–7097.

Another excellent source of information is the U.S. Copyright Web site, the official Web site of the U.S. Copyright Office: www.lcweb.loc.gov/copyright. On this site you will find copyright statute, new legislation, registration forms, international copyright information, and FAQs.

Music, in any form that is under copyright, may only be used for strictly personal use. If it is used for any other purpose, including broadcasting, printing, playing or performing to audiences, or including for use with other media, royalties are due. Distribution refers to creating any duplications or providing for it (copies), even when not for profit. When you have made available more than one or two copies for personal use (or backup) you are in violation of the copyright law. This also applies to tapes, CDs, and music in Web pages or other files.

The exception to the above is if the recording artists make no claim to the production/performance and the music used is in public domain. Public domain means the copyright has expired. This is the case where the creator is dead for more than 50 (fifty) years, in most countries now even 75 (seventy-five) years. An exception is made if the music was published under pseudonym, in which case the work is protected for the period from the year of first publication.

Software Training and Certification

Many software vendors, e.g., Novell® and Microsoft®, provide certification training for their software products. This training includes certification based on a series of examinations that test one's mastery of critical competencies. By becoming certified, one is recognized as an expert in the designing, developing, and implementing of software support solutions. Typical certification designations include, Certified System Engineer, Certified Solution Developer, Certified Product Specialist, Certified Trainer, Certified LAN Specialist, Certified Systems Administrator, Certified Database Administrator, and Microsoft® Office User Specialist.

Office supplies such as pens and pencils, file folders, and paper are consumable, disposable, and easily replaced. Changes in technology and an increased variety of equipment found in offices, however, have resulted in an increase in the number and type of supplies. Knowledge of inventory control, vendors, and the different types of products available helps in organizing supplies for efficient office use, in identifying the best sources, and in purchasing with the qualities and features needed in a particular office.

CHAPTER 9

OFFICE

SUPPLIES

PURCHASING OFFICE SUPPLIES

Office supplies can be purchased through a variety of sources, including office supply stores, salespeople representing dealers and stationers, mail-order firms, warehouse stores, on-line and discount merchants. Some manufacturers also sell directly to large customers.

Additional methods of purchasing supplies are outsourcing and group purchasing. Outsourcing is the process of arranging with a firm specializing in placing orders for others. Group purchasing involves different businesses joining together to purchase supplies. Both methods allow opportunities for discounts not available to a smaller business and provide just-in-time ordering to avoid storage problems. Another way to avoid storage problems is contracting directly with a supplier. A central storage area is then no longer needed since supplies are delivered directly to the department when they are needed.

Choosing the Best Source

Choosing a distributor requires comparison shopping. Using two or three distributors gives greater flexibility and keeps distributors competitive. Smaller, independent dealers are more likely than larger dealers to help manage your space and enhance workplace performance and may be better for larger purchases like office furniture.

Small businesses and home-office buyers can comparison-shop on-line or in person at office supply superstores. Specialty suppliers are another source and often give better prices than large suppliers.

Larger businesses might consider using an on-line purchasing system, which can eliminate the need for a stockroom because many orders are received within 24 hours. Negotiation of prices may reduce costs by 10 to 15 percent as well as eliminate purchase-order processing and requisition costs and reduce inventory costs.

HINT: *Ask a new supplier for a catalog before placing the first order.*

The following factors should be considered when choosing a source for office supplies:

Price

- Is the price full retail or discounted?
- Are prices guaranteed?
- Are prices published or is it necessary to call each time an order is placed?

HINT: *Good values and competitive prices should be available on most of the items needed.*

HINT: *Choose a supplier based on overall price levels rather than by price shopping on one item.*

Placing an order

- Is ordering convenient, whether by phone, by mail, by fax or by computer? Is the Web site easy to use?
- Does the sales representative suggest alternative products to save money or suggest quantity discounts?
- Is the catalog index easy to locate and use?
- Are prices clearly marked?
- Is the same price given for a single item as for a larger order?
- Does the sales staff have the technical competence to meet your company's supply needs?

Receiving an order

- How quickly are orders shipped?
- Do the freight charges increase if the order is partially shipped?
- Is the order consistently accurate?
- Are you notified of substitutions ahead of time?

HINT: *Most orders should be shipped within 24 hours.*

HINT: *Do not accept unordered quantities or extra merchandise.*

Billing

- How long does it take to receive the bill?
- Is a discount available for payments within 10 days?
- Is on-line transaction data readily available for tracking orders?

HINT: *A bill should be sent within a week of delivery.*

HINT: *Become familiar with credit policies in order to maintain a good credit standing and to take advantage of discounts.*

Returns

- How many days do you have to return merchandise without penalty?
- Is there a simple return policy?
- Are warranties honored?
- Is there a guarantee of 100 percent satisfaction?

HINT: *A good supplier may allow up to 90 days to return merchandise with no penalty.*

Generic Supplies

Buying generic supplies can mean a 15 to 50 percent savings. Some good generic products are available, but some generic products that appear to be the same as name brands do not have the same quality.

The cost savings realized by purchasing a generic product often may be offset by the lack of a guarantee or a major manufacturer backing the product. The only way to tell whether or not to use a generic product is by trial and error and having a willingness to take a risk.

PAPER

Paper accounts for a major part of most company supply budgets. There are many types of papers for different purposes, including paper for copiers, fax machines, computers, and special printers, prepunched, and letterhead for correspondence. Purchasing paper that can be used on more than one kind of equipment, such as paper that can be used for copy machines and laser printers, simplifies ordering, handling, and stocking of paper. It can also save your company a significant amount of money. Below are some considerations to bear in mind when selecting paper.

Grades

Paper can be purchased in economy, standard, or premium grades. Better grades provide increased brightness and greater contrast between copy and paper, an important paper characteristic for laser printers because the text appears more legible. Table 9-1 describes paper grades, their brightness, and their uses.

HINT: *Coordinate the brightness levels of all paper for consistent good appearance.*

HINT: *A lower level of brightness makes the paper appear yellowish.*

Table 9-1
PAPER GRADES

GRADE	BRIGHTNESS	USES
Economy	81	Suitable for everyday use and internal correspondence; used when appearance is less important than economy.
Standard	84	Gives a professional but not a formal look; suitable for interoffice communications.
Premium	86½	Company letterheads; good for laser printers or copiers.

Content

The content of paper is the amount of wood pulp it contains, which affects durability and appearance. Office paper is either cotton fiber bond or sulphite bond.

HINT: *If paper is acid-free, it will not turn yellow when stored for archival purposes.*

Cotton fiber bond (or "rag") is made of cotton pulp combined with chemically treated wood pulp. It is available in grades indicating the amount of cotton pulp combined with the wood pulp: 25 percent, 50 percent, 75 percent, 100 percent, and extra 100 percent. Cotton bonds have a watermark, which is an impression, pattern, or symbol on the paper that signifies its quality. The higher the cotton content, the more durable the paper. Table 9-2 describes the uses of different types of cotton fiber bond.

Table 9-2
USES OF COTTON FIBER BOND

CONTENT	USES
100% cotton	Legal documents, certificates, prestige stationery, and vital records.
75% cotton	Permanent records, prestige letterhead, and executive correspondence.
50% cotton	Semipermanent records and letterhead.
25% cotton	Most popular letterhead bond; also used for price lists, report forms, circulars, and bulletins.

Note that cotton bond may not perform well on laser printers and copiers, although some manufacturers make a 25% cotton paper specifically designed for laser printers.

Sulphite bond is made from chemically treated wood pulp. This paper is also known as xerographic paper, because it is typically used for copiers and laser printers. It is smoother and less expensive than cotton-content bond, so it has less of a tendency to curl up and jam in a copy machine or laser printer.

Although sulphite bond comes in five grades, numbered 1 through 5, only #1 and #4 are recommended for general office use. Table 9-3 gives the characteristics of these two commonly used paper types.

Table 9-3
GRADES OF SULPHITE BOND

GRADE	CHARACTERISTICS
#1	Has a watermark; looks so good it is difficult to distinguish from a more expensive cotton bond; cost-effective for letterheads, especially if the letterheads are used in a copier or a laser printer, where permanence is not essential.
#4	Most popular for copying and laser printing; only available in a smooth finish; least expensive since it is made from lower quality pulp and has a very white appearance.

Finish

Paper comes in a variety of finishes, which determine the paper's look and feel. Smoother finishes are less expensive and work better with most office machines. Generally a smooth, regular finish communicates an impression of higher quality than a rough surface. However, the choice of finish is often based on personal preference. Table 9-4 describes three commonly used finishes.

Paper with a textured surface typically does not work well in laser printers or copiers because of its greater potential for misfeeding and paper jams. Smoother paper avoids these problems and also ensures sharper resolution of details. Laser printer paper specif-

Table 9-4
PAPER FINISHES

FINISH	DESCRIPTION	USES
Smooth	Few irregularities.	Works well with copiers and laser printers; most popular for letterhead.
Linen laid	Embossed with a linen design, with a fairly rough feel and appearance.	Creates superior impression. High-quality letterhead.
Ripple	Wavy, glossy finish, with the indentations darker than the higher spots.	Document papers, certificates.

ically designed for certificates and documents and with the look and feel of parchment is also available.

Weight

Paper weight is the weight of one ream (500 sheets) of paper, which is called the basis weight. The weight is a measure of the thickness and density of paper. In English units, the basis weight is the weight of 500 sheets of 17-by-22-inch paper. Measured in metric units it is the weight in grams of one square meter of paper. Office paper weights range from 9 to 28 pounds. In general, paper specifications should follow the recommendations of the equipment or paper manufacturer. Table 9-5 gives paper weights for common office uses.

Table 9-5
PAPER WEIGHTS FOR COMMON OFFICE USES

USE	WEIGHT (LB.)	DESCRIPTION
Copier paper	20	Recommended: Xerographic (#4 sulphite). Refer to the section in this chapter on *Copier Problems Caused by Paper.*
Envelopes	24	Opaque; heavier weight than letterhead paper; check user's manual for compatibility with postage meters, mailing machines, and printers. Refer to the section in this chapter on Envelopes for additional details.
Laser printer	16–28	Refer to user's manual for weight specifications. Most laser printers cannot accept extremely heavy paper stocks and work best with a very smooth sheet of paper such as xerographic or specially formulated laser printer paper. Colors and cotton bond are available.
Inkjet printer	20–24	Choose 90–95+ brightness for better color printing quality. A heavier weight paper has less show-through.
Photo paper	24	Choose a coated paper with a color receiving layer to print photos and color images. Glossy finish has look and feel of regular photographs.
Letterhead		Recommended: 25 percent cotton bond; 86½ brightness. Note: Not all letterhead works well with laser printers.
	20	Most popular weight.
	24	More body, generally used for special purposes.

Color

Many companies prefer neutral colors such as ivory, off-white, and gray for important correspondence. Firms that use colored paper, letterhead with color, or color printers or copiers want their message to stand out from others. Research has shown that direct mail in color increases readership, retention of detail, and response from readers.

Color can make the following materials more effective:

- Annual reports.
- Brochures.
- Color-coded documents.
- Direct-mail pieces.
- Dividers for reports.
- Letterhead.
- Memos.
- Product information.
- Sales materials.

Color can also improve interoffice communication by using it to:

- Distinguish department correspondence (e.g., green paper for accounting, yellow paper for personnel, and so forth).
- Avoid wasting time; this can be done by color-coding documents that look similar (e.g., color-code legal documents that look alike but have different contents).
- Call attention to information. Use a bright, visible color for information that must be read immediately, such as companywide information posted on bulletin boards. Reserve tan or gray for confidential information; such a document will stand out if it is in the hands of the wrong person.
- Add a festive mood to holiday announcements or party flyers.

Bear these points in mind when using colored paper:

Equipment compatibility: Check the user's manual for specifications to be sure the paper is compatible with the equipment.

Laser printers: Not all colored paper can withstand the heat of laser printers. Avoid paper with a colored coating that has been added after the paper is produced. The paper should be of the same quality as white paper used in the laser printer.

Letterhead: Use light-colored paper for letterhead because it has the best contrast and readability.

Photocopying: Try photocopying any document on colored paper before ordering large quantities to see if the result is a shadowed copy.

Multipart Forms

Carbonless paper produces copies without the use of carbon paper. Chemical coatings in the paper form an image when a pen, pencil, or stylus is used. It is used especially for forms needed by several departments.

Fax Paper

Most fax machines use plain paper. (See the section Fax Machines in Chapter 7 for more information.)

Copier Problems Caused by Paper

Copy paper should be properly placed in paper trays. Most paper manufacturers provide loading instructions on their packages (usually an arrow indicating which surface is to be printed on). Some copiers discharge the sheet the same way it is placed in the tray, while others turn it over.

HINT: *To test how a copier works, mark one side of a sheet and run it through to determine the imaging side.*

HINT: *When purchasing a copier, it is important to have a demonstration on the various thicknesses of paper to determine the minimum and maximum possible.*

Table 9-6 provides a quick reference for solutions to copier problems.

Recycled Paper

More people are aware of the limited supply of natural resources and recycle office paper. To facilitate recycling, offices have recycling containers for used white and colored paper next to wastepaper baskets and near copiers. Building maintenance staff collect the paper for recycling.

Recycled paper is available for copiers and computers, as well as for writing and memo pads. File folders and mailers may also be made from recycled fibers. Recycled paper may be white or colored, and it may have some cotton content.

Buy a small quantity at first, then check the results. From an environmental point of view, the best recycled paper is 100 percent recycled with a high post-consumer content

Table 9-6
SOLUTIONS TO COPIER PROBLEMS

PROBLEM	CAUSE	SOLUTION
Feed difficulties	Heavy-stock paper, such as letterhead, may cause static buildup.	Use lighter-weight paper.
Misfeeding	Uneven edges or excessive curl; mixing different paper weights in the same tray or cassette.	Turn the paper over or use another ream.
Jamming in the finish bins or sheets sticking together	Excessive curl. Moisture. Low humidity.	Turn the paper over. Check storage conditions. Ask vendor to check static eliminator.
Wrinkling	High moisture content if the paper has been incorrectly wrapped or stored in a damp location; paper has been left too long in the copy machine.	Check storage conditions; use another ream.

(paper that was recycled after use at home or in the office) and is either not de-inked at all (i.e., the ink was not removed from the printer's waste) or is bleached without chlorine.

Some points to consider when buying recycled products are as follows:

- Test the product with your equipment and see if it meets your needs.
- Compare bids from vendors of virgin products to see if a switch is worth it. Some recycled paper products (such as legal pads and copy paper) may be comparable in price to virgin products, but the costs of some recycled and virgin products can vary greatly.
- Explore the possibility of purchasing recycled products with money the company earns from selling recyclable waste materials.
- Promote the program. Make sure company employees, customers, and vendors know your company is recycling and buying recycled products. Include statements like "Printed on recycled paper" on all publications. Develop news releases, advertising, and public service announcements.

ENVELOPES

Envelopes come in hundreds of styles and sizes to accommodate all mailing purposes. Although other sizes are available, Table 9-7 shows the most common types and sizes of envelopes. Listed below are the characteristics and typical uses of business envelopes.

Commercial and official envelopes (also called business or regular)

- Usually 24 lb. bond for first-class, airmail, or bulk-rate mail handling.
- No. 9 envelope fits into a No. 10 envelope.
- Available with an inside blue tint for confidentiality.
- Cotton fiber bond envelopes should always match letterhead stationery.
- May have a window to use for invoices, statements, addressed documents, or payroll checks. A window eliminates retyping, reducing errors and saving time.

Kraft envelopes: These envelopes come in a wide variety of sizes for a wide variety of uses. Kraft envelopes also have different types of closures. String and button and clasp envelopes can be reused. Clasp envelopes have gummed flaps for extra strength and security. These envelopes have wide usage, from storing small coins to mailing large catalogs.

Tyvek™ envelopes: Available in No. 14 size and made of polyolefin fibers bonded together by heat and pressure, these envelopes are rip-proof, puncture-proof, and water resistant. Because they weigh about half as much as paper, they can save postage. Tyvek™ envelopes may incorporate a seal in the closure to reveal tampering, and a window on the flap changes to the word "opened" if the flap is lifted.

Interdepartment delivery envelopes: These envelopes save paper because they are used over and over again. The most economical interdepartment envelopes have transmittal information printed on both sides. They may close with either a string and button tie or resealable adhesive. Some have drilled holes to make contents visible, and others are available in Tyvek™.

Printer envelopes: Good construction, with a well-creased fold and no more than two thicknesses of paper, is critical for a printer's envelope. The paper weight should not be

---

Table 9-7
COMMON ENVELOPES

TYPE	SIZE	DESCRIPTION
No. 6 3/4	$3\frac{5}{8}$ by $6\frac{1}{2}$ inches	Commercial
No. 9	$3\frac{7}{8}$ by $8\frac{7}{8}$ inches	Official
No. 10*	$4\frac{1}{8}$ by $9\frac{1}{8}$ inches	Official
No. 11	$4\frac{1}{2}$ by $9\frac{1}{2}$ inches	Document/policy
No. 12	5 by $11\frac{1}{2}$ inches	Document/policy
No. 14	9 by 12 inches	First-class mailer
	10 by 13 inches	
	10 by 15 inches	
	12 by $15\frac{1}{2}$ inches	

*The envelope used most often for correspondence.

greater than 24 pounds. Before purchasing envelopes for printers, check the user's manual for envelope use. Poorly constructed envelopes may result in a jammed printer or a wrinkled envelope.

See the following section on Labels for an alternative to envelope use with printers.

LABELS

Labels are available in many sizes, shapes, and widths for a variety of different labeling needs. Labels often include preset layouts for use with most software programs and printers. In addition, specialty label software can be purchased and installed. Most labels are self-adhered to $8\frac{1}{2}$-inch by 11-inch paper.

Envelope labels created by a computer and printed on a printer are easy to use. White labels are common; however clear, patterned, and colored labels are available.

HINT: *Do not feed labels through a laser or ink-jet printer more than once. The tight paper path of the ink-jet printer and the heat in the laser printer can cause the labels to jam or peel off.*

TRANSPARENCIES

A wide variety of overhead transparency film is specially developed to work on printers and copiers. Check the transparency box for compatibility with your printers and copiers since transparencies require a surface coating.

FILING AND RECORDS MANAGEMENT SUPPLIES

Most manual filing systems use file folders, labels, and guides. These products are available in a variety of sizes, shapes, colors, and styles. Filing supply choices depend on individual preferences and needs.

File Folders

There are two basic types of file folders. (1) Manila file folders are made of heavy-weight stock that resists tearing, folding, and bursting. They are typically a light creamy color but are also available in a variety of colors. (2) Kraft file folders are made of unbleached sulfite stock in a dark tan color and are preferable when strength and rigidity are required. They look clean longer than manila folders, but they are more expensive.

Letter-size file folders are $9\frac{1}{2}$ by $11\frac{3}{4}$ inches. The $9\frac{1}{2}$-inch height includes the tab.

Both manila and kraft folders are described by the thickness of the folder, measured in points. One point is equivalent to 0.001 inch. As the point size increases, so does the durability and price of the folder. Typical weights for manila folders are 9½- and 11-point stock. Typical Kraft folders weights are 11- and 17-point. Table 9-8 lists the various sizes and uses of file folders.

In order to be cost effective, the minimum weight of folders for a task should be used. When transferring files for storage, information should be transferred to lighter-weight, less expensive folders. The heavier folders should be reused for active files.

Table 9-8
FILE FOLDER SIZES

WEIGHT	POINT	USE
Medium	$9\frac{1}{2}$	Two or three times a week (semiactive) or less (inactive).
Heavy	11	Several times a day (active).
Extraheavy	17	Numerous times a day (very active); a common weight for guides.
Superior rigidity	25	Guides; available in pressboard (a hard, dense stock).

TAB CUTS

A basic file folder has a tab made out of the same material as the folder. Most styles of folders are made with front flaps undercut to create the tab heading area. Special-purpose folders may have tabs that double the thickness of the folder from the top of the tab to the top of the undercut (called "double tab" or "two-ply" file folders). These tabs are good for active files. Other tabs are made of stronger material such as plastic.

The tab cut determines the number of tabs across the top edge of the file folder. Table 9-9 describes the different cuts. Folders usually are packaged with an equal number of tabs so the labeled tabs in the file drawer are staggered evenly.

OTHER FOLDER TYPES

There are several other important types of file folders:

Plastic file folders: Made of durable and flexible polyethylene or polypropylene, these are good for heavily-used folders because they resist spills and stains and are rarely damaged by handling. Many have a nonslip surface to prevent sliding when stacked. They come in a variety of colors and are good for a color-coded system.

Hanging file folders: Most file drawers are equipped for a hanging file system or can be converted with a metal frame. Files hang at a uniform level from rodlike projections or hooks at the top, allowing tabs to remain visible and preventing folders from sliding down into the drawer. Many have removable plastic tabs into which paper labeling tabs can be inserted—and removed and changed, and tabs can be used in a variety of positions. They are available in a range of colors and thus can be used in a color-coded system.

Interior manila folders: Shorter than regular manila folders, these are specifically designed to be used inside hanging file folders to make it easy to remove material from

Table 9-9
TAB CUTS

CUT	DESCRIPTION	USE
Straight	Tab length is the full width of folder.	Multiple labels; extra long headings.
Half	Tab length is one-half the width of folder; tabs are staggered in sets of two.	Long headings.
Third	Tab length is one-third the width of folder; tabs are staggered in sets of three.	Most common; most folder labels are designed for this folder and do not fit other cuts.
Fifth	Tab length is one-fifth the width of folder; tabs are staggered in sets of five.	Less room for writing; most popular for numerical filing systems.
Two-fifths	Tab length is two-fifths the width of folder; tabs are either right of center or far right.	Long headings.
Shelf or end cut	Tab is on the end of the folder instead of the top; scored expansion bottoms accommodate more material.	Open shelf filing systems where records are stored in horizontal rows rather than in file drawers.

the hanging folder without taking the folder out of the drawer. The height and tabs are designed so as not to block or interfere with hanging folder tabs.

Bellows (expansion) folders: These are available with pockets and may be labeled alphabetically or numerically.

Box bottom hanging folders: These folders have flat, reinforced bottoms for filing heavy, bulky material; closed sides keep smaller items from slipping out.

File folders with fasteners: Folders are available with fasteners attached in various positions to secure papers inside them; self-adhesive varieties are available as well as the standard version with plastic or metal prong fasteners that thread through the folder.

LABELS FOR FILE FOLDERS

File folder labels are available in preset layouts for popular software programs and printers. They may be white or white with a color border. A wide range of border colors is available. Removable file folder labels are also available.

Preprinted inserts are also available for tabs; they eliminate typing of labels. The inserts are usually alphabetical, numerical, daily, monthly, or by states. Legal exhibit labels are also available preprinted.

GUIDES

File guides are used for dividing file drawers into categorized sections, thus preventing misfiling and wasting time. File guides can be 18-point manila, for inactive to semiactive files, or 25-point pressboard for semiactive to active files. Manila guides cost less than pressboard but are less durable. Guides are available with plain tabs, and monthly, daily, or alphabetic preprinted tabs. File guides are available for hanging file folders. Tabs are either made of the same paper as the guide or made of plastic or steel.

Out guides indicate that an entire folder has been removed from the files. Out guides range from 11- to 17-point paper with either end or tab cuts. Usually they are a bright color such as red or orange, The guide may include a printed form on which to write the date and by whom the file was removed or it may have a small pocket for a charge-out card.

COLORS

Color folders allow the classifying and coding of files by color. Color coding can be done with colored labels, file folders, or hanging file folders. Color coding has several advantages, including the following:

- Guiding the eye to correct files and reducing filing and retrieval time.
- Increasing filing accuracy because misfiled items stand out.
- Providing additional subdivisions of filed material beyond label headings.

Storage Boxes

Corrugated cardboard filing boxes can be used for long-term storage of checks, documents, cards, forms, printouts, and tapes. The boxes usually need to be assembled. They have built-in handles and can be ordered with a color-coded system, which can save as much as 50 percent in filing and retrieval time. Some boxes are constructed to stand up under more than half a ton of stacking pressure, which maximizes storage floor space.

WRITING INSTRUMENTS AND CORRECTION SUPPLIES

New colors, improvements in style, a variety of types, and a wide range of prices provide many options. Because each writing instrument has advantages for its recommended use, it is likely that you use several different kinds. Many formerly low-end products have been developed with high-tech, aesthetically pleasing designs.

Pens

Pens are available in the following types:

Ballpoint: Most popular office pen, ballpoints may either be disposable or have a changeable refill. The ink dries quickly and does not smear, it writes through carbon copies, and it may be erasable. Store ballpoints point down for longest life.

Fountain: Enjoying a resurgence in popularity, fountain pens have a prestigious look. They can use a variety of brightly colored inks. Some are disposable, while others are refillable or have disposable ink cartridges.

Rollerball: These are popular for office use. They are available in several colors. The tips have a metal ball encased in a plastic or metal stem. Because they write darker and smoother than ballpoint pens, they are good for drawing, ruling, and detail work as well as writing. They can write through carbon copies; they are usually nonrefillable. Some rollerball pens are available with permanent waterproof ink, which is popular in banks and financial and legal offices as well as in humid climates.

Porous point or *felt tip:* These flow easily and have the crisp, precise lines of a ballpoint; however, their points are made of plastic, which may soften with age. The ink is often brighter in color than that of a ballpoint, and they are usually disposable. Although they will not write through carbon, they are good for detail work, ruling, sketching, and labeling floppy disks.

Markers

Markers are available for highlighting information, writing on surfaces, and writing on white boards and transparencies. Below are descriptions of various markers:

Highlighters: These are often used to call attention to information in reading material with bright see-through colors such as yellow, pink, and orange. They can make very fine or very bold lines, depending on the tip. Some can highlight on thin paper without bleeding through; some are nonsmearing and thus can be used to highlight over ink; some will not show up on copies.

Permanent markers: These are good for writing on nonporous surfaces such as cellophane, glass, metal, and transparent tape. They are suitable for mailing labels since the ink does not run when wet. They are not recommended for ordinary writing because the ink bleeds through paper. The ink dries quickly and will not smear. They are available in a wide variety of colors, but some have a distinctive irritating odor. Chisel (or wedge) tips can make fine, medium, or bold strokes; bullet tip (pointed) makes a heavier mark.

Easel pad markers: Designed to write on easel pads, these are available in a variety of colors. Look for chisel tip and waterbased ink that will not bleed through paper.

Dry erase markers: These are designed for use on whiteboards only; they cannot be used on paper because they dry out quickly. They are available in many colors and have little odor, and they erase with a dry cloth or eraser. Some may also be used on glass, unpainted metal, and glazed ceramics. Whiteboards and dry erase markers are popular because they eliminate chalk dust around computers.

Visual aid markers: Available in both permanent and erasable (if waterbased) forms, these are used for writing on acetates, such as transparencies. Available in a wide range of colors, they are designed to remain brilliant and clear under heat and light.

Pencils

Traditional woodcase lead pencils are still found in many offices, although mechanical pencils are also popular because they have different lead thicknesses and low prices.

The older turn-type mechanical pencils held only one lead at a time and needed frequent reloading. The newest and best mechanical pencils advance the lead automatically and insert new leads as old ones are used up. Lead is available in widths of 0.5, 0.7, and 0.9 millimeters. The 0.5-mm lead is the most popular and is used for general writing and detail work; heavier lines can be drawn with 0.7- and 0.9-mm lead. Mechanical pencils are good for drafting, accounting, and general office work.

COMPUTER, FAX MACHINE, AND COPIER SUPPLIES

Changes in technology have resulted in a greater variety of equipment in the office, and a resulting wide range of supplies for that equipment, which includes computers, fax machines, and copiers.

Computer Disks

Computer disks come in various sizes, depending on the computer used. The most popular sizes are the 3½-inch disk, the ZIP™ disk, and CD-ROM/-R/-RW (compact disk, recordable/rewritable), and DVD (digital video disk). The 3½-inch disk holds approximately 1.4 megabytes, is preformatted, and is available in colors that allow for color-coding data. The ZIP™ disk, used with either a built-in or portable ZIP™ drive, is also preformatted and can hold hundreds of megabytes of information.

Compact disks (CDS) hold close to a million megabytes of information. CD-R media writes one time, and CD-RW media allows recording over and over. DVD disks have more than seven times the storage capacity of a CD. Because of the large size, law databases, accounting software packages, government regulations, and product catalogs are available on DVD.

Disks are vulnerable to fingerprints, heat, and "laser rot" (the deterioration of the aluminum layer due to oxidation). Experts say smaller scratches can be worse than larger ones if the scratches follow the circular curve of the disk where the data is stored. Therefore, proper storage containers are necessary.

HINT: *Kits are available to clean and repair CD/DVD scratches.*

Disk Storage

A wide variety of storage boxes are available for disks and CD/DVDs. CD/DVD disks should be stored in jewel cases or Tyvek™ or paper sleeves. Specially designed boxes for DVDs are fitted with hubs to secure DVDs. ZIP™ disks are sold in plastic cases for storing and transporting.

Traveling diskette and disk holders come in a range of sizes.

Disk Mailers

Disk mailers are designed with a sturdy construction to offer protection from bending, static, and moisture. The mailers provide a preprinted address area with first-class postal identification and a warning such as: "Caution: Do not bend or fold. Avoid exposure to all magnetic fields."

Surge Protectors

Computers are sensitive to problems with the power supply. Such problems include surges, spikes, drops, noise, brownouts, and blackouts. Surges generally last longer than spikes, but both usually occur so fast that they are not noticed. Noise interference can be transmitted to the power line by things such as nearby radio and TV stations, loose electrical connections, and fluorescent lights. (See Table 9-10 for power problems and causes and Table 9-11 for protective devices.)

A loss of power or a sudden surge of power can cause serious damage to the circuitry of a computer, disk drive, printer, and communications equipment as well as erase valuable data. A surge protector is a cost-effective method of insuring that computers, printers, and fax machines are protected from unpredictable weather or current changes. Surge protectors divert any excess electricity out the ground line and away from electrical equipment. They also prevent hardware damage and data transmission errors.

Table 9-10
POWER PROBLEMS AND CAUSES

PROBLEM	EFFECT	POSSIBLE CAUSES
Surge	Increase in voltage	Switching of other equipment on or off.
Spike	Sudden increase in voltage	Lightning, utility company load-switching, power coming on after outage.
Outage	No voltage	Weather, power-line breaks, power system failures.
Sags/brownout	Decrease in voltage	Power company reduction during high demand periods, overloads.
Noise	Interference	High-frequency voltages from local electrical devices, including fluorescent lights.

Table 9-11
POWER PROTECTION DEVICES AVAILABLE

DEVICE	SURGE	SPIKE	SAG	OUTAGE	NOISE
Surge protector	Yes	Yes	No	No	Some
UPS (uninterruptible power systems)	Yes	Yes	Yes	Yes	Some
SPS (standby power systems)	No	No	No	Yes	No
Power conditioner	Yes	Yes	Yes	No	Yes

Some surge protectors have desktop remote controls and alarms to warn when the voltage drops below safe levels. Other surge protectors protect against spikes coming over the phone lines and are ideal for fax machines, modems, and answering machines.

Fax/Phone Line Sharing

Instead of adding another phone line, equipment is available to add a fax machine to an existing telephone line without interfering with the phone or answering machine already there. Models for single-line, two-line, and multiple-line phone systems are available. They are compatible with tone and rotary (pulse) dialing, which allows continued phone operation during power failures.

Printer and Copy Machine Toner Cartridges

Toner cartridges are used by laser printers and some copy machines. Toner is a dry, powdered substance that is attracted to electrically charged areas on the machine's photosensitive revolving drum. Toner cartridges can be ordered in color for some copy machines.

Toner should not be exposed to direct sunlight or room light for more than a few minutes because it uses a developing process similar to that of film in a camera. Light can cause the developing roller inside the cartridge to be damaged.

Ink-jet cartridges are available in black and color and are used with printers, fax machines, and combination machines (printer/scanner/copy/fax). Some service bureaus can recharge cartridges, either locally or through the mail. If the recharging is done by mail, the empty cartridge is shipped in its original box, recharged, and returned.

Recycling programs are available for cartridges, either through the cartridge manufacturers or other companies. Recycling cartridges reduces the amount of solid waste in landfills.

RIBBONS

Ribbons for the same machine may look alike or took totally different due to packaging, colors, and design features. Different part numbers in the user's manual represent differences in design, ink color, length of ribbon, and material, so it is possible for one type of ribbon to have more than one part number. If a ribbon was manufactured by the original equipment manufacturer and made in strict compliance with the device, it carries the abbreviation "OEM."

One way to avoid duplicating orders of ribbons is to establish an in-house list of machines and their ribbons. The list would include statements such as "Margaret's typewriter in Personnel takes X ribbons."

Ribbons for printing calculators and cash registers are nylon and are available in black, purple, or a combination of black and red.

Typewriters use correctable ribbons with lift-off tape or tabs, and nylon or poly ribbons, depending on the model type and manufacturer's recommendations.

Printers use nylon ribbons. The width, length, caliper, and thread count vary with each specific ribbon. For the highest performance of printer ribbons, check the owner's manual for complete instructions on installation. Most ribbons have safety clips installed on the ribbon for protection during shipping and storage. It is important to remove all clips before installation or the ribbon might not advance, causing light printing, jamming, or breakage of the ribbon.

CONTROLLING OFFICE SUPPLIES

Every organization needs a method for controlling office supplies. Keep a minimum number of supply items on the shelves to avoid stockpiling. The following are some steps to take in establishing a system for controlling office supplies:

1. Frequently used, inexpensive items such as paper clips or staples can be located in an unlocked closet or drawer that is readily accessible to all office workers.
2. For each order, a designated employee should issue either an electronic or written purchase order to the supplier with an authorized signature and a purchase order number. Request that the supplier place the purchase order number on the invoice and bill of lading. The buyer should send a copy of each purchase order to the accounts payable department.
3. Determine typical usage of supplies. Estimate monthly and annual usage.
4. Establish a budget. Break the budget down into product categories. The budget will help in future planning.

HINT: *Breaking down the budget into items is also a way to compare costs. Toner cartridges, for example, can be itemized and yields determined for different printers.*

HINT: *If you know how much is spent on individual items each year, you can negotiate prices with dealers.*

Store office supplies with in-house labeling of categories. Here are some suggested categories: *Paper products*—writing paper, forms, file folders, envelopes, labels, computer and copy paper. *Writing instruments*—wood pencils, mechanical pencils, all types of pens, and markers/highlighters. *Computer/copy supplies*—disks and cartridges. *Ribbons*—ribbons for all office machines. *Miscellaneous supplies*—rubber bands, staples, paper clips, and other small items.

HINT: *Label products in stock according to the machines they fit.*

Keep the supply storage area in order. Arrange supplies so the most often used ones are easily accessible—and do not pile supplies so high that stacks of items have to be moved to obtain what is needed. Small items should be stored in labeled boxes.

Be sure that supplies are labeled with expiration dates when applicable.

HINT: *A supply area can look messy if items do not have designated storage locations.*

HINT: *Check the supply area at least once a week.*

When a supply is low, call or fax the order or order on-line. Place new supplies behind or beneath the other supplies.

Have the current office supply catalogs available for employees.

Check each incoming order to be certain the items received are the ones that were ordered. Do not pay for supplies and services not ordered. Do not return unordered merchandise. According to the Federal Trade Commission, you may treat unordered merchandise as a gift. By law, it is illegal for a seller to send bills or dunning notices for unordered merchandise or to ask that the merchandise be returned. If the seller sends items that differ from the original order in band name, type, quantity, size, or quality without your prior express agreement, the substitutions may be treated as unordered merchandise.

Do not pay a supplier unless the invoice has the correct purchase order number. The information on the invoice, the purchase order, and the bill of lading should match.

Order by phone, on-line, or fax for faster service.

SPECIAL STORAGE REQUIREMENTS AND SHELF LIFE

Paper and copier and laser printer cartridges all have special storage requirements.

Paper

Paper is susceptible to atmospheric conditions. Paper has a shelf life of over a year.

Forms and printed products have shelf lives of six months to a year. These storage suggestions for paper will help increase its shelf life:

- Immediately replace the lid after removing reams from a packing box.
- Keep paper sealed in its original, moisture-resistant wrapper.
- Never store more than one partially unwrapped ream on an open shelf, since fading can occur. Color stock fades more easily than white.
- Avoid cold, damp rooms, areas of high heat or humidity, and exposure to direct sunlight.
- If the paper storage area is not climate-controlled, keep a relatively low inventory for infrequently used sizes and colors. Extreme changes in the environment can cause paper to warp.
- Keep stocks of paper on pallets, off the floor. Stack no more than six cartons high, with each carton upright. Improper stacking of cartons or dropping a carton on its corner can damage paper.
- Move paper from storage to user areas at least 48 hours before it is needed to allow the paper to adjust to the temperature in the operating environment. The greater the temperature difference, the longer this adjustment period will be. Some paper manufacturers recommend stabilizing unopened cartons one hour for every degree of difference between the storage and user areas.
- Use older paper first.
- Do not place other objects on top of paper, whether it is packaged or unpackaged.

Laser Printer and Copier Toner Cartridges

A laser printer or copier toner cartridge should be stored in the aluminum bag in which it was originally packaged. Keep cartridges in a dark cabinet away from direct sunlight and rest them in a horizontal position, not vertically. Room temperature should be between 32 and 95 degrees Fahrenheit, and cartridges should be protected from high humidity.

CHAPTER 10

THE

OFFICE

WORK

SPACE

A basic element of every office is the workstation. The workstation is a place where the worker can think and perform an assigned set of tasks. For the office professional the workstation is the action center for organizing and processing information, telephone calls, electronic messages, and files; greeting visitors; maintaining reference materials; and performing other executive-support activities.

TYPES OF OFFICE WORKSTATIONS

The development of open-space planning has changed the look of offices. Open offices use panels to create a maze of workstations consisting of systems furniture. Systems furniture includes partitions, desks or work surfaces, storage units, and accessories. Although offices with fixed walls and conventional furniture are still prevalent, the open office concept provides the greatest amount of flexibility for meeting changing business and financial trends.

A workstation is designed according to the needs of each individual office professional. There are workstations for receptionists, secretaries, administrative managers, supervisors, middle managers, and executives. Each workstation is designed to provide the necessary privacy, work surface, and storage for the task(s) being performed.

The workstation must support a variety of daily tasks. One's physical and psychological well-being are upset by bad design or poorly adjusted office components, such as the desk, chair, and computer. "Syntonic" is a term that means receptive to and in harmony with the environment. Syntonic design integrates or "harmonizes" all aspects of planning to create an office support system that maximizes productivity while meeting human needs. The integration of people, tools, and the workplace is necessary for efficient offices.

COMPONENTS OF A WORKSTATION

The workstation is composed of office seating, work surfaces, storage containers or files, and privacy panels.

Seating

The most important component is the office chair. (See Figures 10-1 and 10-2a.) It has to support office profes-

CHAIR EVALUATION CHECKLIST

	YES	NO
A. HEIGHT		
1. Is the range of height adjustment adequate?	___	___
2. Can the chair height be easily adjusted?	___	___
3. Can the adjustment be made from the seated position?	___	___
4. Are adequate footrests available?	___	___
B. BACKREST		
5. Does the chair have a high backrest?	___	___
6. Does the backrest interfere with arm movements?	___	___
7. Is the lumbar support adequate?	___	___
8. Is the tension of the backrest adjustable?	___	___
9. Does the backrest tilt back?	___	___
10. Docs the backrest lock in position?	___	___
11. Can the backrest be adjusted up and down?	___	___
12. Can the backrest be adjusted forward?	___	___
C. ARMRESTS		
13. Does the chair have armrests?	___	___
14. Are the armrests appropriate for the job?	___	___
15. Are armrests optional?	___	___
16. Do armrests interfere with movement?	___	___
D. SEATPAN		
17. Does the seatpan have a rounded front edge?	___	___
18. Does the seatpan tilt?	___	___
19. Is seatpan tension adjustable?	___	___
20. Does seatpan lock in position?	___	___
E. SAFETY		
21. Is the chair stable?	___	___
22. Does the chair have a 5-leg base?	___	___
23. Are casters matched to the floor?	___	___
24. Can casters be changed?	___	___
25. Are all adjustments safe against self or unintentional release?	___	___
26. Does chair meet all applicable fire codes?	___	___
F. COMFORT		
27. Is the chair adequately padded?	___	___
28. Are materials appropriate?	___	___
29. Is the chair comfortable?	___	___
G. OTHER		
30. Can the chair be easily maintained?	___	___
31. Can maintenance be performed in the field?	___	___

Figure 10-1 chair evaluation checklist.

Figure 10-2a: X99™, manufactured by Haworth, Inc., offers many ergonomic adjustments for the user: pneumatic seat-height adjustment, tuck-away tilt tension, three-point tilt, free-loading forward tilt, and back stop. Figure 10-2b PREMISE® and if™ components combine panel-hung and freestanding work surfaces, mobile storage, tables, and collaboration tools to create a collaborative environment.

sionals in the performance of most office tasks. Lower back pain, the number-one office health problem, is often caused by improper seating. Some researchers believe that there is no one correct seating position. The user, therefore, should be able to adjust the chair to his or her specific anatomical or physical characteristics and favorite seating positions.

Work Surfaces

Much office work is done on the most important work surface, the desktop. (See Figure 10-3.) Other work surfaces may hold equipment, paper-flow sorting trays, telephones, and writing and reference materials.

Because there are various sizes and shapes of paper and office equipment, the surfaces must have adequate depth. A surface must be a minimum of 24 inches deep, for example, to hold binders with printouts, and 30 inches deep to accommodate a personal computer. Sometimes it is possible to adjust the height of the work surface to better accommodate an individual's needs.

Storage

Adequate storage space improves the organization of an office's workspace. Recorded information is stored on many media, such as paper, magnetic disks, microfilm,

GUIDELINES FOR WORK SURFACES

	YES	NO	N/A
1. Is there adequate space to perform all tasks?	___	___	___
2. Is there adequate space for all equipment?	___	___	___
3. Can any workspace be shared?	___	___	___
4. Can the workspace be adapted for either right or left hand use?	___	___	___
5. Are all items of equipment and job aids which must frequently be used within the normal arm reach of the worker?	___	___	___
6. Does the arrangement of the work area allow access to all equipment and job aids without excessive twisting?	___	___	___
7. Are equipment, documents, writing surfaces, telephones, and so on, arranged in the most efficient way?	___	___	___
8. Is adequate space provided for storage of copies, handbooks, documents, and personal belongings?	___	___	___
9. Are different heights necessary for different tasks?	___	___	___
10. Are the heights of all working surfaces correct?	___	___	___
11. Are working surfaces adjustable in height?	___	___	___
12. Are surfaces user-adjustable?	___	___	___
13. Can working surfaces be tilted?	___	___	___
14. Is the surface thin enough to allow adequate leg space and a correct working height?	___	___	___
15. Is there adequate legroom so the worker can adopt different postures?	___	___	___
16. Is the area under the work surface free of obstructions that might interfere with movements between different tasks?	___	___	___

Figure 10-3 Guidelines for work surfaces.

microfiche, CD-ROM, and optical disks. Each medium requires its own unique type of storage container. Fixed or mobile pedestals, binder bins, overhead flipper door cabinets, and lateral or vertical file cabinets help in organizing and storing information media, reference manuals, and supplies. (See the sections on Managing Paper-Based Records and Computer Software in Chapter 12 for more information.)

Privacy Panels

Privacy panels are movable walls that can be as short as 40 inches high or as tall as the ceiling. Open-plan offices use movable panels that are lower than ceiling height to provide privacy. Since all desks, partitions, and other equipment can be moved easily, the workstations can be rearranged in a matter of hours, instead of days. (See Figure 10-2b.)

WORKSTATION ADJUSTMENT

Ergonomics is the study of the relationship between the worker and the work environment. (The term comes from the Greek words *ergon* meaning "work" and *nomos* meaning "law.") It takes into account the individual characteristics of the worker. Ideally, every office workstation should meet the physical, psychological, and work requirements of the individual.

Ergonomic principles are partly based on the study of anthropometrics. This involves the measurement of size and proportions of the human body. The height of a table and the width of a seat pan, for example, should fit the bodily dimensions of workers.

Ergonomic principles are also based on biomechanics, the study of the human body's structure and functions. Activities such as sitting for long periods, bending, tilting, and reaching can strain various body parts. Working positions should try to minimize fatigue and wear and tear on the body caused by such activities.

To conform to these principles, five focal points of adjustment are essential in any workstation: seating, work surface, video display terminal, lighting, and storage.

Seating

Office professionals spend most of their time seated so comfort and efficiency are crucial in selecting the right chair. The proper chair fits the individual and the job. Learn to adjust your chair to accommodate multiple positions within a comfortable range rather than sitting in a single "correct" position. The following guidelines will help:

Height adjustment: Your feet should rest comfortably on the floor or, if necessary, should be supported by a footrest. Most office chairs can be raised or lowered so the user's feet touch the floor. Height adjustment is also important so the sitter's arms maintain a correct angle for keyboard use. A starting point for determining correct chair height is to measure the distance from the floor to the crease behind the knee. The height of the chair should distribute body weight as evenly as possible, and optimum chair heights are 14 to 17.5 inches for women and 15.5 to 19.2 inches for men. Very short people can use a slanted footrest to support their feet.

Lumbar support: The curve of the backrest should support the natural curve of your back to minimize lower back pain. The normal alignment and the natural curve of the lower spine should be supported in a manner similar to the standing position.

HINT: *A thin pillow will provide support if the back of the chair is flat.*

Armrests: A chair with arms or armrests takes pressure off the wrist when keyboarding and also supports leaning positions. The armrests should adjust so you can match your elbow height when your elbows are relaxed at your sides. If you find your armrests forcing your shoulders into a hunched position, consider removing the arms from your chair.

Seat pan: Prolonged sitting cuts off blood circulation to the legs. A sloping, rounded front edge on the seat takes strain off the thighs. Such a seat, called a waterfall seat, improves circulation. There should be at least 2–3 inches between the back of your leg and the seat of the chair. If not, the seat pan can create pressure points and discomfort in the back of the thigh. Shorten or lengthen the seat pan if possible.

Forward tilt: This feature locks the seat in a forward tilting position, which is helpful if you are keyboarding for long periods of time.

Back tilt: This feature helps one recline, which is at times comfortable and necessary. Several manufacturers' chairs allow the user to lock two or three angles. Adjust the chair into an upright position for keyboard activities. You can adjust the mechanism to allow rocking or reclining when not keyboarding.

Base and casters: A five-star base prevents tipping. Dual-wheel or single-wheel casters allow easy movement over both hard and soft surfaces.

Work Surfaces

Most work surfaces are 26 to 29 inches high. Since people vary in height, this is not always satisfactory. Most office professionals prefer a work surface located slightly above elbow height. This allows the arms to rest on the surface but does not require the office professional to lean forward too far.

Video Display Terminals

Office workers often spend many hours a day looking at video display terminals (VDTs). Prolonged work at the terminal can lead to repetitive stress injuries (RSIs). Pain in the lower back, carpal tunnel syndrome, forearm pain, and upper shoulder strain are examples of RSIs. Other keyboarding-related complaints include headaches, eyestrain, and worry about electromagnetic frequency (EMF) from the VDT screen.

Here are guidelines for working at a VDT:

- The VDT should rest on the work surface and preferably not on top of the CPU (i.e., the disk drive). Most workers prefer the centerline of the screen to be slightly below eye level.
- Provide for keyboard height adjustability so the wrists can be kept in a neutral position and the feet are flat on the floor.
- Ensure that the lower arm and extended hand form a straight line parallel to the keytops. For maximum safety and comfort, specify a keyboard tray that slopes

downward in a negative slope away from the operator to offset the positive slope of most computer keyboards. Research finds the tilt-down keyboard tray to be the best in providing for optimum comfort and low RSI risk.

- Specify a palm rest, not a wrist rest. Consider products that are integrated into the keyboard tray. This allows for micro breaks and support of the forearm.

- To minimize neck strain and headaches, use a copy holder to provide for the proper alignment of copy with the VDT.

- Use a mouse platform that allows the mouse to be positioned within the elbow zone to eliminate shoulder abduction.

HINT: *Adjustable VDT tables with two surfaces ensure good posture by allowing the keyboard and screen to be adjusted independently to the appropriate levels.*

HINT: *CRTs generate light, certain inaudible sound waves, radio-frequency radiation, X-rays, electromagnetic fields, and static electricity. Few of these emissions are reported to be harmful in the levels emitted. The general guideline is to sit at least 36 inches away from the backs and sides of the VDT monitor and up to 30 inches or an arm's length, away from the front of the monitor. Also, purchase a low-radiation VDT screen.*

HINT: *Hundreds of products identified by the manufacturer as ergonomic are now on the market. Be selective by identifying the problem you wish to solve and by asking for research to support the manufacturer's ergonomic claims.*

Lighting

Glare and brightness in a work environment, especially where VDTs are used, can cause eye fatigue and hamper employee productivity. (See Figure 10-4.) Appropriate lighting can reduce if not eliminate most problems. Workers need to have as much control as possible over their individual workstation lighting to assure visual and physical comfort. Ways to adjust the lighting within a workstation include (1) the ability to dim overhead lighting and (2) the addition of a desk lamp for lighting specific tasks.

Indirect, ceiling-mounted or ambient light in combination with adjustable, task-specific lighting works best to help eliminate computer lighting problems. Light levels should serve for all tasks within the office and conference rooms, including video conferencing.

HINT: *The National Lighting Bureau is a good source of information on lighting issues and working with lighting consultants. This bureau has published a number of guides related to VDTs and lighting systems. The NLB is located at 2101 L Street NW, Suite 300, Washington, DC 20037.*

CHECKLIST FOR OFFICE LIGHTING

	YES	NO	N/A
1. Is the level of illumination proper for hard copy tasks?	___	___	___
2. Is the level of illumination proper for VDT use?	___	___	___
3. Are task lights provided as necessary?	___	___	___
4. Are lights flicker-free?	___	___	___
5. Are lights clean and well maintained?	___	___	___
6. Is the worker's field of view free of sources of glare?	___	___	___
7. Is the worker's field of view free of reflections from display screens, keyboards, desk, papers, and so on?	___	___	___
8. Are windows covered with blinds, drapes, or other means of controlling light?	___	___	___
9. Are lights covered with glare shields?	___	___	___
10. Are panels used to block glare and reflections?	___	___	___
11. Are workstations positioned to avoid glare and reflections?	___	___	___
12. Are VDTs fitted with filters to reduce reflections?	___	___	___
13. Are VDTs equipped with brightness and contrast controls?	___	___	___
14. Can VDTs or tables be tilted to reduce reflections?	___	___	___
15. Are contrasts within the visual field within recommended limits?	___	___	___
16. Are reflectances of walls, floors, and ceilings within recommended limits?	___	___	___

Figure 10-4 Checklist for office lighting.

ORGANIZING THE WORKSTATION ENVIRONMENT

An office space plan shows the organization and placement of workstation components, including work surfaces, filing and storage cabinets, and chairs. Office space plans should meet the psychological and physiological needs of workers. As the users of workstations, office professionals should have some say in such planning.

A worker's state of mind can directly influence his or her efficiency. For example, when a worker perceives his or her office space to be unsatisfactory, poor morale is the result. Personal preferences regarding placement of the telephone, personal computer, and other office tools are also essential.

HINT: *Most people do not like to sit with their backs to the hallway nor to have more than one entrance into a workstation.*

Environmental disturbances from lighting, noise, and climate (including heat levels and air quality) can cause physiological stress. (See Figure 10-5 for a workstation comfort checklist.)

Planning Office Space

Space planning for administrative staff workstations in large companies is usually done by interior designers or facility managers. However, administrative staffs should have some input into the design of their workstations, to help arrange the work space

---

A "yes" response to any of the following questions indicates the need to make an adjustment in your workstation environment and may require an accessory:

1. Do you use a visual display terminal (VDT) more than 4 hours per day?
2. Are you required to maintain stressful body positions for extended periods of time (examples might include using a mouse or a digitizing tablet)?
3. Are the height, location, and orientation of the workstation furniture, computer, and other features fixed and not able to be adjusted to accommodate your body size and posture preferences?
4. Do you constantly lean forward rather than sitting back in your chair when keying at the computer?
5. Do you have itching or dry eyes?
6. Does the room lighting cause glare or make the VDT screen hard to read?
7. Is the room temperature uncomfortable—too hot, too cold, too stuffy? Do you experience fatigue, especially by two or three o'clock in the afternoon?
8. Does the office environment seem excessively loud and noisy from equipment sounds or workers talking?
9. Are you continually getting out of your chair to get reference manuals or other source materials when working at the VDT?
10. Do you experience extreme bending and reaching for files, manuals, and other information in your workstation while working at the VDT?

Figure 10-5 Workstation comfort checklist.

properly to match the tasks. In small offices, administrative assistants may set up their own workstations.

To organize a workstation for maximum task support, begin with a task analysis. This is a process that profiles what people do and maps this onto a physical setting to see how people do it. Demands associated with different activities will fall into common categories. This information aids the planner in determining proper lighting, acoustics, and work-space requirements.

The next step in the design of a workstation space plan is to divide the workstation into work focus zones. These are the locations in the workstation where a specific type of work is done. Office tasks can be put in six basic categories: data entry; information acquisition; information transaction; analysis and problem solving; creative and imaginative thinking; and meeting and conferring. An office space plan should allow space for each type of work that will be done there.

The third step is to plan the arrangement of work resources, equipment, and materials within each zone. Resources should be positioned for ease of equipment operation, with materials easily reached and visual displays comfortably placed for ease of viewing.

Managing Cables

As advances in information technology continue, the changes in today's office equipment continue at a pace faster than most offices can handle. This sometimes requires the rearrangement of office interiors, including reorganization of wiring. Managing the cables is usually left up to the electricians and facilities design managers. It is important that electrical and LAN ports be provided at the work surface level to accommodate laptops, PDAs, and other equipment that may require frequent connecting and disconnecting from these ports.

LAN Management

Vital to a successful office is the ability to tie all company information together. In order to achieve that goal, a local area network (LAN) usually needs to be established. A LAN allows people in a department to share information with each other electronically as well as to share common resources such as printers and large hard disks.

LANs are comprised of cables—twisted-pair, coaxial, and fiber optics—connected to controller cards installed at each computer. Wireless LANs use radio frequencies or infrared light instead of cables.

WORKSTATION ACCESSORIES

There are many accessories that add to the efficiency of a workstation and that can personalize it. These range from paper management accessories to computer support accessories.

Paper Management Accessories

By aiding the storage and retrieval of paperwork, paper management accessories help to control paper usage within the workstation. Paper management accessories include desk racks with paper holders, as well as vertical and horizontal paper trays and organizers that mount onto wall panels or inside a cabinet. Forms, computer printouts, and reference material can easily be stored in these accessories. Some accessories can be transported to the next workstation. Other accessories include paper holders for computer printer paper and paper catchers for continuous form paper as it moves through the printer.

Computer Accessories

Computer accessories are intended to help users save space, protect data, and increase comfort. Accessories include antiglare filters or screens, monitor arms and swivel bases for adjusting monitors to user comfort, articulating drawers for keyboards, and workstation furniture designed specifically for computers.

HINT: *Glare can be reduced and contrast improved with a light background and dark text or graphics.*

Additional accessories include copy holders, disk files, switching systems, static mats, computer tool kits, footrests, surge protectors, and security and antitheft devices.

Personal Accessories

The way a workstation is decorated and maintained reflects its user's efficiency, professionalism, taste, and status. Policy on personal accessories varies from company to company and department to department.

Here are guidelines to follow when personalizing the workstation:

- Minimize clutter. A work surface that is bare except for the project being worked on and a few stylish accessories conveys an image of control and taste.
- Only those items being used should be on the primary work surface. Calculators, business card files, paper clip containers, extra pens and pencils should be put away when not in use.
- The "in" box should be well managed. An overflowing "in" box represents its owner's lack of efficiency, besides taking up valuable work space. A wall-mounted "in" box is more efficient but it, too, needs to be properly managed.
- Keep projects organized. Projects should be neatly labeled and filed out of the way, not kept in a heap on the corner of a work surface.
- When selecting art for the workstation, restraint and respect for the corporate culture are paramount.

- Fabric panel walls should be kept clear. Mounting things to the fabric panels will keep it from absorbing sound.
- Use fabric art on solid walls to improve acoustics.
- Accessories that are permanently on the work surface should be chosen for utility and style. An accessory should pass the following test: Does it give its owner pleasure to use it and look at it? Is it in good taste?

HINT: *Diplomas and certificates on the wall usually advertise insecurity and lack of taste, except for doctors and lawyers.*

Team Office Environments

Today's work environment is constantly changing, and it is having a profound effect on today's office professionals. Organizations often use teams to solve problems related to achieving competitive advantages that should be confidential including new products, new strategies, and new technologies. Conventional office space—where most of this collaboration is supposed to take place—does not meet the needs of the workers using it. Team members are often in cubicles at remote ends of the facility, or the nearest meeting space is three floors up, or there is one conference room per hundred employees.

Team spaces are helping to effectively provide support of collaborative work. There are three different types of team spaces:

- *Project rooms:* Large, hard-walled areas where the group works together for the duration of a project, with or without individual workstations elsewhere in the facility (good for teams that meet for a defined period and then disperse).
- *Caves and commons:* Small, individual workstations or offices surrounding a group area outfitted with meeting tables and equipment owned by the team. Best for ongoing, cross-functional work.
- *Bullpen:* Open-plan workstations with low barriers between workstations promoting face-to-face communication without moving to a team area. Good for fast-paced work tied to computers or telephones, like financial trading rooms or some types of telemarketing.

Team spaces are often outfitted with break-apart tables that can be moved or reconfigured easily by the team members, as well as chairs with casters. Sometimes a component of the individual workstations is on wheels, so it can combine with other mobile work surfaces to form the team's group table. Flip charts, whiteboards, tackboards, and so forth are used to share and display information and may also be on wheels. Sound-masking systems provide an inconspicuous whooshing sound to muffle conversations and aid in acoustical privacy. Casual communication areas are supported as quick collaboration areas. Pleasant lunch rooms and even outdoor break away spots are also provided as a change of work environment and a positive place for employees to work together. Some corporations include nap rooms, day-care facilities on site, and concierges to arrange for dry cleaning or entertainment reservations.

Telecommuting or Virtual Worker Spaces

Many companies allow their workers to telecommute. The office space requirements of telecommuters is similar to the needs of workers who travel frequently. To meet these needs, personnel who are in the office for just a few days or weeks at a time are often given mobile storage pedestals with file and drawer space. The lockable units can easily be transported about the office to open workstation areas or a quiet room. Enclaves or small private rooms with doors are also often incorporated into floor plans. These spaces are available for short blocks of time so virtual office employees may have a getaway for quiet work or study when in the office.

PART III

SPECIALIZED

OFFICE

PROCEDURES

Successful companies keep their employees informed and involve them in decisions that affect employee welfare. Publications such as policy and procedures manuals, job description manuals, and company newsletters can have a positive impact on employer-employee communication. Office professionals may become members of work groups that formulate and evaluate the publications. Since office professionals have good organizational and computer skills, they often assume major responsibilities for preparing these documents.

POLICY MANUALS

A **policy manual** incorporates general guidelines governing how a company will operate to accomplish its purposes. Policies may be covered in one manual, and procedures that describe how to do certain activities or tasks may be covered in a separate manual; or they may be combined in one manual. If they are combined, policy statements and procedures must be clearly separated and identified.

Although the board of directors makes the final decisions regarding company policies, top-level managers are responsible for seeing that the policies are written and carried out. They may write the policy statements themselves, hire technical writers, or assign the writing to someone else within the company.

Even a small company will find a policy manual helpful to communicate employee responsibilities and outline the firm's mission and goals. Middle management, supervisory, union, and employee input is always necessary and is especially important in the initial and evaluative stages of the process. To lessen the possibility of an employee initiating an unfair treatment action against the company, and to be sure the policies comply with state and federal laws, an attorney should always review policy statements and prepare any disclaimer notices the company includes in the manual.

Purpose

To function effectively, employees need a good overall understanding of what the organization hopes to accomplish. Policy manuals are given to employees to provide that information and to explain the guidelines under which they must function.

CHAPTER 11

OFFICE

MANUALS

AND

PUBLICATIONS

Since policy manuals are written documents, all employees will receive the same information. If managers apply the policies uniformly, employees should receive fair and equal consideration. In turn, a policy manual gives companies some protection from legal suits that may result from employee dissatisfaction.

Content

The amount of information in a policy manual varies with the type and size of the company and with the level of its employees. Exceptions to policies will sometimes occur, so do not try to incorporate every case into one general statement. The following are policy manual topics, divided into two categories, company information and general personnel policies:

COMPANY INFORMATION

- Historical summary
- Company goals/mission statement
- Philosophy and basic beliefs

HINT: *Include how the company got started and what it stands for today. Include a human interest note about the founders.*

- Board of director's policies—authority, organization, meeting notification, and conduct
- Conflict of interest—board members, management, employees
- Stockholders—voting rights, responsibilities
- Organization chart
- Departmental responsibilities
- Company organization/subsidiaries/branch offices—location, function
- Commitment to customer service
- Commitment to employees
- Public relations—handling confidential information, information clearance
- Product lines and services
- Building usage/building names
- Budget and finance—responsibility, financial reports, distribution of reports
- Company closings/takeovers/mergers
- Political activity
- Ethics/theft
- Commitment to a safe workplace

- Commitment to environmental concerns
- Involvement with local community
- Disaster recovery

GENERAL PERSONNEL POLICIES

- Affirmative action and equal opportunity position
- Recruitment standards/applications/reference checks
- Personnel files—content, maintenance, access

HINT: *Under the Americans with Disabilities Act (ADA) and the Family and Medical Leave Act, employers must place medical information in a separate file. Prepare explicit guidelines for accessing medical or personnel files.*

- Benefits, such as insurance, pension, and savings

HINT: *Be very clear which benefits apply to full-time employees, union members, and part-timers.*

HINT: *Avoid phrases that guarantee benefits. Make certain that the wording allows for benefit modifications.*

- Retirement/vesting/401(k) plans/profit sharing
- Vacation schedules/accrued vacation
- Company services, such as company store, merchandise reductions, education, child care, and elder care
- Performance appraisals/promotions/incentives/transfers
- Grievance procedures/probation/termination
- Leaves, such as emergency, illness, personal, jury duty, bereavement, maternity, paternity, family care, adoptions, military, and educational
- Hours of operation/overtime/comp time provisions/outside employment limitations
- Attendance and punctuality—expectations, disciplinary action
- Dress codes
- Holidays
- Payroll provisions, such as pay periods, and exempt or non-exempt status
- Part-time work/student employment/temporary help/outside business centers
- References—liabilities/format
- Work-related injuries/insurance/compensation limits
- Substance abuse—prohibited use, testing, disciplinary actions

- Illness in the workplace/life-threatening diseases/confidentiality of medical records/AIDS/HIV issues
- Sexual harassment—definition, disciplinary actions

HINT: *Do not use the phrase "termination or discipline for good cause." It is often misinterpreted.*

- Safety/building security
- Use of building for outside groups
- Office furniture and decor
- Copyright protection
- Internet/e-mail usage—ownership, privacy, inappropriate use, monitoring

HINT: *An Internet usage policy should include (1) the permissible uses, (2) the monitoring procedure and extent, (3) the discipline that occurs with unauthorized use.*

HINT: *Always ask employees to sign an agreement that acknowledges their consent to the monitoring of electronic messages.*

- Patents/inventions/trademark usage
- Purchasing—equipment requests, vendor selection, contracts
- Disaster plan
- Travel—approval, restrictions, ownership of frequent-flier miles
- Mail services/telecommunications/printing—availability, restrictions
- Records retention/destruction guidelines
- Working at home/mobile offices
- Use of off-site equipment—restrictions, authorization, purchase
- Conference attendance/speaking engagements/honorariums
- Civic responsibilities/jury duty/membership in local professional organizations
- Charity/office contributions/office celebrations

If a policy is new or controversial, such as extended leaves, employee Internet/e-mail use, or drug testing, a short factual statement justifying the policy is helpful. (An example of a policy appears in Figure 11-1.) In such cases, send a cover memorandum along with the policy to all employees explaining the rationale for the new or changed policy. To emphasize the importance of e-mail ethics and practices, companies may specifically wish to address e-mail policies in a separate manual.

All policy changes must have appropriate approval. Check all changes for content with a lawyer. Also check to determine whether a disclaimer notice protecting the com-

---

XYZ COMPANY

3000 SERIES PERSONNEL AND AFFIRMATIVE ACTION

A. Personnel

3920   Drug-Free Workplace

Congress signed the Drug-Free Workplace Act of 1988 into law on November 18, 1988. XYZ Company receives federal money and is, therefore, subject to the provisions of the Act. In an effort to comply with the Act and to continue to provide employees with a safe, drug-free environment at XYZ Company, the Board of Directors has adopted Board Policy 3920, Drug-Free Workplace.

> Employees are prohibited from engaging in the unlawful manufacture, distribution, possession, or use of a controlled substance in any building or on any property under the control and use of XYZ Company. (See Health and Safety Code 11007 for a definition of the term "controlled substance.")

> Any violation of this policy by an employee of XYZ Company may result in (1) requiring the employee to participate satisfactorily in an approved drug abuse assistance or drug rehabilitation program; or, (2) carrying out disciplinary action up to and including termination.

Reference: Health and Safety Code 11007

                        Drug-Free Workplace Act of 1988

Adopted: July 31, 20—

Figure 11-1 Policy in report form.

pany is necessary. Do not write or distribute a memorandum concerning a change in policy to employees before that policy change has been cleared by all the necessary parties. Always include an effective date on new or revised policy statements.

HINT: *Review* The E-Policy Handbook: Designing and Implementing Effective E-mail, Internet, and Software Policies, *published by AMACOM, to help you become more knowledgeable about writing policies.*

The tone of a policy reflects management's attitudes toward employees. If you have input into policy wording, avoid using phrases that sound autocratic or condescending. Use a positive approach when writing policies.

HINT: *Use: All full-time employees are entitled to ten days of sick leave per year. Do not use: No more than ten days apply toward sick leave per year.*

All policy changes are made in writing, and employees must receive adequate notice. Be certain to clarify that any changes made supersede the previous policy.

Format

The first policy manual produced by a company takes considerable time to develop and compile. (For a comprehensive discussion on formatting and designing manuals, see Chapter 18.) Specific guidelines for organizing the final copy of the policy manual follow:

- Check policy manuals from other companies for format possibilities.
- Store policy manuals in three-ring binder notebooks. Store a copy of the policy manual and any changes prepared electronically in an off-site location.
- Use policy manual notebooks with attractive cover designs that can be used for more than one year. Collect policy manuals when employees leave the firm.
- Begin each policy statement on a separate sheet of paper. A new policy statement should always begin on a right-hand page. Continuation pages may be printed on both sides or on one side only. Since pages in a policy manual may change because of insertions of new policies or increases or decreases in the number of pages in a revised policy, do not number policy manual pages consecutively. Instead, indicate the number of pages devoted to each policy:

3005 Equal Employment (page 2 of 2)

- Highlight disclaimers by placing them on a separate sheet of paper or in a boxed format at the beginning of a document. Use bold or larger typeface to separate the disclaimers from the rest of the text.
- State the name of each policy in a title line. If using a memorandum to inform employees of a new or revised policy, show the exact title of the policy and its number in the subject line of the memo.

3680 Memberships in Local Civic Organizations

SUBJECT: Board Policy 3680 Memberships in Local Civic Organizations

- Create a template for policy formats. Your company may use such headings as purpose, policy, definitions, provisions, and references.
- Organize the manual so policies involving similar topics are near each other. Cross-reference those items that pertain to more than one policy:

Leaves: Sickness
Leaves: Emergency
Leaves: Personal
Leaves: Jury (See also Civic Responsibilities)

- Use dividers to set apart major categories of policies within the same manual, such as Board of Directors, Management, and Personnel.
- Develop a numbering system that uses numbers and letters and allows for expansion.

1000 Series   BOARD OF DIRECTORS
                  A. Organization of the Board
                     1000 Authority
                     1005 Officers
                     1010 Meeting dates
                     1015 Agendas
                     1020 Meetings
                  B. Conflict of Interest
                  C. Compensation
2000 Series   MANAGEMENT
3000 Series   EMPLOYEES

- Indicate whether the policy statement is new or whether it is a replacement for a previous policy. Indicate the date the policy becomes effective at the bottom of each page.

Replacement for Policy 3020, dated 8/27/97
or
New Policy _____
Effective Date _____1/2/02_____

- Include codes, references, or regulation numbers that apply to the policy at the bottom of the last page of the statement. Omit lengthy references to the law within a policy statement.

Reference: Section 703, Title VII of the Civil Rights Act.

HINT: *Keep a master list of major policies. Include the names and numbers of the procedures that pertain to each policy. When the policy is changed, check the master list, and, if necessary, make the appropriate changes in the procedures that apply to the policies.*

- Prepare a detailed index of the policy manual. Keep the index current as new policies or changes are made. Distribute the updated index material with each new policy or policy change.

Evaluation

A company may involve personnel other than top management in the process of evaluating policy statements. Office professionals may be asked to review the policies on an individual basis, or they may be asked to review them as members of a committee. The following questions will assist office professionals in providing input into the evaluation process:

- Were suggestions and ideas solicited from employees? The more involved the employees are in the process, the more support they will provide when the time comes to implement the policies.

HINT: *To simplify this involvement process, provide employees with suggestion forms that include spaces for the policy number and title and for the suggested change(s). Names and departments are optional. Recommend a separate suggestion form for each policy. Provide a convenient central location or e-mail address for employees to return their suggestions.*

- Is the manual attractive? The way material is packaged makes a statement about the importance of the policies as perceived by top management.
- Are the policies clearly stated? Is the language direct and simple?
- Is the reason for a new or controversial policy explained?
- Is it easy to locate the policy by topic? Is the manual organized logically?
- Are there any omissions in the policy statements? Are there statements that could be misinterpreted?

HINT: *Do not include a phrase indicating that "employees agree to abide by" anything in the manual. This could be interpreted as creating a contract.*

- Is the manual concise? Excessive reading material can be intimidating, and employees may therefore ignore it.
- Has the manual been checked for proper grammar, punctuation, word usage, and capitalization?
- Are the policies up to date? Is there a plan for a periodic revision and review of the policies?

HINT: *When employees make suggestions about policy statements, file them in an appropriate subject folder and use them for the next revision or review. Maintain a file for each subject covered in the policy manual.*

- Is a policy manual distribution list maintained?

HINT: *If your department is in charge of distributing manuals or policy statements, assign that responsibility to one person or do it yourself. Prepare a list of employees to whom the manuals must be distributed and have these employees sign their names as they receive their copies. Regardless of the form—paper or electronic—obtaining an employee's signature indicating that the policy or policy change has been received is necessary. These forms become a part of an employee's personnel file and may be important in a legal situation.*

Policy Manual Software and Technology

Software based on expert system technology is available to assist policy writers in identifying policies as well as in writing them. (See Chapter 3 for expert system information.) The user selects the policy topics and then responds to preprogrammed questions about these policy selections. Based on the answers given and the software's stored information, a policy for a specific company can be written. The user can edit, accept, or change this policy by using the word processing feature of the program or by exporting the material to another word processing program.

On-line in-depth background material that includes explanations, pros and cons, and legal requirements for most of the policies eliminates much of the basic research that is usually necessary in writing policy manuals. The software creates a table of contents and formats the policies. It provides periodic updates to comply with state and federal laws. The software may be written for a certain state, so caution is necessary when working with legal information.

When manuals are created on-line, stored electronically, and then sent via a network, the costs of printing, distributing, and storing manuals decreases. With this technology, office personnel retrieve and print sections of the manual as needed. Groupware programs allow managers and employees to exchange ideas about policy issues and give policy writers the opportunity to collaborate and share opinions.

HINT: *State clearly that the policy manual can be modified only by certain people in the company. If the manual is redrafted or if any policy is changed, provide new copies with new acceptance forms to all employees.*

PROCEDURES MANUALS

Written procedures are necessary for policies to be carried out effectively. A **procedures manual** provides employees with instructions for implementing policies and for performing specific activities or tasks. An **employee handbook** is another term to describe this type of manual. Supervisors or the people usually doing the tasks write the procedures.

Purpose

Well-written procedures manuals are simple and easy to understand. Since all employees receive the procedures manual, everyone has the same instructions, and therefore policies should be followed and tasks should be performed similarly in all departments.

Specific written procedures save time since new employees need not ask coworkers or supervisors for assistance if they can refer to their procedures manual. Experienced employees use procedures manuals to remind them how to do tasks or activities that they perform infrequently or as a reference when training others. Being consistent with documentation details and avoiding procedural mixups will leave favorable impressions on clients and customers. Procedure manuals like policy manuals may be in paper or electronic form.

Content

The content depends on the policies established by the board and the type of procedures manual being written. One type of procedures manual may deal only with a specialized topic area, such as a company correspondence manual. Another may involve procedures for one department area, such as the accounting department or the mailroom. Yet another may include general information and procedures that apply to everyone in the organization. Some sample topics for the latter type of manual include the following:

INTRODUCTORY INFORMATION

- Organization chart
- Responsibilities of departments/divisions
- Floor plans/office numbering systems/maps
- Names and telephone numbers or extensions of top management and department heads and their principal office professionals.
- Hours of operation
- Glossary of frequently used words, trademarks, and accepted abbreviations

PERSONNEL INFORMATION

- Time cards/paychecks/payroll tax information/payroll data changes
- Vacation requests/holidays
- Leaves—procedures, forms, notification
- Jury duty
- Resignations—timelines, forms, notification

- Tardiness/absenteeism—notification
- Insurance—coverage, forms, claims
- Company library use/recreational facilities
- Education—tuition reimbursement, on-site training
- Physical examinations/substance abuse testing
- Child care/elder care—applications, costs
- Performance evaluations—probation, procedures, timeliness, forms
- Grievances—appeals, procedures, timeliness, forms
- Retirement—benefits, pension fund disbursements, forms, contributions
- Breaks/lunch—cafeteria privileges, hours, infractions
- Parking/keys/security/passwords/company visitors
- Injuries—reporting procedures, forms
- Relocation—benefits, family provisions
- Work away from office—responsibility, evaluation
- E-mail—ownership, personal use, responsibility
- Safety—access to building, identification, attack/storm procedures

TASK-RELATED INFORMATION

- Supplies purchase and control—authorization, forms
- Equipment—selection, purchase, repair, operation
- Fax/electronic mail—restrictions, user directions
- Software—backup, selection, copyrights
- Document creation, including e-mail
- Computer assistance—on and off premises
- Reprographics—forms, services, approval, copyrighted materials
- Travel—approval, reports, reimbursement, forms
- Records disposal/transfer
- Mail services
- Telephone/voice mail—coverage, services, protocol
- Meetings—notice, room reservations, catering requests, forms
- Files—access, security, control, coding
- Company vehicles—responsibility, reservations, forms
- Recordkeeping—banking, billing, receipts, payments
- Forms/letters used company-wide

Writing Procedures

When the procedures apply to the entire organization, managers and supervisors usually write the procedures for their particular areas of responsibility. When the procedures are task related, office managers, supervisors, or their designees write the procedures. When the procedures concern office tasks, the designees are often office professionals. They perform the tasks and have the most knowledge about the steps involved.

Writing clear procedures requires logical thinking and attention to detail. The following suggestions will assist in writing procedures.

- Clarify the reasons a procedure is necessary by answering these questions before beginning to write:
    - ▲ Who will perform the task?
    - ▲ What is the purpose of this procedure? Why is it done *this* way?
    - ▲ What equipment and supplies are required?
    - ▲ With what work area or areas is this task associated? Who is involved in the activity?
    - ▲ What is the first step? The next?
- Examine the current company procedures manual. Prepare a list of changes or recommendations made since the last revision. If preparing a manual for the first time, review other company manuals to determine how these organizations write or format procedures.
- Request assistance from coworkers. For example, if you are writing a procedure for handling petty cash, ask the person who performs the task to list the steps in consecutive order.

HINT: *Before describing how to do a task, watch it being done. If necessary, use a tape recorder to record notes while the person is working.*

- Include only the information needed to complete the tasks. Excessive explanatory material slows a worker's progress in completing a task. Note, however, that although a subtask may seem obvious to someone who does it regularly, a new worker will not necessarily know that each step is necessary.
- Select a title for the procedure carefully. The most effective titles are brief but clear. For example, "Educational Benefits Process" is not a clear title; a more definitive title is "Educational Tuition Reimbursement—Applications."
- Divide the task into its logical parts. For example, a procedure might be necessary to clarify changes in reprographic services. In this case, a logical breakdown is to write instructions for using the convenience copier, the centralized printing center, or off-premise commercial services. Use subheadings and list the procedures by service area.

- Select a numbering system and use it consistently throughout the procedures manual. One example of a numbering system for a section of a procedures manual follows:

> 36. **Travel**
>   F. . . .
>   G. **Company Automobiles**
>   1. **Approvals and authorizations for use**
>   2. **Timelines**
>   3. **Reservation procedures**
>   4. **Accident reporting**
>   5. **Automobile care and maintenance**
>   6. **Forms (attached)**
>   H. . . .

This example identifies "Travel" as a section heading. Within that section, one subheading is "Company Automobiles." Under that subheading are suggested paragraph headings involving procedures for requesting the use of a company automobile.

- Identify who is to do the task. Divide the procedure into two parts: *Who performs the activity?* and *What action is required?* Another format identifies who is to perform the task and then lists responsibilities below.
- Use short, imperative sentences rather than lengthy narrative ones.

HINT: *Use: Obtain Form No. 942, Educational Benefits Approval, from the assistant personnel director in the Human Resources office. Do not use: Educational leave is available to employees and may be applied for by obtaining Form No. 942, Educational Benefits Approval, from the assistant personnel director in the Human Resources office.*

- Use a job title, as in the above example, rather than the name of the individual, since an individual may change his or her position.
- Indicate the meaning of an abbreviation the first time it is used, such as Purchase Requisition (PR). Place the abbreviation in parentheses. The abbreviated form is then acceptable in the remaining steps of the procedure. Define all the technical terms used in a procedure.
- Present only one step at a time. Number each step in chronological order as it should occur.
- Do not begin an instruction on one page and continue it on the next page. Complete the entire instruction on one page.
- Use graphs, flow charts, and equipment diagrams when applicable. Scanned graphics reproduce well in electronic copy.

- Provide samples of the forms required to do a task.
- Identify *very* clearly any warnings for dangerous jobs or precautions about possible problems. Place the warnings at the beginning of the instructions and repeat them if they are part of one of the procedural steps. In order to draw attention to the warning, highlight it, place it in bold type, or capitalize it.

HINT: *If language appears to be a barrier to understanding any activity, write the entire procedure in the languages needed.*

- Have an employee who is unfamiliar with the task try to do it by reading the procedure. Rewrite and clarify if necessary.
- Summarize the steps at the end of each procedure. Since experienced workers may forget how to do a step, a summary can be helpful so as to avoid starting at the beginning and reading each step to locate the problem.
- Indicate the status of the procedure—new or revised. (See information on format under Policy Manuals section.) Include an effective date.
- Refer the user to additional manuals, such as special forms manuals or correspondence manuals, to complete a task. Include cross references when needed to clarify the procedures.
- Identify the policy or government regulation that pertains to the procedure. When the policy or law changes, procedures are likely to change also. More than one procedure may be affected. The policy or regulation identification on *all* the affected procedures makes it less likely that a procedure will be missed in the revision process. The following example of a reference line shows a regulation code number and also a company policy number:

Reference: California Education Code 72292, Governing Board Policy 3110

- Proofread procedures for punctuation, capitalization, grammatical accuracy, and spelling. Edit content and avoid wordiness. Conciseness saves disk space and production costs.

HINT: *Avoid sexist language. Use "his or her" or the plural form "their." Strive to be neutral.*

- Update the procedures regularly based on workers' and managers' suggestions. Maintain a file of these suggestions and send them to the appropriate managers for discussion or approval.

HINT: *A procedures manual must be current to remain effective; therefore, use your organizational skills and volunteer to monitor the procedures manual process as one of your projects.*

XYZ COMPANY

Reference:	Board Policy 3920
	Drug-Free Workplace
Effective Date:	April 20, 20—
Previous Revision:	NA
Procedure:	Drug Abuse Violations
Distribution:	Department Managers

DRUG ABUSE VIOLATIONS (page 1 of 2 pages)

PURPOSE

XYZ Company is committed to providing a drug-free workplace for its employees. To ensure this commitment, department managers need to be aware of employees exhibiting behaviors that may be drug-related and follow these procedures.

DEPARTMENT MANAGERS

1. Contact the Director of Human Resources immediately if an employee is suspected of drug dependency. Document your concerns and outline a plan of action.

2. Confront the employee displaying behaviors of being under the influence of drugs. (See Attachment A for a list of behavioral clues.) Determine whether the employee is at risk to self or other employees.

3. Release an employee who is at risk or who is unable to complete the remainder of his or her assigned activities for the remainder of the day or shift. Arrange for transportation to the employee's home.
   a. Ask the employee to contact a friend or family member to drive.
   b. Drive the employee home yourself.
   c. Request taxi service to take the employee home. Complete a taxi voucher form and submit it to Accounting.

Figure 11-2 Procedure in report format.

Format

The report is the most common format used to announce a revision in a procedure or a new procedure.

A report is usually divided into two sections—the heading (which includes background information) and the instructions. A sample of a portion of a procedure written in report form appears in Figure 11-2. An accompanying memo or e-mail message reminds employees to remove the old procedure and add the new one in its place or to insert the new procedure.

The following suggestions apply to the report design and maintenance. (For a comprehensive discussion on formatting and designing reports, see Chapter 18.)

- Use a looseleaf binder for procedures. Use 8½-by-11-inch paper. Looseleaf binders offer the greatest flexibility since new pages can be inserted easily. These binders are easy to use, since they open flat and are easy to store upright on a desk.
- Consider laminating the materials or placing them in plastic sheet holders if the procedures are used regularly in areas where dust and dirt accumulate.
- Place procedures on-line so employees can access them via their computers.

HINT: *Create subdirectories for company-wide procedures as well as division/department/unit procedures. The latter subdirectory also includes forms. Establish a separate subdirectory for company-wide forms.*

- Use a font size that is large enough to be read easily; for example, 10 point or larger. In some areas where machines are used, the procedures may be posted at a distance and therefore require large type. (See Chapter 19 for more information.)
- Position the visual aids so they are close to the related text. Label the visual aids consistently throughout the document; for example, "Figure 7: Completed Expense Report." A visual aid is effective only if it adds to the written material and if each part is clearly labeled. If the part is not referred to in the text, do not label it in the diagram.

HINT: *If a diagram is reduced in the duplication process, be sure it remains readable.*

- Use a list format. Indent the steps from any narrative that precedes them. The visual effect emphasizes organization and helps the reader follow instructions easily.
- Identify the summary steps by indenting the abbreviated steps or by placing a box around the summary.
- Prepare a detailed table of contents and an index for your notebook or computer file when organizing the procedures.
- Identify pages as follows: "Page 2 of 4 pages."
- Display any forms as originals or in reduced formats and place the instructions for completing the forms on separate pages. Place the forms on the left and the instructions on the right to facilitate their use.

JOB DESCRIPTION MANUALS

A **job description manual** is a compilation of specific jobs within a company that describes the jobs and lists duties and requirements. In large companies, the Human Resources Department is usually responsible for preparing and maintaining the manual. In all companies, input is necessary from those who perform the jobs and from their supervisors. Job descriptions must be in compliance with state and federal laws.

Purpose

Job descriptions provide management with information that is helpful in hiring, placing, and promoting personnel or useful in restructuring or eliminating positions. Supervisors use job descriptions when they evaluate employees' work. Ideally, supervisors should compare actual work performance to the specifications listed in the job description. In large companies, Human Resources personnel do the initial screening of applicants and rely heavily on job descriptions. The screening process becomes easier if job descriptions are clear and identify specific requirements for specific areas. Companies are very aware of discrimination charges and other legal consequences that can result from hiring or termination decisions. Well-written job descriptions communicated to employees can assist in the defense of these decisions.

Content

Job descriptions from other companies may be good models for determining format and content for your manual. Other content information sources include interviews with workers and supervisors, observations by Human Resources personnel, formal job analyses by outside consultants, or job description software. The best information sources are the people who do the jobs.

Two ways to facilitate the collection of information from employees are (1) questionnaires and (2) task diaries completed during a specified period of time. The advantage of the questionnaire is the inclusion of the same questions for all employees doing the same tasks, which makes data categorization and interpretation easier.

HINT: *As you perform new tasks or assume responsibilities for additional activities, you should record information about these tasks. This information is useful not only in writing or revising job descriptions, but also in presenting your added responsibilities to your supervisor in a performance appraisal.*

Job descriptions should include the following information:

- General information, such as name, department, job title, classification, work area location, and supervisor's title. Job titles are important because they lend prestige to positions and are used to compare jobs with similar titles. Assign a title that is definitive; for example, "payroll benefits analyst" rather than "accounting clerk."

HINT: *The* Dictionary of Occupational Titles *is one source of job titles. The publication and periodic supplements are available at most libraries; from the U.S. Department of Labor, Employment and Training Administration, 200 Constitution Avenue NW, Washington, DC 20001, or on-line.*

- Salary structure information, such as salary range, regular and overtime hours, full- or part-time status, and exemption status. An *exempt* status means that some positions are not subject to certain provisions of the Fair Labor Standards Act (FLSA); for example, overtime and minimum wage. Managerial and professional positions often fall into this category.

- Job overview. The overview is a brief summary of the job. Using one description for "similar" jobs can be misleading; therefore, some companies prepare a job description for each position in the company. For example, an overview of an entry level sales division assistant position might be "provides data entry support for the Software Sales Division. Communicates with customers and sales personnel."

HINT: *One side of the job description sheet includes the general information, summary, and duties; the reverse side outlines the job qualifications and specifications. Follow a similar format for all job descriptions. (A sample job description appears in Figure 11-3.)*

- Duties. Duties are those which the job now entails. Do not list duties that have been changed or eliminated. Identify duties by the frequency with which they are done—daily or monthly—and in order of their importance. An unrealistic list of responsibilities or qualifications can hinder finding good employees. Such a list may also be in violation of equal-opportunity laws.

HINT: *When describing duties, use action verbs, such as those listed in the section Work Experience in Chapter 2. Describe duties rather than specific tasks; for example, "organizes monthly conference meetings" rather than "prepares monthly agendas" or "sends out notices of meetings."*

- Supervisory responsibilities, such as number of employees supervised and the type of supervision provided.

- Intercompany contacts; for example, daily contact with a specific department or with customers.

- Working environment; for example, size of office; single workstation or multiple workstations; job safety; travel requirements; physical requirements; type or level of pressure, such as the requirements of high production quotas.

- Education required for the position; for example, high school, four-year degree, special licenses, and certifications.

- Experience and skills required for the position. Job standards require careful analysis and identification and must comply with the ADA and the Equal Opportunity Act. Do not include standards that are unrelated to job duties.

- Date of job description's last revision.

HINT: *Job descriptions require reviews. Rather than updating a job description when it is needed for a job announcement, establish a timeline for periodic evaluations of all job descriptions, such as once every six months.*

Position title:	Administrative Office Professional
Division:	Sales and Marketing
Department:	Marketing Research
Reports to:	Department Manager
Salary status:	Exempt

JOB SUMMARY:

The administrative office professional under the general supervision of the department manager, performs routine office duties as well as a variety of tasks that require planning and organization to meet deadlines and quality standards. The position requires interpersonal skills necessary to coordinate the work flow among the six to eight office support staff members in the department.

DUTIES AND RESPONSIBILITIES:

- Composes routine correspondence and e-mail messages
- Opens, routes, sorts, and prioritizes the department manager's mail
- Maintains the department manager's calendar
- Responds to mail, other messaging input, and telephone inquiries or to surveys from other agencies
- Gathers information and prepares sales reports
- Maintains confidential files
- Prioritizes departmental work
- Delegates tasks to clerical staff
- Supervises department office support staff, temporaries, and student interns
- Edits product releases and brochures to maintain consistency in format and content
- Schedules conference and exhibit assignments
- Makes all travel arrangements for staff
- Organizes weekly materials for department meetings and maintains file for agenda items
- Prepares press releases
- Recommends staff procedure changes
- Collects, compiles, and delivers office payroll time sheets to Personnel
- Conducts online research
- Effectively uses PowerPoint™ to prepare visuals
- Arranges conference calls, meetings on-site/off-site/video/computer

—Continued—

Figure 11-3 Job description.

Job Description
Administrative Office Professional
Page 2 of 2 pages

QUALIFICATIONS:

* A.A. degree
* Certified Administrative Professional (CAP) preferred
* Five years' support staff experience or administrative office professional experience
* Advanced English usage, proofreading, and editing skills
* Decision-making and management skills
* Detail-oriented
* Software proficiency in _____.
* Basic office equipment operation skills
* Written and oral communication skills
* Interpersonal and problem-solving skills
* Report-writing skills
* Knowledge of advanced public relations procedures
* Keyboarding skill of 70 words a minute
* Ability to organize, schedule, and follow instructions
* Ability to maintain confidential or sensitive information

PHYSICAL DEMANDS AND WORKING CONDITIONS:

Positions are primarily sedentary.
Worker may be required to attend off-premises meetings or conferences.

LICENSE REQUIRED:

Possession of a valid and appropriate driver's license

CAREER LADDER:

Executive assistant
Office professional

Approved: Richard Bennett
Date of Approval: January 26, 2001
D.O.T. Reference: NA

Figure 11-3 (continued.)

HINT: *Documentation of tasks performed and of time spent on these tasks is helpful information at performance review time. By writing your own job descriptions, you should be able to negotiate for a title change, increased pay, or a promotion.*

Job Description Software

Job description software provides a good starting point for writing job descriptions. It decreases the research, writing, and input time. The sizes of the databases vary from the *Dictionary of Occupational Titles* to specialized libraries for specific occupations. The software allows you to search by keyword as well as by job title; some even allow job description searches by aptitude.

Other software creates job descriptions similar to the way policy manuals are written. (See section Policy Manual Software and Technology in this chapter.) The software includes job descriptions with prewritten summaries and essential duties, which may be revised or accepted by the user. The user then responds to questions concerning such areas as physical requirements, supervisory responsibilities, language and math skills, and qualifications. The type and number of questions may vary with the software. Based on the answers to the questions, the software provides standard wording for each subsection. The user may also accept or change these statements or add comments.

Other software features include headline and section customization and ADA adaptations. The software is helpful in writing first drafts. It provides a consistent writing pattern and covers topics that may otherwise have been omitted.

HINT: *Companies using job description software must edit the prewritten descriptions carefully. Someone who understands the job and requirements is the best person to do this task.*

WORKSTATION MANUALS

A **workstation manual** or **desk manual** provides a source of information unique to a specific position. The employee at the workstation prepares the information. The manual does not circulate throughout the company and is not an official company publication.

Purpose

The workstation manual serves as a guide for a temporary worker substituting for an absent employee or as an introduction for a new employee. Referring to the manual when questions arise will save time and create less tension in the office. In addition, the manual provides the supervisor with an overview of the many tasks that are performed at a particular workstation.

Content

Some information in a workstation manual may also be included in a procedures or special-topics manual. The following items are recommended when compiling a workstation manual:

- Overview of the position.
- Organization chart.
- Products/subsidiaries.
- Location of personnel/telephone numbers/e-mail:
    - ▲ Immediate supervisor/duties
    - ▲ Supervisor's superior
    - ▲ Supervisors for whom work is performed
    - ▲ VIPs within the department or organization
    - ▲ VIPs outside the organization, such as customers, clients, suppliers, and lawyers
    - ▲ Key personnel responsible for specific areas
    - ▲ Office personnel to contact for assistance
    - ▲ Frequently called phone numbers and e-mail addresses
    - ▲ Distribution lists including names of people who receive copies of the typical documents produced in your office

- Tasks to be completed daily with recommended timelines.

HINT: *To identify typical daily tasks, refer to your time management logs. (See Chapter 3.) Indicate whether the tasks are typically completed in the morning or in the afternoon.*

- Tasks completed periodically; for example, the monthly replenishment of petty cash.
- Current committees/projects in progress.
    - ▲ Chairpersons
    - ▲ Meeting dates
    - ▲ Responsibilities/special procedures
    - ▲ Timelines

- Telephone etiquette.
    - ▲ Standard office greeting/number of rings allowed before answering
    - ▲ Long-distance and conference call procedures and charges
    - ▲ VIP calls—those which the supervisor always takes
    - ▲ Transfer procedures
    - ▲ Outside call procedures
    - ▲ Message taking and distribution procedures
    - ▲ Screening preferences

▲ Paging and forwarding procedures

▲ Personal use of office telephone

▲ Responses to frequently asked questions

HINT: *A quick reference outline is helpful in explaining how the telephone system works; for example, how to transfer or forward a call. Keep it simple so information can be quickly obtained.*

- Postal mail procedures.
    ▲ Times of delivery and collection
    ▲ Incoming mail/mail register
    ▲ Distribution responsibilities/items to route
    ▲ Outgoing mail
    ▲ Overnight/courier services

- Fax Procedures.
- Network protocol
    ▲ Fax
    ▲ Intranet

- Electronic mail procedures.
    ▲ Personal use
    ▲ Netiquette
    ▲ Formats
    ▲ Distribution lists
    ▲ Folder creation
    ▲ Message priorization
    ▲ Virus protection

- Web site Procedures.
    ▲ Personal use
    ▲ Access
    ▲ Purchasing procedures
    ▲ Design
    ▲ Privacy

- Paper filing.
    ▲ System explanation
    ▲ Coding procedures

  ▲ File label preparation
  ▲ Charge-out procedures
  ▲ Tickler file maintenance
  ▲ Shredding or disposal procedures
  ▲ Confidential information
  ▲ Directory arrangement/contents of directories/template directories

HINT: *If files are in a locked drawer or cabinet, identify the people who have access to specific files. Keep the list of people up to date.*

• Electronic Filing.
  ▲ Use of filters
  ▲ Rules
  ▲ Folder preparation
  ▲ Folder maintenance

• Correspondence.
  ▲ Formats
  ▲ Special terminology, trademarks, and abbreviations
  ▲ Signatures required
  ▲ Stationery and envelopes
  ▲ Copies—number and distribution
  ▲ Form letters

HINT: *Sample formats of letters, memos, reports, and envelopes are helpful. Identify formatting requirements and the use of special notations, such as attention, subject, distribution, and attachment lines.*

• Forms.
  ▲ Purpose
  ▲ Samples
  ▲ Location
  ▲ Required copies/distribution
  ▲ Approval/required signatures

HINT: *A completed form is more helpful than a blank form. Identify the source of information for completing each form. If calculations are necessary, give instructions to show how to obtain the figures.*

- Supplies.
  - ▲ Location
  - ▲ Requisition procedures
  - ▲ Purchasing sources
  - ▲ Purchasing procedures

- Travel.
  - ▲ Travel requests
  - ▲ Travel preferences of supervisor
  - ▲ Frequent flyer numbers
  - ▲ Travel agents/electronic ticketing/online travel arrangements
  - ▲ Itineraries
  - ▲ Ticket pickup/delivery
  - ▲ Mileage reimbursement
  - ▲ Expense reports

- Equipment repair.
  - ▲ Reporting procedures/forms
  - ▲ Telephone numbers

- Computers.
  - ▲ Operating procedures
  - ▲ In-house assistance/hotline numbers
  - ▲ Security
  - ▲ Log-on instructions/backup procedures
  - ▲ Instruction manual location

- Software.
  - ▲ Access codes
  - ▲ File naming procedures
  - ▲ File location
  - ▲ Precautions/security
  - ▲ Instruction manual location
  - ▲ In-house staff who have different software expertise

- Reprographics.
  - ▲ In-company services/location
  - ▲ Copy limitations/chargebacks

▲ Request forms/rush requests

▲ Repair service

▲ Overhead transparencies/special requests

▲ Publication and copyright guidelines

• Visitors.

▲ Frequent visitors—names and positions

▲ VIP visitors (those whom the supervisor will always see)

▲ Security procedures

▲ On-site accidents—reports, steps to take

• Meetings.

▲ Minutes/agendas

▲ Scheduling procedures

▲ Room/food requests

▲ Presentation software

• Recordkeeping.

▲ Bank deposits/reconciliations

▲ Timecards

▲ Petty cash

• General.

▲ Technical terms, abbreviations

▲ Special reference materials

▲ Breaks/lunch

▲ Parking/office keys/security

▲ Dress/office appearance

▲ Precautions

▲ Efficiency hints

• Employer information.

▲ Professional memberships—meeting dates and dues

▲ Anniversaries/birthdays

▲ Family—names and telephone numbers

▲ Social security, passport, and credit card numbers

Writing Procedures

A workstation manual requires attention to detail and constant review. The following procedures will assist in organizing the manual:

- Make a list of all the tasks performed and responsibilities involved with the position before beginning to write. Include information on material locations as well as hints or precautions. Index cards work well for this initial step. Sort the cards and place them in categories; for example, place all telephone-related tasks together. When you do a new task, include instructions in the manual. If procedures change, be sure to bring the desk manual up to date. Date each sheet and check periodically to see if information is still accurate.
- Obtain input from your supervisor. Prepare a copy of the manual for his or her desk.
- Use cross-references. For example, a specific task may require the shredding of all draft copies. Rather than describing the shredding procedure each time it is needed, direct the user to the one section where it is described in detail.
- Compile the materials into a three-ring looseleaf notebook. Arrange the material by subject. Use dividers to separate the sections. Number pages consecutively.
- Store the instructions on a separate disk or create a training directory on the hard disk. A new employee will then have access to up-to-date instructions.

HINT: *A temporary agency may help its employees by preparing disks of workstation instructions for those companies who are its major clients. Temporary workers could then become familiar with procedures before beginning a job.*

- Prepare a detailed table of contents. The person relying on the manual wants the information quickly.
- Obtain input from the people who use the manual. Include a "comments" sheet at the front of the manual for this purpose. Consider these comments when making revisions.
- Review the tasks periodically, and note any changes in the margins of the manual. This eliminates preparing new sheets each time a change occurs, yet it keeps the manual up to date. Prepare new inserts as needed.

INSTRUCTION MANUALS

A new piece of equipment or a software package comes with an **instruction manual** or an **owner's guide. A quick reference guide,** which is a shorter version of the instruction manual, may also be available.

Department supervisors should keep at least one copy of all instruction manuals in a centralized location. Each user should have access to the instruction manuals.

Purpose

Instruction manuals explain how to use specific products. These manuals also include answers to repair questions. Checking the manual before calling the repair center can save time and expense. When you call a hotline number for assistance, the person who responds to your question may refer you to a section in the instruction manual for future reference. Instruction manuals are also useful in training sessions and often serve as the textbooks.

Content

Instruction manuals vary in format, size, and style, but they all include similar topics, such as the following:

- Disclaimer notices
- Warranty and liability statements
- Copyright protection
- Table of contents
- Unpacking/setup procedures
- Installation procedures
- Equipment diagram and list of parts
- Care and handling of equipment
- Getting started
- Standard operating procedures
- Precautions
- Advanced operations
- Glossary
- Appendices
- Troubleshooting pointers
- Warranty registration
- Site-license agreement

Evaluation

Well-written instruction manuals can be helpful in learning how to operate new equipment or software, whereas poorly written manuals cause frustration and wasted time. The following questions can help to determine the potential effectiveness of an instruction manual:

- Is the language simple and clear?

HINT: *Before a salesperson leaves the demonstration, ask to see a copy of the manual. Work through the steps of the first several procedures. Omissions or difficulties in following the first few procedures usually are signs of a faulty manual.*

- Are terms explained?
- Is the material written logically? Is it arranged from the simplest to the most complex tasks? Is it direct or is there excess information that causes confusion?
- Is it readable? Are the steps in a procedure numbered? If not, are there lead-in statements such as "To make a copy of a volume, choose option B"? Are there sufficient headings and subheadings to divide topics? Are the paragraphs short?
- Do diagrams accompany instructions? Showing what happens after an instruction has been followed is helpful.
- Is there an index and is it easy to use?

HINT: *To test the thoroughness of an index, select several items and see if the pages provide the necessary information.*

- Is there a hotline number that can be called for information?
- Does it permit a beginner to get started with the main task and learn others as needed?
- Is a quick reference guide available? Is each procedure summarized for easy reference or review?
- Is the manual well bound so it will not fall apart with use? Is it a convenient size? Does it stay open and lie flat?
- Does it have a section listing error codes? Are cautions clearly identified?
- Are care and handling instructions clear?
- Are peripheral devices and limitations identified?
- Are there appendices for extra information that is not found in the instructions?

CORPORATE STYLE GUIDES

Style guides are useful to companies for maintaining quality and consistency in their documents. If a company wants a style guide, it must commit the time and resources to develop its own since each guide is unique.

Purpose

A company style guide sets standards and answers those questions that always seem to cause problems. Well-designed style guides eliminate guesswork and provide a consistent and time-saving writing tool; however, they do not replace such writing aids as dictionaries or grammar and spell checkers.

Style guides are also helpful for project work. If a corporate guide is not available, develop a style sheet for the project. You can also make one for use at your own desk and include all those troublesome spellings or word-usage questions that frequently occur.

Content

The style guide originates in-house with input from many potential users. The content and size of the guide vary. Although the *process* involves the differing opinions of how "things should be done," one person should coordinate the final version of the style guide. Some items to consider include the following:

- Purpose of the style guide
- Copyright material
- Guidelines for preparing tables, graphs, and diagrams
- Labeling graphics in text
- Creating graphics for presentations
- Use of logos
- Gender-neutral writing
- Acceptable ethnic designations
- Document report formats
- Use of boxes, bullets, numbers
- File and directory naming conventions
- Accepted abbreviations and formats
- Use of acronyms
- Proofreading symbols
- Scientific math formula formats
- Spelling of frequently misused words
- One-word, two-word/hyphenated words
- Word usage
- Number writing
- Active/passive voice
- Reading levels

HINT: *Organizing and writing a corporate style guide could be a challenging project for office professionals in a firm. They have access to samples of documents and are*

aware of successful styles and procedures. A style guide needs to be used and fol-
lowed in order to be effective in saving time and in producing quality documents.
Actively seek out evaluations and comments. Hold seminars explaining the use of
the guide. Be certain management supports the style guide.

REFERENCE MANUALS

A **reference manual** is a source for checking specific information. Examples of reference manuals include dictionaries, atlases, office manuals, directories, and thesauruses. Since office professionals refer to these reference manuals frequently, they should be kept within easy reach. Computerized versions of such reference sources as dictionaries and thesauruses may also be accessible as separate software packages, on CD-ROMs, or as integral parts of many software programs. Databases with directory information are also available. See the section on Reference Sources for Home-Based Businesses in this chapter.

Dictionaries

Standard unabridged and abridged dictionaries are indispensable for spelling, definitions, word division, and pronunciation. In addition, some dictionaries include foreign words and phrases, grammar rules, abbreviations, forms of address, directories of colleges and universities, weights and measures, metrics, signs and symbols, and common English names. Unabridged dictionaries can include twice as many words as the standard abridged dictionary. Specialized dictionaries are available for such areas as law, medicine, accounting, insurance, electronics, and education.

HINT: *Use the Web site yourdictionary.com, which includes more than 1,500 dictionaries in over 200 languages.*

Thesauruses

A thesaurus can be helpful in writing or editing documents. It provides alternatives for words that are used frequently. Instead of repeating the same word in a sentence, a synonym can be selected from the thesaurus.

HINT: *Dictionaries and thesauruses should be up to date. Check for new editions in* Books in Print, *which is available at most libraries. Recommend new editions when these references become five to seven years old.*

HINT: Roget's *is a well-known thesaurus, and you can also find it online at thesaurus.com.*

Atlases

An atlas provides geographical information in the form of maps (often in color), with names of large cities and capitals. An atlas has information on climate, air routes, the solar system, and the economy, in addition to census data and other statistical and demographic information. An atlas is useful in making travel arrangements, setting up geographic files, checking world locations, verifying spellings, and determining mileage.

Directories

Directories contain names, addresses, and special data about people or businesses. Types of directories include telephone directories, toll-free number directories, ZIP code directories, and city directories, as well as various types of professional membership directories.

Telephone directories for large cities are on file in libraries or online— www.teldir.com, for instance. Companies can also rent telephone directories that include addresses from telephone companies. Another resource is Pacific Bell Smart Resource Center (800–848–8000), from which you can purchase state and specialty telephone directories, some of which are national in scope. Omnigraphics publishes a toll-free telephone book that covers 44,000 U.S. businesses and organizations. Listings include mailing addresses, telephone and fax numbers, and e-mail and Web addresses. Additional information about this directory is available at www.omnigraphics.com.

The National Five Digit ZIP Code and Post Office Directory is a valuable reference source for checking the accuracy of ZIP codes on outgoing mail. The directory is arranged by geographic location. A copy may be purchased at the counter in your main post office, or you may contact the U.S. Postal Service or your local library.

City directories list names, addresses, and occupations of the residents in a city or area. They may also contain a list of businesses and their officials or owners. Private companies collect the information and publish the directories.

Polk's Directory lists entries by specific city. Entries may be accessed by the entrant's name, address, telephone number, and place of work. You may obtain copies by writing to Polk's, 7168 Envoy Court, Dallas, TX 75241. Haines and Company publishes *Haines Criss-Cross Directory,* which covers an area rather than a specific city. Copies can be ordered from Haines at 8050 Freedom Avenue NW, North Canton, OH 44720. Check with your local public library for additional information.

HINT: *To locate a particular directory, check the local library for the* Guide to American Directories, *which describes the many trade and professional directories published in the United States, or the* Directory of Directories, *which identifies business directories by country, state, and region, as well as by the type of business or the products available.*

Computerized reference services are valuable sources of information. Your public library is an excellent place for locating such sources. The Directory of All On-Line Databases from Cuadra Associates in Los Angeles or Computer Readable Databases from Gale Research in Detroit give the names of thousands of accessible databases available on-line throughout the world.

Office Reference Manuals

An **office reference manual** is an indispensable source of information for office workers. This type of manual offers suggestions and information on a variety of office topics. The use of one office reference manual throughout the organization is more efficient than having separate manuals for each department.

Appropriate selection of a reference manual requires research and input from the prospective users. Once input has been obtained, recommend that a committee of office professionals use this information to make the final selection.

If all office professionals use the same office reference manual, they should have the opportunity to attend training sessions regarding the contents and the effective use of these manuals. Recommend that a group of office professionals be responsible for presenting information on the reference manuals at all orientation sessions for new employees.

Other Reference Materials

Other useful references include books of quotations, etiquette guides, and parliamentary procedure manuals. For matters of editing and printing style, consult *The Chicago Manual of Style* (University of Chicago Press) and the U.S. Government Printing Office's *Style Manual.*

For interesting statistics for research or publications, such as newsletters, visit the Fedstats Web site at www.fedstats.gov. This site covers information published by more than 75 federal agencies.

SPECIALIZED LIBRARIES

Some companies establish their own specialized libraries. These libraries are usually private and available to company employees. Although some specialized libraries may be limited to a few major subject areas, their specific holdings are comprehensive and current. Even small companies can create mini-libraries by using a centralized location to keep such items as specialty magazines, brochures, newsletters, workshop notices, and employee manuals. However, someone must keep the library materials current. The materials may be in different formats; e.g., annual reports or job openings may be on video or minutes may be on audiotapes. Access to a specialized library that does not contain classified or confidential information may be possible for people who are not company employees or members of an association. An explanation that outlines the need for the specialized information (preferably in writing) should be prepared before requesting access to any special collection.

Several reference indexes are available to assist in locating special library information. *The Directory of Special Libraries and Information Centers* provides addresses, telephone numbers, and the titles of those in charge of special libraries, archives, research libraries, and information centers. Another directory, *New Special Libraries,* provides regular updates to this directory. Large document collections are also available in electronic form with search and retrieval features.

REFERENCE SOURCES FOR HOME-BASED BUSINESSES

Online services, local libraries, and printed materials provide home-based business owners with many sources of business-related information. The costs vary. Some sources may be more reliable than others.

Internet

Check your local telephone directory for Internet providers and compare costs and services. Scrutinize the data you obtain from the Internet; consider carefully the source of the information. In your search for information, you can print the data or you can download the material to a disk and print it later. See Chapter 22 for more information on the Internet and World Wide Web.

CD-ROMS

Compact disks with read-only memory store huge amounts of data at relatively low costs. You cannot change the data or write to the disk. If you have CD-ROM capabilities on your computer, you can subscribe to such information services as dictionaries, telephone directories, encyclopedias, reference manuals, clip art, and shareware. Disks are updated at regular intervals. Any program can be loaded into memory while you are working on an application; therefore, you can mark data and transfer it to your current task.

Printed Materials

The Government Printing Office has many publications on a variety of business subjects. Order them from the Superintendent of Documents, U.S. Government Printing Office, Washington, DC 20402. For a copy of AT&T's toll-free directory, *Business Edition,* contact the National Association for Information Services, 1150 Connecticut Avenue NW, Suite 1050, Washington, DC 20036.

U.S. Small Business Administration (SBA)

The SBA provides information and service to small businesses at minimal or no cost. Small Business Development Centers, which are sponsored by the SBA, offer the expertise of university personnel, local businesspeople, and government workers through counseling and workshops. Access to the services is by computer and modem through online programs, through SBA's bulletin board, or by contacting a local SBA office. Your local SBA office also has information on the Service Corps of Retired Executives (SCORE), a group of business retirees who assist small business owners.

Professional Associations

In addition to contact with other professionals, professional association membership includes such items as publications, seminars and conferences, insurance, and equipment and software information. The *Encyclopedia of Associations* at local libraries gives contacts for and descriptions of the organizations.

Local Libraries

Books as well as current magazine articles in specific interest fields are available through public, community college, or university libraries. University libraries often have separate business libraries. Nonstudents may have to pay a minimal fee. Public libraries keep clipping files of local businesses. If materials are not available locally, libraries may order materials from other libraries through interlibrary loans.

Service Bureaus

Information services and bureaus will do the research or survey that a company needs. These bureaus are helpful when time is short or specific area expertise is limited. Information on market demographics, shopping patterns, government regulations, and international markets are a few areas in which information bureaus specialize.

Radio/Television

Radio and TV broadcasts are available for home-based business owners and cover such topics as government regulations, equipment, financial advice, marketing, business opportunities, and telecommunications. Check local listings for time and topics.

COMPANY NEWSLETTERS

Company newsletters provide businesses with opportunities to communicate with employees, or with vendors and current or potential customers or clients. Management determines the purposes of the newsletters and approves their final publication. The emphasis in this section is on internal newsletters.

Because of their organizational skills and their knowledge of word processing or desktop publishing, office professionals assume a major role in producing internal newsletters. They may have responsibility for collecting the information, editing the material, writing articles, or printing and distributing the final copy. Desktop publishing software allows companies to produce newsletters of high quality at a low cost. Simple layouts with attention paid to design details give a professional appearance to company-produced newsletters and other materials published in-house. Local bulletin board or on-line services as well as shareware and freeware offer clip art, fonts, and software for newsletter preparation. See Chapter 19 for newsletter design suggestions.

A firm may wish to create an intranet home page for staff only. Up-to-date announcements, job listings, directory updates, employee news, and computer techniques are some uses for such a page, which, in turn, would decrease e-mail clutter. After one month or some other designated time, there should be an automatic deletion of the material. Establish at the beginning who will be responsible for developing and maintaining the intranet.

The next section deals primarily with the content and writing of the newsletter. For a discussion of its graphic design, see the section on designing a newsletter in Chapter 19.

Content

Determining newsletter content requires a clear understanding of management's goals in publishing the newsletter and the number of issues to be published. For example, is the immediate goal to introduce new ideas? To boost morale? To communicate management's activities? To make announcements? To provide information? To feature individuals in personal or work activities? Is one general issue published monthly or quarterly, or is this a weekly bulletin? Knowledge of these goals not only clarifies the content but also determines the order of the articles in the newsletter.

HINT: *Keep a folder of newsletters from other companies to see what is appealing. Check the local library for books on writing interesting newsletters.*

HINT: *Use anti-virus programs when downloading data from on-line sources or disks.*

Examples of content ideas and possible headlines for newsletter articles include:

▲ Messages from management.
  Example: "A Message from the CEO" or "Straight from the Top."
▲ Forecast reports.
  Example: "A New Year: What Does It Hold for XYZ Company?"
▲ New products/services.
  Example: "XYZ Company Receives Recognition by Chamber of Commerce."
▲ Policy changes and explanations.
▲ Current legislation or news items that impact the company.
  Example: "Water Conservation—Our Responsibility."

▲ General company information.

> **Example:** "Your Financial Future/New Savings Plan for XYZ Employees."

▲ New technology.

▲ Personnel moves.

> **Example:** "Roberts Named Sales Operations Manager" or "Donaldson Promoted."

HINT: *Rather than simply featuring an employee who has moved along a career ladder, go a step beyond and include advice from the individual. For example, "Roberts, XYZ's New Sales Manager, Gives 12 Tips for Getting Customers."*

▲ Education/training.

> **Example:** "Check Out These New Courses." ___✓___ Internet Basics, ___✓___ Presentation Graphics

▲ Employees' work-related achievements/team accomplishments.

> **Example:** "We Do It Best as a Team" or "The Suggestion That Worked."

▲ Presentations made by employees.

> **Example:** "Peters Addresses IAAP®."

▲ Health and safety reminders.

> **Example:** "Take Time to Check for Safety."

▲ Cost-saving reminders.

▲ Ethics issues.

▲ Feature articles on employees/new employees

> **Example:** "Inside XYZ Company" or "Profile/A Closer Look."

HINT: *It is often difficult to become acquainted with coworkers. Distribute a form for employees to complete (voluntary) and include one or more "features" in each issue.*

▲ Calendar of events/activities within the company.

▲ Surveys/suggestions.

> **Example:** "What Employees Need at XYZ Company."

HINT: *Once a survey has been taken, always report the results. Follow-up articles are also interesting; for example, the above survey can be followed with an article on how XYZ Company is meeting these needs.*

▲ Employees' personal achievements/awards.

> **Example:** "On Our Own Time."

▲ Attendance/longevity records.

▲ Employees' participation in community events or in volunteer activities.

▲ Announcements—births/deaths/retirements.

▲ Recreational activities/scores.

▲ Request for newsletter items.

HINT: *Get ideas from as many employees as possible at all levels. Include a form each time the newsletter is published that makes it easy for employees to respond.*

Editing/Writing Newsletters

The editing task is less demanding if writers are carefully selected or if one person does the writing. Rewriting poor copy is often more difficult than writing the original copy. Rewriting can also cause friction with the author and, if clumsily done, may change the original intent of the article. Several suggestions for writing and/or editing articles follow.

* Answer the basic reporting questions—who, where, when, what, why, and how—in the first paragraph. Articles must be informative and creative and yet practical for the readers.

* Write a headline that highlights the action in the first paragraph; for example, "Dayton Corporation Sponsors $3000 Scholarship." Use secondary headlines in smaller type.

* Rank information in a story. After the lead sentence, which is the attention getter, continue to write the material as you have ranked it. If space runs out, you still have the most important parts of the story included.

* Establish a timeline and monitor it regularly. Include articles that are timely. The calendar of events must be up to date and should not include dates of past events.

HINT: *New programs may create interest and appear timely but do not include them unless their progress can be described. An announcement of a program in the planning stages can be premature and can confuse readers.*

* Use the language of the audience for whom the newsletter is written.

* Write short paragraphs—four to six lines—to maintain interest. Use one new idea in each paragraph. Subheadings and captions are effective. Keep the sentences short.

* Distinguish opinions from facts. If it is an opinion, state this in the article. Avoid superlatives and your own judgmental statements.

* Avoid using customer or vendor names unless you have authorization to do so. Some companies may interpret the use of their names as product endorsements.

* Place regularly occurring material in the same location each time the newsletter is printed. Use the same heading for the column. For example, the "Calendar of Events" may be boxed on the lower left corner of the last page of each issue.

- Indicate the approximate number of words an article should have when you ask others to write. Request that the articles be double-spaced, have headlines, sub-headings, and captions, and include photographs or illustrations if applicable.

HINT: *Publish a schedule and clearly indicate your deadlines to other contributors.*

- Request vertical black and white glossy photographs. They are easier to use in columns where space is limited. Try to obtain action photos rather than still photos. If using two photographs on the same page, vary the sizes.

HINT: *A company may obtain permission to use photographs of its employees at the time employees are hired. Check with the Human Resources Department or with your supervisor to be sure proper procedures for photo releases are followed.*

- Consult with the author of an article before making extensive editorial changes. If writing the article, check the accuracy of all facts. Get written permission before writing about a person and a sign-off acceptance signature after it is written or after it has been changed extensively.
- Proofread carefully. Be careful with substitutions like "in" for "it" or "your" for "you." Use your software spell checkers as well as a reference manual and dictionary. If interviewing for a news story, check spelling and details before leaving the interview. It is especially important to check the spellings of names and products. Use a style guide for consistency.
- Put the date, volume, and number on the front of each issue in the same location.
- Include the name, address, telephone and fax numbers, general e-mail address, and Web site of the company as well as the name of the editor. Include the dates of publication. Box the information on the first or last page. Note the example that follows.

Published biweekly for present and retired XYZ Company employees. For additional information, contact the editor, (Name).

AMC
1220 Becker Road
Eau Galle, FL 32611
Telephone (407) 296-5433
Fax (407) 756-6586
E-mail: amc@aol.com
Web site: www.iaap-hq.org

CHAPTER 12

RECORDS

MANAGEMENT

Records management includes management of paper records, micrographics, magnetically stored documents, and optical information systems. Records management starts with the creation or receipt of information and ends with the destruction or storage of the information. Office professionals must be aware of available systems and options to manage records with the most efficient and productive methods.

TYPES OF RECORDS

Records can be either paper or electronic. Electronic records include computer files on a computer disk, hard drive, or LAN (Local Area Network); e-mail; or voice mail.

RETAINING RECORDS

Records retention requirements vary among industries and states. Each organization should develop a records retention schedule to avoid keeping information longer than needed. A retention schedule tells how long to keep records in the office, when to destroy them, and when to transfer them to inactive storage facilities. In determining how long to retain records, consider the following:

- The activity and use of the record. Move inactive records to another storage area.
- Legal retention requirements for federal, state, and local government agencies. Research these requirements carefully and consult with an attorney.
- Long-term value to the organization for research or to the community for scholarly purposes.

HINT: *Charitable and religious organizations usually retain a recorded history of their development. Contact state historical societies for recommendations.*

- The cost of keeping the records (purchasing/leasing file cabinets, supplies, square footage costs) versus the cost of destroying the records. Ask how the organization might be affected if the document/record were destroyed.

Store records according to the following guidelines:

1. Files consulted several times a month or more must be conveniently accessible in the main file area. These records must be organized logically so they can be retrieved quickly. If others share the filing system, the system must make sense to all users.

2. Semiactive records, referred to approximately once a month, may be stored in less-accessible drawers or cabinets.

3. Records used less than once a month should be stored in a storage unit or warehouse off-site, or in natural underground caves specifically used for long-term storage. Off-site storage maximizes space, uses less expensive storage containers, and costs less per square foot than office floor space.

Vital Records

Approximately 1 to 3 percent of business records are vital. Vital documents are those necessary for continuous operation of the business in the wake of fire, flood, earthquake, arson, terrorism, or other disaster. These records can be used to reconstruct a company's legal or financial status and to preserve the rights of the organization, its employees, customers, and stockholders.

Vital records include:

- Insurance policies.
- Documents of incorporation or partnership, certifications, licenses, leases, deeds, and titles.
- Tax returns and supporting materials.
- Warranties for office equipment, computers, and machinery.
- Copyrights.
- Personnel records.
- Financial records such as accounts receivable balances.
- Banking and payroll records.
- Pension and profit-sharing documents.
- Word- and data-processing backup tapes or disks.
- Company policy manuals and departmental procedures manuals.

Not all vital records are stored forever; only the most recent update of some information, such as accounts receivable, is considered vital.

Copies of vital records should be made for protection. Vital records can be protected using one of the following methods:

Dispersal: Copies may be stored at different locations during routine distribution of materials. This method is often used when companies have several locations. Dispersal may also be to banks, insurance companies, government agencies, or accounting firms.

Duplication: Copies of vital records can be made as part of regularly scheduled duplication; they may be in any medium, whether disk, microfilm, or paper.

On-site storage: Vital records can be stored in fireproof cabinets, vaults, or rooms; this is normally acceptable only for temporary storage. There must be proper environmental controls and sufficient security.

Off-site storage: Off-site storage facilities could be company-owned, commercial, or shared with others. They must have environmental controls for temperature, humidity, air circulation, and control of insects and rodents. Access should be restricted to ensure security.

TYPES OF FILING SYSTEMS

Most offices use several different filing systems. There are five major ways to store records, whether those records are on paper or on micrographics or magnetic media. Some offices may use a combination of one or more of the following systems:

Alphabetic: Files are kept under the names of individuals, businesses, and government organizations and filed by the sequence of letters in the alphabet. This is the system used in most offices. It is better for small companies and for individual files. Use standard filing rules for consistency in filing and retrieval.

Numeric: In this system, a code number is assigned to individuals, businesses, or subjects. Once the code number is assigned, no decisions have to be made as to how to file records. They are simply filed in numeric order. However, this method requires an index to find material. A numeric filing system works well for records that can be filed by policy numbers, product numbers, patient billing numbers, or customer account numbers. It is also easily learned by those not familiar with English. Numeric filing increases the confidentiality of records.

Subject: Records are filed alphabetically by topic or category rather than by individual name or business name. This method is best for companies that store records by inventory or merchandise names. It is often combined with an alphabetic system. Such a system can be one of the most difficult to design and maintain. Major filing categories often are: Accounting, Advertising, Associations, Budget, Conferences and Conventions, Credit Department, Equipment, Expense Account, Finance, Insurance, Inventory, Legal, Office Systems, Personnel, Property, Records Management, Safety, Sales, Travel, Vacations.

Geographic: Records are arranged alphabetically according to names of geographic locations. This system works best for sales data broken down by geographic territories. Each geographic territory can be separated by file guides.

Chronological: Records are arranged by date (usually year/month/day). This system is used especially for temporary filing and tickler or reminder files.

If material may be filed under one or more names or subjects, a cross reference should be made. File the material under one name or subject and file a cross reference to that name or subject under the other. Insert a permanent guide in the proper alphabetical position among the regular file folders for cross-reference information.

For example, Dan Imler has a painting service called Dan & Son Painting. All materials are filed in the folder labeled Imler, Dan. A cross reference is placed in the files under Dan & Son Painting. The cross reference reads as follows: Dan & Son Painting, see Imler, Dan.

HINT: *Remove the front of a folder and color-code the label. Staple the cross-reference sheet to the remaining portion of the folder.*

FILING RULES AND STANDARDS

ARMA, the Association of Records Managers and Administrators (www.arma.org), is a professional organization for the records management field that develops and promotes standards for records management.

ARMA Simplified Filing Standard Rules* are:

1. Alphabetize by arranging files in unit-by-unit order and letter-by-letter within each unit.

	AS FILED		
AS WRITTEN	UNIT 1	UNIT 2	UNIT 3
Professional Artists Inc	Professional	Artists	Inc
Professional Speakers Association	Professional	Speakers	Association
Rapid Messenger Service	Rapid	Messenger	Service

2. Each filing unit in a filing segment is to be considered. This includes prepositions, conjunctions, and articles. The only exception is when the word "the" is the first filing unit in a filing segment. In this case, "the" is the last filing unit. Spell out all symbols; e.g., as &, $, #, and file alphabetically.

	AS FILED			
AS WRITTEN	UNIT 1	UNIT 2	UNIT 3	UNIT 4
Brinker & Pisenti	Brinker	and	Pisenti	
The Buffy Antiques	Buffy	Antiques	The	
Campbell & Associates	Campbell	and	Associates	
Creative Journeys of Napa	Creative	Journeys	of	Napa
$ and Cents	Dollars	and	Cents	
Flights of Fancy	Flights	of	Fancy	

*Based on ARMA International "Alphabetical Filing Rules." Copyright © 1972, 1985, 1986, 1995. All rights reserved. Published with permission of and by arrangement with the Association of Records Managers and Administrators, Inc.

3. File "nothing before something." File single unit filing segments before multiple unit filing segments.

	AS FILED			
AS WRITTEN	UNIT 1	UNIT 2	UNIT 3	UNIT 4
A Grand Innovation	A	Grand	Innovation	
A to Z Bookkeeping Bookkeeping	A	to	Z	
Able Auto Painting	Able	Auto	Painting	
C & W Ford	C	and	W	Ford
C G Products	C	G	Products	
Cooperfield Books	Cooperfield	Books		

4. Ignore all punctuation when alphabetizing. This includes periods, commas, dashes, apostrophes, and so forth. Hyphenated words are considered one unit.

	AS FILED		
AS WRITTEN	UNIT 1	UNIT 2	UNIT 3
Brides 'n Maids	Brides	n	Maids
Cody's Books	Codys	Books	
Cluckler All-Steel Building	Cluckler	AllSteel	Building
Parker-West Advertising	ParkerWest	Advertising	
Sonoma Package Co.	Sonoma	Package	Co

5. Arabic and Roman numbers are filed sequentially before alphabetic characters. All Arabic numerals precede all Roman numerals.

	AS FILED			
AS WRITTEN	UNIT 1	UNIT 2	UNIT 3	UNIT 4
1 Hour Photo	1	Hour	Photo	
4 Star Foods	4	Star	Foods	
49er Pet Warehouse	49er	Pet	Warehouse	
355 Park Hotel	355	Park	Hotel	
V Star Foods	V	Star	Foods	
A-1 Equipment Rental	A1	Equipment	Rental	
Four Star Foods	Four	Star	Foods	
One Hour Photo	One	Hour	Photo	

6. Acronyms, abbreviations, and radio and television station call letters are filed as one unit.

	AS FILED			
AS WRITTEN	UNIT 1	UNIT 2	UNIT 3	UNIT 4
Am. Patent Services	Am	Patent	Services	
GE Consumer Service	GE	Consumer	Service	
KOLB TV	KOLB	TV		
WSRO 1350 AM	WSRO	1350	AM	

7. File under the most commonly used name or title. Cross-reference under other names or titles which might be used in an information request.

	AS FILED			
AS WRITTEN	UNIT 1	UNIT 2	UNIT 3	UNIT 4
Dan & Son Painting	Dan	and	Son	Painting
	(See Imler, Dan)			
Cellular Car Service	Cellular	Car	Service	
	(See Sonoma Communications Inc.)			
The Violin Shop	Violin	Shop	The	
	(See Loveland, Mike)			

Examples for Applying the Simplified Filing Rules

PERSONAL NAMES

1. *Simple personal names:* Use the last (surname) as the first filing unit. The first name or initial is the second filing unit. Subsequent names or initials are filed as successive units.

	AS FILED			
AS WRITTEN	UNIT 1	UNIT 2	UNIT 3	UNIT 4
A. Miriam Harms	Harms	A	Miriam	
Deanna Pebbles	Pebbles	Deanna		
Paul B. White	White	Paul	B	

2. *Personal names with prefixes:* Surnames which include a prefix are filed as one unit whether the prefix is followed by a space or not. Examples of prefixes are: D', Da, De, Del, De la, Della, Den, Des, Di, Du, El, Fitz, L', La, Las, Le, Les, Lo, Los, M', Mac, Mc, O', Saint, St., Ste., Te, Ten, Ter, Van, Van de, Van der, Von, Von der.

	AS FILED		
AS WRITTEN	UNIT 1	UNIT 2	UNIT 3
Gary D'Alois	DAlois	Gary	
Jesse Del Moral	DelMoral	Jesse	
Andrea C. LaDow	LaDow	Andrea	C
Peter J. McCabe	McCabe	Peter	J
Terry V. O'Connor	OConnor	Terry	V
Linda St. Andrew	StAndrew	Linda	
Jane C. Van Der Slice	VanDerSlice	Jane	C
Albert Vander Werf	VanderWerf	Albert	

3. *Personal names with personal and professional titles and suffixes:* Suffixes are not used as filing units except when needed to distinguish between two or more

identical names. When needed, a suffix is the last filing unit and is filed as written, ignoring punctuation.

	AS FILED			
AS WRITTEN	UNIT 1	UNIT 2	UNIT 3	UNIT 4
John P. Lynch, C.P.A.	Lynch	John	P	CPA
John P. Lynch, Jr.	Lynch	John	P	Jr
John P. Lynch, M.D.	Lynch	John	P	MD
Mr. John P. Lynch	Lynch	John	P	Mr
John P. Lynch, Ph.D.	Lynch	John	P	PhD
Senator John P. Lynch	Lynch	John	P	Senator

4. *Personal names which are hyphenated:* Ignore the hyphen and file the two words as one unit.

	AS FILED		
AS WRITTEN	UNIT 1	UNIT 2	UNIT 3
Peggy Davis-Farrell	DavisFarrell	Peggy	
Danielle Griffin-Amcor	GriffinAmcor	Danielle	
Carol Lytle-John	Lytle-John	Carol	

5. *Pseudonymous and royal and religious titles:* Pseudonyms are filed as written. Personal names which start with a royal or religious title and are followed by only a given name(s) are filed as written.

	AS FILED	
AS WRITTEN	UNIT 1	UNIT 2
Dr. Seuss	Dr	Seuss
Prince Charles	Prince	Charles
Sister Mary	Sister	Mary

6. *Foreign personal names:* If the surname is identifiable, file the name as any other personal name is filed. If there is a question about the surname, use the last name as the first filing unit and make a cross-reference from the first name.

	AS FILED		
AS WRITTEN	UNIT 1	UNIT 2	UNIT 3
Mohammed Abdullah	Abdullah	Mohammed	
	Mohammed	Abdullah	
	(See Abdullah Mohammed)		
Yang Mo	Mo	Yang	
	Yang	Mo	
	(See Mo Yang)		
Yew Cong Wong	Wong	Yew	Cong
	Yew Cong Wong (See Wong Yew Cong)		

7. *Nicknames:* When a person commonly uses a nickname as a first name, file using the nickname. Cross-reference from the given name only if necessary.

	AS FILED	
AS WRITTEN	UNIT 1	UNIT 2
Susie Sziber	Sziber	Susie
Bob Tagnoli	Tagnoli	Bob
Buck Wood	Wood (See Wood John C)	Buck

BUSINESS AND ORGANIZATION NAMES

1. Business and organization names are filed as written according to the Simplified Standard Rules and using the business letterhead or trademark as a guide. Names with prefixes follow the example for personal names with prefixes above.

	AS FILED			
AS WRITTEN	UNIT 1	UNIT 2	UNIT 3	UNIT 4
A & T Automotive	A	and	T	Automotive
Aardvark Transmissions	Aardvark	Transmissions		
Dee-Jay's Sash & Glass	Deejays	Sash	and	Glass
Kelly Kline Photo Studios	Kelly	Kline	Photo	Studios
U-Save Auto Rental	USave	Auto	Rental	
Van Koonse Glass Co.	VanKoonse	Glass	Co	

2. Subsidiaries of businesses will be filed under their own name with a cross-reference to the parent company if needed.

	AS FILED			
AS WRITTEN	UNIT 1	UNIT 2	UNIT 3	UNIT 4
Comstock Michigan Fruit	Comstock (See also Curtice Burns Foods Inc.)	Michigan	Fruit	
Curtice Burns Foods, Inc.	Curtice (for Divisions see: Comstock Michigan Fruit; Iowa Fresh Foods; Nebraska Produce, Inc.)	Burns	Foods	Inc

3. Place names in business names will follow the Simplified Filing Standard Rule that each word/filing unit is treated as a separate filing unit.

	AS FILED		
AS WRITTEN	UNIT 1	UNIT 2	UNIT 3
California Parenting Institute	California	Parenting	Institute
Oakland Coliseum	Oakland	Coliseum	
Sonoma County Transportation	Sonoma	County	Transportation

4. Each word/unit in a filing segment containing compass terms is considered a separate filing unit. If the term includes more than a compass point, treat it as it is written. Establish cross references as needed.

	AS FILED			
AS WRITTEN	UNIT 1	UNIT 2	UNIT 3	UNIT 4
North Bay Regional Center	North	Bay	Regional	Center
North Coast Drywall	North	Coast	Drywall	
North West Design	North	West	Design	
Northwest Community Center	Northwest	Community	Center	

GOVERNMENT AND POLITICAL DESIGNATIONS

When filing governmental and political material, the name of the major entity is filed first, followed by the distinctive name of the department, bureau, and so forth.

This rule covers all governmental and political divisions, agencies, departments, and federal to county/parish, city, district, and ward level.

1. *Federal:* Prefix with the name of the government and eliminate the department; e.g., of the Interior, Department of the Treasury, and so on. File titles of the office, or bureau, and so on, by their distinctive names.
   - ▲ United States Government; Army
   - ▲ United States Government; Federal Bureau of Investigation
   - ▲ United States Government; Interior
   - ▲ United States Government; Treasury
   - ▲ United States Government; Veterans Administration

2. *State and local:* State, county, parish, city, town, township, and village governments and political divisions are filed by their distinctive names. The words "county of," "city of," "department of," and the like, if needed and as appropriate, are added for clarity and are considered filing units. Note: If "of" is not part of the official name as written, it is not added.

	AS FILED		
AS WRITTEN	UNIT 1	UNIT 2	UNIT 3
Iowa Highway Patrol	Iowa	Highway	Patrol
Marin County Library	Marin	County	Library
City of Healdsburg	Healdsburg	City	of

3. *Foreign governments:* The distinctive English name is the first filing unit. If needed, the balance of the formal name of the government forms the next filing unit(s). Divisions, departments, and branches follow in sequential order, reversing the written order necessary to give the distinctive name precedence in the filing arrangement.

States, colonies, provinces, cities, and other divisions of foreign governments are filed by their distinctive or official names as spelled in English. Cross-reference written name to official native name where necessary.

	AS FILED			
AS WRITTEN	UNIT 1	UNIT 2	UNIT 3	UNIT 4
Brazil	Brazil			
Paris, France	Paris	France		

MANAGING PAPER-BASED RECORDS

Paper accounts for 95 percent of the filing in the United States, and approximately 80 percent of filed information is never used again.

The advantages of paper records are that they are affordable for an office of any size; they are an acceptable form of record for legal purposes; and people are comfortable working with paper. On the other hand, paper records can take up a great deal of space; they are vulnerable to water and fire damage and to loss; file security can be a problem; and only one person at a time can use a paper document.

Paper filing systems should meet the following guidelines:

- Records necessary for daily operations are easily retrieved. Active files are the ones closest to the user.
- Records accessed infrequently are stored in a separate, less-accessible location.
- Access to confidential information is restricted.
- A retention schedule is developed; records are destroyed when they are no longer of value to the company. (See the sections on Retaining Records and on Transfer and Disposal in this chapter.)

Because storing paper files is so expensive and cumbersome, consider the answer to the following questions before filing paper:

- Must the record be retained in paper form?
- Is it possible to convert the paper record to electronic or micrographic form?
- Is it necessary to have both a printed copy and an electronic copy? Some industries require that certain items be kept as paper. Research whether you need to keep printed or electronic copies. Create clear, logical directories and subdirectories to allow fast electronic retrieval.

- Is the information obtainable from the Internet or from the originator?
- What is the cost of maintaining the paper-based system? For paper records, consider floor space and labor for handling, filing, and retrieving records. For electronic and micrographic systems, consider time and labor to convert paper records to another format and the cost of any special equipment.

Reorganizing an Existing Paper-based Filing System

If information cannot be accessed quickly and stored easily, it can be organized following these steps:

1. Prepare a written list of existing files.
2. Categorize files as active or inactive. Remove inactive files from the list.
3. Decide whether any materials (speeches, public relations material, client files) need to be separated from the main filing system.

HINT: *A special file should contain enough material to fill up half a file drawer.*

4. Organize the inventory list by broad categories. Usually one heading and two subheadings per category are sufficient. Get suggestions from others who are using the files.
5. Make any cross references needed. (See the section on Types of Filing Systems earlier in this chapter.)
6. Prepare a summary list, which is a map of the contents of the drawers with broad categories of material contained in each.

HINT: *Use a database or spreadsheet program or the table feature in a word processing program to create the lists.*

7. Prepare labels to put on the actual files. (See the section Preparation of File Folders below for additional information.)
8. Train those who will use the filing system. Distribute the summary list.

Equipment

With the ever-increasing amount of paper in the office, storage has become a major problem for many companies. Filing equipment is available in a wide range of designs and sizes. No more space should be allocated for records than is necessary.

The following are some of the major types of filing equipment and their uses.

Desk-size filing units and two-drawer file cabinets: These are used for files that are accessed daily; they do not, however, utilize space efficiently.

Four- or five-drawer vertical file cabinets: These are the most popular format for active files. A disadvantage is that they can be used by only one person at a time and may not be accessible to those with disabilities.

Lateral cabinets: These are lengthwise units whose drawers or shelves are opened broadside; they are available with two to six drawers or shelves. When open, all records are visible. They may be used as barriers between working areas, and they require 40 percent less floor space than a four-drawer vertical file cabinet.

Open-shelf file units: These lateral units have open shelves like a bookshelf. They are good for high-volume filing and have the advantage of being accessible to more than one person at the same time. All records are visible. Filing and retrieval can be done approximately 20 to 40 percent more quickly than with file cabinets, and they require 50 percent less floor space than a four-drawer vertical file cabinet. Security, however, is a problem.

High-density mobile filing units: These vertical units make a large number of active documents readily accessible. Floor space is saved by not having aisles between the file units; since the units are on tracks or rails, and they are mobile, only one aisle is ever created at a time. Units can be moved either manually (the user pushes the units back and forth) or mechanically. They can increase file space by as much as 200 percent.

Rotary files: Rotation brings records close to the user with little user movement; some versions are automated. Records may be filed vertically or flat. Only one request can be processed at a time, however.

Heavy cardboard boxes: These boxes (12 by 10 by 15 inches) are used for inactive files; they are sealed and labeled and usually stored away from the main work area. Two letter-size file drawers are equivalent to three boxes. The same size is capable of storing both legal- and letter-size documents, as well as odd-size documents and cards. They are structurally secure over a long period of time and provide some degree of waterproofing.

Selection of Equipment

The selection of filing equipment for paper-based records depends upon determining the following information:

1. The amount of floor space available. Vertical file cabinets take up the most space, followed by lateral and open-shelf cabinets. High-density mobile filing units take the least amount of space. Make sure there is adequate aisle space between cabinets. In addition, determine whether moving inactive files to storage will increase the floor space.

2. Number of people accessing the files at one time. Note that vertical cabinets may be used by only one person at a time. As density increases (seven or eight shelves high), accessibility decreases.

3. The method of filing. Determine the most appropriate method: alphabetical, numeric, subject, or geographic. Decide whether to use top or side tabs or bar codes.

4. Number of files pulled each day.

5. Number of refiles each day.

6. Type and size of records.

7. Security concerns. Open shelving is appropriate in a filing area that is accessible only to authorized personnel. In other areas, use cabinets with doors that lock to restrict access.

8. Weight capacity of existing floor. Consult with a structural engineer for load capacity before purchasing new equipment.

9. Corporate growth plans. Are there plans to merge or consolidate operations? Are there plans to move? If at all possible, purchase standard-sized equipment that is usable in other offices or departments in case of reorganization.

10. Corporate budget for filing and storage.

11. Environmental requirements.

12. Accessibility by persons who have disabilities as required by the Americans with Disabilities Act (ADA).

To determine the cost of a system, follow these steps:

1. Compute the current filing inches of space. 175 pieces of paper = 1 file inch; vertical file cabinet = 25 filing inches per drawer; lateral file cabinet = 50 filing inches per shelf.

2. Convert filing inches to square feet needed for equipment.

EQUIPMENT	AISLE SPACE (INCHES)	TOTAL SQUARE FEET OF OFFICE SPACE NEEDED
Letter-size vertical file	28	7.5
Legal-size vertical file	28	9.0
30-inch lateral cabinet	6	6.5
36-inch lateral cabinet	6	7.0
42-inch lateral cabinet	6	7.5

3. Multiply square feet times the cost of office space per square foot.

For example, Company A requires 2,000 inches of filing space. If approximately 20 four-drawer vertical file cabinets are used, 150 square feet of floor space is needed. If floor space averages $30 a square foot, the total annual floor space costs are $4,500.

In the same example, if high-density mobile files are used, 2,000 inches of filing space would fit in 42 square feet of floor space. If floor space averages $30 a square foot, total annual floor space costs are $1,260.

Filing Supplies

The type of folders you should select depends on the following:

- Size of records
- Length of time the file is active
- Need for special features such as fasteners, pockets, or closed sides
- Anticipated volume

Descriptions of typical types of file folders are in Chapter 9, Office Supplies.

Preparation of File Folders

Follow these steps in preparing file folders:

1. Select folder type (see the previous section, Filing Supplies).
2. Choose third, fifth, two-fifths, shelf, half, or straight cut folder tabs. (See the section on Filing and Records Management Supplies in Chapter 9 for tab descriptions.)
3. Decide on folder weight. (See the section on Filing and Records Management Supplies in Chapter 9 for more information on folder weights and uses.)
4. Determine the organization of the tabs. There are three main types of organizations (see Figure 12-1):

   - *Type one:* Use a set tab position for each category of information to allow for quick retrieval. For example, for an alphabetical list of customers, reserve the first tab position for customers in Arizona, the second position for those in California, and the third position for everyone else.
   - *Type two:* Use the first position tab, then the second position tab, and then the third position tab. This is good for a file system that does not change. If it does change, new file folders are added and items are no longer in order. Finding folders then becomes more time-consuming.
   - *Type three:* Place all title information on the same position on each file folder. Filing new folders in this system is easy.

5. Use a computer to prepare labels.

HINT: *Helvetica bold type font style works well. Use 24-point for headings, 18-point for major subheadings. Capitalize the first letter of each word; headings in all capital letters are difficult to read.*

6. Prepare file labels uniformly.

HINT: *Always start label names in the same location close to the top of the label, with a one- or two-space left margin.*

7. Use simple words, such as "Advertising," "Legal," "Personnel."

HINT: *Omit punctuation.*

8. Use file guides. File guides serve as dividers, precede the file folders, and identify the major or subject headings. Guides are made out of heavy pressboard, fiber, or manila stock. (For additional information, see Chapter 9.)

HINT: *Precede every five to ten folders with a guide.*

9. Include a general or miscellaneous folder for each letter of the alphabet to file any material that has no folder. Place it behind the last name folder under that particular letter, and file material in it alphabetically. Review four times a year to purge

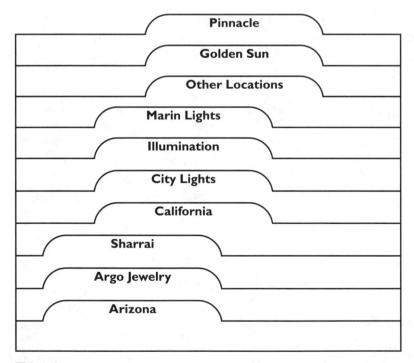

Type I

Figure 12-1 Three types of tab organization.

Type 2

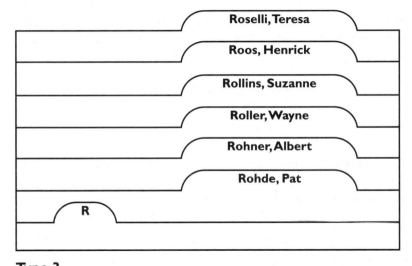

Type 3

Figure 12-1 (continued.)

or refile documents if possible. Start a new folder when a subject has five to ten pages of related documents.

10. Label file drawers.

Color Coding

Color coding may be used with any type of filing system. Colored file folders and labels allow quick identification and location of folders.

Use labels with a color bar at top by assigning a specific color bar to specific file groups. For example, personnel files could be red, customer files might be green, and creditor files could be yellow.

HINT: *Use the same color for labels, binders, and folders if appropriate.*

Use letters or numbers preprinted on a colored and/or patterned background to identify a partial name or subject. For example, the first three letters of a customer's name could be color coded. All customers with names beginning with these first three letters are easily identified as a group. This color-coding system adds an extra step in file preparation.

HINT: *Use the same brand of labels for color-coded alphabetical or numerical labels. Each brand has its own color-coding legend.*

Solid color labels are recommended only when confidentiality is needed; use pastel colors for easy reading. For example, all personnel files could have yellow labels.

The following should be kept in mind when using color:

- Keep the system as simple as possible; e.g., make all the A's one color, all the B's one color, and so on.
- In a numeric filing system use ten colors, since the most common system is based on ten digits.
- Use color folders to indicate certain types of files; e.g., blue could be for correspondence.
- Use different color labels for folders with the same name; e.g., "Steven White, Jr." could have a yellow label; "Steven White, Sr.," a green label.

Filing Documents

Not everything must be filed. Information that will not be used in the future should be thrown away or recycled. Company newsletters, bulletins, newspapers, and vendor catalogs are best placed in a notebook on a bookshelf.

The following tips are helpful when filing:

- Underline or write file headings on documents. Then if an item is removed from the files, it will be refiled in the same folder.
- File documents daily to avoid accumulated filing.
- Remove rubber bands and paper clips; discard envelopes, routing slips, cover memos, and duplicates; staple multipage records together; mend tears with tape.

HINT: *Keep one copy of each draft until the final document is inactive, then discard all previous drafts.*

- Rough-sort documents into major categories; for example, a rough-sort for alphabetic documents is A–L and M–Z.

HINT: *Both alphabetic and numeric sorting organizers are available from office supply sources.*

- File the most recent papers in the front of the folder; place the document facing up, with the top of the page at the left edge of the folder.
- Crease the score marks at the bottom of manila folders when papers are a quarter of an inch thick (about 25 sheets of paper). Manila folders hold approximately 100 pieces of paper. If the folders are not scored for every quarter inch of paper, the file label cannot be seen and the folder will slide into the file drawer or shelf and damage the contents.
- Replace worn folders with new ones.
- Allow 3 to 4 inches of working space in vertical files.

Retrieval and Charge-out

A file can be quickly located if employees charge out files before using them. The following charge-out methods can be used:

Charge-out request: Write down the name of the file (either on a 3-by-5-inch slip of paper or a printed charge-out request); place the charge-out request in an out guide, which is a folder with a pocket for filing documents when the file is missing; remove the charge-out paper when the folder is returned. If the folder is to be used at the filing cabinet, a charge-out request is not necessary.

Out guide: Write on the out guide the name of the folder, when it was removed, and who removed it; place the out guide where the file was located; remove the out guide when the folder is returned. Out guides would be used in the following circumstances in small offices: (1) the file is loaned to someone outside the office; (2) the file is taken outside the office by an employee; or (3) an employee expects to use the file for a week or more. The advantages to using charge-out procedures are as follows:

- Identifies employees using the files.

HINT: *If employees are in a hurry and do not feel they can take the time to complete the charge-out information, assign a special color out guide to be placed in the files in case of emergencies.*

- Allows monitoring of the time a file was taken.

HINT: *Use a color charge-out guide for each week of the month to help identify files missing for longer than necessary. For example, week 1 could be yellow; week 2, red; week 3, green, and so on.*

- Determines activity levels for use of the files.

Safety

The following safety precautions should be observed:

- Close all drawers or reference shelves after using them.
- Open only one drawer of a vertical cabinet at a time to keep the cabinet from tipping over.

HINT: *Newer cabinets are equipped with counterbalances to avoid this problem.*

- Weight the bottom shelf of lateral equipment before loading the top shelf. Once the cabinet is loaded past the middle shelf, it will not tip over.

HINT: *Store paper or folders on the bottom shelf while loading the cabinet for the first time.*

REDUCING PAPER WASTE

Each day American businesses use billions of pieces of paper. Office professionals are constantly dealing with mounting piles of paper and a diminishing amount of storage space. Below are suggestions for reducing paper waste:

- Review and change documents on the computer screen before printing to reduce the number of hard copies and paper drafts. Create only the number of copies actually needed.

HINT: *Use the Print Preview feature of your word processing program.*

- Use e-mail whenever possible; avoid printing unimportant e-mail messages. Review drafts and include comments onscreen and return electronically. Instead of printing a Web page, bookmark it or save the page on your hard drive and access it when needed.

- Adopt policies concerning the desired length of reports, memorandums, and other documents. Single-space the text of final reports.
- Use computer projectors, overhead transparencies, and whiteboards in meetings instead of paper handouts.
- Order supplies on-line.
- Use Internet publishing and electronic forms.
- Store information on computer disks instead of making hard copies.
- Use reusable inter- and intra-office envelopes.
- Reuse paper printed on only one side to print drafts or staple the sheets together to make no-cost scratch pads.
- Use double-sided photocopying whenever possible. Use the size reduction feature offered on many copiers. Train employees on avoiding waste and using the copying machine economically.
- Route general information-type documents instead of making copies for each person or post notices on a bulletin board.
- Check number of copies selected or press reset before copying to avoid getting multiple copies when you need one copy. Help minimize misprints by posting a diagram on how to load specialty papers so documents will be printed correctly.
- Buy small stick-on notes to use in place of full-page fax cover sheets.
- Donate computer printouts and other paper to preschools or elementary schools. Students can use the clean side for painting and drawing.
- Adopt a recycling program and adhere to it.

Nearly half of typical office paper waste is comprised of high-grade office paper, for which there is strong recycling demand.

OBJECT FILING

Video tapes, CDs, and other unusually sized objects need to be organized and filed so they are easily retrievable. These objects are typically filed using a category, name, or date in a specially created cabinet or shelf.

HINT: *Visit stores that specialize in storage containers.*

A cross-reference system may be necessary. The cross-reference system can be computerized using a relational database, which allows sorting by a variety of different categories.

MANAGING ELECTRONIC FILES

Electronic Filing Systems

All software programs have files that need to be stored. It is essential that electronic files be managed properly. Some of the important steps in managing these files are the following:

- Use consistent standards for creating folders or directories and naming files. Follow the same rules as you do with paper files (for example, last name first). Keep the name to approximately 20 characters. If the company frequently corresponds with one customer, add additional information such as dates, author, importance, or subject.
- Periodically clean up electronic files—either eliminate them or store them on disk. A crowded hard disk slows the access speed of finding information because the hard disk head must move farther across the disk to find files.
- Back up important documents. The backup method you should use is determined by the amount of data that you need to store. (See section on Backing Up Software in Chapter 8 for additional information.)
- Store disks and tapes properly, using diskette trays or lateral filing. (See the section on Disk Storage in Chapter 9 for additional information.)

Automated Records Management Systems

Computer software programs known as automated records management systems are used when a paper-based filing system becomes overwhelming to maintain because of the volume of records. These systems can track and analyze the status of documents. The cost of an automated records management system can vary widely.

Automated records management software usually can be operated on existing computer hardware. Imaging and full-text systems may require additional hardware, such as scanners, and a high-capacity storage system, such as optical disks (optical disks are discussed later in this chapter). Networking capabilities make the system accessible to a wide range of employees. The user can see the contents of records.

The advantages of using an automated records management system include the following:

- It provides a method to track files that are not in the filing cabinet.
- It reduces the possibility of misplaced or lost files.
- It generates reports showing who has taken out files and when they are due.
- It helps in making decisions about which records are to be moved to long-term storage.
- Files require less storage space.

- Files can be retrieved quickly.
- Data are easily transportable.

The disadvantages include security problems that stem from unauthorized access, the fact that electronic files are easier to destroy than paper records, the ease of alteration, and the initial cost of the hardware and software.

MICROGRAPHIC TECHNOLOGY

Microforms are photographic reductions of larger documents. Microforms have several advantages. They are an excellent method for storing both active and inactive records, since they take up only a third of the space needed for paper documents. Once recorded, information cannot later be misfiled, since a microform is either a roll or a sheet of film. In addition, microforms are more durable than paper as well as being easily and economically duplicated and economically mailed.

Microforms also have their disadvantages. The initial cost of equipment is high. Readers are necessary (note that readers for microfilm and microfiche are different). Also, microforms must be stored in a controlled environment, and they cannot be updated without refilming.

A microfilm is a roll of film with miniature pictures of pages. A microfiche is a sheet of film with miniature pictures of pages. Both microfilm and microfiche are referred to as microforms.

Microfiche is better for smaller databases; one sheet can store hundreds of images. It is read by placing the fiche on a platen and scanning for the proper index.

Microfilm, although more expensive than microfiche, is one of the most cost-effective methods of storing documents. It is usually used to store large databases of information (typically several thousand images can be stored on one roll of film).

Another way of creating microforms is a method called computer output microfilm/microfiche (COM). Information from the computer is transferred directly to the microfilm/microfiche—it is not printed on paper first. The major advantage of using COM is its speed and the amount of work that can be handled. A COM recorder can film at the rate of 585,000 lines per minute.

Computer-assisted retrieval (CAR) systems can help operators find specific microform images accurately and quickly using a computer. CAR systems consist of (1) a microfilm reader, (2) microfilm cartridges storing the images, and (3) a computer storing the image database. The computer operator enters the document ID number, the database tells the operator which microfilm cartridge to load, and the computer searches for the image.

OPTICAL DISK TECHNOLOGY

Optical disk technology is used with computer systems that communicate with and display images from the optical disk. The disk also works with database software, which organizes and searches the optical disk for the requested images.

Optical disks have several advantages. They are not affected by magnetic fields or other problems that might affect a hard disk. They take up less space than paper storage. Information cannot be misfiled because the computer does the filing and searching. Data can be accessed by a number of authorized operators at the same time.

As with other electronic systems, one disadvantage is the initial cost of equipment. In addition, optical disks may not be acceptable in courts of law in some states as a storage medium. They are also not acceptable to tax authorities as a storage medium.

CD-ROM: The oldest optical disk technology is the CD-ROM. The acronym CD-ROM stands for "compact disk, read-only memory." About the size of a floppy disk, they can store as much as 450 floppy disks. Once recorded, however, a CD-ROM cannot be updated.

CD-R or WORM: CD-R means "CD-Recordable." Recordable CDs are WORM (Write Once, Read Multiple) media that work just like standard CDs. The data on CD-R disks can be read by most CD players, making it a practical way to archive or share data with others. In some cases, a CD-R disk can be written to more than once, but not all drives can read these disks. Data cannot be erased from a CD-R disk for reuse once it has been written. Disks are more durable than tape cartridges and cannot be destroyed by coming into contact with a magnetic field. A number of forms of data can be stored on a CD-ROM, making it possible to mix video, photo-CD images, graphics, sound, and conventional data on a single disk.

CD-RW: CD-RW means Compact Disk-Rewritable. Any particular spot on a CD-RW disk can be erased and rewritten. CD-RW allows a user to record over old data or delete individual files; however, CD-RW disks may not work in all players.

DVD: The acronym DVD stands for Digital Versatile disk. A DVD can store so much data that vendors fit a variety of applications on a single disk. DVDs are available as rewritable. DVD-ROM drives can read CD-ROMs; however, DVD-ROMs are not readable by CD-ROM drives.

Check with an attorney for specific guidance on whether documents stored on optical disk technology can be considered a legal archive.

TRANSFER AND DISPOSAL

When records are transferred from the active filing area to less expensive inactive filing areas, two transfer methods are most commonly used.

The *perpetual* method is used for records that are no longer active because the files have been closed by an event or a date (e.g., legal cases). This method is not suitable for files of a continuous nature. The periodic method is used for records that are regularly transferred after a given time period (e.g., semiannually or annually). Ultimately, vital records are transferred to permanent storage and all other records are destroyed.

HINT: *Create an inventory list of files in each storage box. Place a list in a plastic sheet protector and tape it to the front of the box so you can check the contents without opening the box.*

HINT: *Pack cardboard storage boxes tightly. Records in tightly packed cardboard boxes frequently survive fires.*

A signed authorization is needed to destroy records that have legal retention requirements. This authorization itself becomes a vital record and is proof that destruction was part of normal business operations. If destroyed records are subsequently subpoenaed by a court, the authorization is proof that the records are no longer available. Records that are kept after the legal destroy date can be subpoenaed and used in court.

Three methods of disposal are available. Nonconfidential records can be discarded as wastepaper or recycled. Confidential records can first be shredded, then discarded or recycled. If the volume of records to be disposed of is large, a records management service firm can be hired to eliminate them.

FORMS MANAGEMENT

Forms are either on preprinted paper or on a computer screen. They contain permanent information with blank spaces for variable information. From 85 to 90 percent of the costs of filling out forms are for the personnel who complete, process, and use them. The goal of forms management is to minimize the cost of forms and at the same time increase work efficiency and effectiveness. These goals can be accomplished by following these steps:

- Consolidate or eliminate unnecessary forms. Determine if the form is needed. Analyze other forms to find relationships or duplications. Decide whether the forms or items on the form can be combined, eliminated, or simplified.
- Automate forms applications and systems. Maintain a computer listing of all approved forms. Investigate forms design software packages. Become familiar with designing forms using the features of a word processing package. Allow employees to fill in business forms on-line.
- Maintain a forms file that includes specification sheets, design copies, order histories, and copies of all forms.

- Centralize purchasing and printing for cost savings.
- Review all forms annually or when equipment or procedures change.

DESIGNING FORMS

The following are components of effective business form design:

- Use an existing form to create a document template with the form feature of your word processing program. Create Web-based forms using HTML or an on-line forms builder. Use Adobe Acrobat Reader.
- Design forms so they look proper when printed. A printed version is necessary for users who do not wish to use the computer form.
- Avoid creating documents in sizes that are difficult to file or microfilm. Make certain that the form fits in a business envelope. If the form is printed, use paper of appropriate weight and quality.
- Include requests for all important information (e.g., area code, ZIP code). Make certain the instructions are adequate. Avoid unnecessary information and illegal questions.
- Group items so the user can concentrate on one small area at a time. It is best to put the most frequently used items at the top of the form.
- Use checklists and boxes for information. In addition, use radio buttoms and dropdown menus for online forms. Place instructions above the lines or the boxes.
- For printed forms, avoid having too many words and lines on a page, and use a combination of dark and light lines to guide the reader's eyes through the form. Use light single lines as guides; use heavy lines for major breaks; use double lines to break up the form into distinct sections or for totals.
- Use several type sizes and styles, including bold and italic, to draw attention to important items.
- Avoid wide margins unless they are needed for binding, because wide margins waste paper.
- Make sure lines and boxes are of adequate size to enter data.
- Include a form number and revision date in a standard location, such as a lower corner; identify forms with the organization's name and address. Include the company logo if the form is used outside the organization.
- Use color only if it serves a purpose.
- For printed forms, multipart forms are often the least costly way to duplicate information.
- Number all pages of multipage forms.

Identify each copy on its face if appropriate; for example, Copy 1—Office; Copy 2—Customer; Copy 3—Accounting.

SECURITY OF RECORDS AND DISASTER PROTECTION

Maintaining the security of records is an important part of protecting the assets of an organization. The following tips help secure written, oral, and computerized data:

1. Lock files when they are not in use; secure the office and file keys.
2. Audit who uses the files and for what reasons.
3. No matter the size of the business, a records retention schedule is necessary. Before shredding documents, follow the organization's records retention schedule and consult with an attorney to resolve any questions about the legality of shredding documents. Smaller businesses should shred banking information, corporate financial data, sales plans and strategies, legal documents, customer identification numbers, social security numbers, credit card receipts, canceled checks, and billing statements.
4. Avoid leaving confidential information on desks accessible to the public, on the computer screens, in the fax output tray, or in the copy machine.
5. Protect computer passwords and system dial-in phone numbers; change passwords often; do not post passwords in the work area.
6. Consider purchasing a screen privacy filter, which eliminates side viewing of the computer monitor.
7. Log off the computer system before leaving the terminal.
8. Use tamper-proof interoffice envelopes.
9. Use virus protection software and update virus definitions frequently.
10. Never launch any e-mail attachment that contains software programs or macros without checking with the sender to see what the attachment contains. Suspicious files end in .vbs (Visual Basic Script, a software coding language) or .exe (executable, a software program). Files that end in .doc (word processing files) or .xls (spreadsheet files) can contain macro viruses and also warrant caution.
11. Exercise caution when downloading files.
12. Don't allow all employees to load their own software. An unskilled person may inadvertently damage software while loading it onto their computer, thereby creating or increasing the likelihood of a virus.
13. Watch out for hoaxes before forwarding virus warnings to your entire mail list.
14. Establish a backup schedule for data. Do a backup before every new installation. Consider a backup service.

15. Store backup copies off-site.
16. Make certain security systems are functioning properly, keep a sufficient number
    of lights on at night, and pay attention to the trash bins and other closed objects.

Loss from natural disasters such as earthquakes, floods, hurricanes, and tornadoes can be
minimized by storing the original vital documents at a remote site and keeping only copies
on-site. Consider locations with temperature and humidity control and file protection that
sprays the inert gas Halon instead of water.

Business records provide management with information to make sound decisions. They also provide a measurement of an organization's stability and its potential for growth.

Office professionals often have the responsibility to collect and present the data required for accurate records. In smaller companies, these responsibilities may include handling cash, checking accounts, bank reconciliations, payroll, and billing as well as journal entries and posting transactions and preparing financial statements. In larger companies these financial responsibilities are more time-consuming and complex; they require a greater level of specialization. Most office professionals use specialized software applications ranging in complexity from simple checking account management to fully integrated systems.

Regardless of the size of the company or the amount of technology used, office professionals must understand basic bookkeeping principles. Owners of home-based businesses need a working knowledge of bookkeeping procedures to communicate with their accountants or to handle the bookkeeping work on their own. Realizing *why* a process is done a specific way will help a worker avoid or locate errors that may occur and make the work more meaningful, challenging, and profitable.

CHAPTER 13

FINANCIAL

RECORDKEEPING

UNDERSTANDING TERMS

The accounting/bookkeeping field uses a language of its own. To do simple bookkeeping tasks or select accounting software, you should know the vocabulary.

General Terms

Financial and managerial accounting are the two major accounting classifications. The goal of **financial accounting** is to prepare financial statements and present them to interested individuals outside the company. **Bookkeeping** involves procedures for recording financial data and is part of the financial accounting process.

Managerial accounting requires much of the same information accumulated in the financial accounting process, but management uses the information to plan, schedule, and control the company's internal activities. Cost accounting, financial forecasting (budgeting), auditing, and income tax accounting involve additional specialized accounting functions. For an understanding of these advanced levels, office professionals need additional classes or study.

Companies operate on either an accrual basis or a cash basis. Operating on an **accrual basis** means that all revenue and expenses are recorded at the time they are incurred regardless of when cash is actually received or expended. Companies operating on a **cash basis** record revenue only when cash is received, and they record expenses only when cash is disbursed.

In the **double-entry** system of accounting, both a debit entry and a credit entry are required in the **journal** and the **ledger** for any transaction that involves an exchange of money or property or that adjusts or corrects existing information. A debit is entered on the *left side* of a ledger account; a credit is entered on the *right side*. When recording transactions, the total debits must equal the total credits.

Most businesses use the double-entry system of accounting, whether they record their entries manually or electronically. However, some small businesses use the simpler **single-entry** system, in which each transaction is entered only once as a sum due to or owed by the company.

To be consistent and provide an orderly recording of financial information, a company must identify the accounts it expects to use and give a number to each account. This **chart of accounts** is used to identify the accounts that must be charged when making entries in journals and ledgers. (See Figure 13-1.)

HINT: *Most software programs provide numerous choices for a chart of accounts. Select one or customize one that fits your specific business.*

A **journal** is a diary in which daily business transactions are recorded from source documents such as checks, invoices, and cash register tapes. Journal formats vary. Some companies use a **general journal** and record *all* transactions in it. (See Figure 13-2.) Others use a combined journal form. (See Figure 13-3.)

Each account in the chart of accounts has a space in the **general ledger**. (See Figure 13-4.) In addition to a general ledger, companies may use **accounts receivable ledgers** (records of customers who owe money) (see Figure 13-5) and **accounts payable ledgers** (records of creditors to whom money is owed).

Account Classifications

There are several standard classifications of accounts. **Assets** are items that are owned by a company. **Current assets** include cash, inventory, and other assets that have a high probability of being turned into cash readily, usually within a year. **Plant assets** are long-term assets, such as equipment and land, with benefits that carry over into future accounting periods. Asset accounts increase on the debit side and decrease on the credit side of a ledger.

Liabilities are amounts owed or services yet to be rendered by a company. They also are broken down into current and long-term accounts. Accounts payable and salaries

CORNER BOOKKEEPING SERVICE
Chart of Accounts

100–199 ASSETS
110	Cash
111	Petty Cash
120	Accounts Receivable
130	Prepaid Insurance
140	Prepaid Rent
150	Office Supplies
160	Office Equipment
161	Accumulated Depreciation on Office Equipment
170	Office Furniture
171	Accumulated Depreciation on Office Furniture

200–299 LIABILITIES
210	Accounts Payable

300–399 OWNER'S EQUITY
310	D. R. Johnson, Capital
320	D. R. Johnson, Drawing
399	Income Summary

400–499 REVENUE
410	Service Fees

500–599 EXPENSES
510	Salaries Expense
520	Supplies Expense
530	Insurance Expense
540	Rent Expense
550	Utilities Expense
551	Telephone Expense
560	Depreciation Expense/Office Equipment
561	Depreciation Expense/Office Furniture

Figure 13-1 Chart of accounts for a service company/single proprietor.

GENERAL JOURNAL   Page_____

Date		Entry Description	Ref.	Debit	Credit
20–					
Sept.	4	Equipment		1995 00	
		Accounts Payable/ Donnelly Corp.			1995 00

Figure 13-2 General journal/double-entry system.

Combination Journal for Month of_____ 20_____   Page_____

Cash		Ck #	Date	Explanation of Entry	Ref.	General		Accounts Receivable		Accounts Payable		Service Income	Salaries Expense	Utilities Expense
Dr	Cr					Dr	Cr	Dr	Cr	Dr	Cr	Cr	Dr	Dr
	$1,800	4	June 3	Rent Expense		$1,800								
$980			June 4	Sales				$2,000				$2,980		

Figure 13-3 Combined journal/double-entry system.

payable are examples of **current liabilities.** A mortgage is an example of a **long-term liability.** Liability accounts decrease on the debit side and increase on the credit side of a ledger.

Equity, which is also called capital or net worth, represents the owner's claim (single proprietorship) or owners' claims (partnership) against the firm's assets after subtracting the liabilities. In corporations, owner's equity is called *stockholders' equity* or *shareholders' investment* with a breakdown of common and preferred stock. Owner's equity accounts decrease on the debit side and increase on the credit side of a ledger.

Revenue results from the sale of goods, the rendering of services, or the use of money or property. Revenue accounts decrease on the debit side and increase on the credit side of a ledger account. **Expenses** are the costs involved in an effort to produce

ACCOUNTS PAYABLE   **ACCOUNT NO. 210**

Date		Explanation	Ref.	Debit		Credit		Debit Balance		Credit Balance	
20–											
Sept.	4	Inv. 9920A	G201			1995	00			1995	00

Figure 13-4 Accounts payable account in the general ledger.

Wm. Weiler Associates   Credit Referrals: _____

2092 North Oak Street _____

Des Moines, IA 50301 _____

Telephone: 515-633-9201   Checking Account Reference: _____

Fax: 515-633-9222 _____

e-mail: msmith@wmweil.com

Comments:

Date		Entry Description	Ref.	Debit		Credit		Balance	
20–									
Oct.	1	Balance	✔					83,000	89
	18	Sales Invoice AJ965	SJ90	396	40			83,397	29
	29	CK9065	CR550			83,000	89	396	40

Figure 13-5 Customer's record in accounts receivable ledger.

revenue. Expense accounts increase on the debit side and decrease on the credit side of a ledger account. Categories of expenses may include general, selling, and administrative.

Financial Statements

Financial statements are reports on the operations or financial position of a business during a given fiscal (or financial) period or on a given date. An **income statement** shows

SPORTING GOODS, INC.
Income Statement
For the Month Ended March 31, 20__

Operating Revenue

Sales		$327,000.00	
Less Sales Returns and Allowances	$800.00		
Sales Discounts	500.00	1,300.00	
Net Sales			$325,700.00

Cost of Goods Sold

Merchandise Inventory, March 1, 20__		$80,000.00	
Merchandise Purchases	$150,000.00		
Less Purchases Returns and Allowances	$3,000.00		
Purchases Discount	6,900.00	9,900.00	
Net Purchases		140,100.00	
Merchandise Available for Sale		220,100.00	
Less Merchandise Inventory, March 31, 20__		85,000.00	
Cost of Goods Sold			135,100.00
Gross Profit on Sales			$190,600.00

Operating Expenses

Selling Expenses			
Sales Salaries Expense	$85,000.00		
Supplies Expense	6,000.00		
Delivery Expense	1,500.00		
Advertising Expense	12,000.00		
Total Selling Expense		$104,500.00	
Administrative Expenses			
Office Salaries Expense	$22,000.00		
Rent Expense	15,000.00		
Utilities Expense	3,000.00		
Insurance Expense	3,000.00		
Office Operations Expense	550.00		
Telephone Expense	1,200.00		
Depreciation Expense/Equipment	500.00		
Total Administrative Expenses		45,250.00	
Total Operating Expenses			149,750.00
Net Income			$40,850.00

Figure 13-6 Income statement.

SPINNETI LAWN AND GARDEN SUPPLIES
Balance Sheet
March 31, 20___

ASSETS

Current Assets

Cash		$25,000.00
Petty Cash Fund		100.00
Notes Receivable		3,000.00
Accounts Receivable	$30,000.00	
Less Allowance for Uncollectible Accounts	600.00	29,400.00
Merchandise Inventory		83,000.00
Supplies		200.00
Prepaid Insurance		2,500.00
Total Current Assets		$143,200.00

Plant and Equipment

Equipment	$15,000.00	
Less Accumulated Depreciation/Equip't.	4,000.00	11,000.00
Total Assets		$154,200.00

LIABILITIES

Notes Payable		$18,000.00
Accounts Payable		39,000.00
Salaries Payable		9,500.00
Sales Tax Payable		5,900.00
Total Liabilities		$72,400.00

OWNER'S EQUITY

Tony Spinneti, Capital	$81,800.00
TOTAL LIABILITIES AND OWNER'S EQUITY	$154,200.00

Figure 13-7 Balance sheet for a single proprietorship.

whether a firm operated at a profit or at a loss during a fiscal period, which may be a year, a quarter, or a month. If revenue is greater than expenses, there is a net income; if expenses are greater than revenue, there is a net loss. The **cost of goods sold** section of the income statement represents what you paid for the items you have actually sold.

A **balance sheet** includes three major classifications of accounts: assets, liabilities, and owner's/shareholders' equity. It shows the financial picture of a business on a specific date rather than during a fiscal period. The balance sheet tells a firm's story through financial ratios, which can be used to compare present performance with past records and with records of other firms in the industry. For example, to determine whether a firm can cover its debts, determine the current ratio. To calculate a firm's current ratio, divide its current assets by its current liabilities. If the current ratio is two, the firm could cover its debts twice.

HINT: *Dun and Bradstreet, Inc., publishes industry averages for more than 100 industries. The* Annual Statement Studies *of Robert Morris Associates contains ratios for more than 300 industries.*

A **statement of owner's equity** shows any changes in the owner's claim as a result of additional investments, net income, or net loss; it also shows any draws against the company by the owner. A **statement of retained earnings** shows the changes in income that have occurred but that have not been paid out as dividends to stockholders. The **statement of cash flow** shows the status of cash to cover liabilities. The cash flow statement identifies the changes in cash balances caused by doing business.

Headings are very important on financial statements. Each heading must include the company name, the name of the statement, and the date or time period of the statement. Dollar signs should be next to the first figure in a column and next to all totals. Decimals must align. Double rules indicate that a process is complete.

HINT: *Some accounts may be of more interest than others to your supervisor. Highlight these accounts on any financial statements or reports directed to your department.*

Business Structure

The way a business is organized determines its tax and legal liabilities. A **sole proprietorship** is owned and operated by one individual. It is the simplest structure, since all profits or losses as well as all tax and legal liabilities are the owner's. A sole proprietor must meet all local or state licensing and permit requirements and pay quarterly estimated income taxes. If there are employees, the owner must collect payroll taxes like any other employer.

A **general partnership** is a joint venture with the partners sharing skills, profits, responsibilities, and liabilities equally or on a percentage basis. Each partner is liable for the actions of the other partners, and this applies whether the partner is directly involved in the action or not. Partners report profits or losses on their personal tax returns, but the partnership must have an IRS identification number. In a **limited partnership,** a partner invests a specific amount and limits losses to that amount. Profits are distributed according to the partnership agreement. A legal contract is a wise investment when establishing any type of partnership.

A **corporation** is a separate taxable and legal entity; therefore, personal assets are usually protected. Corporations pay income taxes that are separate from those of the investors. Corporations are also able to obtain capital through the issuance of stock offerings. Two types of corporations primarily used by small family businesses or home-based businesses are the **close corporation** and the **Subchapter S Corporation.** All corporation structures require completion of an Articles of Incorporation form. The Secretary of State's office provides the forms and outlines the requirements to establish a corporation. Legal assistance is helpful when establishing a corporation, especially if other investors are involved.

SELECTING SOFTWARE FOR FINANCIAL RECORDKEEPING

Computerized accounting programs range from programs that produce checks and reconcile bank statements to multiuser, fully integrated systems on a network. There are computer applications for point of sale, accounts receivable, accounts payable, inventory control, payroll, job costing, billing, order entry, and general ledger. Software applications are also available for specific industries and job tasks.

Depending on a firm's needs, the software may be a single application or several integrated applications. Integrated programs allow additional functions to be added as these functions become necessary. Multiuser software depends on a network that allows many users to be online at one time.

General Accounting Software Considerations

Numerous accounting packages are available, so it is important to investigate them thoroughly before purchasing one. Analyze what works well and what weaknesses exist in the present system.

Here are some questions to ask when you select accounting software:

- What are the hardware or system requirements? Is there enough storage capacity to run the program and handle the number of transactions the business requires?
- Do modules operate individually or do they rely on a general ledger package? Are the modules interactive? Is it a single entry or double entry program?
- Is the chart of accounts flexible? Can you mask account format? *Masking* allows a user to specify general ledger account numbers of varying lengths, which permits departmental or other types of subaccounts.
- Are forms predefined or can you create your own formats?
- Do the financial reports provide information for comparative balances, such as budget to actual or current year to previous year? Do they provide year-to-date balances and indicate percentages of increase or decrease in the various accounts? Does the software provide reports on both cash and accrual operations?
- Are transactions automatically posted to the general ledger immediately after they have been entered? Are recurring and reversing entries made automatically? For example, by coding entries that should be reversed, the software makes and

posts the reversing entry on the first day of the next month. Does it allow for batch or real-time posting?

- Is there an effective audit trail procedure?
- Does the program allow data to be exported from or imported to other software programs? If so, which ones? Can the data be displayed in colorful, graphic formats?
- Does the software application require other programs, such as a specific operating system? Can you select the type of business, such as a dental office or a photography studio?
- Does the software offer contact management features to allow tracking information about customers and suppliers? Is the program capable of printing mailing labels? Will it allow printing on standard business forms? Does it include electronic postage?
- How long has the software company been in business? How frequently does the software company update its software? Do the updates add new features or do they just fix the inconsistencies?

HINT: *Other companies may already use the software application you are investigating. Ask for their input before you make a final decision. Check on-line services for accounting software information as well as discussion forums.*

- How difficult is the application to learn? Some applications require an extensive accounting background; others make it easier for nonaccountants to establish a system. Are there onscreen help menus and tutorials? Is the documentation easy to understand and indexed for quick reference? Does the software manufacturer have a toll-free number to call for assistance?

HINT: *A software program exists that analyzes a company's needs, compares accounting software programs, and lists several packages that meet the company's specifications. For information about this software, Software Compare, call PTC, 800–323–8724.*

- Is the software designed specifically for handling global transactions? Is it capable of dealing quickly with multiple currency conversions? Is there foreign language support onscreen and in the documentation? Can the program print checks and other business forms in the language and currencies of different countries? Can it convert English measurements to metric and vice versa? Does the program collect tax information by country and cover international tax regulations?

(Additional help for choosing accounting applications may be found in Chapter 8.)

Spreadsheets

Managers need well-designed spreadsheets to analyze such areas as budgets, sales performances, and inventory levels. Spreadsheets show how different variables or figures affect the end results without reentering data for each process. Users enter formulas and sets of figures to arrive at percentages, totals, or correlations.

Some guidelines for preparing spreadsheets include:

- Find out what your spreadsheet can and cannot do. Check its graphics capabilities if your supervisor uses the information for presentations.

HINT: *Spreadsheet software produces many types of graphs, including bar and pie graphs. Check for a feature that tells you which type of graph works best for the data displayed.*

HINT: *Specialized add-in software reads a spreadsheet file and displays the data in unique ways. For example, a map add-in can display sales volume ($1–$2 million, less than $1 million, etc.) in color by regions or by states.*

- Check the accuracy of the figures. If a total does not seem accurate, check the formula again or bring it to the attention of your supervisor.
- Maintain notes detailing how you arrived at spreadsheet data and its sources. This is especially helpful when you do the spreadsheet infrequently and forget the procedures.
- Find out if the totals are to be placed at the bottom or on the right of the page. Ask your supervisor if percentages or ratios are necessary or if there is a preference for graphs or another type of display.
- Ask questions if you do not understand the basic spreadsheet concepts or the purpose of the spreadsheet. Elaborate graphics cannot camouflage unclear thinking.
- Design the spreadsheet for its end use. Know the group who will view the spreadsheet. Determine fonts, page breaks, spreadsheet name, and type size. To save setup time, try to use similar formats for other work required in spreadsheet form.
- Purge spreadsheets that have formula errors so they are not imported into other documents. Keep a list showing what files are linked to which spreadsheets.

HANDLING CASH RECEIPTS/ACCOUNTS RECEIVABLE

When a business uses a cash register to record its sales, a tape or computer data inside the register shows each sale and the total sales for the day. When a business issues receipts for the cash it receives, the receipts should be prenumbered for security purposes. Cash register tapes and copies of the receipts to customers are the source documents for recording sales and cash receipts. Cash and checks should be deposited daily.

If you obtain funds for others, place the money in a sealed envelope and separate it from other cash. Handle checks made payable to cash with extreme care. Indicate the amount on the outside of the envelope and on a sheet of paper that goes inside the envelope with the money. Insist that the money be re-counted by the person accepting it.

Checks

The party who signs the check is known as the **maker** or **drawer.** The financial institution upon which the check is drawn is the **drawee,** and the party who will receive payment is the **payee.**

When checks are received in payment for goods and services, check for signatures, correct dates, and correct amounts. The figure on the check must match the written amount. If it does not, return the check to the maker or obtain written verification of the correct amount.

If the payee's name is written incorrectly on the face of the check, the payee should endorse it as written and then endorse it again correctly before depositing. If a check is received and funds are not available to cover it, call the maker of the check immediately to determine how payment is to be covered. If there is no check after three days, ask for 24-hour payment in cash, money order, or certified check. Retain the dishonored check in your files.

HINT: *A company may call the bank to verify that sufficient funds are available to cover the check at that specific time. The caller will not be told how much money is in the account.*

Endorsement

All checks require immediate endorsement. An **endorsement** is a signature that transfers ownership of a check or other negotiable instrument. All checks, as well as traveler's checks, money orders, and bank drafts, require a blank, full, or restrictive endorsement. The place for an endorsement is at the left end of the back of a check.

A **blank endorsement** means only the signature of the payee appears. (See Figure 13-8.) A check with such an endorsement should never be sent through the mail and is not recommended for general business use.

Occasionally, a business will use a **full endorsement.** A full endorsement transfers ownership of a check to someone other than the payee. The payee endorses the check and in addition writes "Pay to the order of" and the name of the party to whom the check is being transferred. (See Figure 13-9.)

A **restrictive endorsement** is the most common type of endorsement used by businesses, since it limits the way a check can be used. A typical restrictive endorsement includes "For Deposit Only," the bank's name, depositor's name, and account number. This

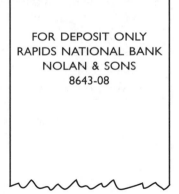

Figure 13-8 Blank endorsement.

Figure 13-9 Full endorsement (also, qualified endorsement).

Figure 13-10 Restrictive endorsement.

type of endorsement provides the safest method of transferring a check. (See Figure 13-10.) Most companies use a stamp or machine to endorse checks quickly and safely. For security purposes, keep the stamp for endorsing checks in a locked drawer.

Procedures for Making Bank Deposits

A **deposit ticket** preprinted with the identification number of the bank and the account number of the customer provides a record of the deposit for the bank and for the depositor. A signed **signature card** on file at the bank gives an employee the authorization to make deposits as well as to sign checks. It is necessary to have a signature card on file at the bank for each employee who has this authorization.

The following procedures for handling bank deposits should help you to speed up banking transactions.

- Use coin wrappers, provided by banks, for large quantities of coins. Write the amount, name, and number of the account on the outside of the wrapper before filling it with coins. Inexpensive counters are available that automatically sort coins.
- Place bills of the same denomination face up in the bill wrappers supplied by the bank. If the bills are not all the same denomination, arrange them so the largest denominations are on top and the smaller denominations are on the bottom. Secure these bills with a rubber band. Record the amount of money included in each wrapper.
- Prepare deposit slips in duplicate. Keep one copy until the bank reconciliation process is complete and all deposits are acknowledged.
- List the coins, currency, and amounts for each check on the deposit slip. If checks are drawn on the same bank, list them together. To identify checks, use the name of the bank on which the check is drawn or use the numbers on the top half of the

American Bankers Association (ABA) number. ABA numbers indicate the state or city of the bank and the bank number. The numbers in the bottom half of the ABA number indicate a Federal Reserve number and are not necessary on the deposit slip. Arrange the checks so they are in the same order as they are listed on the deposit slip.

- Total the currency, coin, and check amounts and place the total in the appropriate location on the deposit slip and also in the checkbook or check register. A check register not only has check forms but also space to record detailed information about the checks.

- Deposit the money by taking it directly to the bank or by using the night depository. Never mail coins or currency, only checks. Banks provide special bags to customers for making night deposits. Do not use the bank's drive-up facility if transactions are complicated. Most banks have commercial windows for their customers.

Procedures for Handling Customer Billing/Collections

The accounts receivable function is an area that is often turned over to an outside vendor. Many companies also have added e-commerce as a retail venue. In both situations, the customer may have no direct personal contact with the company from which they purchased the merchandise or received the service until a problem occurs—and often the problem is in the billing process. Companies must remember that efficient customer service is more important than fancy products, logos, or Web sites.

The billing task is one of the final steps in a sequence that begins with selling merchandise to a credit customer. The **sales invoice** includes all the details of the sale and is the source document necessary for making journal and ledger entries. A company's favorable cash flow depends on prompt payments by its customers. The longer accounts are outstanding, the longer it takes to collect them; some will remain uncollectible. The following are useful guidelines for office professionals who handle the various stages of paper billing and collections:

- Review each item of merchandise on the customer's purchase order to be certain descriptions match stock numbers and prices. Update telephone and address changes.

- Number all invoices, as numbered invoices are easier to track.

- Check the pricing options and the credit terms for approval.

- Verify the extensions and recalculate the totals on the customer's purchase order.

- Initial the purchase order after completing a task. A purchase order that has a verification stamp with each task listed in sequence is helpful in tracking the sequence of responsibility.

- Prepare multiple copies of the sales invoice and distribute the copies as follows: sales representative/sales, inventory control, shipping and transportation, accounts receivable/accounting, and two copies for the reminder file. To eliminate errors in filing and distribution, use different colors for each copy.

- Post the information on the sales invoice to the accounts receivable subsidiary ledger, which is a record of a customer's new sales as well as payments on previously purchased merchandise.
- Maintain a chronological file to control the dates when payments are due.
- Send invoices promptly. Include penalty clauses for late payments in bold print on the invoices. Some companies prefer cycle billing and send bills to certain preestablished groups throughout the month. Arranging groups by sections of the alphabet, by account numbers, or by geographic locations works equally well for cycle billing. Some companies believe that sending invoices to arrive by the first of the month improves on-time payments. Others invoice the same day they ship the goods or perform the service.
- View the collection process from the customer's point of view. Assume that the customer who does not pay has a valid reason for nonpayment.
- Send one of the reminder invoices to notify a customer that payment was due five days after the due date. Include a short note, such as: "We noticed that your invoice is X days old. We are sending a copy of the original sales invoice so you can review the details of the purchase you made with us. We hope that you found the shipment satisfactory. Please call us if we can help you." Include a name and telephone number.

HINT: *Use colorful stickers on reminder messages to clients or small-sized companies. Stickers such as "Thank you for your prompt payment" also show appreciation to the clients who pay on time.*

- Call the customer two weeks after an invoice due date to inquire if the merchandise was satisfactory and if the invoice and reminder were received and approved for payment. Ask, "Have we been delivering service the way that you expected?" If clients are known to be slow in paying, make this call the *day after* the due date. Have the necessary information available, such as the invoices that have not been paid, amounts of discounts, and returned merchandise credits so you can answer all questions and do not have to make another call.

HINT: *Before making the call to a customer, think positively. Your voice should not sound harsh or angry.*

HINT: *In order to remember nonpayment reasons or conversations, use the computer to take notes or write them on the invoice or aged report. Report any changes in a customer's payment pattern to your supervisor.*

- Send the second of the reminder invoices (if payment is still ignored) three weeks after the first reminder. Include a short note indicating that you reviewed the account and noticed that the customer always paid promptly. Again, extend an offer to help. You may also call to ask for a specific amount by a certain day. Do not sound desperate or apologize for asking for payment. Do not question a customer's reasons for not paying. Do not harass or threaten the customer; your company may still want their business.

- If necessary, follow this notification with a series of reminder letters. Each letter becomes more insistent, and the time between letters becomes shorter. Do not bother sending notices by special mail services; delinquent payers can simply refuse delivery.
- Send a collection letter that is both courteous and specific. Gimmick letters, such as the "string attached" theme, may work once, but only if a specific course of action is outlined and a direct request for payment is made. Never overwhelm the message with the gimmick.

HINT: *Write clearly. The reader should be able to read and grasp the meaning of the letter in 10 seconds.*

- Get to know the people in charge of handling your invoices. Give the process a personal touch. Keep a list of each company's employees who are authorized to charge for merchandise or service. If an invoice is sent to the wrong person, it may have to be rerouted. Along the way, it can be misplaced or even ignored.
- Prepare reports to assist management in identifying credit problems and slow-paying customers. An aged accounts receivable report shows those accounts that are overdue by 30, 60, 90, or more than 90 days. (See Figure 13-11.) An aged accounts receivable report arranged by salesperson flags problems unique in specific areas or with specific personnel. A report that arranges outstanding balances from

HICKSON DISTRIBUTORS
Aged Accounts Receivable
August 31, 20—

Customer Name	Inv	Inv Date	Terms	Days			
				0–30	31–60	61–90	90+
Arnold, C.L.	89651	June 15	n/30		359.00		
Bixby Metal	90311	July 15	n/30	865.20			

Figure 13-11 Aged accounts receivable report.

the highest to the lowest identifies those to be collected first. Companies must make prompt decisions concerning continued sales to slow-paying customers.

- Select a reputable credit collection agency with a proven collection record as a last step. Some law firms specialize in debt collection and may be as reasonable with their fees as the collection agencies. In normal economic times, anything 90 days and beyond is material for special collectors or an agency. Agencies work on a contingency basis, sometimes keeping a substantial portion of the collections as their fee. If a customer files for bankruptcy, do not request payment after you receive the filing notice. You can be held in contempt of court.

- If mail is being returned and the client's phone has been disconnected, turn over the account to a collection agency or lawyer immediately.

Considerations for E-Commerce Sales and Collections

Many companies are aggressively pursuing the e-commerce trend, and company managers expect their sales, finance, and purchasing employees to have an awareness of e-commerce basics. Office professionals often have the task of troubleshooting problems in e-commerce.

HINT: *The* E-Commerce Question and Answer Book *is available through the American Management Association (212–586–8100).*

The following suggestions apply to e-commerce transactions:

- Provide a toll-free number for customers to call for specific answers to questions. Many clients still prefer a person's voice responding to their requests.

- Include a Frequently Asked Questions section on your Web site.

- Provide a Web callback link. Customers can click on the link, enter their number, and connect to someone in the company.

- To decrease the number of client questions, post product information and user manuals so customers can download them.

- Verify the customer's credit history. Use a credit reporting firm such as Equifax (www.equifax.com) or Trans Union (www.transunion.com). Business data is easy to obtain, but information about an individual's creditworthiness is more involved. Your application is carefully screened before you obtain access to areas such as employment, educational background, and previous addresses.

HINT: *You can obtain credit reports by phone, fax, postal mail, or on-line. Be aware that companies have different ways to report the items.*

- Update tax calculations, shipping information, e-mail addresses, and catalog product information when and where necessary.

- Include the company's Web address on all correspondence to existing customers and encourage them to use the Web site. Be sure there is a support system in place once customers do decide to use the Web site. Send e-mail notices to customers announcing new products or special services that are available at the place of business or on the Web.

HINT: *Even if users do not order on-line, they often research the products on-line before they buy.*

ACCOUNTS RECEIVABLE/BILLING SOFTWARE

Companies use accounts-receivable software applications to encourage prompt collections and therefore increase their cash flow. With the increase in the number of service-oriented businesses, time-on-task billing is becoming critical for their success. In these instances, time spent on each process needs to be monitored to see how much it costs to produce the revenue being generated. Although the monitoring may be documented manually, it is more effectively controlled by using a computer program.

Accounts receivable and billing functions may be two separate application modules or they may be combined. The following questions will assist office professionals as they research this software:

- Have I browsed the Web site of the software publisher before making recommendations or decisions to purchase?
- Is there a limit to the number of receivable accounts the software can handle? Is the numbering system flexible? Are the customer database records customizable? Do the invoice and sales receipt forms look professional?
- Does the software automatically update such records as inventory, job costing, and the general ledger? Is invoicing done within the accounts receivable module or is a separate module for billing necessary? Does the software application include credit-card authorization?
- Does the software provide the option of handling customer accounts using either the balance-forward method or the open-item method (each invoice a separate record)? Does it allow the user to identify codes for terms and credit lines so selected customers may receive payment terms different from other customers? Can it figure freight charges on pretax amounts? Does it automatically calculate finance charges and discounts? Does it compare discounts offered to discounts actually taken?
- When are invoices printed—at the time they are entered, at the end of the fiscal period, or periodically according to the billing cycle? Does the software application provide alerts when customers exceed credit limits?

- Are aged reports printed? If so, for how many periods (30 to 60 days, 61 to 90 days, and so forth)? Are there other reports showing collections, amounts outstanding, payment due dates, sales by item, individual customer ledgers, and a general ledger control listing? Are prior-year comparisons possible? Is there a graphics option for reports?

- Does the software application issue a warning when a customer is a slow payer or has an overdue balance? Does it generate appropriate notices and collection letters? Can you move easily between the accounts receivable application and a word processing application?

- Is it possible to keep track of the number and amount of sales made by each salesperson? Can data be sorted by such items as ZIP code, customer type, or volume of sales? Can data be reported showing the most popular products and the customers who provided the most revenue?

- Does the software application automatically handle repetitive billings? Does it automatically apply finance charges and sales taxes? Can it handle multiple states' sales taxes and prepare the quarterly sales tax returns?

- Is data entry fast? After the initial entry, an operator should have to enter only a customer number, an item code, a shipping code, and quantity. Names, addresses, dates, and calculations should be filled in automatically.

- Can the software application keep track of time spent on multiple clients' work? Can it bill in 10-, 15-, or 20-minute units? Can it produce invoices from this timekeeping?

HANDLING CASH PAYMENTS/ACCOUNTS PAYABLE

The processing of accounts payable is one function that companies often turn over to an outsourcing firm. These firms not only process accounts payable, but they send invoices to suppliers, record transactions in a general ledger, and generate reports. Even though the accounts payable function may be outsourced, successful businesses will double-check the reported information. The office professional, therefore, should understand the recording process and the forms involved with accounts payable. The manual process is explained in the paragraphs that follow.

Companies still pay for many purchases by check. Check forms and stubs vary. Some companies prefer to use their own printed check forms; others use the checks supplied by their banks. A separate **check register** may be used to record information about checks that are issued.

HINT: *Always complete the stubs and entries in a check register before writing the check. If several invoices are paid with one check, list each invoice number and amount on the stub.*

Check stubs or check register entries are the major source documents for making journal entries for cash payments. Information for any of these forms must include the amount of the check, the date, the payee's name, the reason for the check (invoice number, reference notation, brief explanation), the balance before the check was written, and the new balance after the check is written.

If it is necessary to stop payment on a check, call the bank immediately with the date and number of the check, the payee's name, the drawer's name, the amount, and the reason for the stop payment. Keep a supply of stop-payment forms in the office; these forms satisfy the bank's request for written verification within two weeks of the transaction. Banks usually charge for stop-payment service. Once the payment is stopped, don't forget to add the amount to the checkbook balance and make the correcting journal entries.

HINT: *Check with the bank to determine how long the stop payment lasts; you may have to renew it in six months.*

Procedures for Preparing Checks

Many checks are computer generated or are produced with check-protector equipment. A **check protector** prohibits someone from making changes in check amounts. The device imprints the amount in figures and words (often in color) on the check. There may still be a need, however, to prepare some checks with a typewriter or a pen. Never use a pencil or erasable ink to write any part of a check. Use a check protector with a counting feature so you can monitor the number of checks imprinted.

The following suggestions are helpful in writing checks:

- Use the current date on checks; do not postdate or predate them.
- Enter the payee's full name as far to the left as possible. Draw a line or type dashes to fill in any remaining blank space to prevent the insertion of other names on the check. Titles such as *Ms., Mr.,* or *Dr.* are not necessary. Verify the spelling of a payee's name.
- If a check is made payable to an individual who is acting in an official capacity for an organization, such as a county treasurer, write the name of the payee followed by a specific title on the check. This makes it clear that the money is going to the organization and not to the payee's own account.
- Place the check amount in figures as close as possible to the dollar sign to prevent the insertion of any additional numbers.
- Express the amount of the check in words beginning at the far left of the space provided on the check. Only the first letter of the first word needs to be capitalized. The figures 21 (twenty-one) through 99 (ninety-nine) are the only ones that require hyphens. The word *and* is used only between the dollars and cents amount. If the check is for an even dollar amount, fill in zeros for the cents:

<u>Five hundred twenty-nine and 00/100   —————————— DOLLARS</u>

- Express amounts using as few words as possible. For example, the amount $1645.29 takes up less space if written "Sixteen hundred forty-five and 29/100" rather than "One thousand six hundred forty-five and 29/100."
- Circle any amount following a dollar sign that is less than $1. In addition, write "only" before the amount written in words and place a line through the word "Dollars."

<u>Only seventy-five cents   ——————————— ~~DOLLARS~~</u>

- Do not erase, cross out, or make changes on a check. Write "VOID" on any check that has an error. Make a notation on the stub or in the check register when a check has been voided. File the voided checks.

Check Fraud

Employers are responsible for preventing check fraud and may be held liable if they do not initiate controls or review bank statements on a timely basis. Some reminders for handling checks and initiating controls include:

- Always follow the company's or department's internal control procedures. If there are none, suggest that some be placed in writing. *Never* assume *sole* responsibility for receiving cash, making deposits, writing checks, entering transactions, or reconciling checking accounts.
- Keep blank checks, endorsement stamps, debit cards, authentication signature stamps, and check registers in locked drawers. Notify the financial institution immediately if these items are lost.
- Update the signature cards on file at the company's financial institutions. Promotions, terminations, or resignations mean changes in signature authorizations.
- Reconcile the bank statement monthly. Match the list of payables against the bank statement. Report discrepancies in reconciling or in balancing the books to your supervisor immediately.
- Be aware of suspicious-looking checks or checks that appear altered. Some checks are printed on paper treated with chemicals so if checks are altered, the paper changes color. Other checks will have the word *void* appear when the check is photocopied. KPMG Peat Marwick offers a *Fraud Awareness Guide*. Call 212–872–5850 to receive a free copy.
- Report any excessive complaints from suppliers who are not being paid. Check for inconsistent cash-flow deficiencies. Watch payment requests for goods you never

received. Dishonest employees can prepare extra checks or set up dummy vendors to siphon company funds.

- Purchase check stock from reputable suppliers. Consider shrink-wrapping the check stock; order in small multiples to reduce tampering. Keep the check stock in locked cabinets.
- Shred leftover check stock on closed accounts.

Procedures for Handling Petty Cash

Sometimes a payment is too small to justify writing a check; a petty cash fund is a practical way to handle these small expenditures. Over a year, these expenditures may add up to a considerable amount. Usually management designates one person to be in charge of petty cash. The procedures for handling petty cash are as follows:

- Have management establish procedures and amounts for the petty cash fund. Once established, the designated amount in the petty cash fund does not vary unless management decides to increase or decrease it.
- Always keep the petty cash and the blank voucher forms in a locked box or drawer.
- Limit access to the petty cash fund.
- Complete a voucher form for every request for petty cash. (See Figure 13-12.) The person who makes the request must sign the voucher. Obtain a receipt for the money spent and attach it to the voucher.

```
PETTY CASH VOUCHER              No. _____ 86 _____

Date _____          Amount _____
Paid to _____
_____
Purpose _____
_____
Account(s) charged _____
Issued by _____
Amount of purchase _____   Received payment
Cash returned _____
Cash owed _____      _____
                                Signature
```

Figure 13-12 Petty cash voucher.

Petty Cash Record for Month _____ 20—										Page _____
			Petty Cash		**Payment Distribution**					
Date	**Explanation of Entry**	**Vou. #**	**Received**	**Paid**	**Supplies**	**Advertising Expense**	**Delivery Expense**	**Other Accounts**		
								Acc't. name	**Amount**	
20—										
May	1	Established	—	200 00						
		Fund with ck #8196								
	1	Labels/ PWP Project	1		8 00	8 00				
	2	Floral rental/ OpenHouse	2		30 00				Misc. Exp.	30 00

Figure 13-13 Petty cash record.

- Maintain control by prenumbering the voucher forms. If a mistake is made, write "VOID" on the voucher and in the petty cash record.
- Record every disbursement in a petty cash record. (See Figure 13-13.) Check the chart of accounts to identify the appropriate general ledger accounts to charge.
- Verify that the cash remaining in the petty cash fund and the total of the vouchers equal the amount for which the fund was established. Complete this verification once a week.
- Replenish the petty cash fund at the end of a specified time period by preparing a check request (or the check) for the amount that will bring the fund to its original amount. The check should be made payable to Petty Cash. Cash the check in the accounting department or business office; add the amount to the petty cash box and record the receipt on the petty cash record. Use the cash short and over account when the cash on hand in the fund and the voucher totals are not equal. The cash short and over account accommodates overages or shortages that result from errors made in paying or receiving cash.
- Prepare a summary petty cash report for management. The petty cash report lists the amounts charged to *each* general ledger account and the total petty cash expended for the time period. Stamp the vouchers "Paid" and attach them along with receipts to the report.
- Prepare a journal entry debiting the accounts charged for the disbursements and crediting cash.

HINT: *Replenishing the petty cash fund does not change the original size of the fund. Do not debit or credit the petty cash account at the time you replenish the fund.*

Special Payment Forms

When an ordinary company check is not appropriate or acceptable, one of the following forms of payment may be appropriate:

Certified check: A bank employee stamps "Certified" on the face of an ordinary company-prepared check. This stamp indicates that the amount is available for payment and the bank has earmarked the funds. There is a fee for the service, and a depositor cannot issue a stop-payment order on a certified check. Certified checks need to be included when reconciling the bank statement.

Cashier's check: A bank employee prepares a cashier's check written on the bank's own account rather than on the depositor's account. The depositor reimburses the bank with a payment equal to the cashier's check plus a fee paid to the bank for issuing the check. The depositor may be the payee on a cashier's check and in turn may endorse it to the appropriate creditor, or the cashier's check may be made payable directly to the creditor to whom the payment is due.

Bank draft: A bank draft is helpful when large amounts of money are being transferred from one location to another, when a payment is due in another location, or when payment is due in foreign currency. A bank employee issues a bank draft on funds in another bank rather than on its own funds. The depositor reimburses the bank that issued the draft for the amount and pays the bank a fee.

Money order: Money orders are negotiable instruments and are used most frequently by people who do not have checking accounts. Banks place restrictions on the amount for which individual money orders may be written; however, more than one money order may be purchased for a fee and made payable to a creditor. Money orders are also available for a fee at post offices and at various retail stores.

Traveler's checks: Traveler's checks are useful when it is inconvenient to carry large amounts of cash. At the time of purchase, the user signs the check in the presence of a representative of a financial institution. Each time a traveler's check is cashed, the user signs the check again in view of the person who accepts it as payment. The checks come in various denominations and are also available in many foreign currencies. The numbers on a set of traveler's checks provide a record in case the checks are lost or stolen.

Direct deposit service: Direct deposit service may be used for payroll and many government payments. The company is authorized by the employee to deposit the employee's net pay in a designated financial institution. This eliminates the need for a payroll check. The employee receives only a record of the payment listing such items as regular and overtime hours, gross and net wages, individual tax deductions, and voluntary deductions. A one-time authorization is necessary for an employee to participate in direct deposit of his or her payroll check.

Automatic withdrawal: A company may authorize the bank to deduct certain designated payments from its checking account. The bank transfers these payments to the parties to whom they are due.

Electronic Bill Payment

Paying bills electronically is another way for businesses to make payments. A description of several of these electronic methods follows:

ONLINE BANKING SERVICE

Online banking services require a touch-tone telephone and personal finance software or special software obtained through financial institutions. Companies or individuals have the benefits of transferring funds between accounts, sending wire transfers, obtaining account balances and statements, and paying bills electronically.

DEBIT CARDS

To use a debit card, the buyer swipes the card through an electronic reader and enters a personal identification number (PIN) on a keypad. This action signals immediate transfer of funds from the customer's account to the seller's account. If the customer does not have enough money in the account, the transaction becomes void immediately.

A debit card is convenient but also carries some risks. By law, debit card holders are not responsible for more than $50 of fraudulent charges. Some issuing firms still hold to the $50 amount; others, such as Visa® and MasterCard,® have zero liability. If the merchandise or service is unsatisfactory, a debit cardholder may find it more difficult to negotiate a refund than will a credit card holder.

ELECTRONIC CASH (E-CASH)

Electronic cash refers to paying electronically for a service or product purchased over the Internet. Electronic cash moves quickly through multiple networks other than the present banking system. An example of e-cash is the smart card. Consumers "load" the card's embedded microchip with the cash amount. As purchases are made, the amount decreases until it is time to buy a new card.

Electronic cash has ramifications for the banking industry as well as global trade. It will change the way we handle business transactions in the future.

E-COMMERCE PURCHASING CONSIDERATIONS

Office professionals are often responsible for purchasing office items such as supplies and gifts for clients and employees. They may find it convenient to do this shopping on-line. Here are several e-retailer characteristics to check before ordering.

- Is the site easy to navigate? Are the products visually and accurately represented?
- Are there e-mail and telephone customer service addresses and numbers included? Is there a knowledgeable person to call when something goes wrong?

- Are the policies and procedures for product returns clearly stated?
- Is there a section labeled "How to Order"? Is there an on-line order form? Is a confirmation received upon purchase?
- Is a delivery guarantee stated? What procedures should be followed if the delivery is not made as promised?
- Are the payment terms specific? Are the procedures for handling out-of-stock items and back orders available for customers to review?
- Has the vendor secured sensitive or proprietary information? Is transaction security identified in the site? Does the Web site use encryption to prevent hackers from intercepting credit data?

HINT: *Encryption is used if the Web site's address begins with "https" rather than just "http". The "s" is for "secure." Also, check for the Better Business Bureau (BBB) Online Reliability seal on the site.*

HINT: *Some sites require information about the person or company doing the ordering. Review your firm's policy on revealing data about the company to outside sources before you fill out forms, even if there is a privacy notation on the site.*

Procedures for Reconciling the Bank Statement

Each month a depositor receives a statement from a bank showing the beginning and ending account balances and any additions or subtractions from the account. Included with the statement are the **canceled checks** (those checks presented and cleared for payment), deposit slips, and credit and debit memos. Credit memos are reminders to add amounts to the ledger accounts and checkbook; debit memos require subtractions.

Some banks retain canceled checks and simply list the check numbers and amounts on the statements. The depositor has a checkbook in which either carbons or entries are made each time a check is written so a record of the check is available. If a copy of the original check is needed, the depositor may obtain one for a fee from the bank.

Reconciling the bank statement is the process of identifying the differences between the checkbook balance and the bank balance and bringing these two balances into agreement. Companies often use software programs to reconcile their statements. Reconciliation takes place monthly, as soon as possible after the statement arrives.

HINT: *The bank reconciliation process is not a task to treat lightly or to postpone until time permits. The paperwork, or lack of it, provides auditors with important clues about a firm's financial arrangements. Do not delegate this responsibility to a new or inexperienced employee without training the person and supervising the work.*

Banks provide reconciliation forms on the back of the statements mailed to their depositors. Some companies prefer to use their own reconciliation formats. (See Figure 13-14.)

GRAEBER NURSERY
912463-09
Reconciliation of Bank Statement
June 15, 20___

Bank Statement Balance		$29,642.00
Add Deposits		
June 14		8,320.00
		37,962.00
Less Checks Outstanding, June 15		
No. 2078	$5,815.00	
No. 2082	1,655.00	
No. 2083	62.00	7,532.00
Adjusted Bank Balance		$30,430.00
Checkbook Balance		$31,581.00
Less: Bank Service Charge Expense	81.00	
NSF	1,220.00	1,301.00
		30,280.00
Add: Interest Received		150.00
Adjusted Checkbook Balance		$30,430.00

Figure 13-14 Bank reconciliation company format.

The following steps are helpful in reconciling bank statements.

1. Use an appropriate heading that gives the date, account number, and account name, whether you use the bank's form or the company's.
2. Enter the balance found on the bank statement.
3. Verify that all deposits in transit from last month's reconciliation as well as all deposits made since the last reconciliation are listed on the statement. **Deposits in transit** are deposits that are already recorded in the depositor's books but that did not reach the bank in time to be included in the statement. List any deposits still in transit and add the total to the bank statement balance.
4. Compare the canceled check amounts with the bank statement amounts. If they agree, place a checkmark next to the statement amount. Examine the signatures on returned checks to make sure they are legitimate.
5. Place the canceled checks in numerical order. Compare the canceled checks with the check stub or check register entries. Also, compare the canceled checks with any outstanding checks listed on last month's reconciliation form. Use a check-

mark, preferably in color, on the stub or register to indicate that the check has cleared the bank for payment. Checks without checkmarks are **outstanding checks** and have not been deducted by the bank at the time the statement was prepared.

6. List the amount of each outstanding check along with its number. Obtain a total amount and subtract it from the bank statement balance. This figure represents the **adjusted bank balance.**

7. Enter the current balance from the checkbook. Be sure the balances in the checkbook and in the cash account in the general ledger agree before doing the reconciliation.

8. Look for any credit memos listed on the bank statement. Credit memos include such items as collections made for the depositor by the bank or deposit slip errors in the depositor's favor. Compare the list with the entries on the stubs or in the check register. Add those items not yet recorded to the checkbook balance. Give a brief explanation of each credit memo.

9. Add any interest that has been earned on the checking account to the checkbook balance.

10. Look for any debit memos listed on the statement. Debit memos include such items as payments the depositor has authorized the bank to deduct automatically, such as mortgage or insurance payments, deposit slip errors that decrease the depositor's cash, or insufficient funds notifications. These latter notices let the depositor know that a check that was accepted in good faith was not payable by the drawer's bank due to lack of funds. Subtract those items not yet recorded from the checkbook balance. Include a brief explanation for each debit memo.

11. Subtract fees for overdrafts and for credit card discount fees. The latter are charges made by the bank for handling bank charge card slips.

12. Once these additions and subtractions are completed, the result indicates the **adjusted checkbook balance.** Compare the adjusted bank balance and adjusted checkbook balance.

13. Place the notation "reconciled," the date of the reconciliation, and any corrections, including reasons, on the next available stub in the checkbook or on the next available line in the check register. Write "Correction made (date) from ($x) to ($y)" on the check stub on which the error was made.

14. Journalize and post any adjustments pertaining to the checkbook side of the reconciliation. All debit memos result in a decrease to cash.

15. File the bank statements in chronological order by date with the most recent form on top.

16. File the checks in numerical order in a separate file designed for check retention. Legal requirements for retaining financial records are not the same in all states due to different statutes of limitations.

HINT: *As canceled checks are filed each month, color code them to identify the retention periods. For example, code all checks that must be kept permanently with a red sticker. A column indicating the retention period for records is also helpful in a check register.*

HINT: *Review each month's outstanding checks to investigate checks that have not cleared. Write or telephone the payee to find out if the check was received. If a deposit is not listed on the bank statement and is not in transit, contact the bank as soon as possible to locate the deposit.*

Personal Finance/Accounts Payable Software Applications

Single proprietorships often find that personal finance software for single-entry or double-entry accounting is adequate for monitoring cash flow and reconciling bank statements. For other companies, stand-alone or fully integrated accounts-payable software works best. Answers to the following questions will be helpful in assessing accounts payable or personal finance software applications.

- Is the application designed for single-entry or double-entry bookkeeping? How much accounting theory is required to operate the program?
- Is there automated check writing? Once check information is entered, are the amounts transferred automatically to a check register or to the general ledger? Is there an option to indicate reminder dates for cutting the checks? Are discounts automatic or is there an option for an operator override?

HINT: *Every bill should be paid within 30 days to avoid late charges. Company policy determines early payments to take advantage of discounts. Analyze every invoice when it arrives to verify the billing information.*

- Are checks printed in order of voucher number or due date? If multiple invoices are paid with one check, are all invoice numbers listed?
- If a check is sent out monthly (for example, the rent payment), is there a shortcut so the entire check does not have to be reentered? Is it possible to set up levels and dates for payments? For example, the first level might include the payroll and other fixed expenses.
- Are transactions categorized into deductible and nondeductible tax items?
- Does the application produce cash forecasts, general ledger, accounts payable ledger, and cash flow reports? Do the statements provide year-to-date analyses as well as current fiscal period information?
- Does the application record and print purchase orders? Can the purchase orders be organized by type; for example, order items, services, professional, pending, or

no purchase order needed? When purchases are received, is the inventory automatically updated? Does the inventory tracking feature support multiple purchase costs for the stock?

- Do vendors' accounts indicate such items as name, address, phone number, terms offered, and payment deadlines? Is there online vendor account inquiry so you can determine how much was paid to date? Is it possible to print a report of all vendors as well as selected vendors? Can the vendors' lists be prioritized?

HINT: *An interactive voice-response system allows vendors to ask questions about when they will be paid or when a check was mailed. The vendor punches the purchase order number to receive current account information that the accounts payable department downloads each night.*

- Are reports available for late shipments or returns and allowances? Is there a report for discounts lost (discounts not taken because of employee neglect or management's lack of interest)?
- Does the software perform the bank reconciliation or is separate home-banking software needed? Does it flag unusual transactions? Can the reconciliation changes be posted to general ledger accounts?

HINT: *Overdrafts, bounced checks, and debit/credit memos cause unnecessary service charges and decreased cash flow. Analyze the bank statements and update the checkbook and general ledger promptly.*

- Can the software still be used if the business expands? Can the software support multiple checking accounts?

HANDLING PAYROLL

Every company needs a record of the time its employees work, the amount of wages or salaries paid, and information necessary for completing budgets and tax reports. Office professionals assume various levels of responsibility for payroll tasks, ranging from completing their own time cards to completing federal tax documents. Many companies use computers to do payroll or have contracts with commercial payroll service organizations. Others use their bank's or accountant's payroll services or the software these organizations provide to them. Some small companies still do their payroll manually. Those who understand the concepts of payroll accounting have a level of expertise that is helpful when interacting with CPAs, accountants, managers, and outsource providers and when supervising other employees.

Payroll Records

Most companies find that several types of records will provide them with the information they need to meet the requirements of federal and state regulations affecting payroll. Whether the payroll is done manually or on the computer, the same information is needed.

A **master employee list** of all employee names, numbers, addresses, Social Security numbers, phone numbers, departments, hourly rates, overtime rates when applicable, and the number of exemptions provides the basic source of information for the payroll and personnel departments.

A **time card** or **report** shows the hours worked by each employee. This manual procedure requires careful review and a supervisor's signature. Formats for time reporting vary widely for employees paid hourly wages, for those paid weekly or monthly salaries, and for those hired on a commission, piece-rate, or job-costing basis.

Some companies issue employees plastic time cards with magnetic strips. Employees insert their cards in a card terminal; the machine recognizes the code, records the appropriate in and out times, and links the information to the payroll processing software. Managers can request a printout of everyone who is working at any hour. Workers have the advantage of confidentiality and accurate recording.

The **payroll register** or journal summarizes information for a specific payroll period and includes time and earnings information on every employee on the payroll. The totals on the payroll register provide the data needed for journal entries. (A sample register appears in Figure 13-15.)

An **employee earnings record** is maintained by most companies. (See Figure 13-16.) This record provides a place to accumulate payroll data from one period to the next so that at the end of a fiscal year Wage and Tax Statements, or W-2 forms, may be sent to each employee. When recording the payroll manually, the earnings record helps to determine the date that an employee reaches the maximum deduction for such taxes as FICA (Federal Insurance Contributions Act), state unemployment, or federal unemployment. Once

PAYROLL REGISTER

WEEK ENDING JANUARY 14, 20—   **DEPARTMENT: SALES**

Emp. no.	Employee name	Marital Status	W.H. Allowance	Earnings			Taxable Earnings				Deductions								Net Paid	Ck. No.	Accounts Charged	
				Reg.	O.T.	Total	FICA	Medi-care	FUTA	SUTA	FIT	FICA	Medi-care	SIT	Union dues	Other	Total			Sales Salaries	Office & Adm. Sal.
Totals																					

Figure 13-15 Payroll register.

Employee Earnings Record

Employee: _____   Employee #: _____

Address: _____   Date Employed: _____

_____   Withholding Allow.: _____

_____   Marital status: _____

Telephone: _____   Regular Rate $: _____

Department: _____   Overtime Rate $: _____

Social Security Number: _____   Date Terminated: _____

Hours		Earnings				Deductions								
Reg.	O.T.	Reg.	O.T.	Tot.	Accumulated Earnings	FIT	FICA	Medi-care	SIT	Union dues	Other	Tot.	Net Pay	Ck. No.

Figure 13-16 Employee's earnings record.

these maximum deduction limits have been reached, taxes are no longer deducted from the employee's earnings, and employer contributions and tax expenses are no longer computed.

Payroll Taxes and Other Deductions

Some payroll deductions, such as income taxes and FICA taxes, are mandatory. Other deductions may be optional, such as union dues, charitable contributions, insurance premiums, and savings plan contributions.

FEDERAL INCOME TAX (FIT)

The employee's number of exemptions (earnings not subject to income taxes), marital status, payroll time period, and gross wages determine the amount of that employee's FIT deduction. Form W-4, completed by the employee, provides the authorization for deducting an appropriate amount of federal income tax from an employee's gross wages. The federal government furnishes tax-withholding tables in the booklet *Circular E: The Employer's Tax Guide*. Income taxes withheld by the employer are recorded as liabilities of the company.

STATE, COUNTY, OR CITY INCOME TAX (SIT)

The same procedures for determining federal income tax deductions also apply for calculating state, county, or city income taxes. The forms to fill out vary in each state and locality. Special tax-withholding tables are available from the appropriate government agencies.

FICA TAX

The FICA tax (Federal Insurance Contribution Act) covers Social Security, old-age, disability, and survivor benefits as well as Medicare for persons over 65 years of age. The federal government sets the percentage of gross wages to be taxed and the maximum base on which the tax must be paid. FICA and Medicare have different bases. The base and/or the percentage usually increase from year to year.

The employer is responsible for paying FICA taxes to the government equal to the total amount contributed by all employees in each payroll period. To determine the amount, multiply the total in the FICA taxable earnings column of the payroll register by the current FICA percentage rate. The contributions withheld for employees are liabilities of the business, and the employer's matching contribution is a payroll tax expense.

HINT: *The employer must deposit federal income taxes withheld and the FICA taxes (employees' and employer's contributions) in a timely manner with a bank authorized to accept such payments. If the deposit is not made according to the rules, the employer faces a fine.*

UNEMPLOYMENT TAXES (SUTA/FUTA)

State unemployment taxes (SUTA) temporarily assist employees who become unemployed as a result of changes they cannot control, such as mergers, layoffs, and cutbacks. SUTA rates and tax bases vary from state to state.

Federal unemployment taxes (FUTA) help defray the costs incurred by the states in administering unemployment programs. Employers receive a credit (the maximum percentage is designated by law) against their federal unemployment tax for monies they pay to the state.

To determine the SUTA and FUTA amounts, multiply the totals in the FUTA and SUTA taxable earnings columns of the payroll register by the appropriate tax rates. For information on bases and rates, contact the state unemployment commission. Unemployment taxes are expenses of the business.

OTHER PAYROLL DEDUCTIONS

Deductions other than those mandated by law include such items as contributions to retirement accounts or plans, insurance premiums, and union dues. Retirement plan vesting rights and payroll termination dates must be carefully documented so payouts are accurate. The employer records pension payments as an expense of the business and records employees' contributions as a liability.

In the case of insurance premiums, the employer records any amounts withheld from the employees as a liability. Employees often pay their union dues through payroll deductions. The employer records this deduction as a liability and at the appropriate time transfers the dues to the union treasurer.

PAYROLL FORMS AND REPORTS

The employer records and transfers to the appropriate agencies the amounts deducted from employees' earnings or contributed by the company. The following forms and reports are necessary to document employees' authorizations for deductions and the prompt transfer of contributions.

Form SS-4: If an employer does not have an employer identification number, which is used on all payroll forms and reports, Form SS-4 must be completed. It is available at any IRS or Social Security office.

Form SS-5: If an employee does not have a Social Security number, he or she must complete Form SS-5. The Social Security Administration provides the forms.

Form OOAN-7003: Employees must complete this form if they change their names.

Form W-4: All new employees must complete a Form W-4 (Employee's Withholding Allowance Certificate), on which they indicate the number of withholding allowances they wish to claim. The employer files these forms and uses the number of allowances the employee indicates to compute federal and state income tax deductions. Each exemption represents an amount of income that is not taxable. Employees—not the people in the payroll office—are responsible for requesting any changes in the number of withholding allowances.

Form W-2: Each year on or before January 31, the company must provide its employees with W-2 forms (Wage and Tax Statements) for the preceding year. Employees need these multipart forms to prepare their personal federal and state income tax returns. The employer distributes copies to the Social Security Administration; state, city, or local tax agencies; and employees, who receive several copies to file with tax returns and to retain in their files. The employer retains a copy in the office files. If an employee loses a W-2 form, the company reissues another form with the word "reissued" on the new statement. A reissued Form W-2 should not be sent to the Social Security Administration but given to the employee as a record.

Form W-3: An employer must send a Form W-3, the Transmittal of Income and Tax Statements, along with copies of all the W-2 forms to the Social Security Administration. The due date for the W-2 forms and the W-3 transmittal form is the last day of February.

Form 8109: Each time employers deposit income tax and FICA deductions and contributions, they complete Form 8109 (Federal Tax Deposit Form). Once a company obtains an employer identification number, federal tax deposit coupon books are mailed to the company automatically. Form 8109 must include the amount deposited, the tax period, and the type of tax being deposited.

Form 941: Every three months, employers report the amount of income taxes and FICA taxes deducted or contributed on a Form 941 (Employer's Quarterly Federal Tax Return). Form 941 is due at the regional IRS office one month after the quarter ends. For example, the first quarter ends March 31, and the report is due April 30. Any undeposited tax amounts for the quarter are also due at this time.

Form 940: The employer reports FUTA taxes already submitted during the year on Form 940 (Employer's Annual Federal Unemployment Tax Return). The form is due on January 31 of the next year. Any undeposited tax amounts are also due at that time.

Payroll Software Applications

Payroll is often one of the first areas that companies or home-based companies computerize or outsource. A payroll application can operate as a separate system or be integrated with the general ledger system. Personal finance software is not adequate to handle payroll. The following questions will be helpful in selecting the best payroll software:

- Is there a limit on the number of employees the application can handle? Is there a limit on the number of deductions that can be handled? Are reports generated for each type of deduction per pay period?
- Can different compensation modes be accommodated, such as salary, commission, hourly wage, tips, piece rate, pay advances, vacation pay, bonus, per diem, and contract?
- Are sufficient tax tables available? Which taxes are included? Does the software company offer tax updates each year? What is the cost for the updates? Are both manual and automatic calculation modes available? Can the user set any of the tax rates?
- Are costs of payroll materials and supplies allocated to the appropriate project with updated figures? Are employees able to record their hours spent on projects in real time from their desktop computers so instant project costs are available?
- Is direct depositing available? Does it support multi-frequency payroll periods?
- Can payroll expenses be distributed by department? For example, an employee may be assigned to more than one department with different pay rates. Can departmental time card reports be generated? Is the software capable of handling multiple state requirements?
- Does the software application maintain quarterly, monthly, weekly, and year-to-date earnings and deduction accumulations? Are W-2 forms automatically prepared at the end of the year? Can they be prepared automatically at other times as well? Does the software application automatically update each employee's earnings and deductions? Does it support electronic filing of tax payments and reports?

- Is a check register prepared specifically for payroll each period? Is the general ledger automatically updated? Are there reports categorized by job classification, department, and employee?
- Does the application track sick time and vacation time so that when a person leaves the company the amounts he or she is owed are available? Does it handle clocking time when employees work with several clients on a consulting or freelance basis?
- Can payroll data be exported to spreadsheets?
- If using a payroll outsource service vendor, is the system compatible with yours?
- Can the outsource vendor safely and confidentially dispatch payroll data over the Internet?

OUTSOURCING

Outsourcing began as a strategy used by large companies to cut costs. Today, businesses of all sizes, including home-based businesses, use outsourcing to move work previously done in-house to suppliers or outside service-provider firms that manage the entire operation. These firms provide expertise that many companies cannot afford or provide for themselves. Such areas as payroll, travel planning, benefits administration, retirement plans, loan applications, printing, and mail distribution are office services that are commonly outsourced.

Advantages

If keeping pace with competitors requires huge investments of time, money, and personnel, companies may find an expert outsource provider who will do the work or portions of it more economically. Here are some additional advantages of outsourcing:

- Administrative, recruitment, training, and supervision costs as well as behavior and attitude problems are the responsibilities of the outsource provider.
- Outsource providers supply the resources and assume the liabilities.
- Funds designated for high-cost updated equipment are now available for research or product and service improvement.
- Managers or small business owners can concentrate on their product by limiting their need for in-depth knowledge of technical operational details or constantly changing regulations.
- Companies can gain access to expert specialists and high-level technology they may not have in-house.
- A contract determines the length of a commitment to an outsource provider.
- Employees may receive better health insurance coverage with fewer hassles for the employer.

- Since hiring and terminating become more stable, the work force has a consistent core and is not oversized at off-peak times.

Disadvantages

Outsourcing is not the same as downsizing, although they often occur at the same time. Some disadvantages of outsourcing include:

- Employees are unsure about job security. They may not be pleased with losing their work to the outsource firm.
- Companies find it difficult to develop a team spirit or expect company loyalty or pride from the outsource workers.
- Managers and small business owners relinquish some controls they once had over their operations.
- Because managers often fail to analyze costs of doing the job in-house, comparisons with costs of outsource providers are inaccurate or nonexistent. Discrepancies may exist in the data produced. You may still have to double-check the information.
- Managers view outsourcing as temporary measures and do not plan for long-term outsourcing commitments. They are often in a rush and do not research their providers.
- Employees feel a loss of self-esteem when managers single out their department's function as less important to a firm's central core of operations.
- The quality and ethics of the outsource workers may not meet a company's standards.
- Employees are not a part of the decision-making process and thus view outsourcing as a management strategy. On the other hand, management views unions as stumbling blocks in the outsourcing process.
- Security of the company's information may be at risk at off-company premises.

Outsourcing Considerations

To save costs and trouble later, a Statement of Work should accompany an outsourcing contract. To prepare the statement, managers need answers to numerous questions.

- Which operations are best provided by an outside provider and which should be retained by the business?

HINT: *Office professionals need to be in the loop that makes these decisions. Recommend areas for outsourcing that free you for more management responsibilities. Do some research on outsource providers in your community to get answers to the questions in this section.*

- What are the tasks and responsibilities of each party? Who is responsible for the reports management requires? Are rates competitive with those of other firms?
- How quickly are jobs needed? Can the provider meet the deadlines, handle rush jobs, and make last-minute changes?
- Is the provider financially stable? Does it have competent staff? Who does its backup work? Can it provide the training for new procedures and equipment? Is it fully bonded and insured?

HINT: *In dealing with Web-based outsourcing services, choose an established vendor which has expanded its business into on-line services.*

- What is the quality of similar work done by the outsource company? Does the outsource company have sufficient experience with the jobs or processes that you want outsourced? Are companies that are using or have used the outsource company satisfied?

HINT: *Ask for samples to review as well as references from other users. If the vendor is too new to provide references, request a trial period.*

- How will the data be accessed and downloaded by the business and the provider? Is the equipment compatible? How will the processes interface with each other?
- Who is responsible for monitoring the performance standards? What is the process to be pursued if the outsource vendor does not meet minimum requirements?

HINT: *Office professionals are logical evaluators of many outsourced jobs. Design the procedures for monitoring completed jobs and discuss them with your supervisor.*

- Does the vendor use encryption for data transfer? Does the vendor provide firewalls to keep out hackers and viruses?
- Who owns the materials produced by the outsourcer? Is the outsourcing firm or individual paid by the hour or by the project?

HINT: *Your company's code of ethics and performance standards need to be communicated. Take the time to develop a congenial working relationship with the workers and the agency or the person to whom the work has been contracted. Volunteer to be one of the company's liaisons with the outsource provider, and use the opportunity to communicate successes and criticisms.*

OTHER RECORDS FOR HOME-BASED BUSINESSES

In addition to financial records, several related topics such as taxes, permits, insurance, and loans require the attention of home-based business owners. Pricing decisions and ways to cut costs are also concerns. See the checklist for starting a new business (Figure 13-17).

Permits/Licenses

Most incorporated areas have zoning regulations, zoning laws, and ordinances governing a business operating from a home in a residential neighborhood. These regulations, if ignored, can result in substantial fines for the owner. Since the regulations vary, check with a county and/or city zoning authority to be sure you are not breaking any laws. You may need a professional license to operate in your state. Before paying the fee, be sure that you can obtain a license for a business with a residential address.

The Chamber of Commerce may have a set of materials that includes all the necessary forms for new business owners. If it does not, obtain a fictitious-name statement or d/b/a (doing business as) form and file it with the county clerk's office. The form, required by law, identifies the sole proprietor responsible for the company. Display one in your place of business and give one to your bank when you open a business checking account.

HINT: *Always open a business account. Do not mingle personal and business funds.*

The government requires an identification of your business by Social Security number or an **employer identification number (EIN).** Sole proprietors usually use their Social Security numbers, but if you have employees, use independent contractors, or pay sales tax, you need an EIN.

You may need other business permits. Your state and city offices have that information. These permit requirements vary for different cities and states.

Loans

Most small business owners fail because they underestimate expenses or it takes longer to make a profit than they expected. Plan to have reserve money to cover your fixed expenses for at least 18 months and to cover living expenses of 6 to 8 months. If you need additional money, apply for a loan from a bank or the Small Business Administration's Microloan Demonstration Program (202–205–6490). Try to locate a bank that offers business loans for small borrowers but does not treat the loans as consumer loans with the attendant higher interest rates. Less appealing sources of capital are loans from relatives or friends or from credit cards.

HINT: *When granting loans to service businesses, banks will generally look at accounts receivable and give a credit line of 70 to 80 percent of the value of the current receivables.*

HINT: *Interest rates mount quickly on loans. Never place your credit rating or the family home at risk because of out-of-control borrowing.*

CHECKLIST FOR STARTING A NEW BUSINESS

1. Check zoning regulations.
2. Select the type of business structure.
3. Name the business.
4. Check if duplicate name exists.
5. Develop a business plan.
6. Obtain sufficient capital.
7. Open a business checking account.
8. Register the name with appropriate authorities.
9. Select an accountant or tax adviser.
10. Determine fiscal year.
11. Obtain permits and licenses.
12. Obtain an Employer ID Number if applicable to business.
13. Select office space.
14. Obtain quotes for equipment and supplies.
15. Check lighting and electrical requirements.
16. Design the office layout.
17. Select equipment and supplies.
18. Purchase appropriate insurance.
19. Order business cards.
20. Install a telephone line for the business.
21. Establish a pricing policy.
22. Set up a bookkeeping system.
23. Advertise your product.
24. Release an announcement to local media.
25. Establish answering machine or voice-mail conditions.
26. Hire personnel if necessary or use an outsource provider.

Figure 13-17 Checklist for starting a new business.

Business Plan

Banks require a business plan from loan applicants. The plan should reflect sound thinking, documented information, and an understanding of cash flow. Write your business plan or use a business planning software program that leads you through the following sections:

- Cover sheet. Identify the business name, address, telephone number, and your background.
- Business description. Describe how the business will be structured, the startup date, the experience you have, and the reasons it will be successful. Describe your product or service in detail. Include a capital equipment and supplies list.
- Purpose of plan: Include the form of business, how much money is needed and for what purpose, and how the funds will be spent.
- Marketing strategy. Identify your prospective clients and the reasons they will buy your services or products. Compare your plan with your competitors' offerings. Describe the promotional and pricing plans that will distinguish your business from similar businesses that already exist.
- Financial goal. Include fixed and indirect expenses and monthly net profit-and-loss projections for the first year in addition to your sources of startup capital. Include a personal income statement, balance sheet, and latest tax return. Indicate how the lending institution will be repaid.

Taxes

The government does not deduct federal taxes from the self-employed; therefore, you must pay estimated quarterly income taxes and a self-employment tax. The self-employment tax includes not only your contribution to Social Security and Medicare taxes but also the matching amount an employer would have paid you. If you hire an independent contractor, you do not have to withhold income taxes or Social Security and Medicare amounts from the employee's wages. The IRS has specific rules for identifying independent contractors versus employees, so be sure to review its guidelines.

Home-based-business owners are entitled to certain tax deductions. Some of the major deductions include:

- Equipment and supplies. The IRS sets a limit of dollar amounts every year. You may deduct the entire purchase price of business equipment the year you put it in service. This is true for "listed property" (items used for recreation as well as business) as long as it is used for business more than 50 percent of the time.
- Health insurance. The deduction is a percentage of your premium and is an adjustment to your income. The deductible percentage reaches 100 percent in 2007.
- Home office expenses. The IRS allows the deduction of such expenses as utilities, telephone, trash removal, insurance, mortgage interest, property taxes, and main-

tenance. To deduct these expenses, you must use the office for business only. However, the office no longer has to be an entire room; it may be part of a room as long as it is used exclusively for business. To determine the percentage to use to figure your deduction, calculate the square footage of your office and then the percentage of the office space as compared to the square footage of your entire home.

HINT: *The simplest way to deduct telephone expense is to have a separate line.*

HINT: *A tax accountant can offer good advice about home office deductions and any changes that occur in this sensitive area. For a free copy of* Tax Strategies, *a self-employment survival letter, write to Barbara Brabec Productions, Box 2137, Naperville, IL 60567.*

- Business expenses. You can deduct travel and entertainment expenses, but keep detailed records such as an appointment list and a gas and mileage log.
- Business loss. If you have a loss on your books for the year, you may write it off against income claimed that year or you can carry it back or forward several years.
- Self-employment tax on a yearly established amount of income: one-half of the taxes paid are deductible. Tax preparation fees, if taxes are completed by a professional tax preparer.
- Contributions to a retirement plan, which you can invest as you wish.
- Tax-deferred retirement plans. Home-based business owners are eligible for a Simplified Employee Pension (SEP) plan or a Keogh plan. Both plans allow a contribution of a certain percentage of your net earnings.
- Sales taxes. State regulations vary in taxing service businesses. Some states may require a sales tax, so check with the state office to determine whether you have to file a sales tax report.

Pricing

Pricing a product or service is a challenge. If you charge too much, your clients will get their work done by someone else. If you do not charge enough, your expenses may exceed your income or prospective clients will question the quality of your service or products. Ask these questions as you determine your pricing strategy.

- Who are my potential clients? What authority do they have? What economic class, education level, age group, gender, and occupation do they represent?

HINT: *Your clients will likely be different depending on whether your business is full-time or part-time or whether you work in the evenings or on the weekends only.*

HINT: *Set your own time and customer service standards. Provide your services for the people who meet these standards. Avoid those who are always encountering "emergencies."*

- What will it cost me to produce, advertise, sell, and deliver my product or service? What are my overhead costs? How much do I need for living expenses? How much do I want beyond living expenses?

HINT: *You can always offer a special rate once you have established your price. Do not set the price too low and then raise it immediately. Customers do not appreciate this tactic.*

- What are my competitors charging? Does higher price mean better work in my field? Do prospective clients have other choices in my area? How does my product differ from that of my competitors?

HINT: *Perhaps you can offer additional services such as free pickup and delivery or guaranteed on-time satisfaction. Find a marketing tactic that will work for you, but make it somewhat different from your competitors'.*

- What prices are outside provider companies charging for similar services? Does my professional organization publish suggested rates?

HINT: *For consulting, accounting, or office assistant rates, check with former employers to find out how much they paid temporary agencies or outside contractors for similar services.*

- What type of rate is best for my work—daily, project, or hourly?

HINT: *Do not forget to include planning time in your rates. To be precise in hourly billing time, use a software program designed for time and billing purposes.*

Insurance

Home-based businesses require several types of insurance coverage, such as property, liability, and loss of income. Here are some suggestions for securing adequate business insurance.

PROPERTY INSURANCE

You can obtain an endorsement to your homeowner's policy, which would extend personal property coverage to business property, or you can obtain a full commercial business policy. More insurance companies are beginning to offer specific home office policies that include property coverage, accounts receivable, lost valuable papers, and business income. Cost and extent of coverage will determine your choices.

HINT: *The best "insurance" for data loss and payment records is backing up your completed work or making copies of records and storing them away from your home office.*

HINT: *Maintain a list of all office equipment and furniture that is purchased. Include information such as manufacturer's name, model and service number, place and date of purchase, and technical support numbers.*

LIABILITY INSURANCE

Coverage requirements depend on the type of business. If you have clients coming to your home, you will need insurance for personal liability. Your homeowner's umbrella policy or renter's insurance may not cover business liabilities. If your business is part-time or of a nature whereby clients are not on your premises, an endorsement to your homeowner's policy may suffice.

MEDICAL INSURANCE

Federal law (COBRA) allows you to continue a company's medical insurance coverage for 18 months after you leave your employment with that company. For this to apply, the company that you leave must have at least 20 employees. You pay the premiums to your former employer. Check your spouse's or partner's policies to see if you can qualify for coverage. Contact the Chamber of Commerce or your professional organization; they may have access to group plans.

You will also need disability insurance, which replaces a portion of your income if you cannot work because you are disabled.

Workers' Compensation

If you have employees, you need workers' compensation insurance, which pays employees for costs that involve job-related injuries. The cost depends on occupation and salary. Check with a workers' compensation office in your state.

Cost Considerations

Home-based business owners need practical suggestions for cutting costs and preserving capital. Some ideas follow:

- Have the wiring system in the office area and all ground wiring around the house checked. Faulty wiring can damage equipment or cause a fire.

- Buy a quality surge protector to avoid sudden shocks to the electrical system.

- Build up a financial reserve to cover yourself during slow periods.

- Use the free Small Business Administration resources, including their on-line services.

- Save mailing costs by sending invoices with products or advertisements.

- Order checks from mail-order companies. Be sure they look professional.

- Compare costs of telephone service. Time telephone calls and faxes to take advantage of lower rates.

- Purchase antivirus software to avoid unnecessary downtime and repair. The software scans files and e-mail attachments when they are downloaded.

- Use a business center when you need access to equipment or services that you cannot afford or that you use only occasionally, such as a conference room or mail and fax services.

- Download shareware or freeware software from one of the on-line services.

- Use a lockbox to speed up cash flow. All payments go to a post office box that you rent. The bank picks up checks several times during the day and processes them immediately. The bank photocopies the checks and forwards them to you for recording. Another way to improve cash flow is to ask for partial payment when the contract is signed or the job begins, or you might consider dealing primarily with cash customers.

- Use the advertising pages in the telephone directory as a major advertising source. The most cost-effective advertising method is word of mouth. Do not hesitate to ask for referrals. A presence on the Web is also useful, especially if you are capable of setting up and designing your own site. Compare outsource vendors for Web design or advertising service if you prefer to use your time elsewhere.

- Use volunteers from job centers to do labeling or stuffing tasks. Rely on family members to assist in busy periods.

- Buy only equipment, supplies, and inventory that you need. Look for used furniture in good condition that fits the room which you plan to use as an office. Always buy a quality office chair that is comfortable and supports your body. Consider leasing your equipment, which allows you to use capital for other purposes and provides some protection against obsolete equipment. Know how much lease interest you are paying and check the buyout clause carefully.

- Become well acquainted with your equipment. In a home-based office, you will usually not have a technical specialist nearby to respond to your problem. Repair costs and home calls can be expensive.

- Check the information about reducing the costs of a home-based business in the book *Outfitting Your Home Business for Much Less* by AMACOM (ISBN 0-8144-7993-6). You can order direct from AMACOM (800–714–6395) or from your local bookstore.
- Become an expert before you begin your business so you know what your competition is doing and what your actual costs will be.

Company representatives who travel must have economical, informative, and accurate travel plans. Office professionals have an active role in travel planning; they make the travel arrangements, obtain and organize the information, and handle the follow-up tasks after the traveler returns. At times, office professionals may accompany their managers or the project team on business trips or handle preliminary arrangements, which require travel away from the office.

OBTAINING TRAVEL INFORMATION

Sources to use in making travel arrangements include a commercial travel agency, an in-house travel manager, a transportation department acting as a travel service, or on-line electronic travel services. Some companies outsource travel arrangements. In addition, you can make reservations or obtain schedule and information by calling airlines, hotels or motels, and car rental agencies directly. Numerous travel-oriented magazines and other publications also provide excellent reference sources.

Commercial Travel Agencies

Commercial travel agencies can efficiently arrange business or personal trips. A company usually selects a travel agency and then establishes an open credit account with that agency. Especially if you work for a small company, you may play a major role in selecting a travel agency and agent. You can seek travel information on-line, but a good travel agent is invaluable in planning complex trips, helping with special needs such as canceling or rebooking flights, and assisting when things go wrong while traveling. To select a good travel agency, you should answer the following questions:

- What agency or agencies are other local firms using? Are they satisfied with the services they receive? Will the agency match a lower fare that is found in another source?
- Have any complaints about poor service been filed against the company? The local Better Business Bureau can supply this information.

CHAPTER 14

TRAVEL

PLANNING

- Is the agency a member of a travel trade association such as the American Society of Travel Agents (ASTA) or the Association of Retail Travel Agents (ARTA)? Membership in ASTA, for example, indicates that criteria governing an agent or agency's financial status and ethical practices have been met and the agency has been in business with the same owner for at least three years.

HINT: *If a problem occurs with a travel agent or agency, immediately send copies of all correspondence, dates of telephone calls, names of people contacted, agencies involved, and any documentation involving the action to the ASTA Consumer Affairs Department, ASTA World Headquarters, 1101 King Street, Alexandria, VA 22314. Ask for their free booklet, "Avoiding Travel Problems."*

- Is the agency currently approved by the International Air Transport Association (IATA)? Is it a member of the Airline Reporting Corporation (ARC)? These organizations regulate travel agencies' operations and collect their money.
- Are the agents certified? The Institute of Certified Travel Agents offers two types of proficiency designations: the Certified Travel Counselor (CTC) and the Destination Specialist (DS). To obtain a CTC rating, agents must complete an advanced program in travel management and have at least five years' experience in the travel industry. To receive the DS rating, agents must have expertise in one or more specific destination areas of the world and have a year of travel experience.
- Have the travel agents traveled extensively themselves? Do they appear willing to investigate alternative arrangements, give you the best schedules and prices, and take the time to answer questions? How many years of experience do they have? How can you reach them if there is an emergency?
- Is the agency independent, part of a national franchise, or a member of a consortium? A **consortium** is a number of smaller agencies who have formed a group to obtain benefits that the larger agencies receive.
- Is there a charge for any part of the service or for extra service? Are these fees waived for repeat customers or for company accounts? Are the fees negotiable?
- Does the agency specialize in business travel? Does it book hotel accommodations for large groups? Can it compare costs of meeting rooms and make conference arrangements?
- Does the agent keep looking for lower fares or better seating arrangements and inform you before the date of travel? Be insistent about getting low fares. Ask your travel agent two or three times for this information as you make your reservations.
- Is the appearance of the travel agency professional? Is the layout of the office inviting? Are the brochures current and attractively arranged?
- Are the billing procedures acceptable? How are refunds handled if flights are canceled? Are summary statements prepared that list each trip, date, and cost of trip by employee? Is it possible for the agency to track mileage to be applied to frequent-flyer benefits? Is it possible to provide expense account analysis?

- Does the agency sell tickets on discount carriers? Does it sell discounted or consolidator tickets? Check the restrictions and prices on consolidator fares.
- Does the agency offer e-mail alerts about bargains or extra services?

In-House Travel Departments/Travel Management Firms

Because travel costs are a significant budget item, companies require detailed records of money spent. On-site travel managers can provide immediate attention to travel needs and expenses. Some companies outsource all their travel work to firms specializing in travel. In addition to contracting with travel suppliers for low-priced reservations, these firms provide a variety of reports to management that can help track a company's preferences and costs. Either arrangement allows companies to contract for lower costs and maintain the caliber of services they need.

Online Travel Services

Travel information is readily accessed on-line. Each airline, hotel, and car rental company may be contacted directly. An on-line travel agency such as Travelocity (www.travelocity.com) or Biztravel (www.biztravel.com) also provides travel information and the opportunity to purchase tickets on-line. Some on-line travel agencies offer agent availability as well as e-mail service 24 hours a day, seven days a week. Other travel information includes:

- Up-to-date flight information; flight restrictions.
- Lowest airfares; on-time statistics.
- Delays, gate changes, cancellations within an hour of flight time.
- Credit card arrangements.
- Airline meal selections; seating preferences and availability.
- Priority mail ticket delivery; e-ticket confirmation.
- Flight changes; layover times; baggage allowance.
- Hotel and restaurant information for the United States and overseas; banquet and meeting room facilities; videoconferencing facilities.
- Security precautions; safety updates.
- Weather information and U.S. Department of State travel advisories.
- Car rental information.
- Frequent-flyer tracking/recommendations.
- Local events; city guides; virtual tours of areas.
- Overseas travel information; weather; holidays.
- Tourism offices.
- Travel discussions.
- Suggestions and tips on travel.

CD-ROMs also provide sources of travel information. These include specialized information on such topics as attractions, scenic routes, road atlases and maps, and area guides. In addition to their own Web site information, tourist bureaus may also organize their promotional materials for CD-ROM distribution.

Published Travel References

State travel and tourism departments provide information on outstanding features of their states. Chambers of Commerce, as well as local tourism and convention bureaus, are excellent sources for local information. Public libraries and bookstores have copies of consumer travel publications as well as tourist guides. Auto clubs supply information on lodging, restaurants, and places of interest to its members.

Travel reference guides provide detailed information about domestic and foreign air and rail transportation and accommodations. To use these references effectively, it is necessary to keep them up to date. Their use can save e-mail time or telephone contact time with a travel agent; however, the references are expensive, and the price may be too high for a small firm. Following are several published travel references:

Official Airline Guide® (OAG®): This guide provides subscribers with detailed airline schedules. Cities are arranged alphabetically and listed by destination and origin with the airlines that service them. Information for each flight is arranged chronologically by the time of departure. Times are stated in local times. Additional information includes flight numbers, days the flights operate, number of stops and in which cities, food service, types of aircraft, baggage allowances, and the airline's toll-free number for reservations. Ground information includes distances to the city from the airport, types of airport transportation available, car rental agencies and their toll-free numbers, and helicopter services. An electronic edition is also available.

HINT: *You may call the Official Airline Guide (800–323–4000) or check its Web site (www.oag.com) for products and services that may be purchased.*

OAG® Pocket Flight Guide and *Executive Flight Planner:* These pocket guides are quick references for checking scheduled direct flights and are especially helpful when there are delays or flight cancellations. They also include airline reservation telephone numbers of all carriers in each listed city, departure and arrival times, names of airlines and flight numbers, class of service, type of aircraft, and stops en route. The guides are updated monthly.

Official Frequent Flyer Guidebook: This book lists airline, hotel, and car rental frequent flyer programs. Updated yearly, it gives information on joining and how to claim awards, as well as frequent-flyer tips. A periodical is also available. Information about services, cost, products, and shipping can be obtained by calling 800–487–8893.

OAG® Travel Planner Hotel and Motel Redbook: Published four times a year, this reference contains detailed hotel listings (some with ratings), airline and ground information, car rental and rail directories, airport diagrams, country and city maps, and currency conversion rates. A section for each country features a calendar of events, banking and business hours, consulate office information, and travel document requirements. A North American edition, *OAG® Business Travel Planner*, is also available. The *OAG® Worldwide Hotel Directory*, an electronic source, is especially helpful for non-U.S. locations.

Official Hotel and Resort Guide: Several volumes contain descriptive information about hotels, motels, and city attractions. Maps, room rates and ratings, number of rooms, fax and Telex information, e-mail addresses, and telephone numbers are useful when trying to determine the best accommodations. The guides come in a looseleaf format with updated pages mailed regularly to subscribers.

Hotel and Travel Index: The listings in this reference are arranged alphabetically by country, state, and city. Publication of this large, comprehensive index is on a quarterly basis. It is available in single issues or by subscription and includes telephone numbers, e-mail addresses, Telex and fax information, addresses, number of units, and credit cards accepted.

Official Railway Guide: Rail timetables and fares for Amtrak as well as for trains in Canada and Mexico are available in this guide, which is published eight times a year. Information on large-city commuter rail transit services is useful to business travelers.

Thomas Cook Timetables: Schedules for Europe are available in the *Thomas Cook Continental Timetable*. The *Thomas Cook Overseas Timetable* lists schedules for all other worldwide railway systems. Both guides show maps of the area traveled, visa requirements, and time zones.

The Official National Motorcoach Guide/The Official Canadian Guide: These guides include fares and schedules for bus lines in the United States, Canada, and Mexico. Copies are available monthly. Single issues may be purchased.

UNDERSTANDING TRAVEL TERMS

Regardless of your source for professional travel assistance, you should understand the terms and acronyms you will encounter. Most important are terms used in airline travel, accommodations, and car rental.

Airline Travel Terms

Business travelers have three classes of airline service from which to choose:

First class: offers wider seats and more space than other classes of service. It also offers quality food service, free drinks, and attentive, personalized service. First class is the most expensive seating.

Business class: less expensive than first class, but the passenger also receives special benefits, such as a quiet working atmosphere.

Coach class: seats are not as wide as other classes of service, and there is limited legroom. With more passengers moving around the cabin, coach class is less quiet and less appealing as a working area. It is the least expensive class of service.

With a **direct** flight, the plane makes stops in one or more cities, but passengers do not change planes. A **nonstop** flight has no stops between the departure and arrival cities. A **connecting** flight requires a plane change.

Fare structures are determined by destination and also by such factors as the amount of advance purchase time required, the class of seating, the refundable status of the ticket, and the day of the week and time of travel.

HINT: *Nonrefundable tickets have penalties attached if plans change and the trip is not made. The entire cost of the ticket may be lost. In some cases, the ticket may be used within a year of the date the ticket was issued. If the cancelation is due to a family medical emergency, a physician's letter will void the penalty. When making reservations, be sure to request information about the penalties for canceled trips.*

For a traveler on **standby status,** there is a possibility that a seat will become available at the time of the flight. If one is available, the person travels as a regular customer. A traveler on a **waiting list** is one who wants to fly at a time when the flight is already filled. The traveler's name is placed on a numbered list. If a seat becomes available as the result of a cancellation (within 24 hours of flight time), travelers are accepted from the waiting list in the order of the assigned number and type of booking.

A **stopover** involves spending more than 12 hours in a location that is an interruption in the trip. An **open-jaw** trip is one in which the passenger returns to a city other than the one in which the trip originated. An **open ticket** is valid between two cities but indicates no specific reservation. For example, it may be used if a return trip cannot be finalized at the time the reservations were made.

Most airlines offer **frequent flyer** incentives to encourage customers to use their services. Members may take free upgrades in class of service, or save the miles and take a discounted fare trip or a free trip later, or use the credits toward other gift awards.

Airline club services are available for an annual fee. Members may use airport facilities for making telephone calls (local calls may be free), using the computer or fax, photocopying, storing luggage, or working or relaxing in a quiet area. Meeting rooms may also be booked, and refreshments are available. For a fee, some clubs allow travelers to get day passes. In a few of the busiest airports, a few companies are also offering travelers mini-office space (cyber cubicles) for rent by the minute. Quarters are cramped, but they are equipped with PCs, faxes, phones, and printers.

Accommodation Terms

Hotel rates and service depend on the type of plan offered. **Budget hotels** have low prices and cater to the traveler on a limited budget. **Executive** rooms are deluxe accommodations and expensive. **Business-class/corporate-class** rooms often have in-room work-stations with up-to-date equipment. The cost is higher than the usual corporate rate. Some businesspeople prefer **all-suite** hotels, with living room, bedroom, bath, and often kitchen facilities. This type of arrangement is useful when meetings are to be held in hotel rooms, for extended stays in one location, or for foreign business visitors. Rooms are often advertised with ratings; a four-star rating is very high. A **concierge** is a hotel employee who assists guests with such tasks as obtaining and trouble-shooting electronic equipment, making theater reservations, or suggesting restaurants. A concierge may be assigned to a specific floor or floors in a hotel. A **business center** provides guests with access to centralized office equipment and assistance.

The **American plan (AP)** is a rate that includes, in addition to the room, all meals daily. The **modified plan (MP)** offers breakfast and dinner. The **breakfast plan (BP)** includes full breakfasts each day. The **Continental plan (CP)** includes a Continental breakfast (often muffins or sweet rolls, juice, and beverage) each day. The **European plan (EP)** offers no meals. A **rack rate** is the official posted rate of a hotel room. **Corporate rates,** which must be requested, are available to business travelers and are less than the quoted normal daily hotel or motel rates. The **frequent-stay benefit** allows regular customers to receive discounted rates or extra services such as upgrades in rooms, late check-outs, car rental discounts, and special attention to reservations. Some frequent-stay programs have incentive ties to frequent-flyer membership programs. **Adjoining** rooms are next to each other but may not have a door between the rooms. **Connecting** rooms have a door between rooms.

Car Rental Terms

Car rental agencies use different classifications when describing their cars. Most agencies use the term **deluxe** to describe their largest, most expensive model. A **standard** model is a full-size car. A **compact** is regular size, and a **subcompact** is a small car.

A **drop-off charge** is the amount a car rental agency charges when a car is rented at one location but returned to another. Most contracts include **unlimited mileage,** and the driver pays a set amount for a designated time period; with a **limited mileage** plan, the payment is based on the number of miles traveled.

A **collision damage waiver** increases the cost of a rental car. Most travelers will not need these waivers since they are covered by their own personal automobile insurance policies, by their companies' policies, or by their credit card plans. Even with the purchase of a collision/damage waiver, a considerable deductible may still be owed if the car is damaged.

MAKING RESERVATIONS

When making reservations of any type—airline, hotel, or car—the preferences of the person traveling, as well as company policies, are important considerations. If other company employees are also traveling, you may be required to work with others in different offices to coordinate travel arrangements. To ensure a trip free from annoying distractions, reservations must be accurate and complete. You should handle these tasks prior to making reservations:

- Research the travel policies of the company. Well-written policies specify such items as whose signatures are required for travel approval, per diem allowances, travel restrictions, procedures for using company credit cards, and the documentation necessary for expense reports.
- Identify travel agencies, airlines, car rental agencies, and hotels and motels that the company prefers to use. Your travel agency, an on-line service, or a travel outsource firm should have this information in its database. Keep a file to update these preferences regularly along with telephone numbers and contacts.
- Maintain a permanent file of traveling preferences that includes these items:

  - ▲ Preferred days of the week for travel.
  - ▲ Departure times (early morning, midday).
  - ▲ Type of airline and seating arrangements.
  - ▲ Frequent-flyer/frequent-guest numbers and information.
  - ▲ Restrictions on costs.
  - ▲ Location of hotel; type of accommodations; services needed at hotel or motel; type of room and location of room.
  - ▲ Type and size of car; ground transportation.

HINT: *Membership in associations such as the American Management Association or the American Automobile Association allows special hotel and car rental rates. Some companies also have accounts or contracts with specific hotels and car rental agencies that allow them special rates for their employees. Always give the name of the organization and member number for which a special rate is available when making the reservation.*

- Verify the trip details, such as destination, dates, and meeting times and places with the traveler.
- Prepare a planning preference guide to use when making reservations (See Figure 14-1). Before making the final reservations, be certain the traveler approves the arrangements. Include two alternate flight reservation plans unless the traveler specifies one specific time period only. Most Web sites give you numerous choices.

HINT: *Box in or highlight the information that must be given to the travel agent or reservation assistant so you do not forget information when making reservations. Record every detail about the reservation made.*

TRAVEL PLANNING GUIDE

Name: _____ Department: _____

Credit card: Type: _____   Card #: _____   Exp. date: _____

Frequent flyer info.   Airline: _____   Number: _____

Preferences of traveler: Place a check mark in the column labeled "Information Given" each time a reservation is made through a travel center. Many travel agencies also keep this information on file for their clients

TRAVELER'S PREFERENCES

Information Given

Airline

_____   Carrier: _____

_____   Seating: _____

_____   Days of week: _____

_____   Departure times: _____

_____   Special needs: _____

_____   Other: _____

Accommodation

_____   Hotel/motel/other: _____

_____   Hotel/motel location: _____

_____   Floor/room location: _____

_____   Type of accommodations: _____

_____   Services needed: _____

Car rental

_____   Model, type, size: _____

_____   Services needed: _____

TRAVELER'S ITINERARY

Departure

Date	Departure		Arrival		Airline/Flight #	Airport
	City	Time	City	Time		

Restrictions _____
_____

Return Trip

Date	Departure		Arrival		Airline/Flight #	Airport
	City	Time	City	Time		

Restrictions _____
_____

Figure 14-1 Travel Planning Guide.

Class of service: _____ Seat: _____ Type of plane: _____

Special meals: _____ Verified: _____

Booking date: _____ Option: _____ Name of agent: _____

Confirmation date: _____ Name of agent: _____

Airline telephone: _____

Cost: _____ Method of payment: _____ Ticket pickup: _____

Flights preceding option selected: _____

Flights following option selected: _____

Transport to destination: _____ Distance to destination: _____

Comments: _____ Traveler's approval: _____

Hotel/Motel Accommodations

Hotel/motel name: _____

Address: _____ Telephone: _____

Booking date: _____ Confirmation #: _____

Date of arrival: _____ Date of departure: _____

Type of room: _____ Number of people: _____

Check-in time: _____ Check-out time: _____

Meeting facilities/size: _____ Banquet facilities/size: _____

Directions to/from hotel: _____

Courtesy transportation: _____

Cost: _____ Guaranteed arrival: _____ Method of payment: _____

Special services: _____ Cancel by: _____

Reservations agent: _____ Traveler's approval: _____

Car rental

Company name: _____

Name of driver(s): _____

Car model, type, size: _____ Special services: _____

Dates car needed: _____ Incoming airline/flight number: _____

Pickup location: _____ Drop-off location: _____

Cost: _____ Method of payment: _____ Date of reservation: _____

Agent: _____ Traveler's approval: _____

Figure 14-1 Travel Planning Guide (continued)

HINT: *To make the planning guide easily recognizable, use colored paper. Keep a copy of the guide in the files. It is an excellent source for preparing the itinerary.*

- Begin a trip folder for each person who is traveling. Collect all materials that pertain to the trip and file them in the folder. Place all written confirmations, appointments, addresses, and telephone numbers in a large envelope that fits in the folder. Include hotel brochures, restaurant suggestions, maps of the city, and transportation options that will be helpful when the traveler arrives at a destination. This trip folder will be the basis for organizing the materials that will accompany the traveler on the trip.
- Weather information (current and three-day forecasts) is available for U.S. and foreign cities by dialing 900–WEATHER or by checking online at www.weather.com. There is a per-minute charge. You may order a wallet-size card with telephone access codes for every country by calling 800–222–0300 or by accessing the Web site www.att.com/traveler.
- Confirm all meeting dates, locations, and times two days before the traveler leaves. Request directions to the meeting locations as well as directions within the building, such as floor and room numbers. Document travel arrangements as well as addresses and telephone numbers that might be used while at this destination.
- Keep profiles on each traveler for whom you make arrangements. Include telephone numbers, people to contact in emergencies, physicians, passport numbers or copies, and credit card data.

Airline Reservations

The airline reservation is usually the first reservation made after the trip has been approved and tentative appointments have been scheduled. The following information is needed before finalizing a booking:

- Departure city, date, and time.

HINT: *When booking a flight, request information on flights scheduled before and after the one that is actually being booked. Include this information as a note on the itinerary so alternative arrangements can be made in case a flight is delayed or there is a seat on an earlier flight. Rather than waiting for a reservations agent at the ticket counter when a flight is canceled, call directly the canceling airline or a travel agent.*

HINT: *To save time and to obtain the best selection of fares, indicate general departure times, such as early morning, rather than exact hours. Most airports are busiest from 9 a.m. to 11 a.m. and from 4 p.m. to 7 p.m.*

- Arrival date, time, and destination.

HINT: *Distances from cities to airports vary. Allow sufficient time between scheduled meetings and airline departure and arrival times. Be especially careful with scheduling during rush-hour traffic periods.*

HINT: *Nonstop flights to the destination city are most desirable, but check the costs. If a flight requires a connection in cities where the weather may be bad or where a terminal change is necessary, allow sufficient time between flights.*

- Restrictions on costs; special rates for conference groups.

HINT: *Companies may request that employees stay over a Saturday night to save on airline fares. Be sure to consider the extra hotel charges when comparing these rates. These fares are usually nonrefundable. Always request the airline's regulations for restricted or discounted fares.*

- Number of people traveling.
- Names, addresses, and telephone numbers of travelers.
- Frequent-flyer mileage information.

HINT: *When using frequent-flyer credits for free trips, make reservations directly with the airline. Maintain a list of frequent-flyer mileage numbers so they are available when reserving the flights. Make sure the travel agent or travel manager has the frequent-flyer numbers.*

- Type of ticket; paper or electronic (e-ticket).

HINT: *Security concerns require all passengers (including e-ticket holders) to produce photo identification and to check carry-on luggage.*

- Class of service; type of flight; seating preference; smoking or non-smoking; accommodations for the disabled if applicable; baggage limits and carry-on restrictions.

HINT: *The number and size of carry-on bags vary from airline to airline and rules are enforced rigorously. A typical carry-on item should measure no more than 22" in length by 14" in height by 9" in width.*

- Arrival time for flight check-in.

HINT: *At some airports, the recommended airport arrival for check-in for domestic flights is 2 hours before flight time; for international flights, 3 hours.*

HINT: *Curbside luggage check-in may be limited, and checking baggage at off-airport locations will likely remain prohibited.*

- Special meals, such as vegetarian, all fruit, low fat, low sodium, kosher, Hindu, and Muslim.

HINT: *Verification of special-request meals should be made approximately 48 hours before flight time to assure availability of the meals. Order the speciul meals at the time the reservation is made.*

- Electronic equipment availability.

HINT: *Airlines have various electronic services available. Some airlines have fax services. Check with the airlines to determine their restrictions for operating electronic equipment, including computers, while on the ground or in the air.*

- Airline and flight numbers.

HINT: *Avoid selecting e-tickets as a ticketing option during times of heightened security. E-tickets can cause delays when travel routes are changed or flights are canceled.*

- Name of destination airport or airports.
- Type of ground transportation and where to get it; cost; and mileage to city center.

HINT: *Find out about insurance on rental cars from the company insurance agent. What coverage does the company provide for collision and liability? Are there places where the coverage is not valid? In case of an accident, who should be contacted? Are any types of cars not covered by the company's policy? Does the policy cover all drivers?*

- Air shuttle service.

HINT: *Air shuttle reservations are not necessary. Passengers purchase tickets through a machine or en route. Check for luggage restrictions since some shuttle flights allow only carry-on bags.*

- Arrangements to pick up tickets; method of ticket payment.

HINT: *When using an e-ticket, record the confirmation number and ask for an itinerary. If a reservation is lost or there is a billing mistake, such information is crucial since you have no printed ticket to back you up. Check with the airline to see if seat selection is available before arrival at the airport. Call the airline to check what ticket documentation will be required by the airlines and their security screeners.*

- Airline telephone service.
- Airline club availability.
- Airline service centers.

HINT: *Airline service centers offer services similar to those of airline clubs; however, travelers do not have to be members. Travelers pay only for the services they use. Since charges vary from center to center, check costs carefully.*

- Name of agent making the reservation.
- Date of booking.
- Date of confirmation.

HINT: *Some airlines require that you confirm a return flight 24 to 48 hours before departure. This is always a standard procedure on international flights. Include a reminder note on the itinerary that reconfirmation is necessary.*

- On-schedule information.

HINT: *A travel agent or your on-line travel service can provide ratings on airlines' on-schedule performances. The higher the number on a scale of 1 to 10, the better the airline's on-schedule performance. Specific flight information is available on-line, along with gate changes and cancellations, up to an hour before flight time.*

- Safety information.

HINT: *Aisle seats are best if a quick departure is necessary. More legroom is available with bulkhead or exit (emergency) row seats. Travelers in emergency row seats must be willing to open emergency doors if a need arises.*

Hotel or Motel Reservations

Travel agents or travel management firms can reserve hotel or motel accommodations. You can also call the hotel or motel directly or use toll-free reservation numbers provided by the larger hotel and motel chains. On-line services provide you with accommodation locations, price ranges, ratings, number of rooms, and in some cases, virtual tours of the rooms and hotel. The following information will be helpful in making hotel or motel reservations:

- Name of person and company.
- Arrival date and time; departure date and time; whether you want a guaranteed late arrival.

HINT: *If the reservation is guaranteed late arrival, the hotel charges the customer whether the room is used that evening or not. If changes in accommodations are made while en route, the person traveling must inform the hotel or motel to avoid charges. Some hotels require one to three days' notice if reservations are canceled. When making the reservation, inquire about the cancellation policy of the hotel or motel.*

HINT: *For hotels around the world, check the Web site www.hotelguide.com. Hotel Reservations Network at 800–964–6835 or www.hoteldiscount.com is useful for booking accommodations in major cities at discounted prices. Their service is especially useful when hotel space is difficult to locate. When dealing with hotel clearinghouses, be sure to clarify who is to be paid and how cancellations are handled— through the clearinghouse or the hotel.*

• Cost restrictions.

HINT: *Promotional rates may be available. Ask for these rates when making the reservation. Call the hotel directly rather than the toll-free central reservations number to check on special rates. Do not accept rack rates. Hotel or motel room taxes as well as costs for extra amenities such as parking or equipment rentals can be expensive. Always request this information when comparing lodging accommodations.*

• Number of persons per room; bed size; smoking or no-smoking room or floor; separate secure floor for women; room location (e.g., away from vending machines); top, first, or concierge service floor.
• Method of payment (credit card number).

HINT: *Since credit cards are used so frequently, keep a list of personal and corporate credit card numbers in a special file. Mark it "confidential" and keep it in a locked drawer.*

• Frequent-guest information.
• Specific location of hotel or motel.

HINT: *Careful booking is required since there may be several hotels in the area that are part of the same chain. Request specific location information—city, address, telephone numbers, and proximity to meeting location. Online services provide directions and maps.*

• Type of plan, such as European, Continental, or modified.
• Courtesy airport pickup and return; hours of operation; pickup location; procedures to obtain the service.

HINT: *Some hotels provide complimentary transportation to certain nearby business locations. A rental car may not be necessary.*

- Check-in and check-out times; express registration and check-out availability.
- Laundry/cleaning services; barbers or hairdressers (appointments necessary?); evening drinks/refreshments; room-service hours; telephone service/extra charges; pool; exercise facilities; Continental breakfast.

HINT: *If travelers arrive late and have to leave early the next morning, they may not use the extra services. Select hotels or motels that match a traveler's needs.*

- Office assistant services; private office suite availability; equipment availability; modem capabilities; Internet access, especially high speed.

HINT: *Some hotels offer high-speed wireless Internet access. A card obtained from the hotel desk connects a laptop to the hotel's network, which offers access to the Internet from anywhere on the hotel property (not just from a room).*

HINT: *Specific information may not be available by calling a toll-free number when making reservations. To be certain of equipment and its compatibility with the items that the traveler plans to bring, call the cyber concierge at the hotel. This concierge will also help solve technology problems such as accessing the Internet or copying files to ZIP disks. The service is usually complimentary.*

HINT: *Some hotels reserve a floor for business travelers. There is usually an executive lounge where guests can relax, obtain concierge assistance, and mingle with other businesspeople. Others have business centers with up-to-date equipment and software, telephone and fax services, and secretarial assistance.*

- Health club facilities.
- Business advisors for briefings on protocol in foreign countries; access to on-line news services.
- Suites or conference rooms; banquet and meeting facilities.

HINT: *Hotels are very helpful in arranging group meetings or conferences. Contact the hotel sales manager or convention sales coordinator for information.*

- Confirmation number.

HINT: *Hotels may overbook or lose a reservation. Always request written confirmation of a hotel reservation. Obtain the name of the reservation clerk and the confirmation number.*

Car Rental Reservations

Car rental agencies have rental locations at airports or short distances from airports, at some hotels, and at downtown or suburban locations. When making car rental reservations, the following items of information will be helpful:

- Dates for which the car is needed; pickup and drop-off times; pickup and drop-off locations.

HINT: *Agencies typically do not charge for cancellations; however, some do for popular models such as vans or convertibles. Pickup and drop-off locations off the airport premises may be less expensive than those at the airport. Be sure to obtain addresses and directions for nonairport locations.*

- Name of person renting and names of drivers; age limitations of drivers.

HINT: *Drivers need to be 25 years old. A few agencies rent to drivers under 25, but the cost is higher. Check for additional drivers' charges if several people are traveling together. All drivers must be present at the car rental desk to be designated as first or second drivers.*

- Flight number of arriving flights if applicable.
- Cost restrictions; discounted rates; out-of-state or out-of-country restrictions.
- Limited or unlimited mileage; gas charges.
- Model, type, and size of car; smoke-free or not.

HINT: *When renting a car for use abroad, you may encounter unknown models. Ask the agent to identify a U.S. car that would be similar to the foreign model. Obtain the agency's fleet sheet, which indicates such items as the type and size of cars available, size of trunks, and fuel capacities.*

- Drop-off charge; late drop-off charge.

HINT: *Rental firms charge a fee for late returns. When reserving the car, ask about such penalties. Make a note on the itinerary to indicate the time a car must be returned.*

HINT: *Pickup and return procedures often take time, especially when the airports are busiest or when security checks are thorough. When reserving a car, include express check-in on the list of your comparison features.*

- Frequent-flyer coupon restrictions and information; frequent-renter information.
- Cellular telephone availability and cost.
- Computerized maps.

HINT: *Car rentals with computerized directional systems are helpful in unfamiliar territory. A user identifies the location and destination and a map shows directions (including multilanguage directions) on a screen on the dashboard. There is an extra charge for this feature. Another feature, the police alert device, is useful in an emergency. Pushing a button enables police to identify the location of the car.*

- Insurance coverage.

HINT: *If a car is rented outside the United States or Canada, additional insurance may be needed. Document and date all contacts you make with insurance carriers or credit card companies regarding insurance coverage.*

HINT: *Obtain a final bill before leaving a foreign car rental agency. Request that a car rental employee write on the rental contract that the car has been returned undamaged.*

Company Cars, Planes, Charter Flights, and Trains

A company may provide a car for an employee to use for business travel. Someone in the company is responsible for reserving the cars and keeping maintenance records on them. Since other employees also use company cars, it is important to reserve the car as early as possible in the trip-planning process so one is available when needed.

Automobile manufacturers are experimenting with installing electronic equipment and work areas into cars and minivans so they can be converted into mobile offices.

State or city tourist bureaus issue road maps and city maps as well as general information about the area. It takes time to obtain these materials; therefore, such information needs to be requested early in the planning process. On-line access provides up-to-date information that you can download and use.

HINT: *If a person travels to certain locales frequently, maintain a file of maps, lists of good restaurants, limousine services, and other information for those areas. Arrange the materials by city or state and keep the files up to date.*

HINT: *To make expense reporting and record keeping easier, prepare a mileage chart showing the number of miles between cities to which the person often travels.*

If a company has its own planes, consult the person who keeps the records for reserving a seat. This person is usually responsible for contacting the pilots, verifying departure dates and times, and following the guidelines for determining which employees (and family members, if applicable) are eligible to use the service.

When a number of people travel to the same meeting or when they go to cities not served by commercial airlines, chartering a small plane may be economical and time-efficient. To identify companies that operate charter flights, check the Yellow Pages of the local telephone directory under "Aircraft Charters and Rentals" or a similar heading. To obtain information about the cost of a charter flight, you must indicate the length of the trip, the number of stops, size of plane, overnight stays for crew members, in-flight catering, jet or nonjet, and the number of passengers.

Other information you should request includes insurance coverage, safety and experience records of the pilots, amenities available on the plane, and arrangements for ground transportation.

For those who wish to avoid airport traffic and lines and who have short distances to travel, rail service is an alternative. Stations are usually in the center of the city, making arrival at business appointments more convenient. Train travel in many foreign countries is fast and comfortable, and significantly less costly than travel by air.

ARRANGING INTERNATIONAL TRAVEL

With international business activity expanding, more company employees are traveling to destinations outside the United States. As you organize the details involved in international travel, you will need information about travel documents requirements, customs, security, medical assistance, and currency payment options.

Sources for Obtaining Travel Documents

The documents necessary for travel vary from country to country. Sources of information about a country's entry requirements or travel restrictions include the following:

- Airline offices serving the countries being visited.
- Travel agents; travel management firms.
- Foreign government tourist bureaus with offices in the United States.
- *Foreign Entry Requirements* (U.S. Government Publication M-164), which includes such information as required travel documents, immunizations, embassy or consulate addresses and telephone numbers, time required for processing travel documents, and currency regulations.
- *U.S. Consuls Help Americans Abroad* (A U.S. government publication).

HINT: *For free copies of both booklets, write to the U.S. Department of State, Bureau of Consular Affairs, Room 5807, Washington, DC 20520. Another more general publication, Your Trip Abroad, is available from the Superintendent of Documents, U.S. Government Printing Office, Washington, DC 20402-9371.*

- Embassies or consulates.

HINT: *Embassies are located in capital cities. Contact the embassies of the countries being visited and request entry requirements in writing. Consulate generals are branches of embassies, and consulates are offices with limited responsibilities; the officers are consuls or vice-consuls. For locations of these embassies or consulates, check The Congressional Directory; a copy is available at most public libraries. Consulates and embassies are helpful in emergencies or when trying to contact a person traveling in a foreign country.*

- Citizens Emergency Center for Travel Advisory Information, Department of State, Washington, DC 20520, which issues warnings about areas of political unrest, terrorism, currency restrictions, and hotel shortages in specific regions or countries.

HINT: *Visit www.travel.state.gov for worldwide travel warnings and bulletins. Immediate threats are listed as Public Announcements, which are drafted by consular offices in the country, and Travel Warnings, which are drafted by the U.S. State Department. The latter listing is considered to be more serious.*

- On-line travel forum services.

PASSPORT

A **passport,** issued by the U.S. Department of State, is required for every U.S. citizen who plans to travel in a foreign country. It is valid for ten years and gives a citizen the right to leave the United States, receive protection, if necessary, within the country being visited, and reenter the United States after traveling. A passport is not necessary for a citizen traveling to Mexico, Canada, the West Indies, the Caribbean, and some South and Central American countries, although requirements may change over time. It is wise to apply for a passport well in advance since it may take three to six weeks to obtain.

First-time passport applicants need to appear in person at a State Department passport office, at an appropriately designated courthouse (federal, state, or county), or at a post office. Everyone in a family needs an individual passport. The applicant needs to complete a form (DSP-11) and bring the following:

- Proof of identity—driver's license or government identification card.
- Proof of citizenship—birth certificate, certificate of naturalization, certificate of citizenship, or report of birth abroad of a citizen of the United States. If these are not available, secondary proof, such as a baptismal certificate, voter registration verification, elementary school records, or insurance papers, is also acceptable.
- Photographs—two identical 2-by-2-inch color or black-and-white photographs taken during the past six months. The Yellow Pages in the local telephone directory will indicate studios or stores where passport pictures are taken and processed. The date of the photograph and the owner's signature should be written on the

backs of the two photographs. Make several extra copies of the photographs. In case a passport is lost in a foreign country, extra photographs can expedite getting a replacement passport from the U.S. consulate.

- Fee.

If a person had a passport in the past and now wishes to renew it, a shorter form (DSP-82) mailed to the nearest passport agency is acceptable. The necessary documents include the application form, the old passport, two photographs, and the fee. If a passport has expired and an immediate foreign trip is necessary, applying in person at a U.S. Passport Office (located only in major cities) with proof of departure will be sufficient to get a passport issued on the spot.

HINT: *If you are not near a passport office, call 800–272–7776 or fax 202–462–2335 (Washington Passport and Visa Service). They will process applications in 24 hours to ten business days. Fees vary and shipping charges are extra.*

HINT: *Passport numbers and dates for renewal should be recorded in the "travel preference" folders maintained for all managers to remind the users of dates when passports must be renewed.*

HINT: *Order a 48-page passport with space for numerous visa stamps if the person travels a great deal to foreign countries.*

VISA

A **visa** is a permit to enter a certain country for a specific purpose on a specified date. If a visa is required in a country, the consulate of that country issues one by stamping the passport. A travel agent can obtain a visa for a traveler by sending the passport, an application, and any necessary fees to the appropriate consulate office. Many countries in Asia, the Middle East, Africa, and Eastern Europe require visas. In a very limited number of cases, a visa may be issued upon arrival in a country. Passport offices do not issue visas. Some countries require letters of reference or proof from travelers that they have transportation in and out of the country; some restrict the length of stay. Apply for a visa early; it takes time for the document to be processed.

TOURIST CARD

The tourist card grants entry to a country without a passport or visa. Tourist cards for a country such as Mexico are available from the country's embassy or consulate office, official tourist offices in the United States, some travel agencies, airlines serving that country, or at the port of entry. To get the card, travelers need proof of citizenship, such as a passport or birth certificate.

INTERNATIONAL DRIVING PERMIT

The permit verifies that the data on a regular driver's license is valid; the information is written in the language of the country in which it is needed. Many countries now allow driving with just a U.S. or Canadian license. To obtain a permit, a fee, a completed application, and two passport photographs are required. Permits remain in effect for one year from the date of issue and are available from the American/Canadian Automobile Associations (AAA/CAA). These associations can advise you of the countries where permits are necessary. Even with the permit, you will need a valid U.S. or Canadian driver's license. Association membership is not necessary to get a permit.

INTERNATIONAL CERTIFICATE OF VACCINATION

The United States does not require vaccinations before returning; however, some countries do request documentation of certain vaccinations for such diseases as cholera or yellow fever before entering. **International certificate of vaccination** forms are available through local or state public health offices or passport agencies. The form requires a physician's signature and the health department's stamp.

HINT: *For up-to-date international health information, order a copy of* Health Information for International Travel, *U.S. Government Printing Office, Washington, DC 20402. It lists required and recommended vaccinations by country and recommends ways to maintain health while traveling. Always use a current copy since regulations concerning proof of vaccination change. There is a fee for the booklet. The Centers for Disease Control (CDC) International Travelers Hotline, 404–639–3311, is another source for region-by-region information concerning required vaccinations. The Public Health Office may also have this information, but always ask the date of their sources.*

HINT: *If vaccinations are needed, remind the traveler to allow time for the vaccinations to become effective, such as five days for cholera. If multiple vaccinations are required, time may be needed between inoculations. Maintain an office record of these vaccination dates.*

CERTIFICATE OF REGISTRATION

The **certificate of registration** allows a traveler to register any personal foreign-produced item, such as a watch or camera so it does not become subject to duty. Documents, such as a bill of sale, jeweler's appraisal, or receipt are proof of prior possession. When proof is not available, travelers should take the item to a customs office, port of entry, or international airport to obtain a certificate.

CUSTOMS DECLARATION

Articles purchased in certain foreign countries and brought back to the United States are subject to **customs declaration;** there are, however, exemptions. The Department of the Treasury, U.S. Customs Service, publishes *Know Before You Go* and *Customs Hints for Returning U.S. Residents,* which are designed to assist travelers who have made purchases in foreign countries. For additional customs information, call a U.S. customs office in a major city.

HINT: *Checkpoints between the countries that make up the European Community no longer exist, simplifying passport checks and customs clearances. Remind travelers to keep their merchandise receipts in case they are needed for U.S. customs.*

Foreign Currencies

Once travel plans are completed, there may be a need to obtain foreign currency. Traveler's checks in dollars or a foreign currency are two ways for business travelers to handle money. Worldwide travel companies, such as American Express, banks with foreign exchange facilities, and some travel agents, through airline-sponsored reservation systems, sell traveler's checks in foreign currencies. The customer may receive foreign traveler's checks by registered mail or, for an additional fee, by overnight delivery, or they may be picked up in person.

Credit cards are accepted in most foreign countries. Charges are based on the day's exchange rate, which may be more favorable than the conversion rate involved with traveler's checks. Some hotels and car rental agencies do not accept debit cards for check-in or reservations. They do accept them for payment, however.

Large banks and American Express® or Thomas Cook offices usually have certain currencies available for those travelers who want cash before they arrive in a country. For example, Thomas Cook (www.us.thomascook.com) makes foreign currency available online for approximately 100 different countries. There is a charge dependent on the amount requested and a minimum delivery charge. For currencies of less frequently visited countries, call Ruesch International (800–424–2923) for speedy delivery. Current exchange rates are published in some local newspapers, in the *Wall Street Journal,* and online at OANDA (www.oanda.com). Rates may also be obtained by calling the bank or the reference librarian at the public library.

Medical Emergency Procedures

As firms expand trade with less-developed countries, they will need to provide their employees with information not only on the country's culture but also on its potential health and safety hazards. Business travelers also need information about the medical assistance that is available in the countries in which they will be traveling. Office professionals can help with this research and share the information with others in the firm.

Travelers with health conditions need to carry sufficient medication on their person—*not* in their checked baggage. They also need such items as their doctor's telephone number and a medical summary of problems, treatments, prescriptions (pharmacist/physician proof may be necessary), and allergies. Medic Alert® tags, which are available by calling 800–344–3226, identify a traveler's medical problem and provide an identification number and an emergency toll-free number.

All raw food, salads, and fruit with their skins can cause illness. Contaminated water should not be drunk (no ice cubes) or used for brushing teeth. Research the details carefully before departure as each may have individual health issues.

The State Department's Citizens Emergency Center (202–647–5225) provides material on health conditions throughout the world. Current troubled locations as well as travel safety and warnings are available. The Center for Disease Control (CDC) hotline at 404–639–3310 (www.cdc.gov/travel) provides information on possible health hazards in specific countries. The CDC also publishes *Health Information for International Travel,* which is available from the Superintendent of Documents, U.S. Government Printing Office, Washington, DC 20402.

U.S. consulate offices maintain lists of certified local English-speaking physicians and specialists and will contact family members when there are emergencies. Credit card companies and travel assistance companies have emergency hotlines and offer similar services. Some additional services include making evacuation arrangements, monitoring hospital care, translating medical information, and locating blood that has been properly screened. The State Department does not pay to airlift someone to a stateside hospital, although it does help with the details involved in arranging payment.

HINT: *There is space in the passport for identifying people to call in case of an emergency. Keep a copy of this page from all travelers' passports in the office. It is especially helpful to assistance groups when they have to contact family members.*

HINT: *The International Association for Medical Assistance to Travelers (IMAT; www.iamat.org) is a nonprofit organization that publishes a list of English-speaking doctors worldwide and gives free information about food and water risks, as well as diseases for many countries. This information should be less than a year old; therefore, do not rely on an old copy in your files.*

Foreign medical offices may want payment at the time of service. Therefore, travelers should carry information on their policy type, group or individual policy number, and type of coverage. Not all medical costs incurred outside the United States are reimbursed by U.S. insurance companies, so purchasing travel health insurance as well as insurance for emergency medical care and evacuation can be helpful. Short-term emergency insurance may be purchased from International SOS™ by calling 800–523–8662 or going online at (www.internationalsos.com) or through Worldwide Assistance® (www.worldwideassistance.com). Be sure to check the evacuation procedures for location and costs carefully. Long-term emergency medical assistance plans are available through WorldClinic® at

781–744–3170 or on-line at (www.worldclinic.com). WorldClinic® is a 24-hour medical practice staffed by physicians trained in the United States. Registration and association with this practice guarantees reliable medical help and, when necessary, evacuation to an appropriate U.S. hospital for treatment.

Cultural Awareness

Company employees who represent their firms in foreign countries will find it helpful to acquire general information about the countries as well as knowledge of the customs and values of the people with whom they will be working. Office professionals can assist in collecting and organizing this information so it can be used by anyone who travels internationally or associates with foreign visitors. In addition, office professionals need this information since they are often directly involved when foreign visitors arrive at their companies for business meetings or visits.

GENERAL INFORMATION

Find out as much as possible about a given country by reading about or searching on-line for such topics as economic climate, history, the political party in power, education, recreational facilities and events, business ethics, and negotiation strategies. A current atlas will provide general information about a country. People who have visited the country, businesspeople who have done business there, or college professors who teach language or area studies courses are also excellent resources for general information about specific countries. International travel training videos are often appropriate learning tools.

LANGUAGE

Everyone appreciates a visitor's attempts to communicate in the language of the host country. Small electronic language translators are available, often with correct pronunciations. Practice the pronunciations for such courtesy phrases as "Thank you" and "It was a pleasure meeting you." If business is to be conducted in English, the English used must be understandable. Superlatives such as "fantastic" or "absolute disaster" are confusing. Two-word verbs, such as "break up" or "win back" should be avoided. Acronyms, slang, and jargon, such as "ballpark figures," are difficult for non-English-speakers to interpret. Translation software includes document translation and vocabulary aids for several languages.

HINT: *Be patient and give individuals time to understand your comments. Speak in a normal tone; speaking louder sounds harsh and impatient.*

HINT: *International hotels may have business centers that provide interpreters and translators. Check with the U.S. hotels that have international branches.*

GREETINGS/ADDRESS

Greetings range from handshakes to bows to friendly slaps on the back. For example, handshakes are a common form of greeting and saying goodbye in the western European countries. Japanese businesspeople often bow and then shake hands. Refrain from using the left hand in greeting someone from a Muslim country.

Addressing someone with his or her title and last name is appropriate in most countries. Chinese names often appear in last name, middle name, and first name order. Place this information in the appropriate meeting folder.

HINT: *Determine the names of people who will be visited or who will be visiting, and write down the pronunciation of each name.*

CONVERSATION

Politics, money, and religion are inappropriate topics. It may be rude to discuss business during a social occasion. Express an interest in the traditions and culture of the country. Do not stereotype foreign clients or make assumptions about their cultures.

EYE CONTACT

To Americans, eye contact signifies honesty; but in some countries, such as India, avoiding eye contact signifies respect.

BUSINESS CARDS

Business cards are very appropriate in international situations. It is courteous to print one side of the card in English and the other side in the language of the country visited. When a visitor presents a business card, accept it graciously and review it carefully before placing it on your desk.

TIME

In some countries, meetings and appointments often begin late; however, this does not devalue the importance of the business to be conducted or provide a reason for others to be late. In other countries, however, promptness is imperative. Afternoon breaks of two hours or more are common in many European countries. In such cases, appointments are best made for the morning hours.

Central European businesses may close during July or August for vacation. Long weekends are also customary. Banks and some businesses in the Middle East are open on Saturday and Sunday but closed on Friday.

Time differences between various parts of the world affect travel preferences as well

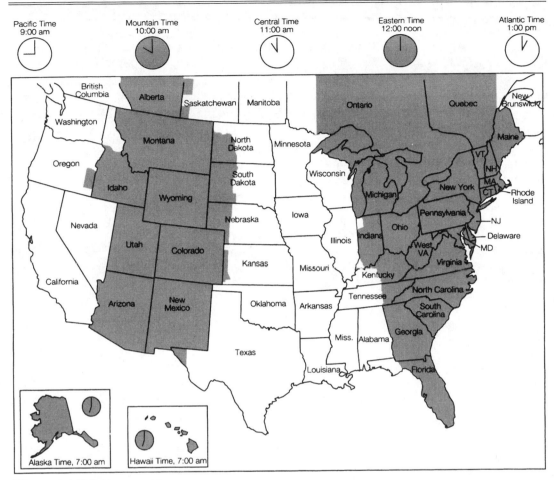

Figure 14-2 U.S. time zones.

as optimum meeting times. (For a map of U.S. time zones, see Figure 14-2; for worldwide time differences, see Table 14-1.) ClockRack is a software utility that shows current times around the world. It may be downloaded at www.pcmag.com/utilities.

HINT: *Jet lag may make it necessary to allow some time for readjustment. Avoid scheduling meetings too close to arrival time at the destination city.*

Holidays vary from country to country. Some are regional or local only. To avoid scheduling appointments on holidays, check with the country's consulate or embassy in the United States or the Web site www.religioustolerance.org.

Table 14-1
TIME DIFFERENCES AROUND THE WORLD

COUNTRY	TIME ZONE			
	EST	CST	MST	PST
American Samoa	-6	-5	-4	-3
Argentina	+2	+3	+4	+5
Australia (Sydney)	+15	+16	+17	+18
Austria	+6	+7	+8	+9
Belgium	+6	+7	+8	+9
Bolivia	+1	+2	+3	+4
Brazil	+2	+3	+4	+5
Chile	+1	+2	+3	+4
Colombia	+0	+1	+2	+3
Costa Rica	-1	+0	+1	+2
Cyprus	+7	+8	+9	+10
Denmark	+6	+7	+8	+9
Ecuador	+0	+1	+2	+3
El Salvador	-1	+0	+1	+2
Fiji	+17	+18	+19	+20
Finland	+7	+8	+9	+10
France	+6	+7	+8	+9
Germany	+6	+7	+8	+9
Greece	+7	+8	+9	+10
Guam	+15	+16	+17	+18
Guatemala	-1	+0	+1	+2
Guyana	+2	+3	+4	+5
Haiti	+0	+1	+2	+3
Honduras	-1	+0	+1	+2
Hong Kong	+13	+14	+15	+16
Indonesia	+12	+13	+14	+15
Iran	$+8\frac{1}{2}$	$+9\frac{1}{2}$	$+10\frac{1}{2}$	$+11\frac{1}{2}$
Iraq	+8	+9	+10	+11
Ireland	+5	+6	+7	+8
Israel	+7	+8	+9	+10
Italy	+6	+7	+8	+9
Ivory Coast	+5	+6	+7	+8
Japan	+14	+15	+16	+17
Kenya	+8	+9	+10	+11
Korea	+14	+15	+16	+17
Kuwait	+8	+9	+10	+11
Liberia	+5	+6	+7	+8

EST: Eastern Standard Time; MST: Mountain Standard Time; CST: Central Standard Time; PST: Pacific Standard Time.

COUNTRY	EST	CST	MST	PST
Libya	+7	+8	+9	+10
Luxembourg	+6	+7	+8	+9
Malaysia	+13	+14	+15	+16
Monaco	+6	+7	+8	+9
Netherlands	+6	+7	+8	+9
New Zealand	+17	+18	+19	+20
Nicaragua	-1	+0	+1	+2
Nigeria	+6	+7	+8	+9
Norway	+6	+7	+8	+9
Panama	+0	+1	+2	+3
Paraguay	+1	+2	+3	+4
Peru	+0	+1	+2	+3
Philippines	+13	+14	+15	+16
Portugal	+5	+6	+7	+8
Romania	+7	+8	+9	+10
Saudi Arabia	+8	+9	+10	+11
Senegal	+5	+6	+7	+8
Singapore	+13	+14	+15	+16
South Africa	+7	+8	+9	+10
Soviet Republic (Moscow)	+8	+9	+10	+11
Spain	+6	+7	+8	+9
Sri Lanka	$+10\frac{1}{2}$	$+11\frac{1}{2}$	$+12\frac{1}{2}$	$+13\frac{1}{2}$
Sweden	+6	+7	+8	+9
Switzerland	+6	+7	+8	+9
Tahiti	-5	-4	-3	-2
Taiwan	+13	+14	+15	+16
Thailand	+12	+13	+14	+15
Tunisia	+6	+7	+8	+9
Turkey	+8	+9	+10	+11
United Arab Emirates	+9	+10	+11	+10
United Kingdom	+5	+6	+7	+8
Vatican City	+6	+7	+8	+9
Venezuela	+1	+2	+3	+4

Table 14-1 (*continued*)

MEALS AND TIPPING PRACTICES

In some countries, such as Greece or Spain, the time for the evening meal is relatively late. In other European countries, the main meal may be eaten at midday. Huge banquets are often given in China. Travelers to Asian countries may wish to learn to use chopsticks. Pork is not eaten in the Middle East. Toasting is very common in European countries.

Tipping practices vary. Prepare a list of tipping suggestions for each country the traveler plans to visit and include it with the materials to be taken on the trip. Current tourist manuals found in bookstores or public libraries are useful sources of information for tipping practices. In many countries, a percentage tip is included on the bill, so additional tipping is not necessary.

BODY LANGUAGE

Head shakes may have different meanings or even opposite meanings in various countries. A nod may simply mean that the message has been heard; it does not necessarily indicate agreement. Requesting feedback is appropriate and wise at various stages of a discussion.

In Japan, it is polite to use both hands when receiving or giving items, such as business cards. In India, it is inappropriate to use the left hand for such purposes.

HINT: *The book* The Do's and Taboos of Body Language Around the World, *by Roger Axtell, deals specifically with gestures and body movements.*

GIFT GIVING

Appropriate gifts include products from the United States or an illustrated book. The quality of the gift is important. If the people involved have visited the United States in the past, notice what they admired or find out about their hobbies. In some western European countries, a gift is not given at the first meeting. Giving a banquet for Chinese businesspeople is an appropriate gift, but receiving a clock as a gift is considered bad luck in China. In Mexico, a gift of a desk clock or a fine pen or lighter is acceptable, but sterling silver items are not appreciated. No gifts of liquor should be given in the Middle Eastern countries, since alcohol is forbidden by the Islamic religion. Return dinner invitations or theater invitations are customary forms of gifts in most countries. In cultures where group work is respected, give a gift that all members of the group will enjoy.

Colors are significant and should be considered when choosing gifts; for example, white and black are associated with mourning in Japan. The same is true of purple in Latin American countries. Red and gold are good colors in China.

AGE, SEX, AND DRESS

Age is highly honored in some countries. A younger person, therefore, may be less successful in business negotiations. In other countries women may find it difficult to conduct business transactions. Visitors from some countries may not even be comfortable with seeing women in offices. In Saudia Arabia, women of any nationality are not permitted to drive. Dress for both men and women should be conservative for business meetings.

CORRESPONDENCE

Generally, business letters from foreign countries are formal and courteous; use correct titles. Review letters from your foreign correspondents and use similar phrasing when writing to them. Do not send a form letter; write an individual response.

The tone of your own business correspondence should not be overly familiar. The use of clear, precise English is helpful to a foreign reader. Short sentences limited to one idea and paragraphs of seven to eight lines will clarify major points. If several points are made, precede them with "first," "second," and so on. To avoid confusion in dates, write them out; for example, use "October 8, 2002," rather than "10/8/02" which may be interpreted as August 10.

If measurements or money are mentioned in correspondence, use metric units and current monetary conversion rates. To avoid misunderstandings, indicate both the dollar amount and the amount in the appropriate foreign currency. (For metric equivalents and conversions, see Table 14-2.)

DECISION MAKING

A company's trustworthiness is an important factor in conducting foreign business. To establish a favorable perception of trustworthiness, such items as the history of the com-

Table 14-2
APPROXIMATE CONVERSIONS TO METRIC MEASURES

WHEN YOU KNOW	MULTIPLY BY	TO FIND
Length		
Inches (in)	2.5	Centimeters (cm)
Feet (ft)	30.0	Centimeters (cm)
Yards (yd)	0.9	Meters (m)
Miles (mi)	1.6	Kilometers (km)
Area		
Square inches (in2)	6.5	Square centimeters (cm2)
Square feet (ft2)	0.09	Square meters (m2)
Square yards (yd2)	0.8	Square meters (m2)
Square miles (mi2)	2.6	Square kilometers (km2)
Acres	0.4	Hectares (ha)
Volume		
Teaspoons (tsp)	5.0	Milliliters (ml)
Tablespoons (tbsp)	15.0	Milliliters (ml)
Fluid ounces (fl oz)	30.0	Milliliters (ml)
Cups (c)	0.24	Liters (l)
Pints (pt)	0.47	Liters (l)
Quarts (qt)	0.95	Liters (l)
Gallons (gal)	3.8	Liters (l)
Cubic feet (ft3)	0.03	Cubic meters (m3)
Cubic yards (yd3)	0.76	Cubic meters (m3)
Mass (weight)		
Ounces (oz)	28.0	Grams (g)
Pounds (lb)	0.45	Kilograms (kg)
Short tons (2,000 lb)	0.9	Tonnes (t)

Source: U.S. Department of Commerce, National Bureau of Standards, Washington, DC.

pany, its founders and personal information about the people attending the meeting are helpful and may be sent to the foreign company before the visit.

In some countries the most important matters are left until the end of a meeting; in others, omitting details suggests evasiveness. Knowing such differences before a meeting and organizing the materials accordingly can aid in negotiations.

In some Asian countries decisions are often made by a group, not left to one person. The time needed to make decisions, therefore, may be lengthy, which can be a factor in scheduling meetings or business trips.

References for Foreign Travel

Numerous guides exist on customs, etiquette, and general information about foreign countries. Some provide terms and pronunciations for specific industries. Other resources include airline magazines, travel guides, a foreign country's tourist office, and on-line references. For a general perusal of on-line references, use a key phrase such as "cultural diversity" to begin the research.

Two excellent sources of information are the Business Council for International Understanding, The American University, Washington, DC 20016, and the "Culturegrams," brochures from the David M. Kennedy Center for International Studies, Brigham Young University, Provo, UT 84604, at 800–528–6279 or on-line at www.culturegrams.com. *The Business Travel Survival Guide* by Jack Cummings is a good source for tipping practices and gift-giving suggestions. *Do's and Taboos Around the World, Do's and Taboos of International Trade,* and *Do's and Taboos of Hosting International Visitors* are helpful guides for acceptable etiquette in foreign countries. Another travel site with a large listing of cultural topics is www.webofculture.com. The site includes addresses of people throughout the world who will answer questions about their country's customs and cultures.

ARRANGING TRAVEL FUNDS

Company guidelines for obtaining travel funds are usually very specific and require strict adherence to established schedules and procedures. Company credit cards, cash advances, and personal payments to be reimbursed later are ways to fund travel.

Corporate Credit Cards

A company often issues corporate credit cards to individual employees. These cards remain the property of the company. Prepare a list of the designated official in charge and all employees who are issued individual credit cards for travel purposes. This list must be kept up to date so that if an employee leaves the company, the expenses charged to that credit card are cleared before another employee receives the card privileges. Corporate credit cards that allow access to cash via ATMs decrease the need for cash advances. Credit card receipts provide an audit of travel expenses when they are matched against the monthly report from the credit card company. American Express®, Diners Club®, Visa®, and MasterCard® are major providers of corporate credit cards.

HINT: *Review the policy manual for corporate credit card rules. Be certain each credit card holder receives a copy of the policy when the card is assigned.*

Cash Advances

A cash advance allows a traveler to receive funds before leaving on a business trip. Since all costs are not known in advance, it is necessary to estimate such expenses as food and business entertainment. A typical cash advance form requires a manager's approval.

To be sure the amount received matches the amount requested, count the money received and do not sign a receipt form until this has been verified. Place the cash or check in an envelope for the traveler, include a copy of the signed request form, and obtain a signature from the person who accepts the money. File that signed copy in the preliminary trip folder; it will be helpful in preparing the expense claim. Someone has to document to whom a cash advance was given, how much was actually spent, and when unspent funds were returned. Expenses on corporate credit cards are simpler to track.

Personal Payments

When payments for travel expenses are handled personally by the traveler, receipts for all expenditures are necessary for reimbursement. Be sure there is sufficient credit available on a personal credit card to cover costs when entertaining clients. Since some of the payments may have been on the traveler's personal credit card, it is advisable to make copies of all receipts. The traveler's copy accompanies the expense claim.

HINT: *For IRS and expense claim purposes, request cash register receipts for food and miscellaneous expenses rather than a fill-in-the-blank tab.*

HINT: *For information about foreign exchange rates, call a local bank or check online at www.oanda.com for a listing of more than 150 different currencies and current conversion rates. Know the currency of the traveler's destination, including smaller denominations. It is helpful to obtain a small amount of the local currency before the trip for tips, cabs, or meals upon arrival.*

HINT: *Exchange rates are usually better overseas than at home. Once abroad, banks rather than airport agencies or hotels often offer the best rates. Advise travelers to exchange money as needed; some countries will not reexchange leftover currency when a traveler leaves.*

HINT: *Austria, Belgium, Finland, France, Germany, Ireland, Italy, Luxembourg, Netherlands, Portugal, and Spain now use Euros.*

Letters of Credit

Handling travel funds with a letter of credit allows a traveler to obtain funds up to a designated amount from banks. Such a letter states that the person is a customer in good standing at the bank issuing the letter. The letter acts as an introduction in financial institutions and allows the bearer to make withdrawals up to the amount of the specified credit line.

Automated Teller Machines (ATMs)

Users punch in their personal identification numbers (PIN) and receive the amount in the local currency. Banks deduct the amount withdrawn (U.S. dollar conversion) and a service charge from users' home bank accounts.

HINT: *ATMs are popular in Europe, but they may not always accept another country's cards. Check with the company issuing the ATM card for a list of its usable ATM locations and its charges. Check, too, that the user's PIN has the correct number of digits for use abroad.*

Traveler's Checks

Some banks or corporate travel companies sell traveler's checks without a commission. American Express accepts telephone orders for traveler's checks and mails them first-class. If traveler's checks are lost or stolen, they can be replaced. Unused checks may be used on other trips. Travelers may purchase traveler's checks in foreign currency and thus eliminate the need for currency exchange. Since some countries impose surcharges for cashing traveler's checks, purchase the checks in larger denominations to limit the number of transactions.

Smart Cards

The card resembles a credit card in size. A traveler buys an amount of money, and this amount is digitized on a microchip on the card. When the card is used, the amount of the purchase decreases the card's balance.

Reducing Travel Costs

Companies constantly evaluate travel and entertainment expenses to determine how to cut costs. Office professionals need an awareness of these travel management strategies:

- Travel policy. Developing a comprehensive travel policy is the first step in establishing a travel management program. The following are suggested areas to include in a travel policy:

▲ Who may travel/booking procedures.

▲ Who approves travel/credit card authorization.

▲ Designated travel company.

▲ Class of travel/designated airline, hotel, and car rental agency.

▲ Expense ranges/per diem rates.

▲ Reimbursement procedures.

▲ Insurance coverage.

▲ Meals and entertainment.

▲ Frequent-flyer benefits/ownership.

▲ Miscellaneous expenses.

The policy needs to be communicated to employees in such a way that they accept it, and it needs to be enforced in such a way that all are treated fairly. See Chapter 11 for additional information on policy manuals.

- Travel consolidation. Consolidating travel arrangements with one agency or on-line provider or with one hotel, airline, or car rental agency generates savings and upgraded services because of the volume of travel purchases. If the travel agency provides detailed reports on travel spending habits and suggestions for saving money, companies can analyze their travel needs and make adjustments.

- In-house travel manager/designated employee. Centralizing travel responsibilities with a designated employee or manager eliminates the time consumed by individuals planning their own trips. An in-house manager can obtain better prices and prepare contracts with travel firms in line with the company's travel policy. The company can also prevent travel policy abuses.

- Corporate charge cards. Companies issue these cards to travelers to control expenses and make it easier and faster to track and report major expenditures. The card reduces the need for large cash advances. Companies can select and code restrictions to prevent misuse. One check or transfer covers the costs each month. Discount dining cards for participating restaurants also produce savings.

- Frequent flyer, hotel, car rental programs. Taking advantage of these programs offers such perks as service upgrades or free trips or rooms. The programs are interrelated; for example, frequent flyers may receive hotel savings and car rental coupons.

- Conference calls/teleconferencing/videoconferencing. Once initial meetings are over, companies often find that they can conduct the rest of their business with a conference call. A videoconference may also be acceptable. Both alternatives require clear objectives and a block of uninterrupted time. Sending several employees to an off-site conference is costly; a teleconference may be more cost-effective.

Other cost-saving suggestions regarding travel arrangements include:

- Reserve flights as early as possible. The biggest discounts are for 14 to 30 days in advance. Reserve the least expensive flight even if it is not with the individual's frequent flyer airline.
- Investigate Saturday night stay-over requirements. They may not result in savings if lodging and food costs are expensive.
- Reserve a flight that lands at a smaller or less congested airport. Try to schedule meetings at hotels/motels near the airport to eliminate the costs of car rentals or other ground travel. Taxes on car rentals are especially high in foreign countries; taxis and limousines may be less expensive.
- Start a database of the best hotels in each city to which company employees travel most frequently.
- Ask for upgrades on every reservation. Established customers often receive extra amenities.
- Downgrade the size of the rental car unless the car's safety record is worse than average.

PREPARING THE ITINERARY

The **itinerary** is a chronological outline of travel plans prepared for each person who is traveling. Even though the airline prepares a flight itinerary, it is helpful for the traveler to have more detailed information presented on a day-by-day basis.

The planning guide provides an excellent source of information for the itinerary. Itinerary formats may vary, but the information is similar on all. (See Figure 14-3.) This information includes:

- Dates and times of departure and arrival.

HINT: *Include the day of the week as well as date. If the international date line is crossed, be sure the dates are accurate. If the flight crosses time zones, use the local arrival time. Indicate the number of hours of flying time between destinations.*

- Departure and arrival cities.

HINT: *A city may have more than one airport. For example, New York has both La-Guardia and Kennedy. Choose the airport closest to the meeting location. Clearly identify the destination airport on the itinerary.*

- Airline; flight numbers; seat assignment; services provided.
- Airport transportation; cost; times of operation; telephone numbers of limousine services.
- Car rental agency; type of car; charge card used.

ITINERARY
SANDRA MCNEELEY
May 6–8, 20—
National Pharmaceutical Sales Conference

WEDNESDAY, MAY 6

1:30 p.m.	Leave Chicago/O'Hare Field American Airlines Flight No. 836 Nonstop
5:10 p.m.	Arrive Boston/Logan Int. Hotel Transportation Provided Phone: 617-267-9314 Hotel: Revere Square Hotel, 9135 Revere Square Dates: May 6 and 7 Confirmation No. 156J92CD (by Joan) Guaranteed Arrival

NOTE: Upon arrival, contact Tom Kennedy regarding conference presentation.

THURSDAY, MAY 7

7:30 a.m.	Breakfast meeting with Donald Hallahan and Courtney Watson, Revere Square Coffee Shop Advertising Review Promotion Campaign

NOTE: Contact conference headquarters for conference handouts.

10:00 a.m.	Presentation to National Pharmaceutical Sales Conference, Decker Hall, Revere Square Hotel
11:45 a.m.	Luncheon with Jon Blake, new account, Pullman Room, Regency Square Hotel
4:00 p.m.	Meeting with all regional sales managers, Hall B, Revere Square Hotel
7:30 p.m.	Conference Banquet, Boston Room, Revere Square Hotel

FRIDAY, MAY 8

7:30 a.m.	Breakfast meeting with Tom Kennedy, Hotel Coffee Shop
10:00 a.m.	Exhibits Review with Sandra Milo, Grand Ballroom, Revere Square Hotel
12:00 noon	Conference Luncheon, Boston Room, Revere Square Hotel
3:10 p.m.	Leave Boston/Logan Int. American Airlines Flight No. 462 Nonstop
5:30 p.m.	Arrive Chicago/O'Hare Airport

Figure 14-3 Sample itinerary.

- Accommodations; confirmation numbers; written confirmations; telephone, fax, or Telex numbers; e-mail address; guaranteed arrival time; date reservation was made; name of person who made the reservation; credit card used; services available.
- Daily appointments; address; room and building; time of meeting; names of people involved; reason for meeting; contact persons and their office and home telephone numbers.

HINT: *If social engagements are scheduled, indicate the type of dress required.*

- Reminders for each appointment, such as where to find materials needed for each meeting or personal information about the people at the meeting.

HINT: *If an appointment is some distance away from the airport, indicate its distance so the meeting can end on time. Highlight times when a connection time is short or extra materials are needed. Leave a reminder if a task must be completed, such as making a reservation if a return time or date was left open.*

When the itinerary is up to date, prepare two copies for the traveler (one to carry and one for the luggage), one copy for the office files, and one copy for the manager left in charge. The traveler may also wish additional copies for family and/or friends.

ORGANIZING TRAVEL DETAILS

Even though materials may be collected as soon as the initial plans for a business trip are in place, it is not always possible to complete everything before the trip begins. Some last-minute tasks include the following:

- Check the tickets against the information in the trip planning folder. Check the itinerary to be sure times, dates, and locations match the tickets.
- Organize materials and supplies that will be needed for the trip. A checklist for each traveler is helpful. The following are examples of items to include on the list:
    - ▲ Copy of itinerary.
    - ▲ Tickets.
    - ▲ Motel or hotel information.
    - ▲ Money, letters of credit, or traveler's checks.

HINT: *If traveler's checks are used, give the traveler a list of the check numbers, to be kept separate from the checks. Keep a second list in the office. Each time a traveler's check is spent, it should be recorded. In case of loss, the check numbers will be avail-*

able for a refund. (See the section Special Payment Forms in Chapter 13 for a discussion of traveler's checks.)

▲ List of airline, hotel, and car rental toll-free numbers.
▲ Speeches and reports.

HINT: *In case the original copy of a speech gets misplaced, e-mail or fax a copy to a specified individual at the location of the meeting. Send handouts ahead of time so they will not have to be carried on the plane. Allow sufficient time for the items to reach their designated locations and verify that they were received. If the materials are sent to a hotel, indicate the name, date of arrival, and specific meeting for which they will be used. If they are sent to a business, address the package to a specific person in that organization.*

▲ Business cards; company letterhead and envelopes, preaddressed mailing envelopes; company forms, Post-it® notes, manila envelopes, legal pads, folders; paper clips, stamps, notepads, tape, rubber bands, calendar.
▲ Notes on the area, on special customs, and on etiquette (for foreign countries).
▲ Items that must be delivered; wrapped gifts.
▲ Airline timetables; maps.
▲ Expense account forms; office checks.
▲ Passport; visa.
▲ Vaccination certificates; international driver's license or permit.
▲ Medical prescriptions/medications.

HINT: *Prescriptions should have a professionally printed pharmaceutical label identifying the medication.*

▲ Names and telephone numbers of doctors and emergency contacts.

HINT: *Since medical and eyeglass prescriptions are important and difficult to replace, be sure they are in the materials to be carried by hand. Include a personal health information card with blood type and allergies.*

▲ Credit cards; lost card telephone numbers.

HINT: *A list of card numbers and toll-free customer service numbers of the credit card companies is helpful in case the cards are lost. Prepare a list for the office and one for the traveler.*

▲ Frequent-flyer numbers.

▲ Telephone smart card; emergency telephone numbers.

▲ Portable slide projector or overhead projector.

▲ Slides, transparencies, handouts.

HINT: *Audiovisual presentations are less frustrating if the materials are sequenced and numbered before the trip begins. Include relevant instructions for setting up equipment when a presentation is to be given, as well as troubleshooting tips.*

▲ Calculator.

▲ Laptop computer; batteries; charger; extra disks, software; summary of keystrokes to activate the modem, fax, printer, and programs.

▲ Cell phone; handheld organizer; pager.

HINT: *Handhelds (PDAs) can synchronize travel schedules, daily appointments, expense reports, and so forth, with a PC. Some also allow slide-in modules such as pagers and cell phones.*

HINT: *E-mail is available with a cell phone. When e-mail is received, the program calls a traveler's cell phone. The traveler calls the number that appears on the phone to read his or her message. The traveler can reply vocally; the person being called gets an e-mail message with directions on how to retrieve the message.*

▲ Adapters for three-prong plugs (some locations may have only two-prong outlets); car battery adapters for electronic equipment, adapters for use in foreign countries.

▲ Surge protector; battery packs.

HINT: *Prepare a list of computer repair locations in each of the areas the traveler plans to visit. Check on-line for ways to access good connections with a modem while traveling.*

HINT: *Make copies of this list for use in organizing travel materials. Ask the traveler to check the items that need to be packed. Include one completed copy in his or her files and keep one in the office.*

• Contact the airline, travel agency, hotel or motel, or car rental agency if any changes in travel plans are made. Confirm the airline reservation a day before departure.

• Place materials for each appointment in a separate folder and place them in envelopes with clasps. Prepare a label with the company name and date of appointment for each folder as well as for the envelope. Number each envelope in consecutive order according to the information on the itinerary. In case the envelopes are mixed up, the numbers will make it easy to rearrange. Include helpful information such as recent correspondence, an annual report of financial information, names of people contacted previously, officers' names, and product or service updates for each company.

- Place airline tickets and confirmations in a special envelope labeled "Tickets." Do not pack the tickets, passports, visas, or traveler's checks in the luggage that is to be checked. If a ticket is lost or stolen, the traveler must buy a new one. The airline will reimburse the traveler for the cost of this purchase, but it may take as long as four months to receive the refund.

- Contact the airline to determine the number, weight, and size restrictions for luggage that may be carried on the plane. Sort materials in two groups—one for hand-carried luggage and one for checked luggage.

- Make photocopies of airline tickets, passport identification page, driver's license, and credit cards. Keep one set at the office and give the other set to the traveler.

- Remind the traveler to review carefully everything being carried on the plane. The FAA has prohibited all knives and cutting instruments, but airports may impose additional and stricter limits.

- Obtain a list of people who should be given the traveler's out-of-town number. Make arrangements for contacts with you at regularly scheduled times. Cybercafés are widely available to international travelers and often offer a more reasonable way to keep in touch with the office than the expensive hotel provision. Check the Internet Café Guide (www.netcafeguide.com), which includes hundreds of listings of connected cafés all over the world.

HINT: *With the help of an e-guide and the online Café Guide list, the cafés that are near the traveler's hotel can be identified. By subscribing to a special service such as Mail2Web, a traveler can also access accumulated e-mails from home at a cybercafé.*

- Maintain a list of the items packed and hand carried. This list will be helpful in the event that luggage is lost.

TRAVEL EMERGENCIES AND SAFETY

Travelers can minimize travel safety problems if they are prepared to handle emergency situations. Office professionals can assist travelers by identifying potential hazards and suggesting precautions. Some suggestions are:

- Recommend that an international traveler register with a nearby U.S. embassy or consulate. A family may leave messages with the Citizens Emergency Center,

202–647–5225. The consulate contacts the traveler and follows up with the family. Suggest that the traveler write names of contact people on the pages provided in the passport.

- Establish a procedure for financial emergencies in case of loss or theft of a wallet, handbag, or airline tickets. In foreign countries, consulate offices will assist a traveler in contacting employer or family. Travelers' aid desks at airports can provide some help if money and all identification have been lost or stolen. Funds may be wired through a bank or through Western Union.
- Clarify company legal assistance. In foreign countries a consul can provide names of attorneys but cannot obtain jail releases. If there are complications, call the Citizens Emergency Office at the State Department (202–647–5225) or the International Legal Defense Council (215–977–9982).
- Determine the location of the U.S. embassy or consulate office.
- Check out kidnapping and ransom (K&R) insurance if the firm does a considerable amount of travel in unsafe locales.

HINT: *If a passport is stolen or lost, it should be reported to the police and to the passport division of the nearest U.S. consulate. The consul will need the police report and positive proof of citizenship.*

- Record airline ticket numbers and date and place of issue on the itinerary. This information is also helpful if the airline ticket is lost or stolen and a replacement is necessary—the traveler reports the loss to the airline's refund department, completes a form, and sends it to the credit card company for reimbursement.
- Record numbers of traveler's checks and keep the list at the office. Request the telephone numbers and the procedures for reporting and replacing lost or stolen traveler's checks from the company selling them. All companies do not have the same procedures. Report the loss to police and the company that sold the checks.
- Report credit card losses to the police and to the company issuing the card. Keep a list of these corporate credit card telephone numbers available. Send a copy with the traveler so card losses can be reported promptly.
- Make reservations at hotels and motels with good security. Travel agents can check safety factors for you. Concierge floors or business centers often have restricted access or special security features. Other security features include plastic access cards (instead of keys), 24-hour front desk service, and inside entry to motel rooms.
- Remind travelers to take these precautions while staying at hotels:

  ▲ Do not open a hotel/motel door to a stranger. Verify with the front desk if a potential visitor announces "Room service" and nothing has been ordered.

▲ Use the door locks and chains. Never leave the door to the room ajar.

▲ Check the locks on deck or patio doors and windows to be sure they work and have locks.

▲ Schedule meetings in a public area rather than in your room.

▲ Locate a fire escape. Check the number of doors to the escape (in case of poor visibility because of smoke).

▲ Check with the concierge or front desk about the safety of areas around the hotel before walking or jogging alone.

▲ Use the hotel safe for important papers and valuables.

▲ Request that check-in personnel write the room number on paper rather than announce it.

▲ Try using another form of identification besides the passport when checking into a hotel in a foreign country, especially if the hotel is required to hold a piece of identification while you are a guest.

▲ Do not use the "Make Up Room" sign. Call housekeeping to tell them when to make up the room. (This sign is an obvious disclosure that no one is in the room.)

▲ Do not use cabs that are not legitimate. Ask someone at the hotel to suggest a reputable taxi company.

▲ Carry the name of the hotel with you. It helps with pronunciation or if you forget the hotel's name and address.

▲ Use luggage labels with last name and initials only and the company address.

• Remind travelers who are driving to take these precautions:

▲ Keep doors locked and windows closed when driving and when leaving the car. In foreign countries, be sure that the car has air-conditioning.

▲ Avoid rest areas that are unattended or that have few people in them. Choose well-lit gas stations and pay phones.

▲ Rent a vehicle that does not advertise "rental car" by license or company identification.

▲ Request an in-car telephone or an e-guide when reserving a rental car. E-guides identify your location and can provide exact directions to any location in the city.

▲ Contact the police in case of a breakdown. Do not leave the car if someone stops to help. Know how the rental car works *before* you leave the car rental agency.

▲ Understand metric speed and mileage used in other countries. See Tables 14-2 and 14-3.

▲ Inform the office of any route or destination changes.

▲ Hire a reputable driver/guide in congested areas.

- Include identification and an itinerary inside checked luggage as well as in carry-on items. Keep a list of the makes, models, and serial numbers of all electronic equipment. Do not leave baggage out of sight.

- Keep luggage between your feet while waiting in check-in lines or queues. Keep a firm grasp on laptops at all times. Hand the laptop to a security agent at the luggage checkpoint rather than place it on the conveyor belt.

- Travelers should contact the airline when bags are missing and complete a written report. It is necessary to have the claim checks and to describe the luggage. Airlines reimburse passengers if baggage is lost or damaged.

- Recommend that expensive jewelry and watches be left at home when traveling. Dress should be conservative. Outward displays of wealth attract criminals.

- Do not discuss travel plans with callers or people coming in to the office. Take their messages and relay the information to appropriate individuals. This practice protects both the traveler and the family.

- Book flights that do not make connections in airports with unacceptable security. Open areas and areas around lockers and telephone booths are not the safest places in airports.

- Ask the airlines for details on their security information. Check if they perform bag-to-traveler check-and-match operations. Ask how old the aircraft is. Even planes that are less than two years old still need to have their glitches checked.

- Contact the American consulate if serious disturbances break out while you are in a foreign country.

COMPLETING FOLLOW-UP TASKS

Well-planned business travel includes monitoring the office tasks that must be completed during a manager's absence. While the manager is away, the office professional assumes responsibility for the daily office tasks necessary to operate efficiently. When the manager returns, the office professional often prepares the expense report and follows up on the tasks resulting from the trip.

Handling Tasks During a Manager's Absence

You should decide which tasks the manager must handle upon returning to the office and which you can handle without immediate supervision. The following suggestions will assist you in organizing work so time is used efficiently.

- Maintain a day-by-day activities list. Highlight the priority action items to alert the manager who contacts the office regularly. Compile questions that need to be asked when he or she calls. Identify the best time to contact the manager. Obtain fax numbers and e-mail addresses for the places where the manager has scheduled meetings. Clarify how paychecks or money transfers should be handled *before* the trip begins.

HINT: *If a manager is traveling overseas, consider bringing a laptop home in the evenings. Time differences often require alerting travelers of airline changes or reading or handling e-mail at other times than during the hours of a normal working day.*

- Understand the parameters of authority while the manager is away from the office. Discuss emergency procedures and delegation of tasks *before* he or she leaves. Know who has been authorized to handle emergencies and to make major company decisions. When another manager has been designated to be in charge, be sure all pertinent items and telephone calls are directed to that person. Know who has the authority to sign paperwork.
- Maintain folders for mail and e-mails received and the actions taken. Label the folders as follows:
    ▲ Immediate attention.
    ▲ Actions completed.

HINT: *Maintain a log of each task or action taken. For easy reference, attach this log to the inside of the "Actions completed" folder. Include a copy of the paperwork connected with each action.*

    ▲ General reading.
    ▲ General correspondence.
    ▲ Signature/approval required.
    ▲ Phone calls; visitors; appointments made; activities in the office.

- Compose routine correspondence as needed. Sign the letters as follows:

    Sincerely yours,
    Barbara Williams
    Executive Assistant to J. T. Todd

- Forward mail, use e-mail, or fax items to predesignated locations. Maintain a record of these items along with dates they were forwarded. Keep copies in a folder labeled "Items sent to (name)." If mailing items, number each item and inform the manager of the number of items enclosed. Indicate the number and type of items being forwarded and keep a list for the office files.

- Maintain a list of all telephone calls and all appointments made each day. Prioritize the calls and keep a list that will be helpful to a manager. Always update the appointment calendars. As directed, cancel and reschedule appointments and committee meetings during the manager's absence.

Completing Expense Reports

Completing expense reports is another task that requires attention. Some businesses require receipts for all company money spent; others have per diem allowances, which require only receipts for expenses above the limits. For information about IRS per diem standard allowances, order IRS Publication 463 or call 800–829–367. For per diem listings in various cities, call the Government Printing Office at 202–512–1800 or go on-line at www.policyworks.gov./perdiems. Follow explicitly the company guidelines for categorizing travel expenses. If questions arise about travel expenses, discuss them with the person submitting the expenses. Study company policy and ask for clarification when needed.

Here are some suggestions for completing expense reports:

- Complete the expense claim paperwork as quickly as possible. If a traveler used a PDA while away from the office, expenses can be entered immediately and transferred to the office. When foreign travelers complete expense reports, software that converts foreign currencies to U.S. dollars is useful. If a receipt is missing or a gap in activities is evident, it will be easier for the manager to remember the event now rather than later.
- Use spreadsheet software or a software application designed to set up expense reports.
- Review the receipts and notes made while traveling. If any part of the trip was canceled, check the monthly credit card statements carefully for excess charges.
- Categorize the receipts by transportation, registration, food, lodging, business entertainment, and miscellaneous (tips, tolls, parking, telephone and fax charges, office assistant services, postage charges).
- Attach all required receipts to the expense claim forms. Make copies of each receipt for the files. Keep these receipts for five years. Legitimate business expenses include the following:

  - ▲ Transportation (airline, shuttle, railroad, bus, taxi, limousine, or rapid transit); car rentals; automobile costs at the current IRS rates or established company rates per mile; parking fees; flight insurance.
  - ▲ Lodging; laundry and cleaning costs.
  - ▲ Telephone, fax, mail, and shipping charges; business supplies.

▲ Exhibit charges; conference registration fees.

▲ Conference room charges.

▲ Business entertainment expenses.

▲ Meals, tips.

- Indicate the type of entertainment, names of clients (titles and companies repre-sented), dates, location (city, state, and street location), duration, and the purpose of the meeting when itemizing the business entertainment expenses on the claim form. The IRS reviews these amounts very carefully and specifies that they must relate to the business being conducted. The expenses may be incurred directly be-fore or after a business activity takes place as well as during the activity. File the detailed written documentation with a copy of the expense report.

HINT: Travel, Entertainment, and Gift Expenses, *a booklet published by the IRS, lists rules for handling deductible travel expenses. You can obtain a copy from the IRS or, in many cities, from the public library. For up-to-date rulings on spousal travel deductions and requirements, refer the traveler to a tax adviser.*

- Compare the total expense incurred with the cash advance made. If money is owed to the company, get a check for the difference from the traveler and attach it to the expense report.
- Review the completed expense claim carefully. Check all calculations at least twice. Obtain the necessary signatures and submit the claim for payment. It is important to have the necessary documentation and to be sure the claim is accurate the first time it is submitted so reimbursements will not be delayed.

Handling Post-Travel Tasks

When the traveler returns to the office, numerous tasks will need completion. Some suggestions for handling these follow-up activities include:

- Avoid scheduling lengthy, important meetings the first day or two after the trip.
- Review the activities that have taken place during the time away from the office. Schedule time on the appointment calendar to discuss the items in the "Immediate attention" and "Actions completed" folders.
- Compose thank-you letters for courtesies that were extended during the trip. Write the appropriate follow-up letters. Send gifts when appropriate.
- Replace all materials that were removed from the files for use during the business trip. The checklists of materials that were packed for the trip provide a reminder of those items that were taken out of the office. If necessary, prepare computer files or folders for new contacts or subjects that were the result of the trip.

- Record comments about travel and hotel preferences in the travel preference folder.
- Contact the airline's consumer affairs office to file a complaint or report on good service. Complaints may also be made to the U.S. Department of Transportation, Consumer Affairs Division, Room 10405, 400 Seventh Street SW, Washington, DC 20590 (202–366–2220). To report safety matters, call the Federal Aviation Administration (800–255–1111).

Successful meetings are the result of careful planning and management. There are two types of meetings. A **formal meeting** is a structured, planned meeting with a prepared agenda, such as an annual sales meeting, yearly conference, or convention. An **informal meeting** is generally held on company premises and can be held regularly or called at the last minute.

PLANNING A MEETING

Whether the meeting is formal or informal, the process of planning for a meeting is the same. Certain questions must be answered by the person calling the meeting so the meeting planner can act:

- What is the purpose of the meeting?
- How long will the meeting run?
- Who should attend?
- What equipment and aids will be needed?
- Where should the meeting be held?
- When is the best time to hold the meeting?

To determine the time and place of the meeting, you need to notify participants of the meeting and determine their availability. Reserve at least three convenient dates and times. Ask them to hold these times open until they are called back later in the day to confirm the meeting's date and time. After contacting all participants, review the schedule to see what date and time are acceptable to all. You may have to undertake this process several times to arrive at an acceptable date and time.

Depending on the complexity of the meeting, scheduling, budget, and other forms may be necessary. Such meeting forms may be available through the company or, if not, an office supply store may carry standard forms.

Meeting Functions

The functions involved in planning and running a meeting depend on how the organization operates, the type of meeting, and whether the planning and execution

CHAPTER 15

MEETING

PLANNING

AND

MANAGEMENT

of the meeting rests with one person or with committees. All or some of the following functions must be addressed in planning a meeting:

- Budget.
- Agenda.
- Attendees.
- Meeting notices and agendas.
- Guests, speakers, or program participants.
- Site and facilities.
- Equipment and audiovisuals.
- Exhibits and demonstrations.
- Refreshments and meals.
- Minutes and proceedings.

Notification of Meeting Participants

Notification of participants can be made by telephone, mail, or computer through e-mail or network communication system, if available. The meeting planner should make a list of those to be notified, make sure all have been informed, and check responses so a final list of attendees can be prepared. Participants should be informed of the day, time, and place of the meeting, the topic to be discussed, and the identity of other participants. An agenda and supplementary material should also be distributed; for example, directions to the meeting location are often provided.

In addition, supplementary material should be gathered for the meeting. The meeting room should have enough chairs, pads, pencils, and paper. All charts and graphic material should be displayed, and any audiovisual equipment and/or computer technology should be checked and set up for use.

Agenda

An agenda is a list of all matters to be brought up at the meeting. Agendas vary with the type of meeting. Informal meeting agendas simply list the items to be discussed during the meeting. Formal meeting agendas detail times, events, speakers, and locations of events.

HINT: *All papers and documents pertaining to matters that will be discussed at the next meeting should be kept in a meeting folder. The folder should contain copies of the meeting notice, a list of those to whom notices were sent, drafts of resolutions to be taken up at the meeting, and an outline of the minutes of the last meeting. An agenda can be prepared from material accumulated in the current meeting folder.*

In formal meetings, the bylaws of an organization usually state the order of business of the meeting, and an agenda can be prepared from this model. A typical agenda for a directors' meeting might include:

- Reading of the minutes of the last directors' meeting.
- Presentation of reports of officers and committees.
- Adoption of a resolution approving the minutes of executive committee meetings.
- Current business.

The agenda should list each item to be acted upon. The agenda with copies of all minutes, reports, handouts, visuals, and resolutions attached should be furnished to each participant. (See Figure 15-1.)

Meeting Coordination Software

The personal computer is a valuable tool when planning meetings. Spreadsheets, project management software, personal information management or desktop management software, and scheduling software can be used to coordinate and keep track of the many details. (Refer to Chapter 8 for detailed information on these software programs.) A scheduling program specifically designed for meeting planners is recommended for anyone who spends considerable time with this type of activity. This type of software integrates e-mail, calendaring, and scheduling functions. Generally, you can have access to meeting participants' schedules, confirm room space, arrange for equipment, and send meeting notices via e-mail. Some schedule software programs include a "meeting wizard" function to guide you through the steps of the meeting planning process. In addition to dedicated scheduling applications, programs such as Microsoft Outlook® can also be utilized for this purpose.

Meeting Room Facilities and Supplies

As soon as a date for the meeting has been determined, a meeting room must be selected. Most companies have conference rooms available for small meetings of company personnel. For large meetings, an off-site area may be selected. This may entail reserving a ballroom in a hotel or teleconference rooms in a number of cities. In selecting a meeting site several factors must be considered:

- Size of group and purpose of meeting.
- Budget.
- Ambience, acoustics, privacy.
- Ventilation.

(a)

MEETING OF THE HIGHER EDUCATION ADVISORY COMMITTEE

May 17, 20___

AGENDA

1. Discuss latest product proposal.
2. Review new product literature.
3. Update list of potential clients.
4. Report on previous sales calls to top six universities.

(b)   **SALES MEETING CONFERENCE**

Monday, March 16, 20___

8–9 a.m.	Breakfast	Tiffany Room
9–10:30 a.m.	Opening Session	Ballroom A
	James Hughes, Senior VP	
10:30–11 a.m.	Break	
11 a.m.–Noon	Selling to Higher Education	Ballroom A
	Peter Mann, Consultant	
Noon–1 p.m.	Lunch	Terrace Room

Tuesday, March 17, 20___

8–9 a.m.	Breakfast	Terrace Room
9–10 a.m.	Marketing Communications	Ballroom A
	Tina Sanford, Mgr.	
10–Noon	Individual seminars (Consult packet for seminar information and locations)	
Noon–1 p.m.	Lunch	Evergreen Room

Figure 15-1 Sample agendas for (a) informal meeting, (b) formal meeting.

- Support services (e.g., catering, audiovisual equipment).
- Dependability of service.

Once a meeting room has been selected, you must determine how the room is to be set up. There are numerous arrangements to select from, depending on the number of people participating and the size of the room itself. Common room setups include:

Theater style: Suitable for large audiences; designed for lecture presentation and/or audiovisuals; speaker is visible, on raised platform.

Classroom style: Suitable for taking notes; works well with long, narrow room; attention directed to speaker.

Boardroom style: Good for small groups; communication facilitated; formal setting.

U-shape style: Allows speaker access to each participant; good for medium-size group; promotes interaction.

T-shape style: Good for panel discussion; accommodates small groups.

Round-table style: Informal; prompts discussion; good for small group work.

Meeting room facilities should be checked for audiovisual support, Internet connections, lighting, heating and ventilation. Microphones, slide projectors, computers, overhead projectors, multimedia equipment, video machines, screens, and the like need to be properly set up and working. During the meeting, be sure to provide enough memo pads, pencils, water and glasses, and ashtrays (if smoking is permitted). If coffee or tea is to be served, check your supplies and equipment (if the meeting is held at the company's facilities) or arrange for them to be served by someone else.

HINT: *Several publications are available as references for meeting facilities. They include Successful Meetings, published by Bill Communications, Inc., 633 Third Avenue, New York, NY 10017, www.billcom.com, and Official Meeting Facilities Guide, published by New Concepts Canada, 7311 Schaefer Ave., Richmond, BC, Canada V6Y 2W7, 604–272–1174 or 888–975–7888, fax 604–272–4574, sales@new concepts.ca, www.newconcepts.ca/omfg.htm.*

APPLICATIONS OF ELECTRONIC COMMUNICATIONS

Communication systems can be used to hold informal or formal meetings, ranging from 2 people to 25,000. In each case, technology can play a vital part in relaying information.

One form of meeting is teleconferencing. With the rising costs of travel, the increased demands on executives' time, and the global emphasis on business, teleconferencing allows people at different locations to hear and see one another without leaving their offices. Teleconferences can be broken into three general categories: audiographic, audio, and video. Although these methods differ in the technologies used, they have several things in common. They:

- Link people at multiple locations.
- Are interactive, providing two-way communications.
- Are dynamic, allowing the active participation of users.

Audiographic Teleconferences

Audiographic teleconferences transmit words, numbers, or graphics. Such teleconferences include the following:

Desktop computer conferences: Individuals use computer terminals and various types of telecommunication connections, including phone lines, ISDN, or T1 lines, to access a host computer to communicate with one another. Participants do not have to be gathered at telephones or in conference rooms at the same time. They input their comments on the computer at their convenience, as long as the comments are given prior to the deadline established by the conference manager. The advantage of a computer conference is that all participants can review and comment on any material filed in the host computer on their own schedules, in their offices.

Slow-scan video: A camera scans an image from top to bottom for transmission over a phone line to a receiving monitor. It is best used for transmission of documents such as blueprints and schematics.

Freeze-frame video: Freeze-frame or slow-scan television adds visuals to an audio teleconference. Graphics are placed in front of a standard closed-circuit TV camera. The camera is connected to a scan converter that changes the picture into a still image that is then sent over a telephone line or other link.

Faxes: Faxing involves the transmission of an exact copy of something over communications lines.

Electronic blackboard: Similar to a classroom blackboard, this device sends graphics over an ordinary telephone line. Meeting participants write on the board, and the writing appears on a monitor (screen) in the other locations.

Electronic mail (e-mail): This is a message system for sending information from one person to others. E-mail systems are usually programs on computer networks.

Instant messages: On-line chats are used to communicate with associates on the Internet. They are similar to e-mail because they consist of text that is sent back and forth. However, unlike e-mail, users don't have to wait hours or days for an answer. As the name suggests, messages usually arrive instantly. Files can be sent or shared using an instant message. Also, users can talk to multiple associates at the same time.

Teleconferences

Telecommunications technologies play a vital role in linking business executives worldwide. Electronic meetings take place in the office or in the conference room and are referred to as **teleconferencing.** Computer, audio, and video teleconferencing involves specialized equipment that links two or more locations and provides for interactive participation among the users. Office assistants often have the dual roles of meeting facilitator and technology expert.

Computer-based conferences allow participants to work together on a variety of documents from any distance via the personal computer and a computer modem using *groupware software.* (See Chapter 8 for details on this type of software.) This type of meeting lacks the advantage of face-to-face communications. To counter this disadvantage, graphical images called *avatars* (also referred to as agents, characters, or bots) are used to represent each person on the computer screen. *Virtual chat rooms* can be created, using the *avatars* to represent participants in an electronic meeting working on group projects. Digital photographs or any graphic can be used for an *avatar.*

Audio teleconferences involve the transmission of sound only. Generally, the office professional's role is connecting a number of people from various locations at a given time. This is usually done through the company's telephone carrier or a telecommunication company's bridge service. Typical equipment requirements include an ordinary telephone for an individual or a speakerphone when two or more persons are present in a room. Larger audio conferences use a special microphone, such as the Polycom SoundStation™, to effectively facilitate a group audio conference. This type of system provides full 360-degree coverage within a room. Voice-over IP (Internet Protocol) phones are also used for this type of conference. These phones allow for the convergence of both voice and data networks.

Video teleconferencing allows one or more people to interact via a television camera from the *desktop* or a *conference room.* **Desktop videoconferencing** has the advantage of allowing participants to see one another and concurrently interact on documents, such as spreadsheets or reports. Participants use a PC equipped with a videoconferencing software package, a video camera built into the video display screen or attached to it, and a headset for voice communications. The minimum components of a desktop PC videoconferencing system include a suitable area that will not disturb coworkers. The office should be wired with at least a category 5 cable, which provides a real-time conference at 30 frames per second, sufficient electrical power, telephone, and access to a local and wide area network. An H.323 standards-based codec and video software, camera, speakers/headphones, and microphone are also required. Video bridges are used for multipoint connectivity, as well as a scheduling software package.

Video conference rooms have more sophisticated cameras and audio equipment, and they accommodate larger numbers of participants. Two pieces of specialized hardware are often used in conference rooms: (1) a *video visualizer,* which is used to input documents, photographs, slides, and 3-D objects directly into the video production equipment, and (2) a *smart whiteboard,* which uses lasers to scan the surface and report any digital input to an attached computer. Most whiteboard software incorporates special tools for annotating images and connects one site to another via a pair of modems. Using a special modem and software, voice and data can be combined into one simultaneous connection, allowing participants to send a file or a remote presentation and talk at the same time.

Web-based conference services (also referred to as webinars, on-line seminars, cyber-meetings, or Web conferencing) assist organizations with communicating both internally and externally on a global scale. Interactive audio and videoconferencing technologies facilitate this type of activity. Customers use these services for meetings, training, sales, support, and marketing activities. Generally, two types of conferencing environments are available: large virtual auditoriums that can hold up to 2,500 participants, or highly interactive on-line meeting rooms for smaller groups. Participation in Web-based conferences requires a computer, Web browser, microphone, earphones or speakers, and an on-line connection. To set up an account with a conferencing company, a customer usually provides a name, telephone number, and an e-mail address, plus a credit card number or a business address for billing purposes.

DOCUMENT COLLABORATION

If your team has a project that involves word processing or spreadsheet documents, vendors such as Microsoft provide features for document collaboration. This feature is especially important for geographically dispersed team members. For example, documents that require input and editing from a number of sources can use Office XP's review and workflow tools. Users can choose to show the document before and after changes, as well as any alterations made.

With Office XP versions that include FrontPage® 2002, you also get SharePoint® Team Services, which allow you to set up a group resource Web site. SharePoint® team members can be notified when changes to content occur and save data from the Web site directly into their Outlook 2002 calendar. Documents can be submitted to the SharePoint® Portal for review, archived, discussed and approved before they are made available to others for viewing.

Using Electronic Equipment in the Meeting Room

The workplace is shifting from one-person, one-task operations to group interactions and meetings. As a result, technology is being used more and more to bring people together. Meetings now include sophisticated electronic equipment. Videoconferencing is becoming the affordable alternative to project reports, planning sessions, sales training, product development meetings, and financial reviews.

A number of organizations specialize in teleconferencing, providing services ranging from consulting to installing a complete system. The use of outside sources depends on the degree of involvement expected of office professionals as well as their knowledge of the equipment. Users of such equipment should expect to be trained by professionals. Training includes control panel operations (the "buttons" used to operate the equipment), graphics capabilities, seating arrangements, room scheduling, and troubleshooting.

As an office professional, you may be expected to prepare the visuals to be used during the meeting. Try to keep them simple, bold, colorful, accurate, and informative. Always make them easy to read by mixing upper- and lowercase letters and justifying the left margin. The following guidelines will help to make your visuals more readable:

- Minimize complexity; use one idea per visual.
- Do not be wordy.
- Keep the text short, about six or seven lines per visual.
- Do not crowd the visual with more than one illustration.
- Use short words.

- Keep the letters large and bold so they can be read from the back of the room.
- Keep the number of type sizes per visual limited to a maximum of three.
- A maximum of four colors per visual is recommended.
- Incorporate video clips if needed to amplify a point. Keep the clips to one minute in length.

Several table shapes have been developed for teleconferencing. They include the following:

- Canoe-shaped—an oval table with participants seated side by side along one side.
- Keystone—a solid "V" shaped table, with users sitting along both outside edges facing one another.
- Curved—a table bent in a crescent shape, with users seated on the long edge of the curve.

The canoe and curved formats have the advantage of placing every person the same distance from both cameras and video monitors.

General guidelines for watching a video on a monitor are as follows:

- People should be seated about 10 feet from a 19-inch image and about 9 feet from a 27-inch screen.
- Minimum viewing distance from a standard monitor is two to four times the width of the image. For color monitors, however, viewers must be at least six feet from the image.
- Maximum viewing distance from a monitor is estimated to be between 12 and 14 times the image width.
- Seat placement within 45 degrees of the center of the screen is acceptable.
- A screen should be angled 5 degrees below a viewer's straight vertical line of sight for the best results.
- Seats should directly face a monitor.

PROJECTION TECHNOLOGY

Two computer projection systems are available: liquid crystal displays (LCDs) and digital light processors (DLPs). Both have their advantages. By relying on three liquid crystal display panels, one each to create the red, green, and blue components, an LCD creates color images continuously. DLPs require only one imaging device to create bright, full-color images, making them somewhat lighter than their LCD counterparts. When evaluating a projector, consider brightness. The higher the brightness, the better the image that will appear on the screen. Look for the ANSI lumens rating. The higher the number, the brighter the projector. Contrast ratio is another factor to consider. This is the difference between the brightest bright and the darkest dark in an image. For example, a contrast ratio of 400:1 means the possible picture area is 400 times brighter than the darkest. Resolution—the number of horizontal and vertical picture elements in an image—is also important. Most projectors support VGA (640 by 480 pixels), SVGA (800 by 600 pixels), and XGA (1024 by 768 pixels). Another feature to consider is built-in digital keystone correction. This feature corrects the image to its proper rectangular shape.

Taking Minutes

Minutes are an accurate recording in outline form of the actions that occurred in a meeting. For informal meetings, the minutes should be brief and simple. Formal meetings require more complex minutes.

You may be asked to take minutes during the meeting. Skillful minute-taking is an art that takes practice to develop. Here are some guidelines to follow:

- Get a copy of the agenda beforehand if you were not the person who prepared it. If technical or unfamiliar jargon is used, familiarize yourself with common terms. Minutes of past meetings, handouts for the meetings, and glossaries of relevant subjects are appropriate sources.
- Take thorough notes.

HINT: *Consider using a small tape recorder. You will have to get permission to do so from every participant. If even one objects, do not use it.*

- Record verbatim all resolutions, amendments, decisions, and conclusions.

HINT: *A resolution is a formal statement of the group, approved by a vote of the group. After a resolution is drafted and approved, it must be signed, distributed, and incorporated into the minutes. Resolutions may be for achievements, sympathy, promotion of special events, and so forth. Each paragraph in a resolution begins with the words WHEREAS or RESOLVED, either in capital letters or underlined.*

- Use eye-catching symbols to mark any item that may need action.
- Write a rough but complete draft as soon as possible and submit it for review to the supervisor in charge of the meeting.
- Transcribe the minutes as soon as possible after the meeting. Do not add your own opinions. Be sure you have the chairperson approve and sign the minutes before they are distributed.
- Send handouts to anyone who was absent from the meeting.
- Include any follow-up meeting information at the bottom of the minutes, such as the date, time, and location.
- Correct the minutes at the next meeting, if necessary. For formal meetings, corrections are made on the official copy with red ink (if possible) and initialed in the

margin. Minutes should never be erased or rewritten. If corrections are extensive, they should be written on a separate page and attached to the original minutes. A marginal note should be included at the side of the item in the original minutes indicating a correction is attached.

When putting formal minutes into their final form, use the following outline:

1. Name of group, place, date, and time of meeting.
2. Listing of those present, identifying officers and other officials.
3. Call to order; approval of minutes of previous meeting as is or with corrections and/or amendments.

MEETING OF PLANNING COMMITTEE
September 7, 20___

ATTENDANCE
The monthly meeting of the planning committee was held in the conference room of Manville Hospital at 10 a.m. on September 7, 20___. Dale Stetzer, Vice President of Marketing, presided. Present were Mary Farr, George Rowen, Sue Gates, Ted Smith, and Larry Taylor.

REPORTS/MOTIONS/NEW BUSINESS
1. Sue Gates presented a report on the proposed east wing renovation. Further information is to be given at the October 9 meeting.
2. George Rowen reported on the progress of the sewer project. Completion is expected by early spring, 20___.
3. A new service contract was approved for the computer equipment.

MEETING DETAILS
The next meeting of the planning committee will be held on October 9 at 10 a.m., Conference Room A, Manville Hospital.

ADJOURNMENT
The meeting was adjourned at noon.

_____
Peter Ren, Recorder

Figure 15-2 Sample minutes.

1. Three months prior to meeting:
_____a. Book a meeting location.
_____b. Identify and contract with support services.
_____c. Notify attendees regarding details of meeting.
_____d. Prepare travel arrangements for attendees.
_____e. Identify local events and get information.
_____f. Plan a program of formal and recreational events.
_____g. Plan a topical program and identify speakers.
_____h. Invite speakers and VIPs.
_____i. Order needed audiovisual equipment.

2. Three weeks before meeting:
_____a. Confirm menus, room setups, audiovisual requirements, and supplies
         with the hotel, in writing.
_____b. Reconfirm speakers, formal and recreational events.
_____c. Mail agendas and other pertinent information.
_____d. Reconfirm attendees.

3. One week before your meeting:
_____a. Ship material to meeting location for delivery at least 24 hours ahead
         of your arrival. Label the boxes with the name of the contact person,
         the group's meeting name, and the date of planned arrival.
_____b. Confirm arrival of materials prior to your departure to the meeting.
_____c. Make arrangements to collect from the meeting location, pack and ship
         back to your office any unused materials.
_____d. Bring a master set of handout materials with you and make arrange-
         ments for duplicating additional materials if necessary.
_____e. Confirm food and beverage requirements at least 48 hours prior to
         the meeting.
_____f. Bring your own supplies of tape, shipping labels, paper clips, pens, pen-
         cils, note pads, badges, scissors, masking tape, magic markers, and so
         forth.

Figure 15-3 Meeting planner's checklist.

4. Reports of officers and committees.
5. Unfinished business; discussion, motions.
6. New business and action taken.
7. Motions, including names of those involved in total motion, if amended, and names
   of seconders.

4. Upon arrival at the meeting location:

_____a.   Meet with the convention coordinator, confirm all details, and walk through the meeting site.

_____b.   Confirm with the audiovisual coordinator that needed equipment will be available.

_____c.   Meet with the bell captain and the maitre d'.

_____d.   Confirm the attendees list with the front desk and the room assignments if possible.

_____e.   Arrange for any gifts that are to be delivered to the attendees' rooms, e.g., fruit basket.

_____f.   Double-check that meeting room locations are posted in the hotel lobby on the hotel monitors.

5. Meeting day(s):

_____a.   Walk through meeting spaces at least one hour before start of program.

_____b.   Confirm that speakers have checked into the hotel. Leave notes in their mailboxes to contact you.

_____c.   Check with the audiovisual coordinator regarding equipment and supplies for each meeting room.

_____d.   Be available at all times should an emergency develop.

6. Final meeting day:

_____a.   Meet with the hotel conference coordinator to review invoices, receipts, and arrangements for returning unused materials.

_____b.   Disburse appropriate gratuities. Gratuities should total 1 to 2 percent of the cost of the event.

Figure 15-3 (continued).

8. Date and location of next meeting.
9. Adjournment and time of adjournment.
10. Signature of secretary and, if required, the chairperson.

Corporate minutes should be typed on plain white paper (watermarked for official corporate stockholders' and directors' meetings). If the minutes are brief, double-space the body and triple-space between paragraphs. If the minutes are long, they should be single-spaced for the text and double-spaced between headings. When side subheadings are used, it is not necessary to indent the paragraphs. Allow a one-and-one-half-inch left margin and a one-inch right margin. The title should be capitalized and centered. (See Figure 15-2.)

When filing the minutes, be sure to include all handouts and the agenda for future reference. By law, corporations are required to keep minutes of stockholders' and directors' meetings. Such minutes are considered legal records and should be guarded against tampering.

Follow-Up Activities

After the meeting, you must follow up on a number of details, including distribution of the minutes to proper individuals, collection of any extra materials, review of charges and receipts, and writing of thank you letters to speakers, participants, and hotel staff (if appropriate). It is also important to maintain an accurate meeting folder for reference.

The checklist in Figure 15-3 is a helpful reminder to keep in front of you throughout the process of planning for a meeting.

Once documents have been created, they must be distributed efficiently and economically. Postal rates keep increasing, so companies must monitor their mailing costs and consider ways to reduce them. Whether the documents are coming into the company or leaving the company and whether they are distributed by the U.S. Postal Service or transmitted electronically, office professionals must know the guidelines for each method of delivery.

U.S. POSTAL SERVICE™

The U.S. Postal Service (USPS) offers several classes and subclasses of domestic and international mail delivery services. Domestic mail service covers all classes of mail handled in the United States, its territories and possessions, the areas comprising the former Panama Canal Zone, and Army/Air Force (APO) and Navy (FPO) post offices. It also includes mail for delivery to the United Nations in New York City. International mail service covers mail received from or posted to foreign countries.

For updated information about the U.S. Postal Service, check the *Domestic Mail Manual*, which is available by subscription from the Superintendent of Documents, U.S. Government Printing Office, 710 North Capital Street NW, Washington, DC 20402-9371 (202–512–1800). Local post offices have copies of the *Quick Service Guide* and *Postal Addressing Standards* as well as *Time-Saving Information for Your Business*. The *Postal Explorer* is a new service that is available on the Internet at http://pe.usps.gov as well as on CD-ROM. It contains manuals for domestic and international mail, zone charts, bulk mail guidelines, and rates.

To be placed on a mailing list to receive a free USPS newsletter, write to Memo to Mailers, National Customer Support Center, U.S. Postal Service, 6060 Primacy Pkwy, #101, Memphis, TN 38188-0001.

First-Class Mail

First-class mail consists of such items as letters; stamped cards (sold by the post office); postcards (sold commercially); bills; typewritten, handwritten, or photocopied messages; price lists; statements of account;

CHAPTER 16

MAILING

DOCUMENTS

checks; printed forms; and computer-generated matter with the characteristics of business or personal messages.

Sealed first-class mail items are not subject to postal inspections. First-class mail may be sent certified, COD, or registered. The sender may also obtain a certificate of mailing. (See Special Services for Domestic and International Mail.)

To qualify as first-class, items must weigh 13 ounces or less. Items that are ¼ inch thick or less must be at least 3½ inches high, at least 5 inches long, and rectangular in shape. First-class postal rates are based on weight, with the charge for the first ounce higher than the charges for the second and succeeding ounces. Rates for postcards and stamped cards are less than for regular first-class items.

The USPS forwards all first-class mail without charge for one year if it is informed of the new address.

HINT: *Less confusion results when companies inform their clients of address changes and complete the change-of-address forms furnished by the USPS before they move. Remind employees within the department to complete change-of-address forms if they leave the company and want their mail forwarded.*

First-Class Subclasses and Categories

The two current subclasses of first-class mail are (1) stamped cards and postcards and (2) letters and sealed packages. Each subclass has an automation rate category and a presorted rate category. To qualify for reduced rates in these two categories, a single mailing must contain a minimum of 500 items. Each piece must include a complete delivery address with correct ZIP code, ZIP +4 code, or the numbers in the barcode. All customer addresses on automation and presort mail must be updated periodically by using a U.S. Postal Service–approved address update procedure. To encourage companies' use of barcoding, automation rates are lower than presorted rates. To obtain the automation rate, mail must be 100 percent delivery-point barcoded. The bar code must be on the addressed side of the envelope or package within the bar code read area. All the Postnet bars must have the same width and spacing.

HINT: *If you use a software program or an outsource service provider, be sure that the services or products meet USPS accuracy standards. Call the National Customer Support Center (800–238–3150) for a list of certified suppliers.*

Priority Mail

Priority mail is first-class mail that weighs more than 13 ounces. The mailer also has the option of using priority mail for items that weigh 13 ounces or less for faster delivery. The maximum weight for priority mail is 70 pounds. Delivery time is generally two days. Rates depend on the weight of the item and the zone to which it is being mailed. The 2-pound rate is charged for all the material that can fit into a priority mail envelope provided by USPS, regardless of the actual weight of the item. Priority mail boxes, envelopes, labels, and stickers may be ordered by phone (800–222–1811) or on the Internet at http://supplies.usps.gov/.

Customers may request pickup service and pay one fee per call, not per item. Priority mail packages may be insured or sent COD. Signature confirmations, delivery confirmations, and certificates of mailing are available with priority mail. Mailers can also send business reply mail as priority mail. For extra fees, mailers can use return receipt/restricted delivery, special handling, certified, and registered services with priority mail.

Express Mail (Post Office to Addressee Service)

Express mail is U.S. Postal Service's fastest service for mailing documents. (See Figure 16.1.) If a package is mailed at a USPS express mail location on or before a specified time for overnight delivery, it will be delivered the next day. A signature to indicate that the item was received is necessary. If the item does not arrive as promised, the mailer may file a claim for a postage refund.

Rates depend on weight and destination. Express mail is not acceptable for mailings of more than 108 inches in length and girth combined or for packages weighing more than 70 pounds. The cost includes insurance against loss or damage. Express mail also offers a flat rate for all material that can fit into a special envelope. This flat-rate service saves time since the envelope does not have to be weighed at the post office but may be placed with the company's outgoing mail or in a USPS collection box.

Express mail may be scheduled for pickup, and tracking services are available at www.usps.com or by calling 800–222–1811. Express mail may be sent COD (collect on delivery). By paying an extra fee, mailers may also request a return receipt, which offers proof of delivery. Express mail is available for international service.

Periodicals Mail

Periodicals mail is a class of mail that consists of magazines, newspapers, or other printed material published at least four times a year and at specified times. Publishers and news agents use this service to mail newspapers and periodicals in bulk. To mail single issues of newspapers or magazines, use standard mail (A) or (B).

Publications should have informational printed sheets that are not designed primarily as advertising or as promotional pieces. Circulation records must be available for periodic examination by postal service personnel. Subscription orders and receipts are the only enclosures allowed in periodicals mail; other types of enclosures require additional postage.

Standard Mail

Standard mail is material that does not require first-class or express mail service. Both standard mail (A) and standard mail (B)–Parcel Post have several subclasses with specific eligibility and preparation requirements.

Figure 16-1 USPS Express Mail Form.

STANDARD MAIL (A)

Circulars, catalogs, booklets, printed matter, and photographs may be sent as standard mail (A). Standard mail (A) rates are available to businesses and qualified nonprofit organizations. The rates for the nonprofit groups are lower than the rates for business mailers. To qualify for standard mail (A) rates, items must weigh less than 16 ounces. Postal Service personnel may inspect standard mail (A), whether it is sealed or unsealed.

Standard mail (A) rates may be used for material with the same general message sent to different addresses. At least 200 pieces or 50 pounds will qualify for bulk-mail rates. The greater the degree of automation assumed by the mailer, the lower the rate for bulk mailings. Special services, such as certified or registered, do not apply for bulk mailings.

For volume mailings, standard mail (A) must be properly sorted, bundled, labeled, and put in trays or sacks. Mailers have numerous sorting options, so it is wise to check with the local post office for assistance. Payment is due before postal employees can accept and verify the accuracy of bulk mailings. With each mailing, mailers must complete a USPS form that requires the number of pieces per ZIP code and accurate calculations.

STANDARD MAIL (B)

Standard mail (B), also known as parcel post, consists of mailable matter that weighs 16 ounces or more. Parcels exceeding size (108 inches combined length and girth) or weight (70 pounds) limits are not mailable using USPS services. Standard mail (B) does not include a guaranteed arrival time, and it may be subject to Postal Service examination. Rates for standard mail (B) depend on weight and distance mailed. There are eight postal zones in the United States; zone charts are available from local post offices.

Under the standard mail (B) parcel post category, instructions, packing slips, or invoices may go inside a parcel at no extra cost. Attach a letter to the outside of a parcel and pay the first-class rate for the letter and the standard mail (B) rate for the package. Another way to include a letter is to place it inside the package, mark "Letter Enclosed" on the outside of the parcel, and pay the appropriate postal rates for the parcel and letter.

Another standard mail (B) category, bound printed matter, includes promotional, advertising, and educational items. Material must be permanently fastened with at least 90 percent of the sheets imprinted with letters, figures, or characters.

International Mail

The USPS offers land (surface) mail and airmail services to most foreign locations. Companies with extensive international communications should have a copy of the *International Mail Manual,* which is available from the Superintendent of Documents by subscription.

HINT: *Check the Postal Explorer at the USPS Web site at http://pe.usps.gov. One of the major sections gives information on international mail standards. Another section shows the calculation of postage rates and prints postage for international mail as well as domestic mail.*

SPECIAL SERVICES FOR DOMESTIC AND INTERNATIONAL MAIL

As an office professional, you should understand the special services provided by the USPS. These services often involve fees. The forms for domestic and international special services are not the same.

Business Reply Mail/Courtesy Reply Mail

Business reply mail (BRM) consists of postage-paid envelopes or stamped cards that are enclosed with other mailings. The major purpose of business reply mail is to encourage recipients to respond. The service is available for first-class and priority mail. Mailers pay an annual fee for a BRM permit. These permits allow mailers to pay postage only for the items that are returned by the recipients. The words "First-Class Mail Permit No. xxx" and the name of the post office issuing the permit (city and state) must appear on the address side. (See Figure 16-2.) The design of the BRM card must be planned with and approved by the local post office.

WINDOW SERVICES
UNITED STATES POSTAL SERVICE
126 NORTH BARSTOW STREET
EAU CLAIRE WI 54703-9998

NO POSTAGE
NECESSARY
IF MAILED
IN THE
UNITED STATES

BUSINESS REPLY MAIL
FIRST-CLASS MAIL   PERMIT NO 73026   WASHINGTON DC

POSTAGE WILL BE PAID BY ADDRESSEE

WINDOW SERVICES
UNITED STATES POSTAL SERVICE
126 NORTH BARSTOW STREET
EAU CLAIRE WI 54703-9998

B - 1105 - 1206465

Figure 16-2 Business reply mail.

Courtesy reply mail requires no fees. The mailer sends pre-addressed cards or envelopes, but the receiver must add the postage before returning the item.

Certificate of Mailing

The certificate shows that the Postal Service accepted the item and provides proof that an item was mailed. It does not indicate that the item arrived at its destination and does not include insurance. The certificate is available with first-class, priority, and standard mail, and it applies to domestic and international mail. The person sending the item completes the certificate of mailing and pays the fee.

Signature Confirmation/Delivery Confirmation

These services provide confirmation of a delivery date or attempted delivery date when a sender inquires about an item. (See Figure 16-3.) If the mailer requests a signature confirmation, USPS will provide a copy by fax or mail. Both confirmations are available only with priority and standard mail (B) categories. There is a cost for the services. These confirmations do not provide automatic insurance coverage; insurance must be purchased. Inquiries by senders can be made by calling 800–222–1811 or by accessing the USPS Web site at www.usps.com. Be sure to have the confirmation number available.

Certified Mail

Certified mail is a domestic mail service that provides proof of mailing and delivery for items sent by first-class or priority mail. No insurance coverage is provided. A signature is obtained upon delivery, and a record of delivery is kept by the Postal Service for two years. You must have the certified mail receipt when you make an inquiry.

Figure 16-3 Delivery confirmation.

For an additional fee, a return receipt or a restricted delivery receipt is available to the mailer as evidence that the delivery occurred. Mailers of certified mail may request special delivery service for an extra fee.

Enter the certified number on the return receipt card, self-address it, and attach it to the item being certified. Mark the date, attach the correct postage, and mail at any post office or deposit in any USPS mailbox. (See Figure 16-4.)

Return Receipt/Restricted Delivery

A return receipt signifies to the mailer that delivery of an item took place. The return receipt may indicate to whom and the date the package was delivered or it may indicate to whom, date delivered, and delivery address. A restricted delivery allows a mailer to designate the addressee who should receive the item. Return receipt/restricted delivery services are available for certified, registered, insured, express, and COD mail. They apply to domestic and most international mailings. Fees for return receipts do not cover damages or losses to the items sent. (See Figures 16-5.)

Return Receipts for Merchandise

Return receipts for merchandise are available only for priority mail and standard mail (A) and (B). They allow the mailer to obtain a mailing receipt, a return receipt, and a record of delivery. The record of delivery is kept by the post office. Return receipts for merchandise are not available for international mailings. Special handling is available for

Figure 16-4 Certified mail.

Figure 16-5 Domestic return receipt.

standard (B) mail. Articles with return receipts for merchandise must be mailed at a post office; they cannot be deposited in collection boxes.

Registered Mail

Registered mail is the most secure means of delivering valuable and important mail. The post office gives the mailer a receipt, and a USPS employee records the arrival of registered mail at each point along its way. When delivery is made, the mailer receives notification. (See Figure 16-6.) You must declare the full value of the items registered whether or not you purchase insurance. First-class, priority, and COD mail may be registered. Insurance and return/restricted delivery receipts are available for additional fees. Domestic and most international mail may be registered.

HINT: *Valuable items such as stock certificates, merchandise, or jewelry should be registered. Send any item that cannot be replaced, valuable or not, by registered mail.*

Figure 16-6 Registered mail receipt.

Insured Mail

Insurance is available to guard against loss or damage to items mailed at standard mail (A) and (B) rates or to standard mail (A) and (B) matter mailed at first-class rates for actual value of the items. Do not overstate the value. Return receipt/restricted delivery services are available for extra fees; special handling is also available. Domestic and international mail may be insured. Maximum coverage varies according to the country. (See Figure 16-7.) Insured mail must be taken to the post office; it cannot be deposited in a collection box. An appropriate endorsement for insured mail is stamped on the parcel.

The receipt is necessary if a claim for loss or damage is ever made. Write the name and address of the addressee on the receipt and file it until you know that the parcel arrived safely.

Special Handling

Mail marked "Special handling" receives preferential handling in dispatching and transporting. Special handling applies to first-class, priority, and standard mail (A) and (B). It also applies to COD, insured items, and return receipts for merchandise items. It

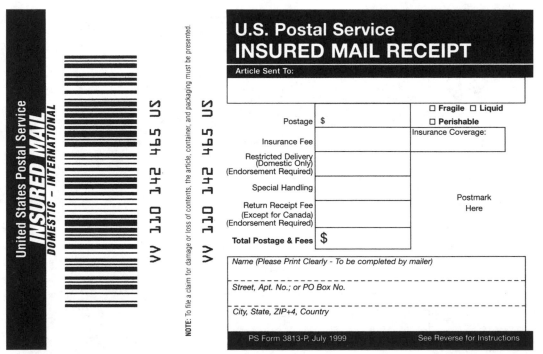

Figure 16-7 Insured mail receipt.

does not include "special" care in handling fragile or breakable items. The weight determines the fee. The special handling fee is in addition to standard mail (A) and (B) postage. The service is available for international mail.

Collect on Delivery (COD)

COD service allows mailers to send merchandise for which they have not been paid; payment for the merchandise and cost of mailing are collected by USPS when the package is delivered.

First class, standard (A) and (B), and express mail may be sent using COD service. Registered mail, return receipt, and restricted delivery services are all available with COD. COD service is not available for international mail. The COD fee includes insurance against loss or damage and an amount to cover the potential failure of the addressee to pay for the merchandise.

Payment may be in cash or by a check payable to the sender. When cash is involved, the sender receives a money order from the Postal Service for the amount collected. There is a limit on the amount that may be collected.

Other USPS Services

Other USPS services include electronic bill payment and stamps over the Internet. USPS also offers tracking service. It contracts with printing and mailing services so mailers have access to the USPS database of delivery addresses for CASS (Coding Accuracy Support System) certification on the Internet. Users get real-time access to change-of-address information, which ensures up-to-date mailing lists and provides compliance with USPS regulations.

HINT: *Since USPS rules and regulations do change, check with your local post office for the latest mailing information.*

Electronic Postage (E-postage)

E-postage programs are available from companies on the Internet such as Stamps.com, E-Stamp, or Pitney Bowes. A company representative sets up an account with an Internet postage company and purchases a postage meter license from USPS. The amount purchased is credited and recorded on an Internet postage server. Postage is available 24 hours a day, 7 days a week. Users fill in the return and delivery addresses, type of item, type of item on which to print (envelope size, label), weight, and type of service (first-class, priority). The address is checked with USPS's CASS system for accuracy, and postage is deducted from the company account.

Use the following list of options to help you decide which on-line vendor you will use for electronic postage:

- Do you prefer software or a CD-ROM?
- Is the software compatible with PCs and Macs?
- Is the software free? If not, what are the costs?
- Is the software available from a Web site or can you buy it at a retail store also?
- Is there a monthly fee? Is there a minimum or maximum charge?
- Is there a fee if no postage is purchased during a month?
- Is there a storage vault to download stamps without connecting to the Internet each time you want a stamp?
- Does the software analyze shipping rates and services?
- Can you print international postage?
- Does the software print labels?
- Can domestic addresses be verified with a USPS database?
- Is a postal scale sold with the software so users can set the amount of postage, class of service, envelope size, and other shipping details?
- Does the service offer free shipping and tracking tools?
- Are there reports that track how much postage you purchased and used?
- Can you import logos and graphics to print on envelopes or cards?

ALTERNATE DELIVERY SERVICES

Other delivery services are available besides the USPS. The costs, delivery times, and types of services offered vary. The advertising pages of a local telephone directory include companies that offer freight, delivery, and shipping services under such headings as air cargo, package express service, and delivery service. Individual companies can provide information on rates, service charts, and limitations on items transported.

Air Express

Other major delivery companies, such as FedEx® and DHL, provide air express or courier express service for domestic and international deliveries. These companies will pick up a firm's or individual's letters, parcels, or heavy freight items and provide same day, next day, or second day delivery. Same day services are the most expensive. In addition to speed, charges depend on the size and weight of the parcel. Volume discounts are often available.

HINT: *FedEx® (www.fedex.com) has free software (also available on the Internet) that allows you to connect to FedEx®, obtain complete shipping and billing information, call for pickup, and print labels and bar codes.*

Most courier companies are expanding their domestic and international markets. Some operate their own planes; others rely on commercial flights. To increase convenience, firms are developing 24-hour branch office services with other companies; for example, Kinko's® offers FedEx® service. USPS also has an agreement with FedEx® that allows FedEx® drop boxes in some post offices. In turn, FedEx® planes will transport certain postal items for USPS. Other firms are competing by adding more hubs, offering faster service, adding additional services, or expanding to more cities. All major firms can track a lost item. Guaranteeing the arrival of the shipment or returning the fee for a lost item is part of the service offered by most companies.

Since costs and arrival times vary, go over these details when calling for service:

- Value of the parcel(s).
- Delivery date.
- Number of packages.
- Service; for example, same day, overnight, international, or second day delivery.
- Pickup service, latest time to call or to drop off items, charges.
- Weight of each parcel.
- Destination.
- Type of merchandise.
- Day of the week for pickup as well as delivery.
- Money back guarantee.
- Customs requirements for international service.
- Tracking system information available.
- International service reliability.
- Online storage for package history information.
- On-time delivery performance.

HINT: *Organize your work so it is not necessary to use expensive delivery services at the last minute. Use these services only for documents that must be delivered the same day or overnight.*

Some air express advisers will help companies analyze their needs at no charge. To assist them, keep records of where deliveries go, when and how often they are sent, and how much it currently costs.

The major carriers now offer logistics services (warehousing) so companies can store products at the carrier's location rather than maintaining four or five regional warehouses themselves. When a product is needed, carrier employees pull the product from the inventory and ship it according to company instructions by the carrier's transport system.

United Parcel Service (UPS)

United Parcel Service (UPS) delivers packages to individuals and businesses. In addition to ground service, air service—next day or second day—is available to destinations within the United States and many other countries.

Mailers can request door-to-door service or they may drop off the item at a UPS facility or collection box. Fees differ depending on the service.

The sender must fill out a form with the sender's name and address, the recipient's name and address, and the contents of the parcel. The package must weigh 70 pounds or less. The size limitation for a package is 108 inches, length and girth combined. In addition to the protection against theft or damage already included in the basic UPS rate, the mailer may purchase additional insurance coverage. UPS offers package tracking on its Web site, and it is linked with commercial on-line services.

HINT: *The UPS tracking system allows the sender and receiver to trace the location of an item throughout the shipping process. The system indicates the time that the item arrived and the person who signed for it. To activate the tracking process, select the tracking area on the delivery company's home page on the Web. Enter the package's tracking number and follow the instructions to start the process.*

UPS's customer automation system electronically manages package and billing information, so it can produce the financial reports that a user needs.

Independent Mail Firms

Companies specializing in mail services have become popular. A firm may contract with one of these companies for special services such as bulk mail. Most of them will pick up and deliver.

Stores such as Pak Mail Centers of America® offer all types of mail service—USPS, UPS®, FedEx®—and give the sender costs and options for each service.

Local Transport Services

Companies located in small cities may have to depend on local bus service for some deliveries. The cost is reasonable, and insurance is included in the basic charge. Depending on local schedules, same day service as well as Sunday and holiday service may be possible. In addition to rate information, the local bus company offices can indicate any limitations concerning the size and weight of a parcel.

Small businesses or individuals contract for local delivery services. Local messenger services make intracity deliveries the same day. In foreign cities, these deliveries may be by barge or bicycles. Some promise delivery within the hour.

ELECTRONIC MAIL

Electronic mail (e-mail) is a cross between a telephone call and a letter. Standard features of an e-mail system allow a sender to use the computer keyboard to input a message. Once the address or mailbox of the recipient is entered, the message is transmitted to the addressee's computer by activating a transmit key. At the receiving workstation, the recipient checks the mail received, selects a message to view, displays it on the monitor, and then answers it, downloads it for printing, or routes it to someone else. Some advantages and special concerns of e-mail are discussed below.

Advantages

Advantages of e-mail include:

- Speed. A message arrives quickly, and the recipient has the option of responding immediately or prioritizing messages for later action.
- Convenience. Messages do not have to be written or received during normal business hours; the system is operable 24 hours a day. E-mail is good for reaching people who are difficult to contact or who are in other time zones. It minimizes telephone tag. Telecommuters can stay in touch with their coworkers and supervisors.
- Idea exchange. Ideas flow more spontaneously than with formal meetings with planned agendas. Appearance, age, shyness, and speaking ability seem less important.
- Scanning capability. Subject lines give a recipient an opportunity to review the messages and select those requiring immediate action.

HINT: *Use short, descriptive phrases in the subject line.*

- Cost. Messages are inexpensive when compared to alternative forms of communication.
- Sender identification. Most e-mail software automatically places the sender's name in the FROM line, which authenticates the origination of the message.
- Destination reliability. If the addresses are accurate, there will be minimal transmission errors. Messages do not have to go through another individual.
- Simplicity. Using e-mail requires some basic instructions, but it does not require in-depth computer expertise.
- Information access. Office professionals have access to information they can share and respond to simultaneously. One message may go to numerous recipients, which eliminates routing information or sending memos.

- Document linkage. "Threading," or attaching keywords to messages, allows their integration with other documents or computer files for accurate retrieval. Threading informs people about the relationship of various projects.
- Universal use. Keeping in touch with the office with wireless e-mail is easy while traveling.

HINT: *Be aware that some systems cannot reach behind security walls to get corporate mail. Some systems may not work with a phone but do work with a handheld PDA (personal digital assistant).*

Special Concerns

Special concerns of e-mail use include:

- Privacy. Even the use of a personal password is no guarantee that a message will not be read by management. Messages may be altered and/or forwarded to others beyond the person you contacted without your knowledge.
- Delayed response. Although a sender may expect an immediate response, the receiver may not prioritize the message in the same manner.
- Message impact. E-mail cannot provide cues such as body language, tone of voice, and use of humor or sarcasm. Situations involving personnel problems are handled more effectively with face-to-face contacts. A letterhead carries more weight and prestige for important correspondence.
- Inappropriate messages. Because of e-mail's simplicity, people send messages that are not clear or are written in anger. Poor communicators will not become good communicators because of e-mail. Because of the inherent insistence of e-mail, messages are often hurriedly prepared and questions are answered with little in-depth consideration. Electronic mailboxes become clogged with general information or lengthy documents that seem more appropriate for a company bulletin board or paper form for later reading.
- Volume. Information overload may cause the recipient to filter messages identified by keywords and send the others to a "folder" for later attention—or just ignore them. Message senders tend to become wordy with a blank screen in front of them. It becomes easy to send messages to people who really do not need them.
- Overwork. People tend to be "on call" 24 hours a day at home, in the office, on vacation, and while traveling. There is a "need" to check e-mail for messages, which may then generate other tasks.
- Junk mail overload. *Spam* is a Web term for unsolicited and unwanted bulk e-mail such as product advertisements, get-rich gimmicks, or pornographic or other offensive material. Most popular e-mail programs come with filters that can sort mail as it arrives into different folders, including one for "Trash."

HINT: *Internet service providers (ISPs) usually reprimand spammers who have misused e-mail privileges, so unwanted material should be forwarded to the originating ISP.*

- Employee misuse. Employees waste time using the system for messages unrelated to work.
- Carelessness. Because of e-mail's informal style, those sending messages may be careless in proofreading or using correct grammar and style, in organizing material logically, and in keying e-mail addresses.

Message Composition

Office professionals often must compose e-mail messages for their supervisors or send their own e-mail. For guidelines on proper message composition, see Chapter 17, Written Correspondence.

E-Mail Procedures and Etiquette

Companies need to implement procedures and etiquette guidelines for creating, distributing, and storing e-mail documents. Office professionals should take the initiative and recommend training sessions in which message content, format, style, and etiquette are covered. Some suggestions for e-mail procedures and etiquette protocol include:

- Do not leave e-mail messages onscreen when you are away from your desk. Sign off even if it is for a short time. Most e-mail programs allow you to save a document that you have started but do not complete immediately. Place your screen so that visitors or coworkers cannot view the document on which you are working.
- Do not copy or send software or information that is copyright-protected.
- Avoid attaching lengthy files to e-mail messages. Unless the file is essential, it often takes the recipient more time to download than it is worth.

HINT: *Limit the size of attachments by using a file compression software program, which can be downloaded from the Web. If your ISP server limits the size of individual e-mail messages, break lengthy text messages into two or three blocks.*

- Do not open attachments unless they are sent by a reliable source. Attachments create catastrophes when they contain viruses.
- Use the search function found in most e-mail programs to locate misfiled material in folders. Most programs will have a "Find" or "Search" command with additional toolbars to lead you through the process. Search under date received or date sent, recipient name, or words in the subject line or body.
- Most options screens have a checkbox that you can mark to instruct the software to connect with the ISP at whatever interval that you desire. The software alerts

you when e-mail arrives. This saves you time, since you are not always clicking "Check for new mail." Check and respond to messages several times a day, if only to indicate receipt. When you cannot respond to an e-mail message, acknowledge receipt with a brief return note indicating an approximate time that you will respond.

- Use a screening technique or "filtering" process that automatically routes a document according to its content, priority, or date. The receipt of hundreds of e-mail messages a day requires using filters or rules to sort messages into folders. Subject lines or project names are effective folder names.

HINT: *Take the time to learn the filtering techniques for your e-mail program. Some are more limited and will allow filtering by address or subject line only.*

- Set up your e-mail application to "Send" at preset times during the day or set it so when you click "Send," it goes to a "send later" file. This is especially helpful if you want to retract a message that you already sent or one in which you misspelled a name.

HINT: *Think twice before sending an immediate response to an angry e-mail message.*

- Set up a receiver's group list when sending the same e-mail to multiple recipients. Key the list only once; it then becomes one address book entry. After that, key the name of the list and send additional messages to every recipient without keying the addresses each time. In most systems, click on "Address Book" and use the tools that follow.
- Use the BCC: field to hide the distribution list. Place e-mail addresses to whom information goes in the BCC: field. Each recipient's address should be hidden from the other recipients.
- Be aware of the existence of e-mail viruses. E-mail messages, especially attachments, are the sources through which many computers become infected with viruses. Some viruses also infect a user's address book, so all e-mail addresses in that book become infected as well.

HINT: *Use an antivirus program such as Norton AntiVirus® 2001. As incoming e-mail is being received, the program scans for viruses; if one is found, the program intercepts it and issues you a warning.*

- Control spam. To identify spam, watch for messages that do not include your name in the To: line or that use all capital letters or X's in the subject line or that have no return address.

HINT: *Do not try to unsubscribe from spam mail. The address given may be a fake one, and all you will do is confirm that yours is indeed an active e-mail address.*

- Do not use e-mail for personal or sensitive messages; it is not private. Supervisors or colleagues may see messages by accident or on purpose. Avoid gossip, sexual innuendos, or critical remarks about another person or group. Do not use e-mail to discuss proprietary information.
- If it is necessary to keep an item of information private, use an e-mail encryption service available on the Web such as UPS Document Exchange (www.exchange. ups.com). Encryption delivers communications through the service Web site and scrambles a message so no one (except the recipient) can read the e-mail.
- Inform a sender when a message reaches you by mistake rather than ignoring or deleting it. Forward it with a note that you received the message by mistake.
- Establish e-mail storage procedures similar to those for filing paper documents. For example, a procedure might be to purge documents within 30 to 60 days and archive important messages on disk, tape, or paper. (See Chapter 12, Records Management, for information on archiving e-mail.)
- Maintain distribution lists by adding or removing names promptly upon request. Include only those people who have a need to receive the information from your office. Request that your own or your supervisor's name be removed from other senders' lists when information is not needed.
- Do not attach an unauthorized message to another person's message. Do not print and distribute another person's message without approval.
- Include e-mail addresses on letterhead and business cards. A suggestion to use the company e-mail address may be left on the voice-mail answering message.
- Send your message as text only. Some older versions of e-mail programs may not be HTML compatible, and the recipient will get a scrambled, unreadable message. Send graphics and other enhanced materials as an attached file.

HINT: *HTML (Hypertext Markup Language) is the code used to display Web information; it allows such additions as colored text and graphics.*

- Always know how an e-mail address will be used. Read the fine print in the use and privacy statement on each Web site. The site may be selling your e-mail address to other vendors.

Legal Issues

Legal conflicts occur over e-mail ownership and privacy rights when specific guidelines are not published and communicated. Establishing an e-mail policy and having employees sign a form indicating they have read it can prevent many of these problems. Here are some suggestions to include when writing a policy on e-mail:

- Employer property. The e-mail system is company property—not employee property. Companies should monitor their system with caution. Employers feel that they must monitor e-mail and Internet activities because they are concerned not only with the loss of employee productivity but also with their own liability in discrimination and harassment situations. They also must guard against trade secret exposure or an invasion of viruses. Some companies do not monitor their employees' use of the Internet and e-mail during lunch hours or breaks. Most companies, however, do make porn sites off limits to all employees. Other companies operate on the basis of trust with the expectation that morale will remain high and that trust will prevail.

HINT: *Contact an attorney for consultation.*

- Business use. The e-mail system is for business use only. Using it for harassment, flaming, or making illegal or other inappropriate comments is prohibited. Companies may be liable for their employees' e-mail messages and conduct.
- Proprietary information. Use of the system to transmit trade secrets, share confidential information with competitors or other employees, or solicit personal business is prohibited.
- Privacy. Personal passwords do not guarantee privacy. If e-mail is allowed for personal use, be specific about acceptable and unacceptable use. No laws protect the privacy of employees' e-mail to date.

HINT: *If the terms "excessive" or "inappropriate use" appear in a company e-mail policy, ask for a clear explanation so you do not inadvertently violate the policy.*

- File retention. Establish erasure policies and regular file-retention periods for e-mail. In dealing with sensitive information, include hard-drive reformatting and backup devices as part of retention procedures.
- Discipline. Violations of the e-mail policy result in discipline, including discharge. Avoid sending an e-mail message that you would not want everyone to read. Even if mail is deleted, it can be read and perhaps be used as evidence in a court of law.

INCOMING MAIL

Incoming mail includes USPS mail, special courier deliveries, intercompany correspondence, and electronic messages. Although incoming mail may arrive throughout the day, most USPS mail arrives at specified times. Office professionals facilitate the handling of these documents by prioritizing, opening, and distributing them as soon as possible after they are received.

Sorting Incoming Mail

In companies with centralized mail departments, USPS mail is delivered by mailroom messengers or robotic mobile delivery carts programmed to stop at designated locations. In other companies, postal carriers deliver the mail to each person's desk or to one person who then distributes it.

Once the mail is delivered, arrange it according to importance. Check the address of each item to be sure it has been delivered to the correct location. Return all mail that does not belong to the department to the mailroom or to the post office.

Materials may be prioritized differently in different types of businesses, but the following are useful suggestions for sorting mail by priority:

First priority: express, certified, priority with confirmation, registered, or insured mail; special courier deliveries.

HINT: *The term "accountable mail" is any incoming mail for which a record has been kept in tracking its progress to your office. For safety purposes, more companies will continue the tracking progress from the time the mail reaches the mailroom until it is distributed to the recipient.*

Second priority: personal or confidential mail. If a supervisor gives you permission to open personal, confidential, or private mail, attach a note to indicate that the envelope was marked as such.

Third priority: first-class mail, e-mail messages, interoffice mail, priority mail, airmail.

Fourth priority: packages.

Fifth priority: periodicals mail—newspapers and magazines.

HINT: *Magazines and newspapers may be important to a supervisor. Do not put periodicals mail aside for later handling, but include it in each mail distribution.*

Sixth priority: Standard mail (A)—catalogs, advertising materials, pamphlets, and booklets.

Supplies for Opening the Mail

Several supplies are helpful in opening the mail:

- Letter openers. Small mail opener machines, either manual or electric, can save considerable time. Some models automatically feed the envelopes, even ones of various sizes. In addition, such equipment can open the envelopes on one end (or on one side and one end), stack the envelopes, and count them.
- Date and time stamp.
- Mail record, special services record, mail-expected record, or a combination of these records. (See the section on Recording Incoming Mail.)
- Stapler, paper clips, adhesive message pad, pencils, and transparent tape.

- Mail stop directory. If mail needs to be routed to another location, include the mail stop location (if applicable) as well as the name.
- Routing slips.

Procedures for Opening the Mail

The following procedures are recommended for opening mail and removing the contents:

- Arrange the envelopes so the flaps face the same direction before opening them by hand or machine. Open all envelopes first; then remove and unfold the contents. To prevent discarding an enclosure, hold each envelope to the light to make sure the envelope is empty. Clip each envelope's contents together. Do not discard the envelopes until you have verified the addresses.
- Tap the lower edges of the envelope to allow the contents to fall to the bottom and avoid cutting them. If an item is cut, use transparent tape to repair the damage.
- If an envelope was opened when it should not have been, write "Opened by Mistake" on the envelope and initial it.
- Use a date stamp to record the receipt date of each item. Once the contents have been removed, stamp the document in the same location; for example, in the upper right on correspondence or on the back of catalogs. Include the time a document is received if it is important. The date and/or time may be handwritten, hand-stamped, or machine-stamped.
- Review each document for the sender's name and address, enclosures, and date. If the address on the envelope and document differ, clip the return address from the envelope and staple it to the letter. Make a note to verify the correct address with the sender. Once verified, change all mailing list notations and circle the correct address on the correspondence just received.
- Record an omission of a date or a major discrepancy between the date on the letter and the date of the postmark on a piece of adhesive notepaper. Attach the note to the correspondence for your supervisor's attention. Staple the envelope to the document. Any discrepancies may have consequences in legal matters.
- Verify the receipt of all enclosures. If an enclosure is missing, circle the enclosure line and indicate that the item is missing. If the amount in the message is different from the amount on an enclosed check, indicate the discrepancy next to the enclosure notation. Record the missing item(s) on the mail record and make a note to contact the sender as soon as possible.
- Attach an enclosure to a document with a staple or a paper clip. Attach small enclosures to the front of documents and attach enclosures that are the same size or larger to the back of documents.

HINT: *A staple may damage an attachment, such as a photograph. Fold a small sheet of paper in half and place the attachment between the fold and document. Use a paper clip to attach them together.*

- Check suspicious-looking packages for bombs or contamination. Things to look for include no return or fake return addresses; bulky, sloppy, or lopsided packaging; childlike printing in the address; misspelled addressee; too much postage. Call the Postal Inspection Office and the police if you receive a suspicious package. Store the item in a remote area until it is checked by a technician.

- Recommend to your supervisor that workshops be set up to advise employees on mail security precautions and handling questionable items.

- Check parcels for first-class mail, such as an invoice or letter, that may be attached to the front of the package or enclosed inside.

- Verify that the contents of the package match the packing slip or invoice as well as the original requisition. Indicate the acceptance of the materials listed on the invoice with a signature or other designated approval before sending the invoice to accounting for payment. Note on the mail record that the ordered materials were received.

- Indicate that enclosures have been distributed to another location by writing a note on the original copy of the letter and on the mail record.

Recording Incoming Mail

In addition to recording the date and time that materials arrive, keep a record of the mail. The mail record is a daily list of mail received with follow-up actions and dates. The list is easily maintained on the computer. A review of the record indicates how a document is being handled and to whom a document was routed. It helps in locating and tracing correspondence. Record those items that appear to need additional handling as well as certified, registered, expedited, priority, and first-class mail; interoffice mail; airmail; e-mail; and personal mail.

A special services record lists only those documents requiring the sender to pay additional fees, such as certified or registered. The mail expected record lists mail that is still expected, such as materials that have been ordered or items that are being sent under separate cover. If the mail expected is very limited, a note on your "to do" list is sufficient. File these mail records in an 8½-by-11-inch notebook at your desk. Establish separate records for each special one-time event, such as a special publication or a conference that requires registration fees.

Check mail management tips in *1001 Tips for Better Mail Management,* by Allen A. Curtis Jr., published by Excelsior Book Division (607–746–700).

Annotating Mail

In addition to reviewing and recording mail, reminders or comments may be placed in the margins of the correspondence, with underlining or highlighting of key facts. Refer only to the items that require your supervisor's attention; excessive annotation is ineffective. Before making notations on the correspondence, obtain your supervisor's consent. If the documents are distributed to other departments, the marginal notations or underscores may not be appropriate.

Nonreproducing pencils are useful when annotating correspondence since the notations do not reproduce when photocopied. Adhesive notepaper also works since it is easily removed before copies are made for distribution. Use a highlighter only with your supervisor's approval.

Many incoming documents require only brief acknowledgments or transmittal of material. Draft responses to such correspondence for your supervisor's signature or under your own name. Discuss your ability to handle certain types of correspondence with your supervisor. Prepare a list of the actions you take ("Items I Handled") and place it with the incoming mail distribution for your supervisor to review.

Distributing Incoming Mail

Once the mail is sorted by importance, it can then be divided into such categories as:

- Immediate action required.
- For reply/routine mail.
- For reply/other employees.
- For reply/office assistant.
- No reply needed—information only (e.g., thank-you notes, acknowledgment letters).
- Magazines, newspapers, publications.
- For reading (e.g., announcements, reports not included in the first two categories, advertisements).

The earlier the mail reaches the right desk, the more time there is to respond to those items that require immediate action. Try to set aside the same times each day for handling the mail. Use these procedures for quick, effective distribution:

- Sort the first-class mail into such categories as invoices, client concerns, orders, or correspondence from suppliers.
- Use a consistent system for presenting the mail. Place it in folders or arrange it according to priority, with the most important documents on top.
- Place incoming mail in the same location on the supervisor's desk each time it is delivered. If folders are not appropriate, place a bulky item such as a book on top of the mail. Place the top sheet face-down so the materials are not visible to others.

- A supervisor may request assistance in handling the magazines and trade publications that he or she receives. Request a prioritized list of topics and publications. Prepare a list of articles in each magazine that correspond with these subjects. The supervisor can then select the magazines and articles to read. A second method involves preparing file cards for the articles that fall in an interest area. File these cards in the subject folders for each interest topic. A third method is to photocopy the table of contents of a magazine and highlight those articles in which the supervisor may be interested. Place this list in a folder marked "For Reading." Always keep reading files and subject lists up to date.

- Ask for assistance in determining which advertisements and catalogs to save, if any. Store them in a separate location away from general files. Discard the older editions as soon as new ones are received.

- If an employee has left the company, forward personal correspondence to the employee's home. Cross out the company address on the envelope and write the forwarding address and the words "Please forward." If the document appears to be business related, forward it to that person's replacement, or to the immediate supervisor if a replacement has not been named.

OUTGOING MAIL

Efficient handling of outgoing mail speeds the communication process. Processing the mail so it is not delayed and following the USPS guidelines for addressing mail are responsibilities of office professionals. Under the 1996 Classification Reform, the Postal Service offers considerable discounts for mail that is properly screened, addressed, and bundled.

Processing Outgoing Mail

Before sending the mail to the mailroom or depositing it for delivery, several steps are needed to process it:

- Check that all letters have a signature. Be sure all attachments and enclosures are included.

- Address mail so it is readable by the USPS's OCR (optical character recognition) system. (See the section on addressing mail.) Readable mail moves through the system more quickly; nonreadable mail must be handled manually.

- Combine mailings. If there are two letters to one company, place them both in the same envelope. Use both sides of the paper for lengthy reports; this practice saves paper and also postage costs. An envelope holds four to six sheets of paper.

HINT: *Recommend that a company-wide check be done to verify addresses. Thousands of dollars are wasted because of incorrect or duplicate addresses. Outsource providers can do this service. Check with the USPS if you mail using automation rates. Numerous software programs are available to update addresses to meet USPS requirements. If the volume of mail does not justify the program, verify the accuracy of the addresses manually by checking the current address list and making the appropriate changes.*

- Check that all correspondence has been dated and that the address on the envelope matches the inside address. When inserting the material in the envelopes, be sure the correct letter goes in the proper envelope.
- Verify the ZIP code with the address on the original correspondence or locate it in the ZIP code directory. Check that each piece of mail meets USPS dimensions and weight limits.
- Deposit all metered mail on the date stamped. Do not place metered stamps on the envelopes one day and wait until another day to do the mailing. If the mail does not make the last pickup, take it to another collection box or to the post office.
- Change the date on the postage meter each morning before other tasks are started. Electronic metering systems automatically advance the date, give accurate readings for whatever item is on the scale, and allow you to compare postal rates with FedEx® and UPS®. Metered mail is processed faster than stamped mail, since it does not have to be canceled at the post office.

HINT: *For security reasons, always review postage usage reports. If postage meters are accessible in offices during evening or weekend hours, unauthorized use can occur. Keep the meters locked when possible.*

- Avoid waiting until the end of the day to deposit mail. Take mail to the mailroom several times during the day. Mail deposited by 2 P.M. has a chance of being processed by 5 P.M. for next day delivery.
- Use the USPS order forms to order stamps or order on-line at www.shop.usps.com.
- Use window envelopes only if the address has four or fewer lines. More than four lines will not be fully visible in the window section. If any part of an address is unreadable, the item is rejected and must be handled manually.
- Inform mailroom personnel when a large mailing is planned.
- Weigh all mail. Do not guess. Use a scale that measures to a fraction of an ounce. In addition to setting accurate postage values, most scales will print self-adhesive labels. Small desktop scales are ideal for home-based businesses.
- Place tape over a metal clasp on an envelope. This avoids damage to the envelope if it gets jammed in the sorting machine. Write "Please hand stamp" on the outside of the envelope if it contains bulky items. Use pressure-sensitive seals rather than staples when mailing announcements or newsletters.

HINT: *If materials must be clipped together or stapled, fold so the paper clips or staples are in the inner fold of the document. Paper clips can get bent and cause a jam in a sorting machine.*

- Mark envelopes with the notation "Do Not Bend" when you send photographs, certificates, or transparencies. Use cardboard for extra protection.
- Obtain full value for the amount of postage used. If paying for one ounce, weigh the letter to determine if another announcement or promotion piece can be included. This eliminates two separate mailings.
- Use the smallest and strongest containers possible for wrapping packages. Do not use string and wrapping paper, since packages may also be processed by machines; use a filament tape. Do not use newspaper for protecting the contents; use lightweight stuffing.
- Include a letter with any disk that is being transmitted through the mail. Identify the contents of the disk and the sender in the transmittal letter and on the disk label. This procedure causes less confusion should the disk and letter be separated. Also, identify the software program and the hardware used.
- Prepare disks for mailing by placing them in cardboard or heavy plastic wrap before putting them in a box or padded envelope. On the outside of the box or envelope, indicate a disk is enclosed.
- Consider using a service bureau to handle bulk mailings or considerable amounts of international mail. Foreign postal services have established centers in the United States to deliver mail abroad.
- Stay up to date on mailing standards. Request a tour of the local post office. Check the USPS Web site at www.new.usps.gov.
- Subscribe to *Mailers Companion,* a publication that includes mailing guideline changes. The postal address is *Mailers Companion,* U.S. Postal Service, 475 L'Enfant Plaza SW, Room 6830, Washington DC 20260-2450, or e-mail for information at rlovell@email.usps.gov.

Folding and Inserting Mail

Machines are available to fold, seal, and stamp mail. Correct folding and insertion give letters a professional look and make them easy for the reader to open and unfold. The steps involved in folding and inserting materials for the No. 10, No. 6¾, and window envelopes follow. Always use a flat surface for neater folds.

No. 10 Envelope
- With the document face-up on the desk, fold up the bottom third of the page first.
- Fold the top third of the letter down over the bottom third so the top edge is ¼ inch from the first fold.

- Insert the item so the open side of the document is at the back (side to be sealed) and to the top of the envelope.

No. 6¾ Envelope

- With the document face-up on the desk, fold the bottom half of the paper to ¼ inch from the top. Leaving the ¼ inch makes it easier for the reader to separate the pages.
- Fold the document in thirds. Start with the first one-third fold from the right side. Continue with the second one-third fold from the left side so the edge is ¼ inch from the right side.
- Insert so the last fold is toward the bottom of the envelope and the open edge faces the back of the envelope (the side to be sealed). Insert the document so the open edges are on the stamp side of the envelope.

HINT: *If the folds are not parallel with the top and sides, the letter will look sloppy when unfolded. Fold the sections so they are exactly the same width. Avoid uneven edges and folds that are at angles.*

Window Envelope

- With the document face-up on the desk, fold up the bottom third of the page first.
- Fold the top third of the document in the opposite direction so the edge touches the first fold.
- Insert the document so the last fold is at the bottom of the envelope and the address shows through the window.
- Postal guidelines call for a space of ¼ inch between the side and bottom edges of the window and an address.

HINT: *Fold enclosures with the document or insert them so they are in the fold of the document.*

Addressing Envelopes

The USPS has provided guidelines for addressing envelopes so its electronic equipment can read the addresses and speed the delivery of mail. (See Figure 16-8.)

State abbreviations: Use the standard two-letter abbreviations as given in Table 16-1.

ZIP codes: Use nine-digit ZIP codes, if known, or the five-digit ZIP code. Letter-sorting machines sort envelopes by ZIP codes. Optical character readers read the last two lines of an address. Bar code readers can process mail with imprinted bar codes at extraordinary speeds. Most countries have postal code systems. Canadian and British postal codes consist of numbers and letters arranged in two groups of three characters each; for example, F3N 4B2.

Mailpiece Clear Zones (White Areas)

Figure 16-8 Format for addressing an envelope.

Address placement: Mail can be processed more quickly if the address is placed in a designated location on the envelope and arranged in a specific sequence. The USPS recommends the following for address placement:

- Locate the address lines within the OCR read area. This area is $\frac{5}{8}$″ to $2\frac{3}{4}$″ from the bottom of the item and $\frac{1}{2}$″ margins from the side.
- Align the address so each line is straight.
- Do not mark anything within the bar code boundaries. This area is $\frac{5}{8}$″ from the bottom and $4\frac{3}{4}$″ from the right side of the item.
- Use dark ink on light backgrounds. Bright colors and reverse printing are not recommended.
- Use USPS abbreviations. (See Table 16-2.) See *Postal Addressing Standards*, available at your local post office, for more information.
- The return address should appear on the front of the envelope, not on the back. Block the return address two lines from the top and three spaces from the left side of the envelope,

HINT: *When logos or graphics are printed on envelopes, be sure they do not block the OCR read area and skew the scanning process.*

Table 16-2
STANDARD ADDRESS ABBREVIATIONS

UNITED STATES AND POSSESSIONS

Alabama	AL	Montana	MT
Alaska	AK	Nebraska	NE
Arizona	AZ	Nevada	NV
Arkansas	AR	New Hampshire	NH
American Samoa	AS	New Jersey	NJ
California	CA	New Mexico	NM
Colorado	CO	New York	NY
Connecticut	CT	North Carolina	NC
Delaware	DE	North Dakota	ND
District of Columbia	DC	Northern Mariana Islands	MP
Federated States of Micronesia	FM	Ohio	OH
Florida	FL	Oklahoma	OK
Georgia	GA	Oregon	OR
Guam	GU	Palau	PW
Hawaii	HI	Pennsylvania	PA
Idaho	ID	Puerto Rico	PR
Illinois	IL	Rhode Island	RI
Indiana	IN	South Carolina	SC
Iowa	IA	South Dakota	SD
Kansas	KS	Tennessee	TN
Kentucky	KY	Texas	TX
Louisiana	LA	Utah	UT
Maine	ME	Vermont	VT
Marshall Islands	MH	Virginia	VA
Maryland	MD	Virgin Islands	VI
Massachusetts	MA	Washington	WA
Michigan	MI	West Virginia	WV
Minnesota	MN	Wisconsin	WI
Mississippi	MS	Wyoming	WY
Missouri	MO		

CANADA

Alberta	AB	Nova Scotia	NS
British Columbia	BC	Ontario	ON
Manitoba	MB	Prince Edward Island	PE
New Brunswick	NB	Quebec	PQ
Newfoundland	NF	Saskatchewan	SK
Northwest Territories	NT	Yukon Territory	YT

DIRECTIONAL ABBREVIATIONS

North	N	Northeast	NE
East	E	Southeast	SE
South	S	Southwest	SW
West	W	Northwest	NW

ARMED FORCES

Armed Forces Europe, Middle East, and Canada	AE
Armed Forces Pacific	AP
Armed Forces Americas (except Canada)	AA

Address format: The USPS recommends the following guidelines for formatting the address:

- Align each line of an address at the left.
- Put the address in all caps.

HINT: *Lowercase letters in standard type styles are acceptable if they meet postal guidelines for OCR readability.*

HINT: *Titles of respect should be used when appropriate. Do not combine titles and degrees; for example, "Dr. Mary Smith, M.D." is redundant.*

- Omit punctuation marks but include the hyphen in the ZIP + 4 code; for example, 94702-6401.

HINT: *Although omitting punctuation is preferred, including it is acceptable.*

- Limit the address to four to six lines. Use standard word abbreviations rather than two lines for a firm name. See accepted abbreviations in Appendix G in *Postal Addressing Standards,* available at your local post office.
- Single space the address.
- Avoid nonstandard print fonts, such as script, and styles, such as italic or condensed.
- Use the last line of the address for the city, state, and ZIP + 4 code. Leave two spaces between the state and ZIP code.
- Use the line above the last line for the street address or post office box number. It is not necessary to use both. Use the correct ZIP code for either the delivery address or the post office box number. Do not place any information below the ZIP code; this just delays the item at the post office.

HINT: *If a return address includes both a street address and a post office box, address your correspondence to the post office box. Mail may be picked up from the box earlier in the day and on weekends. If the business moves to another location, the box usually stays the same. If you are shipping via an air express service, you may be required to use the street address only.*

- Put suite numbers or apartment numbers on the same line as the street address. If the address is too long, put the suite or apartment number on the line above the street address.
- Identify the addressee on the top line of the address. The department name, if applicable, should appear on the second line and the company name on the third line.
- Place the "Attention" line on the line above the name of the firm.

- Put special service notations such as special delivery, certified, or registered two lines below the stamp in all capital letters. Underscores are not necessary. The information must be above the OCR read area.
- Put handling instructions such as Confidential and Personal three lines below the return address and above the OCR read area. Capitalize the first letter of each word and underscore.
- When addressing mail to foreign countries put the name of the country on the last line in all capital letters. Do not underline or abbreviate the country name. Do not place postal codes of foreign countries on the last line of the addresses. However, for mail addressed to Canada, place either "Canada" or a postal zone on the last line. Both options are acceptable.

HINT: *Address formats differ in foreign countries. In European countries, the street name often appears first with the number following it. Write the address exactly as it appears on the letterhead.*

INTEROFFICE MAIL

Interoffice mail may be delivered by mailroom personnel or intercompany transport or by e-mail via the computer. Most companies have distinctive envelopes for interoffice mail. Light brown envelopes with space for names and departments/locations of the recipients are the most common. They are 9½ inches by 13 inches or 4 inches by 9½ inches. The smaller size is appropriate for small notes. Avoid using the smaller envelopes for documents that must be folded to fit inside.

HINT: *If the material is confidential, use an ordinary envelope and seal it. Label it "INTEROFFICE MEMO" in the upper right corner so it will not get mixed in with the other classes of mail. Some companies have special envelopes for confidential interoffice mail that are labeled as such.*

DIRECT MAIL

Before investing time and money in a direct-mail campaign (postal or e-mail), you should set objectives and select target markets. Once the market is targeted, obtain mailing lists that are accurate and current. Effective mailing lists are easy to reuse and manipulate.

You can prepare your own in-house lists, or rent, buy, or lease them. The lists may be rented for one-time use or more than once if stated in the original agreement. Use the list only as specified in the rental agreement. The best source for direct e-mail is a subscriber list. Each person on the list completes a form on the company's Web site. For generating a broader base of participants, use a service that collects names of people who want to be on lists to receive e-mail.

HINT: *When ordering a mailing list to be sent through USPS, allow at least six weeks to order and receive the list, sort the names, and prepare the mailing. Time the mailing so it reaches potential clients at the beginning of the week or at seasonal slack times. During the holiday season and around tax deadlines or accounting closing periods, direct-mail literature receives less attention.*

Mailing lists can be compiled from such sources as the following:

- Customer list.
- Company sales invoices.

HINT: *Customers expect invoices; therefore, a marketing message can be included as a subtle marketing reminder.*

- Company payroll records.
- Consumer and trade publications.
- Replies to advertisements.
- Business license applications.
- Professional organizations; for example, Kiwanis, Chamber of Commerce.
- Utility companies.
- Voting lists.
- Auto registration lists.
- Magazine subscribers.
- Tax lists.
- Warranty registrations.
- City directories.
- Telephone directories.
- Responder lists (people who have bought by mail from someone else).
- Newsletters.

HINT: *A newsletter often softens a blatant sales pitch and provides better results.*

- Special sales bulletins.
- Bank and credit unions.
- Credit bureaus.
- Warranty product cards.
- Discount offers.

HINT: *Avoid words such as "free" or "win." These words suggest spam in e-mail messages and are easily filtered to a "Trash" folder.*

Mailing lists may be maintained on address labels, address plates, file cards, computer printouts, a database, or in an e-mail address book.

HINT: *Printing directly on an envelope is more personal; a recipient will be more likely to open it rather than toss it away.*

HINT: The Directory of Directories, *an annual publication from Gale Research Company, has listings for organization and business directories.*

In-house preparation of mailing lists requires time and planning. Begin by identifying the appropriate fields to include in setting up a database. Then revise the fields as necessary once the database is established. In addition, use information from mapping or data mining research to target people.

Specific information to help target a base list includes:

- Name/address/telephone number/e-mail/fax.
- Social Security number (if known or applicable).
- Income level/sales volume.
- Job title of the person making the inquiry or purchase.
- Number of years the organization has been in business.
- Age category of individuals (when applicable).
- Geographic area.
- Product areas.
- Amount of order.
- Date of first purchase; date of last purchase.
- Frequency of orders.
- Peak buying times.
- Code for products in which an interest is shown.
- Category of the company; for example, manufacturing, real estate, finance.
- Level of inquiry; for example, branch office, department, project group.

Companies using a direct-mail approach should always have a definite goal in mind before they target their participants. Is this a one-time promotion? Is it to advertise a new product? Is it a newsletter? If the latter, how many times will it be sent? They also must be ready to handle the response from the direct-mail campaign and have sufficient staff, products, and supplies available.

Periodic newsletters are effective promotional tools. Direct postal mail marketing is expensive and time-consuming, so e-mail direct marketing can more easily take advantage of this format. Newsletters should be written in a friendly, easy-to-read format. Attention must be paid to grammar and punctuation. Use underlines or color to highlight major points.

HINT: *Begin with a quarterly or monthly newsletter. Evaluate results to decide if a weekly communication is feasible. Remember that a newsletter does not need multiple pages to be effective.*

Graphics may add appeal to a direct mailing if the graphics are done tastefully and if they relate to the reason for sending the direct mail piece.

HINT: *Not all customers may be able to receive HTML e-mail; therefore, send the document in HTML and in plain text so the customer may choose which version to open.*

List-processing or mail-management software allows users to prepare and sort lists more efficiently. Select software that verifies your mailing lists against the USPS National Database (USPS CASS-approved ZIP + 4). Most software programs have a change-of-address system utility, a database that has all address changes filed during the past three years.

To stop the massive influx of catalogs, write instructions on the mailing label and send this label to the company. Always mark the correspondence to the attention of Customer Service. If you call a catalog company, use the toll-free number and have that mailing label available.

You may find that organizing direct mail campaigns and maintaining mailing lists are not productive tasks. Outsource providers can handle these jobs effectively, which allows you more time to concentrate on filling the needs of the responders.

To remove your name from nonprofit mailing lists, contact the Mail Preference Service of the Direct Marketing Association, 1120 Avenue of the Americas, New York, NY 10017. Another way to decrease the influx of direct mail is to request companies with whom business is transacted to stop selling the company name to other organizations.

PART IV

OFFICE

COMMUNICATIONS

Well-written correspondence is one of the most important factors in communicating a strong, positive corporate image. The office professional is expected to know how to correctly and attractively format correspondence for maximum impact using the most productive means available. In addition, many office professionals are expected to compose written communications for others.

For years the formats of memos and letters did not change. Computers, however, now allow the design of personalized form letters, printing of envelopes from prepared address lists, and discovery of errors by spelling, grammar, and style checkers. All of these advances in technology have brought about streamlined, uncluttered correspondence designed to improve operator productivity.

The Internet and e-mail are valuable, cost-effective tools for employees. Although some correspondence still requires memorandums and letters, e-mail is the preferred method of communication within companies and to many customers. E-mail is more conversational than traditional letters and the style of the writing and formatting is more casual.

CHAPTER 17

WRITTEN

CORRESPONDENCE

TIPS ON COMPOSING CORRESPONDENCE

Before going into the specifics of various types of correspondence, below are general guidelines regarding all types of correspondence.

- Write only when circumstances are appropriate. In some instances, it may be better to place a phone call, handle in person, or send an e-mail message or fax.

- Be aware that anything put in writing may be shown to others, even if it is not intended for them. Therefore, do not put anything in writing that you would not say publicly or you would not want published with your name. Never send correspondence in anger.

HINT: *Wait 24 hours before sending a negative reply or something written in anger. After cooling off, you may decide not to send a response. This hint especially applies to e-mail messages.*

HINT: *Understand the needs of your receiver. Some people respond more quickly to e-mail than written correspondence; others prefer telephone communications.*

- Know your audience. Determine what relationship exists or what relationship you wish to achieve. Demonstrate sensitivity to the needs and interests of the reader. Personalize correspondence if possible. You may need to know the following items for audience analysis: occupation or position, gender, age range, education, income, and experience.
- Have a specific objective. For example, ask for information or attempt to make a sale. Every piece of correspondence should have the subtle objective of building goodwill for your organization.

HINT: *Always know the purpose before writing. It helps to answer this question: What do I want my reader to do (or know) when they finish reading what I have written?*

- Use the active voice. Voice shows whether the subject acts or is acted upon. In the active voice, the subject performs an action: Our accountants completed the audit; We shipped your order on Friday, December 3. In the passive voice, the subject is acted upon: The audit was completed by our accountants; The order was shipped on Friday, December 3. The active voice is more direct, even though both sentences state the same information.

    The passive voice is often used to soften the impact of negative news: Your order will be shipped when the enclosed order blank is returned. This is less negative than the active voice: We will ship your order when you return the enclosed order blank.

HINT: *Many computer grammar and style checkers can analyze sentences for active or passive construction.*

- Be concise. Use specific, concrete words. Eliminate unnecessary words. Avoid clichés and jargon.

HINT: *The average sentence should have fewer than 20 words.*

HINT: *Keep paragraphs to three or four sentences.*

HINT: *Computer thesaurus programs can suggest synonyms and help you avoid repeating the same words. Computer grammar and style checkers can point out unnecessary words or statements.*

HINT: *Use lists. All items must be parallel.*

WORDS AND PHRASES TO AVOID:	USE:
accompanied by	with
according to our records	(avoid)
acknowledge receipt of	(avoid)
as of this day	today
at the present time	now, presently
at your earliest convenience	(be specific)
attached please find	enclosed
be cognizant of	know that
consensus of opinion	consensus
deliberate upon	think about
disbursements	payments
due to the fact	because
enclosed please find	enclosed
forward	send
free of charge	free
herewith	(leave out)
increment	increase
in compliance with your request	as requested
in reference to	about
in the amount of	for
in the event of	if, in case
kindly	please
to our previous . . .	when we last
per your request	as requested
re	regarding
scrutinize	read, examine
subsequent to	after, since
take the liberty of	(avoid)
thanking you in advance	thank you
this is to acknowledge	(avoid)
up to this writing	until now
utilize	use
vitally essential	vital or essential

- Be polite and courteous. Be positive by stressing what you can do instead of what you cannot do. Use the "you" attitude to convey warmth and friendliness. The "you" attitude is writing from the reader's point of view by emphasizing "you" and minimizing "we" and "I."

HINT: *Some companies prefer the use of "we" rather than "I" to show that the writer is speaking for the company. Use "we" or "us" to show others share the message.*

- Get straight to the point unless the news is bad. Make the purpose of the correspondence obvious. Arrange material from general to specific. Start with a general statement and add facts that explain the statement.

HINT: *The last paragraph is remembered the longest, so important information should be stated or restated there.*

- Reply promptly. If you cannot respond to a letter or e-mail, acknowledge it immediately and say when the requested information will be available: Thank you for your letter (or e-mail). The information you requested will take several days to research. As soon as we have the information, . . .

HINT: *When saying "no" to a request or job applicant, delay the reply for a week so it does not appear that little thought was given to the response.*

- Use proper grammar, spelling, and punctuation. A computer grammar and style checker helps point out potential problems with sentence structure, punctuation, and writing style. A computer spell checker locates many (but not all) misspellings and typographical errors.
- Check the accuracy of dates and figures.
- Use simple type fonts such as Times New Roman or Arial and a font size of 12 points (10 points is difficult for some people to read).

E-Mail Writing Tips

E-mail is substituting for paper mail because of its speed. E-mail creates a "paper trail" that increases the lifespan of the message and may leave either a positive or negative impression with the reader. Many people with e-mail access have not been trained to use it, have poor writing skills, or think they can ignore the formalities of writing. See also Chapter 16, Mailing Documents, for additional e-mail writing suggestions.

The following tips help in writing e-mail messages:

- Practice the same rules of writing you would use if you were sending the correspondence through traditional channels; but at the same time, keep the message short.
- Keep the line length to approximately 60 characters. Know whether your system has word wrap or not. Some e-mail programs will wrap the text at wrong points or not wrap it at all.
- Avoid sarcasm, pomposity, and anger.
- Proofread carefully onscreen. Set the Spell Check feature on your e-mail program to automatically check spelling before the e-mail is sent.
- Avoid all caps, which has the effect of "screaming" to the receiver.
- Avoid fancy fonts, colors, graphics, and animated graphics. Not all e-mail clients and servers can handle messages in these formats.
- Leave a blank line between paragraphs.

- Only use abbreviations common to the English language (for example, FYI) or to your business. Not everyone is experienced with e-mail jargon, and they may not want to admit their confusion.
- Use emoticons only in informal correspondence and sparingly. The most common example of an emoticon is :-).
- Use the salutation that you normally would use. For example, if you address someone as Ms., Mrs., or Mr., use that salutation in an e-mail. If you normally call someone by their first name, omit the title. If you are unsure, use the formal salutation.

HINT: *Observe how someone signs his or her e-mail and reply accordingly.*

- Use a signature line, which is the letterhead of an e-mail message. Sign your e-mail with your name, title, and company name, address, e-mail address, and fax and voice numbers.

HINT: *Set your e-mail program to automatically add this information at the end of an e-mail message.*

- Avoid adding quotations at the end of the e-mail in business communication (for example, "Most people are about as happy as they make up their minds to be." Abraham Lincoln).
- Reply to an e-mail message instead of starting a new message. Users on each end can easily follow the sequence of messages, especially after several exchanges.
- Create folders and store messages instead of printing them.

HINT: *Set your e-mail program to automatically sort e-mail and put it into folders instead of having all e-mail delivered to your inbox. An automatic e-mail sort function is only as good as the program's filters, however, so mail can go astray. And, of course, you have to remember to check each file for new mail.*

- Restrict yourself to one subject for each message. Send multiple messages for multiple subjects.
- Be tolerant of others' mistakes in writing and using e-mail.
- Always use the "http://" prefix when keying a Web site address. Some e-mail programs will permit the user to click on a Web address to go right to the address. Without the "http://" prefix, these programs do not have that capability.

E-mail software programs often come with many time-saving features, including:

- address books (e-mail addresses that can be automatically inserted into the To line or the message)

- distribution lists (addresses of people associated with a group, which eliminates keying each e-mail address separately in the To line)
- filters (automatically sort mail, delete mail, reply to mail, and so on)

HINT: *Periodically check your e-mail filters to be sure they are still meeting your needs and not misdirecting important mail.*

Be aware that many organizations feel e-mail composed and sent at work is the property of the company. Some companies regularly check e-mail messages with the justification that the company can be liable for your e-mail. It is also possible for your e-mail to be altered without your knowledge. In addition, if someone else has access to your password, they can send e-mail in your name. With most e-mail systems, it is easy to send copies to others without your knowledge.

When sending electronic information to customers, give an option for removal from your mailing list. For example, "If you do not wish to receive this information, click on *unsubscribe.*"

International Communication Suggestions

The global nature of communications demands an understanding of how people in other cultures communicate. Americans are typically more informal than the rest of the world, deemphasizing rank, status, and position.

When communicating with individuals in cultures where formality is expected—such as Latin America, Europe, and Japan—follow these suggestions:

- Use last names, titles, and other indications of rank and status. Never use first names unless invited to do so. In many Latin American countries, the title is more important than the name.
- Write individual letters to people of higher status. Avoid mass mailings and form letters. Know who should receive copies of correspondence.
- Avoid trying to "cut through the red tape" to get the job done. Red tape is honored in some cultures.
- Demonstrate some knowledge of other languages, even though individuals in other cultures may be communicating in English.
- Avoid using words that have more than one meaning, industry-specific jargon, or abbreviations. Humor typically does not translate well. Be cautious when using sports-related terms, such as "give me a ballpark figure," or terms that might not be understood in other cultures, such as "keep your nose to the grindstone."
- Avoid references to exclusively American holidays such as Thanksgiving or the Fourth of July and avoid references to religious holidays.
- Find out if the recipient uses British English or American English. A reader who is unfamiliar with the variations between the two may presume that your writing

contains typos. Most European companies use British English. Most American companies—no matter where they are based in the world—use American English.

- Paper sizes are different in different countries. The United States standard is 8 ½ by 11 inches whereas the European A-4 standard is 210 by 297 mm.
- Short, concise sentences are easier for someone who is interpreting English. For international business e-mail, write in a formal tone. You can progress from formal to friendly, but it is difficult to move back from friendly to formal.

American messages are sometimes too direct for individuals in cultures where it is important to get to know a person before doing business. To overcome this difficulty, use faxes, e-mail, and letters to share information in order to build a relationship. The professional or personal information shared depends upon the culture of the other country.

COMPONENTS OF LETTERS

Letters may include some or all of the following:

- Date.
- Inside address.
- Salutation.
- Subject line.
- Complimentary closing.
- Writer information.
- Initials of typist.
- Notations.

The inclusion of a component depends on the purpose of the correspondence and the letter style used.

Date

All letters should include a date. Write the date as, for example, January 15, 20__. Spell out the month. Or use the military or international style of 15 January 20__ to avoid punctuation and save keying time. Place the date two or more lines beneath the letterhead; the shorter the letter, the more space is needed beneath the letterhead. Place the date either at the left margin or the center of the page, depending upon the letter style used (see the section on Letter Styles later in this chapter).

HINT: *Use the date feature of your word processing program to insert the date into document templates. The date feature inserts the current date every time you open a document. If preserving the original date the letter was sent is important, type the date into the document.*

Inside Address

The inside address contains everything necessary for delivery of correspondence: the name, job title, company name, street address or box number, and the city, state, and zip/postal code.

NAME

- Check on the correct spelling of the recipient's name.
- Use a courtesy title if it is known. Courtesy titles include Dr., Mr., Mrs., and Ms. (See the section on Salutation below for determining whether to use Ms., Mrs., or Miss.)

HINT: *If you do not know whether you are addressing a man or a woman with first names like Lynn or Pat, omit the title of Mr. or Ms.*

- Omitting earned titles such as Dr., M.D., or the Reverend may offend the reader, especially if that person has written your company using his or her title. Courtesy titles are not used if the earned title is included, and only one earned title is used: e.g., Louise F. Granger, M.D. (not Dr. Louise F. Granger, M.D.).
- Esquire (abbreviated as Esq.) can be used after the name of a lawyer, but no courtesy title should then be included: e.g., Shannon A. Duff, Esq. (not Ms. Shannon A. Duff, Esq.). Many lawyers do not use this courtesy designation, so follow the lead of the receiver when you draft your document: If the recipient uses Esquire on his or her letterhead, include it in your document.
- Use a job title if the name of the person is not known.
- Use a period after most courtesy and earned titles (except Miss).
- Spell out Professor and Reverend.

HINT: *If you do not know the recipient's name, use the name of the department (for example, Human Resources Department) and use the proper salutation (see Salutation section). Addressing correspondence this way eliminates the need for an Attention line.*

JOB TITLE

- Omit the job title if the exact title is not known.
- Place it either on the same line with the name, separated by a comma, or on the next line.

COMPANY NAME

- Check on the exact spelling and punctuation of the company name.
- Type the name exactly as it appears in the company's official letterhead, including The, Inc., or Co. If the name is long and requires another line, indent the second line 2 or 3 spaces.

STREET ADDRESS OR POST OFFICE BOX

- Spell out numerical names of streets and avenues if they are numbers less than 10: e.g., Seventh Street, Third Avenue, 15th Street.
- Use figures for all house numbers except One: e.g., One Commerce Boulevard, 2 Park Avenue, 102 Sunnyslope.
- Spell out Avenue, Street, Boulevard, and so forth.
- Place a box number after the street address:

3489 Westwood Road

Box 4388

HINT: *Use the street address for overnight delivery. If both the box number and the street address appear on the envelope, the U.S. Postal Service delivers to the address directly above the city, state, and ZIP code information.*

HINT: *Remember that air express companies may not deliver to box numbers.*

- Omit periods after abbreviations: e.g., Box 34, Elm Street, NW

  The trend toward dropping periods in the inside address is a result of U.S. Postal Service requests to eliminate punctuation on envelopes. Also, addresses on computer databases generally do not include punctuation.

CITY, STATE, AND ZIP

- Include the full name of the city with no abbreviations. For example, San Francisco instead of SF.
- Use the two-letter state or province abbreviation recommended by the U.S. Postal Service. (See Table 16-1 in Chapter 16.)
- Place the ZIP or postal code two spaces after the state or province abbreviation.
- Use the ZIP + 4 code if known.
- A comma is not necessary between the city and the state, but one may be used.

The inside address should be single-spaced and placed at the left-hand margin. Locate it not less than two lines nor more than twelve lines below the date; placement depends on letter length. For longer letters, place closer to the date; for shorter letters, avoid extending the inside address beyond the middle of the page. Avoid going beyond the center of the page with the inside address. If necessary, carry over information to the next line, which should be indented five spaces. Avoid having more than six lines in an address; it may be necessary to combine lines.

Here are some examples of inside addresses:

Ms. Sarah Raintree
Sales Manager
Interim Personnel, Suite 203
4378 Southwest Boulevard
Chicago, IL 60637

Dr. Gail Radtkey
Vice President
Lawrence Galleries
3892 Independence Avenue
Phoenix, AZ 85773

Cameron Jacobson, M.D.
968 Lakeville Highway
Napa, CA 94943

Credit Manager
Creative Leisure
5948 Industrial Road
Trenton, NJ 38943

Alexandra T. L. Freeman, Personnel Coordinator
Cowan & Associates
4783 Redwood Highway
Box 5012
San Rafael, CA 94530

INTERNATIONAL ADDRESSES

When keying an international address, spell out the full name of the country on a separate line in all capital letters.

Ms Gertrud Baumann
AR Research
Doblinger Hauptstrasse 38

**1190 Wien
AUSTRIA**

When writing to Canada, the territory or province may be spelled out or abbreviated. The Canada Post prefers the abbreviated form for the province or territory for an envelope or text label.

**MR. HENRY SMITH
14 MERRIWETHER LANE
OTTAWA ON CANADA
K1A 0B1**

Salutation

A letter should always be addressed to an individual if the name is known. Below are suggested salutations.

ADDRESSED TO AN INDIVIDUAL

The most common salutation is Dear. Whether the first name or last name with title is used depends on the relationship between the writer and the recipient. Most people find it annoying to be addressed by their first name if they do not know the writer.

Use Ms. when addressing a woman, unless previous correspondence indicates she prefers the title Mrs. or Miss. Many women prefer the neutral term of Ms. over a term that denotes marital status.

If a person has an earned title such as M.D., Ph.D., or Ed.D., use Dr. in the salutation. Spell out the title Professor.

Avoid substituting a designation of business rank or position for a name; use "Dear Mr. Jones," not "Dear Personnel Director Jones." Similarly, write "Dear Ms. Reynolds," not "Dear Editor Reynolds."

The Honorable is used for individuals with high offices at the federal, state, or city levels. This title is still held after retirement. Table 17-1 provides sample salutations used for clergy, elected officials, military officers, and education officials.

WHEN RECIPIENT'S NAME OR GENDER IS NOT KNOWN

Traditional salutations of Dear Sir or Madam are inappropriate if the recipient's name is not known. You may address the recipient by title: e.g., Dear Screening Committee, Dear Board Members, Dear Credit Manager. If the recipient's gender is not known, you may use the first and last name, as in "Dear Lynn Crichton."

A salutation can use either open or closed punctuation. Either is correct, but the style

Table 17-1
SAMPLE SALUTATIONS

PERSON	INSIDE ADDRESS	SALUTATION
Elected Officials		
Chief Justice	The Chief Justice Supreme Court	Dear Mr. Chief Justice
Governor	The Honorable Richard Swan	Dear Governor Swan or Dear Governor
Judge	The Honorable Rosa Bezzari	Dear Judge Bezzari
Mayor	The Honorable Carolina Jung	Dear Mayor Jung
President	The President	Dear Mr. President Dear Madam President
Speaker of the House	The Honorable José Perez The Honorable Julia Payne	Dear Mr. Speaker Dear Madam Speaker
State Senator	The Honorable Lisa O'Leary	Dear Senator O'Leary
State Representative	The Honorable Mary Carter	Dear Representative Carter
U.S. Representative	The Honorable Betty Hamilton	Dear Representative Hamilton or Dear Ms. Hamilton
U.S. Senator	The Honorable Sam Nelson	Dear Senator Nelson or Dear Mr. Nelson
Vice President	The Vice President	Dear Mr. Vice President Dear Madam Vice President
Education Officials		
	Dr. J. Barbara Hall	Dear Dr. Hall
	Professor Quinlan Jones	Dear Professor Jones
Clergy		
Protestant clergy	The Reverend Sarah Gilligam	Dear Dr. Gilligam (with a doctoral degree) Dear Ms. Gilligam (without a doctoral degree)
Bishop of the Episcopal Church	The Right Reverend Randolph Jones	Dear Bishop Jones
Methodist Bishop	The Reverend George Rojas	Dear Reverend Rojas
Mormon Bishop	Mr. Gerald Hornaby	Dear Mr. Hornaby
The Pope	His Holiness, The Pope	Your Holiness
Cardinal	His Eminence, Paul Cardinal Bernardi	Your Eminence or Dear Cardinal Bernardi
Priest	The Reverend Father Peter Smoll	Dear Father Smoll
Nun	Sister Mary Margoilis or Mary Margoilis, R.S.C.J.	Dear Sister
Rabbi	Rabbi Benjamin Stein	Dear Rabbi Stein
Imam, Islamic (from a Muslim)	The Honored Sheikh (name)	Brother Sheikh (name) or Hujjat al-Islam Sheikh (name)
Imam, Islamic (from a non-Muslim)	The Honored Sheikh (name)	Dear Sheikh (name)

(Continued)

Table 17-1 (*continued*)

Military		
First Lieutenant	First Lieutenant, Craig Garcia	Dear Lieutenant Garcia
Lieutenant Colonel	Lieutenant Colonel, Samuel Jacobson	Dear Colonel Jacobson
Noncommissioned officers in Army, Air Force, and Marine Corps	Master Sergeant Roger Webb	Dear Sergeant Webb
Enlisted person in Navy	SN Charles Brown	Dear Seaman Brown

must be consistent in a letter. Open punctuation means there is no punctuation after the salutation or closing. Closed punctuation uses a comma after the salutation when the first name is used; a colon after the salutation when a title and last name are used; and a comma after the closing.

Abbreviate the titles Mr., Mrs., Ms., Messrs., and Dr. Spell out all other titles. Key the salutation two lines below the inside address. If you will use a standard window envelope, start two inches from the top of the page.

HINT: *Use the simplified letter style and omit the salutation.*

Subject

The subject line describes the purpose for writing a letter. The subject line is not necessary in business letters but is used when drawing the reader's attention to the contents of the letter. It is particularly helpful if recipients, such as government agencies, receive a volume of correspondence. No punctuation is needed.

HINT: *Avoid* re, *an outdated Latin expression meaning the same as "subject."*

Complimentary Closing

The most popular and appropriate closing is Sincerely. Sincerely yours and Cordially are also well-accepted closings. Respectfully yours is used when writing to a high official, including the President of the United States or a high church official. If a closing has more than one word (such as Sincerely yours), capitalize only the first word.

Place the closing two lines below the last line of the letter. Use a comma after the closing if using closed punctuation in the salutation; use no punctuation if using open punctuation. (See the section Salutation earlier in this chapter for a definition of open and closed punctuation.)

Writer's Name and Signature

All letters should include the name and title of the writer. Enough space should be left between the complimentary closing and the typed name of the writer for a signature.

NAME

- Place the writer's name four lines under the closing to allow space for the signature.

HINT: *Reasonably priced software is available to replicate actual handwriting. This software can be used to place signatures on documents.*

- Use the first name with or without the middle initial as preferred by the writer; place a period after a middle initial if used.
- Place earned titles after the name; place periods after earned titles if appropriate: e.g., Karen Fisher CPS®; Martin Pena, M.D.

JOB TITLE

- Place the writer's job title on a line below the typed name:

Sincerely,

Ronald Rubik
Sales Manager

Sincerely,

Debbie Paulsen CAP
Administrative Assistant
to Ronald Rubik

- If the letter is signed by someone other than the writer, sign the writer's name and use your initials.

Sincerely,

Sylvia J. Crinski
gk
Sylvia J. Crinski
Vice President

- Professional, military, or academic titles appear after the writer's name:

Sincerely,

John Toten M.D.

Sincerely,

Leslie Duggins CPS

Reference Initials

The typist's initials are often included but may be omitted. Use lowercase initials at the left margin and place them two lines below the writer's title. If desired, the author's initials can be put in all caps preceding the typist's initials.

SJ/ms
ms

Enclosure Notation

Enclosure notations include information such as the number and nature of enclosures.

- Place notations at the left margin two lines below the last notation.
- Enclosure may be written out or abbreviated Enc. More than one enclosure can be noted as follows:

Enclosures 2
Enclosure—Software
Enclosures
    Software
    Documentation Manual
File Name Notation

File Name Notation

The use of computers has made it necessary to include file name notations on correspondence. The file name needs to be as meaningful as possible, with the length depending upon the operating system software used. Place it on the line below the reference initials.

HINT: *Reduce the font size to make it less noticeable.*

Delivery Notation

If the correspondence will be delivered in a way other than first-class mail, include that information below the file name notation. Place it on the line below the file notation. Notations may appear as By FedEx, By certified mail, By fax, By messenger, By registered mail.

ser
drrison.doc
By FedEx

If a letter has been faxed first and then mailed or e-mailed, include a "confirmation" notation on the letter so the recipient realizes it is the original. Place this information on the second line below the date line.

Confirmation of fax sent on June 5, 20–
Confirmation of e-mail message sent on June 5, 20–.

Copy Notation

- "cc" means carbon copy. Since carbons are obsolete in many offices, the notation "c" for copy followed by a colon is commonly used. The notation "bcc" or "bc" is used for "blind" copies, that is, for copies that the recipient of the document will not necessarily know about. If only one person is receiving a copy, space two times after the colon. If more than one person is receiving a copy, tab once after keying the notation; otherwise the names may not align when fonts are changed.

c: Adele Richards
Marvin O'Leary

HINT: *Place a check mark next to the name or highlight the person or department for whom the copy is intended.*

Postscript

A postscript is used to strongly express an idea deliberately omitted from the body of the letter. The postscript is keyed two lines below the last notation. Key "PS:" or "PS." and space two times.

ser
drrison.doc

PS: Send your registration materials back today for preferred reservations!

LETTER STYLES

Most companies have designated letterhead and developed a letter style to identify, communicate, and project a corporate image. Letter styles are typically based on their perceived impact on others. Many office support personnel use software to create their own letterheads.

The most common letter styles are the block, simplified block, and modified block letter. Because of word processing software, the block letter style is the most frequently used. The less centering and indenting in a letter, the easier it is to keyboard and revise, which increases productivity. Productivity can also be increased by having one standard letter format instead of having different styles for different writers.

The following general formatting rules apply to letters, no matter what style is used:

- Use a standard line length, which is typically 6 inches (left and right margins of 1.25 inches). Line length can be decreased for shorter letters. A line length longer than 6 inches is difficult to read. Start a new page if the letter runs long rather than increase the margins to more than 6 inches.
- Press Enter four times after the date. The space may be increased or decreased depending on the length of the letter.
- Single-space the body; leave a blank line between paragraphs.
- Use short sentences averaging no more than 20 words.
- Include at least two sentences in a paragraph.
- Keep paragraphs approximately the same length. Avoid more than 10 lines of type in a paragraph; divide a longer paragraph into two shorter ones.

- Use left justification only. Research shows that full justification is more difficult to read.
- Use numbered or bulleted lists to make a letter look more interesting. Discreet use of italics or bold print also adds interest.
- Use the automatic numbering feature for proper placing and indenting of succeeding lines of lists.

Block Letter

In a block letter, all lines are flush with the left margin. (See Figure 17-1.)

FORMATTING SUGGESTIONS

- Press Enter two times after the inside address, salutation, the subject (if any), and before the closing.
- Press Enter four times after the closing for the writer's information.
- Press Enter two times after the writer's information for the initials of the typist and notations.

Simplified Block Letter

This letter style reflects a trend toward eliminating the salutation and complimentary close. All lines are flush with the left margin. A subject line is used in place of the salutation. The simplified letter is the most efficient letter style to keyboard. (See Figure 17-2.)

- Key the inside address with initial caps or in all capital letters.
- Press Enter three times after the inside address.
- Omit the salutation and use a subject line. The subject line may be initial capped or in all caps.
- Press Enter three times after the subject line and begin the body.
- Omit the closing.
- Press Enter four times after the body for the writer's information. The writer's name and title may be initial capped or in all caps.

Modified Block Letter

The modified block letter is somewhat more traditional. The date, closing, and writer's information start at the center. All other lines are flush with the left margin. This format looks balanced on the page. (See Figure 17-3.)

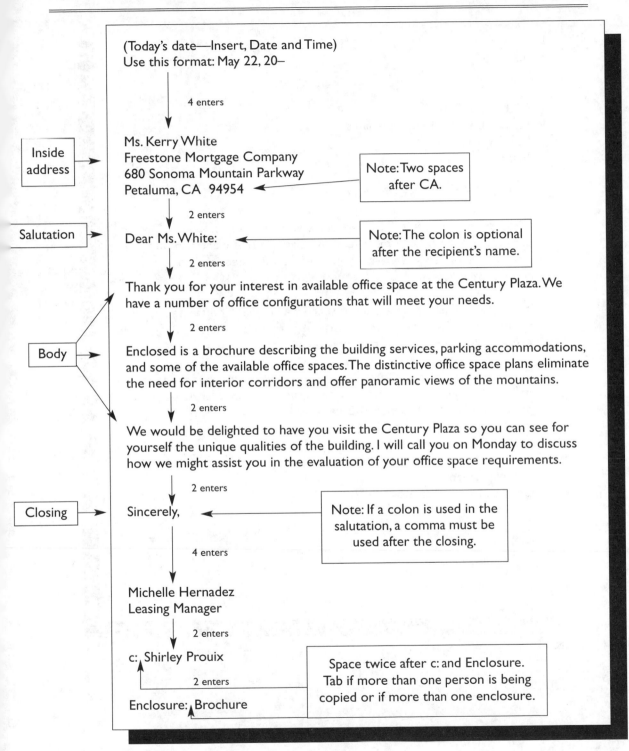

(Today's date—Insert, Date and Time)
Use this format: May 22, 20–

↓ 4 enters

Inside address →

Ms. Kerry White
Freestone Mortgage Company
680 Sonoma Mountain Parkway
Petaluma, CA 94954 ←

Note: Two spaces after CA.

↓ 2 enters

Salutation →

Dear Ms. White: ←

Note: The colon is optional after the recipient's name.

↓ 2 enters

Thank you for your interest in available office space at the Century Plaza. We have a number of office configurations that will meet your needs.

↓ 2 enters

Body →

Enclosed is a brochure describing the building services, parking accommodations, and some of the available office spaces. The distinctive office space plans eliminate the need for interior corridors and offer panoramic views of the mountains.

↓ 2 enters

We would be delighted to have you visit the Century Plaza so you can see for yourself the unique qualities of the building. I will call you on Monday to discuss how we might assist you in the evaluation of your office space requirements.

↓ 2 enters

Closing →

Sincerely, ←

Note: If a colon is used in the salutation, a comma must be used after the closing.

↓ 4 enters

Michelle Hernadez
Leasing Manager

↓ 2 enters

c: Shirley Prouix

Space twice after c: and Enclosure. Tab if more than one person is being copied or if more than one enclosure.

↓ 2 enters

Enclosure: Brochure

Figure 17-1 Block letter.

June 5, 20—

Mr. Michael Troy
Human Development Associates
203 S. Willits
Visalia, CA 93291

YOU DID AN OUTSTANDING JOB!

"Thanks" hardly seems like an adequate word to express our appreciation for all the time, effort, and planning that went into our conference, Mike. You were so responsive to our needs and so willing to be flexible.

You did an excellent job again this year. I had a million details to worry about, and it was a relief not to worry about you or your presentation. I knew you would do a great job!

The enclosed evaluations are our best ever and reflect your ability to deliver the training we wanted. Thanks again, Mike, for everything you did to make our conference a success.

Michelle Bryant
Conference Coordinator

ik
troy.doc
c: Caroline Hing
Enc.

Figure 17-2 Simplified block letter

June 11, 20–

Ms. Michelle Bryant
Conference Coordinator
The Learning and Guidance Center
6543 Lincoln Way
San Francisco CA 94367

Dear Michelle:

Thank you so much for letting me observe your conference at Lark
Creek Inn on June 1. Your leaders did a marvelous job of relating to
the participants as well as educating them in leadership, presentation
styles, and problem-solving skills.

I will communicate my experience to our training department. With
your conference as a model, we have a high standard to meet.
Congratulations on a wonderful conference!

Sincerely,

Sandra Mandici
Project Consultant

lp
bryant.doc
c: Ben Louis
Enc.
P.S. I am using Mick's delegation suggestions.

Figure 17-3 Modified block letter.

- Press Enter two times after the inside address, salutation, and the subject (if any) and before the closing.
- Press Enter four times after the closing for the writer's name and title.
- Press Enter two times after the writer's name and title for the initials of the typist, if any.
- Press Enter two times after the typist's initials for any notations.

Multipage

The first page of a multipage letter should be keyed on letterhead. The rest of the pages should be keyed on plain paper of the same size and quality as the letterhead. At least three lines of the letter should go on the last page with the closing (if used) and the writer's signature.

A heading should be placed at the top of the page that includes the name of the addressee, page number, and date in either of the following formats:

Dr. Christine Davis   2   **April 19, 20–**

Dr. Christine Davis
Page 2
April 19, 20–

FORMATTING SUGGESTIONS

- Leave a 1-inch top margin unless word processing software is used and the heading is in a header, in which case the heading would be ½ inch from the top of the page.
- Start the body three lines below the heading.
- Use the same side and bottom margins as on the first page.

FORM LETTERS

A form letter is a letter sent to many people, usually about a frequently occurring or routine situation. Form letters save time in letter writing and keyboarding. A form letter is useful when people repeatedly ask for the same information. Form letters about products or the company can be prepared in response to customers who write with questions, requests, or complaints. They are also useful when the same information needs to be sent to more than one person, company, or group; for example, a letter sent to a list of customers.

Form letters should appear as if they were written for the recipient. This is easily done with the mail-merge function of many word processors. (See Chapter 8, Office Computer Software.) The following are suggestions for personalizing form letters:

- Use company letterhead and matching envelope.
- Include the recipient's name, title, and address in the inside address.
- Use a personalized salutation; for example, "Dear Ms. Jackson."
- Customize by adding specific information if known; for example, "I enjoyed talking with you this morning."
- Personally sign each letter.

E-mail autoreply

A cost-effective method to distribute information about a company to potential clients is to set up an e-mail autoreply or autoresponder. An e-mail autoreply is an e-mail alias (for example, webmaster@yourcompany.com) that executes an autoreply program that automatically replies to any e-mail sent to it. The e-mail autoreply can be configured to send any message, such as a FAQ or product listings, in the automated reply. The autoreply reduces the need for a human to answer e-mails individually and shortens the time customers must wait to get answers.

MEMO STYLES

A memorandum, or memo, is a short, informal message used in-house. The tone depends upon the relationship between the reader and writer. Because memos are sent to people in the same organization, jargon and technical terms may be used and the tone may be more informal than correspondence leaving the company.

A heading such as Memorandum, Memo, or Interoffice Correspondence is printed or keyed at the top of the page. Most memos contain the headings To, From, Date, and Subject instead of an inside address, salutation, closing, and signature line. (See Figure 17-4.)

HINT: *Word processing software programs have a memo template that can be used or modified.*

To

This line includes the name and job title of the individual(s) who will receive the memo. When a memorandum is sent to a group, a distribution list identifying the individuals who are part of the group can be keyed after the reference initials. If copies of the memo are to be sent to other individuals, the notation "c:" is keyed below the distribution list and followed by the name(s) to whom the copies will be sent.

Memorandum

To Steve Posgate, Allan Brody, Tracy Brennan, Brett Rouzer, Antonio Ruiz, Janet Sandberg

From Michelle Bryant, Conference Coordinator

Date May 23, 20–

Subject Finalizing Conference Details

The registrations are arriving and plans are under way for the fifth Leadership Conference to be held June 1–4 at Lark Creek Inn, Lake Tahoe.

Enclosed is the form confirming your attendance. Please complete this form and return it to me by May 28 so I can proceed with the room reservation list and make other necessary arrangements at Lark Creek Inn.

mj
Enclosure

Figure 17-4 Memo.

bj

Distribution:

Cynthia Cramer
Jerry Eastman
Deborah Lesniak

c: Elizabeth Rea-Medina

From

This line includes the writer's name and title (if necessary). Writers sign their name or initials to show they have read and approved the contents.

Date

The month is written out with a comma separating the day from the year: e.g., January 20, 20–. Military style of 20 January 20– is acceptable to avoid punctuation and save keying time.

HINT: *Create a template using your word processing program and set up the date as a coded field so you do not have to key the dates. Remember that the date feature updates itself each time you open the document, so key the date if preserving it is important.*

Subject

Use a concise phrase with action verbs if possible on this line. The following general formatting rules apply to memos, no matter what style is used:

- Use a 6-inch line.
- Begin the first line 1 inch from the top of the page unless letterhead paper is used. If letterhead is used, begin at least two lines below the letterhead.
- Key TO, FROM, DATE, and SUBJECT in all capitals or initial caps. A colon after each heading is optional. Leave one blank line between lines of the heading.
- Leave two blank lines after the last line in the heading before the body.
- Single-space the body; leave a blank line between paragraphs.
- Align paragraphs at the left margin unless using a memo template.
- Place the typist's initials two lines below the last line of the body.
- Place the enclosure notation two lines below the typist's initials.

ELECTRONIC SIGNATURES

The traditional validity of hand-signed documents applies to electronic e-commerce signatures. On-line and faxed documents have the same force of law as paper contracts and records. A consumer must consent to the use of electronic notices and records, and no person is required to use electronic records, signatures, or contracts. Paper is, however, still required for certain documents such as eviction notices, wills, and court orders. The problem with e-signatures is that an unauthorized person may "sign" documents.

ADDRESSING ENVELOPES

Mail addressed according to the U.S. Postal Service guidelines helps ensure accurate delivery. (See Chapter 16, Mailing Documents.)

- Use paper with a minimum basis weight of 20 pounds.
- Include a return address in the upper left-hand corner if preprinted envelopes are not used.
- Line up addresses flush left.
- Allow at least 1-inch left and right margins.
- Place address horizontally.

HINT: *Use word processing software to address envelopes. The bar-code feature is also available. The software package will automatically place the address on the envelope at the location suggested by the U.S. Postal Service.*

- Put address in all capital letters with no punctuation or initial caps with punctuation.

HINT: *For many years, the U.S. Postal Service preferred addresses to be in all uppercase letters with no punctuation. Now lowercase letters with punctuation are acceptable.*

- Use easy-to-read fonts, not italics or script. Securely fasten stickers and labels to prevent damage by automated equipment.

Mailing Labels

Word processing packages provide predefined label options for laser printers. Mailing labels can also be created using the mail merge feature.

HINT: *Do not use labels that are separating from the backing sheet or that are wrinkled or damaged in any way. The printer may be damaged.*

HINT: *Do not feed a sheet of labels through a laser printer more than once. The label adhesive is designed for only one pass through the printer. Damage to the printer may occur.*

SAMPLE CORRESPONDENCE

Books containing sample business letters are available. In addition, numerous sample business letters are available on-line. Use a search engine and enter the kind of letter you want (for example, sympathy letter) and choose among the different letters available. Be aware that letters found in books or on-line may contain dated expressions (see the list of Words and Phrases to Avoid in this chapter).

Announcement Letter

An announcement letter is similar to a press release. It is a way to improve visibility and provide a reminder of a firm or products. An announcement may be made for the following reasons:

- Opening of a company or division.
- New product or service.
- Change of address.
- New staff.
- Promotion.
- Anniversary.
- Acquisition.
- Merger.

SUGGESTED FEATURES

- Communicates pride; some are very formal with only a few sentences.
- Gives appropriate information such as names, dates, and addresses; has a clear purpose.
- Addressed to the public or a company; envelopes addressed to individuals.
- Uses company letterhead or a specially printed white or cream card with black ink.

SAMPLE ANNOUNCEMENT OF NEW SERVICE

Milan, Inc., is pleased to offer 24-hour customer service for your convenience. Call toll-free 1-800-489-5984.

SAMPLE ANNOUNCEMENT OF NEW EMPLOYEE

Hirschfield and Nadler Law Office is pleased to announce that Patricia Issel has joined our staff as an associate in our probate department.

SAMPLE ANNOUNCEMENT OF A PROMOTION

The President and Board of Directors of AMS Industries, Inc., are pleased to announce the promotion of Charles Leoni to Vice President. Mr. Leoni has been the Sales Manager for AMS in San Francisco for the past ten years and will join our corporate staff in Houston.

Letter of Apology

Mistakes do occur, and it is important to apologize for them in a prompt letter of apology.

SUGGESTED FEATURES

- Blames the company, not a specific person or department.
- States what is being done (or was done) to correct the error.
- Explains how the error was made.
- Apologizes for the error.
- Reassures the customer that steps are being taken to reduce the chances of error in the future.
- Closes positively.

SAMPLE LETTER OF APOLOGY

Your book order was shipped air express on November 2. You should have the books by now.

In investigating the problem, we discovered your order code was entered incorrectly in the computer. Consequently, your order was shipped to another school. Since we pride ourselves on our data-entry procedure, mistakes like this are very infrequent. However, our computer programmer is adding an extra safeguard to our order program so we can avoid errors like this in the future.

I appreciate receiving notification of the problem in enough time to send the books before classes started. We believe you will be pleased with the revised edition of *Administrative Procedures.*

Please accept our apology for this inconvenience. Best wishes for a successful school year.

Confirmation of Appointment

A confirmation of an appointment need not be sent for every appointment, but it can be used to verify a verbal conversation.

SUGGESTED FEATURES

- Is brief and limited to appointment information, including date, time, place, and names.
- Is sent out immediately after the appointment is made.

SAMPLE LETTER OF CONFIRMATION

This is to confirm our appointment on Monday, September 2, at 9 A.M. in Room 4026, 4th Floor, of the Economic Development Building, 722 Capitol Mall. A public parking garage is located directly across the street at 7th and Capitol.

I look forward to continuing our discussion on your proposal.

Letter of Congratulations

Letters of congratulation build goodwill. They may be sent for the following occasions:

- Promotions and appointments to new positions.
- Achievements.
- Awards and honors.
- Introduction of a new product.
- Marriages, births, and anniversaries.
- Retirements.

SUGGESTED FEATURES

- Expresses interest sincerely and enthusiastically.
- Avoids negatives.
- Begins with the expression of congratulations.
- Mentions the reason for the congratulations.
- Ends with an expression of goodwill.

SAMPLE LETTER OF CONGRATULATIONS FOR RECEIVING AN AWARD

Congratulations for receiving the Distinguished Achievement Award from the National Media Association! I was so proud when they announced your name and the audience gave you a standing ovation.

No one is more deserving of this award than you. Congratulations on your consistent accomplishments. We are all celebrating for you.

SAMPLE LETTER OF CONGRATULATIONS FOR RECEIVING AN APPOINTMENT

Congratulations on your appointment as Vice President of The Travel Center. You have worked hard, and I am thrilled your efforts have been rewarded. You will bring dynamic leadership to your position.

Please accept my best wishes for success in your new position.

Employment Rejection

Examples of sample cover letters to use in a job search are in Chapter 2. Unsolicited letters of application should be answered briefly and immediately.

SUGGESTED FEATURES

- Conveys thanks for the interest in the firm.
- Indicates positions are not available.
- Expresses luck in job search.

SAMPLE LETTER OF REJECTION TO JOB SEEKER

Thank you for your interest in North Bay News. Presently we do not have any positions available that match your background.

We will keep your resume on file and contact you if your experience meets our needs. We wish you success in your job search.

SAMPLE LETTER OF REJECTION TO EMPLOYER

Thank you for your offer of employment. Unfortunately, I have accepted another position.

I enjoyed meeting you and your staff and appreciated the time that you spent interviewing me and describing the position.

Perhaps we will have an opportunity to work together in the future.

Meeting Notification

Meeting notifications should be in writing. If the meeting will always be on the same day, same time, and same place, notification is sent when the meeting time and place are set, along with a listing of all the dates. If any dates are altered from the original schedule, notification should be in writing.

SUGGESTED FEATURES

- Is brief and limited to meeting information, including date, time, place, and names.
- Is sent out immediately after the meeting date is set.
- Includes any special items to be brought to the meeting; for example, budget figures, reports, or personnel manual.
- Includes a tentative agenda and asks for input.

SAMPLE NOTIFICATION LETTER

The date for our regular staff meeting has been changed to March 15 at 1 P.M. in the Board Room because many of us will be involved in planning for our national convention.

Attached is a tentative agenda. If you have any item you would like to add, please let me know by March 10. We will be discussing sick-leave policy, so bring a copy of the regulations distributed on January 20.

Letter of Resignation

The letter of resignation is used to notify your supervisor that you are resigning from a position. Generally the letter should be positive, since these letters typically stay in a personnel file. If you resign because of a lack of promotional opportunities or because you did not receive a promotion, you may prefer to express those disappointments in the letter of resignation. Derogatory comments about the staff or company should be avoided.

SUGGESTED FEATURE

- Includes the effective date, which is typically two weeks in advance of leaving.

SAMPLE FRIENDLY LETTER OF RESIGNATION

I am resigning effective June 1, 20–, after five years of stimulating and productive work at Ferraris, Inc. As you know, I will be moving to Seattle to take a position as administrative assistant to the president of Environmental Controls.

Moving back to Seattle fulfills a dream of being able to work in an environmental field in my hometown. I will miss all the good friends I have made at Ferraris, and I will particularly miss working with you. Thank you for making me part of the team.

SAMPLE LETTER OF RESIGNATION FOR LACK OF PROMOTIONAL OPPORTUNITIES

I am resigning as your administrative assistant effective June 1, 20–. Although I have learned a great deal working at Ferraris, I had hoped to have an opportunity to expand my responsibilities. I feel I need to find a position that will give me the chance to use more of my talents.

Thank you for all your help and support during these past three years.

Request Letter

A request letter should be clear and precise. Be brief and specific; cover only the information requested. If information is needed from two separate departments, write two letters.

SUGGESTED FEATURES

- Include all information necessary, such as item number, quality, price, color, and where to ship.
- Use list form, which is easier to read than a letter.

SAMPLE SIMPLE REQUEST LETTER

Please send me 15 copies of your free brochure, "Telephone Techniques." We plan to use this brochure in training our support staff.

Thank you.

SAMPLE REQUEST LETTER

The Harrison House is recommended as a good meeting facility near the Kansas City Airport. Our Board of Directors is meeting October 5–8, 20–, and we need a meeting room and accommodations.

Date	October 4–8
	Arriving October 4. Staying the nights of October 4, 5, 6, 7; departing October 8.
Number	15. Need a room with a large enough table to comfortably seat 15; video projection and overhead projection availability. 15 single-occupancy rooms.
Food Service	One evening banquet; four luncheons. If possible, meals in a room separate from the meeting room.

Please send rates, meeting room sizes, recreational facilities, and catering menus. We will be making a decision on the meeting by March 1. I look forward to hearing from you.

Sympathy Letter

Sympathy letters are written when a colleague (no matter what position in the company) has lost someone to death.

SUGGESTED FEATURES

- Expresses your sorrow at the news.
- Recalls something positive about the deceased.
- Makes an offer to be of help or comfort.
- Uses a sympathy card or is handwritten on personal stationery.

SAMPLE SYMPATHY LETTER

Jeff was a wonderful, supportive man. He was always calm, even in times of crises. We all know how close you were and how much you will miss him. I have lost not only a coworker but also a good friend.

I am thinking of you at this difficult time. Please let me know if there is anything I can do to help.

CHAPTER 18

REPORTS

Reports provide essential information for everyday operations and decision making. Businesses could not function without written reports. A fundamental component of many office professionals' jobs is to correctly format reports for their supervisors. In addition to formatting, some office professionals decide on content and write reports.

Reports range from informal interoffice memos describing seminar attendance to bound formal reports such as feasibility studies. Reports are categorized according to subject, intended audience, and length. Each type of report requires a different format and organizational style, and these vary widely from one organization to another.

SHORT REPORTS

Short reports are also called informal, semiformal, or semitechnical reports. They get right to the point, with objective reporting of facts in one to three pages. The subject of the report determines the number of subdivisions it has, if any. Short reports are typically routine and have a limited audience of coworkers or an immediate supervisor.

A short report will answer the questions who, why, where, when, what, and how. Some companies follow a specific procedure for organization of reports, while others leave the organization up to the author. A short report typically includes the following components:

- Purpose.
- Findings.
- Conclusion or Summary.
- Recommendations.

HINT: *Some employers prefer to find the recommendations at the beginning of the report instead of the end to avoid having to read the entire report.*

Detailed information such as drawings, charts, or cost analyses are usually placed at the end of the report in a section referred to as "Attachments" or "Appendices."

If a report is for in-house use, it is usually in memo format or as an e-mail attachment, while those reports going outside the company are typically written in the form of a letter. Memos or e-mail attachments are the least formal type of report format. Some companies may use standard, printed, letterhead forms.

MEMO FORMATTING SUGGESTIONS

Memos use a heading with the following lines: To, From, Date, Subject. There is no need for an inside address, salutation, complimentary close, or signature line. Be sure to include the name and job title of individual(s) who will receive the memo or a copy of it. (See Figure 18-1.)

- Use a 6-inch line (1.25-inch left and right margins). Leave a 1-inch top margin unless using letterhead.
- Start the body of the report on the third line after the last line of the heading.
- Use single spacing with block paragraphs.

(For more detailed information on memos, see the section on Memo Styles in Chapter 17.)

LETTER FORMATTING SUGGESTIONS

A letter has to appear more formal, especially if the report is directed to someone outside the company. It should be on company letterhead. (See Figure 18-2.) If letterhead is electronic, the letter may also be transmitted as an e-mail attachment.

- Use a 6-inch line (1.25-inch left and right margins). Lines of more than 6 inches are tiring to the eye.
- Allow a top margin of 2 to 2 ½ inches, depending upon the depth of the letterhead.
- Allow a bottom margin of 1 inch.
- Use single spacing with block or indented paragraphs and one blank line between paragraphs.
- Begin the body on the second line after the salutation.

(For detailed information on letters, see the section on Letter Styles in Chapter 17.)

MULTIPAGE REPORT FORMATTING SUGGESTIONS

If the report is more than one page, type the continuation page on a blank sheet of paper. Leave a 1-inch top margin. Begin the body on the third line after the heading.

HINT: *A header command on a word processing program can add the required information and the page number.*

TO   Maria Gravelez, Supervisor

FROM   Judith Witmore CPS, Administrative Assistant

DATE   August 3, 20–

SUBJECT   Evaluation of IAAP® Convention in Salt Lake City

After attendance at the International Association of Administrative Professionals® Convention in Salt Lake City, July 20–25, 20–, I recommend that at least one support staff member have the opportunity to attend each year. The information distributed at the convention is extremely valuable and will be beneficial to all support staff at Western Bank.

The sessions ranged from technical to practical to personal. Even with the variety of the sessions, nearly all workshops focused on the central theme of expanding and enhancing the contribution of office professionals in the workplace.

The sessions I attended were as follows:
1. Improving Electronic Communications
2. Collaborating with Virtual Teams
3. Effective Web Page Design
4. Keeping E-systems Free from Copyright Violations

More than 100 companies exhibited the latest in office technology, demonstrating everything from office products to teleconferencing services.

The convention was outstanding and a highlight of my professional career. I will be sharing what I learned with the other office professionals at Western Bank at our monthly meeting.

Figure 18-1 Short report in memo form.

December 7, 20–

Mr. Gary Thomas
Public Relations Director
Clemmons, Jones, and Grantz
3894 South Geary
San Francisco, CA 94132

Dear Mr. Thomas:

This is the third issue of your company newsletter that I have coordinated and edited. I have the following recommendations, which I think will enhance this communication.

Format
The two-column format does not provide much flexibility in layout and design. We are restricted in placement of pictures and columnar headings. It is my recommendation that we move to a three-column format.

Pages
The number of pages has ranged from four to ten. The first newsletter had ten pages, and subsequent issues gradually decreased to four. I recommend that a standard number of pages, preferably four, be set for the newsletter. If there is any additional information that needs to be included in an issue, it can be added as an insert.

—Continued—

Figure 18-2 Short report in letter form.

Gary Thomas
Page 2
December 7, 20–

Printing
We have used Mountain Printers because they gave the best quote.
As you know, we had to reprint the last issue because of the poor
quality of the photos. I have previously worked with Zenith
Printers. The cost is approximately 10 percent higher, but the quality
is consistently excellent.

Use of Color
We have used color in every headline. This format seems to make
the newsletter look "busy." I recommend we use color only on the
masthead, dates, and flag sections. It will not only reduce the cost
but also improve the appearance.

It has been a pleasure working with your professional staff. I am
eager to hear your reactions to these recommendations. I will be
out of the office until December 15. Please call me at 415-555-1257
any time after that date so we can talk.

Sincerely,

Sarah Williams

Sarah Williams, CPS
Consultant

Figure 18-2 (continued.)

- Leave at least two lines of a paragraph at the bottom of a page. Carry over at least two lines to the next page.
- Do not divide the last word on a page.
- Always include at least two lines of copy after a heading before starting a new page.

LONG REPORTS

A long or formal report gives detailed information about a subject and usually requires extensive research. The audience may include stockholders or top-level managers. Such reports may influence long-range financial or organizational decisions. Often they are designed and printed out-of-house if they are important enough.

Long reports may include some or all of the following components:

Preliminary Pages: Cover, letter of transmittal, title page, table of contents, list of illustrations, abstract or executive summary.

Body: Introduction, background, problem, purpose, scope, main discussion (70 percent of the report), conclusions, recommendations.

Back Matter: Glossary, references/bibliography, appendix.

Many businesses have a standard format, described in a style guide, to follow in writing a report. A standard format minimizes misunderstandings between the author and the person or persons keying and/or designing the report.

Table 18-1 gives details on a format typically used in business reports. Word processing software programs provide report templates and styles to use or modify. These features allow some flexibility in appearance and spacing (see Chapter 19). For additional formatting suggestions, see the specific topics in this chapter.

Text Flow Suggestions

Standard typography rules are used to control the minimum number of paragraph lines displayed on a page and the lines of text that should be kept on the same page. The following are the standard rules:

1. Leave at least two lines of a paragraph at the bottom of a page. Carry over at least two lines to the next page.

HINT: *Use the Widow/orphan feature of your word processing software to eliminate this problem.*

2. Keep headings and sideheads with the first line of the next paragraph.

HINT: *Use the Keep With Next or Block Protect feature of your word processing package.*

Table 18-1
BUSINESS REPORT FORMAT

Margins	
Bound	1.5-inch left margin; 1-inch right
Unbound	1.25-inch left margin; 1.25-inch right
Top of first page	2-inch margin
Succeeding pages	1-inch margin
Bottom	1-inch margin
Page Numbers	
Preliminary pages	Use sequential lowercase Roman numerals beginning with i for the title page. Center folios at the bottom of the page. The title page has no number.
Body	Use sequential Arabic numerals beginning with 1 for the first page. Folios may be in one of two styles:
	1. At the top of the page at the right margin.
	2. Centered at the bottom of the page. When using word processing software, the default position for page numbers is .5 inches from the top and bottom of the page.
Spacing	
Body	Double-spaced with .5 inch paragraph indentions or use the report template in your word processing software. To save paper, a report may be single-spaced with one blank line between paragraphs and no paragraph indention.

   3. Avoid dividing a short paragraph.

HINT: *Use the Keep Lines Together or Block Protect feature of your word processing package.*

HINT: *When keying a report, insert a page break before the chapter title.*

   4. Begin chapter titles at the top of a page.
   5. Indent quoted material ½ inch from both margins. Either double- or single-space.
   6. Avoid dividing a quote or list of items unless at least two lines are at the bottom of a page and two lines are on the next page.

COVER

The cover should reflect the style of the rest of the report. An attractive cover helps persuade the reader to open the report and read it. A well-designed cover makes it easy to understand the subject of the report. For an important report, these elements should appear on the cover:

- Title of the report.
- Name(s) of report writer(s).
- Name and address of the company.

COVER FORMATTING SUGGESTIONS

- Illustrations and/or graphics should be used only if they are relevant and of high quality.
- Simple typography should be used, and it should be stronger than the type size and typeface chosen for the inside.
- The paper should be heavier than the paper used for the report itself.
- Standard covers can be preprinted and should include the company name and address and a cut-out window. The title of the report appears on the title page and will show through the window.
- The top margin should be 2 inches and the bottom margin should be 1 inch.

HINT: *Your word processing software may have a cover page template.*

- The same elements that appear on the title page can also be printed on the cover. (See the section on Title Page below.)
- A cover is not necessary for less formal reports. A title page can be used as the cover for such reports.

LETTER OF TRANSMITTAL

A letter of transmittal may be used to convey a report from one organization to another, or from one person to another. It may be bound as part of the report or it may be attached to the front. A letter of transmittal summarizes the purpose, scope, and major recommendations of the report. (See Figure 18-3.)

A cover letter may be used instead. A cover letter includes a simple statement such as "Enclosed is a copy of. . . ." If reports are regularly distributed inside a company, a letter of transmittal is not necessary.

TITLE PAGE

A title page is usually the first page of a document after the cover. (See Figure 18-4.) It usually contains the following elements:

February 10, 20–

Mr. Louis Johnson
President
Pacific Telecommunications
4783 South Pima
Tucson, AZ 85745

Dear Mr. Johnson:

Enclosed is the report "Improving Computer-User Comfort,"
which you asked our company to prepare. The report summarizes
current research on the effects of computers on health and
recommends changes for your computer users.

We interviewed over 500 Pacific Telecommunications employees in
the past six months and consulted with health experts in eye and
wrist fatigue. We also reviewed all the current literature available
for computer health hazards.

Our recommendations are as follows:
1. Reduce room illumination or consider antireflection screens.
2. Purchase standard keyboards for notebook computers.
3. Replace existing chairs with adjustable chairs and firmer back
   support.

You should find our report useful in reorganizing your
workstations for maximum comfort. If you have any questions or
would like to discuss our recommendations, please let us know.

Sincerely,

Janet Wong
Consultant

Figure 18-3 Letter of transmittal.

Making an Effective Presentation
The Art of Business Communication

Benjamin Strom
20–

International Association of Administrative Professionals®

Kansas City, Missouri

Figure 18-4 Sample title page.

- Title. The title should be brief yet informative.
- Name(s) of report writer(s). Include the title(s) of the writers and their contribution to the project or report (e.g., coordinator, editor, analyst).
- Name and address of the company or organization preparing the report.
- Date the report was written.
- Any agency or order numbers.
- Name of the firm for which the report was prepared (e.g., *Prepared for International Association of Administrative Professionals®*).

TITLE PAGE FORMATTING SUGGESTIONS

- Not all title page elements must be included, nor must they be placed in the order given above.
- The layout should be consistent with the document, however. If the chapters start on the same line on each page, the title should start on that same line.
- A 6-inch line length is typical.
- Position the title approximately 2.5 inches from the top of the page.
- Avoid putting the longest line at the top of the page or below the visual center.
- Allow enough space for the left margin given the binding that will be used.
- The title page is counted as small Roman numeral i, even though no number is typed on the page.
- Format titles with bold print and initial caps.

HINT: *Your word processing software may have a cover page template that can be used as a title page.*

TABLE OF CONTENTS

The table of contents lists the major sections of the report and the page numbers as well as all appendices. It allows the reader to see how the report is organized, what topics are covered, and where to find specific information. The table of contents may include a list of subdivisions and any subheadings that may be included under each subdivision. Include subheadings only if there are two or more, but do not include *any* subheadings if their inclusion would make the table of contents too long. (See Figure 18-5.)

Include a brief summary of the contents of each chapter if the subdivision titles are not sufficiently descriptive or if the contents need to convince the reader to look at the report.

If space is limited, the title page and table of contents may be combined on the same page.

TABLE OF CONTENTS FORMATTING SUGGESTIONS

- The left and right margins may be different from those of the report. The subdivisions and page numbers should be close together so the eye can link the two.
- Rules (lines) can be used to separate subdivisions instead of leader lines (rows of dots).

HINT: *Use the tab leader feature of your word processing program.*

Table of Contents

Introduction
  Why Communication Is Important 1
  Your Goals in Communicating 2
  How Personality Affects Communication 3

Section 1: Communication Model
  The Communication Model 5
  Barriers to Effective Communication 8
  Overcoming Communication Problems 9

Section 2: Nonverbal Communication
  Eye Contact 11
  Gestures 15

Section 3: Interpersonal Communication
  Appearance 17
  Voice 20
  Facial Expressions 25

Section 4: Summary 28

ii

Figure 18-5 Sample table of contents.

- The top margin should be 2 inches from the top of the page and the bottom margin 1 inch from the bottom of the page.
- This page is counted as Roman numeral ii, which should be centered on the bottom of the page.

HINT: *Use the table of contents feature of your word processing software to generate the table of contents.*

LIST OF ILLUSTRATIONS

A list of illustrations and tables is necessary only if the report contains a number of these special features (see Figure 18-6). If the report contains few illustrations or tables, include these items in the table of contents.

ILLUSTRATIONS LIST FORMATTING SUGGESTIONS

- It is not necessary to use the same margins as in the report, but you should use the same margins as in the table of contents.

Illustrations

iii

Figure 18-6 List of illustrations.

- If there is a list of illustrations, the page's folio is Roman numeral iii, centered on the bottom of the page.
- The top margin should be 2 inches and the bottom margin 1 inch.

HINT: *Use the table numbering feature in your word processing software to automatically number tables and illustrations. This feature will also generate separate lists of tables and illustrations.*

ABSTRACT OR EXECUTIVE SUMMARY

The abstract or executive summary is a summary of what the report contains, including problems and conclusions. It may contain a listing of key points in sentences or miniparagraphs. Readers can see the contents of the report without having to read it. The abstract or executive summary immediately precedes the text, but it does not have to appear on a separate page. Sometimes it is included in the cover letter preceding the document. If space is available, it may be on the title page or cover.

ABSTRACT FORMATTING SUGGESTIONS

- The abstract may be less than a page; an executive summary is often two or three pages.
- If these elements are used, their pages are folioed as the next Roman numeral, centered on the bottom of the page.
- The top margin should be 2 inches and the bottom margin 1 inch.

Here is a sample summary:

"Improving Computer User Comfort" summarizes the current research on the effects of computers on health and recommends changes for computer users. Employees were interviewed and health professionals were consulted. Current literature was reviewed.

We recommend that the following changes be made for computer users: reduce room illumination or consider antireflection screens, purchase standard keyboards for notebook computers, and replace existing chairs with adjustable chairs and firmer back support.

BODY OF THE REPORT

The body is the main text of the report and should be organized according to the nature of the report. Listed below are the sections included in most reports.

Introduction: An introduction tells the reader why the report was written and helps interpret what follows. It can be in a larger type size than or have different line spacing from the rest of the report.

Main discussion: The main discussion should be organized according to major topics and subtopics. Headings help readers identify major subjects and are included in the table of contents.

Conclusion: The conclusion ties everything together for the reader by presenting the findings of the report. Conclusions should be based on the information and documentation in the report and contain no new information.

Recommendations: Recommendations suggest what should be done based on the findings or point out areas in which further study is needed. Not all reports have recommendations.

TEXT HEADINGS

Headings are important because they allow the reader to see how a report is organized. Headings can be one of the following types:

Centered on a line by itself. Leave two blank lines above and one below the heading, which should be all capitals or initial caps and bold.

Flush left on a line by itself. Leave two blank lines above and one below the heading, which should be all capitals or initial caps and bold.

Paragraph headings are on the same line with the text. One blank line goes before the paragraph heading, assuming that the text is double spaced. The heading can be bold or italic and should be followed by a period. Begin the text two spaces after the period.

Before selecting a subheading style, decide how many levels of subheadings are needed. Headings should be limited to a maximum of three levels.

If one head level is used, it should be flush left.

If two head levels are used, one should be flush left and the other a paragraph heading *or* one should be centered and the other flush left.

If three head levels are used, one should be centered, one flush left, and one a paragraph heading.

TEXT HEADINGS FORMATTING SUGGESTIONS

- Use either upper- and lowercase or all capitals. The choice is determined by the length of the majority of headings; long headings are more difficult to read in all caps. When using upper- and lowercase, use lowercase for articles and prepositions, such as "the," "a," "to," "of," "with," "for," "by."

- The report title should be bigger and/or bolder than the strongest subheading.

HINT: *Use the style headings available with your word processing package.*

- A heading can be one size larger in the same weight as the text.

HINT: *Use the outlining feature of your word processing program to review your headings.*

HEADERS AND FOOTERS

Multipage documents include headers and/or footers. A header is information that prints at the top of the second and the following pages; a footer is the same information, but printed instead at the bottom of the page. Headers and footers typically are not printed on the first page of a document. They may have more than one line of text.

By using word processing software, different headers or footers can be created for even pages, odd pages, and (if appropriate) the first page. For example, the chapter title can be printed on the even pages and the text of the first head level on the odd pages. Page numbers are appropriate in either the header or the footer.

HINT: *If the fonts are changed for the entire document, the fonts of the header and/or footer must be changed also.*

HINT: *If a multipage document is printed two-sided, odd and even headers or footers are more professional.*

TABLES

Tables present statistical data to explain written text. All tables present data in vertical columns and horizontal rows. (See Figure 18-7.)

Table I
Workstation Components
(rounded to the nearest dollar)

Component	Quantity Needed	Average Price
Ergonomic Chair	40	$69–350
Keyboard	35	20–60
Monitor	35	180–500
Computer Desks	42	75–450

Figure 18-7 A sample table.

TABLE FORMATTING SUGGESTIONS

- Maintain equal space between columns.
- Leave at least half an inch of white space above and below the table.
- The table's typeface may differ from that of the report. Sans serif figures are often preferred to serif figures (see the section on Type and Printing Styles in Chapter 19 for an explanation of serif/sans serif). Times Roman and Helvetica are usually legible and narrow, which means more information can be placed in the table.
- Try to keep the table vertical so readers will not have to turn the page to read it. Use a double spread over two facing pages for a wide table.
- If the table will not fit on the same page as the text referring to the table, put the table on the page immediately following the reference in the text. If necessary, reduce the size of the table so it will fit on the same page as the reference to it.
- Use margins equal to or wider than the report's margins.
- Use consistent line spacing for all tables in a report. If you are using a word processing program, experiment with spacing between lines.

Table Numbers

Tables can be numbered Table 1, Table 2, Table 3, and so on, in the order they are mentioned in the text and with "Table" capitalized. It is not necessary to number tables if a report has only one table, widely scattered tables, or tables that can be easily described and found.

Tables should be numbered separately from illustrations, such as Table 1, Illustration or Figure 1. If the report has many tables, graphs, and charts, they can all be called Exhibit and numbered in sequence.

Tables can also be placed in an appendix. Tables in an appendix are numbered separately from those in the text. For example, Table A-1 would be Table 1 in Appendix A.

FORMATTING SUGGESTIONS

- Use either all capitals or an initial capital, i.e., TABLE 1 or Table 1, and bold.
- The table number can be set flush left on a line by itself with the title directly below it or centered.
- The table number can also be on the same line with the title, followed by a period or a dash, or sometimes both: Table 1. Annual Salary Ranges by Title; Table 1—Annual Salary Ranges by Title; Table 1.—Annual Salary Ranges by Title.

HINT: *Use the table numbering feature of your word processing software.*

Table Titles

The title of a table should be short and direct. Omit articles such as "the" and "a" and phrases such as "summary of."

FORMATTING SUGGESTIONS

- Center the title or place it flush left.
- Do not use punctuation after a title unless it is a full sentence.
- Words should be capitalized with letters in both upper- and lowercase, except for articles and short prepositions, which should be in lowercase. Titles in all caps are difficult to read and take up more space.
- If a title runs two lines, the lines should be similar in length, with the first slightly longer than the second. If the title is flush left, the second line may be either flush left or indented. Otherwise both lines must be centered.
- Leave white space before the body of the table.
- Use bold type for an effective table title.

Subtitles

A subtitle gives an explanation of the table. It may list abbreviations or explain how the data were obtained. The subtitle should apply to the entire table and not just to one or two columns. Place specific information about columns in footnotes. (See the section on Footnotes, Endnotes, and Text Notes, below, for additional information.)

FORMATTING SUGGESTIONS

- The subtitle may be in the same style as the title or in parentheses.
- Place the subtitle on a separate line below the title.
- The type size is usually smaller than that of the title.

Column Headings

Single words or concise phrases are used above all columns in a table. Two lines may be necessasry to explain columns.

FORMATTING SUGGESTIONS

- Use enough white space between column headings so the table does not look crowded.

- Use bold type for effective column headings.
- A column heading spanning two or more columns is called a spanner head. The spanner head may be separated from column heads by a space, a rule, or a different typeface.
- Use upper- and lowercase letters.
- Avoid abbreviations and symbols that may not be understood by the reader.

Figures

Align columns of numbers at the right:

$$4504$$
$$23$$
$$2$$

Dollar Amounts

Omit decimal points and zeros when the figures are whole amounts. However, if one amount contains a cents figure, every amount requires the cents. Place the dollar sign next to the first amount. Align the dollar sign vertically with the column containing the longest figure. (See the examples below.) Do not use commas in four-digit numbers unless the numbers appear in the same column with larger numbers.

$ 20	$ 20
1000	1,000
350	35,000

Decimals

Align the decimal points of every figure in a column. All figures should have the same number of decimal places.

$$10.000$$
$$5.535$$
$$7.750$$

Percentages

A percent sign follows the first figure in a column of percentages. However, percent signs are not necessary if you use the word *percent* or *percentage* in the column heading:

MEMBERS RESPONDING	PERCENTAGE OF MEMBERS RESPONDING
50.2%	50.2
30.7	30.7
28.2	28.2

Parentheses

Parentheses around figures signify a negative amount. If some, but not all of the figures include parentheses, the figures should still align on the right:

(340,400)
2,500
(50)

Dates

Right align a column of dates by the last figure:

January 5, 20–
June 12, 20–
October 2, 20–

Total Amounts

The total is usually shown as the last row in a table of figures. The total should be clearly labeled and easy to find. However, it may be omitted if it is obviously a total. When a percentage adds up to 100, using the word *total* is optional. If the percentages do not add up to 100, a total should be given with a note such as "Percentages do not add up to 100 percent because of rounding."

	35
	2,365
	796
TOTAL	3,196

The word *total* should be indented from the left margin of the table and may be in all caps and bold.

HINT: *If using a word processing package, add shading to the* total *row.*

Word Tables

Word tables should be simple. Entries should be brief, with or without rules. Runover lines can be flush left as shown or indented several spaces.

FORMATTING SUGGESTIONS

- Set in all caps and indent.
- Use bold type for heading and title.
- Set off with one blank line above or below.
- Do not use periods.

Footnotes

Footnotes include source notes, spelling out of abbreviations in a table, and explanations of specific items in a column. They are placed immediately below the table.

Source notes are required when the table is reprinted from another source or when the table has been created using data from another reference. Source notes should be placed before any other table notes:

Raised symbols in a table refer the reader to notes. Common symbols are *, †, ‡, and §.

FORMATTING SUGGESTIONS

- Set footnote in a smaller type size than the table.
- Set the words *Note* or *Source* in italics.
- Begin footnotes flush left.
- Place a period at the end of each note.

CHARTS AND GRAPHS

A chart or graph shows numbers in picture form. This representation of data can often have a greater impact than a table of figures. Tables are used when readers need precise statistical details; charts and graphs are used when readers are concerned with the overall effects of statistics. But note that too much information in one diagram is confusing; it is better to have two small charts than one large chart.

Charts and graphs are easy to produce using computer software. The following information is entered into the computer:

- Title of the chart.
- Subtitle (if needed).

- Heading for the x-axis (horizontal axis) and y-axis (vertical axis) if creating a bar or line chart.
- Numbers for each entry in the chart or graph.
- Footnotes, if needed.
- Appropriate type of graph.

The software then creates the graph on screen.

The three most popular ways of presenting statistical information in graphic form are pie charts, bar charts, and line graphs.

Pie Charts

Pie charts are used to show budgets, sales, and costs at a particular time. They are not effective for showing trends over a period of time. And if there is a large gap between the highest and lowest figures, it is difficult to show the smallest numbers accurately in a pie chart. The size of a section or wedge of the pie chart is proportional to the quantity the wedge represents. (See Figure 18-8.)

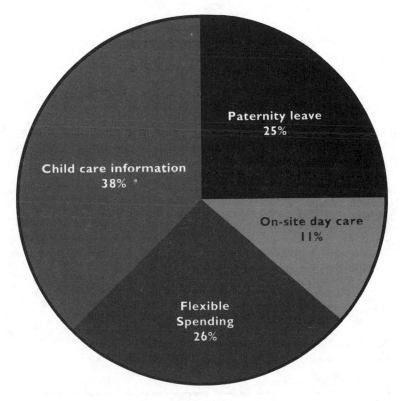

Figure 18-8 Sample pie chart.

Do not use more than six sections in a pie chart; it is difficult to read a pie chart with more sections. Avoid listing small slices of the pie separately; combine small slices into a category called "Other" or "Miscellaneous." Make the slices add up to an exact figure: 1, 100%, $1, or a rounded multiple of one of these.

Bar Charts

Bar charts are used to show information over a period of time or to make comparisons. Bar charts allow for more complex comparison of information by presenting data in multiple bars. The height of a bar is proportional to the quantity it represents. Vertical bars are used to show increases in quantities. Horizontal bars are used to show increases in distance. As on pie charts, if there is a large gap between the highest and lowest figures, it is difficult to show the smallest numbers accurately. (See Figure 18-9.)

Line Graphs

A line graph is effective in illustrating trends or comparisons over a period of time. Limit the number of lines to three if they cross one another. (See Figure 18-10.)

Figure 18-9 Sample bar chart.

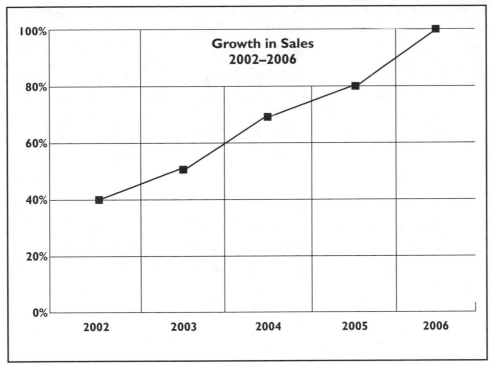

Figure 18-10 Sample line graph.

PHOTOGRAPHS

Photographs in reports increase interest and readership. Usually the best photographs of people are candid shots, as opposed to posed shots. The most skillful photographs are those taken by professionals. Photographs can be scanned and used in office publications.

HINT: *Hire photographers who work part-time for local newspapers.*

FOOTNOTES, ENDNOTES, AND TEXT NOTES

Footnotes, endnotes, and text notes document the following:

- Direct quotes.
- Paraphrases of written works.
- Opinions of persons other than the author.
- Statistical data not compiled by the writer.
- Visuals such as photographs, tables, or charts not constructed by the author.

Many formats exist for documenting sources used in a report or to provide information outside the main text. Footnotes are positioned at the bottom of a page, endnotes are placed at the end of a report, and text notes are notes in parentheses within the body of the material itself.

Footnotes and endnotes are easy to insert using word processing software. The footnote will be automatically positioned on the page in the appropriate place with a superscript (raised number) in the text. If there are many footnotes on a page, the report will look unattractive; the reader's eye must move from the body of the text to the bottom of the page. The endnote feature puts endnotes at the end of the document. Endnotes necessitate flipping back to the end of the report to find the reference.

FORMATTING FOOTNOTES

- Use a type size two sizes smaller than that of the text, if possible.
- Single-space the footnotes; double-space between footnotes.
- Indent the first line of each footnote .5 inches or place it flush left.

FORMATTING ENDNOTES

- Place endnotes after appendices. If there are no appendices, the endnotes follow the body of the report.
- Center the heading "Notes" 2 inches from the top of the page.
- Begin keying the first endnote two blank lines below the heading.
- Single-space endnotes; double-space between endnotes.
- Indent the first line of each endnote .5 inches or place it flush left.
- Use the same margins as in the report.
- Number the pages as part of the report.

FORMATTING TEXT NOTES

- Text notes immediately follow the information given in the report.
- If there are only a few references in the report, all bibliographic data can be placed in parentheses. (See Figure 18-11.)
- When there are numerous references in the body of the report, give the name of the author and the page number of the text in parentheses immediately after the information presented in the report. List the sources in full at the end of the report.

REFERENCE NOTES, REFERENCE LIST, AND BIBLIOGRAPHY

Several different styles may be used for citing sources in footnotes, endnotes, or text notes. The style shown below is for business reference notes. (Academic style differs

Salary Review
The PC workstation manager is paid less than the telecommunications man-ager; typically, the security specialist is paid more than the Web developer (Barbara Carlson, *Salary Comparisons,* Universal Publishers, New York, 2002, p. 85). These statistics are reviewed and revised each year, and can serve as a general guide for analyzing salary schedules.

Figure 18-11 Text notes in a report.

slightly in that the place of publication precedes the publisher and date, with a colon after the place.)

BOOK WITH NO AUTHOR

Compilation of Statistics, Brock Publishing Co., New York, NY, 2001.

BOOK WITH ONE AUTHOR

1. Carolyn J. Mullins, *The Complete Writing Guide to Preparing Reports, Propos-als, Memos, Etc.,* Aaron Publishing Co., Englewood Cliffs, NJ, 2000.

TWO OR MORE BOOKS BY THE SAME AUTHOR

2. Carolyn J. Mullins, *The Complete Writing Guide to Preparing Reports, Propos-als, Memos, Etc.,* Aaron Publishing Co., Englewood Cliffs, NJ, 2000.
3. ———, *Report Writing,* Cooper Press, New York, 2002, p. 54.

BOOK WITH TWO AUTHORS

4. Mark Louis and Margaret Emke, *Successful Writing,* Cooper Press, New York, 2002.

BOOK WITH THREE OR MORE AUTHORS

5. Milton Hoover and others, *Report References,* P. J. Thomas Co., Boston, 2001.

BOOK TITLE WITH EDITION NUMBER

(The edition number is given when the book is not in its first edition.):

> 6. Harry Shadle, *Economics of Business*, 3rd ed., Iowa State University Press, Ames, 2001.

BOOK WITH CORPORATE AUTHOR

> 7. International Association of Administrative Professionals®, *How to Get Your Article Published in OfficePRO*, Kansas City, MO 2002.

ARTICLE IN A MAGAZINE OR PROFESSIONAL JOURNAL

> 8. William Smith, "Accessories Improve User Comfort," *OfficePRO*, 50:8, October 2002.
> 9. Ron Zemke, "The Ups and Downs of Downsizing," *Training*, 27:11, November 2002, p. 27.

ARTICLE IN A MAGAZINE OR PROFESSIONAL JOURNAL WITH NO AUTHOR CITED

> 10. "Green Ballots vs. Greenbacks," *Time*, 136:22, November 19, 2002, p. 44.

ARTICLE IN A NEWSPAPER

> 11. Sabin Russell, "Dow Advances 36 Points in Strong Session," *San Francisco Chronicle*, December 13, 2001, C1.

TECHNICAL PAPER PRESENTED AT A CONFERENCE

> 12. Diane B. Hernandez, Amy Chang, and Leah Abdul, "Electronic Communications in the Virtual Office," International Association of Administrative Professionals® Convention and Education Forum, San Diego, CA, March 4, 2002.

SPEECH OR CONVERSATION

> 13. Bernard F. White, U.S. Department of Labor, Washington, DC, speaking to the 59th annual American Society for Training and Development, Cincinnati, OH, December 5, 2002.

CITING A WEB SITE

From the World Wide Web: http://www.iaap-hq.org/ResearchTrends/research__trends.htm

CITING A DOCUMENT FROM A WEB SITE

Brown, Alexandria, "Hiring a Virtual Assistant Can Help You Grow Your Business," Guru Worldwide, Inc. Retrieved December 21, 2001, from the World Wide Web: http://www.guru.com/channel/start/guide/G11502.jhtml.

Malone, Thomas, W., "The Future of E-Business," *MIT Sloan Management Review*, 43:1, Fall 2001. Retrieved December 21, 2001, from the World Wide Web: http://mitsloan.mit.edu/smr/past/2001/smr43112.html.

Walker, Rob, *"Accounting and Accountability,"* *Slate*, December 18, 2001. Retrieved December 21, 2001, from the World Wide Web: http://slate.msn.com/?id=2059908.

Note: Personal e-mail correspondence is not listed in the reference list. Cite these in the text with the initials and surname of the communicator and as exact a date as possible. For example, S. Fenner (personal communication, January 24, 2002).

A bibliography lists all the references relevant to the report, while a reference list gives just the ones cited. In a reference list, an author's first name precedes the last name; in a bibliography, the name of the initial author is reversed, with the last name appearing first. The works are numbered in a reference list but unnumbered in a bibliography. Works appear in a reference list in the same sequence that the information they contain appears in the report, while in a bibliography they are listed alphabetically by author. Reference lists and bibliographies are usually punctuated and capitalized in the same way, and both are positioned at the end of the report, before attachments.

FORMATTING SUGGESTIONS

- Place the title 2 inches from the top of the page.
- Use the same margins as in the report.
- Begin each reference at the left margin.
- Indent the second line five spaces.
- Single-space each reference; double-space between references.
- References without authors are alphabetized by title.

Here is a sample bibliography:

Brown, Alexandria, "Hiring a Virtual Assistant Can Help You Grow Your Business," Guru Worldwide, Inc. Retrieved December 21, 2001, from the World Wide Web: http://www.guru.com/channel/start/guide /G11502.jhtml.

"Green Ballots vs. Greenbacks," *Time*, 136:22, November 19, 2002, p. 44.

Hernandez, Diane B., Amy Chong, and Leah Abdul, "Electronic Communications in the Virtual Office," International Association of Administrative Professionals® Convention and Education Forum, San Diego, CA, March 4, 2002.

Hoover, Milton and others, *Report References.* P.J. Thomas Co., Boston, 2001.

International Association of Administrative Professionals®, *How to Get Your Article Published in OfficePRO,* Kansas City, MO, 2002.

Louis, Mark and Margaret Emke, *Successful Writing,* Cooper Press, New York, 2002.

Mullins, Carolyn J., *The Complete Writing Guide to Preparing Reports, Proposals, Memos, Etc.,* Aaron Publishing Co., Englewood Cliffs, NJ, 2000.

———, *Report Writing,* Cooper Press, New York, 2002.

Russell, Sabin, "Dow Advances 36 Points in Strong Session," *San Francisco Chronicle,* December 13, 2001, C1.

Shadle, Harry, *Economics of Business,* 3rd ed., Iowa State University Press, Ames, 2001.

Smith, William, "Accessories Improve User Comfort," *OfficePRO,* 50:8, October 2002, p. 31.

White, Bernard F., U.S. Department of Labor, Washington DC, speaking to the 59th annual American Society for Training and Development Conference, Cincinnati, OH, December 5, 2002.

Zemke, Ron, "The Ups and Downs of Downsizing," *Training,* 27:11, November 2002, p. 27.

GLOSSARY

A glossary is an alphabetical listing of specialized vocabulary and definitions. A glossary is necessary if the readers will be unfamiliar with the terms used in the report.

FORMATTING SUGGESTIONS

- The heading "Glossary" is centered 2 inches from the top of the page.
- Leave two blank lines after the heading.
- Use one of the following styles: (1) Two columns—put the terms in alphabetical order in the left column and definitions in the right. (2) Hanging indentation—begin each term at the left margin, followed by a colon, then give the definition; indent the second line five spaces from the left margin. (3) Paragraph style—indent each term five spaces from the left margin, followed by a colon, then give the definition; the second line is flush with the left margin.

- Terms may be in bold.
- Use periods at the end of definitions if they are written as sentences.

HINT: *Use the glossary feature of your word processing package to create the glossary.*

APPENDICES

Appendices include the supporting material for the report. Items in an appendix may be questionnaires, statistics, detailed test results, descriptions of data, or cost comparisons. Appendices appear in the order referred to in the report. Each appendix is assigned a letter; e.g., Appendix A, Appendix B, and so on.

FORMATTING SUGGESTIONS

- Type the heading "Appendix A" centered 2 inches from the top of the page.
- Leave two blank lines after the heading.

COMPUTER PRESENTATIONS

Graphic presentation software makes it easy to develop professional presentations. Presentations can be used with a group or in a booth at a trade show to attract the attention of participants. The presentation can also be sent on disk to customers or off-site employees or posted on the Internet.

FORMATTING SUGGESTIONS

The following are suggestions when designing a computer presentation:

- Select a background that will project well. Use consistent color schemes and formatting conventions for all the slides in the presentation. The colors of the text and the background should contrast for clear visibility.

HINT: *Blue backgrounds make words easy to read when projected. Red is the most difficult text color to read.*

- Use 32 point as the minimum size in a sans serif font such as Arial, Helvetica, or CG Omega. Serif fonts such as Times New Roman or Courier may be more difficult to read.

- Less information on a slide is easier to read. Use a maximum of six lines on a slide and six words on a line.
- Use a combination of upper- and lowercase letters. Avoid using capital letters exclusively.
- Avoid the temptation to create complex visuals, which will distract from the message.
- Include one major idea in each visual. When presenting, paraphrase rather than read the visual.
- Include transitions (an eye-catching way to move from slide to slide) and builds (the highlighting of one subtitle at a time).
- Print copies of the visuals as handouts. Most computer presentation programs will automatically reduce the size of the visuals so several can be printed on a page.
- Place a black visual at the end of the presentation so you know you have finished.
- Include graphs, charts, graphics, and tables to increase visual interest. Poor image quality will be particularly noticeable and may detract from the presentation.

HINT: *Invest in a software clip art collection; such collections will greatly increase the number of graphics available, and they are reasonably priced.*

HINT: *Numerous graphics and photographs are available on-line. To copy a graphic or photograph from a Web page, right-click and save it to disk. Make certain that the image is not copyrighted.*

- Use the spell check feature and proofread carefully. The visuals should be perfect.
- Check the location where the presentation will be given to make certain the presentation projects properly.

HINT: *When using equipment in a remote location, plan to arrive at least 45 minutes ahead of time for troubleshooting.*

HINT: *If you are presenting in a place you are not familiar with, always have a hard copy of the visuals made into transparencies in case the equipment does not work properly.*

HINT: *Bring an extension cord with three-way adapter plugs. If you are using an overhead and projection plate, bring an extra transparency bulb.*

A disadvantage of computer presentations is the inability to personalize them. If you wish audience input, bring along a flip chart or make certain a board is available for writing. Also, the audience can be distracted by the transition from one slide to another.

Many office professionals are determining content for publication and using computers and software to create and design publications and Web pages. Office publications have four functions:

- To capture attention
- To focus interest
- To create a desire
- To motivate to action

Each step of the publishing process should contribute to one of these functions.

ADVANTAGES OF IN-HOUSE PUBLISHING

Designing publications in-house eliminates the need to hire outside professionals to produce publications and Web pages and offers the following advantages:

- It speeds up production because it is no longer necessary to accommodate the schedules of specialists.
- It saves money after the initial equipment purchase because some or all of the work is completed in-house.
- It is easier to make changes and corrections.
- It offers more internal control over the design and production schedule.
- It provides greater security for confidential or sensitive documents.
- It allows a business to have more professional-looking everyday documents.

Small printing jobs can be printed out and then reproduced on a copy machine, with larger publications completed by a professional printer.

Designing Web pages has become easier because many software programs can save in a Web page format. In addition, special Web page design programs are easy to learn and use without learning HTML (Hypertext Markup Language).

Companies may offer Web space on the network server where employees can upload Web pages. If this op-

CHAPTER 19

OFFICE

AND

WEB

PUBLISHING

tion is not available to employees, in-house computer specialists can upload Web pages. Using the intranet for publishing newsletters, memos, and manuals saves paper, ink, and money in addition to making information available faster and avoiding distribution problems.

TYPE AND PRINTING STYLES

Various typefaces, or shapes of type, and sizes of characters are used in publishing. Different typefaces can greatly affect the appearance and legibility of a document and help deliver the appropriate message.

Typeface

Different typefaces convey characteristics such as casual, formal, modern, traditional, friendly, or serious. Companies use different typefaces to reflect a style and corporate identity.

The major distinction between typefaces is the presence or absence of serifs. **Serifs** are the small curves added to the ends of strokes; **sans serif** typefaces lack these small curves. Here are two different typefaces, one with serifs and one sans serif:

Office Publishing (serif)
Office Publishing (sans serif)

Most of the differences among typefaces are in the lowercase letters. The one letter that most often differs from typeface to typeface is the lowercase *g*. Listed below is the letter *g* in a variety of typefaces:

g   Garamond
g   Times Roman
g   **Bookman**
g   Gothic

For written documents, research has shown that a sans serif typeface is harder to read than serif. Sans serif is also difficult to read in boldface or italics. Sans serif type is recommended mainly for headings and headlines. For digital documents, body text is usually sans serif, while headings are serif. Avoid using two serif faces together or two sans serif fonts together. Table 19.1 lists some typefaces that convey certain images.

Table 19-2 lists the recommended typefaces for various sorts of publications. Here are a few miscellaneous but important facts about typefaces to bear in mind:

- Typefaces with different names can be identical because although a typeface *itself* cannot be copyrighted, the typeface *name* can be.

Table 19-1
TYPEFACE CHARACTERISTICS

CHARACTERISTIC	SERIF	SANS SERIF
Classic	Garamond, Baskerville, Bodini, Book Antiqua, Garamond, Goudy Old Style, Palatino, Utopia	Arial, Helvetica, Univers
Clean, Modern	Bookman, Century Schoolbook, Cooper, Times New Roman, Truesdell	Bernhard Gothic, Futura, Gill Sands, Goudy Sans ITC, Metro
Common	Bookman, Century Schoolbook, Palatino, Times New Roman	Arial, Helvetica, Futura, Optima

Table 19-2
TYPEFACES FOR DIFFERENT PUBLICATIONS

PUBLICATION	TYPEFACE
Advertising	Sans serif (e.g., Helvetica)
Charts	Sans serif (e.g., Helvetica, Arial)
Digital documents	Sans serif
Documents (lengthy)	Serif
Magazines	Serif
Newsletters	Serif (e.g., Times Roman, Bookman, Trump, Palatino)
Reports	Sans serif
Signs	Sans serif
Table	Sans serif (e.g., Helvetica, Arial)

- Typefaces with geographic names (Venice, New York, Geneva) may cause problems when brought into page layout software. The characters are wide, with wider spacing between letters, and they look less attractive when printed.
- Times Roman, Arial, and Helvetica are usually standard in software packages; others can be purchased on disk or downloaded from the Internet.
- Fonts suitable for print do not always translate well to the screen for Web use.

Type Size

The size of the type determines whether people read a publication. A small type size is doomed to failure. The size of type is measured in picas and points. The pica and point system dates back to the time when all type was produced in metal or wood. A *pica* is one-sixth of an inch. Each pica is divided into 12 **points**. A point is $\frac{1}{72}$ of an inch. The size of type is called the **point size,** and is approximately equal to the distance from the top of an h to the bottom of a q.

1 inch	=	6 picas
1 pica	=	12 points
72 points	=	1 inch

Twelve-point type, for example, is type that measures 12 points from the top to the bottom of the letters. Software programs provide measurements in fractions of points and sometimes in centimeters and millimeters. The range of type sizes available depends on the printer used and the fonts available.

Table 19-3 shows examples of Times Roman and Helvetica in different point sizes. Notice that Helvetica tends to look larger than Times Roman, although they are the same point size. For a document with a lot of text, the characters per line make the number of pages; i.e., the more characters on a line of text, the shorter the document. Listed below are some common uses of common type sizes:

Brochure to fit in No. 10 envelope	14–36 point
Copyright notice or other fine print	6 point
Formal announcements and invitations	10, 12, or 14 point
Newsletter body	10 or 12 point
Text	10 or 12 point
Overhead transparency	18 point or larger
Digital documents	12 points or larger

HINT: *For the heading text, use a larger point size than for the text, and use an even larger size for the main title. If 12-point type seems too large, use a lighter weight type (see next section). For printed documents, type of headings should be 12 or 14 points. For digital documents, the headings should be 16 points or larger.*

Table 19-3
DIFFERENT POINT SIZES OF TWO TYPEFACES

TIMES ROMAN (SERIF)	HELVETICA (SANS SERIF)
This is 7 point.	This is 7 point.
This is 10 point.	This is 10 point.
This is 12 point.	This is 12 point.
This is 18 point.	This is 18 point.

Type Style

Each typeface usually has a series of different **weights,** or letter thicknesses. Most computerized typefaces have at least a bold weight and an italic. Tables 19-4 and 19-5 show different weights of Helvetica and the uses of different styles.

Fonts

A font is a particular style and size of a typeface. It is also called a **type family.** A font includes capitals, lowercase, small caps, punctuation marks, and mathematical symbols. Below is a font of Times Roman:

ABCDEFGHIJKLMNOPQRSTUVWXYZ
abcdefghijklmnopqrstuvwxyz

Leading

Leading is the distance between lines of type; it is often called line spacing. Line spacing does not alter the size of the typeface or lengthen the line; it merely moves the lines farther apart. Short lines (e.g., 45 characters on a line) need less space between them

Table 19-4
WEIGHTS OF HELVETICA TYPE

This is an example of Helvetica typeface in lightface.
This is an example of Helvetica typeface in boldface.
This is an example of Helvetica typeface in italic.

Table 19-5
USES OF DIFFERENT TYPE STYLES

STYLE	USE
Bold	Main titles and subtitles; used to draw attention to the most important thing first. Avoid setting large blocks of text in bold because nothing will stand out.
Italics	Quotations, names of books and magazines, emphasized words. Avoid setting large blocks of text in italics because research shows people read italic type up to 20 words per minute more slowly than regular type.
Capital letters	Only used if a few individual words need emphasis. A long title in capitals may take up too much space or be difficult to read.
Underlining	Avoid (left over from the days of typewriters); use italics or bold for emphasis.

than long lines (e.g., 80 characters on a line). Software usually has a 2-point leading default, which is acceptable for most publications.

Extra leading for bold type increases legibility and may be needed to lighten its color or weight. Sans serif type might also need extra leading to help the reader's eye drop to the next line of text. Below are two sample pieces of text with different leading:

> A type set on its own body size without
> additional line feed is said to be
> "set solid."

> A 12-point type with 3 points of extra space
> is called "12 on 15 pt" or $^{12}/_{15}$ pt.
> Printers refer to this as 3-point leading.

Suggestions for a Professional Appearance

Here are some suggestions to guide you in making type choices:

1. Use no more than two typefaces (a headline face and a body copy face). The two typefaces should be different enough to be distinguishable from one another. Often the best mix is a serif typeface with a sans serif one. The typeface for body and headlines can be the same. You can alter a typeface's appearance by varying the weights and widths. Use the regular weight for body and bold or bold italics for heads.
2. Choose the most readable typeface. Ornate typefaces are difficult to read, as this example shows:

Holiday Greetings

Type should be determined by the audience. Young or older readers need larger text type so documents can be read easily, while busy people need type that can be scanned quickly. Avoid using a script typeface, which looks like handwriting, for more than a few lines of copy, because it is tiring to the eye.
3. Determine the reading distance before determining the type size. Posters, for example, take a larger type size than a booklet.
4. Lengthen the line or reduce the type size to save space, rather than changing the typefaces.
5. Type may be either right-justified (even along the right margin) or ragged right (uneven at the right margin). Justified text is associated with typeset copy; however, some people feel justified text is harder to read than ragged right. If text is ragged right, paragraphs should have one line of space between them and not be

indented. If the text is justified, paragraphs should have one line space between them and be indented.

HINT: *Use your software to leave additional space above and below paragraphs.*

6. Use one rather than two spaces after the period at the end of a sentence.

HINT: *Use the search and replace feature to change two spaces to one space.*

7. Do not use asterisks to begin items in a list; instead, use bullets or other symbols.

Columns

The width of the column depends upon the purpose of the publication. The following table suggests uses for different numbers and widths of columns:

COLUMN WIDTH	USE
One	Newsletters, pamphlets
Two	Newsletters
Three	Newsletters, publications that mix text with graphics and or boxes
Four	Indexes, lists, dictionaries
Five or Six	Newspapers

GRAPHICS AND ILLUSTRATIONS

A graphic or illustration in a publication or on a Web page enhances the text and makes it seem more interesting. Graphics and illustrations can include original drawings, photographs, charts, and graphs. Research shows twice as many people will read a publication if it is supported by photos or artwork.

Original Drawings

Original drawings can be created with paint or draw programs on computer or by hand. They should correlate with items to be emphasized in the text. Cartoons can be added for humor but should not be overused. The drawing should be of the same quality as the publication.

Clip Art

Clip art is art done by professional artists and is copyright-free. It is typically arranged by topic or by themes, such as business or holidays. A wide variety of clip art is available on CD-ROMs and on-line.

It is very important to be aware that most drawings in newspapers, magazines, on-line, and other commercial publications are copyrighted; they are *not* clip art. Check with the publisher before reproducing.

Charts and Diagrams

Charts and diagrams not only provide visual interest, but also supply information in a smaller amount of space than would be used by a verbal explanation. Diagrams should be kept simple and not used if they require a great deal of explanatory information.

Photographs

Scanners and digital cameras can be used to add photographs to publications. When using photographs, avoid pictures of people holding trophies, shaking hands, or a group just smiling into the camera. Try to use candid shots of people doing their jobs. Readers enjoy human interest. Readers also prefer large photographs.

If you must include head shots of people, try to use a similar format. The same amount of head and shoulder should appear in each photo, and the relative sizes should be similar. If you are identifying people in a line, identify as "From left: . . ."

Use captions to describe or explain the action in the photo. The caption should be below the photo it describes and run a maximum of four lines.

Pull Quotes

Pull quotes are quotations used as a graphic device, especially when no graphic art-work is available. Pull quotes summarize surrounding material and draw attention to it. Pull quotes are set in a larger type with boxes or rules around them.

Design Graphics

Rules are lines for borders or boxes. They are used to separate categories of infor-mation (e.g., numbers and words), to draw attention to information, or to decorate. They are best used sparingly. Use vertical rules to separate columns and horizontal rules to separate topics within a column.

Screen tints are shadings or fill patterns that look like light versions of the ink. They are useful in highlighting blocks of type, such as a table of contents, and in helping organize data in calendars.

Reverses consist of printing the background rather than the image (e.g., white words on a black background). They are hard to read and are best used for display type in cal-endars or nameplates.

Special Concerns About Using Graphics and Illustrations

Before adding any graphics or illustrations to a publication, ask the following questions:

- Are words adequate or are graphics needed to bring attention to the message?
- Will graphics help explain part of a text?
- Is there a place, person, or event frequently referred to in the text whose illustration would aid the audience's understanding?
- Is there a step-by-step process that could be illustrated?
- Is there a mood or style that could be captured by graphics?

The following suggestions should be kept in mind when using graphics and illustrations:

- Use them only if they add to the message.
- Mix them with text instead of isolating them at the beginning or end of a page.
- Avoid complicated graphics—keep them simple.
- Place the graphic or illustration on or near the same page as the text that it depicts.
- Unless they are purely decorative, illustrations should be accompanied by captions. Captions should be in a smaller type size than the text; if they are in the same type size as the text, they should be in bold, italic, or a different typeface.
- Include a source line (reference) for an illustration if appropriate.
- Use illustrations that are in different sizes and shapes to add interest. At least one visual on a page should be substantially larger than others to attract reader interest. Readers usually see visuals first and move from print to visuals while reading.

Video Clips

If your company promotes itself or its products with video, that video should be on the company's Web site. Video can also be effective on intranets or internal corporate networks. Questions to ask before including video clips on Web sites are:

- What value does the video add to the Web site?
- Does the value justify the effort spent digitizing the video and making it ready for the Web?
- Will the site's users actually spend time downloading the video clips?

Uploading video clips to a Web page varies in complexity, the type of authoring software (or lack of authoring software) being used, and video format. The optimal video clip needs no local installation of software applications on individual computers. Prepare the video clip to be viewed on the most common speed of Internet connection for your customers.

If no one on the staff has the time or expertise to be involved in this process, service companies can take corporate videos, digitize them, and provide Web space.

DESIGNING PUBLICATIONS

Publications that best accomplish their goals are ones that have both their content and the audience clearly identified. Whether designing a brochure, advertisement, Web page, or newsletter, it is important to ask and answer the following questions:

- What is the goal? To persuade? impress? explain? boost morale? If goals are high, higher-quality publication may be necessary. Quality is determined by the design, paper, and photography.
- Who is the audience? Employees? Association members? Investors?
- What are the budget constraints?
- How will it be distributed? Mailed in an envelope? Sent as a self-mailer? Inserted in other publications? If it will be a self-mailer, leave part of the back page for the return address and a mailing label. Make certain to check placement of the back page before printing, so the newsletter does not appear to be upside-down when opened.
- Is art needed? Not all publications need art. If costs are limited, clip art or scanned art can be used.

Whether a brochure, newsletter, Web page, or advertisement is being created, the following steps are suggested:

- Make a rough layout using pen and paper before using the computer. Drafting ideas on paper helps visualize and formulate objectives as well as accounting for the design limitations of the publication.
- Select the typeface. (See the section on Typeface earlier in this chapter.)
- Determine type size for the body copy, headings, and other text blocks.
- Decide whether to use right-justified or ragged right text.

HINT: *Most readers find ragged right text easier to read.*

- Determine what graphics will be used.
- Avoid bias based on gender, race, age, ethnic background, physical ability, or sexual preference.
- Use the active, not passive, voice.

HINT: *Use the grammar checker on a word processing package, which will search for the passive voice.*

- Keep the writing simple.

HINT: *The grammar checkers on most word processing packages indicate the grade level of your writing. Write at about the seventh grade level for general understanding.*

HINT: *Reduce the grade level by decreasing the number of complex sentences and eliminating multisyllable words.*

- Keep sentences short.

HINT: *A sentence of 17 words is considered standard. Long sentences make content more difficult to understand.*

- Check for correct spelling, grammar, punctuation, inconsistencies, and inaccuracies.
- Decide on color. Research shows about three times as many people will read a publication if it is in color. People in all cultures attach meanings to color (i.e., blue may mean power in some cultures and sadness in others). Colors should make some relationship—either symbolic or literal—to the product or service. Avoid using unusual colors and keep the audience in mind. Younger people generally like brighter colors, whereas other consumers may prefer subtle colors. Color, however, should be used sparingly. Ordinary text should not be printed in color; rather, color should be used for nonverbal elements, such as boxes or rules.

Most popular software programs have prepared templates designed by professionals. These templates are for newsletters, brochures, flyers, business cards, and numerous other common publications. The templates help you to be consistent within each page and within a publication and help add balance to a page. Templates have specific margins, columns, fonts, and type sizes already selected; however, these elements are all easy to modify.

Designing a Brochure

Brochures are intended to present a positive image of the company. The rules for designing a brochure are fairly simple:

- Writing should be clear and concise.
- The typeface should be easy to read.
- The title will be more prominent if it is set in a sans serif typeface.
- Since either the front or back will be seen first, benefits should be listed in both places.

- Contemporary colors should be used. Effective colors are off-white, light yellow, buff, goldenrod yellow, pink, and very light tan. Avoid green (unless it is bright teal or turquoise)—it is too restful to elicit action.
- Shading is frequently used to draw attention to layout elements.
- Price information and graphics, if appropriate, should be included to allow the reader to see what is being described. If price information changes frequently, include that information as an extra sheet. Always position benefits before the price.
- The company logo should be in a prominent position, usually on the cover, to promote the name. If the logo is purely graphic, the name should be repeated near the logo.
- Company name, address, and fax and phone numbers should be included.
- Bullet points can be used with hanging indentations.
- Photographs should be contemporary. Use action shots and crop unnecessary background to eliminate distractions.
- Leave sufficient white space.

When creating a brochure, keep in mind how the document is to be folded. The type of fold chosen should be one that can be handled by the printer's machine. (Figure 19-1 shows two suggestions for folds.) Panels must be unequal to accommodate folds.

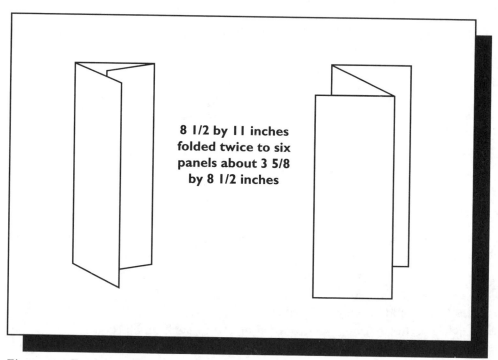

Figure 19-1 Two types of brochure folds.

Any folded brochure must be designed carefully so there is no artwork or copy on the folds. A brochure using either of the folds shown in Figure 19-1 can be used as self-mailers or inserted in a No. 10 business envelope. These brochures can also be included with a one-page letter and still be mailed at the one-ounce postal rate. Envelopes may not be available to fit odd-size folds.

HINT: *The tear-off registration portion of a brochure should not include important information on the other side.*

Designing a Flyer

A flyer is used to publicize an event or product. Flyers are usually read quickly and often read at a distance. Because of this, type should be large and spare. Type too large, however, may detract from the message. The usual flyer is printed on 8½-by-11-inch paper.

Laser printers need ¼-inch to ⅜-inch margins. If you are printing small numbers, using a color printer with good-quality paper will make flyers look professional. It is also possible to print one original on the color printer and then have full-color photocopies made on a color copier machine. You can purchase a variety of paper with preprinted, colorful borders to add visual interest.

Designing an Advertisement

Because there are so many ways to lay out information for an advertisement, there are no typical page layouts and few rules. Simple one-page advertisements are usually on 8½-by-11-inch paper.

The design of a poster is different from the design of a magazine advertisement. The poster must use attention-getting visuals with little text. The visuals for a magazine advertisement do not need to be so striking, since the advertisement will be seen up close and will probably contain more text than a poster.

The following are suggestions for designing advertisements:

- The design should immediately get the reader's attention, either with a headline or an image. Visuals should reinforce the message in the copy.
- Avoid unnecessary words. Either get right to the point or lead up to the point in a way that captures the reader's interest.
- Do not use too many images or large-type headlines.
- Avoid a typeface that is hard to read.
- Use the company logo consistently for continuity.
- Use rules, not underlining, for a coupon response advertisement. And make certain there is enough space for the coupon to be filled out legibly.
- Use plenty of white space.

- Use thin-lined borders to make a wide ad appear taller.
- Center headlines.
- Make certain that information is accurate. It is illegal to give false or misleading information in an advertisement.

Designing a Newsletter

Newsletters are designed to provide information to readers on a regular basis. Most are four or eight pages long on 8½-by-11-inch paper. Understanding the audience is critical in writing and designing a successful newsletter. Listed below are some suggestions:

Know the audience: If the publication has reluctant readers, use design techniques such as large type combined with extra white space.

Design a nameplate (the top of the front page): The nameplate is also called the flag. The nameplate should include the name and subtitle of the newsletter and the publication date. The inclusion of the following elements is optional: logo, illustration, photo, issue number, slogan, publisher, editor.

Include a masthead (the area with business information): The masthead should have the same content and stay in the same location (typically the second page) from one issue to the next. The masthead includes the name and address of the sponsoring organization and the editor's name. The inclusion of the following elements is optional: frequency of publication, subscription costs, names of key officers and contributors, copyright notation, and International Standard Serial Number (ISSN) (used by librarians to catalog publications). Newsletters mailed second class must display either an ISSN or post office identification number in the nameplate, masthead, or return address.

Determine the content: A table of contents on the front cover draws attention to articles in the newsletter. Some content suggestions for a company newsletter are as follows:

- Job-related information.
- Personnel policies and practices.
- Effect of external events on job.
- News of departments and divisions.
- The organization's stand on current issues.
- Stories about employees.
- Personal news (births, birthdays, and so forth).
- Training and professional development.
- Technical information.

Compose headlines: Before writing articles, lay out headlines to help focus the article. The headline must:

- Convey the point of the article.
- Be from the reader's point of view.
- Relate to the story.
- Be in the present tense with an action verb and subject.
- Be specific.

Do not capitalize every word in a headline—only the first word and proper nouns.

Determine the writing style: The writing style should be consistent with company or association image. Newsletter articles are usually less formal than magazines, books, and reports. Use natural conversational tone, with concentration on "you, yours."

Choose the number of columns: Look at newsletters produced by others for ideas and inspiration. And bear the following format hints in mind:

- Most readers look at headlines, photos, and captions first while skimming.
- The inside pages are seen together, so the layout should be tied together with design graphics. Headlines can be set across a whole page, for example.
- Once the basic format is determined for a newsletter, keep it for succeeding issues. Consistency makes content easier to find and lets the designer concentrate on content for each issue.
- More than 90 percent of newsletters in the United States are 8½ by 11 inches. If the publication is four pages, print on an 11-by-17 sheet folded once to become 8½ by 11. An eight-page publication is made with two 11-by-17 sheets or one 17-by-22 sheet folded and trimmed.
- Bottom margins are always slightly larger than top and side margins to make it appear that copy is centered on the page.
- Run main stories over two columns in a three-column newsletter to gain impact.
- The newsletter title, page number, and date are often repeated across the top of every page. Page numbers may also be printed at the bottom of a page.
- Author identification can be placed at the beginning or end of an article. An author's background can be summarized at the end of an article.
- Use headers and footers to repeat the publication title, name of author, and page number. Page numbers are appropriate at either the top or bottom of the page.

Select typeface and size: Bear the following points in mind:

- Stay with just a few typefaces and sizes. Serif type is easier to read for long sections of type. Sans serif type can be used for headlines or captions, as long as it is compatible with the typeface used for the body.
- Make the most important headlines large and place them near the top of the page.
- Choose a thin typeface, such as Times Roman or News Gothic, for narrow columns.

Decide on graphics: Refer to the section on Graphics and Illustrations earlier in this chapter, and follow these suggestions:

- Graphics should contribute to a specific objective.
- Use rules and screen tints to organize information that is not text or in captions.

Do not crowd the page with text and/or graphics: Leave plenty of white space (blank space between text and graphics). The average length of sentences should be about 15 words; paragraphs should be three to four sentences and no longer than seven lines long.

HINT: *Avoid white space in the middle of a page. Add emphasis to headlines by surrounding them with white space.*

Decide whether text will be right-justified or ragged right.

Design calendars carefully: The calendar should appear in the same place in each issue and should not have important items that may be clipped out on its reverse side. When properly designed, a calendar serves as an advertising tool. Include the location and date for each listed activity. Categorize by location activity, or date based on the readership. The design should make it easy for readers to find what they want.

Consider using graphics:
- Use trivia facts, boxed quotes, or clip art for filler if the text does not end at the bottom of the page.
- Divide long articles and place them on more than one page.
- Choose color. Most newsletters are printed in black with a second color used sparingly.
- Use bullets and dingbats (typographical design elements).
- Add oversize initial caps to help mark new sections of copy.

Designing a Web Page

A Web page should provide content that is useful to its audience. The content should be updated regularly, including a thorough check of any links connected to the Web page. Since the typical user has a 56K modem, the Web page must be responsive to that user. Therefore, use graphics sparingly and size them to fit in a typical user's window (a maximum of 465 to 532 pixels wide). If a site has been designed on a PC, the pages will look too wide on a Macintosh®.

Keep the following design and formatting suggestions in mind:

- Use a simple design. Busy backgrounds detract from content and make text illegible. Too many colors or fonts can also be distracting and give the site a cluttered feel. The easiest text to read is black type on a white background.

- Use one design throughout the site. Be consistent in your choice of fonts. Sans serif fonts of at least 12 points are best for digital documents.
- Use headings, lists, and consistent structure. Heading typefaces should be at least 16 points.
- Use short sentences, short paragraphs, headings, and bulleted lists so content can be easily scanned. Each line of text should be kept to about a dozen or so words.
- Use ragged right alignment.
- Provide descriptive links. For example, avoid "click here."
- Use frames cautiously.
- Preview the page in various browsers, including older versions.
- Organize and summarize data in tables.
- Make the page short enough so it does not require a great deal of vertical scrolling.
- If a hyperlink takes the users to another site, you may lose them. When adding hyperlinks to your site, it is better to have the link appear in a new window so the user will remain in your site.
- Avoid complicated graphics that take a long time to download. Readers will lose interest and exit the site if it takes too long to download a page.
- Look at other Web sites to get design ideas.

PRINTING METHODS

Printed output can be produced either with a laser printer or with phototypesetting equipment.

Publications produced on a computer can be stored on disk and printed at a typesetting service bureau that has a professional quality printer. Some bureaus are self-service and charge by the hour for computer rental time. Other bureaus charge for each finished page. Before sending a large project to a typesetting service bureau determine the file formats and platforms the printer can support. Obtain quotes from printers to get the best price.

Preparing to Print

Before you print through a service bureau, the printer should be consulted about resolution, lines per inch, and whether to print on paper or film. The following steps should be taken before sending work to a bureau:

1. Take carefully proofread hard copy (laser-printed) to the service bureau. (If the publication is sent electronically resend a fax or e-mail message as confirmation.)
2. Deliver a list of fonts with the publication. Ask ahead of time how the service bureau wants the fonts set up.

Table 19-6
BINDING SYSTEMS

BINDING METHOD	NUMBER OF SHEETS
No equipment:	
Two-pocket portfolios	15
Prong-style report covers	100
Punchless	125
Slide lock	30
Paper punch:	
Two-piece plastic and pressboard report covers	600
Vinyl ring binders:	
½ inch	100
1 inch	200
1½ inches	325
2 inches	500
3 inches	600
Stapler needed:	
Stapled report cover	15
Plastic ring punch-and-bind machine:	
Either manual or with an electric motor; binds on side or top.	12–425 (depending on equipment)
Adhesive tape machine:	
Uses adhesive tape to bind punched reports to special report covers designed for the machine.	Short reports
Thermal binding system:	
Uses a heat-sealing process to adhere pages to a one-piece, preglued spine and cover.	40–600

3. Ask whether the version of software they are using is compatible with the software you used to create the file.

4. Bring the original graphics file if the document was created with a page layout program.

5. Proofread the copy again once it has been printed.

Methods of Printing

The choice of a printing or copying method depends on the following factors:

- Number of copies
- Budget
- Deadline
- Print quality

The two main ways to print multiple copies of office publications are by photocopying and offset printing. Printing by office copier is quick and convenient. Lines and large areas of black can be copied adequately, but fine details or photographs do not reproduce well. This method is not recommended for more than 100 copies.

Offset printing involves making photographs or film of the camera-ready copy. A plate is made from the photographic film; separate plates are made for each color. Note that once the film is made, it is extremely expensive to make corrections. This method results in much better quality than printing by copier. *Quick printers* are good for short runs needed quickly. *Commercial printers* are used for longer runs and more complicated jobs.

Paper

Paper costs can represent half the cost of the printing and influence the quality of a publication. Printers usually make suggestions on weight and type of paper because these decisions can be very technical.

Binding

Binding contributes to the overall impression created by a publication. There are binding methods that are mechanical and others that do not require equipment. Table 19-6 describes binding systems that can be used in the office without sending the material to a printer.

Printers and binders offer a wide range of binding options. The type of binding should be decided on before the material is printed so the publication's margins are appropriate. Word processing and page layout programs can be used to adjust margins appropriately.

HINT: *Custom binders are available for camera-ready artwork. View binders with plastic overlay on the front, back, and/or spine can help you customize binders quickly and economically.*

HINT: *Thermal binding systems are used to improve the appearance of sales presentations, reports, and other important documents.*

HINT: *Since printers usually subcontract binding work, it may be less expensive to contact a binder initially.*

DESKTOP PUBLISHING GLOSSARY

Printers and graphic artists use certain terms that may be unfamiliar. Figure 19-2 lists some definitions.

ALLEY: Space between two columns of typeset material.

BOXED COPY: Text with horizontal and vertical lines (or rules) around it.

CAMERA-READY: Of a quality appropriate for final copy and ready to be printed or photographed.

CLIP ART: Art designed by professional artists that is copyright-free and commercially available. The art may be printed on paper or stored on a disk.

CROPPING: Cutting an illustration to fit a given area or to remove unwanted background along the edges.

DESKTOP PUBLISHING: The process of designing and producing a publication with a computer.

DTP: An abbreviation for desktop publishing.

FLAG: See NAMEPLATE.

FONT: A typeface in a particular style and size. Some software programs use this term in place of TYPEFACE.

GRID: A skeleton of the finished printed page showing vertical columns, margins, and the space between horizontal lines.

HALFTONE PROCESS: A photograph broken up into fine dots for reproduction.

LASER PRINTER: A computer printer that uses a laser beam to form images on paper, a page at a time.

LAYOUT: The arrangement of text and images on a page.

LEADING: The distance between type lines, measured in points from the baseline of one line of type to the baseline of the next line. Also called line spacing.

MASTHEAD: The information in a newsletter that includes the business information, such as name and address of sponsoring organization.

MOUSE: A hand-controlled input device that gives commands to the cursor or icon on the screen.

NAMEPLATE: The top of the front page that includes the name and subtitle of the newsletter and publication date. Also called flag.

NETWORK: A system of interconnected computer systems and terminals.

PAGE LAYOUT PROGRAM: A program that allows placement of text and pictures on the screen before printing.

POINT: Unit of type measurement. One point is approximately equal to 1/72 of an inch.

RAGGED RIGHT: The uneven alignment of text along the right margin.

READABILITY: Relative ease with which a printed page can be read.

RIGHT-JUSTIFIED: The even alignment of text along the right margin.

RULES: Lines of various thickness and pattern used to divide and box text on a page.

SANS SERIF: Characters of a typeface without SERIFS.

SCANNER: Hardware that reduces an image into a grid of dots that can be stored in the computer.

SERIFS: The short lines terminating the main strokes of certain letters in a typeface.

TEMPLATE: A page grid that has been created as a guide and can be used repeatedly for similar documents.

TYPE STYLE: An assortment of styles of a typeface, such as italic and bold.

TYPEFACE: An assortment of characters of one particular kind of type. Some software programs use the word FONT instead.

TYPESETTING: The preparation of characters in a printed typeface created by a traditional metal type or by the photocomposition process.

WHITE SPACE: The blank space between text and graphics on a page.

Figure 19-2 Desktop publishing glossary.

Printed office documents should be written correctly and formatted attractively. Office professionals with excellent proofreading and editing skills can take pride in meeting professional standards. Reference books, dictionaries, and English grammar and usage manuals are essential sources for answering proofreading and editing questions. Some proofreading and editing jobs may be effectively completed by outside service providers.

Editing and proofreading are separate but integrated skills; both require concentration on the details involved in producing error-free documents. **Editing** is a process to ensure that the content of a document is accurate, clear, and complete; that the material is organized logically and free of grammatical errors; and that the writing style is appropriate for the purpose. Editing should be completed before the final copy is printed to avoid the cost of revising or rewriting. **Proofreading** entails checking copy for errors in spelling, punctuation, capitalization, statistical data, and format. It takes place at two stages—first while editing the material and again after printing the final document.

CHAPTER 20

EDITING

AND

PROOFREADING

EDITING DOCUMENTS

Productivity increases when a minimal number of document revisions are necessary. If the writer and the office professional work as a team, the editing process should be smooth. If the writer is inexperienced or careless, an office professional who has an excellent grasp of basic grammar, an understanding of the content of the material, and an appreciation for appropriate writing style can be invaluable. Be aware, however, that some writers do not appreciate having their work changed.

Language Usage

Well-written communications reflect a company's competence and reliability. Try to ensure that the principles of grammar are consistently followed.

- Review the rules of grammar by taking refresher classes at a local college, by reviewing English grammar books at the public library, or by using an up-to-date handbook for office professionals.

- Use a thesaurus to avoid repetition or overuse of a word, but be sure that the substitution does not change the meaning of the sentence.

HINT: *Sometimes you know the meaning of a word but not the word itself. Check the* Random House Word Menu *by Stephen Glazier, which organizes material by topics.*

- Check for parallel structure; e.g., that all items in a list begin with a verb.
- Check that all sentences are complete.
- Be aware of language-usage problems in areas such as: (1) noun/verb agreement; (2) homonyms; (3) word usage, such as *less* versus *fewer* or *that* versus *which;* (4) dangling participles and split infinitives; (5) pronouns/antecedents; and (6) active/passive voice.
- Use the services offered by grammar hotlines. Faculty members and graduate students at many universities and colleges answer questions from callers about spelling, punctuation, capitalization, number style, and grammar. These services are usually free.

Content

A well-written communication contains complete information and follows a logical thought pattern. Suggestions to achieve this clarity include the following:

- Be sure the document answers the who, what, when, where, why, and how questions.
- Identify the purpose of the document succinctly and directly. Will other documents follow or have other documents already been written? If so, the format and style should be similar.
- Determine whether the document is an informational piece, a sales announcement, or a new product description.
- Begin new paragraphs when introducing new ideas.
- Eliminate vague statements that lack precision or completeness. Be sure the intent of the document is clear.
- Eliminate excess verbiage; keep the facts and ideas new.
- Make the transitions from point to point smooth rather than abrupt.
- Ask a layperson to read the material to see if it makes sense.

See Chapter 17, Written Communications, and Chapter 16, Mailing Documents, E-mail Message Composition, for additional guidelines.

Style

An appropriate writing style stimulates a reader's interest in the message. To attain this goal, try to do the following:

- Present information in a logical format, with a smooth flow from sentence to sentence and from paragraph to paragraph.
- Strive for an *average* sentence length of 16 to 20 words. If successive sentences are very short, a communication may seem curt. If sentences are too long, they may be difficult to follow because they bury information.
- Use a writing style that is appropriate for the reader. Evaluate the situation to determine whether the tone of the document should be formal or informal. It pays to know your audience.
- Use words that clarify rather than confuse. Avoid unfamiliar words. Short words are preferable to long ones.
- Eliminate archaic, trendy, or slang expressions. Do not use emoticons in business communications.
- Select the correct verbs. If necessary, use a thesaurus to find verbs that are appropriate. Eliminate long runs of adjectives and adverbs.
- Use the active voice in most business communications.
- Avoid overusing a word. Check your thesaurus to locate another word.

PROOFREADING DOCUMENTS

Whether proofreading copy on a computer screen or on a printed page, it is easy to miss errors on your first review of the material. The efficient proofreader makes separate checks for format, mechanical accuracy, and statistical data.

Format

An attractive document can affect a reader's impressions of a company. Do the following when checking the overall appearance of a document:

- Scan all pages to be sure headings and subheadings as well as the spacing between these headings are consistent. If one heading begins with a verb, use verbs for other headings at the same level. Check the paragraph indentations for consistency.
- Check that page numbers are consecutive and in the same location on each page.
- Check enumerations for omissions or inaccurate numbering or lettering.

- Check that the top, bottom, and side margins are in proportion to each other. Bound reports require a wider left margin than unbound reports. (See Chapter 18, Reports.)
- Follow the company style manual if there is one. However, take the initiative to recommend companywide adoption of new formats if a document's appearance can be improved or productivity increased with the recommended changes.
- Scan outlines for number and letter accuracy. Avoid an A without a B or a 1 without a 2.
- Compare figure and table labels to the reference in the text. When you move, add, or delete material, the references may shift or get out of sequence.
- Determine whether consistent type styles and fonts were used.

Mechanical Accuracy

Producing quality documents requires precise and careful attention to details. The following points should be helpful:

- Learn basic spelling, word usage, and punctuation rules to avoid repeated checking of reference sources. Constant checking is a time waster. However, do check the dictionary or a reference manual if you are in doubt. Never guess.

HINT: The Elements of Style *by Strunk and White is an excellent usage and style manual. Another source is* Grammatically Correct: The Writer's Guide to Punctuation, Spelling, Style, Usage and Grammar *by Anne Stilman.*

- Use an on-line dictionary or thesaurus to quickly look up a word while working on a document. Many on-line dictionaries can determine what you mean even if you misspell the word initially.
- Be aware that errors often occur in certain types of words or locations in a document. Check the following areas carefully: (1) items that are enumerated; (2) long words (syllables are often omitted); (3) words at the margins or at the bottom of a page; (4) words with double letters; (5) proper names; (6) headings, subheadings, and titles; (7) word endings, such as *-tion, -ed,* or *-s;* (8) sentences with beginning and closing marks of punctuation, such as quotes and parentheses; (9) words or phrases printed in all caps; and (10) words that are similar, such as *than* for *that* or *now* for *not.*
- Check carefully for transposed letters, figures, or words.
- Check e-mail addresses for correct letters, numbers, and punctuation.
- Compare the inside address of a letter with the original source, and then check the inside address with the address on the envelope to be sure they agree. Check that

all enclosures are included and all copy notations are identified. Be sure that mailing instructions have been noted.

- Examine line endings and beginnings to be sure a word like *to* or *the* has not been printed twice.
- Recheck proper names to be sure they are spelled correctly. Titles must be accurate. If words are not familiar, proofread letter by letter.
- Check that illustration identifications match text references.
- Make sure all dates are correct by checking them against the office calendar; make sure the days of the week mentioned match the dates given.

Statistical Data

Errors in figures suggest carelessness and may cause embarrassment for a company. Proofreading numbers takes special care. Here are some suggestions for ways to proofread statistical data.

- Count the items in a series or in a tabulation on the original copy; then compare this count to the number of items on the final copy.
- Verify the accuracy of the arithmetical functions on both the original and the printed copy. Take the extra time to verify extensions and all totals.
- Verify the accuracy of all numbers by checking them twice. Check for transposed numbers. Check the decimal alignment within tabulations. Be sure the number of zeros is correct. A spell checker will not identify these types of errors.
- Check with the writer when you are not sure about spacing or using upper- or lowercase letters in formulas.

Proofreading Marks

Both you and the writer should be able to interpret and use proofreaders' marks. To use the marks, identify the location of the error in the copy itself and note the type of error in the margin closest to the error. Table 20-1 shows the standard marks proofreaders use to indicate changes on printed matter.

PROOFREADING BY YOURSELF

Teaming up with a coworker is the best way to proofread lengthy documents or statistical information. One person reads aloud to a second person who checks the copy. However, since a coworker is not always available, the following suggestions are for proofreading alone.

Table 20-1
PROOFREADERS' MARKS

EXPLANATION	NOTATION IN MARGIN	EXAMPLE
Add space	#	our tuition#plan
Align vertically	‖	‖A. Software B. Hardware
Capitalize	caps	Mary harrington
Center copy	] [	]CHAPTER I[
Close up space	⌒	a recent let⌒ter
Delete	൧	proofreading ൧
Double space	ds	ds ⌐to work. ⌐Thank you for
Insert	∧	two requests∧merit (have)
Insert apostrophe	˅	company˅s payroll
Insert colon	⊙:	Include the following items⊙
Insert comma	∧	your prompt∧helpful response
Insert hyphen	=/	well=/equipped
Insert parentheses	(/)	to obtain ten(10)
Insert period	⊙	We have her check⊙
Insert quotes	˅/˅	She said, ˅I will increase sales.˅
Insert semicolon	ˆ;	She spoke; we listened.
Let it stand	stet	arrive today at 5 p.m.
Move down	⊔	⊔Table 12-2
Move left	⊏	⊏ proofreader can use
Move material	⟲↑	(Last month's sales)↑
Move right	⊐	⊐facsimile services
Move up	⊓	⊓SECTION 2
New paragraph	¶	¶We will attend
No paragraph	no ¶	no ¶Next fall
Single space	ss	ss ⌐Please return the ⌐office supplies.
Spell out	sp	sp (Jan) 19
Transpose	tr	the last payment
Underline	___	The word their
Use boldface	bF	The task of editing
Use italic typeface	ital	a bona fide transaction
Use lowercase	lc	My recent Request
Verify data	?	The 10 a.m. meeting ?

- Place a 3- by 5-inch card or a ruler below the line you are proofreading on your final copy and your finger below the line on the original copy. This forces you to slow down your proofreading rate as you move from line to line.
- Read the copy character by character and then reread it for content. Finally, scan the entire document for format consistency.

HINT: *If the document is not too lengthy, read the material from right to left rather than the usual direction of left to right. This forces you to read each word.*

- Count lines to compare the number of printed lines with the number of lines on the original copy.
- Listen to machine-dictated material a second time while proofreading the printed copy.
- Do your proofreading during a quiet period so you can concentrate on the copy. When you are proofreading a lengthy document, take frequent breaks to prevent your eyes from getting tired.

PROOFREADING COPY ONSCREEN

Proofreading onscreen immediately after putting the information into a computer is more productive than bringing it back onscreen later. The more editing you can do onscreen, the less time it will take to review the final printed copy. The following suggestions should prove helpful for onscreen proofreading:

- Strive for "first printing, final copy." Revising always takes time.
- Use the spell checker as a routine check for obvious errors. (Update the dictionary in the program to include terms or acronyms unique to your specific company or area.)

HINT: *Remember that most e-mail programs include spell check features.*

- Use a plastic ruler to remain on the correct line when proofreading onscreen, or move the cursor from line to line as you proofread. If possible, ask someone else to proof the screen as you slowly read aloud from the original copy.
- Divide the document into convenient viewing sections for proofreading; for example, paragraph by paragraph or 10 to 12 lines at a time.
- Check a revised document carefully. Words are often omitted or rekeyed, or a new paragraph is inserted without deleting the old. Or a paragraph can be moved without deleting it at its original position. Review the copy that comes immediately before and after the revisions as well.

- Make sure references to other pages are accurate. For example, your text might refer to a list on page 8, but after you revise the copy, it's on page 7.
- Have a coworker read/spell information while you make corrections at the keyboard.
- Always proofread the final printing. Spell checkers just call attention to possible misspellings.

HINT: *A manual edit is always necessary. Some words may not be misspelled, but do not represent the words that you want; for example, omitting the "t" on "the" or using "effect" for "affect."*

SPECIAL CONCERNS ABOUT EDITING AND PROOFREADING

A current reference manual, dictionary, and thesaurus are invaluable aids. To ensure uniformity in style and English usage, recommend that everyone in your company use the same reference books.

If space does not permit an addition or revision on a page, use a separate sheet of paper on which each insertion is identified; for example, 121.1, which refers to the first correction on page 121. Correlate each correction with the appropriately numbered page and identified insertion location in the document. Make editing remarks in another color. Use a pencil so it is easier to correct your comments.

Never rely solely on your memory; always verify pertinent facts, such as dates, figures, and times. Errors in dates often occur at the beginning of a new year.

If letters sit on a desk or in an e-mail folder or inbox, the material can be confusing if there is a reference to "next week" or "within a few days" in the documents. Check the dates before sending the documents.

Prepare a style sheet that outlines the format, shows correct spellings of proper names, and lists words that cause spelling or hyphenation difficulties. Style sheets are also valuable to keep on file for future use with similar documents.

It is often advisable to put the copy aside for a while and come back to it later with a fresh eye to proofread the final copy.

Review all notations made by someone who proofreads your copy. These notations are suggestions, not "corrections." You do not have to accept all the suggestions.

USING SOFTWARE TO EDIT AND PROOFREAD

Numerous software programs and Web sites offer assistance on grammar, usage, spelling, and word usage. These programs are not substitutes for good proofreading and editing skills.

Reference Software/CD-ROMs

An electronic dictionary, like a traditional dictionary, contains word definitions, syllabification, inflected forms, and part-of-speech labels. It may include pronunciations and foreign language translations. An electronic thesaurus offers numerous synonyms for words. These software references can be called up while you are working on a document. Specialized versions for such areas as law, medicine, and engineering are helpful. Always check the copyright date of the source material. You will want the versions with the most recent dates.

Another type of dictionary software can help you locate a word you may have forgotten. If you can think of only a vague meaning or concept, key in a descriptor or two; the program provides a list from which you can select. This type of dictionary includes idioms, word origins, spelling, parts of speech, and definitions.

CD-ROMs provide numerous resources for office professionals to use while working on other documents. Because they can hold so much data, most CD-ROMs include a dictionary, thesaurus, world atlas, ZIP code directory, business writing style guide, book of quotations, and world almanac. Other features vary with the packages.

Spelling, Grammar, and Style Checkers

Spell checker, grammar, and style checker software programs are available as stand-alone applications. The stand-alone packages may or may not work with other software that you use.

Word processing software has its own built-in spell checkers; some also include grammar-check and style-check features as well as thesauruses.

Spell checkers are expandable, so you can add abbreviations, company-specific terms, and acronyms. Legal, medical, and scientific dictionaries can be included. Some spell checkers check for unintentional repetition of a word, capital letters, and singular or plural word endings. Spell checkers will only check for correct spelling; they do not check for correct use of the word. For example, spell checkers do not tell you when to use "fewer" or "less" or when to use "its" or "it's."

Grammar and style checkers identify certain types of writing deficiencies by using rule-based expert system techniques. On this basis, the checkers can only offer tips for improvement; specific corrective actions are still the author's or proofreader's responsibility. Different grammar/style checkers often produce different results and recommendations, so it is imperative that the user be competent in the use of the language.

HINT: *Grammar applications will not identify all errors and may indicate that some words or sentences are wrong when they are actually correct. Do not accept suggested corrections without question.*

The following checklist illustrates the many decisions facing potential users of applications for checking spelling, grammar, and writing style. Be especially cautious in selecting grammar programs on Web sites. Use a recognized source.

- Is the program easy to use? Is the documentation easy to understand? Are you able to download from the Internet?
- Does the program check spelling only? Does it check spelling as well as grammar and style?
- Does the program check the spelling as the document progresses or does it check the spelling in a batch mode when the document is finished?
- Is the program capable of checking foreign language documents?
- Does the critique indicate excessive use of jargon? negative terms? difficult words? clichés? abstractions? Is there a critique of sentence structure? Is a summary of the criticisms for the entire document available?
- Are the following language usage areas included?

  ▲ Subject/verb agreement
  ▲ Passive voice
  ▲ Awkward phrasing
  ▲ Sentence structure
  ▲ Plurals and possessives
  ▲ Double negatives
  ▲ Long-sequence prepositional phrases
  ▲ Long-sequence noun modifiers
  ▲ Article usage
  ▲ Superlative versus comparative usage, e.g., best versus better
  ▲ Split infinitives
  ▲ Number agreement
  ▲ Pronoun usage
  ▲ Compound adjectives
  ▲ Capitalization

- Does the spell checker automatically correct a misspelled word, or does it present a list of words from which to select, or does it highlight and allow you to correct?
- When grammatical errors are identified, are there comments explaining the rules? For example, "This sentence may be in the passive voice." Are replacement sentences offered? Are you able to change rules? Can you add rules? If a company has its own guidelines regarding style, it will want to obtain software that allows changes or additions to the rules.
- Does the program perform a second evaluation of a sentence after it has been rewritten? (The second attempt may be worse than the first one.)
- Is a readability grade-level analysis available? How many formulas or indexes are available for this readability level? (A readability level indicates the number of

years of education the reader needs to understand the document.) Index levels vary from program to program.

HINT: *Most people are more comfortable reading at one or two grade levels below their top reading level. Know the audience that will be reading the document.*

- Are the average number of words per sentence and syllables per word as well as the number of sentences per paragraph shown?
- Can the software be customized? Are you able to select the kind of writing you plan to do—for example, proposal, business letter, memo, advertising, or technical?

CHAPTER 21

ORAL

COMMUNICATIONS

The ability to speak clearly and well is essential in today's office. All office professionals must be able to listen actively to people inside and outside the company and respond with accurate information to questions and requests. Good communication requires a positive attitude that recognizes the needs of others.

RECEPTIONIST TECHNIQUES

The receptionist is often the first contact visitors have with a company, so it is vital that the receptionist create a positive impression. Larger offices usually have a reception area with a trained receptionist; in smaller offices, an office professional handles these responsibilities.

Waiting Area

Any waiting area, no matter the size, must be clean and comfortable. The following suggestions help make waiting more pleasant.

- Include current magazines with subjects that appeal to both men and women, a daily newspaper, an annual report, and/or company brochures.
- Make coffee and tea available or indicate their location.
- Have a place for coats with ample hooks or coat hangers.
- Do not allow visitors to wait in private offices unless permission has been given.
- Have a separate area for children to play if they are frequent visitors. Even if children visit infrequently, have a few children's books and toys available.
- Check the reception area every hour or so to straighten it up.

Greeting Visitors

All visitors should be treated as important guests, with courtesy and respect. You should stop what you are doing, smile, and greet the visitor. Below are some tips for making the visitor feel welcome.

- Greet the visitor with "good morning" or "good afternoon." It is not necessary to rise or shake hands, unless the visitor extends his or her hand first. If you are on the telephone, acknowledge the visitor with a nod and smile.
- Greet people by name. Use Mr., Ms., or a professional title and the visitor's last name, unless you are on a first-name basis with the visitor. Refer to your supervisor by title and last name.

HINT: *Take a business card if offered and file it. If necessary, write the visitor's name phonetically on the card to avoid mispronunciations. Brief written notes will also help you remember the visitor.*

- Offer to take the visitor's coat; indicate seating verbally or with a hand gesture.
- Keep your work area free of food or drinks and other items that detract from your professional image. Make certain that your screen saver represents the company in a positive manner; keep all personal reading material off your desk, and eliminate clutter and irrelevant personal items from your desk.

HINT: *If you must eat at your desk, make certain it is not in view of anyone who might be visiting; avoid foods with strong odors or that have been microwaved.*

- Treat everyone, including suppliers and vendors, with dignity and respect.
- Avoid initiating conversations; however, respond to visitors who wish to talk. Talk about company business in generalities and avoid controversial subjects. In answering direct business questions, it is always acceptable to say, "I'm sorry, I don't know the answer to that."
- Follow company policy in allowing unscheduled visitors to see your supervisor. Find out the reason for the visit. If the person refuses to state the reason for the visit, it may be necessary to say something like the following: "I'm sorry, but I'm unable to make an appointment without telling Ms. Garcia the purpose of your visit." When in doubt, ask your supervisor.
- Stop unknown people from going beyond the reception area. Know company policy for handling sales representatives and solicitors. Be familiar with what to do in the case of emergencies or dealing with suspicious characters.
- Keep a list of employees who speak other languages in case a visitor does not speak English. If you have difficulty understanding someone's name, ask him or her to spell it for you.

Workplace Violence

Employees, supervisors, and managers have become victims of physical assaults in the workplace. Reducing the risk of workplace assaults requires strong management commitment evidenced by a refusal to tolerate violence and the assurance that every effort will be made to prevent violent incidents. Employers should develop procedures for workplace security and appropriate training for all employees. Emergency action plans should be in place.

Employers who need assistance in addressing workplace security hazards can contact the Division of Occupational Safety and Health (OSHA), which has available pamphlets, samples of model programs, and videos. The following are violence prevention suggestions:

- Report any threat ("I wonder what would happen if . . .," "I'll get even with him," or "If they fire me, someone will get it.") to your supervisor.
- Report stalking, shouting, or otherwise intimidating behavior.
- Clearly mark exits. Have a plan for escape should a violent incident occur. This plan should be the same as the fire evacuation plan to minimize confusion.
- Observe what is going on outside the workplace and report any suspicious persons or activities to security or the police.
- Post emergency police and fire department numbers and the company's address by the phone. Ensure that telephones have direct-dial 911 access. Any delay in contacting security or emergency medical services could cost lives.
- Have a code word that informs other employees there is potential trouble. Consider a panic button and cell phones for employees in remote locations.
- Avoid meeting in a private office with anyone whom you suspect may react in a negative manner to suggestions about behavior or quality of work. Have a witness available if possible and alert another employee or security personnel.
- Invest in metal detectors, bulletproof glass, entrance controls in certain parts of the building, closed-circuit TV cameras, a ban on working alone, or private security guards if workers are engaged in a potentially dangerous occupation.
- Limit accessible cash to a small amount. Use a time-access safe for larger bills and deposit them as they are received.
- Do not fight or argue with a violent person; offer no resistance whatsoever.
- Always move slowly and explain each move before you make it.
- Make no attempt to follow a violent person from the workplace. Lock the door when he or she leaves and immediately call the police. Do not unlock the door until police arrive.
- Write down everything you remember about the person while you wait for the police to arrive.

Keeping a Record of Visitors

Some offices keep a register of visitors for security reasons or to help prepare client billing. The register should include the date, time, name and company, purpose of visit, and other information necessary for record keeping. Smaller offices typically use the appointment notations in a calendar for keeping information.

Introducing Visitors

The visitor should be escorted to the office door. If the supervisor's door is closed, knock before entering.

Proper etiquette requires introducing the visitor first. If the visitor is a lower-ranking company employee, introduce the supervisor first; for example, "Mr. Supervisor, I would like you to meet Mr. McLean, who is in the Graphic Arts Department." For frequent visitors say, "Ms. Manager can see you now; please go right in." (For additional information, see Chapter 6, Business Ethics and Etiquette.)

Delayed Appointments

No matter how carefully scheduling is done, appointments may be delayed. If the supervisor is running later than scheduled, explain the delay to the visitor. If possible, try to give the approximate length of the delay so the visitor can decide whether to wait or reschedule the appointment. If possible, call visitors ahead of time to notify them and explain the delay. If a visitor's meeting is taking longer than scheduled, call and remind the manager about the next appointment or take in a reminder note.

TELEPHONE PROCEDURES

The telephone should be used properly by everyone in a firm. What is said over the telephone and how it is said helps or hurts a company's image. Proper use of the telephone establishes a positive impression that the company's employees are friendly, efficient, and helpful.

Telephone Courtesy

Telephone etiquette is vital to creating a courteous and pleasant company image. Below are general suggestions for telephone usage:

- Speak directly into the telephone, holding the mouthpiece about an inch and a half from your lips. Do not eat, drink, or chew gum while on the telephone.
- Keep background sounds, such as a radio, low or use earphones, especially in shared areas. The clicking of the keyboard keys can be heard over the telephone. Avoid keyboarding while talking with someone unless you are entering their information in the computer.

- Avoid talking on the telephone and with a coworker at the same time. The telephone receiver will transmit sound even though the mouthpiece is covered.

- Use a pleasant, professional tone of voice. Convey through your voice that you are confident, reliable, and capable. Avoid slang, "yeah," and "OK," as well as technical words a caller may not understand.

- Be cheerful and positive.

- Vary your pitch. Keep your pitch just above your best note to open a phone conversation. Use a lower pitch when emphasizing words. Lower your voice and pitch when making telephone calls in an open room.

- Speak loud enough to be heard.

- Enunciate clearly. Use words to identify letters in spelling names and places.

A as in Able	N as in November
B as in Boy	O as in Ocean
C as in Charles	P as in Peter
D as in Dog	Q as in Queen
E as in Edward	R as in Robert
F as in Frank	S as in Sugar
G as in George	T as in Thomas
H as in Henry	U as in Uniform
I as in India	V as in Victor
J as in John	W as in William
K as in King	X as in X-ray
L as in Lincoln	Y as in Young
M as in Mary	Z as in Zero

- Use careful pronunciation.

- Talk slowly enough to be understood. Talk at about the same pace as the caller.

- Address people by their names and titles.

- Use courteous phrases such as "thank you," "please," and "you're welcome."

- Respond verbally with "yes" and "I see" when someone else is talking so they will know you are still there and listening.

- Handle as many calls as possible yourself without referring the calls to others.

- End the phone call pleasantly and professionally, preferably using the caller's name; for example, "It's been nice talking with you, Ms. Fortino." Use "good-bye" instead of "bye-bye."

- Let the caller hang up first. Hang up gently and securely.

- Return calls promptly.

- Do not worry about your regional or foreign accent unless others have a difficult time understanding you.
- Follow through with promises.

Answering Incoming Calls

To handle incoming calls effectively, it is important that an office professional and supervisor communicate daily. According to recent research, seven out of ten customers will refuse to do business with a firm again if they were badly treated on the very first encounter. The following suggestions help a supervisor and office professional keep each other informed. (For additional suggestions about time management, see Chapter 3.)

- Meet first thing in the morning to go over the schedule and prepare for the day.
- If your supervisor is working under a deadline, find out if anyone else might handle his or her calls or visitors.
- Find out whose calls are expected in order to help screen calls.
- Know ahead of time names of people whose calls should be transferred, no matter what the situation. Be aware that not every call from an important person is urgent.

Phones should be answered according to company policy, if there is one, and in such a way that a caller never has to guess whether it is the right number. Below are some suggested ways to answer phones:

▲ *Answering for the company:*
"Good morning, International Association of Administrative Professionals."

"International Association of Administrative Professionals, Maria speaking."

▲ *Answering for a department:*
"Sales, Maria Carlson speaking."
"Publications, Ms. Saleh. May I help you?"

▲ *Answering another person's phone:*
"Dr. Fenner's office, James speaking."

▲ *Answering your own phone:*
"Purchasing, Glenn Cushner speaking."

Here are some hints regarding proper phone use:

- Smiling when talking on the phone realigns the throat muscles and causes the voice to be softer, the mouth to be more open, and the jaws to be less tense.
- Keep the pitch of the voice in the medium range, which has a calming effect on callers.
- Giving your name enables the caller to address you in the conversation and imparts warmth and friendliness.
- If you are going to be away from your desk, ask someone to answer your phone or forward it to another phone, voice mail, or an answering machine.

The following suggestions help make a positive impression on incoming callers:

- Answer immediately, preferably on the first ring but before the third ring.
- Be prepared. If you are right-handed, place the telephone on your left so the right hand is available to take notes. Reverse the position if you are left-handed. And always have the following available: pen or pencil, message pad, watch or clock for noting the time, company extension numbers, and telephone book.
- Avoid the use of company jargon.
- Determine who is calling if that information is not volunteered by the caller; for example, "May I ask who's calling, please?" or "May I tell Mr. Manager who's calling?"
- Verify the pronunciation and get the spelling of the caller's name.
- Be discreet. Avoid disclosing personal information; for example, "He's not in yet," "She's still at lunch," "He usually doesn't work on Thursday afternoons—that's his day for golf." Step outside the office if a coworker or host takes an important call while you are there. If they motion you to stay seated, read any materials you may have brought to their office or look out the window. Discretion, however, does not include dishonesty. An office professional should never be expected to lie for colleagues or supervisors; it is unethical.
- Determine which calls are urgent and decide on the appropriate person to handle them. If a call is urgent, it may be necessary to interrupt a meeting or conference discreetly with a note indicating who is waiting on the phone.
- Thank the caller for calling before transferring to the desired destination. (See the section Transferring Calls below for additional information.)
- Develop scripts to cover most common calls.

Dealing with Accents

As the workplace becomes more global, talking with people who may speak differently is common. Below are some tips to improve telephone communications:

- Make prior arrangements with others who might be answering the phone from someone who may be difficult to understand. Be prepared to say, "Dr. Fenner told me to expect your call."
- Ask the person to spell his or her name. Spell it back and write it out phonetically, particularly if you are transferring the call.
- Do not pretend to understand. Ask the person to slow down so you can verify the request. Make certain they understand it is your difficulty, not theirs.
- Slow down and listen to the caller's pattern of speech. Repeat key words back to make certain you have interpreted the meaning correctly.
- Keep your voice well modulated. It is not necessary to raise your voice.
- Have a phrasebook available. Know the names of those in the company who can speak other languages.

Answering Simultaneous Incoming Calls

In order to answer a phone by the third ring, it may be necessary to interrupt one conversation to answer another line. When several incoming calls occur at once, use the following technique:

1. Put the caller on hold. (See the section Holding Calls below.)
2. Answer the next call.
3. Complete the second call only if it can be handled *quickly.*
4. Return to the original call promptly.

Consider a direct approach to answering a call, such as, "Hello, this is Carol at the XYZ Company. How may I direct your call?"

Holding Calls

Being put on hold irritates many callers. Anyone using a telephone needs to be sensitive to this and do everything possible to be polite and attentive. The following suggestions help promote goodwill, even if a caller is put on hold.

- Ask permission to put the caller on hold. For example, say "May I put you on hold?" or "Is it convenient to hold or would you prefer to call back?"; avoid "I have to put you on hold" or "Can I put you on hold?" Always wait for a response.
- Check back every 30 to 40 seconds while the person is on hold. Thank them for holding and ask if they wish to continue holding. Listening to music helps alleviate the stress of waiting. Instead of selecting a radio station or taped music for callers to listen to, consider using company-related information such as, "The 2002 International Convention and Education Forum will be held July 21–24, in Nashville,

Tennessee." Avoid keeping callers on hold for more than a minute or two unless that is their preference.

- Inform the caller if the wait is longer than you anticipated; for example: "Thank you for holding, Mr. Customer. Ms. Manager is still on the other line. Do you want to continue holding or would you prefer to have her call you back?"

Transferring Calls

Know how the transfer procedure works on your telephone system to avoid losing a caller during the transfer process. Remember to give the caller enough information to call back in case the transfer process does not work. When transferring calls, the following procedures are helpful:

- Transfer calls only if you are unable to help the caller. If the business has many incoming calls, consider a voice message that informs the caller that the receptionist is busy helping another caller and giving the caller an option of holding or leaving a message.
- Ask permission to transfer calls.
- If you do not know where to transfer a call, put the caller on hold and ask coworkers for assistance.
- Give the name and complete telephone number to the caller in case the call is disconnected during the transfer process. For example: "Mr. Customer, I think the Service Department is better able to answer your question than I am. If you don't mind, I'm transferring you to Mr. Howe's office. His number is 483–3002 in case you need to call again."
- Ask before automatically transferring to a person's voice mail. Give the name and complete telephone number in case the transfer does not work.
- Suggest having the call returned instead of transferred if the caller complains about having been transferred several times.
- Give the called party any helpful information. For example, "Carol Sekor of North Bay Construction is holding; she has a question about last month's invoice."

Cutting Short a Call

Sometimes it is necessary to terminate a call. It takes skill to end a call with enough tact that the caller feels good about the conversation. The following suggestions are useful for cutting short a call:

- Give a short, sincere explanation for getting off the telephone; for example, "I'm sorry to cut this short, but I have a visitor waiting to see me" or "Let me sum up our conversation. . . ."

- Make plans to get back with the caller if necessary; for example, "We have a staff meeting in five minutes; may I call you back?" or "Excuse me, but I'm trying to get a letter ready for overnight delivery; may I call you back?"

Taking Messages

Taking accurate messages is vital when answering the telephone for others. By some estimates, 90 percent of messages contain incorrect information, with errors ranging from names and phone numbers to reasons for calling.

To avoid taking messages or having someone place a call back, try to help the caller yourself; for example: "Ms. Wong is out of the office. I expect her back after 3:00. I'm her administrative assistant and work very closely with her. May I help you?"

If it is necessary to take a message, keep these points in mind.

- Use a form. In fact, fill out a form even if the caller indicates they will call back.
- Include both the time and date.
- Write legibly.
- Verify the caller's name, company name, and phone number by repeating back the information.
- Include as much information as possible to help the callee return the call. Attach to the message slip any material (e.g., files, invoices) that may be helpful in answering the call.
- Deliver the message promptly.

Screening Calls

The purpose of screening calls is to decide whether to transfer a call or take a message. Screening must not offend the caller. The following suggestions are helpful when screening calls.

- Avoid giving the impression that calls are being screened. Avoid asking the caller's name *first* and *then* saying the manager is unavailable. Instead, immediately state that the manager is unavailable and ask if the call can be returned, in the process finding out who is calling. If it happens to be someone the manager wishes to talk with, the call can be transferred or the following statement can be made, "May I put you on hold while I see if I can interrupt her?"
- Use judgment in determining whether the supervisor needs to talk to every important person (including relatives or higher-ranking people) immediately. It may be necessary to say, "Mr. Nunes is in a staff meeting. Do you want me to interrupt him?"
- Transfer a call if it is an emergency.

Placing Outgoing Calls

All businesses make outgoing calls. The manner of handling outgoing calls is just as important as prompt, courteous service for incoming calls. Before placing an outgoing call, you must have a reason for calling and know what you want to accomplish. This takes planning even before picking up the telephone receiver. Use the following guidelines in placing outgoing calls:

- Know the name of the person you want to reach and how to pronounce it. Check the pronunciation and spelling with others if you are unsure.
- Verify the phone number before calling. Keep frequently called numbers in an address book. Calling Information for a number costs money. Look up unknown numbers in an on-line phone directory database. Locate on-line phone directories by going to a search engine and typing in the keywords "phone numbers."
- If you reach a wrong number, do not just hang up; say, "I'm sorry; I must have dialed the wrong number." If the wrong number is long distance, immediately call the operator to receive credit on the phone bill.
- Plan outgoing calls in advance. Have all materials available and make an outline or rough script (but sound natural when talking).
- Group outgoing calls one after another to save time—but leave some time between each call in case someone is trying to reach you.
- Avoid the hours of noon to 2:00 P.M. and any other times you know to be inconvenient. Take different time zones into consideration.
- Identify yourself immediately; for example, "This is Colleen Peppard of Hargrave and Johnson."
- Ask if it is convenient to talk. If it is not convenient, make an appointment to call back; for example: "Can you talk for a minute? I have three items to discuss about the conference next week."
- Avoid calling people at home unless they request that you do so.
- Insist on calling back if the connection is faulty.
- Determine whether you might save time by sending an e-mail instead of by calling. Only use this option if you know that a person checks e-mail frequently.

Handling Complaints and Angry Callers

Resolving complaints is important to the success of any business. You want to do all you can to retain the customer or client. Angry people may use abusive language, exaggeration, sarcasm, or personal attacks. While you cannot control the angry person, you can control your reaction to the situation.

Here are suggestions for handling complaints and angry callers:

- Listen to the complaint. Listen to both the feelings and the facts. Avoid interrupting until the entire complaint has been stated, getting emotionally involved, reacting to a personal attack, or allowing yourself to get angry.

- Do not interrupt until the caller starts repeating information. This is an important signal.

- Show the caller you understand the problem by opening your answer with a sympathetic comment. "I think I understand the problem and I hear how it has affected you. What can we do to solve the problem?"

- If the caller is angry, pause before you respond and respond politely. If the caller is extremely angry, ask if you can call back. If the caller refuses, ask if you may have some time to collect needed information. This additional time may allow the caller to calm down. Putting angry people on hold may upset them more. Instead, put the phone on the desk. Express regret with a statement such as, "I'm sorry for your inconvenience."

- Find a way to agree with their circumstances. Say something like, "I understand what you are going through; I'd be upset too if it had happened to me."

- Ask open-ended questions that allow people to further explain the problem; for example, "You feel the last shipment . . . ?" Use a checklist or a script. (Allow the other person to finish the sentence.)

- Suggest three or four alternatives for handling the problem that (1) you are able to do and (2) you have the authority to do. Do *not* say, "Company policy says we can't." A statement like this says you do not make decisions, and the caller may demand to talk to a supervisor. An example of giving alternatives is saying, "I cannot give you your money back, but you can pick out another product of equal value or have credit toward another purchase."

- Transfer the call only if you are certain the individual to whom you are sending the caller can and will take responsibility for solving the problem.

- Follow up in a week to make certain the problem is resolved. Ask if there is anything else that would be of assistance.

Arranging a Conference Call

A conference call is a telephone call involving three or more people. Many phones have a conference call feature that allows office professionals to set up a call from the office telephone.

If the phone system does not have conference call capability, operator assistance is necessary. In the front of most phone directories is information on how to set up a conference call using that provider. Charges are added for the number of places connected, distance, and length of conference. If possible, give the operator advance notice of the call.

The steps for setting up the conference call are:

1. Check with the participants on their availability. Do not forget time zone differences.
2. Set the time of the conference call. Either notify the participants by telephone or in writing of the time according to their time zone.
3. Fax or e-mail an agenda ahead of time. This information helps participants gather materials and be better prepared for the call.

If operator assistance is necessary, dial 0 for the operator and explain that you wish to make a conference call. Give the operator the names and phone numbers of those taking part in the call and the time of the day of the call.

Cellular Phone Etiquette

Cellular telephones are a standard business tool. The following are suggestions for cellular phone etiquette:

- Call the work number first and leave a message before calling the cell phone number.
- Use discretion when discussing confidential information such as credit card numbers or calling card numbers.
- Select words carefully and use first names only.
- Avoid annoying melodies for the ringer.
- Use caller ID or voice messaging for your personal cell phone at work. Consider a vibrating battery.
- Take your cell phone with you or turn it off when you leave your desk.
- Turn off your cell phone during meetings and let voice mail record the message.
- Modulate your voice when speaking on a cell phone. Avoid loud, animated conversations.
- Keep conversations brief especially while in a public area or when not alone.
- Keep conversations private.
- Give priority to the people that you are with and not to the cell phone conversation.
- Inform the person whom you are calling that you are using a cellular phone. If the connection fades or drops, the person will know to wait to see if the clarity returns or that you will be calling back.
- Focus on safety first. Do not use cellular phones when they impede your ability to drive or walk. Get a hands-free kit or phone cradle holder for your vehicle or a walk about kit for your phone when out of the car.
- Do not use a cell phone inside an airplane or a hospital ward, as this may interfere with the signals or other sensitive equipment.

HINT: *For those who need added privacy, scrambling devices and enhanced privacy services are available.*

VOICE MAIL SYSTEMS

The message on the voice mail system should take into consideration the following factors:

- Rotary phones cannot access extensions or use the keypad for codes like touch-tone phones can.
- Always provide an option for people with rotary phones, such as, "If you are calling from a rotary phone, please stay on the line for an operator."
- Some people prefer to talk with people instead of machines: Voice mail should make that option available.
- Avoid catching callers in an "endless loop" of pressing buttons so they are not able to reach their intended party or get their questions answered.
- Indicate to callers if your voice mail system allows only a few minutes for a message.

For example, when you call International Association for Administrative Professionals®, you are connected to a recorded voice that says: "Thank you for calling International Association for Administrative Professionals®. If you know your party's extension, you may dial it now. If you are calling from a rotary telephone, please hold. If you are calling from a touch-tone telephone, please dial zero for assistance. Thank you."

- Listen to messages promptly. Act on each message immediately by replying, forwarding, saving, or deleting. If you need to spend more time doing research, let your caller know. Return calls within two hours.
- Delete messages frequently.
- Keep a record of your password in a secure place. Avoid simple security codes such as the same number as your voice mailbox. Use between 5 and 10 digits for your security code. The more digits you use, the harder it will be to decipher your security code.
- Update your greeting regularly, especially for vacation periods or extended absence. Callers feel most comfortable leaving a message when they know when their message will be heard and their call returned.
- Take care when recording your greeting. If you want callers to leave certain information, ask for it in your greeting. Unless reminded, callers sometimes forget to leave their full name, where they are from, or mention what they want. Always listen to you recordings after making them.

- Use distribution lists for multiple copies of messages. Learn how to transfer callers into someone else's voice mailbox. When forwarding messages, add comments so the recipients know why they are receiving the forwarded messages.

Leaving Voice Mail Messages

Voice mail technology has changed the type of messages left. Some people feel they can be as rude as they wish and use any tone of voice they want. Others leave personal, volatile, and potentially devastating messages on voice mail. Researchers think machines make such things easier because they detach people from an event and give permission to do something we would not do otherwise.

When you have a difficult or complex message to deliver and you reach voice mail, it is appropriate to say something like, "I am sorry I did not reach you. Please call me. I have some news."

If the possibility exists that you will have to leave a voice mail message, make an outline of what you have to say and check all facts and figures before placing the call. Avoid sounding like you are reading and include the following information when leaving the message:

- Your name. Spell it if it is not a very common name.
- Your phone number. Say it slowly and leave it at the beginning of the message. Many voice mail systems require listening to the entire message when replaying it.
- Leave a complete message but only one topic per message. Details can help someone begin work on a project or gather information before returning the call; however, avoid giving too many details so the receiver does not have to listen and relisten to the recorded message. Small talk is not appropriate.
- Tell the recipient how you expect him or her to reply by being specific about how you want the matter handled.
- Encourage the caller to e-mail you and give your e-mail address in your message. Suggest to the caller that e-mail messages will get more detailed responses than voice mail messages.

MEDIA RELATIONS

The most cost effective method of publicizing an event or activity is through the media. News coverage can generate additional registrations, help sales, and educate the public about your organization. Larger businesses have public relations professionals but small businesses can still effectively receive media coverage. The following are opportunities to get publicity:

- Anniversaries
- Business news

- Corporate supporters
- Events and activities
- Recognitions
- Seminars
- Technology

Establish a contact from your company. This person should consistently send the news releases and make the personal or telephone contacts with the media.

News releases can be sent to radio, television, or newspapers. The following are guidelines for news releases:

- Use professional letterhead.
- Give the essential information first; use background and additional information later in the announcement. Keep the length to two double-spaced pages.
- Highlight any celebrity or VIP appearance.
- Proofread names carefully. Make certain the news release is free of grammatical, spelling, or punctuation errors.
- Avoid industry jargon.
- Be aware of deadlines and make the contact well in advance.
- Always send a personal note or follow up with a phone call when a publication prints your news release or does a feature story.

For newspapers, send a business announcement to the business editor. If you are trying to get a feature story, contact the features editor or reporter. The most professional contact is to send a news release with a letter attached. Ask if there is a staff photographer who could cover an event. If not, enclose high-quality, black-and-white photographs. Include the name(s) of the person(s) in the picture.

The news assignment editor is the best contact at a television station. Think about what will be interesting to viewers and only contact a television station when you have something special to show.

CHAPTER 22

ELECTRONIC

COMMUNICATIONS

AND

THE

INTERNET

Electronic communications and telecommunications allow data to be electronically transferred from one point within an information system to another. In today's office, computers and other equipment can be linked together to expedite the exchange of information within a business and between organizations.

Computer networks can be set up to distribute information within a department or an office, through a local area network (LAN), or between different locations through a wide area network (WAN). Databases provide computers with an organized means of storing large amounts of information. Public databases are available that make information available to users on a subscription or non-subscription basis.

The Internet is the world's largest computer network. Millions of people use it to send e-mail, search information databases, and conduct electronic commerce. In addition to being used for communications functions, the Internet is a social system inhabited by computer-literate people and shaped by the infrastructures, standards, protocols, expertise, and values that enable these communications.

COMPUTER NETWORKS

A computer network ties different functions together electronically, allowing for improved communication and greater sharing of information among individuals, departments, other offices or satellite offices, and other locations. Networking can also reduce equipment costs because it allows several PC users to share expensive peripheral equipment, such as laser printers and high-capacity disk drives.

The administration and management of a network is usually handled by a network administrator. Any problems arising in a network usually happen because of technical and programming issues. However, it is helpful for office professionals to understand the function of networking equipment and the terms used to describe it.

Local Area Networks

A **local area network (LAN)** is used to distribute information in an office through different terminals, called **nodes,** that are connected to a central information depository, called a **server.** The server manages the flow of information between computers hooked together on the LAN, somewhat like a traffic cop who manages the flow of traffic. The server also enables users to share peripheral equipment, disk drives, and data files.

The server is connected to each terminal or node in the network by some kind of cable (twisted-pair, coaxial, or fiber-optic). The cable is connected to a **controller card** in each computer terminal. The controller card interprets the messages going to and from the network.

The term *bandwidth* (the width of a band of electromagnetic frequencies) describes (1) how fast data flows on a given transmission path, e.g., from node to node on a network, and (2) the width of the range of frequencies that an electronic signal occupies on a given transmission medium. Any digital or analog signal has a bandwidth. Generally speaking, bandwidth is directly proportional to the amount of data transmitted or received per unit time. For example, it takes more bandwidth to download a photograph in one second than it takes to download a page of text in one second. Large sound files, computer programs, and animated videos require still more bandwidth for acceptable system performance. Virtual reality (VR) and full-length three-dimensional audio/visual presentations require the most bandwidth.

Wireless Networks

Wireless LANs use a radio frequency or infrared light to transmit information, eliminating the need for cables. Wireless networks allow data connections to the Internet and other networks from airports and other public areas; quick connections to networks from office conference rooms, cafeterias, and other areas away from employees' desks; cordless connections that allow mobility during a connection; and connections between computing devices and cellular phones for e-mail and other data transfers. The two most popular types of wireless networks use either radio frequency or infrared (IrDA) technologies to transmit data. An emerging technology is Bluetooth, which connects various types of telecommunication devices, including personal computing, networking, industrial, automotive and consumer electronics.

The Wireless Application Protocol (WAP) is a secure specification that allows users to access information instantly via handheld wireless devices such as mobile phones, pagers, two-way radios, smartphones, and communicators. WAP is supported by all operating systems and supports most wireless networks. WAPs that use displays and access the Internet run microbrowsers—browsers with small file sizes that can accommodate the low memory constraints of handheld devices and the low-bandwidth constraints of a wireless-handheld network.

Desktop Management Networking Standards

The Distributed Management Task Force Ltd. (DMTF) is the industry organization that is leading the development, adoption, and unification of management standards and initiatives for desktop, enterprise, and Internet environments. Working with key technology vendors and affiliated standards groups, the DMTF is enabling a more integrated, cost-effective, and less crisis-driven approach to management through cross-platform management solutions.

The DMI [Desktop Management Interface] 2.0 standard is the basis for the industry's first truly open management platform. The DMI standard significantly increases the ease-of-management of desktop systems and servers by reducing platform-specific barriers. DMI-enabled systems can be monitored, accessed, and controlled by DMI-based management tools running in heterogeneous environments. For the first time, systems can be mixed, matched, and managed in a consistent manner across multiple operating system and hardware platforms.

If you have general questions about the DMTF or DMTF Technologies, contact the

Distributed Management Task Force Ldt.,
c/o MacKenzie Kesselring, Inc.,
200 S.W. Market Street, Suite 450,
Portland, OR 97201,
503–416–2116,
503–225–0765,
dmtf-info@dmtf.org

Electronic Mail

A major application of networks is electronic mail. E-mail is the sending and receiving of messages in electronic form between computers in a network. Messages can be stored, saved, and edited. They can also be forwarded or copied to another user or users. A user can also reply to a message. (See section on Electronic Mail in Chapter 16.)

Voice E-Mail

Voice e-mail is more friendly and personal than regular e-mail. It allows a caller to convey emotions on-line by using his or her voice instead of the keyboard. Voice e-mail add-on programs enable you to send and receive voice messages exactly like regular e-mail; the only difference is that instead of typing your messages, you digitally record them. The advantages are obvious: input is faster, there are no editing or spelling issues, you can be creative in providing sound effects, and you can include pictures and photographs in your voice e-mail messages.

Modems and Other Interface Devices

Computers operate using digitally encoded electronic signals (see section on the Computer in Chapter 7). Telephone lines transmit analog electronic signals. For a computer to transmit and receive information over a telephone line, a **modem** is needed at each end. Modem stands for "modulator-demodulator." A modem translates (or "modulates") digital signals into analog signals for transmission over a phone line. At the other end, another modem converts the analog signals back into digital form for the receiving computer. A modem is sometimes also called a **data set.**

The following characteristics distinguish one modem from another:

- **bps:** How fast the modem can transmit and receive data. At slow rates, modems are measured in terms of baud rates. The slowest rate is 300 baud (about 25 characters per second, often abbreviated cps). At higher speeds, modems are measured in terms of bits per second (bps). The fastest modems run at 57,600 bps, although they can achieve even higher data transfer rates by compressing the data. Obviously, the faster the transmission rate, the faster you can send and receive data. For example, a 56-baud modem operates at a speed of 33.6 to 56 kilobits per second. Efficient transmission of voice, graphics, and video images requires even faster modems. A 10-megabyte video clip, for example, takes 28.4 minutes to transfer from one computer to another with a 56-baud modem. This same file could be transferred on a T1 telephone circuit (speed rate of 1.5 megabits per second) in 52 seconds and on a cable modem (speed rate of 4 megabits per second) in 20 seconds. Cable modems are available from cable TV services and are used to connect a personal computer with a coaxial television cable.

- **voice/data:** Many modems support a switch to change between voice and data modes. In data mode, the modem acts like a regular modem. In voice mode, the modem acts like a regular telephone. Modems that support a voice/data switch have a built-in loudspeaker and microphone for voice communication.

- **auto-answer:** An auto-answer modem enables your computer to receive calls in your absence. This is only necessary if you are offering some type of computer service that people can call in to use, for example a computer photographic and digital services company.

- **data compression:** Some modems perform data compression, which enables them to send data at faster rates. However, the modem at the receiving end must be able to decompress the data using the same compression technique.

- **flash memory:** Some modems come with flash memory rather than conventional ROM (read-only memory), which means that the communications protocols can be easily updated if necessary.

- **fax capability:** Most modern modems are fax modems, which means that they can send and receive faxes.

Analog Modem Standard

Older, slower analog modems used a **V.34 modem standard.** This standard has been replaced by the faster **V.90 modem standard.** Modem users are often confused about setting their modem's connect speed at 115,200 instead of a slower speed. These speeds are the Data Terminal Equipment (DTE) speed, which is the speed of the connection between your PC and your modem. The Data Communications Equipment (DCE) speed is often the bottleneck when communicating via modem. The DCE speed is the speed between your modem and the modem to which you are connecting. Prior to V.90 modems, the best speed between two modems was 33,600 bits per second. With the advent of V.90 technology, rates approaching 50,000 bits per second are achievable. It is also important to note that the send and receive data speeds are different when you connect in V.90 mode. High speed (up to 54K bps) is realized in the downstream direction, which is a plus when users are downloading graphics, and large files from the Internet. The upstream direction is limited to 33.6K bps, slower but acceptable, since most of the data Web surfers send is mouse click commands, which don't require much data to be transmitted.

An improvement on the V.90 dial-up modem specification is forthcoming from the International Telecommunications Union (ITU). The **V.92 standard** introduces three features that add convenience and performance for the modem user. The three features are quick connect, modem-on-hold, and PCM Upstream.

- *Quick Connect* shortens by 50 percent the time it takes to make a connection for most calls. It does this by remembering ("training") the phone line characteristics and storing them for later usage. Typically, the modem "handshake" takes from 25 to 27 seconds.
- *Modem-on-Hold* allows you to receive an incoming call and stay connected to the Internet (Call Waiting service from your phone company is all that is required). It also works in reverse; you can initiate a voice call while connected and keep the modem connection. The V.92 specification allows for hold times from 10 seconds to infinite.
- *PCM Upstream* boosts the upstream data rates between the user and Internet Service Provider (ISP) to reduce upload times for large files and e-mail attachments. A maximum of 48K bps upstream rate is supported.

Digital Connections

Anyone who has used a modem knows the problems associated with an analog dial-up access modem: You have to wait for your modem to dial a number and establish a connection to your ISP. A digital connection provides users with a dedicated, "always on" connection. It is also faster and easier to share with a large group of users. There are different types of digital connections:

ISDN (Integrated Services Digital Network): This is considered the next speed step above a 56K modem. The speed increase can be substantial, from 64K bps to 128K bps. But ISDN is not a true "always on" connection. Most ISDN providers will bill per-minute charges for the time you spend connected to the Internet. Many people consider ISDN to be a fading technology.

Frame Relay: Frame relay is a connection to the Internet that is owned by the telephone company and shared by many users. Frame relay ISPs provide a Committed Information Rate (CIR) for the minimum transmission speed they will guarantee. Transmission speeds vary from 64K bps to 1.54M bps.

Satellite: Satellite connectivity is becoming a viable alternative for high-speed Internet access. The problem with satellite is that it is available only for downloading data. Users need a modem to send information out. Downstream speed is up to 400K bps. Upstream speed is related to your modem speed (up to 56K bps).

Cable: Cable connects you to the Internet through a coaxial cable, often using the same line that carries your cable TV service. Cable is heavily marketed to home users, and for many smaller organization without DSL or the budget to get T1, it is the only viable high-speed option. Speeds vary from 200K bps to 30M bps for download speeds and 128K bps to 3M bps for upload speeds.

DSL: DSL describes several types of DSL (Digital Subscriber Line) technologies, including ADSL, which provides different upload and download speeds, and SDSL, which provides the same speed in both directions and is most popular with businesses. Speeds vary from 144K bps to 8M bps for download speeds and 128K bps to 8M bps for upload speeds.

T1: A T1 line can connect an entire office to the Internet. Sometimes referred to as a leased line, a T1 is a private, dedicated line that goes directly from your office to your ISP. If that much speed is not required, fractional T1 leased lines are available. This is simply a T1 line split into segments and divided among users. Leased lines provide guaranteed bandwidth, since they are not shared with other users. Data speed transmission varies from 64K bps to 1.54M bps.

T3: For organizations that need the fastest available connection to the Internet, a leased line connection is also available at T3 speed (45M bps) or fractional T3 speed (starting at 3M bps). T3 is primarily used by ISPs.

Private Branch Exchange

The type of phone system used in the office is important when considering modems and other telecommunication devices. Currently most office phone systems are private branch exchange (PBX) systems. These are telephone facilities within an office or office building that connect to the public phone network. A PBX switches calls between enterprise users on local lines while allowing all users to share a certain number of external phone lines. A PBX includes telephone trunk (multiple phone) lines that terminate at the PBX; a computer with memory that manages the switching of the calls; the network of lines with the PBX; and oftentimes a console or switchboard for a human operator.

Wireless PBX: A wireless PBX system can be integrated into a PBX to provide employees with a portable telephone as an extension to their desktop telephone. This allows employees to keep the same extension number with the freedom of a mobile phone. A wireless system also allows for the integration of mobile cellular service.

ELECTRONIC COMMUNICATIONS THROUGH DATABASES

A database provides computers with a means of storing information. It is a large and continuously updated file on a particular subject or subjects.

Databases can be used for various applications. They are limited only by the user's imagination and needs. Small and large companies use databases to maintain inventories or process orders. Banks use databases to maintain checking and savings accounts. The government uses databases to track income taxes owed by citizens. Databases can be private or public.

Private Databases

A private database is one developed specifically for a company or organization and is not available to the general public. An example of a private database would be the customer list for XYZ Company. This database would contain information on customers, their orders, their addresses, and so forth. It would be used by management and office professionals.

Private databases are generally determined by the computer sophistication of a company. It is important to understand that a well-organized database can help employees quickly analyze, compute, and report what might otherwise take months to do manually. It could be the responsibility of the office professional to help establish a database or work with the management or information system personnel to use and further develop the database.

Public Databases

Information utilities have capitalized on the explosive need for information. An information utility is any organization that will let an individual use its information (or someone else's), usually for a fee. The information utility may use one database or several and offer many services. An individual can search and retrieve information on a variety of topics from airline information, to news and sports, to stock quotes. Different utilities specialize in different types of information.

To reach these information utilities, an individual typically either calls directly or calls through **Telenet**® or **Tymnet**® (two services that save long-distance phone charges). When connected with the utility, a person logs on, using a password and account number. Prices for these utilities range from a few dollars to several hundred dollars per hour. Some have sign-up charges, monthly minimums, subscriptions, consulting fees, and other fees associated with their use. A thorough understanding of the fees is necessary to avoid possible billing problems.

Information utilities are an outgrowth of several different technologies. They combine communications technologies (information delivered by phone lines, cable, or television), space technology (satellites), and computer technology (software and computer programming used to assemble large amounts of information or databases and retrieve them).

Information utilities offer various kinds of service, including transaction-based, communication-based, and information-based. **Transaction-based services** include shopping services, computerized classifieds, theater ticket sales, plane reservations, and at-home banking. It is essentially shopping by computer. Within the office, the service that would probably be utilized most is the one for making plane reservations.

Communication-based services include e-mail (see above), computerized bulletin boards, and on-line conferences. E-mail is a service that is used to send a message to anyone also using the system. A message is sent to a person's electronic mailbox. The next time that person goes to read his or her mail, the message will be there. America Online® (AOL®), for example, provides an electronic mailbox service for its subscribers.

Computerized bulletin boards function like real bulletin boards. A message is "posted" in the system and can be read. Usually bulletin boards are devoted to one subject or group of people, such as all users of IBM® personal computers or individuals with the same hobby. To use them, a modem, telephone, and computer are needed. Users dial an access number and log on to the system. To "log on" simply means that an individual has electronically connected into the system—in this case, the bulletin board.

On-line conferences or forums are written conversations between two or more people. Such conferences can be a club or professional group meeting in different locations by computer.

Information-based services are really electronic libraries. They contain everything from bibliographic research services to stock market quotes to electronic newspapers. These services are particularly useful for doing research. Reference information is available in abstract and/or full-text form.

Using on-line databases requires some special knowledge and involves certain considerations. Professionals are available in many companies to search on-line databases for the necessary information. However, if the responsibility is the office professional's, several tips are offered here:

- Don't be intimidated. The more you use a database service, the easier it gets.
- Check the bulletin board. On-line bulletin boards and communications services can be used for learning more about database searches.
- Be prepared. Know what you are looking for before going on-line.
- Remember that every database is unique and may require special search techniques.
- When searching through full text, first look at headlines and lead paragraphs. Then focus on those that seem most promising.
- If possible, make global searches of all databases that may be of interest.
- Every database is priced differently and some are free. Try the less expensive ones first.

- Download the documents you want and read them later to reduce on-line time. Save the articles on disk instead of printing.
- If your research needs are varied or infrequent, it may make sense to pay a professional to do the searching.

Information Utilities

Just as there are different services offered, there are also different kinds of information utilities. Each uses different technology. They are (1) **teletext,** (2) **videotext,** and (3) **interactive databases**.

TELETEXT

This is an information utility that sends its information by television. Teletext is a generic term that applies to several different specific systems. One of those systems is used by PBS, NBC, ABC, and CBS in their closed-caption system for the hearing impaired.

Each "page" contains one screen of information and is sent along with the regular television transmission. The system puts the teletext information into the black bars that show up between normal television picture frames.

To use teletext, a special adaptor is required. The pages include a table of contents with the page numbers. When the page number is entered into the adaptor, that page shows up on the television screen.

VIDEOTEXT

This is an information utility that puts information into a computer (text or graphics or both), transmits that information, and displays that information on a modified television set (in the form of pages) e.g., WebTV.® Using videotext is much the same as using teletext. An individual sits in front of the television with an adaptor, punches in the numbers of the pages wanted, and the pages show up on the screen. With this system, connection is directly to a computer. The television functions like a computer terminal. The system is asked directly what is wanted, and it will respond.

INTERACTIVE DATABASES

These services are available on-line (i.e., connected by personal computer terminal to the service's mainframe computer) or offline. The latter type is available through CD-ROM disks. The on-line type of system uses time-sharing (technology that allows many people to use the same computer at the same time). An interactive process allows a command to be entered to find all information dealing with a specific topic. It is not necessary to look through menus—the system tells what stories or information fit the description. From that listing, a user can select which items he or she wishes to review. The computer then pulls those articles from the database.

Compact optical disks (CD-ROM) provide interactive information. Instead of connecting on-line using the computer terminal, the subscriber uses a CD-ROM disk that is accessed by a special drive on the personal computer. Many on-line databases, such as Educational Resource Information Clearinghouse (ERIC®), are now available on CD-ROM. The advantage of CD-ROM is that it saves telephone costs. The disadvantage is that information is not always up to the minute.

THE INTERNET

The **Internet** is a network of computer networks connected together world-wide. On these networks are millions of computers, computer terminals, and users. The Internet has become the world's largest group of computers connecting government bodies, universities, libraries, and businesses. Over the Internet, people can send messages to one another, participate in interest groups, gather research information, or even buy and sell.

Browsers or **graphical user interfaces (GUIs)** are software applications based on the Hypertext Markup Language (HTML). These applications make it easy to use the Internet. The two most popular browsers, accounting for 95 percent of the browser market for the desktop/laptop computer, are Internet Explorer and Netscape. Two popular alternative browsers are Opera® and NeoPlanetShort®. All of the above browsers are graphical browsers, meaning they can display both graphics and text, as well as multimedia information, including sound and video.

Mobile equipment, such as personal digital assistants, cell phones, and other pocket PC devices, use a browser based on the Wireless Application Protocol (WAP) that allows cell phones and other mobile devices with tiny screens, displaying text-based interfaces, to retrieve information from the Internet and conduct e-commerce activities. Phones running WAP will conduct wireless stock trading, purchasing from Internet vendors, surfing the Internet, and email send/receive activities. Future wireless browsers will duplicate for users with a handheld device the browsing experience of the desktop. This includes viewing the full text and images of any Web page without excessive scrolling.

Domain Name System (DNS)

Every computer on the Internet has a unique address—similar to a telephone number—which is a complex string of numbers. The sequence is called an IP (Internet Protocol) address. The Domain Name System (DNS) makes browsing easier for users by linking strings of letters (the "domain name"—www.icann.org, for example) to the numerical address (192.0.34.65, for example, which would bring you to the same Web page). This mnemonic device makes addresses easier to remember.

The Internet Corporation for Assigned Names and Numbers (ICANN®), a global, nonprofit, private-sector organization, oversees the processes and systems that ensure that each domain name maps to the correct IP address.

The top level domains (TLDs) most often used are .gov (Federal Government), .mil (military), .edu (education), .org (organization), .net (networks), and .com (commercial). ICANN® is working to add seven new TLDs (top level domains) to the Internet's domain-name system:

- **.biz** (for businesses and corporations): For more information visit the Web site of NeuLevel℠, Inc.: www.nic.biz.
- **.info** (for information-based services such as newspapers, libraries, and so on): More information is available at the Web site of Afilias℠ Limited: www.nic.info.
- **.name** (for individuals and personal Web sites): See Global Name Registry for more information, at www.nic.name.
- **.museum** (for museums, archival institutions, and exhibitions): Contact the Museum Domain Management Association (MuseDoma™ at www.nic.museum.)
- **.coop** (available only to cooperatives): Contact the National Cooperative Business Association (NCBA) at www.cooperative.org for information.
- **.aero** (for services and companies dealing with air travel): Contact the Société Internationale de Telecommunications Aéronautiques SC (SITA) for information at www.information.aero.
- **.pro** (for professions such as law, medicine, accounting, and so forth): More information is available from RegistryPro, Ltd, at www.registrypro.com.

Sponsored domains, such as .coop, are open only to a defined community represented by the sponsor. Unsponsored and restricted domains, like .gov and .edu, can be used only by organizations that meet the eligibility criteria: .gov can only be used by governments, .edu can only be used by four-year educational institutions. Unsponsored and unrestricted domains, like .com, .org, and .net, can be used by anyone. Most noncommercial organizations use .org, and most commercial businesses use .com to characterize their operations. Domain names in .biz, .info, and .name can be registered only through ICANN®-accredited registrars and their resellers. A list of accredited registrars is on the InterNIC® Web site (www.internic.net).

A list of two-letter country-code top level domains, such as .au (Australia) and .uk (United Kingdom), is available at www.iana.org/cctld/cctld-whois.htm. These domains are administered by country-code managers. Information about each country manager is available by clicking the appropriate country code.

Internet E-Mail

A popular benefit of the Internet is the capability to send messages to colleagues around the world without using a postage stamp. Your e-mail address is divided into two parts and is determined by the nature of the Internet account that you established—for example, an on-line service or a direct connection via your LAN through your company's direct, high-speed connection.

The first part of your address is your login name. This is the name of your account or the name you use each time you access the Internet. Usually names are used, such as *jdoe* for *Jane Doe.* However, some people may use a code name.

A domain name comprises the second part of your Internet address. This name identifies computers and groups of accounts. For example, *.gov* is the domain name used by the U.S. government. Subsets or levels of domains are also used. For example, the White House uses *whitehouse.gov* as its address. The higher-level domain is always to the right; the lower-level domain, to the left. Each domain subset is separated by a period, called a "dot." Always check with your service provider or employer, in case of a direct connection, for the correct domain name.

The login name is always to the left of the domain name(s), separated by @, called "at." For example, if you wanted to send a message to the president, you would use this address: *president@whitehouse.gov.* If you are buying access from a service provider for yourself or your company and can pick a domain name, consider your location. For instance, *jdoe@albany.ny.us* refers to Jane Doe of Albany, New York, United States. When sending a message to a group of people, address the message to one person and then cc (carbon copy) and list the addresses of the other e-mail users.

When sending e-mail to someone using an on-line service such as America Online® (AOL®), you need to know the identification (ID) or on-line address of the user, for example, name@aol.com. Other on-line services have their own protocol for using the Internet.

You may wish to attach files to your e-mail messages. Some mail systems also allow you to include a link to a Web site within your message (rather than sending a Web page as an attachment), so the recipient can click straight through to an Internet reference or site that you want to discuss.

A major advantage of the attachment function is that the recipient can store important documents that are sent electronically. When sending files, keep in mind that the recipient has to have a copy of the same software program that generated the document to be able to open it.

A major disadvantage of the attachment feature is that it is the way most computer viruses are transmitted. When unsuspecting computer users receive an e-mail virus, they may accidentally infect their own computer system. Users who connect via Microsoft Outlook® or Outlook Express® can unwittingly send e-mails containing the virus to all the contacts in their address book. You can minimize the danger of infection by always scanning attached files with a good antivirus software program. The two best known antivirus products on the market are McAfee Virus Scan® and Norton AntiVirus.® A good rule of thumb is NEVER to open an attachment that you're unsure about, even if it came from a friend. Ask the sender about it first. Also, never open any file with a .vbs extension. This is a scripting file that most likely will harm your system. Another option is to install a program that alerts you when scripts are going to run on your computer and stops them before they run. One such program is AnaloGX's Script Defender.

Be sure to record and store the Internet and on-line addresses of your colleagues. Keep them in your address file. Also, when sending e-mail messages avoid hard-to-read ALL CAP messages. Be sure to check your messages often.

Junk Mail and Spamming

A business's image can be tarnished if it uses junk mail and spam (massive posting of ads in irrelevant discussion forums) as a means to obtain sales. Junk mail and spam impose massive expenses on unwilling victims. If you encounter unwelcome advertising in a newsgroup, discussion forum, or e-mail, don't post a reply in the same forum and don't reply to the "from" address—it's probably a fake. You can check news.admin.net-abuse.misc, a newsgroup that will allow you to find out what others know about the incident. (See Internet Newsgroups, below.) You can also contact the National Fraud Information Center (http://www.fraud.org) if the spamming appears to consist of illegal activity or fraud.

Major e-mail programs include tools to block spam with filters that scan an incoming message's domain name, subject heading, text, and other elements. You can customize filters based on addresses or text in the spam message. Design the filter to automatically direct any incoming mail containing the letters *XXX* in the body of the message to a folder named *Junk Mail.* Or, set up a filter to sort out e-mail with subjects lines including words such as *Quick Cash.*

Spam filtering utilities work with your e-mail client. Some offer up to 15,000 filters, based on addresses of known spammers or common text strings. Other spam filters delete spam before you download and read it.

Internet Newsgroups

A **newsgroup** is a worldwide bulletin board system of forums or discussion groups. Anyone with an interest in a topic can participate by posting and replying to messages. Newsgroups do not contain separate file libraries and many are unmoderated. They can be used to discuss business, share information on the best restaurants for entertaining clients, and acquire end-user information on computers or software you may be planning to purchase.

A large number of newsgroups are part of a system called **Usenet.** Independent of the Internet, Usenet is also a network of networks. The system's traffic is routed largely over the Internet. Usenet relies on a hierarchical system, going from left to right, for its host addresses. A series of descriptive words is used, separated by periods. For example, the newsgroup *rec.arts.movies* is part of the broader recreational *(rec)* category. Other popular categories include *comp* for computer-related subjects, *news* for information about newsgroups themselves, *sci* for discussions about the hard sciences, *soc* for information about different types of societies and subcultures, and *misc* for all kinds of topics.

Users will encounter a different network culture on Usenet with its own rules and regulations about behavior. Here are guidelines to help you:

- Begin newsgroup surfing by reading the *news.announce.newusers* group for background information.

- Always read messages before you post your own messages to learn what issues have been discussed.

- Read the frequently asked questions (FAQ) lists posted in individual newsgroups.

- Use lines of 80 characters to format your messages and don't right-justify text. Also, never submit messages in ALL CAPS and do not use special control characters or tabs.

- Use clear and descriptive titles to help readers to scan through the messages by subject.

- When replying to a message, summarize the part to which you are responding. Do not repeat the entire message.

- Don't post "me too" messages in response to a query.

Conducting an Internet Search

Finding useful information quickly on the Internet is possible when you use the correct search tools. The number of Web servers and Web pages will continue to grow, making it necessary to take advantage of the excellent tools that are available for finding information. Subject search utilities make it easy to work your way through the Internet. Two categories of search tools dominate: subject indexes and search engines—and combinations of the two.

Subject Indexes: These are lists of links organized into subject categories and may provide the best strategy if you are still figuring out what information you need. They are analogous to a table of contents in a book. Subject indexes include **Alta Vista**®, **WWW Virtual Library, The English Server** (from the University of Washington, concentrating on the humanities), and **Nerd World**®.

Search Engines: Instead of looking through lists of lists (subject indexes), a keyword or key phrase is entered onto a line or into a box and the search engine does the work. All documents containing matching words or phrases in appropriate fields appear on the screen. Keyword searching is a good strategy when you have a specific word or phrase in mind, for example, the name of a technical term or a product. **Lycos**®, developed at Carnegie Mellon University, is one of the most powerful and frequently used search engines. Other popular search engines include Excite℠, WebCrawler,™ and WWW Yellow Pages (one of several "Yellow Page" Web directories offering links to many corporate sites).

Combinations of the above two categories also are available, offering the advantages of both. **Yahoo!**® is one of the largest and most complete centralized subject indexes with a search engine on the Internet. It has categorized Web sites into 14 main topics and hundreds of subtopics. Others include Planet Earth, with a geographic emphasis, and EINet Galaxy, where librarians compile and organize information using a vertical structure within defined subjects.

A meta-search engine can quicken your keyword search through hundreds of databases. Four of the major meta-search engines are: Ixquick, MetaCrawler, Dogpile, and Mamma.com.

When conducting a search, always use more than one index or search engine. Also, when you discover Web pages to which you would like to come back in the future, mark them with your Bookmarks menu, which allows you to add pages to your own personal list.

Citing Electronic Sources

A bibliographic reference for citing electronic sources consists of elements similar to those used in other types of documentation. The citation should include the name of the author, the title, place of publication, publisher's name, date of publication, and a designation of the location, or page number, of a reference. Many styles also include a designation of the publication medium. However, with electronic sources, not all of these elements are always available.

The following examples and supporting rationale are taken, with permission from *The Columbia Guide to Online Style,* by Janice R. Walker and Todd Taylor, and is available from Columbia University Press. This style reference offers many examples and other information of use to the modern writer and researcher. Contact Columbia University Press at www.columbia.edu/cu/cup/sales/order.html for ordering information. This information is continually changing, so consult www.columbia.edu/cu/cup/cgos/idx__basic.html for the latest updates.

Preparing the Bibliographic Material: Bibliographic listings of electronic sources follow the format for whatever style you are using for print sources, i.e., humanities styles, such as *Modern Language Association* or *Chicago Manual of Style,* or scientific styles, such as *American Psychological Association* or *Council of Biology Editors.* The basic formats for citing electronic sources presented here are in the *MLA* style. Other styles are available at the Web site reference cited above.

The following examples are grouped according to method of access, or protocol, which is a key element in locating and accessing electronic documents and files. For a more complete listing and further information, see *The Columbia Guide to Online Style.*

The World Wide Web (WWW): To cite files available on the World Wide Web, give the author's name (if known), last name first; the full title of the work, in quotation marks; the title of the complete work (if applicable), in italics; any version or file numbers; and the date of the document or last revision (if available). Next, list the protocol (e.g., "http") and the full URL, followed by the date of access in parentheses.

> Burka, Lauren P. "A Hypertext History of Multi-User Dimensions."
> *MUD History.* 1993. http://www.utopia.com/talent/lpb/muddex/essay (2
> Aug. 1996).

E-mail, Discussion Lists, and Newsgroups: Cite the author's name (if known) or the author's e-mail or login name (the part of the e-mail address before the @ sign), followed by the subject line of the posting, enclosed in quotation marks; the date of the message if different from the date accessed; and the name of the discussion list (if applicable), in italics. Next, give the address of the list , or the protocol and address of the newsgroup, followed by the date accessed in parentheses.

> Crump, Eric. "Re: Preserving Writing."
> *Alliance for Computers and Writing*
> *Listserv.* acw-l@unicorn.acs.ttu.edu
> (31 Mar. 1995).

Information Available Using Gopher Protocols: List the author's name (if known), last name first; the title of the paper or file, enclosed in quotation marks; the title of the complete work (if applicable), in italics; and the date of publication (if known), including any previous publication information (if applicable). Include the protocol (i.e., "gopher"), the address, the gopher search path or directories followed to access the information (if applicable), and, in parentheses, the date the file was accessed (if applicable).

> African National Congress. "Human Rights Update for Week No. 10
> from 5/3/96 to 11/3/97." gopher://gopher.anc.org.za: 70/00/hrc/1997
> /hrup97.10 (1 Jan. 1998).

Information Available Using File Transfer Protocols (FTP): Give the author's name (if known), last name first; the full title (of a shorter work in quotation marks; of a larger work, in italics); and the document date (if available). Next, give the protocol (i.e., "ftp") and the full FTP address, including the full path needed to access the file. Last, list the date of access, enclosed in parentheses.

> Johnson-Eilola, Johndan. "Little Machines: Rearticulating Hyper-
> text Users." 3 Dec. 1994. ftp://ftp.daedalus.com/pub/CCCC95/johnson-
> eilola (14 Aug 1996).

Information Available Using Telnet Protocols: List the author's name or alias, last name first (if known); the title of the work (if applicable), in quotation marks; the title of the full work or Telnet site (if applicable), in italics; the date of publication or creation (if known); and finally the protocol (i.e., "telnet") and complete Telnet address, any directions necessary to access the publication, and the date of the visit, enclosed in parentheses. Separate commands from the address with a single blank space.

> traci (#377). "DaedalusMOO Purpose Statement." *WriteWell.* tel-
> net://moo.daedalus.com:7777 help purpose (30 Apr. 1996).

Synchronous Communication Sites. Include the name or alias of the author or speaker (if known); the type of communication (i.e., "Personal interview") or, for synchronous conferences, the session title (if applicable), enclosed in quotation marks; the site title (if applicable), in italics; the protocol and address, including any paths or directories, the command sequence (if applicable), and, in parentheses, the date of the conversation.

> Kiwi. "Playing the Jester Is Hard Work." *DaMOO.* telnet://damoo. csun.edu:7777 (4 Dec. 1996).

Online Reference Sources. Give the author's name (if known); the title of the article, in quotation marks; the title of the complete work, in italics; any print publication information, including the date; information concerning the online edition (if applicable); the name of the online service, in italics, or the protocol and address and the path or directories followed; and, in parentheses, the date of access.

> "Fine Arts." *Dictionary of Cultural Literacy.* 2nd ed. Ed. E. D. Hirsch, Jr., Joseph F. Kett, and James Trefil. Boston: Houghton Mifflin. 1993. INSO Corp. *America Online.* Reference Desk/Dictionaries/Dictionary of Cultural Literacy (20 May 1996).

Electronic Publications and Online Databases. List the author's name (if known), last name first; the title of the article, in quotation marks; and the title of the software publication, in italics. Next, list any version or edition numbers or other identifying information, the series name (if applicable), and the date of publication. Finally, cite the name of the database (if applicable) and the name of the online service—both in italics—or the Internet protocol and address, any other publication information, the directory path followed (if applicable), and, in parentheses, the date accessed.

> Christopher, Warren. "Working to Ensure a Secure and Comprehensive Peace in the Middle East." U.S. Dept. of State Dispatch 7:14, 1 Apr. 1996. *FastDoc.* OCLC. File #9606273898 (12 Aug. 1996).

Software Programs and Video Games. Cite the name of the author or corporate author (if available); the title of the software program, in italics; the version number (if applicable and if not included in the software title); and the publication information, including the date of publication (if known).

> ID Software. *The Ultimate Doom.* New York: GT Interactive Software, 1995.

Creating a Web Business Page

Software is available to assist in getting a business onto the Internet. A Web page is similar to a Yellow Pages ad in the phone book, with a major exception. When composing a Web page, the author uses hyperlinked multimedia elements. The standard authoring language is known as **Hypertext Markup Language (HTML).** This language allows your documents to include audio, video, text, graphic, and tables. Links can be made to e-mail, Usenet news, and other Web sites.

Companies of all types use the Internet to promote their products or provide product-related information.

The following suggestions can help you create or update a Web page:

- Create your page for your audience. Keep in mind what type of connection and browser the users will be deploying. Don't create something that is so graphic-intensive that users find it difficult to access the information.
- Include the following items in your home page: title, contact person's e-mail address, copyright information, and the last time the page was updated.
- Organize your Web page so a reader can scan through it. The pages should be simple and self-explanatory so readers do not have to scroll through the entire document to find desired information. Each page should be written and designed to stand alone, and no page should rely on another.
- Graphics can enhance a Web page but too many can be a problem. If images take too much time to download, readers often get tired of waiting and leave the Web site. If your Web page includes many graphics, provide readers with the option of choosing to read the site as text only. Keep audio and video clips to a one-minute viewing time.
- Consider including a search engine on the home page if you have a large database of information to make available.
- Test your Web page on both Internet Explorer® and Netscape® browsers and have different people evaluate it.
- Spellcheck and proofread your site's text, and be sure to test your links, before launching your site. Consider using a testing service such as Net Mechanic® (www.netmechanic.com).

INTRANETS

Because of the increasing availability of encryption and authentication tools, companies can build secure **intranets** (private networks) over the Internet to protect electronic commerce applications. First-generation products, such as firewalls, were insufficient because of their reliance on Internet Protocol (IP) addresses that could be forged. Typically, noncritical, delay-insensitive information, such as e-mail, one-way data transfers and low-bandwidth LAN traffic, is appropriate. Using an intranet to extend a WAN (by linking suppliers, customers, and remote offices) or to communicate internationally is also suitable. Future uses of intranets will include high-bandwidth, two-way communications, including real-time videoconferencing and highly sensitive data.

INTERNET2

Internet2 is an experimental world-wide information network that will permit information to be transferred 600 times faster than is possible using phone lines. A consortium of 60 leading companies, 189 universities, and various governmental agencies are testing new technology applications, such as digital libraries, virtual laboratories, distance-independent learning and teleimmersion. With the capability to transfer huge volumes of data in minutes rather than days, Internet2 is likely to significantly change how we work, learn, and play.

GLOSSARY OF COMPUTER TERMS

access, to locate (data) for transfer from one part of a computer system to another.

acoustic coupler, a device designed to connect a telephone handset to a modem and a computer.

active-matrix, of or pertaining to a high-resolution liquid-crystal display (LCD) with high contrast, used especially for laptop computers.

adapter. *See* expansion card.

add-in, a component, such as an expansion card or chip, added to a computer to expand its capabilities.

add-on, a product, as an expansion card or computer program, designed to complement another product.

address, a label, as an integer or symbol, that designates the location of information stored in computer memory. Also, to direct (data) to a specified location in an electronic computer.

addressable, (of information stored in a computer) capable of being accessed.

alpha test, an early test of new or updated computer software conducted by the developers of the program prior to beta testing by potential users.

American Standard Code for Information Interchange. *See* ASCII.

analog computer, a computer that represents data by measurable quantities, as voltages, rather than by numbers.

AND, a Boolean operator that returns a positive result when both operands are positive.

applet, a small application program that can be called up for use while working in another application.

application, a specific kind of task, as database management, that can be done using an application program.

application program, a computer program used for a specific kind of task, as word processing architecture, a fundamental underlying design of computer hardware, software, or both.

artificial intelligence, the collective attributes of a computer, robot, or other mechanical device programmed to perform functions analogous to learning and decision making. The field of study involved with the design of such programs and devices.

ASCII, a standardized code in which characters are represented for computer storage and transmission by the numbers 0 through 127. A(merican) S(tandard) C(ode for) I(nformation)

assembler, a language processor that translates symbolic assembly language into equivalent machine language.

assembly language, a computer language most of whose expressions are symbolic equivalents of the machine-language instructions of a particular computer.

author, the writer of a software program, especially a hypertext or multimedia application.

backslash, a short oblique stroke used in some operating systems to mark the division between a directory and a subdirectory, as in typing a path.

backup, a copy or duplicate version, especially of a data file or program, retained for use in the event that the original becomes unusable or unavailable. A procedure for creating a backup. Also, to make a backup of (a data file or program).

batch, a group of jobs, data, programs, or commands treated as a unit for processing.

batch processing, a form of data processing in which a number of input jobs are run as a group.

baud, a unit used to measure the speed of data transfer, usually equal to the number of bits transmitted per second.

bay, an open compartment in the console housing a computer's CPU in which a disk drive, tape drive, etc., may be installed. Also called *drive bay.*

BBS, bulletin board system: a computerized facility, accessible by modem, for collecting and relaying electronic messages and software programs, playing games, etc. Also called *electronic bulletin board.*

beta test, a test of new or updated computer software or hardware conducted at select user sites just prior to release of the product.

binary, of or pertaining to a system of numerical notation to the base 2, in which each place of a number, expressed as 0 or 1, corresponds to a power of 2. Computers use the binary number system to store and process information.

BIOS, computer firmware that directs many basic functions of the operating system, as booting and keyboard control. B(asic) I(nput)/O(utput) S(ystem)

bit, a single, basic unit of computer information, valued at either 0 or 1 to signal binary alternatives.

bit map, a piece of text, a drawing, etc., represented, as on a computer display, by the activation of certain dots in a rectangular matrix of dots.

block, a group of computer data stored and processed as a unit. (in word processing) a portion of text or data marked off for deleting, moving, etc. To mark off (a portion of text or data) for moving, deleting, printing, etc., as in word processing.

board, a piece of fiberglass or other material upon which an array of computer chips is mounted. Also called card.

Boolean operation, any logical operation in which each of the operands and the result take one of two values, as "true" and "false" or "circuit on" and "circuit off."

boot, to start (a computer) by loading the operating system.

BPS, bits per second (refers to the number of data bits sent per second between modems).

buffer, a temporary storage area that holds data until ready to be processed.

bulletinboard. *See* BBS.

bus, a circuit that connects the CPU with other devices in a computer. The data bus transmits data to and from the CPU.

byte, a group of adjacent bits, usually eight, processed by a computer as a unit.

cache, a piece of computer hardware or a section of RAM dedicated to selectively storing and speeding access to frequently used program commands or data.

CAD/CAM, computer-aided design and computer-aided manufacturing.

capture, to enter (data) into a computer for processing or storage. Also, to record (data) in preparation for such entry.

card. *See* board

CD. *See under* compact disk.

CD-ROM, a compact disk on which a large amount of digitized read-only data can be stored. C(ompact) D(isk)-R(ead) O(nly) M(emory).

central processing unit. *See* CPU.

character, any encoded unit of computer-usable data representing a symbol, as a letter, number, or punctuation mark, or a space, carriage return, etc.

character set, the numbers, letters, punctuation marks, and special symbols that can be used by a particular device, as a printer, or in a coding method, as ASCII.

chat, to engage in dialogue by exchanging electronic messages usually in real time.

chip, a tiny slice of semiconducting material on which a transistor or an integrated circuit is formed. Also called *microchip.*

circuit board, a sheet of fiberglass or other material on which electronic components, as printed or integrated circuits, are installed.

CISC, complex instruction set computer: a computer whose central processing unit recognizes a relatively large number of instructions.

click, to depress and release a mouse button rapidly, as to select an icon.

client, a workstation on a network that gains access to central data files, programs, and peripheral devices through a server.

clock, the circuit in a digital computer that provides a common reference train of electronic pulses for all other circuits. The clock speed, usually measured in megahertz, indicates how fast the computer will carry out commands.

clock speed. *See under* clock.

code, the symbolic arrangement of statements or instructions in a computer program in which letters, digits, etc., are represented as binary numbers; the set of instructions in such a program.

color monitor. *See under* monitor.

command, a signal, as a keystroke, instructing a computer to perform a specific task.

compact disk, a small optical disk on which music, data, or images are digitally recorded for playback. Abbreviated: CD.

compatible, (of software) able to run on a specified computer. (of hardware) able to work with a specified device. (of a computer system) functionally equivalent to another, usually widely used, system.

compiler, a computer program that translates another program written in a high-level language into a form, usually machine language, that can be executed by a computer.

compression, reduction of the size of computer data by efficient storage.

computer graphics, pictorial computer output produced, through the use of software, on a display screen or printer. Also, the technique or process used to produce such output.

config.sys, a text file that loads at startup and contains DOS (Disk Operating System) commands. Memory device drivers and programs are specified that control hardware devices; enable or disable system features; and set limits on system resources.

configuration, a computer, the equipment connected to it, plus software, set up to work together. Also, the act of configuring a computer system.

configure, to put (a computer system) together by supplying a specific computer with appropriate periph-

eral devices, as a monitor and disk drive, and connecting them. Also, to insert batch files into (a program) to enable it to run with a particular computer.

console, the control unit of a computer, including the keyboard and display screen.

conversion, the process of enabling software for one computer system to run on another. Also, the transformation of data from a form compatible with one computer program to a form compatible with another.

coprocessor, a processing unit that assists the CPU in carrying out certain types of operations. For example, a math coprocessor is a processing unit that performs mathematical calculations using floating-point notation.

copy protection, a method of preventing users of a computer program from making unauthorized copies, usually through hidden instructions contained in the program code.

CPU, central processing unit: the key component of a computer system, containing the circuitry necessary to interpret and execute program instructions.

crash, (of a computer) to suffer a major failure because of a malfunction of hardware or software.

CRT, cathode ray tube: a type of computer monitor.

cursor, a movable, sometimes blinking symbol used to indicate where data (as text, commands, etc.) may be input on a computer screen.

cyber-, a combining form representing "computer," e.g., cybertalk; cyberart.

cyberspace, the realm of electronic communication.

daisy wheel, a small spoked wheel with raised numbers, letters, etc., on the tips of the spokes: used as the printing element in some computer printers. Laser and inkjet printers have almost entirely replaced daisy-wheel printers for producing high-resolution text with personal computers.

database, a collection of organized, related data in electronic form that can be accessed and manipulated by specialized computer software. Also, fund of information on one or more subjects, as a collection of articles accessible by computer.

data bus. *See under* bus.

data highway. *See* information super-highway.

DBMS, database management system: a set of software programs for controlling the storage, retrieval, and modification of organized data in a computerized database.

dedicated, (of a computer) designed for a specific use or an exclusive application: a dedicated word processor.

default, a preset value that a computer system assumes or an action that it takes unless otherwise instructed.

density, a measure of how much data can be stored in a given amount of space on a disk, tape, or other computer storage medium.

desktop computer, a computer made to fit or be used on a desk or table.

desktop publishing, the design and production of publications by means of specialized software enabling a microcomputer to generate typeset-quality text and graphics. Abbreviated: dtp

digital, involving or using numerical digits expressed in a scale of notation to represent discretely all variables occurring in a problem.

digital computer, a computer that processes information in digital form.

directory, a division in a hierarchical structure that organizes the storage of computer files on a disk. Also, a listing of such stored files.

disk, any of several types of media for storing electronic data consisting of thin round plates of plastic or metal.

disk drive, a device in or attached to a computer that enables the user to read data from or store data on a disk.

diskette. *See under* floppy disk.

display, to show (computer data) on a CRT or other screen. The visual representation of the output of an electronic device. Also, the portion of the device, as a screen, that shows this representation.

docking station, a small desktop cabinet, usually containing disk drives and ports for connection to peripherals, into which a laptop may be inserted so as to give it the functionality of a desktop computer.

document, a computer data file.

documentation, instructional materials for computer software or hardware.

dongle, a hardware device attached to a computer without which a given software program will not run: used to prevent unauthorized use.

DOS, an operating system for microcomputers. D(isk) O(perating) S(ystem).

dot-matrix printer, a computer printer that produces characters and graphics by pushing pins into an inked ribbon to form the appropriate pattern, or matrix, of dots.

dot pitch, a measure of the distance between each pixel on a computer screen. A lower number indicates a sharper image.

double-click, to click a mouse button twice in rapid succession, as to call up a program or select a file.

download, to transfer (software or data) from a computer to a smaller computer or a peripheral device.

dpi, dots per inch: a measure of resolution used especially for printed text or images.

drag, to pull (a graphical image or portion of text) from one place to another on a computer screen, especially by using a mouse.

drive bay. *See* bay.

driver, software that controls the interface between a computer and a peripheral device.

dump, to output (computer data), often in binary form, especially to diagnose a failure. Also, a copy of dumped computer data.

edit, to modify (computer data or text).

electronic mail, a system for sending messages via telecommunications links between computers. Abbreviated: e-mail.

e-mail. *See* electronic mail.

emoticon, e.g., a combination of characters used to communicate humor, sarcasm, sadness, etc., in an electronic message.

end-user, the ultimate user of a computer or a software program.

Energy Star Program, a program of the U.S. Environmental Protection Agency encouraging the manufacture of personal computers that can reduce their energy consumption when left idle.

enhance, to provide with more complex or sophisticated features, as a computer program.

enhanced keyboard, a keyboard having 101 keys, with 12 function keys along the top.

environment, the hardware or software configuration of a computer system.

Ethernet, Trademark. a local-area network protocol featuring a bus topology (all devices are connected to a central cable) and a 10 megabit per second data transfer rate.

execute, to run (a computer program) or process (a command).

expansion card, a circuit board that fits into an expansion slot, used to add sound capability, more memory, etc., e.g., a sound card is an expansion card that permits files containing music, voice, or other sounds to be played on a computer. Also called *expansion board*

expansion slot, a connection to which a new circuit board can be added to expand a computer's capabilities.

export, to save (documents, data, etc.) in a format usable by another application program.

fax modem, a modem that can fax data, as documents or pictures, directly from a computer.

field, a unit of information, as a person's name, that combines with related fields, as an official title, address, or company name, to form one complete record in a computerized database.

file, a collection of related computer data or program records stored by name, as on a disk.

file server, a computer that makes files available to workstations on a network.

firmware, software stored permanently on a ROM chip.

first-generation, being the first model or version available to users.

flame, (especially on a computer network) an act or instance of angry criticism or disparagement. To behave in an offensive manner; rant. Also, to insult or criticize angrily.

flash memory, a type of reprogrammable computer memory that retains information even with the power turned off.

flat-file, of or pertaining to a database system in which each database consists of a single file not linked to any other file.

floating point, a decimal point whose location is not fixed, used especially in computer operations.

floppy disk, a thin, portable, flexible plastic disk coated with magnetic material, for storing computer data and programs. Currently, the the 3½-inch disk (sometimes called a microfloppy), housed in a square rigid envelope, is the common size used with personal computers.

flops, a measure of computer speed, equal to the number of floating-point operations the computer can perform per second (used especially in combination with the prefixes mega-, giga-, and tera-) fl(oating-point) op(erations per) s(econd)

font, a set of characters that have a given shape or design.

footprint, the surface space occupied by a microcomputer.

format, the arrangement of data for computer input or output, as the number of fields in a database record or the margins in a report. To set the format of (computer input or output). Also, to prepare (a disk) for writing and reading.

freeware, computer software distributed without charge.

FTP, File Transfer Protocol: a software protocol for exchanging information between computers over a network. Also, any program that implements this protocol.

function key, a key on a computer keyboard used alone or with other keys for operations.

gateway, software or hardware that links two computer networks.

GB. *See* gigabyte

gigabyte, a measure of data storage capacity equal to approximately 1 billion bytes. Abbreviated: GB

gigaflops, a measure of computer speed, equal to one billion floating-point operations per second.

global, (of a computer operation) operating on a group of similar strings, commands, etc., in a single step.

Gopher, a protocol for a menu-based system of accessing documents on the Internet. Also, any program that implements this protocol.

graphic, a computer-generated image.

graphical user interface, a software interface designed to standardize and simplify the use of computer programs, as by using a mouse to manipulate text and images on a display screen featuring icons, windows, and menus. Abbreviated: GUI.

groupware, software enabling a group to work together on common projects, share data, and synchronize schedules, especially through networked computers.

GUI. *See* graphical user interface.

hacker, a computer user who attempts to gain unauthorized access to proprietary computer systems.

hard copy, computer output printed on paper; printout.

hard disk, a rigid disk coated with magnetic material, for storing computer programs and relatively large amounts of data.

hardware, the mechanical, magnetic, electronic, and electrical devices composing a computer system.

hardware platform, a group of compatible computers that can run the same software.

hardwired, built into a computer's hardware and thus not readily changed. Also, (of a terminal) connected to a computer by a direct circuit rather than through a switching network.

Help, a system for supplying documentation for a software program, accessible on line from within the program.

high-level, (of a programming language) based on a vocabulary of Englishlike statements for writing program code rather than the more abstract instructions typical of assembly language or machine language.

hi-res, high-resolution.

home computer, a microcomputer designed for use in the home, as with game, multimedia, and educational software or electronic online services.

host computer, the main computer in a network, which controls or performs certain functions for other connected computers.

HTML, HyperText Markup Language: a set of standards, a variety of SGML, used to tag the elements of a hypertext document: the standard for documents on the World Wide Web.

hypermedia, a system in which various forms of information, as data, text, graphics, video, and audio, are linked together by a hypertext program.

hypertext, a method of storing data through a computer program that allows a user to create and link fields of information at will and to retrieve the data nonsequentially.

icon, a small graphic image on a computer screen representing a disk drive, a file, or a software command, as a picture of a wastebasket that can be pointed at and clicked on to delete a file.

impact printer, a computer printer, as a dot-matrix printer, that forms characters by causing a printhead to strike at paper through an inked ribbon.

import, to bring (documents, data, etc.) into one application program from another.

information superhighway, a large-scale communications network providing a variety of often interactive services, such as text databases, electronic mail, and audio and video materials, accessed through computers, television sets, etc.

initialize, to set (variables, counters, switches, etc.) to their starting values at the beginning of a computer program or subprogram. To prepare (a computer, printer, etc.) for reuse by clearing previous data from memory. Also, to format (a disk).

inkjet printer, a computer printer that prints text or graphics by spraying jets of ink onto paper to form a high-quality image approaching that of a laser printer.

input, data entered into a computer for processing. The process of introducing data into a computer for processing and/or internal storage. Also, of or pertaining to data or equipment used for input, e.g., a computer's main input device.

input/output, the combination of devices, channels, and techniques controlling the transfer of information between a CPU and its peripherals.

install, to put in place or connect for service or use, e.g., to install software on a computer.

instruction, a computer command.

interactive, (of a computer or program) characterized by or allowing immediate two-way communication between a source of information and a user, who can initiate or respond to queries.

interface, computer hardware or software designed to communicate information between hardware devices, between software programs, between devices and programs, or between a computer and a user.

interlaced, of or pertaining to technology that allows a monitor to display an image with higher resolution than it would otherwise be capable of by refreshing half the lines on the screen during one pass of an electron gun and the other half during a second pass. Interlaced monitors are more subject to flicker than noninterlaced ones.

interleaving, a method for making data retrieval more efficient by rearranging or renumbering the sectors on a hard disk or by splitting a computer's main memory into sections so the sectors or sections can be read in alternating cycles.

Internet, a large computer network linking smaller computer networks worldwide.

interrupt, a hardware or software signal that temporarily stops program execution in a computer so another procedure can be carried out.

I/O, input/output.

jaggies, a jagged, stairstep effect on curved or diagonal lines which are reproduced in low resolution, as on a printout or computer display.

job, a unit of work for a computer.

joystick, a lever used to control the movement of a cursor or other graphic element, as in a video game.

KB. *See* kilobyte.

keypad, a small panel of numeric and other special keys on a computer keyboard.

kilobit. *See* kilobyte.

kilobyte, a measure of data storage capacity equal to approximately one thousand bytes (1,024 bytes). Also called *kilobit.* Abbreviated KB.

LAN. *See* local-area network.

language, a set of symbols and syntactic rules for their combination and use, by means of which a computer can be given directions.

laptop, a portable, usually battery-powered microcomputer small enough to rest on the lap.

laser printer, a high-speed, high-resolution computer printer that uses a laser to form dot-matrix patterns and an electrostatic process to print a page at a time.

letter-quality, designating or producing type equal in sharpness and resolution to that produced by an electric typewriter: e.g., a letter-quality computer printer. Abbreviated: LQ.

light pen, a hand-held light-sensitive input device used for drawing on a computer display screen or for pointing at characters or objects, as when choosing options from a menu.

line printer, an impact printer that produces a full line of computer output at a time.

load, to bring (a program or data) into a computer's RAM, as from a disk, so as to make it available for processing. Also, to place (an input/output medium) into an appropriate device, as by inserting a disk into a disk drive.

local-area network, a computer network confined to a limited area, linking especially personal computers so programs, data, peripheral devices, and processing tasks can be shared. Abbreviated: LAN.

log in, to gain access to a secured computer system or on-line service by keying in personal identification information.

log off, to terminate a session on a computer.

loop, the reiteration of a set of instructions in a computer routine or program.

lo-res, low-resolution.

LPM, lines per minute: a measure of the speed of an impact printer.

LQ. *See* letter-quality.

machine language, usually a numerical coding system specific to the hardware of a given computer model, into which any high-level or assembly program must be translated before being run.

machine-readable, (of data) in a form suitable for direct acceptance and processing by computer, as an electronic file on a magnetic disk.

macro, a single instruction, for use in a computer program, that represents a sequence of instructions or keystrokes.

mailbox, a file in a computer for the storage of electronic mail.

mainframe, a large computer, often the hub of a system serving many users.

main memory. *See* RAM.

management information system, a computerized information-processing force offering management support to a company. Abbreviated: MIS.

math coprocessor. *See under* coprocessor.

MB. *See* megabyte.

megabit. *See* megabyte.

megabyte, a measure of data storage capacity equal to approximately one million bytes. (1,048,576 bytes). Also called *megabit.* Abbreviated: MB.

megaflops, a measure of computer speed, equal to one million floating-point operations per second.

megahertz, a unit of frequency equal to one million cycles per second, used to measure microprocessor speed. Abbreviated: MHz.

memory, the capacity of a computer to store information, especially internally in RAM while electrical power is on. Also, the components of the computer in which such information is stored.

menu, a list of options or commands from which to choose, displayed on a computer screen. A menu bar is a vertical or horizontal list of options that can be located on the top, bottom, or sides of a computer display screen. A pop-up menu appears temporarily when the user clicks on a selection. A pull-down menu appears beneath the option selected.

menu bar. *See under* menu.

menu-driven, of or pertaining to computer software that makes extensive use of menus to enable users to choose program options.

MHz. *See* megahertz.

microchip. *See* chip.

microcomputer, a compact computer having less capability than a minicomputer and employing a microprocessor.

microfloppy. *See under* floppy disk.

microprocessor, an integrated computer circuit that performs all the functions of a CPU.

MIDI, Musical Instrument Digital Interface: a standard means of sending digitally encoded information about music between electronic devices, as between synthesizers and computers.

minicomputer, a computer with processing and storage capabilities smaller than those of a mainframe but larger than those of a microcomputer.

minitower, a vertical case, smaller than a tower and larger than a case for a desktop computer, designed to house a computer system standing on a floor or desk.

MIPS, million instructions per second: a measure of computer speed.

MIS. *See* management information system.

modem, an electronic device that makes possible the transmission of data to or from a computer via telephone or other communication lines.

monitor, a component with a display screen for viewing computer data. A monochrome monitor can display two colors, one for the foreground and one for the background. A color monitor can display from 16 to one million different colors.

monochrome monitor. *See under* monitor.

morphing, the smooth transformation of one image into another by computer, as in a motion picture.

motherboard, a rigid slotted board upon which other boards that contain the basic circuitry of a computer or of a computer component can be mounted.

mouse, a palm-sized device equipped with one or more buttons, used to point at and select items on a computer screen, with the displayed pointer controlled by means of analogous movement of the device on a nearby surface.

MPC, multimedia PC, a system conforming to specifications covering audio, video, and other multimedia components, and able to run multimedia software.

MPR II, a standard developed in Sweden that limits to 250 nanoteslas the electromagnetic radiation emissions from a monitor at a distance of a half meter.

MS-DOS, Trademark, a microcomputer operating system. M(icro) S(oft) D(isk) O(perating) S(ystem).

multimedia, the combined use or integration of several media in computer applications, as text, sound, graphics, animation, and video.

multitasking, the concurrent execution of two or more jobs or programs by a single CPU.

multiuser system, a computer system in which multiple terminals connect to a host computer that handles processing tasks.

netiquette, the etiquette of computer networks.

network, a computer or telecommunications system linked to permit exchange of information.

newsgroup, a discussion group on a specific topic, maintained on a computer network.

noninterlaced, of or pertaining to technology that refreshes all the lines on a monitor's screen at one time while maintaining screen resolution. (Noninterlaced monitors are less subject to flicker than interlaced ones.)

nonvolatile, (of computer memory) having the property of retaining

data when electrical power fails or is turned off.

NOR, a Boolean operator that returns a positive result when both operands are negative.

NOT, a Boolean operator that returns a positive result if its operand is negative and a negative result if its operand is positive.

notebook, a small, lightweight laptop computer measuring approximately 8 1/2 × 11 in. (22 × 28 cm).

numeric keypad. *See* keypad.

OCR. *See* optical character recognition.

offline, operating independently of, or disconnected from, an associated computer.

online, operating under the direct control of, or connected to, a main computer.

on-line service, a database service providing information, news, etc., accessed through a modem.

operating system, the software that directs a computer's operations, as by controlling and scheduling the execution of other programs and managing storage and input/output.

optical character recognition, the process or technology of reading printed or typed text by electronic means and converting it to digital data. Abbreviated: OCR.

optical disk, a grooveless disk on which digital data, as text, music, or pictures, are stored as tiny pits in the surface and read or replayed by a laser beam scanning the surface.

optical scanner. *See* scanner.

OR, a Boolean operator that returns a positive result when either or both operands are positive.

output, information made available by computer, as on a printout, display screen, or disk. Also, the process of transferring such information from computer memory to or by means of an output device.

page, a block of computer memory up to 4,096 bytes long. Also, a portion of a program that can be moved to a computer's internal memory from external storage.

page description language, a high-level programming language for determining the output of a page printer designed to work with it, independent of the printer's internal codes. Abbreviated: PDL.

page printer, a high-speed, high-

resolution computer printer that uses a light source, as a laser beam or electrically charged ions, to print a full page of text or graphics at a time.

palette, the complete range of colors made available by a computer graphics card, from which a user or program may choose those to be displayed.

palmtop, a battery-powered microcomputer small enough to fit in the palm.

parallel, of or pertaining to operations within a computer that are performed simultaneously: parallel processing. Also, pertaining to or supporting the transfer of electronic data several bits at a time: a parallel printer.

passive-matrix, of or pertaining to a relatively low-resolution liquid-crystal display (LCD) with low contrast, used especially for laptop computers.

password, a string of characters typed into a computer to identify and obtain access for an authorized user.

path, a listing of the route through directories and subdirectories that locates and thereby names a specific file or program on a disk drive (in some computer operating systems). Also, the currently active list of all such routes that tells the operating system where to find programs, enabling a user to run them from other directories.

PC. *See* personal computer.

PCMCIA, Personal Computer Memory Card International Association: (especially for laptop computers) a standard for externally accessible expansion slots that accept compatible cards for enhancing the computer's functions, as by adding memory or supplying a portable modem.

PDA. *See* personal digital assistant.

PDL. *See* page description language.

pen-based, (of a computer) having an electronic stylus—a pointing and drawing device shaped like a pen. The stylus works with a digitizing tablet or touch screen to communicate with the computer.

peripheral, an external hardware device, as a keyboard, printer, or tape drive, connected to a computer's CPU.

personal computer, a microcomputer designed for individual use, as for word processing, financial analysis, desktop publishing, or playing computer games. Abbreviated: PC.

personal digital assistant, a handheld computer, often pen-based, that provides especially organizational software, as an appointment calendar, and communications hardware, as a fax modem. Abbreviated PDA.

PIM, personal information manager.

pixel, the smallest element of an image that can be individually processed in a video display system.

platform. *See under* hardware platform and software platform.

Plug and Play, a standard for the production of compatible computers, peripherals, and software that facilitates device installation and enables automatic configuration of the system.

plug-compatible, designating computers or peripherals that are compatible with another vendor's models and could replace them.

pop-up menu. *See under* menu.

port, a data connection in a computer to which a peripheral device or a transmission line from a remote terminal can be attached. Also, to create a new version of (an application program) to run on a different hardware platform.

portable, (of data, software, etc.) able to be used on different computer systems.

PPM, pages per minute: a measure of the speed of a page printer.

printer, a computer output device that produces a paper copy of data or graphics.

printhead, the printing element on an impact printer.

printout, computer-output produced by a printer.

print wheel. *See* daisy wheel.

program, a sequence of instructions enabling a computer to perform a task; piece of software. Also, to provide a program for (a computer).

programming language, a high-level language used to write computer programs, or, sometimes, an assembly language.

prompt, a symbol or message on a computer screen requesting more information or indicating readiness to accept instructions.

protocol, a set of rules governing the format of messages that are exchanged between computers.

pull-down menu. *See under* menu.

queue, a sequence of items waiting in order for electronic action in a computer system.

RAM, volatile computer memory, used for creating, loading, and running programs and for manipulating and temporarily storing data; main memory. R(andom) A(ccess) M(emory).

random-access, designating an electronic storage medium that allows information to be stored and retrieved in arbitrary sequence.

random-access memory. *See* RAM.

raster, a set of horizontal lines composed of individual pixels, used to form an image on a CRT or other screen.

read, to obtain (data or programs) from an external storage medium and place in a computer's memory.

read-only, noting or pertaining to computer files or memory that can be read but cannot normally be changed.

read-only memory. *See* ROM.

read-out, the output of information from a computer in readable form.

real-time, of or pertaining to computer applications or processes that can respond immediately to user input.

recognition, the automated conversion of words or images into a form that can be processed by a computer.

record, a group of related fields treated as a unit in a database.

red-lining, a marking device, as underlining or boldface, used especially in word processing to highlight suggested additional text in a document.

refresh, to redisplay the information on (a screen) so as to prevent loss or fading. A refresh rate of many times per second is typical for a computer's display screen.

refresh rate. *See under* refresh.

register, a high-speed storage location in a computer's CPU, used to store a related string of bits, as a word or phrase.

relational database, an electronic database comprising multiple files of related information, usually stored in tables of rows (records) and columns (fields), and allowing a link to be established between separate files that have a matching field, as a column of invoice num-

bers, so the two files can be queried simultaneously by the user.

resident, encoded and permanently available to a computer user, as a font in a printer's ROM or software on a CD-ROM. Also, (of a computer program) currently active or standing by in computer memory, as a TSR program.

resolution, the degree of sharpness of a computer-generated image as measured by the number of dots per linear inch in a hard-copy printout or the number of pixels across and down on a display screen.

response time, the time that elapses while waiting for a computer to respond to a command.

retrieve, to locate and read (data) from computer storage, as for display on a monitor.

reverse video, a mode on the display screen of a computer in which the colors normally used for characters and background are reversed.

RISC, reduced instruction set computer: a computer whose central processing unit recognizes a relatively small number of instructions, which it can execute very rapidly.

ROM, nonvolatile, nonmodifiable computer memory, used to hold programmed instructions to the system. R(ead) O(nly) M(emory).

routine, a set of instructions directing a computer to perform a specific task.

run, to process (the instructions in a program) by computer.

save, to copy (computer data) onto a hard or floppy disk, a tape, etc.

scalable font. *See under* font.

scan, to read (data) for use by a computer or computerized device, especially using an optical scanner.

scanner, a device that converts text or graphic images into a digital form that the computer can use. Also called *optical scanner.*

screen saver, a computer program that blanks the screen display or puts a moving pattern on it to prevent the permanent etching of a pattern on a screen when the pattern is displayed for a long time. Also, any of a selection of moving patterns available through this program, appearing on a screen if there has been no user input for a specified amount of time.

scroll, to move a cursor smoothly, vertically or sideways, gradually causing new data to replace old on the display screen of a computer.

SCSI, a standard for computer interface ports featuring faster data transmission and greater flexibility than normal ports. S(mall) C(omputer) S(ystem) I(nterface)

search, to command software to find specified characters or codes in (an electronic file), e.g., to search a database for all instances of "U.S." and replace them with "United States." Also, to find specified characters or codes in an electronic file by means of software commands.

serial, pertaining to or supporting the transfer of electronic data in a stream of sequential bits: a serial port. Also, of or pertaining to the transmission or processing of each part of a whole in sequence, as each bit of a byte or each byte of a computer word.

server, a computer that makes services, as access to data files, programs, and peripheral devices, available to workstations on a network.

SGML, Standard Generalized Markup Language: a set of standards enabling a user to create an appropriate scheme for tagging the elements of an electronic document, as to facilitate the production of multiple versions in various print and electronic formats.

shareware, computer software distributed without initial charge but for which the user is encouraged to pay a nominal fee to cover support for continued use.

shell, a computer program providing a menu-driven or graphical user interface designed to simplify use of the operating system, as in loading application programs.

slipstreaming, the act of updating a software program without adequately informing the public, as by failing to release it as an official new version.

slot. *See* expansion slot.

software, programs for directing the operation of a computer or processing electronic data.

software platform, a major piece of software, as an operating system, an operating environment, or a database, under which various smaller application programs can be designed to run.

sort, to place (computerized data) in order, numerically or alphabetically.

soundcard. *See under* expansion card.

spell checker, a computer program for checking the spelling of words in an electronic document.

split screen, a mode of operation on a computer that uses windows to enable simultaneous viewing of two or more displays on the same screen.

spool, to operate (an input/output device) by using buffers in main and secondary storage.

spreadsheet, an outsize ledger sheet simulated electronically by specialized computer software, used especially for financial planning.

stand-alone, (of an electronic device) able to function without connection to a larger system; self-contained.

storage. *See* memory.

store, to put or retain (data) in a computer memory unit, as a hard disk.

subdirectory, a directory hierarchically below another directory in DOS or UNIX.

subnotebook, a laptop computer smaller and lighter than a notebook, typically weighing less than 3 pounds.

subroutine, a prepared instruction sequence that a programmer can insert into a computer program as needed.

surge protector, a device that provides an alternative pathway for electrical energy when excessive voltage appears on the power line, shunting the energy away from computer circuits.

system, a working combination of computer hardware, software, and data communications devices.

system.ini, a file that determines a variety of options for the Windows operating environment, including which video, mouse, and keyboard drivers are installed for Windows.

system(s) program, a program, as an operating system, compiler, or utility program, that controls some aspect of the operation of a computer.

systems analysis, the methodical study of the data-processing needs of a business or project.

tag, a symbol or other labeling device indicating the beginning or end of a unit of information in an electronic document.

tape drive, a program-controlled device that reads data from or writes data on a magnetic tape which moves past a read-write head.

telecommuting, the act or practice of working at home using a computer

terminal electronically linked to one's place of employment.

telnet, a protocol for connecting to a remote computer on the Internet. Also, any program that implements this protocol.

teraflops, a measure of computer speed, equal to one trillion floating-point operations per second.

terminal, any device for entering information into a computer or receiving information from it, as a keyboard with video display unit.

text editor, a computer program for writing and modifying documents or program code on-screen, usually having little or no formatting ability.

toggle, to shift back and forth between two settings or modes of computer operation by means of a key or programmed keystroke.

touch screen, a computer display that can detect and respond to the presence and location of a finger or instrument on or near its surface.

tower, a vertical case designed to house a computer system standing on the floor.

track, one of a number of concentric rings on the surface of a floppy disk, or other computer storage medium, along which data are recorded.

trackball, a computer input device for controlling the pointer on a display screen by rotating a ball set inside a case.

tree, a computer data structure organized like a tree whose nodes store data elements and whose branches represent pointers to other nodes in the tree.

TSR, a computer program with any of several ancillary functions, usually held resident in RAM for instant activation while one is using another DOS program. T(erminate and) S(tay) R(esident)

UNIX, Trademark. A highly portable multiuser, multitasking operating system used on a variety of computers ranging from mainframes through workstations to personal computers.

upload, to transfer (software or data) from a smaller to a larger computer.

user, a person who uses a computer.

user-friendly, easy to operate, understand, etc.

user group, a club for the exchange of information and services among computer users.

utility program, a system program used especially to simplify standard computer operations, as sorting, copying, or deleting files. Also called *utility.*

vaporware, a product, especially computer software, that is announced and promoted while it is still in development and that may never come to market.

VDT. *See* video display terminal.

vector graphics, a method of electronically coding graphic images so they are represented in lines rather than fixed bit maps, allowing an image, as on a computer display screen, to be rotated or proportionally scaled.

VGA, video graphics array: a high-resolution standard for displaying text, graphics, and colors on monitors.

video display terminal, a computer terminal consisting of a screen on which data or graphics can be displayed. Abbreviated: VDT.

virtual, temporarily simulated or extended by software; virtual memory on a hard disk. Also, of, existing on, or by means of computers.

virtual reality, a realistic simulation of an environment, including three-dimensional graphics, by a com-

puter system using interactive software and hardware.

virus, a segment of self-replicating code planted illegally in a computer program, often to damage or shut down a system or network.

volatile, (of computer storage) not retaining data when electrical power is turned off.

WAN. *See* wide-area network.

wide-area network, a computer network that spans a relatively large geographical area. Abbreviated: WAN.

wild card, a character, as an asterisk, set aside by a computer operating system to represent one or more other characters of a file name, as in the DOS command "DEL*.DOC," which would delete all files with names ending in ".DOC."

window, a portion of the screen of a computer terminal on which data can be displayed independently of the rest of the screen. Also, a view of a portion of a document bounded by the borders of a computer's display screen.

Windows, trademark. Any of several microcomputer operating systems or environments featuring a graphical user interface.

wired, connected electronically to one or more computer networks.

word processing, the automated production and storage of documents using computers, electronic printers, and text-editing software.

word processor, a computer program or computer system designed for word processing.

workstation, a powerful microcomputer, often with a high-resolution display, used for computer-aided design, electronic publishing, or other graphics-intensive processing. A computer terminal or microcomputer connected to a mainframe, minicomputer, or dataprocessing network. Also, a work or office area assigned to one person, often one accommodating a computer terminal or other electronic equipment.

World Wide Web, a system of extensively interlinked hypertext documents: a branch of the Internet. Abbreviated: WWW.

write, to transfer (data, text, etc.) from computer memory to an output medium.

WWW. *See* World Wide Web.

WYSIWYG, of, pertaining to, or being a computer screen display that shows text exactly as it will appear when printed.

XOR, a Boolean operator that returns a positive result when either but not both of its operands are positive.

INDEX

About the International Association of Administrative Professionals®

The International Association of Administrative Professionals® (IAAP) has more than 60 years of experience in preparing office workers to assume leadership roles in their organizations. IAAP is a nonprofit, membership association with 40,000 members in 600 chapters worldwide. IAAP is the world's leader in developing personal and professional competencies for secretaries, administrative, executive support staff, office managers, coordinators, and others.

IAAP developed and administers the Certified Professional Secretary® (CPS®) examination, a one-day, three-part exam that covers finance and business law, office systems and administration, and management, and the Certified Administrative Professional^{CM} (CAP^{CM}) examination, a one-and-a-half-day, four-part exam. In addition to conducting and disseminating research on office trends, IAAP also works closely with business educators and corporate trainers to prepare individuals for office careers and to increase the proficiency level of employees.

IAAP publishes *OfficePRO*® magazine and sponsors numerous seminars and conferences each year. An educational online resources catalog provides office staff with discounts on self-study materials and online education and training opportunities.

For more information on IAAP, membership, professional certification, educational activities, or contact for local chapters, call 816/891-6600, fax 816/891-9118, e-mail service @iaap-hq.org, or visit www.iaap-hq.org.